THE WORKING MEN'S COLLEGE

AUSPICIUM MELIORIS

ÆVI· MDCCCLIV·

Purchased.

R.E.Tyler Del. 1913. C.H.Perry Sc.

WORKING MEN'S COLLEGE

LIBRARY REGULATIONS

The Library is open every week-day evening (except Saturday), from 6.30 to 9.30 p.m.

This book may be kept for three weeks. If not returned within that period, the borrower will be liable to a fine of 2np per week.

If lost or damaged, the borrower will be required to make good such loss or damage.

Up to three books may be borrowed at a time at the discretion of the Librarian.

SURVEY OF LONDON
VOLUME XXXVII

PREVIOUS VOLUMES
OF THE SURVEY OF LONDON

* Original edition out of print. Photographic facsimile available from A.M.S. Press Inc., 56 East 13th Street, New York.

No. 24 Kensington Park Gardens, 1853
Designed by Thomas Allom for C. H. Blake, the principal building speculator in
Victorian North Kensington, who lived here 1854–9

SURVEY OF LONDON

GENERAL EDITOR: F. H. W. SHEPPARD

VOLUME XXXVII

Northern Kensington

THE ATHLONE PRESS
UNIVERSITY OF LONDON
Published for the Greater London Council

1973

Published by
THE ATHLONE PRESS
UNIVERSITY OF LONDON
at 4 Gower Street, London WCIE 6DR

Distributed by
Tiptree Book Services Ltd, Tiptree, Essex

U.S.A. and Canada
Humanities Press Inc
New York

ISBN 0 485 48237 1

Printed in Great Britain by
WILLIAM CLOWES & SONS, LIMITED
LONDON, BECCLES AND COLCHESTER

Preface

THIS VOLUME describes the northern part of the Parish of St. Mary Abbots, Kensington, and covers the whole of the area to the north of Kensington High Street as far as Kensal Green. Large-scale building development began here during the boom years of the early 1820's, and except in the north-western extremity was virtually completed by the 1880's. This study is therefore largely concerned with nineteenth-century suburban growth, a subject which has not been dealt with in detail by the *Survey of London* since the publication of volume XXVI on Southern Lambeth in 1956. Since then there has been a marked increase of public interest in the nineteenth-century townscape, and this volume forms a natural complement to the recent work of the Historic Buildings Board in the designation and enhancement of conservation areas. Two more volumes, now in course of preparation, will describe the remainder of the Parish of Kensington.

B. J. BROWN
Chairman, Historic Buildings Board
Greater London Council
County Hall

Acknowledgments

The Council tenders its grateful thanks to all those individuals and institutions whose help has made the preparation of this volume possible, and particularly the following:

Lady Teresa Agnew; Mr. Zvi Barlev; Rev. M. F. Barney; Mr. C. B. Berry; Mr. G. C. Berry; Mr. R. T. Bishop; Rev. L. A. Bralant; Mr. J. Brandon-Jones; Mr. Robert Brandt; Mr. F. F. Brickdale; Mr. H. E. Gonne Browning; Rev. F. T. C. Byron; the Prior, Carmelite Church, Kensington Church Street; the Mother Superior, Carmelite Monastery, St. Charles Square; Mr. H. R. Carter; Professor E. M. Carus-Wilson; Mrs. Josephine Cashmore; the Dowager Marchioness of Cholmondeley; Mrs. G. Christiansen; Rev. F. P. Clark; Miss Mae Cooke; Rev. Eldin R. Corsie; Rev. David A. Craig; Mr. Romilly B. Craze; Mr. B. R. Curle; Miss E. M. Dain; Rev. Norwyn Denny; the Mother Superior, Dominican Convent, Portobello Road; Commander C. H. Drage; Mrs. M. P. G. Draper; Mr. A. E. Dunster; Professor H. J. Dyos; Mr. J. U. V. Edwardes; the Egyptian Consul-General; Miss R. Ensing; the Chief Representative of the Commission of the European Communities in the United Kingdom; Mr. P. Filatov; H. E. the Finnish Ambassador and Madame Wartiovaara; Rev. D. Fletcher; the Rt. Hon. Hugh and Lady Antonia Fraser; H.E. the French Ambassador; the Earl of Gainsborough; Dr. Mark Girouard; Rev. J. H. Goodman; Mr. Ian Grant; Mr. A. S. Gray; Mr. A. C. L. Hall; Mrs. Gwen Hart; Rev. John F. Hathway; Miss Hermione Hobhouse; Mr. Peter Hodson; Rev. C. C. Hordern; Mr. Derek Hudson; Mr. J. Huisman; H.E. the Indian High Commissioner; H.E. the Iraqi Ambassador; H.E. the Israeli Ambassador; Rev. P. Jameson; H.E. the Japanese Ambassador; Mr. C. J. H. King; Rev. P. P. Kirwin; H.E. the Laotian Ambassador; H.E. the Lebanese Ambassador; Mrs. Henry Levy; the Mother Superior, the Little Sisters of the Poor, Portobello Road; Rev. J. M. Livingstone; Mr. O. R. W. W. Lodge; Mrs. P. E. Malcolmson; Mr. W. Males; Rev. J. McCarthy; Miss Priscilla Metcalf; Mr. C. B. Mills; H.E. the Netherlands Ambassador; H.E. the Nigerian High Commissioner; the Very Rev. M. Nikolich; H.E. the Norwegian Ambassador and Mrs. Koht; Mrs. N. Parkes; Dr. Stephen Pasmore; H.E. the Philippines Ambassador; the Hon. Claude Phillimore; Major W. T. Pitt; the Mother Abbess, the Poor Clares Monastery, Barnet; Miss E. Poyser; Dr. David Reeder; Rev. H. L. O. Rees; the Registrar-General of Births, Deaths and Marriages; Sir Harry Ricardo; Rev. D. S. Richardson; Mr. F. P. Richardson; H.E. the Russian Ambassador; Mr. and Mrs. D. A. G. Sarre; H.E. the Saudi Arabian Ambassador; Miss Irene Scouloudi; Mr. James Byam Shaw; Professor T. B. Smith; Mrs. Tom Stacey; Miss V. Stokes; Miss Helen Stopien; Miss Dorothy Stroud; Sir John Summerson; Mlle. I. de la Taille; Miss M. P. West; Miss E. C. Wheat; Mr. Michael White; Rev. Cyril Wilson; Mr. Clayton R. Wintrip.

The Ashmolean Museum, Oxford; the Trustees of the Bedford Settled Estates; the British Museum; British Transport Historical Records; the Campden Charities Trustees; Cheltenham Central Reference Library; Messrs. Chesterton and Sons; the Church Commissioners; the Corporation of London, Guildhall Library; the Directors of Coutts and Co.; the Crown Estate Commissioners; the Governors of Dulwich College; the Essex County Record Office; Messrs. Fladgate and Co.; Messrs. Frere, Cholmeley and Co.; the General Cemetery Company; Messrs. Gregory, Rowcliffe and Co.; the Guardian Royal Exchange Assurance Group; the Hertfordshire County Record Office; the House of Lords Record Office; the India Office Library; Kensington Central Public Library; the London Museum; the Metropolitan Water Board; the National Monuments Record; the National Register of Archives; the Trustees of the Phillimore Kensington Estate; the Phoenix Assurance Co. Ltd.; the Principal Probate Registry, Somerset House; the Public Record Office; the Royal Academy; the Royal Institute of British Architects; the Scottish Record Office; the Sun Alliance and London Insurance Group; the Victoria and Albert Museum; Westminster Public Libraries; the Willett Estates; Messrs. Witham, Weld and Co.

Contents

Plates *at end*

Map of Northern Kensington *in end pocket*

List of Plates

(Unless otherwise stated all the Plates are photographs taken since 1946 whose copyright belongs to the Greater London Council)

List of Figures in the Text

Note. In some of the buildings shown in the above drawings the fenestration, glazing-bars, stucco enrichment and ironwork have with the passage of time been altered. In these cases the surviving evidence has been used to show the buildings in their presumed original condition.

General Introduction

QUEEN VICTORIA was born at Kensington Palace in 1819. At that time the population of Kensington amounted to some 12,000 souls, and was already growing fast. During her childhood at the Palace it almost doubled itself, and by 1901, the year of her death, it exceeded 176,000, having multiplied itself over twenty times during the preceding century.

Urban growth on this scale was, of course, commonplace in nineteenth-century England, and particularly throughout the Victorian age. In London itself half-a-dozen other suburbs could stand comparison with Kensington in this respect, but Kensington could, and indeed still can, nevertheless claim a pre-eminent position in the hierarchy of the Victorian metropolis. This claim is founded not merely on the Queen's own personal association, even though that was reiterated at the close of her reign in her intention to confer the title of 'Royal' upon the newly formed Borough of Kensington, at the request of its Council. It rests, rather, upon the more durable foundations of the bricks, mortar, stone and stucco of the houses, churches, museums and other public buildings which arose here during her reign, and most of which still survive. Some of these Kensington buildings may be numbered among the foremost architectural monuments of the time: all of them exhibit for posterity, with a vividness unequalled anywhere else in the capital, both the social structure, habits and assumptions of their Victorian creators, and also the underlying grandeur of their formidable energy and strength. Kensington is indeed the very citadel of Victorian London.

This volume, the first of three projected for Kensington, describes the whole of the ancient parish to the north of Kensington High Street, together with those parts of Kensal New Town and Kensington Palace Gardens which were incorporated into the Royal Borough of Kensington on its formation in 1900.* This area, which will henceforth be referred to here as northern Kensington, measures about a mile or less in breadth and extends some two and a half miles north-westward to Kensal Green. Its eastern and northern parts are in general some fifty to a hundred feet higher than the flat plain to the west, the downward slopes, from Campden Hill and Notting Hill, for instance, being steep by London standards. Almost the whole area was drained naturally by the watercourse known as the Counter's Creek, whose tributaries flowed west and south to the lower ground, and thence along the borders of Hammersmith and Fulham to the Thames.

For centuries two roads, Roman in origin and following the lines of Kensington High Street and of Notting Hill Gate and Holland Park Avenue, provided the only important lines of communication here, their west-east course testifying to the overpowering presence

---

* Neither Holland House, which may form the subject of a monograph at a later date, nor Kensington Palace, which was not within the ancient parish of Kensington, are included.

In this General Introduction sources are not given for statements authenticated in the succeeding chapters.

of London. The narrow twisting lane now known as Kensington Church Street was almost the only ancient north-south highway, and connected the two small settlements which arose beside the two main thoroughfares, one around the parish church of St. Mary Abbots and the other at Notting Hill Gate, where extensive digging for gravel took place from at least the early seventeenth century. Beyond Notting Hill Gate, Portobello Lane (now Road) wound northward as far as Portobello Farm, and until well into the nineteenth century much of the northern extremity of the parish remained remote and inaccessible.

At the end of the sixteenth century most of northern Kensington belonged briefly to Sir Walter Cope, and consisted of the manor of Abbots Kensington and the so-called manors of West Town and Notting Barns. Within this area manorial courts are only known to have been held for Abbots Kensington, and even here part of the copyhold land was being enfranchised, for by about 1600 wealthy Londoners were beginning to buy estates and build houses in Kensington. Cope himself was one of the many members of James I's court who were knighted in 1603. His first 'capital messuage' was probably Campden House, which acquired this name through a later owner, Sir Baptist Hicks, first Viscount Campden, a City mercer: he, too, was one of James's new knights, and had made his fortune by supplying the court with silk. Meanwhile Cope was building 'Cope's Castle', later known as Holland House, and another courtier, Sir George Coppin, was living first at the mansion later to be called Sheffield House, on the east side of Kensington Church Street, and subsequently at what was to become Kensington Palace. Later in the seventeenth century Chief-Justice Sir Robert Hyde had another big house in Church Street (later called Craven House), and when William III bought Coppin's old house in 1689, by then in the possession of the Earl of Nottingham, Kensington's claim to be the 'Court suburb' of London was achieved.

In the half-century after the arrival of the royal court several ranges of houses were built in the vicinity of the parish church, chiefly in Kensington Church Street and Church Court and in Holland Street, a few of which still survive. The parish church itself was largely re-built between 1683 and 1704, a charity school was erected nearby in 1711–12 to the designs of Nicholas Hawksmoor, and in the 1730's twelve houses were built on the site of Craven House in Church Street (Nos. 128–142 and 152–168 even). By this time the maintenance of the two chief highways had been placed under turnpike trusts—Notting Hill Gate/ Holland Park Avenue (the Uxbridge road) in 1714, and Kensington High Street (the Hammersmith road) in 1726, the latter being the responsibility of the Kensington Trust, which in 1741 took over Kensington Church Street.[1] Several more substantial houses were also built in the vicinity of Campden Hill, one of which, later known as Aubrey House, achieved a short-lived fame through the discovery of a medicinal spring there. In general, however, the frequent residence of successive monarchs at Kensington had no great impact on building development in the parish, and when, after the death of George II in 1760 the Palace ceased to be used by the sovereign, Holland House, already in the occupation of the Fox family, became for more than a century the chief resort in Kensington of fashionable society.

In northern Kensington the first recognizably modern suburban building development began in 1788, the ground landlord being evidently prompted by the opportunities presented by mounting metropolitan pressures rather than, as often hitherto, by the fortuitous presence of the royal court. In that year William Phillimore agreed to lease some 750 feet of his land fronting Kensington High Street for ninety-nine years to two City building tradesmen, Samuel Gray, bricklayer, and John Schofield, carpenter, and in due course long terrace ranges of four-storey houses arose, designed by Phillimore's own surveyor, William Porden, who in 1792 himself agreed to take the remaining land on the estate fronting the High Street. Progress was, however, slow, the building of the whole range of sixty-three houses (only two of which, Nos. 98 and 100 Kensington High Street, now survive) being spread over some twenty-five years.

Speculations of this kind were taking place contemporaneously on many other of the principal highways around London. In northern Kensington this was, however, the only one to be commenced before the opening of the nineteenth century, during the course of which almost the whole area was to be developed for building. This transformation forms the principal theme of this volume, and we must now examine some of the principal factors in it.

Enormous increases of population, such as that which took place in Kensington, provided the basic stimulant to nineteenth-century suburban growth. Detailed demographic analysis cannot, however, find a place in this present study, and little more than a simple statement of the figures contained in successive censuses is given below.

GROWTH OF POPULATION

Year	London*	% increase	Kensington parish	% increase	Kensington Town†	% increase	Kensington Town adjusted to exclude area south of High Street	% increase
1801	958,863	—	8,556	—	—	—	—	—
1811	1,138,815	18·8	10,886	27·2	—	—	—	—
1821	1,378,947	21·1	13,428	32·5	—	—	—	—
1831	1,654,994	20·0	20,902	44·9	—	—	—	—
1841	1,948,417	17·7	26,834	28·4	17,369	—	—	—
1851	2,362,236	21·2	44,053	64·2	29,183	68·0	19,733	—
1861	2,803,989	18·7	70,108	59·1	51,910	77·9	39,860‡	101·0
1871	3,254,260	16·1	120,299	71·6	91,645	76·6	76,603	92·2
1881	3,815,544	14·7	163,151	35·6	120,141	31·1	103,879	36·9
1891	4,228,317	9·8	170,071	4·2	122,366	1·8	107,462	3·5
1901	4,536,267	6·7	176,628	3·3	128,037	4·4	115,149	7·2

* London is taken to mean the Metropolitan area as defined by the Registrar-General in the census of 1851. The figures for 1801–41 have been adjusted to cover the whole Metropolitan area.

† The enumeration sub-district of Kensington Town, first distinguished in 1841, comprised most of the area described in this volume but did not include the Southern Row area of Kensal New Town, which was formerly in a detached portion of the parish of Chelsea; Kensal Green north of the canal, now mainly occupied by the cemetery; and a large part of Kensington Palace Gardens, which was formerly in the parishes of Paddington and St. Margaret's, Westminster. On the other hand the Kensington Town sub-district contained a considerable part of Kensington south of the High Street, including almost the whole area north of Cromwell Road and west of Exhibition Road, which is not described in the present volume.

‡ In producing this figure an estimate has had to be made for certain areas south of the High Street for which the enumerators' books are defective.

These figures show, for the whole of the parish, that in the first three decades of the nineteenth century the rate of increase was mounting steadily, but that this gathering momentum was checked in the 1830's, although at 28 per cent it still remained large.

This deceleration was followed by a tremendous resurgence throughout the whole parish, but particularly in Kensington Town (see note † of table above), from the 1840's to the 1860's. Between 1841 and 1871 the population of Kensington Town grew from 17,369 to 91,645, the rate of increase within approximately the area covered by this volume reaching its maximum of over 101 per cent in the 1850's. The period 1841 to 1871 marked, in fact, the climactic years in the making of northern Kensington, and thereafter there was a substantial decline in the volume of growth, both here and throughout the whole of the parish.

Several elements contributed to this increase of population. Expectation of life was increasing, for in London as a whole the annual death rate fell from 25·4 per thousand living in 1846–50 to 18·8 in 1896–1900, while in Kensington it fell from 20·3 in 1861–5 to 16·3 per thousand living in 1896–1900.[2] In both London as a whole and in Kensington natural increase of the existing population, by excess of births over deaths, was proceeding in ever growing volume,[3] but in Kensington's most rapid period of development, in the 1860's, when the population of the parish rose by over 71 per cent, immigration was of course by far the most important source of growth. Of the 50,000 by which the population of the parish increased during that decade, about four fifths were immigrants,* and only about one fifth is accounted for by excess of births over deaths. In Kensington Town, where the building of the Hammersmith and City Railway opened up large tracts of hitherto relatively remote land, some 30,000 migrants settled in this area during the 1860's; and although the volume of increase throughout the parish was slightly lower in the 1870's (43,000, equivalent to a rise of 35·6 per cent), inward migration, at 26,000 for the whole parish (of which 14,000 came to Kensington Town),* still remained the largest source of growth.[4]

About half of the migrants who came to London between 1851 and 1891 had been born in either Middlesex, Surrey and Kent, or in the adjacent counties within about a hundred miles of the capital. As might be expected, however, the length of the migrant's journey to London was related to the depth of his pocket, distance presenting no difficulty for the rich. Thus in Phillimore Walk, in 1861 wholly working-class occupied, two thirds of all the householders born outside London had travelled less than a hundred miles from their birth-place, whereas in the thirty large mansions of Holland Park which by 1871 had been completed and fully occupied, mainly by merchants and fundholders, only three of the householders had been born in London, and only another six within a hundred miles of the capital. Five of the remainder were Scots by birth, and another five were foreigners.

Constant movement of population was also proceeding inside the metropolitan area from one district to another, and from the illimitably complex pattern of this internal migration, two distinct 'social gradients' (to quote Professor Dyos's phrase) may be discerned, 'one leading upwards and outwards; the other leading downwards, if not inwards'.[5] Kensington was, of course, a much-favoured destination for well-to-do Londoners moving upwards and outwards, as the following half-dozen examples chosen at random from among householders to be mentioned later illustrate. John Egg, a member of the West End family of gunmakers, came to Addison Avenue from Pall Mall in about 1850, while George Penson, a cheesemonger or provision merchant with a growing business in Newgate Street, came to

* No allowance is made here for migration out of the parish, but in Kensington this was probably then relatively small.

Ladbroke Square from either the City or from Southwark at about the same time. R. R. Sadler, a lawyer with offices in Golden Square near Regent Street, moved his home during the 1840's first from Westminster to St. Pancras and then from St. Pancras to Norland Square.[6] The property speculator C. H. Blake came in 1854 to Kensington Park Gardens from St. Marylebone, and a few years later the portrait painter Henry Tanworth Wells came from the same parish to Upper Phillimore Gardens. But not all of Kensington's immigrants were well-to-do. Many of the working men who settled during the 1860's and 1870's in the new streets being laid out on the site of an abandoned brick-field adjoining the Potteries are said to have been displaced by clearances elsewhere, both in such central districts as St. Giles in the Fields, and also by those nearer at hand in Campden Place (now Clanricarde Gardens, Notting Hill Gate) and in Jennings's Buildings in Kensington High Street. In Acklam Road and St. Ervan's Road, close to the Great Western Railway, where small terrace houses were being built in the late 1860's, railway and building workers predominated, and most of them had come there from either St. Marylebone, Paddington or other parts of Kensington—suggesting that even within the metropolitan area the distance covered by working-class migrants was often extremely short.[7]

The growth of population was both a cause of and a response to building development. Unlike population-growth, however, which can only be measured at decennial intervals, the volume of building can, for part of the nineteenth century, be measured annually. The diagram reproduced on page 6 shows the fluctuations which took place between 1820 and 1885 within northern Kensington in the number of buildings erected each year, and between 1856 and 1885 within London as a whole. After 1885 building land was becoming scarce in northern Kensington, and the statistical returns of building become blurred by the inclusion of large blocks of flats.

During the building boom of the early 1820's two of the largest landowners in northern Kensington, the third Lord Holland and J. W. Ladbroke, began to develop their estates, and J. F. Hanson, a speculator who had previously been active at Brighton, started work at Campden Hill Square. All these operations were evidently premature, this part of Kensington being still well outside the urban frontier, and after the financial crash of 1825, which hit them with great severity, no new major enterprises were undertaken until the development of the Norland estate was begun in 1839 by Charles Richardson, a solicitor who had recently become the ground landlord.

Except on the Norland estate the upturn in building activity which seems to have begun in the inner suburbs of London in about 1837 did not reach northern Kensington until the early 1840's. Even then the peak of 1843 was largely the result of Richardson's activity, and his difficulties in attracting both investors and tenants to the Norland estate suggest that demand for houses so far out of London was still extremely limited. But the less remote parts of northern Kensington were beginning to establish themselves within the field of suburban speculation in the mid 1840's, and except in the crisis year of 1847 the upward movement of building which began after 1844 continued until 1852–3.

Much of this activity took place on the Ladbroke estate, where Richard Roy, a solicitor with previous experience of building speculation at Cheltenham, organized a spurt of activity in the Lansdowne Road area in the mid 1840's. In 1850–1 he was joined by Charles Henry Blake, a retired Calcutta merchant, and Dr. Samuel Walker, a clergyman 'of a

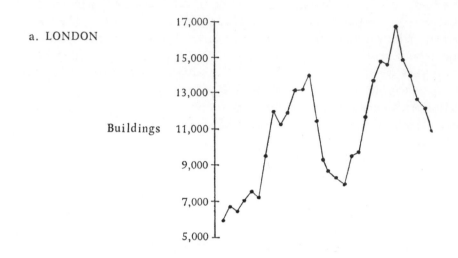

a. LONDON

Buildings

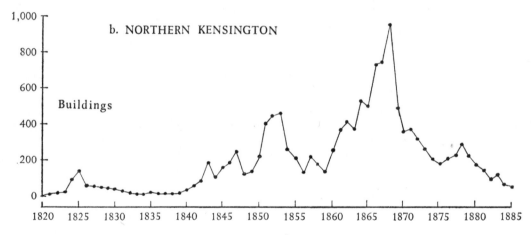

b. NORTHERN KENSINGTON

Buildings

BUILDING FLUCTUATIONS IN LONDON AND NORTHERN KENSINGTON

These graphs show the number of new buildings roofed or 'covered in' during each year in (a) London as a whole, and (b) in the area of Kensington covered by this volume (see page 1). 'Covering in' was the stage in building operations at which the district surveyor could charge a fee and at which building leases were usually granted. The chief sources from which the figures have been compiled are the Middlesex Land Register for 1820–45, the detailed monthly returns of the district surveyors for 1846–55 and 1871–85 (northern Kensington), and the annual summaries provided by the district surveyors based on the fees which they received for 1856–70 (northern Kensington and London) and 1871–85 (London). The annual summaries give the number of new buildings for which fees were paid promptly and the number for which fees were paid 'in arrears', i.e. buildings which had been covered in during previous years. For the purposes of these graphs the total for a particular year has been calculated by adding together the number of buildings for which fees were promptly paid and the number 'in arrears' in the following year.

The detailed district surveyors' returns, which are the most reliable source, are not available before 1845 or for 1856–70, and for London as a whole figures on a comparative scale are not available before 1856. From the nature of these sources the figures cannot be regarded as entirely precise, and they do not distinguish between different types of buildings (most of which in northern Kensington were houses or coach-houses and stables) or between the sizes of buildings.

most amicable disposition', both of whom, abetted by Roy, speculated on a very large scale in the vicinity of Stanley Crescent and Arundel Gardens. With cheap capital readily available it seemed impossible to build too many houses,* but when the Bank rate rose from 2 per cent to 5 per cent in 1853 the principal builder in this district, David Allan Ramsay, became bankrupt, and Blake and Walker were left with scores of empty or half-finished houses on their hands. Blake survived to continue his long and ultimately successful career as a speculator in northern Kensington, but Dr. Walker's fragile empire was totally shattered.

In contrast with the period between the middle of 1848 and the end of 1852, when money in London had never been 'so cheap for so long', the period between the last quarter of 1853 and the beginning of 1858 was one in which credit was scarce and the Bank rate rarely dropped below 5 per cent.[8] In 1857 *The Building News* attributed the depression in the building trades to 'the peculiarity of the finance system which, within the last few years, has run wild, and seeks to make money dear and credit impossible in trading operations'. A correspondent quoted in the same journal explained that 'Persons can now realise 5 to 6 per cent very readily upon loans, or merely by deposits at joint-stock banks, and, therefore, are not willing to be satisfied with 4 or 5 per cent from builders, encumbered with the business of mortgages and other securities.'[9] In northern Kensington there was a substantial fall in the volume of building in 1854–8, and considerable fluctuation from year to year at this lower level.

The rise in building activity which began in northern Kensington in 1859 and eventually reached its highest-ever peak in 1868 formed part of the general rise then taking place throughout the rest of London. But whereas in the metropolis the number of new buildings completed per year doubled between 1859 and 1868, in northern Kensington the number increased over sixfold in the same period, and in 1868 nearly 7 per cent of all new buildings in the metropolitan area were being erected in this part of Kensington. By 1859 the effects of the over-building of the early 1850's were diminishing; empty houses were being occupied for the first time, and half-finished shells were being completed, particularly on and near the Ladbroke estate, where Blake was able, early in 1860, to find reliable new financial backers. With confidence thus restored, the maintenance of the boom in northern Kensington was principally due to the re-opening of the West London Railway to passenger traffic in 1863 and the opening of the Hammersmith and City Railway, which traversed the fields of Notting Dale, in 1864.† In anticipation of these events Charles Chambers, a builder, agreed in 1862 to build 238 houses on the Holland estate near the West London Railway, while in Notting Dale, Blake, who was one of the directors of the Hammersmith and City Railway Company, contracted in the same year to buy all the remaining part of the Portobello estate, then consisting of some 130 acres, where he subsequently organized the building of several hundred houses, many of them being of the small terraced variety.

The sharp downward turn in building after 1868, which took place all over London, may have been partly a delayed reflection of the general loss of confidence engendered by

---

* Something of the heady speculative atmosphere of these years is indicated by the district surveyor's returns for northern Kensington. Of 790 new houses for which notices were given in 1852, 90 were not begun and 195 more were 'suspended', 'abandoned' or were taken over by other builders. In some cases the builder was changed more than once.

† In 1868 the Metropolitan Railway was also extended from Paddington round to South Kensington, but its course was largely through areas already built upon.

the failure of the bill discounting firm of Overend and Gurney in May 1866. The diagram on page 6 suggests that this certainly had some immediate effect in northern Kensington, and a clergyman anxious to build a church in Holland Road, where large numbers of houses were in course of erection, wrote in November 1866 that 'had not the monetary panic . . . taken place, from 300 to 400 more houses would have been erected by this time'. A claim put forward later that the panic of May 1866 had caused negotiations for building on the parkland surrounding Holland House to be abandoned illustrates the probable longer-term effect of the crisis. It seems more likely, however, that after almost a decade of building growth, supply of houses had once again outrun demand—at an auction sale held by Blake in 1870, for instance, the reserve prices for thirteen houses in Ladbroke Grove were not reached—and that capital was being directed from building to more attractive investments, some of them abroad.[10]

In the 1870's the volume of building in northern Kensington fell by over half, reflecting a similar fall in inward migration, and with relatively little building land still available it ceased by 1885 to have any significant correspondence with the general pattern for the rest of London.

Between 1820 and 1885 some 13,000 buildings (most of them houses) were erected in northern Kensington. The monthly returns of the district surveyors show that a very large number of builders engaged in this prodigious operation, but that on average well over half of them built no more than six houses each (and usually less) over any two-year period. Even in the peak years 1852–3,* over a quarter of all the builders working in the area (30 out of 109) erected only one or two houses each. A few of them were firms of some size and metropolitan standing who undertook contract work for specific customers in Kensington, but the vast majority were involved in speculative building. Most of them described themselves as 'builder', and there is no evidence that men trained in the various constituent trades of the building industry (bricklayer, carpenter, glazier, plumber, etc.) joined together in the building of groups of houses, as had often been done in pre-Victorian times. Despite their large numbers, however, the small-scale builders' contribution to the total stock of new houses was comparatively small. In 1852–3, for instance, those builders erecting six or fewer houses each (some 60 per cent of all the builders in northern Kensington) were responsible for only 16 per cent of the new houses begun in those two years.

At the opposite extreme, builders operating on a very large scale were rare in northern Kensington. Even those few who did commit themselves to extensive undertakings usually confined themselves to one locality, and their careers were extremely brief. Both William Reynolds, who began work on 97 houses on the Ladbroke estate in 1845–6, and David Allan Ramsay, who began 72 on the same estate in 1852–3, became bankrupt before they could complete all of them. George Ingersent, who undertook to build 90 houses in the vicinity of Westbourne Grove, also in 1852–3, was in financial difficulty by 1854. Soon afterwards he was building a mere four houses in Palace Gardens Terrace, one of them being Mall Tavern, where he was living in 1856, having evidently exchanged building for the less frenetic trade of licensed victualler.

The mainstay of the building industry in northern Kensington was provided by the builders with establishments of moderate size who built a large number of houses spread

* The monthly returns have not survived for the peak years of the 1860's.

evenly over one or more decades. Among the most successful of these firms was that of the Devon-born brothers, William and Francis Radford, who between 1848 and 1880 built over two hundred houses, mostly large detached villas, around Pembridge Square and in Holland Park. In 1871 they were employing some sixty men. Francis Radford became a prominent local resident, and at his funeral in 1900 there were ten mourning-coaches;[11] his effects were valued at £256,000. Another builder of this class was Jeremiah Little, who was born in Leeds[12] and came to Kensington from St. Marylebone. Between 1848 and 1873 he built some 150 houses in the Campden Hill area, and in 1861 he was employing sixty hands. At the time of his death in 1873 he owned freehold and leasehold property to the net value of £120,000. The career of James Hall, however, indicates the risks involved in larger speculative operations. He came to the Pembridge Villas area from St. Pancras in 1846 and in the course of the next eight years built some sixty substantial houses there. In the uncertain financial climate of the mid 1850's he entered into agreements to build over two hundred houses on the Holland estate, and by 1860, despite the general upturn in building, he was in difficulties which were acknowledged to 'have arisen from the too great extent of his undertakings'. In 1864 he was declared bankrupt.

Builders of this medium class often took several acres of land under agreement with a ground landlord, or even purchased land themselves. Sometimes they built only a proportion of the houses erected on the land, thus providing opportunity for other builders including the very small firms. William Chadwick, who also undertook large-scale contract work, became involved in speculation on the Ladbroke estate through not being paid for work done at the Hippodrome racecourse there. In 1840 he entered into an agreement to build on seven acres of the estate, erected a number of houses himself and later used other builders to whom he granted sub-leases. Jeremiah Little was partner in an agreement to build on most of Stephen Pitt's land in 1844, but he does not appear to have become directly involved in building operations until four years later. In the later years of his career he provided opportunities for his children by purchasing land on which they could build. Three of his sons, Henry, William and Alfred, followed him into the building trade and made sizeable contributions to the development of Victorian Campden Hill. In 1860 G. F. J. Tippett purchased seventeen acres in the vicinity of Powis Square and over the next fifteen years 250 houses were built on his land, some by Tippett himself, but the majority by other builders to whom he granted building leases. He also built on a large scale in Paddington, but this particular attempt to combine the roles of landowner, developer, builder, and even probably architect, was not successful, for in 1883 he was declared bankrupt with liabilities of £860,000.

The capital needed for the building of northern Kensington was supplied from a wide variety of sources. In order to get development under way, or to maintain its momentum, ground landlords such as William Phillimore or Felix Ladbroke often lent money to builders to whom they had previously granted building leases, and in 1853–4 Dr. Walker advanced £66,000 in this way. In order to make such loans, the ground landlords had sometimes had to borrow themselves; in 1826, for instance, Lord Holland had borrowed £6,000 from Coutts' Bank for the use of the solicitor who acted as the steward of his estate, while Dr. Walker was heavily indebted to the London and Westminster Bank. Private banks such as Coutts', however, only rarely lent money for use in building development, and among the joint-stock banks the London and Westminster on the Ladbroke estate and the Union Bank of London on the Holland estate were the most important. In 1859 John Beattie, the manager of the Temple Bar branch of the latter, lent £10,000 (presumably on behalf of the bank) to the builder James Hall on the security of thirty houses on the Holland estate, and after Hall's bankruptcy Beattie became one of the developers of a large part of the estate east of Holland Road.

Between the 1840's and the 1870's insurance companies made a small number of large loans in connexion with the development of northern Kensington. In 1847 the ground landlord Felix Ladbroke borrowed £25,000 from the Sun Fire Office, which he in turn evidently lent to his building lessees, but insurance company loans were more usually made direct to builders of substance, or supposed substance. William Reynolds, for instance, borrowed from the Sovereign Life Assurance Company in 1846 for his speculation in the vicinity of Lansdowne Road, while Thomas Goodwin and William White had £34,450 from the Hand-in-Hand Insurance Society in 1872–4 for building in Linden Gardens and Clanricarde Gardens. G. F. J. Tippett's large-scale building in both the vicinity of Powis Square and in Paddington in the 1860's was largely financed by four insurance companies —the County Fire Office, the Sun, the London Assurance Corporation, and ultimately the Law Life Assurance Society, to which in 1870 he owed over £125,000. Most loans by insurance companies were at 5 per cent interest for five to seven years, but the term was sometimes extended.

The role of the building societies and land societies is more difficult to determine, their individual life-cycles being often comparatively brief in the mid nineteenth century. Their activities in northern Kensington were confined to areas where land and property values were comparatively low. Between 1847 and 1851 five building societies were engaged in the northern part of the Norland estate, and in the 1860's and 1870's two land societies were developing extensive properties on the Portobello estate.

Capital was also provided by commercial men whose business lay elsewhere in London (often in the City), and for whom suburban building speculation was only an incidental activity. Thus, to cite a few examples, a woollen-draper of Covent Garden had an interest in Peel Street in the 1820's, a firm of hat manufacturers of Newgate Street in Campden Hill Square in the 1830's, a poultry salesman of Leadenhall Market in Ladbroke Gardens in the 1850's, and a cheesemonger of Newgate Street in the Ladbroke estate from the 1840's until his death in 1879; and there were numerous other investors who were vaguely described as 'merchant' of the City. Men of this class usually only lent money on security and took little or no part in the day-to-day hurly-burly of building development themselves. The career of Jacob Connop, a bill broker with extensive commitments on the London money market who in 1840 undertook the development of some fifty-eight acres of the Ladbroke estate, with dire results for himself and others, provides a rare exception. Direct dealings between the short-term money market and suburban speculators were, however, comparatively rare, the most notable example being a six-months' loan at an unrecorded rate of interest from the bill dealers Samuel Gurney and James Alexander in association with Sir Moses Montefiore and Lionel Nathan de Rothschild to the builder William Reynolds during the crisis of 1846–7—a costly device which quickly precipitated Reynolds's bankruptcy. Land agents and auctioneers also occasionally made short-term loans to speculators, but they were evidently only resorted to when immediate financial collapse could not otherwise be avoided.

By far the most important channel for capital was, however, provided by the lawyers. In the early nineteenth century the attorneys had been one of the first of the ancient professions to reform themselves, and in the middle of the century, when much of northern Kensington was being developed, they still performed many of the functions which have since been taken over by the accountants, bank managers and building societies. Land owners, speculators and builders in need of borrowed money most commonly turned to their attorneys who, when the field of choice for investment offered by the stock market was still comparatively restricted, often had other clients with money to lend, or could tap other sources of capital, particularly at those times when gilt-edged securities offered low returns. The volumes of the Middlesex Land Registry record thousands of mortgages arranged by attorneys, a single example of which must suffice, that of the Radfords, whose building in the Pembridge Square area has already been mentioned. Their work there in the 1850's and 1860's was financed by a long series of private mortgages arranged by Stephen Garrard, a lawyer who was one of the former ground landlord's executors, and who was able to obtain money from such varied sources as a Member of Parliament, a barrister, a farmer from Southall, a Warwickshire clergyman, a publisher, a Brentford confectioner, and a hatter in St. James's Street.

With builders thus relying so greatly on lawyers for capital, the lawyers often themselves became involved in the business of building speculation. One such was Robert Furniss Long, who applied in 1851 to the London Assurance Corporation for a loan and was able to offer twenty-nine houses in St. Ann's Road as security. At that time he owned about 150 finished or unfinished houses, and in his application he stated that 'Several of my Clients are Builders to whom I lend a temporary assistance until the houses are completed and ready for sale or mortgage'. When they mortgaged through him they paid interest at 5 per cent, and 'effect a Policy on their lives which enables them to have more time to sell the property without submitting to a sacrifice by a forced sale'.[13] A 'rich lawyer' was, in fact, considered to be the ideal associate for a builder to have.[14]

In addition to the arrangement of mortgages, lawyers also often acted for ground landlords as the managers of estates—the Holland, Ladbroke and Jenkins estates are all cases in point. In each of these three examples the lawyer in question himself took leases of part of the estate in due course, and thus became personally involved in the fortunes of the speculation. Lawyers also became personally involved through the misfortunes of a client, and the opportunities for personal gain sometimes presented thereby. In 1840, for instance, John Duncan acquired a short-term interest, already heavily encumbered, in part of the Ladbroke estate after the failure of the racecourse there, which had been promoted by one of his clients. It was, however, much easier to enter the field of suburban speculation than to leave it without loss, and from Duncan's ill-judged opportunism stemmed the life-long involvement on the Ladbroke estate of his partner, Richard Roy. At first Roy was only Duncan's guarantor, but after the latter's bankruptcy he successfully took over the management of Duncan's property on behalf of a bevy of creditors, and ultimately speculated on his own account on other parts of the Ladbroke estate. Occasionally a lawyer even took on the role of ground landlord, as in the previously mentioned case of Charles Richardson, who in 1839 bought the Norland estate and subsequently organized its development under his own personal auspices.

We may now examine briefly such evidence as exists relating to the profits and losses to be made in the business of suburban development. The table below shows that in 1820, on the eve of the first ripple of building in northern Kensington, over two thirds of all the land in the area belonged to four owners, and 94 per cent of it to fifteen owners. High concentration of land-ownership in a few hands was not unusual at this time in the suburbs of London, but this area presents an unusually extreme example of it. All four of the largest proprietors had inherited their estates and so were not burdened by any recent large capital

THE STRUCTURE OF LAND OWNERSHIP IN NORTHERN KENSINGTON, 1820*

acreages based on T. Starling's map of 1822

Size of estates	Number of landowners	Land holdings		Cumulative total of estates as % of acreage of area
		Acreage	% of area	
Over 200 acres	3	661	53·6	53·6
151–200 ,,	1	177	14·4	68·0
101–150 ,,	none			
51–100 ,,	3	163	13·3	81·3
31–50 ,,	1	50	4·1	85·4
11–30 ,,	7	112	9·1	94·5
6–10 ,,	2	16	1·3	95·8
1–5 ,,	8	24	1·9	97·7
remainder†	not known	28	2·3	100

* This table applies only to the part of the ancient parish north of Kensington High Street.

† This consisted of copyhold lands, manorial waste and small freehold estates of less than an acre located in or near to the ancient centres of settlement and mostly already built over.

outlay. They therefore started with great advantages, and might be expected in the long run to have made considerable profit from their good fortune. The two who started to develop in the 1820's, however, failed to do so. These were the third Lord Holland, the extravagance of whose successors led by 1874 to the disposal of the estate, and James Weller Ladbroke, whose heir, Felix Ladbroke, seems to have died in comparatively reduced circumstances in 1869 after selling the greater part of his property. The other two principal proprietors, by contrast, made no attempt to develop their estates until the 1850's and even then were content to wait until the boom years of the 1860's for large-scale building to begin. These were Colonel Matthew Chitty Downes St. Quintin and his son, both absentees living in Yorkshire, whose Kensington property, developed solely by means of long leases, yielded an annual rental of £3,510 in 1885, and the two Misses Talbot, who in 1862 sold the 130 acres of their Portobello estate outright for £107,750.

This seems to suggest that two of the most important ingredients required for success were patience and the ability to choose the right moment to act, whether by granting leases or by straightforward sale. The Phillimores seem to have realized this, for after the slow progress of their first attempts at development virtually no more building took place on their estate for some thirty years after 1825, although Charles Phillimore could (it may be presumed) have found willing builders at least during the 1840's; and when in 1855 he did agree to lease twenty-one acres, his patience was rewarded by a ground rent of £66 per acre—three times as great as that previously obtained by William Phillimore for adjacent land in 1808.

Land values throughout northern Kensington during the first half of the nineteenth century were, indeed, still relatively low. In the 1830's the Great Western Railway paid £112 per acre[15] and the General Cemetery Company £174 per acre, both for land at Kensal Green. In less remote areas the price of freehold ground usually varied in the first half of the century between about £250 and about £400 per acre. The higher prices which were occasionally paid can generally be explained by special circumstances. In 1809–10 the West Middlesex Water Works Company, for instance, paid £450 per acre for a very eligible site on the summit of Campden Hill, and during the hectic building boom of the early 1820's a piece of land near Kensington Church Street was sold twice in the same year, first for £560 and then for £750 per acre. In order to extend the burial ground of St. Mary Abbots Church the Kensington Vestry had in 1814 to pay no less than £2,100 for about one acre of ground.

Agricultural rents seem to have yielded about £4 or £5 per acre, but when a speculator took land on lease for building he generally paid between £18 and £30 per acre. This represented a useful improvement for the ground landlord, but even so rents of this order were still low, for Thomas Cubitt was generally paying around £50 per acre in the 1820's and 1830's for land in Pimlico.[16] As late as 1846 James Weller Ladbroke leased nine acres of his best land (now the site of Kensington Park Gardens) for only £30 per acre, and other parts at still lower rents—a fact which no doubt made possible the exceptionally lavish use of land in the layout of this estate.

Despite the inducement offered by such low prices and rents, the progress of building speculation in northern Kensington in the first half of the century was in general unsteady, and even when it was rapid (as on the Norland estate, where five hundred houses were built in the 1840's, or on William Reynolds's part of the Ladbroke estate), it was not financially successful for the developer. Except in the vicinity of Kensington Church Street, where Stephen Pitt was able to obtain a ground rent of £63 per acre in 1844, the area was still too far out to command full and continuous support from investors; the supply of capital was erratic, and there were many financial failures.

In the second half of the century most of northern Kensington was overrun by the advancing urban frontier, and after the uncertain period in the 'no man's land' of the 1850's, increased confidence produced a less intermittent supply of capital—the third essential ingredient of successful speculation—and substantial fortunes were no doubt made.

On the Ladbroke estate during the brief boom of the early 1850's the price of land fluctuated violently, part of one piece of ground sold in 1852 (with the benefit of a number of building leases) for £1,333 per acre being re-sold in the slump of 1856 for only £795 per acre. The general price level was, however, far above that of earlier years, and the price of £829 per acre which C. H. Blake paid for the 130-acre Portobello estate in 1862 was by that time probably low. Only three years later, when the Hammersmith and City Railway had been opened, he was considering the sale of part of this property for £1,350 per acre, and in 1868 he actually did sell about one sixth of it for £1,816 per acre, followed in the course of the next four years by several other sales at prices ranging between £1,400 and £1,800 per acre. Within little more than twenty years land-prices had, in fact, increased four- or five-fold, and on leasehold land elsewhere in northern Kensington there were, of course, corresponding rises. In 1854 the vicar of Kensington secured a ground rent of £60 per acre from part of the glebe land around Palace Gardens Terrace, but in 1877 a rent of £425 for less than a single acre in the adjoining Vicarage Gate was offered; and at an auction in 1869 £520 per acre was bid for the site of Clanricarde Gardens.

During the boom years leading up to the peak of building in northern Kensington in 1868, when new houses could not be built fast enough to satisfy demand, the business of development evidently yielded a good return for landowners, speculators and builders alike. In marked contrast with previous decades, there are hardly any examples of failure or bankruptcy, even among the builders,* many of whom, particularly on the Portobello and St. Quintin estates, moved on steadily over a period of years from one street to another, providing steady work for the lawyers and safe investments at $4\frac{1}{2}$ or 5 per cent for the lawyers' clients.

It would, however, be very misleading to imply that a profit could be made from suburban speculation as quickly and easily as a loss, and the one well-documented example known in northern Kensington suggests that this was far from being the case. This was C. H. Blake, who, as has already been mentioned, began to speculate actively on the Ladbroke estate in 1850. After ten years, during which he had been compelled to mortgage his entire estate, including even his furniture and plate, his excess of income over outgoings amounted to only about one half of one per cent of his total investment; and at the time of his death in 1872, after twenty-two years' incessant worry and work, this figure had only grown to about $3\frac{1}{4}$ per cent. A few years later, when all the outstanding charges had been paid off, the average annual return mounted to $6\frac{1}{2}$ per cent and his children became the chief beneficiaries of his arduous career as building speculator. If Blake's history has any wider application, it shows that the profits of suburban development were not quickly or easily made, and not unduly great.

By the mid 1880's building development in northern Kensington had been largely completed. Except in the north-western extremity, where a few fields still remained, all the open country shown on Starling's map of 1822 (Plate 1) had been covered with streets, crescents, squares and thousands of houses. This tremendous tide of building also included by 1900 sixteen Anglican churches and a large new parish church. The Roman Catholics had built six convents and two parish churches, most of them at the instigation of Dr. Henry Manning, who prior to his elevation to the Archbishopric of Westminster in 1865 had been superior of the Oblates of St. Charles and had concentrated the energetic missionary efforts of this small religious order upon this district. There were also some fifteen nonconformist chapels, most of them either Congregationalist or Baptist, one of the largest cemeteries in London, and numerous schools of all denominations.

Until the 1850's this whole complex process of building in Kensington had proceeded with a minimum of public control. The parish Vestry, which was of the open variety, was hardly concerned in the business of estate development, and the Kensington Improvement

---

* The case of James Hall, previously mentioned as bankrupt in 1864, provides an exception but this was due to the excessive commitments which he had undertaken in the 1850's.

Commissioners, established by an Act of 1851 for the paving, repairing, lighting and cleansing of the highways,[17] were soon superseded under the terms of the Metropolis Management Act of 1855. Prior to the establishment of the Office of Metropolitan Buildings in 1844 there was no public supervision of building in Kensington, for the London Building Acts had hitherto not applied there. Until 1847 the administration of sewers had been the responsibility of the Westminster Commissioners of Sewers, but as most of northern Kensington was well drained by natural watercourses, no great harm had come from their leisurely management except in the Potteries. In this stagnant low-lying area the almost complete absence of public supervision resulted in the growth of one of the worst slums in London and the creation of social problems which led in recent years, after a century of incessant effort, to large-scale rebuilding. Between 1847 and 1855 the Metropolitan Commissioners of Sewers had to cope *inter alia* with the rapidly mounting volume of building in northern Kensington, but with the more immediate problems of successive visitations of cholera also on their hands little progress was made until the reorganization of the vestries and the establishment of the Metropolitan Board of Works in 1855. The Board took over the regulation of buildings and the construction of main sewers, while the vestries managed the building and maintenance of local sewers and the regulation of nuisances. The foundations of a rational system of public administration were, in fact, only laid in the middle of the most rapid period of building development in northern Kensington (*c.* 1840–*c.* 1870), and a large part of the responsibility for this process was therefore still in the private hands of landowners and speculators.

On most of the larger estates the ground landlord employed an architect or surveyor to provide a layout plan, and in some cases these were at first men of some reputation—William Porden on the Phillimore estate, Robert Cantwell on the Norland estate, or Thomas Allason on the Ladbroke and Pitt estates, for instance. But their plans were often modified to suit the exigencies of changing circumstances, their connexion with a particular estate was sometimes very brief, and their part in the business of estate development was relatively limited. With the notable exception of Thomas Allom, who provided designs for all the houses on C. H. Blake's property in the vicinity of Kensington Park Gardens, few houses seem to have been designed by the estate architects or surveyors, although the speculator-builder often had to obtain their approval for his own designs. Whatever their precise role may have been, it does, however, appear to have been declining in its importance, the surveyors of the 1860's and 1870's, such as J. C. Hukins on the Portobello estate, being in general men of markedly less substance than their predecessors of the previous generation. If any single group can be said to have been the principal progenitors of nineteenth-century northern Kensington, the ubiquitous and ever-busy lawyers have a far stronger claim than the architects or surveyors; and it is an odd quirk of fortune that their activities should have been so quickly and totally forgotten.

After the substantial completion of building development in northern Kensington in the mid 1880's, fresh building did not cease, for redevelopment had already begun. On the Pitt estate on Campden Hill, in Linden Grove (now Gardens) and in Campden Place (now Clanricarde Gardens), for example, the building of the Metropolitan Railway had already resulted directly or indirectly in partial or complete rebuilding in the 1860's and 1870's, while large houses with correspondingly large gardens, which had been surrounded by the advancing urban tide, were being demolished in the 1880's and 1890's for the building of large tall terrace houses or blocks of flats. Most of this early redevelopment was in the area between Kensington High Street and Holland Park Avenue, an early example of it, in the 1870's, being on the site of General Charles Richard Fox's house at the north end of Addison Road. The demolition of Elm Lodge and the building of nineteen tall terrace houses on its site, now called Airlie Gardens, in 1881–3, the erection of flats and houses in the grounds of Campden House in 1894–1900, and the commencement of the building of the flats known as Oakwood Court in Addison Road in 1899, all provide cases in point. Redevelopment is, indeed, a permanent feature of the urban scene, and in more recent years King's College for Women (now Queen Elizabeth College) and Holland Park School as well as more luxury flats have been built in the originally spacious surroundings of the Campden Hill area, while in the Potteries, Notting Dale and Kensal Green whole streets of cheap outworn terrace houses have been razed for the building of Council flats.

The inhabitants of Victorian northern Kensington included all ranks of society, ranging from the dukes on Campden Hill (sometimes called 'the Dukeries') and the great men of commerce in Kensington Palace Gardens ('Millionaires' Row') down to the pig-keepers of the Potteries and the laundresses of Kensal Green. The great majority of them belonged, however, to the middle classes, whose way of life in the Ladbroke locality of northern Kensington could provide Charles Marriott, writing in 1910, with 'a stronger impression of social stability than any other part of London I know . . . Ladbroke upholds the proper dignity of the English middle classes'.[18] Half-a-dozen samples of social and occupational structure, drawn chiefly from middle-class districts, are contained in later chapters. One general point may, however, be made here—namely, that the existence of a predominantly middle-class suburb required many local services for its maintenance, and that these needs created a substantial amount of employment, much of it unskilled or semi-skilled, within the area from a comparatively early date. By far the largest source of such local employment was, of course, domestic service, which in London as a whole in 1851, provided work for about one in every eleven of the entire population. In Kensington Registration District more than one in every six of all women aged over twenty years were servants, the vast majority of whom 'lived in'. Next in importance, in the early years of large-scale development, came building, and there was also a substantial amount of brickmaking, chiefly to the south of Notting Hill Gate and around the Potteries. By 1876, however, the commercial section of the local directory contained over 2,500 entries for northern Kensington, made up of no less than 220 different trades.[19]* The public houses and the shops for the sale of

* The most common trades were:

Bootmaker	153	Dressmaker	57	Gas fitter	29
Publican	121	Tobacconist	55	Cornmerchant	29
Greengrocer	100	Confectioner	49	China and glass dealer	28
Grocer	93	Oilman	46	Hairdresser	28
Builder	92	Decorator	45	Ironmonger	28
Tailor	84	Chemist	43	Fruiterer	27
Baker	76	Cheesemonger	42	Plumber	27
Butcher	75	Stationer	42	Dyer	24
'General shop' keeper	74	Fishmonger	37	Cab proprietor	23
Draper	69	Carpenter	34	Carver and gilder	21
Dairyman	66	Wardrobe dealer	32	Coal merchant	21
Laundryman or		Upholsterer	29	Sweep	20
laundress	65	Milliner	29	Watchmaker	20

food, clothing and household goods, which formed the largest groups, were distributed throughout the whole area, but there were also a number of other trades, such as those of launderer, cowkeeper, cab proprietor and job master, which were heavily concentrated in the poorer areas, chiefly around Golborne Road and (particularly in the case of the launderers) Bramley Road and Kensal Green. The Portobello and Bramley Road districts were both adjacent to the Hammersmith and City Railway, opened in 1864, but a count taken in 1882 showed that only about 560 workmen's return tickets (at 4d. each to the City) were issued daily at all stations along the line. In winter there was only one morning workmen's train, which left Hammersmith at 5.43 a.m., and many of the travellers on it lived in Hammersmith or Paddington, as well as in Kensington.[20] It is therefore evident that daily working-class travel by rail out of northern Kensington to jobs elsewhere was still small in scale, and that very large numbers of the workmen resident in the area lived within walking distance of their jobs. These daily journeys on foot no doubt took many workmen far outside Kensington (as the establishment of no less than 153 bootmakers within the area by 1876 perhaps implies), while other labourers and artisans were employed locally in the more exotic manufacturing industries not dependent only on local demand (e.g. the makers of pianos, umbrellas, hair, plumes, bird-cages and sound-boards for harmoniums, etc.). After reasonable allowance has been made for these various forms of employment, it nevertheless appears that a substantial residuum of local labour was engaged in providing the day-to-day services (chiefly in the fields of food, drink, clothing, household equipment, laundering, domestic service, jobbing building and transport) required for the maintenance of the middle-class residents who formed the majority of the population of northern Kensington. Pockets of cheap labour, such as those to be found in Kensal Green, Notting Hill Gate or the vicinity of the Potteries, were in fact a necessary adjunct of a predominantly middle-class Victorian suburb, and had a vital function to perform within it.

The Fabric

Aerial views of northern Kensington show the pattern of nineteenth-century estates laid out over moderately hilly terrain. The distinctive layouts of some of the larger estates stand out prominently, as do the lines of the two ancient roads from London and the recently completed motorway of the Western Avenue Extension. The parklands of Kensington Gardens and Holland Park are matched by Kensal Green Cemetery and the communal gardens of the squares, more particularly those of the Ladbroke estate with the seven acres of Ladbroke Square itself and the concentric bands of the gardens around St. John's Church—a total of fifteen large gardens on the one estate. The churches take their place amongst the estates which they were built to serve, and St. Mary Abbots marks the old village centre in Kensington High Street, from which Kensington Church Street pursues its twisting northward course to Notting Hill Gate. The great mansions of Kensington Palace Gardens and Palace Green stand clearly defined in their own grounds along the edge of Kensington Gardens close to the Palace. In the extreme north are the landmarks of the gasworks at Kensal Green and the complex of St. Charles Hospital with its central tower, whilst in the area to the south Campden Hill was until recently dominated by the stand-pipe tower of the former Grand Junction Water Works (demolished in 1970).

Other prominent buildings include those of Queen Elizabeth College, Holland Park School, the borough library and a number of substantial blocks of flats built at various times over the last eighty years, but it is the Victorian family houses, ranged in their thousands along the streets of the estates, which provide the major architectural interest of the locality.

The development of the characteristic form of London house from the end of the Georgian period through to the last quarter of the nineteenth century is particularly well demonstrated in northern Kensington. Beginning with the typical terraced dwelling of three to five storeys above a basement, brick faced and dryly reticent in the manner evolved on the estates of Bloomsbury and St. Marylebone, the Kensington house became fully stuccoed and more architecturally ambitious as the nineteenth century advanced, with the terraced layout giving way to individual or paired villas in garden settings, particularly in those areas further from the centre of London where comparatively low land values permitted this less intensive use of sites.

The basic late Georgian Kensington house, such as that built along Kensington High Street on William Phillimore's land between 1788 and 1812, follows directly upon metropolitan precedent and makes no concession to its rural situation beyond the insertion of a small front garden between pavement and basement area. In the elevational view of the High Street in 1811 reproduced on Plate 44 the house fronts rise above low garden walls with small shrubs behind them, and through the breaks between the terraces pastoral views of Campden Hill may be seen.

The design of such houses varied only within the narrowest limits. The main structure can be represented as a stock-brick 'box', covered with a roof of Welsh slates either in the form of a mansard with dormers or concealed behind a neat brick parapet. The internal construction of all but the larger houses was timber framed, not only in the joisted floors which spanned between back and front walls, but also in the internal studded partitions from the ground floor upwards. The need to provide support for a stone wall-hung stair, or additional rigidity in a house of unusual size might, however, call for the sparing use of brick walls internally. Apart from this, brick internal partitions were normally restricted to the basement.

The average sized house was some twenty feet wide and thirty feet deep, with three or four storeys above a basement (Plate 46a). Internally it was organized according to a fixed formula determined and developed during the eighteenth century. The basement contained the kitchen, scullery and pantries, and ample storage for beer and wine was provided, usually in the centre of the house between the back and front basement rooms. The kitchen premises were serviced through a doorway into the front area, which was stone paved and contained stone steps leading up to the small front garden or to a gate in the iron railings along the pavement. The basement doorway was normally situated under the stone bridge which spanned the area at street level to give access to the front door, and the service and social entrances to the front of the house were thus quite separate. Circular iron plates let into the pavement allowed the delivery of coal to be made directly from the merchant's cart into brick-lined vaults which communicated with the area. The low-pressure water supply commonly served a lead storage tank at kitchen level. The placing of the kitchen at this level kept the principal rooms well away from any rising damp in the brick walls. Floors were usually of stone in the basement passages, sculleries and stores, but frequently of suspended timber construction in the kitchens despite the vulnerability of wood to fungus attack—a danger which was also pronounced in the matchboarded dados covering the lower parts of much of the basement walls.

The ground storey contained the dining-room, at the side of a narrow entrance hall, and behind it a smaller parlour or morning-room. The dining-room might be a little deeper than the front rooms on the upper floors and was sometimes finished with a sideboard recess at its inner end. The rear parlour was usually narrower than the dining-room in order to accommodate the extra width of the stairs at the end of the hall.

On the first floor the principal living-room or drawing-room occupied the whole front of the house, its two or three windows usually extending down to the floor and frequently furnished with casements opening on to a balcony or series of balconettes. It became common to unite this room with the smaller room behind it through wide folding doors so as to make one large room for entertaining. The stairs might be in wood or stone according to the ambitions of the builder or speculator, or in stone with cast-iron balustrades to first-floor level, and in wood above.

The bedroom floors were usually similar in plan to the first floor but were sometimes subdivided into smaller rooms, particularly on the top floor. In larger houses the stair to the top floor might take the form of a small accommodation stair outside the main stair-well, and in such cases it was normally of timber construction. The owner's bedroom would usually be on the second floor, with provision for children's rooms and servants' rooms on this or higher floors in accordance with the scale of the house.

The windows, except for casements on to first-floor balconies, were all of the double-hung sash variety, with their cased frames and counter-weights recessed behind the brick-work so as to be invisible when viewed from outside. Windows up to the first floor were furnished internally with panelled shutters which folded back into cased reveals and could be secured across the opening with an iron bar.

The house front was the simplest natural expression of this practical scheme. Generally the brickwork was of London yellow stocks laid in Flemish bond. Stucco was for the most part only sparingly used until the second quarter of the nineteenth century, although the lower part of the house façade up to the string marking the first-floor level might be stuccoed, sometimes with channelling to simulate stone-coursing—a practice still prevalent in the 1830's, as for instance at Nos. 9–11 Holland Street (Plate 38a). Where face brick-work was employed it was customary to apply a stucco rendering to the reveal of the window openings, whilst the heads of all rectangular openings were spanned by flat arches of finely gauged brick applied as a facing with a timber bressumer or lintel behind (Plate 42c, d). The balcony at first-floor level (where it occurred) was usually formed in stone with a cast-iron front in one of the manufacturers' standard patterns. The cornices and other horizontal members were commonly reduced to mere stone or stucco strings but the façades almost always adhered to a Palladian scheme of proportions in which the ground storey represented the base upon which a giant order of architecture might be raised to embrace the first and second storeys so as to support an entablature above the heads of the second-floor windows. This order was seldom present, but even in the most simple sorts of houses it is implied, its ghost regulating the shape and proportion of the house front. The back of the house could be, and commonly was, severely utilitarian. The placing of windows on the stair landings and sometimes small closet projections serving these landings made architectural regularity difficult to achieve.

The house building of the first three decades of the nineteenth century was characterized by a sparse refinement which made the ideal profiles of mouldings as slender as practicable and reduced projections to the minimum. Front doors were placed within round-headed arches without hoods and no more modelling was allowed in the façade than an occasional recession of half a brick to form a round-headed relieving arch or rectangular panel over the heads of the first-floor windows (Plate 38c). Architectural refinement dictated that rainwater pipes should be confined to the rear walls wherever possible, and the gutter behind the front parapet was frequently discharged into a lead-lined trough passing through to the back of the building, an expedient which was also employed to drain the centre valley of M-section roofs.

Gradually, however, the progress of taste led away from the self-effacing restraint of this standard house. Wider use of stucco, following the example of Nash's work in Regent's Park and Basevi's designs for Belgrave Square, made ambitious architectural display economically possible, and face brickwork became less common. An article on Roman cements in *The Architectural Magazine* in 1834 commented that 'In consequence of the discovery of cements of this kind, we are now enabled to erect buildings of brick, coated over with this material, which are as handsome as those of stone, and much stronger and more durable [*sic*] . . . By the aid of cement we are also enabled to display every kind of architectural form and ornament, in many cases at a fifth of the expense that similar ornaments would cost if formed either of moulded bricks or of stone.' Where brickwork was exposed after 1840 it was usually embellished with moulded stucco dressings in window architraves and cornices (Plates 40c, 41e), whilst from the later 1850's the yellow stock brick was largely abandoned in house-front work in favour of smooth gault bricks (white or grey Suffolk gaults). The effect either way was to produce a building of a more 'finished' and highly wrought appearance (Plate 60d).

The emergence of stucco as a material which made display of this kind possible went hand in hand with an increasingly felt need for enrichment, and these trends, occurring just at the time of the great domestic expansion of northern Kensington, gave the area a stuccoed homogeneity within which we can still nevertheless distinguish certain clearly defined architectural trends.

Firstly the standard Georgian terrace house previously described could be given a new stucco disguise. It had been so well suited to its use and was so adaptable to varying family and economic circumstances that it remained throughout the greater part of Kensington's development the orthodox type for the middle-size house. In the 1840's it is to be found with stucco dressings in Ladbroke Square (Plate 61e), and in full stucco dress in Royal Crescent (Plate 72a, b) and Norland Square (Plate 71b), while in the 1850's it became grander in Kensington Park Gardens and Stanley Gardens (Plate 64), where it appeared in extended compositions against a background of extensive communal gardens.

At the same time a desire to create more picturesque forms than the unbroken terrace of standard houses allowed had already begun to find expression in a number of ways. The example of Nash's layout in Regent's Park (1811 onwards) in particular had presented a new ideal for London developers. Its villas in landscaped settings and informal groups, the great terraces with their emphasis on variety and articulation, the circus plan for estate roads and the relationship between buildings and planting, all these made a deep impression on those concerned with the layout of lesser estates. In northern Kensington proposals for a radial layout made an early appearance in the planning of the Ladbroke estate and influenced the final layout of the crescents around Notting Hill (Plates 52, 54–5, 57). On the same estate it is also possible to detect the influence of J. B. Papworth and his work at Cheltenham. James Thomson, one of the designers responsible for the Ladbroke layout, had been a pupil of Papworth and had also worked with Nash in Regent's Park. The semi-detached villa appears in large numbers and in various guises, sometimes bearing a close resemblance to Cheltenham examples (Plates 59, 63). Elsewhere the individual villa occurs in such outer streets as Addison Road and Holland Villas Road (Plate 50a, b), where intensive building was not favoured, and in the special circumstances of the Crown Estate in Kensington Palace Gardens, where the houses are of great size and ambitious treatment. The demand for detachment became, indeed, so strong that in the case of the rows of big detached villas in Pembridge Square and Holland Park (Plates 51d, 69), and even in parts of Oxford and Cambridge Gardens (fig. 79), the spaces between the houses are so narrow that the rows are almost terraces, but the architectural expression is nevertheless that of individual houses.

Where the economics of development did not permit the more extravagant use of land which the semi-detached or detached house required if it was to make its proper picturesque effect, it was still possible to employ devices which would break up the terrace into quasi-independent units and reduce the monolithic appearance of the traditional terrace. Since the latter part of the eighteenth century London designers such as Michael Searles (in his Paragon at Blackheath and elsewhere in South London) had experimented with paired houses connected by lower wings. These wings usually contained the entrances and might be recessed so that the main blocks appeared to be independent when viewed in sharp perspective. In the 1840's this form was employed on the Norland estate in Addison Avenue and St. James's Gardens (Plate 71a, c, d), while on the Holland estate in Addison Road rows in pinnacled Gothic and pedimented classical dress stand side by side (fig. 16).

These various departures from the old standardized terrace plan, whether in the form of individual or paired villas or in the 'articulated' terraces, involved wider frontages and were more extravagant in the use of land. Providing more accommodation on each floor, the houses were lower, and at the same time the excavation of the basements became shallower, giving more light to the kitchen and a greater elevation above pavement level to the ground floor (Plate 68a, b). The principal rooms were now frequently placed on this more imposing ground floor with only the bedrooms above. The old Palladian scheme of a giant order standing upon the ground-storey base was necessarily abandoned in such houses, although it was also being superseded in some of the taller houses for reasons of fashion. Superimposed orders became more common in the 1850's and 1860's in treatments providing that quality of overall enrichment which was becoming admired— Stanley Gardens (Plate 66c, d), Ladbroke Gardens (Plate 65a) and Pembridge Square (Plate 69), for instance—whilst some of the more distinguished designs looked towards the astylar Italianate of Barry's club-houses (Plate 94a). In other cases the orders were so freely treated as to be scarcely recognizable, as in the pilaster strips of many of W. J. Drew's houses on the Ladbroke estate (Plate 62).

The stucco Gothic of the houses in Addison Road (fig. 16) is one of the rare exceptions where this style is employed, although Gothic also appears at Nos. 6–12 (even) Phillimore Place (Plate 48a) and, in a red-brick Elizabethan form with diapered brickwork and shaped gables, in the remarkable ranges of villas along St. Ann's Villas (Plate 72d, e). But the overriding character of the stuccoed houses built in the two middle quarters of the nineteenth century is classical-Italianate, expressed in a variety of manners. Designs may be highly sophisticated, as in the best of the villas in Kensington Palace Gardens (Plates 94–5, 98, 106); picturesque as in Thomas Allom's work for C. H. Blake in Stanley Gardens and Kensington Park Gardens (Plates 64–6); or debased and perfunctory as in some of the later developments and on the more remote and less desirable sites (Plates 67a–d, f, 74a–e).

Towards the middle of the century constructional standards became more robust and there was a more prodigal use of building materials. Walls became heavier, structural timbers more massive, joinery sections and mouldings more lavish in windows and doors, and stone stairs became more common. Cast-iron balustrades replaced wooden ones and marble chimneypieces were more ornate. Damp-proof courses made an appearance in some of the best work. Due to improvements in both the quantity and the pressure of domestic water supplies, water-closets were gradually superseding earth closets during the first half of the century, and in 1855 the builders of new houses were obliged by statute to provide proper drainage and 'sufficient' sanitary conveniences. Thereafter water-closets soon came into more general use, and some houses were built with bathrooms.

It may be said in general terms that the hold of the traditional urban forms grew weaker and the blood of the Italianate movement thinner as the end of the 1860's was reached. The fine double-fronted stucco houses built in the parallel roads of Holland Park by the Radford brothers (Plate 51d) were still going up in the 1870's, but this was the last conservative continuation of a formula which had proved outstandingly successful in earlier years.

In 1864–5 Philip Webb, having designed the Red House at Bexley for William Morris some six years earlier, designed a house in Holland Park Road (now No. 14) for Valentine Prinsep, the painter, in the red-brick style of the new Domestic Revival (fig. 28). At the same time and in the same road George Aitchison was also designing a red-brick house for Frederic (later Lord) Leighton (figs. 26–7), and in 1867–8 the new style of Philip Webb's house for George Howard at No. 1 Palace Green (Plate 108) evoked prolonged antagonism from the Commissioners of Woods and Forests and their classically-minded architect, (Sir) James Pennethorne. These revolutionary houses were to be followed by a number of other individual buildings representative of the advanced aesthetic ideals of the late 1860's and 1870's, most of which were situated on the Holland estate near to the houses of Prinsep and Leighton (Plates 76–91). These houses in Holland Park Road and Melbury Road were all for eminent artists, including G. F. Watts who employed F. P. Cockerell, Marcus Stone and Luke Fildes, who both employed Norman Shaw, and the architect William Burges, who designed Tower House for his own occupation. Together they form a most important group demonstrating the force of the reaction against the Italianate stucco amongst the artistic community of the time. Leighton House and Tower House have interiors of great interest. The demolition of G. F. Watts's house in *c.* 1965, in spite of an attempt by the London County Council to preserve it, is very much to be regretted. The architecture of this artistic colony was an early manifestation of a highly influential movement, but it had little architectural progeny in northern Kensington, for by this time the development of the farmlands of the parish had been virtually completed.

The varied styles of the churches and chapels of northern Kensington (Plates 6–28) provide a measure of contrast from the general background of the domestic buildings, but only in a few cases do they stand out in high relief. Some, such as St. James, Norlands, St. John the Evangelist, Ladbroke Grove, All Saints', Talbot Road, and St. Peter's, Kensington Park Road, are centrepieces of the domestic development, but in most cases, such as St. Mark's, St. Mark's Road, St. Michael and All Angels', Ladbroke Grove, and St. George's, Aubrey Walk, the churches do not dominate architecturally, only their spires and towers indicating their location when seen from a distance. In other instances, such as those of St. Clement's, Treadgold Street, St. Francis of Assisi, Pottery Lane, and St. Pius X, St. Charles Square, they are so modest in scale that they could easily be overlooked, and indeed merge self-effacingly with their surroundings. As would be expected, most of the churches are Gothic, although there are considerable variations of both style and form. The economical structures of Lewis Vulliamy's two churches, the Tudor Gothic St. Barnabas', Addison Road, and the Early English St. James, Norlands, are representative of an early somewhat utilitarian approach to church building, with few concessions to ecclesiological correctness. The church of St. John the Evangelist is a more conscious attempt to re-create a correct Early English building, while (Sir) George Gilbert Scott's great and ambitious church of St. Mary Abbots is representative of a fully developed and mature revival of that style. All Saints' Church, an earlier work by William White, found favour with the Ecclesiological Society, and indeed something of a medieval character was achieved that has not been entirely lost despite war damage and other vicissitudes. One of the most ambitious churches in the area, St. John the Baptist, Holland Road, by James Brooks, is an essay in early French Gothic and is completely vaulted in stone, but the grandeur of the church is now partly masked by later additions by J. S. Adkins.

Both of the churches designed by E. Bassett Keeling demonstrate the eccentricities of his individual interpretation of 'Continental Gothic', although both buildings are considerably mutilated. His particular use of cast-iron columns, the polychromatic brick interiors, and the extraordinary gallery fronts caused the ecclesiologists grave doubts, and Keeling's career as a church architect was brief, though spectacular. Although J. P. St. Aubyn's Church of St. Clement incorporates cast-iron columns, and is constructed of brick with a roof owing more to the vernacular traditions of timber craftsmanship than to stylistic correctness, the architectural effect is more composed and unified than that of the restless eclecticism and brash individuality of Keeling's work. Hard utilitarian design is encountered at the Church of St. Michael and All Angels, a curiosity in the German Romanesque style by J. and J. S. Edmeston, while St. Columb, Lancaster Road, by C. Hodgson Fowler, owes much to Early Christian architecture. St. Peter's, by Thomas Allom, is a classical basilica, quite different from the mainstream of ecclesiastical architecture of the period and probably the last classical building for the Anglican church in nineteenth-century London.

Especially fine among Roman Catholic ecclesiastical buildings are the beautiful brick interior of the chapel of the Carmelite Monastery in St. Charles Square by F. H. Pownall; the chapel of the Dominican Convent, Portobello Road, by Henry Clutton; and the church of St. Francis of Assisi by Clutton and John Francis Bentley. The French influence of the thirteenth century is evident in both of Clutton's works, and the fittings, designed by Bentley, are exquisite examples of Victorian workmanship.

The dissenting chapels offer a characteristic array of preaching-boxes, although some concessions to the outward appearances of fashionable Gothic are found in the Baptist Chapel, Westbourne Grove (an extraordinary galleried building vaguely Early English in style), the Kensington Temple, Kensington Park Road, and the Notting Hill Methodist Church, Lancaster Road, but the stylistic insufficiencies are great.

At Kensal Green, in the extreme north of the area, the once much-favoured necropolis of the General Cemetery of All Souls possesses distinguished examples of the Greek Revival style of architecture in its chapels, entrance gate and lodges, and catacomb arcade. The cemetery itself provides an eloquent commentary on Victorian styles and tastes in the rich collection of sculptured memorials, mausolea and statuary (Plates 29–32).

CHAPTER I

The Village Centres around St. Mary Abbots Church and Notting Hill Gate

THE Victorian church of St. Mary Abbots stands on approximately the same site as its predecessor, a small and modest brick church which had been largely rebuilt between 1683 and 1704, but with a building history dating back to the Middle Ages. A village settlement had grown up around this church, particularly along the highway between London and Hammersmith (now Kensington High Street) and at the southern end of the lane (now Kensington Church Street) which wound its way northwards from the church. By the end of the Middle Ages much of this land was copyhold of the manor of Abbots Kensington, some of it remaining so until the twentieth century.

The Manor of Abbots Kensington

In c. 1100 Aubrey de Vere, who was lord of the manor of Kensington, presented the church and lands in Kensington to the Abbey of St. Mary at Abingdon at the request of his dying son Godfrey, who had previously been cured of an illness by the abbot. This grant, which was confirmed by royal charter, gave rise to the subsequent use of the name Abbots Kensington for the new manor thereby created and to the designation of the church as St. Mary Abbots. There is some doubt about how much land was involved, but the clearest evidence indicates that the grant consisted principally of two hides and a virgate, or approximately 270 acres.[1]

The Abbey of Abingdon was dissolved in 1538 and for most of the sixteenth century the ownership of the manor was vested in the Crown. A succession of tenants held the manor on lease, until in September 1599 it was purchased by trustees acting for (Sir) Walter Cope, a politician of some influence at Court.[2] Cope had already acquired two manors or so-called manors to the

north of the highway now known as Kensington High Street, those of West Town and Notting (Nutting, Knotting) Barns. In neither case do these appear to have been full manors, for there is no evidence that manorial courts were held in either, and in the fifteenth century both seem to have been connected with the manor of Kensington, which was still owned by the de Veres.[3] West Town, which Cope bought in 1591, consisted in modern topographical terms of the area between Kensington High Street and Holland Park Avenue to the west of Holland Walk.[4] Notting Barns, which Cope purchased in 1599,[5] lay to the north of Holland Park Avenue, but its extent is not certain.* By the 1670's, however, the manor of Abbots Kensington was regarded as encompassing the whole of the parish lying north of Kensington High Street.[7] This no doubt over-simplified interpretation of the manorial structure may have arisen because from the early seventeenth century Cope and his descendants owned both of the two main manors in the parish—Kensington (by that time known as Earl's Court[8]) and Abbots Kensington—and the rights and extents of the two manors may have become confused by this common ownership.

When Cope became owner of the manor of Abbots Kensington in 1599, the tenant was Robert Horseman. The two men had been engaged in a lengthy feud,[9] and it was no doubt in order to secure an advantage over his adversary that Cope used his influence in high places to secure a grant of the manor from the Crown. Shortly afterwards, however, the dispute was taken to the Privy Council and Cope was required to sell to Horseman a substantial part of the manor. By the subsequent conveyance in November 1599 Horseman secured the fee simple of the house in which he was living and over two hundred acres of land.[10] This house, which was known as the Manor House or

---

* In 1600 Cope sold the manor or farm of Notting Barns and over five hundred acres of land to Henry Anderson, a City merchant, but whether all of this land was within the 'manor' is not made clear in the conveyance.[6] An account of the earlier history of this 'manor' is given in Florence M. Gladstone's *Notting Hill in Bygone Days*.

Parsonage House, stood a short distance to the north-west of the parish church and was probably the medieval manor house of Abbots Kensington. The name Parsonage House suggests, however, that it may also have been occupied at one time by incumbents of St. Mary Abbots. This was, in fact, the more frequently used name during the seventeenth century and the estate attached to the house came to be known as the Parsonage House estate.[11] The land sold by Cope's trustees to Horseman included not only a large part of the district now known as Campden Hill, but also areas north of the highway to Uxbridge (now Notting Hill Gate and Holland Park Avenue) which were within the manor of Abbots Kensington, particularly the Northlands (Norlands) and the North Crofts (now the area of Pembridge Square and Pembridge Gardens).

Horseman died in 1600,[12] and his son, also named Robert, sold the land to various purchasers. The Parsonage House itself, together with about seventy acres of land, was sold in 1616 to Sir Baptist Hicks (later first Viscount Campden) for £2,679.[13] Most of this land was absorbed into the Campden House estate and later formed the bulk of the Phillimore estate, but in 1656 the third Viscount Campden sold the Parsonage House and approximately eight acres to John Sams, a mercer, for £900.[14] Under the terms of Sams's will the property passed to his wife's family, named Booth.[15]

The Jones-Price estate

In 1722 the Booth family sold the Parsonage House and about four acres of adjoining land for £1,600 to John Jones, a Kensington bricklayer.[16] Four years previously Jones had purchased the freehold of the Crown Inn (formerly the Angel) in Kensington High Street, and in the stable-yard behind he laid out a cul-de-sac (now Kensington Church Court) and built fourteen houses there, ten on the north side and four on the south.[17] These houses were known at first as Jones's Buildings; none have survived. But the arched entrance to the court (originally the entrance to the stable-yard) has been preserved, although the

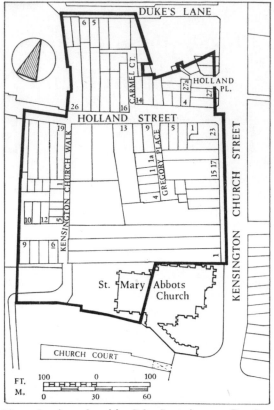

Fig. 1. Land purchased by John Jones in 1722. Based on the Ordnance Survey of 1894–6

arch itself and the adjoining premises to the north (formerly a police station) were rebuilt in 1872–3.[18*]

The extent of the area purchased by Jones in 1722 is indicated in fig. 1.† On a small-scale plan of 1717 the Parsonage House itself appears as a substantial U-shaped building situated close to Kensington Church Street, halfway between the old church and the present Holland Street.[21] But from the evidence of deeds it seems that the house was sited further west, between the modern Gregory Place and Kensington Church Walk, north of the churchyard and south of the now demolished No. 15 Holland Street. On the north side of the house was a large courtyard called Parson's Yard through which passed a public way from Kensington Church Street to Holland

* The police station had been established in Church Court at No. 1 in 1830.[19]

† The piece at the south corner of Duke's Lane and Kensington Church Street not purchased by Jones but formerly part of the Parsonage House estate had been sold previously, partly in 1636 and partly in 1713. Everything here appears to have been rebuilt in the second half of the nineteenth century.[20]

House. The name Parson's Yard was later applied to this way, which was re-named Holland Street in about 1820.[19] Soon after Sams had acquired the Parsonage House in 1656 it was divided in two and leased to tenants, and by 1722 many of the adjoining barns, stables and coach-houses were said to have been converted into houses.[11]

Jones demolished all the buildings on the estate, except the Parsonage House and an old conduit, and with the help of his nephew and son-in-law John Price, another Kensington bricklayer, he began to erect houses.[11] The first to be built, by November 1724, were on the south side of Holland Street (Nos. 3–7 odd), the west side of Kensington Church Street (Nos. 9–23 odd) and in Gregory Place.[22] Of these Nos. 9–17 Kensington Church Street still remain but only the 'double house', now numbered 15 and 17, appears to retain (in its upper storeys) both its original brick front and segmental window openings. A few houses were let by Jones on long leases to building tradesmen who had, presumably, assisted in the work.* The corner house (No. 23), which was rebuilt in 1870, was originally an inn called at first the George and later the Catherine Wheel.[24]

On the north side of Holland Street Jones built Nos. 4–8 (even), since rebuilt, and behind them he laid out a stable-yard, now the site of Holland Place.[25] The original entrance to the yard was in Holland Street; the present entrance from Kensington Church Street was made in 1882 when that street was widened and the houses between Holland Street and Duke's Lane rebuilt.[26] Vestiges of Jones's stable buildings may survive in the weatherboarded house No. 27A Kensington Church Street. Jones may also have been responsible for building a dissenting meeting-house which stood on the site of the present Nos. 10 and 12 Holland Street by January 1725.[25]

The progress of this development was not entirely without incident. In July 1726 Jones pulled down some of the wall along the northern boundary of his estate and began work on four houses fronting on Duke's Lane (formerly Campden Lane). But he immediately encountered opposition from Lord Lechmere, the owner of Campden House, who claimed the lane was private and objected to Jones's using it to bring in cartloads of building materials (the way through Parson's Yard having apparently been blocked by the fall of a house there). Lord Lechmere complained to two justices of the peace that Jones had made a 'forcible and riotous' entry upon his land, and on the following day the justices, attended by a constable, were present when two of Jones's carts, laden with sand, were stopped at the entrance to the lane by workmen from Campden House.[11]

What happened next is disputed. Witnesses hostile to Jones later claimed that an unseemly fracas ensued 'with much rudeness and sauceyness in the lane'. Jones's workmen were said to have made 'very loud Huzzas and Shouts' ridiculing the justices and 'urging disrespectful words of Lord Lechmere', and Jones himself, who had been fetched from a barber's shop, climbed on to the scaffolding, and was seen to be encouraging his workmen to resist. One of the justices fined him £20 on the spot for obstruction and when Jones refused to pay he ordered the constable to take him to Newgate. Jones was 'put into a coach and hurried to Prison', but while the constable was talking to the turnkey 'he slipt away and went as fast as he could towards the Temple to his Lawyer' with one of Lord Lechmere's servants in hot pursuit. Jones later returned to Newgate with his Welsh lawyer, Thomas Vaughan, who paid the £20 and 'prevailed' upon the keeper (for 'a guinea fee') to enter Jones's name in the admissions book. Two days later Lord Lechmere filed a complaint in Chancery and was granted an injunction restraining Jones from proceeding with the building. Jones himself subsequently instituted proceedings against one of the justices for wrongful arrest. He tried unsuccessfully to bribe the constable to give evidence on his behalf, but another witness ('old Jasper Orchard') was persuaded to sign an affidavit in Jones's favour, having previously been plied with glasses of 'Welch Ale' at the George.[11] The outcome of these cases has not been traced; possibly they were still undecided when Jones died a few months later in March 1727.

In his will Jones bequeathed his Kensington property to his wife Rebecca and his son-in-law John Price, who together continued to build on the estate.[27] They completed the four houses in

---

* These were: John Barnard of Kensington, *carpenter*; Thomas Crouch of St. James's, Westminster, *slater and plasterer*; and Thomas Dale of Kensington, *joiner*.[23]

Fig. 2. Nos. 10–26 even Holland Street, elevations

Duke's Lane (since rebuilt);[28] they laid out a passage (now Carmel Court) between Holland Street and Duke's Lane and built a house on the east side (now demolished),[29]* and in Holland Street they built Nos. 1 and 16–26 even (completed by 1728–9),[30] Nos. 10 and 12 (in existence by December 1736), and probably No. 2 [31] (Plate 38b; fig. 2). Of these only Nos. 1, 2 and 16 have been completely rebuilt. Nos. 10 and 12 stand on the site of the earlier, short-lived, meeting-house.

This building activity was followed by a period of about twenty years in which no new houses appear to have been erected. During this time several parts of the estate were sold, including two plots of unbuilt land on the south side of Holland Street—the site of the present Nos. 19–25 (odd) in 1747, and the site of the now demolished Nos. 15 and 17 in 1758.[32] By 1760 the purchaser of the site of Nos. 19–25, Robert Pilkington, a gardener, had built two houses there. These were demolished when the present Nos. 19–25 were erected in the 1850's.[19] The sale of the freehold of No. 26 Holland Street in 1736 included the site of Nos. 6 and 7 Duke's Lane (Queen Anne's

Cottages), which do not, however, appear to have been built until the late eighteenth century.[33]

None of this building had affected the Parsonage House itself, which under the terms of Jones's will had been bequeathed in trust to Price to provide an income for the maintenance of Jones's three grandchildren until the youngest should come of age. The house was then to be sold to raise funds for various bequests.[27] But provided he could pay these bequests Price was not obliged to sell the property, and he evidently did not do so. It is not known when the Parsonage House was demolished, but by 1760 Price had built six new houses (four in Kensington Church Street, and two in Holland Street) with gardens extending over the site.[34] The four houses in Kensington Church Street still survive (now Nos. 1–7 odd), though No. 1 has been refaced. In Holland Street, only one of the two (now No. 13) remains (Plate 38a; fig. 3). These two, originally a semi-detached pair, were first occupied in 1764, No. 13 by Lady Mary Fitzgerald, and the adjoining house by a Colonel Pownall.[19] Pownall's house was rebuilt as two (now Nos. 9 and 11) in 1838–9

* Part of the garden of this house is now occupied by No. 14 Holland Street.

CARMEL COURT

14   12   10

(Plate 38a), and at the same time four more houses were built in the garden behind (now Nos. 1–4 Gregory Place).[35] From 1894 to 1915 No. 13 was occupied by the artist Walter Crane, who decorated the walls with some of his celebrated wallpapers, none of which remains.[36]

In April 1763 Price offered to sell to the Vestry a plot of land on the south side of the estate, formerly part of the Parsonage House garden, for an extension to the churchyard of St. Mary Abbots. His offer was accepted, and in October, some months after his death, the land was conveyed to the Vestry by his executors and trustees.[37] In the following year most of the remaining parts of Price's estate were partitioned by his trustees and sold to Thomas Dade of Soho, carpenter, and Thomas Wilson of St. James's, Westminster, haberdasher.[38]

On the south side of Holland Street the ground between No. 13 and Kensington Church Walk remained undeveloped until 1833 when half the area was purchased by William Outhwaithe of Hammersmith, bricklayer, and the other half by Robert Hartley of Kensington, gentleman.[39] Outhwaithe immediately built No. 15 Holland Street on his plot and some years later, in 1846–7, Hartley built No. 17, a detached house known at first as Hartley Villa and later as Raimond House.[40] The sites of both houses are now occupied by a block of flats, Ingelow House, named after Jean Ingelow, the poetess, a former occupant of No. 15.[41]

The west side of Ingelow House faces Kensington Church Walk which had existed as a cartway leading to the Parsonage House since at least 1726. In 1767 the vicar agreed to allow the Vestry to make 'a constant thoroughfare' through the churchyard from the south-east corner with a gate into Church Walk to be kept open during the day,[42] but the present extension through the churchyard to Kensington High Street was not made until after the Vestry had acquired the southern end of Paramour's Pingle in 1814 (see page 50). None of the present rather undistinguished buildings in Kensington Church Walk appear to be earlier in date than the mid nineteenth century. The little group of seven houses on the west side (Nos. 6–12 consec.) was erected in 1875–6 by Lucas and Son of Kensington Square, builders.[43]

The Conduit Close

Among the lands bought by Sir Baptist Hicks from Robert Horseman in 1616 was a four-acre field on the east side of Church Lane called 'the More', or Conduit Close.[13] In terms of the present topography the area of Conduit Close is bounded on the north by Hamilton House and Vicarage Court, on the south by the buildings on the north side of Old Court Place, on the east by the houses in Palace Green, and on the west by Kensington Church Street. In 1656 the third Viscount Campden sold part of this close to John Sams and another part to Thomas Hodges, the vicar of Kensington.[44] Hodges subsequently purchased some of Sams's piece, and at the time of his death in 1672 he appears to have owned slightly less than half the area of Conduit Close.[45] By this time the rest had passed into the ownership of Sir Heneage Finch, later first Earl of Nottingham, whose son sold it to the Crown in 1689.[46] The barracks in Kensington Church Street now occupy this site (see page 192).

Hodges had built two fairly substantial houses on his part of the Conduit Close, both of which survived until the second half of the eighteenth century.[47] The 'upper house' (the northern, and larger, of the two) attracted some distinguished tenants including Lady Bellasyse (Baroness Osgodby), Sir Thomas Parker, later first Earl of Macclesfield, Sir Robert Eyre, lord chief justice of common pleas, and Anne, Countess of

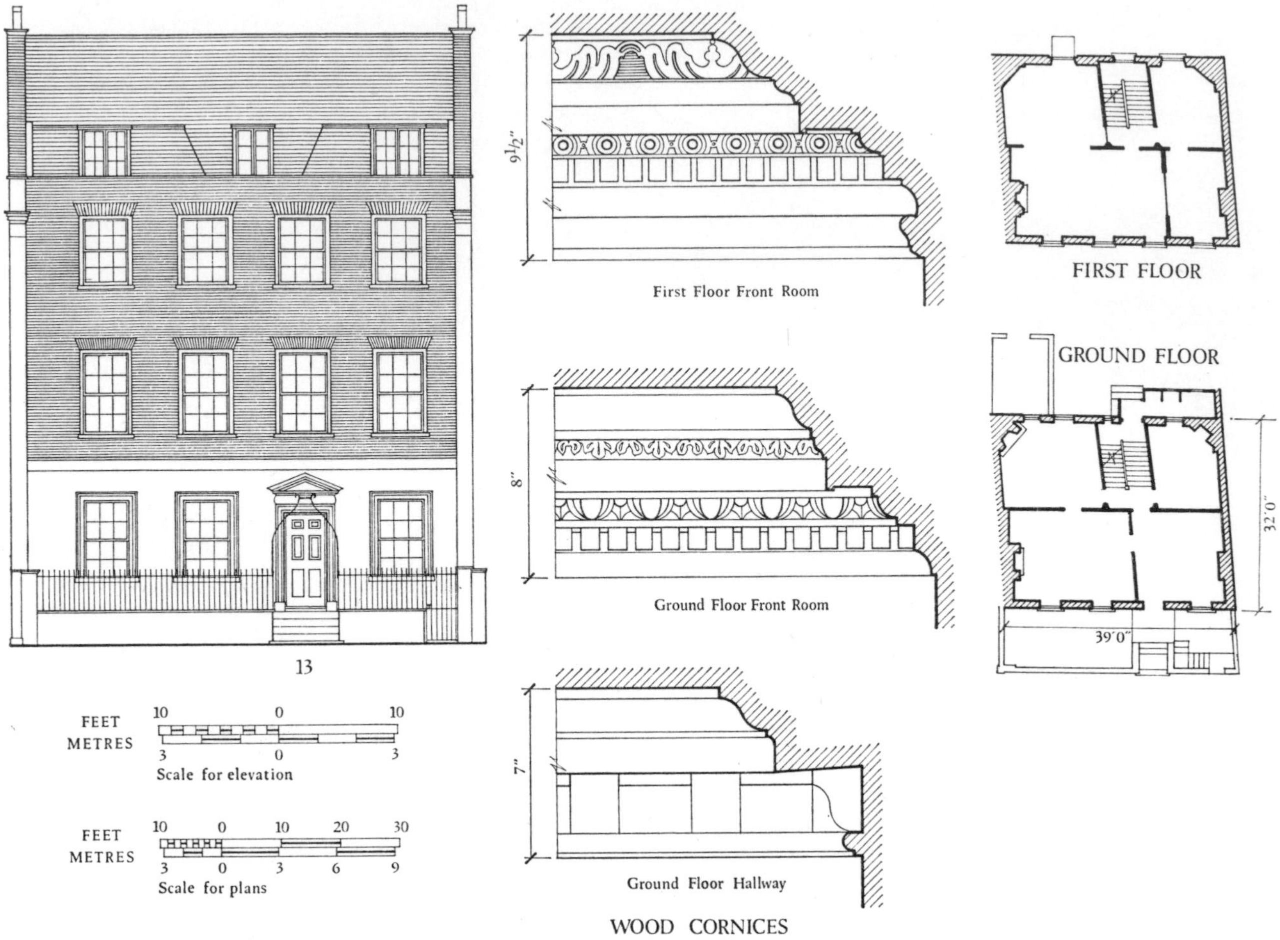

9½"

First Floor Front Room

8"

Ground Floor Front Room

7"

Ground Floor Hallway

WOOD CORNICES

13

FEET
METRES
10   0   10
3   0   3
Scale for elevation

FEET
METRES
10   0   10   20   30
3   0   3   6   9
Scale for plans

FIRST FLOOR

GROUND FLOOR

32' 0"

39' 0"

Fig. 3. No. 13 Holland Street, plan, elevation and details

Salisbury, widow of the fifth Earl.[48] In deeds of the eighteenth century the site of this house was usually described as the Little Conduit Close. The 'lower house' appears from a schedule of fittings of 1717 to have consisted of two storeys and an attic with two principal rooms on each of the first two floors and four rooms in the attic. The fittings at that time included marble fireplaces with Dutch tiles and wainscoted chimney-pieces decorated with 'landskips'.[49]

In 1675 Hodges's widow sold the two houses to Henry Hazard of Kensington, gentleman, though at the time of his death (in 1706) he appears to have retained only the 'lower house'.[50] The ownership of both houses was, however, reunited again in the second half of the eighteenth century under John Gorham of St. Andrew's, Holborn, a bricklayer. In 1764 Gorham bought

the 'lower house', then described as 'lately decayed fallen or taken down', and rebuilt it,[51] and in 1781 he bought and rebuilt the 'upper house'.[52] These two houses were later known as Maitland House and York House respectively. George III's daughter, Princess Sophia, lived at York House from 1839 until her death in 1848. Occupants of Maitland House have included James Mill and his son John Stuart Mill, and Sir David Wilkie, the artist.[41]

Both houses survived, with additions and alterations, until the early years of the twentieth century when the property was acquired for redevelopment.[53] The site is now occupied by York House Place, a block of flats called York House (1904–5, Durward Brown architect),[53] the Gas Light and Coke Company's neo-Georgian showrooms, now the North Thames Gas Board

(1924–6, H. Austen Hall, architect, with stone carving by W. Aumonier, Plate 36d)[54] and Church Close, a Tudoresque block of shops and flats, with a central courtyard (1927–8, Yates, Cook and Darbyshire, architects).[55]

In the remaining area of the old village centre lying to the north of Kensington High Street the original pattern of settlement has been largely obscured by later rebuildings. On the east side of Kensington Church Street Nos. 2–28 (even) occupy the site of a group of copyhold houses of some antiquity, but no evidence has been found that any features earlier than the mid nineteenth century survive. Nos. 14–28 were rebuilt (in some cases possibly only refronted) as a result of road widening carried out in 1913.[56]

Further to the north, where Kensington Church Street curves to the north-west, some sites on both sides of the street (here anciently known as Love Lane) remained copyhold until the nineteenth century. To the west of Vicarage Gate the block of flats called Winchester Court was built on the site of a large house which had been converted into a convent in 1851 or 1852. The convent later became the Orphanage of St. Vincent de Paul.[57] Winchester Court was completed in 1935 to the designs of D. F. Martin-Smith in association with D. Beswick, and was described at the time as 'decidedly the most meritorious building to appear in this district for a long time'.[58] An unusual combination of brick and faience is used in the façades of the building, the ground and first floors being of black faience and the upper storeys of brick relieved by balconies of cream-coloured faience and narrow bands of blue faience.

To the north-west of Winchester Court was a terrace of houses called Wiple Place, now demolished. This was erected shortly before 1800 as a speculation by Charles Wiple of the City, a sugar-baker.[59] Although Wiple owned the freehold of the site when the terrace was built, the land appears at one time to have been copyhold.[60]

On the opposite (west) side of Kensington Church Street several buildings were erected at various dates on copyhold land. Some of these were later incorporated into the Pitt estate and are described in Chapter III. Two of the remainder, later Nos. 49 and 51 Church Street, were adapted in 1849 for use by the Kensington Dispensary (later the Kensington Dispensary and Children's Hospital), an institution which had been founded in a house in Holland Street in 1840 for the care of poor patients. In 1928 a new children's hospital was opened in Pangbourne Avenue (see page 317), the premises in Kensington Church Street having been vacated in 1925. The site is now occupied by Newton Court, a block of flats designed in 1926 by Wills and Kaula, architects.[61]

The drawings prepared for the Kensington Turnpike Trust by Joseph Salway in 1811 (Plate 44) show the north side of Kensington High Street when it still consisted of an attractive group of small-scale buildings of various dates. Of all the buildings depicted, only two, now numbered 98 and 100, survive (see page 61).

To the east of Kensington Church Street a major road widening scheme undertaken by the London County Council in 1902–5[62] involved the clearance not only of nearly all the buildings along the north side of this part of Kensington High Street, but also of the narrow streets and alleys opening out of it, namely Kensington Place, Brown's Buildings and Clarence Place. Among the new buildings erected in place of those demolished were the Fire Brigade Station in Old Court Place to the designs of W. E. Riley, Superintending Architect of the London County Council,[63] Nos. 54–60 (even) Kensington High Street (Old Court Mansions) to the designs of Philip E. Pilditch (ground floor altered in 1963)[64] and Nos. 62–70 (even) Kensington High Street to the designs of Paul Hoffmann.[65]* Two buildings which survived road widening were the then recently completed (1894) Royal Palace Hotel, designed by Basil Champneys,[66] and the late seventeenth-century lodge at the west corner of Palace Avenue. Both were, however, demolished for the erection of the Royal Garden Hotel, which was completed in 1965 to the designs of Richard Seifert and Partners.

The Church of St. Mary Abbots
Plates 6–9, 33a, b; fig. 4

The position of the church which was granted to the Abbey of Abingdon in *c.* 1100 is not known

* For Nos. 26–40 (even) Kensington High Street see page 193.

for certain. That either this church or a successor stood in the thirteenth century on the site of the present building is known from descriptions of the tower of the old church before its rebuilding in 1770–2 and from accounts by the builders of the Victorian church of stonework found when demolishing its predecessor.[67] This medieval church was largely rebuilt, except for the tower, between 1683 and 1704[68] (Plate 6). When a survey of the building was made in 1866, it was found that many of the walls consisted of a thin skin of brickwork encasing a rubble core, indicating that in some cases the medieval walls may merely have been refaced with brick.[69]

The most distinguished part of the old church was the west tower, which was constructed in 1770–2 to the designs of John Smith, clerk of works at Kensington Palace.[70] It was built of brick with stone quoins and stringcourses dividing it into three stages; at the top was a battlemented parapet surmounted by a clock-turret on which stood a cupola containing the bells, the whole being topped by a weather vane. This elegant Georgian tower replaced a low stone structure, with a small spire which barely rose above the roof of the nave.

Despite several repairs to the fabric during the nineteenth century, the brick church was in 1866 declared to be unsafe by two architects—Gordon M. Hills and T. Hayter Lewis. The vicar, Archdeacon Sinclair, decided that a new church should be built on 'a scale proportioned to the opulence and importance of this great Metropolitan parish'. A building committee decided unanimously at its first meeting in May 1867 that the new church should be built on the site of the old, and engaged (Sir) George Gilbert Scott as architect. By the end of June, Scott had prepared plans and elevations. He estimated that the cost of the structure would be £35,000, an expenditure he thought necessary to make the church worthy of the importance of the parish. In July 1868 a meeting of parishioners approved a slightly amended design, and a faculty was secured to rebuild the church.[71]

The successive contracts for the construction of the church were concluded with Dove Brothers of Islington. Demolition of the old church took place in 1869 and the new building was sufficiently far advanced to be consecrated on 14 May 1872. The top stone of the spire was laid in an elaborate ceremony on 15 November 1879 to complete the main structure at a total cost, including fittings, of almost £45,000. Among the specialist firms employed were Farmer and Brindley, sculptors, Clayton and Bell, decorators, and Potter and Sons, smiths.[72]

In 1889–93 an arcaded cloister was built from the corner of Kensington High Street and Kensington Church Street to the south porch of the church. The architect was John Oldrid Scott, who also supervised the completion of the main body of the church after his father's death in 1878, and designed many of the fittings. The contractor for the cloister was John Thompson of Peterborough.[73]

St. Mary Abbots is a solid and impeccably detailed essay in the Early English style, with a six-bay clerestoried nave and aisles, two-bay projecting transepts (each bay under a separate gable), and a three-bay chancel with two-bay north and south aisles. The south chancel aisle is now a chapel, and the north now contains the organ and the sacristy.

The church is faced with Kentish ragstone and Bath stone dressings. The west front (Plate 7a) is symmetrical, flanked by buttresses crowned by octagonal spirelets, and by the low walls of the aisles. It is pierced by three large windows, each containing two lancet lights with a circular window above. A wheel window pierces the tall diapered gable which is surmounted by a cross of stone. The west doorway is richly carved with both foliate and naturalistic designs, and is surmounted by a gable capped by an elaborate cross. There are two wooden doors with great iron hinges and other furniture of foliate design. Between the doors is a trumeau above which is a seated Christus within a quatrefoil panel flanked by suppliant angels. The western walls of the aisles are each pierced by a window consisting of two lights with a sexfoil window above.

The great tower with spire (Plate 7b), unusually placed at the north-east corner of the church, is a conspicuous feature of this part of Kensington.* The massive tower consists of four stages, supported by large stepped angle buttresses slightly set back. Each face of the first, second and third stages is divided by a stepped buttress, and is pierced by small lancets set between the

---

* A recent measurement by nautical sextant showed the height of the tower and spire to be approximately 250 feet. The spire is surmounted by a vane, originally fourteen feet in height.

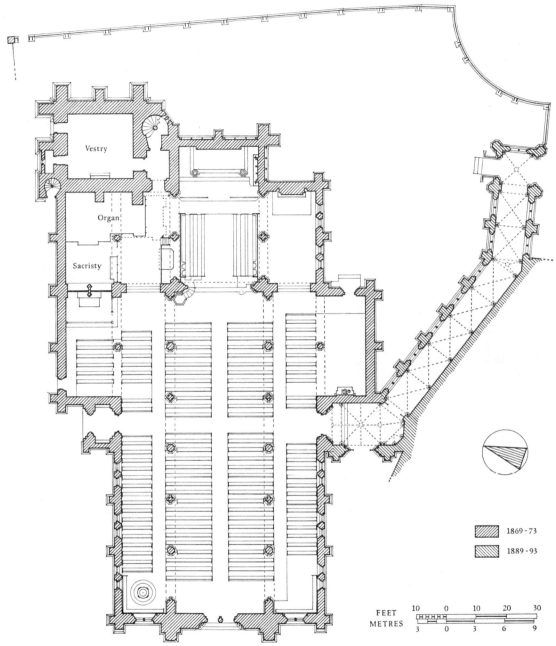

Vestry

Organ

Sacristy

1869-73

1889-93

FEET
METRES

Fig. 4. St. Mary Abbots Church, plan

buttresses. The tall belfry stage is pierced on each face by deeply recessed arches carried on clustered shafts, and flanked by blind panels each containing two ornate niches originally intended for statuary. The central openings contain large pairs of lancets surmounted by roundels. Above the blind panels are quatrefoil panels set within circular frames. The belfry stage is crowned by a neat parapet of open arcading under a ball-flower cornice. The corner buttresses are capped by large octagonal spirelets. Within these spirelets at the base of the spire is an inner tier of crocketed pinnacles, and between these are the steeply gabled two-light openings of the upper belfry. The octagonal spire itself has two bands of lozenge diapering dividing it into three stages.

The arcaded covered way added in 1889–93 (Plate 9b) is entered through a square, vaulted porchway with a gabled front and with octagonal corner turrets having pronounced colonnette shafts. Above, octagonal pinnacles rise from behind a battlemented parapet. The cloister continues at an angle to the porch, and each bay is stepped up slightly, as the floor is ramped, so that the approach to the south porch of the church itself is dramatic and mysterious. There are nine bays of this stone-vaulted covered way, the north side of which has open geometrical tracery with decorative iron-work in each bay, while the south side, apart from the first three bays, is solid. The south door of the church is set in a richly carved portal, with detached shafts supporting a richly carved arch. The dark wooden doors with elaborate wrought-iron hinges are excellent examples of Victorian craftsmanship and of Scott's detailing.

The interior (Plates 8, 9a) is commodious and stately, the walls being faced with smooth-dressed Bath stone. The detail is precise, but lacks variety. The west end of the nave, which is particularly impressive, has a doorway with two massive wooden doors set in pointed arches under rere-arches of flatter pitch divided by a trumeau, the whole being contained within a segmentally arched recess. Over the doors is a stringcourse above which rise three level windows of two lights each with simple geometrical plate tracery and roundels at the tops. Standing proud of this tracery are tall clustered colonnettes divided into three stages by roll-moulded shaft rings, and crowned by foliate capitals which support the rich tracery in front of the windows, giving an open-arch screen effect. In front of the mullions

between each of the two-light windows is a free-standing cylindrical colonnette linked in two places to the mullions by little stone bridges level with the shaft rings. At the apex of each arch in the screen is a quatrefoil opening set immediately before each roundel. Above the central light, in the gable, is a large wheel window of five lobed lights recessed within a circle.

The arcades of the nave have pillars alternately quatrefoil and octagonal in plan. Over the arches is a roll-moulded stringcourse, above which is the clerestory, consisting of twelve windows each of two lancets and a quatrefoil. There is an arcade brought forward from the plate tracery of each window, giving lightness and delicacy to the detail. The aisle windows are pierced with paired lancets.

The nave roof is of wood, erected to designs by Romilly Craze in 1955, and replacing a timber roof destroyed in the war of 1939–45. Scott's original roof had transverse diagonal ribs, and was varnished and dark in colour. The new roof is a simple barrel vault which is canted in sections. The aisles retain their original roofs.

The large chancel arch has columns of marble marked off in four stages by roll-moulded shaft rings, and an elaborate hood mould.

The three-bay chancel has arcades on both sides, each of two bays, much more richly detailed than in the nave. The columns are composed of clustered colonnettes marked off by roll-moulded shaft rings at half their height. Grouped semi-circular shafts carry foliate capitals at stringcourse level, from which springs the quadripartite wooden vault of the chancel roof. The clerestory windows above the arcades consist of sexfoil roundels set in recessed pointed arches supported by attached colonnettes. The spandrels are filled with lush foliate carving.

The east bay of the chancel is richer still. The window mullions consist of several colonnettes, and the arches are fully moulded. There is no arcade as the chancel aisles are only two bays long. The geometrical east window is a lavish composition consisting principally of three main lights with a sexfoil and two small quatrefoil lights over them. This large window is flanked by single lights.

The chancel is furnished with a marble reredos and a finely carved and gilded altar. On the south side is a sedilia projecting forward from the wall, consisting of three cusped arches beneath steeply gabled canopies supported on slim colonnettes. There are iron grilles on either side of the chancel at the rear of the choir stalls.

The handsome wooden pulpit of 1697 comes from the old church. The baptismal font, carved by Farmer and Brindley, stands on a stone base and is carried on columns of polished marble; on top is a fine openwork canopy of wrought iron (Plate 33b).

Several monuments of interest survive from the old church. That to the seventh Earl of Warwick and Holland in the south transept, with a seated figure of white marble, is probably by J. B. Guelphi. Among some elaborate Baroque cartouches are those in memory of Thomas Henshaw, Colin Campbell and Philip and Elizabeth Colby. The severely classical monument to Aaron Mico (who died in 1658) is similar to the work of Joshua Marshall and is a good example of its period.

The stained glass windows were almost all by Clayton and Bell, and were mostly private gifts, although there were several erected by public subscription. The effect of the interior must have been very rich and sombre, but this has been dissipated to a considerable degree by the removal of the background glass, leaving the coloured figures on a clear glass ground in several windows in the nave, and by the pastel colours applied to the roof.

The tomb of Miss Elizabeth Johnstone, which stands in the churchyard to the north-west of the church, was designed by (Sir) John Soane in 1784 and carved by John Hinchcliffe the elder. Soane's own notes and drawings in Sir John Soane's Museum (Plate 33a) show a brick-lined vault covered with slabs of Portland stone on which rests a marble-faced sarcophagus, surrounded by iron railings. Only the sarcophagus is now visible in the churchyard. The monument was commissioned by the Earl of Bellamont, and Soane was paid £10 for his 'trouble'.

The Roman Catholic Church and Priory of Our Lady of Mount Carmel and St. Simon Stock, Kensington Church Street and Duke's Lane

Plate 27

The founder of this Carmelite community was Father Herman, who had been born Herman Cohen in Germany and had become a convert to Roman Catholicism, joining the order of Discalced Carmelites. He came to London in 1862 on the suggestion of Cardinal Wiseman and set up a temporary home with the Sisters of the Assumption in Kensington Square. In 1863 he rented a large house in Kensington Church Street on the site of the present Newton Court. The house, which had at one time been called Bullingham House but is not to be confused with the mansion of the same name on the Pitt estate (see page 50), had extensive grounds on its south side. The property, which was copyhold, was owned by Stephen Bird, a prominent local builder, who sold it to the Carmelites in 1864 for £3,500. The land was enfranchised, and Edward Welby Pugin provided designs for a church to be built in the grounds. Building began in 1865 and the opening ceremony took place on 16 July 1866. The church was built of stock bricks with stone dressings in a predominantly Early English style. It was lavishly fitted out over the course of several years, but was destroyed during the war of 1939–45.[74]

The present church was designed by Sir Giles Gilbert Scott, and was completed in July 1959.[75] The tall, gaunt exterior is faced with reddish-buff bricks and stone dressings. The style is a freely interpreted late Gothic, partly North European and partly Perpendicular in its origins. From the outside the church appears to consist of a very high clerestoried nave with steeply roofed lean-to aisles, each having three gables at right angles to the main body of the church. The interior is, in fact, aisleless, the dominant features being the pointed concrete arches which divide the church into seven bays and carry the steeply pitched roofs and the clerestory (Plate 27c). The ceiling above the clerestory is flat. The bases of these dominant arches are pierced by square-headed openings above which are pointed panels containing gilded and painted Stations of the Cross. Alternate bays of the side walls are occupied by chapels and confessionals.

Although the church is orientated east west, the liturgical 'east' is at the west end. The sanctuary is wide and shallow, lit by two tall windows that illuminate the large gilded angular reredos. The choir and organ gallery is at the 'west' end, over a small baptistry. There is a Lady Chapel 'north' of the sanctuary.

In 1875–6 the community obtained the copyhold interest in the remaining land along the north side of Duke's Lane for approximately £4,600. The property was subject to an existing lease and this may have delayed plans to build a new monastery on the site. In 1886, however, the copyhold was enfranchised, and the priory was built in 1886–9 by Edward Conder of Kingsland Road to the designs of Goldie, Child and Goldie.[76] It consists of a long range of five-storey stock-brick buildings with stone dressings in the Flamboyant style of sixteenth-century northern France (Plate 27a, b), and is connected by a corridor to the church.

Wesleyan Chapel, Clarence Place
Demolished

This chapel was built in 1836–8. It was a small unpretentious building which seated only two hundred people, but it had a pleasing stucco front divided into three bays by Doric pilasters and crowned by a pediment.

Clarence Place was swept away by road improvements in 1902–5, but the chapel itself survived and was afterwards situated on the north side of a new street called Old Court Place. In c. 1905, however, it ceased to be used as a chapel, and the building was adapted for commercial purposes. It was demolished in 1962.[77]

Charity School, Kensington High Street
Also known as the National Schools. Plate 37d. Demolished

One of the best known buildings in Kensington until its demolition c. 1878 was the old parish charity school on the north side of Kensington High Street. The most notable feature of the building was a shallow bell-tower, capped by a broken pediment, rising through an open pediment—a fanciful device which led many authorities to the conclusion that it was designed by Sir John Vanbrugh. It was, in fact, the work of Nicholas Hawksmoor and was built in 1711–12, when he was clerk of works at Kensington Palace.

The charity school was founded in 1707.[78] Previously there had been a parish free school for poor children, which was held in a house on the north side of the High Street called the Catherine Wheel.[79] In 1709 the Vestry resolved that the trustees of the charity school, which appears to

have been originally established in another building, should be allowed to rebuild the parish school-house and to have free use of it thereafter, provided that they agreed to teach the children of the free school there also.[80]

Rebuilding began in 1711, and an adjoining house, conveniently belonging to Richard Slater, a carpenter who was employed on the new building, was purchased to provide a bigger site.* The trustees resolved that 'the Designe of the said Building should be left to the care of Mr. Hawksmore'. Hawksmoor did not charge a fee, but the sum of £5 which he had pledged towards the cost of building was not collected. The total cost, including £97 paid to Slater for his house, was £1,180.[81] The charity school was built of brick with some stone dressings and consisted of three main storeys above a basement. The handsome street elevation was of three bays, the centre one projecting forward to form a porch at ground-floor level. Above the third storey this projection carried the two-stage bell-tower. In 1818 the upper stages of the tower above the roof ridge of the main building were removed.[82] The interior of the building was relatively plain, the only ornamental features of note being some panelling and a chimneypiece with engraved glass over it in the principal room on the first floor.[83]

As the population of Kensington grew the school had to expand. In 1804 a new girls' school was established in a house immediately to the west of the school-house which had been secured by the trustees in 1721.[84] Shortly afterwards the school adopted the teaching methods of the National Society formed in 1811, and in 1817–18 a new school was built to the designs of Thomas Hardwick on the site of a public house called the Coach and Horses, which stood to the west of the new girls' school and which was purchased by the trustees in 1816.[85] Further schools were built in Church Court and Edge Street, and in 1875 extensive new school buildings were erected in Church Court to the designs of Gordon M. Hills, the London diocesan architect. The builders were Stimpson and Company of Brompton Road.[86] The various buildings along the Kensington High Street frontage, including the school-house designed by Hawksmoor, were sold to the Kensington Vestry in 1875 and shortly afterwards demolished to make way for the Town Hall erected

---

* Other tradesmen who worked on the building were: Thomas Callcott and Ferdinand Unsworth, *bricklayers*; Thomas Eustace, *mason*; Francis Parker, *plasterer*; John Watkins and William Taylor, *smiths*. All were apparently local men.

in 1878–80. The stone statues of a boy and a girl which had been made by the mason Thomas Eustace[87] and placed on the front of the charity school, were preserved and erected on the north elevation of the school in Church Court (now known as St. Mary Abbots School) facing the churchyard.

Royal Kent Theatre
Plate 34a, b. Demolished

This small theatre, which had a brief and chequered history, was situated on the west side of Brown's Buildings (now Old Court Place). The site of the theatre, measuring approximately 40 feet from east to west and 80 feet from north to south, was 120 feet north of Kensington High Street. Most of this site is now occupied by the roadway of Old Court Place, for the original street called Brown's Buildings was little wider than an alley, a fact which no doubt helps to explain the theatre's unprepossessing exterior (Plate 34a).

It was first opened in 1831 as the Royal Kensington Subscription Theatre, but within a year the lessee, John Colston, became insolvent. The interior was remodelled on the lines of the Olympic Theatre in Wych Street, the name was changed to the Royal Kent Theatre, apparently in deference to assistance given by the Duchess of Kent in obtaining a licence for public performances, and the theatre re-opened on Easter Monday 1834, when it was described as a 'very handsome little Theatre'. Its history was not happy, however, and it was closed from time to time. Even when performances did take place they were not always noteworthy for the events on stage. In 1838 the company engaged to perform ran off with the takings, and in 1842 the management felt it necessary to inform their customers of the presence of 'police constables in every part of the house to prevent any disturbances'.

The first owner of the freehold was Thomas Wetherell of Hammersmith, who also owned other property in the vicinity. In 1838 the theatre was advertised for sale freehold at an auction and one report stated that 1,100 guineas had been paid for it, but the sale could not have been carried out for Wetherell remained the freeholder until 1843, when another auction sale was forced on him by a mortgagee and the building changed hands for £720. The last known performance took place in October 1846, and in 1849 John Ridgway, a local builder, paid £500 for the building, which was described as 'not now used for Theatrical performances and . . . untenanted'. He demolished the theatre and had erected five houses in its place by the following year.[88]

Vestry Hall, Kensington High Street
Plate 37a

In 1851, when the Kensington Improvement Bill was before Parliament, the Vestry decided to build a new Vestry Hall in place of the room attached to the old parish church, which was no doubt considered unsuitable for the meetings of the improvement commissioners. A faculty was obtained allowing the use of the southern part of the burial ground which had been added to the churchyard in 1814, and the new hall was built there in 1851–2 to the designs of Benjamin Broadbridge, an architect who lived in Ladbroke Square. The builder was Thomas Corby of Pimlico.[89] The style of the building, which is faced with red bricks and stone dressings, was no doubt intended to be in keeping with the older domestic architecture of Kensington, such as Holland House and Campden House.

After the building of the new Town Hall in 1880 (see below) the Vestry Hall continued to be used for municipal purposes and from 1889 until 1960 it housed the central public library of Kensington.[90] In 1880 the elegant iron railings and gate piers in front of the building were removed because the Vestry considered that they impeded the approach to the new Town Hall.[91]

Town Hall, Kensington High Street
Plate 37b

Within twenty years of its opening, the Vestry Hall built in 1851–2 was proving too small, and the Vestry decided to build a new hall in Kensington High Street on the site of the National Schools, which were being moved to Church Court. In 1875 the Vestry bought the school buildings from the trustees for £7,100, and also purchased two houses in Church Court in order to provide a slightly bigger site.[92]

The design of the Town Hall (as the new building was called to avoid confusion with the old Vestry Hall) was the result of an architectural competition which was particularly badly organized even at a time when such competitions were frequently mismanaged. Buildings in the Gothic or the Elizabethan style were specifically excluded and the cost was to be not more than £18,000. Of sixty-five entries received, *The Architect* thought that sixty were 'of commonplace mediocrity'. A professional adviser, John Whichcord, was appointed, but his opinions were entirely ignored by the vestrymen, who disliked his predilection for the Queen Anne style, fearing that a building which looked like a board school might result. They chose a design by Robert Walker, and in so doing fulfilled the worst fear of *The Building News*, which had hoped that 'a commonplace Italian design will not be selected'.[93]

Walker's design was modified somewhat, largely because the purchase of two further houses in Church Court enabled the building to be enlarged. The builders were Braid and Company of Chelsea, whose eventual contract was for £30,549. The foundation stone was laid in December 1878 and the Town Hall was opened in August 1880.[94] In 1898–9 an extension was built at the rear by Leslie and Company of Kensington to the joint designs of William Weaver, the Vestry's surveyor, and William G. Hunt, a local architect.[95]

Notting Hill Gate and Kensington Gravel Pits

In strict usage Notting Hill Gate is the name of a short stretch of the main road which follows the course of the ancient highway from London to Acton and Uxbridge. This stretch extends from Kensington Palace Gardens in the east to Ladbroke Terrace in the west, and its name recalls the presence here of a succession of turnpike toll gates, the last of which was removed in 1864. The name Notting Hill Gate has, however, been commonly applied to the general district on either side of the road, and in this respect it is the modern equivalent of the name Kensington Gravel Pits, which was used into the nineteenth century. The ground on both sides of the roadway now called Notting Hill Gate was dug for gravel from at least the early seventeenth century,[96] and some of the pits survived as large ponds until well into the nineteenth century (Plates 1, 5a). The establishment of a small village settlement here may have preceded the discovery of beds of gravel,

for the point at which the lane from the parish church (now the northern part of Kensington Church Street, formerly Silver Street) joined the Uxbridge highway formed a natural situation for such a settlement. As in the case of the village centre of St. Mary Abbots, much of the land here was copyhold of the manor of Abbots Kensington.

Road widening and large-scale rebuilding has destroyed most of the visual evidence of this village settlement, but it may still be discerned in the pattern of such streets as Kensington Mall, Rabbit Row and West Mall, and in a few old houses on the north side of Notting Hill Gate and the east side of Kensington Church Street. Most of the houses in the area were small cottages, but there was at least one of some size, which is usually referred to as Craven House.

This stood in an acre of ground on the east side of Kensington Church Street, on or near to the sites of the present Nos. 158–164 even (fig. 5). It was purchased in the seventeenth century by William, first Baron (and later first Earl of) Craven, from Sir Robert Hyde (1595–1665), a lawyer who had sheltered Charles II after the Battle of Worcester and who subsequently became chief justice of the King's Bench.[97] When Lord

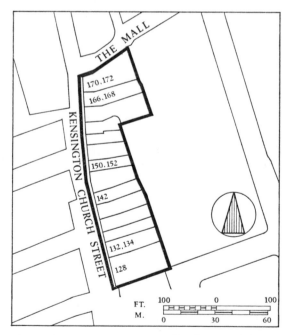

Fig. 5. The Craven House estate. Based on the Ordnance Survey of 1862–72

Craven died unmarried in 1697, this estate passed to another branch of the family under a settlement of 1669.[98]

In June 1736 the two members of the Craven family in whom the estate was then vested sold the property for £360 to the architect Isaac Ware, and six months later Ware conveyed a moiety of it to Charles Carne of St. Martin's in the Fields, glazier.[99] (Ware and Carne were subsequently engaged together in developing an estate in Chandos Street, Covent Garden, in 1737.[100]) In August 1736 they entered into an agreement to let the estate at Kensington for building to Richard Gibbons of Bloomsbury, carpenter. Craven House was demolished and along the Church Street front Gibbons built twelve houses in two blocks of six, formerly Nos. 1–6 and 7–12 High Row, now Nos. 128–142 (even) and 152–168 (even) Kensington Church Street. Ware and Carne let the houses on seventy-one-year leases either to Gibbons, or at his request to the building tradesmen who had evidently assisted with the work.* There is no evidence that Ware exercised any control over the design of the houses. The last leases were granted in February 1737 and shortly afterwards Gibbons became bankrupt.

After the houses were built Ware and Carne sold most of the estate. The southern group of six houses (Nos. 128–142) was bought for £500 in October 1737 by James Allen of Dulwich, gentleman, who subsequently conveyed them in trust to Dulwich College to provide an income for a schoolmaster or schoolmistress to teach reading to poor children in Dulwich. The property is now owned by James Allen's Girls' School.[101] The northern group (Nos. 152–168) was bought by Martin Clare of St. Anne's, Soho, gentleman (founder of the Soho Academy),[102] and the small plot between the two groups (now the site of Yates's timber-yard, Nos. 144–148) was bought by James Swann of Kensington, gentleman.[103] No houses had been built here but by 1742 the site was occupied by a brewhouse.[104] Only a small piece of unbuilt land at the north end of the estate was not sold at this time. A detached house was later built here which may have been occupied at some time by Ware himself.†

Of the twelve houses built in 1736–7 only No. 138 (Plate 38d) retains something like its original appearance. In the adjoining house (No. 136) the window openings have been altered and at No. 152 a shop has been built out in front of the ground floor. The other houses have been either completely rebuilt or refronted. No. 128 (formerly No. 1 High Row) is basically the house built in 1736–7 though its present front is not original. It probably dates from about 1842 when the fourth storey and projecting wing appear to have been added. Residents of this house have included Muzio Clementi, the composer, William Horsley, the organist and composer, and his son John Callcott Horsley, the artist. Felix Mendelssohn, who was a friend of the Horsley family, paid several vists to the house. J. C. Horsley later built a studio behind the house with a large north-facing window which still survives.[106]

The street formerly known as The Mall included not only the short stretch now called Kensington Mall but also the northern part of Palace Gardens Terrace approximately as far south as the present Nos. 57 and 90, where until the 1850's the roadway ended at the edge of the open fields of the glebe lands. The east side of this road is now largely occupied by the ecclesiastical buildings which are described below. Nos. 116 and 118 Palace Gardens Terrace, which are approached by a right-of-way on the north side of the Essex Church, probably date from the early nineteenth century, together with part of No. 126 to the north, for in a will proved in 1833 the buildings on this site were described as 'three Cottages . . . erected and built upon the . . . Ground . . . whereon formerly stood an old decayed Cottage'.[107]

On the west side of the street Nos. 59–69 (odd) Palace Gardens Terrace and Mall Tavern were built as part of the speculations of Thomas Robinson, who was the principal developer of the Glebe and Sheffield House estates. Nos. 59 and 61 were erected on either side of the entrance to stables belonging to the de Murrietta family, who lived in Kensington Palace Gardens. Robinson was granted a ninety-nine-year lease of the sites by Mariano de Murrietta in 1854, and he in turn granted ninety-four-year leases of each house to the builder Thomas Stanway of Paddington, in

---

* These were: Thomas Callcott the younger, *bricklayer*; Richard Gould, *plasterer*; and Edward Smithsend, *painter*, all of Kensington.

† He was said (erroneously) to have died 'at his house at Kensington Gravel Pits' in 1766.[105] The site is now occupied by Nos. 170 and 172 Kensington Church Street and Campden Mansions in Kensington Mall.

1859.[108] Nos. 63–69 and the public house were built on land purchased by Robinson in 1855. Thomas Stanway was also involved in their construction, but the principal builder appears to have been George Ingersent, who became the publican of Mall Tavern as soon as it was completed in 1856.[109]

A piece of land bounded by Kensington Mall, Rabbit Row, West Mall and Palace Gardens Terrace was purchased by Sir Samuel Morton Peto in 1863.[110] On the northern part of this land he had extensive stables built by the contractors Lucas Brothers for use in conjunction with the house which they were building for him at No. 12A Kensington Palace Gardens.[111] The site of the stables is now occupied by Broadwalk Court, a block of flats erected in 1934–5 to the designs of Robert Atkinson.[112]

On the southern part of Peto's land Lucas Brothers erected Mall Chambers (Plate 112b), a block of 'improved industrial dwellings', to the designs of James Murray, the architect of Peto's house. In December 1866, when the building was under construction, Peto sold the freehold of the site to the contractors for £3,350, no doubt because he was then in financial difficulties after the collapse of the firm of Overend and Gurney, and he may also have been indebted to Lucas Brothers for the building of his house. They apparently finished Mall Chambers as a speculation.[113] *The Building News* commented favourably on the accommodation provided, which was 'intended for a class somewhat above ordinary mechanics and labourers', but it considered that the exterior had 'rather the look of a warehouse'.[114]*

In the 1920's and 1930's the rapid growth of motor traffic made Notting Hill Gate a scene of increasing congestion. In 1937 the London County Council obtained statutory power to widen the street, and approved expenditure of over £1,000,000 for this purpose. But the outbreak of war in 1939 prevented the commencement of work, and approval for the project was not given by the Ministry of Transport (a substantial contributor to the cost) until 1957. The scheme involved the reconstruction by the London Transport Executive of the two underground stations as one interconnecting station with a concourse below the road, the widening of Notting Hill Gate for some 700 yards between Kensington Palace Gardens in the east and Ladbroke Terrace in the west, and the widening of short stretches of Kensington Church Street and Pembridge Road. The Council had begun to purchase the properties required for demolition in 1955, and in the following year, after finding that it would be under a statutory obligation to provide other housing for 460 persons who would be displaced, the Council resolved that a housing scheme for the provision of 118 dwellings at the Alton estate, Roehampton Lane, Wandsworth, should be submitted to the Ministry of Housing.

The reconstruction of the two underground stations began in 1957, and the road-works soon afterwards. Altogether some four and a half acres of surplus land became available for redevelopment, and the three largest sites, consisting of three and a half acres, were leased by the Council for ninety-nine years to Ravenscroft Properties Limited and City Centre Properties Limited. These three sites consisted of the area on the north side of Notting Hill Gate between Pembridge Road and Ladbroke Terrace, where shops and 145 dwellings were provided, some of the latter being in an eighteen-storey block; on the south side of Notting Hill Gate between Palace Gardens Terrace and Kensington Church Street, where shops and offices were built; and the area on the west side of Church Street, where offices predominated. The architects for the buildings on these three sites were Messrs. Cotton, Ballard and Blow. The road-works were completed by the end of 1960, and the buildings some two years later.[116]

Essex Church, Palace Gardens Terrace

This red-brick Unitarian church was erected in 1886–7 by John Chappell of Pimlico, builder, to the designs of T. Chatfield Clarke and Son. The site had been purchased in 1873 by Sir

---

* In 1871 the occupations of the residents were as follows: baker, barrister's clerk, bookseller's assistant (2), cab-driver, carpenter (2), carver and gilder, chaff cutter, Civil Service attendant, coach-builder, coachman, dairyman, domestic servant (2), dressmaker (3), dyer and cleaner, fishmonger, fitter at engineering works, fundholder, gasfitter (2), governess (in own school), housekeeper, jeweller (2), laundress, librarian, machinist, milliner, painter and decorator, plumber (2), railway messenger, railway porter, sculptor's porter, shoeshop trader, smith, solicitor's clerk, stationer, stationer's porter, stockbroker's clerk, stone-mason, surgeon, tailor, tailor's foreman, upholsterer, watchmaker, wine merchant.[115]

James Clark Lawrence, M.P., an alderman of the City of London, in order to provide a permanent home for a 'Free Christian Church' which had been founded in Kensington in 1867 and had subsequently met in various rooms and halls.* An iron church, which was opened in 1874, had to suffice until the funds to build a permanent church were provided by the sale of the Essex Street Chapel near the Strand.[118]

Second Church of Christ Scientist, Palace Gardens Terrace

The site on which this church stands has a short but varied ecclesiastical history. A chapel, which was described as 'a large, gloomy-looking structure of the Classical School', was erected here in 1861–2 under a ninety-year lease granted to Robert Offord of Kensington, who was the brother of the first minister, the Reverend John Offord of Plymouth. Although he was nominally a Baptist, Offord's ministry was basically non-denominational. In 1872, after a brief interlude under a Presbyterian minister, who also secured the freehold of the building, the chapel was purchased by a group of Swedenborgians who re-opened it as the New Jerusalem Church. The chapel, which had one thousand sittings, proved too large for the needs of the community and in 1911 it was sold to the Christian Scientists.[119]

Plans for new buildings were drawn up by the architects, Sir John Burnet and Partners, but their execution was delayed by the war of 1914–18. Eventually the hall was completed by 1923 and the church by 1926 from designs by Thomas S. Tait, a partner in the firm.[120]

The complete group of dark-red brick buildings with stone dressings consists of a large church, vestibules, a hall, offices, and a house. The elements are disposed on two sides of an entrance court, the other two sides of which are formed by low walls and a screen of trees.

Externally there are motifs from Early Christian, Byzantine and Romanesque architecture, but the interior owes little to period precedent. The church itself is square on plan, and has raked floors with fixed seats. The principal feature of the interior is the organ, and the décor is uncompromisingly of the 1920's. The large window facing north, which is formed by four equal segmental arches, giving the effect of a shortened *vesica piscis*, is an unmistakable product of the 'Jazz Age'.

Gaumont (formerly Coronet) Theatre, Notting Hill Gate
Plate 34c

The Coronet Theatre was built for Edward George Saunders to the designs of the noted theatre architect, W. G. R. Sprague; the builder was W. Wallis of Balham. Designed to have a seating capacity of 1,143 and costing approximately £25,000, it was described effusively by *The Era* as 'a theatre of which the whole County of London may be proud'. It opened on 28 November 1898 with a performance of 'the celebrated Japanese opera' *The Geisha*, despite the fact that Saunders had not yet been granted a licence by the London County Council on account of the unfinished state of the building. A prosecution was brought against him by the Council and he was fined. In 1916 the theatre was adapted for use as a cinema, and in 1950 the name was changed to the Gaumont.[121]

* Lawrence bought the property from William Hutchins Callcott, the composer, the last of several generations of the Callcott family to own it. Two houses which stood on the site had been occupied by several notable members of the family, including John Wall Callcott, the composer, and Sir Augustus Wall Callcott, the painter.[117]

CHAPTER II

The Sheffield House and Glebe Estates

The Sheffield House estate

The house known as Sheffield House in the first half of the nineteenth century was a late-Georgian mansion on the east side of Kensington Church Street opposite to Sheffield Terrace. It stood on the site of an earlier house of the same name, which had belonged to the Sheffield family during part of the seventeenth and eighteenth centuries.

In 1603 Sir Walter Cope sold a house, which appears to have been in almost exactly the same position as the Georgian house, and two acres of land* for £700 to Sir George Coppin, who, like Cope, was an influential figure at the Court of James I.[1] By 1613 Coppin had sold this house, presumably moving on to the house which was built for him and later enlarged to become Kensington Palace. The purchaser was Lady Jane Berkeley, widow of Henry, seventh Baron Berkeley. In 1613/14 Cope sold a further one and a half acres of land to Lady Berkeley to provide a total holding of three and a half acres[2] (fig. 6). In her will, proved in 1618, she left the house to her grandson, Sir Roger Townshend, but by 1646 it was in the possession of Edmund Sheffield, first Earl of Mulgrave.[3]

The mansion remained in the hands of the Sheffield family until the death of Robert Sheffield, a grandson of the Earl, in 1724 or 1725, and was then known as either Sheffield House or Mulgrave House.[4] Robert Sheffield had no surviving male heirs, but a grand-daughter married Sir John Robinson, baronet, and, after litigation, the estate passed to him.[5] In 1744 he sold or leased the house and its grounds to John Barnard, a builder, and Thomas Callcott, a bricklayer, both of Kensington, who used the grounds as a brick-field and demolished the house. They also built a group of almshouses, possibly on the site of Melon Place, in lieu of an annuity of £10 which Lady Jane Berkeley had left to the poor of Kensington.[6]

In 1791 the Vestry noted that a Thomas Robinson, esquire, had purchased the Sheffield House estate.[7] There is no evidence that he was related to Sir John Robinson, and he is described by Faulkner as gardener to George III.[8] Little is known about him, but at his death he left bequests of over £3,000 as well as his real estate. By 1798 he had rebuilt Sheffield House as a large, if rather plain, brick-faced three-storey house.[9] He demolished the almshouses, no doubt because he did not like their presence so close to his new mansion.

On his death in 1810, Robinson left the house to his wife for her lifetime, with reversion to his nephew Alexander Ramsay Robinson, who already owned other property elsewhere in Kensington.[10] He died in 1824, leaving the house to his eldest son, another Thomas Robinson,[11] who, in 1854, entered into agreements for the demolition of his great-uncle's house and the development of its grounds and of a substantial part of the adjoining glebe land, which he held on a long lease, by speculative building.

The Glebe

The land which constituted the glebe of the parish until 1954, when most of it was sold to the Church Commissioners, belonged to successive vicars of Kensington from at least 1260, and possibly earlier. In that year a composition made between the Abbot of Abingdon and the vicar of Kensington recited the bounds of the land reserved to the vicar, and these correspond with the recent boundaries of the glebe in most respects.[12] The northern boundary appears, however, to have originally been the King's highway (now Notting Hill Gate) and one seventeenth-century vicar advanced the theory that after some of the glebe land had been dug for gravel the pits so formed had been incorporated into the waste of the manor.[13] The extent of the glebe in the

---

* The land had previously been copyhold of the manor of Abbots Kensington, of which Cope held the lordship.

nineteenth century was about thirteen acres (fig. 6), a close approximation to the half a virgate which was mentioned in Domesday Book as the area of the priest's holding in Kensington, and the correlation is even more exact if the land between the glebe and Notting Hill Gate is included.

At least four vicarage houses have been recorded, not all in the same position. By 1610 there was a 'dwelling House for the Vicar' at the south end of the glebe, its site being now occupied by the roadway of Vicarage Gate at its junction with Kensington Church Street.[14] In *c.* 1774 this was rebuilt as a three-storey Georgian house, although parts of the earlier fabric may have been retained.[15] In 1877 a new red-brick vicarage in a Gothic style was built on the south side of the cul-de-sac of Vicarage Gate to the designs of William White. *The Builder* had mounted a campaign several years previously for a better line of communication between Notting Hill Gate and Kensington High Street and had recommended the demolition of the Georgian vicarage so that Kensington Church Street could be continued in a straight line to the north. The site of the old vicarage was, indeed, given up to the Vestry for the formation of a road (now the southern arm of Vicarage Gate), but ironically the main thoroughfare to Notting Hill Gate from the south is still along the old course of Kensington Church Street.[16] The vicarage designed by White was recently demolished and a new vicarage and parish hall, designed by Antony Lloyd, were built at the eastern end of the cul-de-sac of Vicarage Gate and opened in 1968.[17]

Another building which has often been confused with the vicarage was a large house known in the sixteenth century as the Manor House or Parsonage House. This stood between the parish church and Holland Street, and its history is discussed in Chapter I. The fact that it was known as the Parsonage House indicates that it may at one time have been occupied by incumbents of St. Mary Abbots.

The development of the Sheffield House and Glebe estates

In 1853 Thomas Robinson, the owner of Sheffield House and leaseholder of most of the glebe land, arranged with Archdeacon Sinclair,

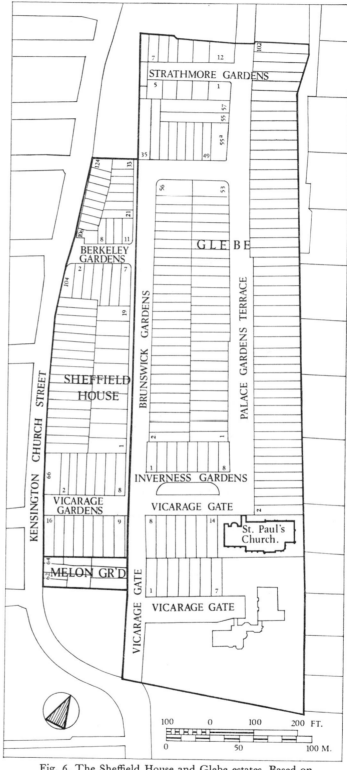

Fig. 6. The Sheffield House and Glebe estates. Based on the Ordnance Survey of 1894–6

the vicar of St. Mary Abbots, that he would surrender his lease, which had forty years outstanding, in return for a building agreement enabling him to develop both his freehold and leasehold property simultaneously. He had threatened to erect 'objectionable' buildings on the glebe if he was not allowed the extension of his term which was necessary to undertake a successful speculation. In April 1854 the vicar entered into an agreement with Robinson whereby the latter was to build houses on the glebe and would be granted leases for terms equivalent to ninety-nine years from March 1854. The elevations of the houses were to be approved by the architect of the Ecclesiastical Commissioners,* and the leases were to contain the usual covenants requiring the occupiers to keep their houses in good repair and decoration. No trade or business was to be carried on that would prove 'hazardous noisy noisome or offensive', including those of bagnio-keeper and sheriff's officer. It was found later that this agreement had not received the consent of the Ecclesiastical Commissioners or the Bishop of London, even though several leases had been granted under it, and a more formal agreement was entered into in 1860.[18]

The tables on pages 47–8 give the basic details of the speculation undertaken by Robinson. The author of the layout plan for the development was probably the architect David Brandon, who submitted applications to the Metropolitan Commissioners of Sewers in 1854 for permission to construct over three thousand feet of sewers in the new streets about to be formed.[19] There is, however, no evidence that Brandon provided any house designs. With the exception of Nos. 106–124 (even) Kensington Church Street, which have stock-brick façades with stucco dressings over ground-floor shops, all of the houses built under Robinson's auspices have stucco façades with an extensive use of ornament and consist of three or four main storeys over basements. They are arranged in terraces, but variations in design, usually reflecting the work of different builders, relieve the monotony. The houses built by William Lloyd Edwards of Paddington are interesting for the Mannerist treatment of the decorative features, which include Doric friezes over Ionic columns or half-shafts in the porches or doorways, pediments perched at the top of bays, and several

narrow windows, sometimes set in niches between paired entrances (Plate 41c, d). The same treatment is given to the façades of Nos. 42–58 (even) Palace Gardens Terrace, where the lessee was Jeremiah Little, but it is likely that Edwards also built these houses for he made the application to the Vestry for permission to connect drains from them to the sewer in Palace Gardens Terrace.[20] Jeremiah Little, who built Nos. 60–102 (even) Palace Gardens Terrace, was a major builder in Kensington from the 1840's until his death in 1873 (see page 53), and these houses are very similar in style to Nos. 9–55 (odd) Argyll Road, which he built on the Phillimore estate at approximately the same time. The only builder who does not appear to have used a distinctive style of his own was Thomas Huggett, a local builder, who was granted sub-leases by Robinson. Nos. 21–33 (odd) Palace Gardens Terrace are very similar to Little's houses on the other side of the street, and the other houses of which he was the sub-lessee, Nos. 22–32 (even) Brunswick Gardens, display some of the decorative features associated with Edwards's houses.

Building operations began on the site of Sheffield House, but instead of granting building leases of the land which he held in fee simple, Robinson sold most of it between 1854 and 1857, retaining only the freeholds of Nos. 1–19 (odd) Brunswick Gardens. The price which he received for the land is not known, but he may have used the money to pay for the construction of roads and sewers, and for the erection of some houses under contracts instead of building leases. Courtland Terrace, now Nos. 35–49 (odd) Brunswick Gardens and No. 55A Palace Gardens Terrace, appears to have been built in this way for Robinson by Jeremiah Little and his son Henry in 1856, Robinson himself not being granted leases by the vicar (the houses were on glebe land) until 1858.[21] These houses are similar to Nos. 3–9 (odd) Pitt Street on the Pitt estate, also built by Jeremiah Little.

Jeremiah Little purchased most of the former Sheffield House estate and granted leases of the majority of the houses erected on the land to his sons Henry and William, both also described as builders, for ninety-nine years from Midsummer 1854 or equivalent terms. In the case of some houses in the terrace originally called Sheffield

---

* There is no evidence that any such approval was ever sought.

Gardens, now Nos. 68–102 (even) Kensington Church Street, it was stated later that Henry and William Little had only been acting as trustees for their father, who had built the houses at his own expense.[22] Whatever the extent of the co-operation between the members of the Little family, Henry Little, at least, built up a flourishing business of his own, which in 1861 employed fifty-four men and thirteen boys.[23]

A piece of ground to the south of the Sheffield House estate, called the Melon Ground (fig. 6), was also purchased by Jeremiah Little. The vendors were Lucy Margaret and Robert Tetlow Robinson, sister and brother of Thomas Robinson; they had inherited the land under the will of their father Alexander Ramsay Robinson and it may, therefore, have once formed part of the Sheffield House estate.[24] Melon Place was laid out across the centre of the site and three houses were built facing Kensington Church Street, of which Nos. 62 and 64 survive, together with four cottages and a builder's yard in Melon Place. All were leased to Henry Little in 1858.[25] Three houses facing Vicarage Gate were erected in place of the builder's yard in 1880–1 by Joseph Mears of Hammersmith, who purchased the site from Little.[26]

The last houses to be built in the first stage of Robinson's development were Nos. 38–46 (even) Brunswick Gardens and Nos. 35–43 (odd) Palace Gardens Terrace. In the agreement of 1854 the ground on which these houses were built had been reserved for a church which Archdeacon Sinclair was planning to build to replace the temporary iron church of St. Paul, Vicarage Gate, but a provision was written into the agreement that if a reasonable time elapsed without the church being built Robinson could demand a building lease of the ground. As the roadways on each side were still awaiting completion, Robinson asked for a lease of the site in 1863 and the legal advisers to the Ecclesiastical Commissioners recommended the vicar to grant his request.[18]

The northernmost part of the glebe (to the north of Nos. 57 and 90 Palace Gardens Terrace) still remained undeveloped, however. The street called The Mall extended southward to this point and on its east side were three old houses and a cottage. These buildings, and the ground on the opposite side of the street, had been included in the long lease granted to the elder Thomas Robinson in 1794, but Alexander Ramsay

Robinson had bequeathed this part of his lease-hold possessions to Lucy Margaret and Robert Tetlow Robinson. They assigned the ground to Thomas Robinson in order that it could be included in the area to be developed under his agreement with Sinclair. He was granted a lease by the vicar in 1858 at a ground rent of £5 per annum, but four years later he sub-let the plot to his brother and sister at the same rent so that they would secure the benefit of any improved ground rents created by development.[27] Building did not take place until 1868–70 when Jeremiah Little built Strathmore Gardens and Nos. 92–102 (even) Palace Gardens Terrace.[28]

The total ground rent secured by the vicar from Robinson's development was slightly over £540 per annum for about nine acres of land.[29] This figure, which is equivalent to approximately £60 per acre, compares favourably with those received for mid nineteenth-century developments on the Pitt and Phillimore estates. Robinson, however, secured a handsome profit in improved ground rents through the sub-leases which he granted to builders. For instance, he was granted one lease of the sites of Nos. 45–53 (odd) Palace Gardens Terrace and Nos. 48–56 (even) Brunswick Gardens at an annual ground rent of £5, but he sub-let the individual houses to William Lloyd Edwards at a total in improved ground rents of £110 per annum.[30]

When the building of a new vicarage in 1877 necessitated the formation of a new street (the cul-de-sac of Vicarage Gate), the opportunity was taken to develop a further part of the glebe to the west of the iron church of St. Paul. Tenders were invited for the highest ground rent offered for the erection of not more than fourteen houses under ninety-nine-year leases. At least £30,000 was to be spent on the construction of the houses. Joseph Mears submitted an offer of £425 per annum which was accepted, and he built Nos. 1–14 (consec.) Vicarage Gate under an agreement made in October 1877.[31] Less than an acre of ground was involved, and the substantial amount which Mears was prepared to offer in ground rent demonstrates the considerable increase in the value of building ground in this part of Kensington since 1854, when the agreement had been made with Robinson. Most of the houses built by Mears were sold leasehold shortly after completion at prices varying between £4,000 and £4,500.

In the 1930's a further part of the garden of the

vicarage was appropriated for building when the block of flats called Vicarage Court was built on the east side of the southern arm of Vicarage Gate under a ninety-nine-year lease granted in 1934.[32]

In 1954 the Church Commissioners purchased the developed portion of the glebe,[33] the vicar of St. Mary Abbots retaining the vicarage and its still extensive grounds. When the new vicarage and parish hall were built in 1966–8, the site of the old vicarage was used for the erection of the block of flats known as Hamilton House.

The Church of St. Paul, Vicarage Gate
Plate 19. Demolished

After concluding the agreement of 1854 for the development of a large part of the glebe land, Archdeacon Sinclair, the vicar of St. Mary Abbots, had a temporary iron church built in the grounds of his vicarage at the southern end of Palace Gardens Terrace, the longest of the new streets being formed. The church, which was constructed by Hemming and Company of Bow of corrugated galvanized iron, was completed by September 1855 (Plate 19a, b). It was the first iron church in the metropolis.[34] The building was paid for out of pew rents over several years, Sinclair indemnifying the contractors against any failure to meet the costs of construction.[35]

The provision of a permanent structure became a pressing necessity when the fabric of the iron church began to deteriorate, and an appeal for funds was launched in 1885. The vicar of St. Mary Abbots at that time, the Honourable Edward Carr Glyn, recognized that the site on which the temporary church stood was by no means ideal, for it was hemmed in by the houses of Vicarage Gate on the west and Palace Gardens Terrace on the north, but he thought that it would be virtually impossible to secure another site in view of the steep rise in the value of land in Kensington over the past two decades. He

therefore conveyed the site as a free gift to the Ecclesiastical Commissioners in 1886.

A limited competition was organized for the design of the new church. The vicar felt that 'a good, well-ordered, and beautiful church is the limit of our ambition' and placed a ceiling of £10,000 on the cost. The assessor was Ewan Christian, and the winner was Arthur Baker, whose motto was 'Hope'. The building committee was not entirely convinced, however, and asked for modified designs from Baker and two other competitors. Eventually a considerably modified design by Baker, who lived in Kensington and had worked as an assistant in Sir George Gilbert Scott's office, was selected (Plate 19c, d). The builders were E. C. Howell and Son of Bristol and Lambeth, and construction began in July 1887. The first service was held in November 1888, and the church was consecrated on 25 January 1889. It was designated a chapel-of-ease to St. Mary Abbots. The total cost, including Baker's fee and other expenses, was £11,000, which had been entirely defrayed by the date of consecration.[36]

The church was built of brick with a very sparing use of stone dressings and the roofs were tiled. The style was French Gothic of the thirteenth century, although the chancel owed much to Early English prototypes. A copper-covered flèche placed over the crossing gave the church a vertical emphasis above the tall terraced houses which dominated its setting, and Baker's amended design provided for two porches flanking an apsidal baptistry at the western end of the north side of the nave, which was the only part of the exterior abutting on to a public highway. The westernmost porch led to a covered atrium beyond the west wall of the nave.

The church was severely damaged during the war of 1939–45 and was not rebuilt. Its site was sold to the Distressed Gentlefolks' Aid Association[37] and is now occupied by a nursing home.

CONVEYANCES AND LEASES ON THE SHEFFIELD HOUSE ESTATE

Except where indicated otherwise, the dates refer to the years in which the conveyances and leases were made: these are not always the date of actual building. The chief sources are the Middlesex Land Register in the Greater London Record Office at County Hall and the Minutes of the Vestry Sewers Committee in Kensington Public Library.

Berkeley Gardens, north side

8–11 consec.   See Nos. 106–124 even Kensington Church Street below.

Berkeley Gardens, south side

2–7 consec.   Ground sold by Thomas Robinson, esquire, to Jeremiah Little of Sheffield Terrace, builder, 1854–7. Houses built by Little in 1857–8.

Brunswick Gardens, west side

1–19 odd   Leased by Robinson to Henry Little of Vicarage Gardens, builder, 1858–9.

21–33 odd   See Nos. 106–124 even Kensington Church Street below.

Kensington Church Street, east side

66–102 even   Ground sold by Robinson to Jeremiah Little. Houses leased by Jeremiah Little to Henry Little, except for Nos. 76–94 which were leased jointly to Henry Little and William Little of Sheffield Terrace, builder, 1854–6.

104   Originally No. 1 Berkeley Gardens. See Nos. 2–7 consec. Berkeley Gardens above.

106–124 even   The freeholds of these houses, together with the ground on which Nos. 8–11 consec. Berkeley Gardens and Nos. 21–33 odd Brunswick Gardens were built, were sold by Robinson to Edward Lambert of St. Marylebone and Edward Brooshooft of Hull, esquires, as security for £3,000 lent by them to Thomas Finlay of Paddington, 1856. Finlay appears to have built all of the houses between 1856 and 1862.

Vicarage Gardens, north side

2–8 consec.   Ground sold by Robinson to Jeremiah Little. Houses leased by Jeremiah Little to Henry Little, 1856–8.

Vicarage Gardens, south side

9–16 consec.   Ground sold by Robinson to Jeremiah Little. Houses leased by Jeremiah Little to William Little, except for No. 10 to Henry Little, 1856–8.

LESSORS AND LESSEES ON THE GLEBE ESTATE

Except where indicated otherwise, the dates refer to the years in which the leases were granted: these are not always the date of actual building. All leases granted by vicars of Kensington were with the consent of the Ecclesiastical Commissioners and the Bishop of London. The chief sources are the Middlesex Land Register in the Greater London Record Office at County Hall, the records of the Church Commissioners and the Minutes of the Vestry Sewers and Works Committees in Kensington Public Library.

Brunswick Gardens, east side

2–20 even   Vicar of Kensington to Thomas Robinson, esquire, 1858–61. Robinson to William Lloyd Edwards of Paddington, builder, 1861.

22–32 even   Vicar of Kensington to Robinson, 1858. Robinson to Thomas Huggett of Dartmoor Street, Kensington, builder, 1861.

34 and 36   Vicar of Kensington to Robinson, 1858. Robinson to Edwards, 1861.

38–46 even   Vicar of Kensington to Robinson, 1863. Robinson to Edwards, 1864.

48–56 even   Vicar of Kensington to Robinson, 1858. Robinson to Edwards, 1861.

Brunswick Gardens, north side

35–49 odd   Vicar of Kensington to Robinson, 1858. Built by Jeremiah and Henry Little in 1856–7.

Inverness Gardens

1–8 consec.   Vicar of Kensington by direction of Thomas Robinson to William Lloyd Edwards, builder, 1860. Nos. 7 and 8 rebuilt after destruction in war of 1939–45.

Palace Gardens Terrace, east side

2–40 even   Vicar of Kensington by direction of Thomas Robinson to William Lloyd Edwards, builder, 1859.

CHAPTER TWO

LESSORS AND LESSEES ON THE GLEBE ESTATE

42–90 even	Vicar of Kensington by direction of Robinson to Jeremiah Little, builder, 1858. Nos. 42–58 probably built by Edwards.
92–102 even	The ground on which these houses and Nos. 1–12 Strathmore Gardens were built was leased by vicar of Kensington to Thomas Robinson, 1858. Sub-leased by Thomas Robinson to Lucy Margaret and Robert Tetlow Robinson, 1862. Houses sub-leased by L. M. and R. T. Robinson to Jeremiah Little, 1871.

Palace Gardens Terrace, west side

1–19 odd	Vicar of Kensington to Thomas Robinson, 1860. Robinson to Edwards, 1860. Nos. 1, 3 and 5 rebuilt after destruction during war of 1939–45.
21–33 odd	Vicar of Kensington to Robinson, 1858. Robinson to Thomas Huggett, builder, 1860.

35–43 odd	Vicar of Kensington to Robinson, 1863. Assigned by Robinson to Henry Bingley Clark of Surrey, esquire, 1863. Sub-leased by Clark to Edwards, 1864.
45–53 odd	Vicar of Kensington to Robinson, 1858. Robinson to Edwards, 1861.
55A	Originally numbered with north side of Brunswick Gardens. See Nos. 35–49 odd Brunswick Gardens.
55 and 57	Vicar of Kensington to Robinson, 1858. Built by Jeremiah or Henry Little in 1856.

Strathmore Gardens

1–12 consec.	See Nos. 92–102 even Palace Gardens Terrace above.

Vicarage Gate

1–14 consec.	Vicar of Kensington to Joseph Mears of Hammersmith, builder, with the exception of No. 7 to Jonathan Pearson of High Street, Notting Hill, ironmonger, by direction of Mears, 1878–9.

CHAPTER III

The Pitt Estate

WHEN first covered with speculative housing on a large scale in the mid nineteenth century, the Pitt estate (fig. 7) consisted of approximately sixteen acres of land surrounding Campden House. Most of this property had formed part of the large estate attached to Campden House in the seventeenth century and had been purchased by Stephen Pitt in 1751, but a small piece of copyhold land (the site of Bullingham Mansions) had been acquired by the Pitt family through marriage.

In 1609 Sir Baptist Hicks, a wealthy mercer much favoured by the King, was admitted as a tenant of the manor of Abbots Kensington to a capital messuage and two closes of land called The Racks and King's Mead.[1] This holding formed the heart of the Campden House estate (the relationship between the 'capital messuage' and Campden House itself is discussed on page 55) and it appears that a substantial part of the estate was originally copyhold land, although it must have been enfranchised at an early date. In 1616 Hicks purchased some seventy acres to the south and west of his original holding from Robert Horseman for £2,679,[2]* and at its greatest extent in the first half of the seventeenth century the Campden House estate must have consisted of over one hundred acres.

In 1628 Hicks was created Viscount Campden, deriving his title from the manor in Gloucestershire which he also owned. As he had no male heirs the title was granted with specific remainder to his son-in-law Edward, Lord Noel.[3] His estates also passed to the Noel family, but the Dowager Viscountess Campden lived at Campden House for several years after his death in 1629. Both the second Viscount, who died in 1643, and the third were active Royalists and the Campden estates were confiscated during the Civil War. They were restored to the third Viscount in 1647 on payment of a composition of £9,000.[4] At this time the property in Kensington formed

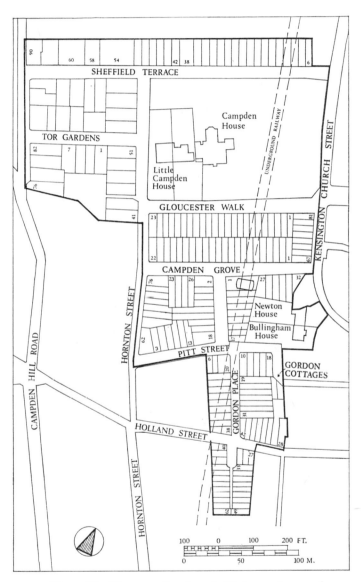

Fig. 7. The Pitt estate. Based on the Ordnance Survey of 1894–6

---

* This purchase, which included a mansion called the Manor House or Parsonage House was of land which Robert Horseman's father had secured from (Sir) Walter Cope in 1599 (see pages 25–6).

only a small part of Viscount Campden's total holdings, most of his estates being in Gloucestershire and Rutland.[5]

In 1662 an Act of Parliament was passed settling the Campden House estate on Viscount Campden and his heirs,[6] but in 1708 the third Earl of Gainsborough* sold the estate, a further Act having been obtained some time previously to enable the property to be sold. The purchaser, who paid £6,800, was Laud D'Oyley of St. Mary le Savoy, a merchant.[7] D'Oyley, who died shortly afterwards, left his property to his son Robert, and in March 1709/10 Robert D'Oyley broke up the estate when he sold Campden House and about thirteen acres around the mansion to Robert Balle, a merchant, for £2,550. In subsequent transactions D'Oyley sold two more pieces of land to make Balle's total holding some sixteen and a half acres.[8] The remainder of the estate afterwards descended to the Phillimore family (see page 58).

Robert Balle did not retain the now much truncated Campden House estate for long, for in 1719 he sold it for £4,000 to Nicholas Lechmere, the attorney-general, who was later created Baron Lechmere. In 1751 Edmund Lechmere, the nephew and heir of Lord Lechmere, sold the estate to Stephen Pitt for £2,800, and, with the exception of some parts sold since, it has remained in the ownership of the Pitt family.[9]

Stephen Pitt was the son of Samuel Pitt, a merchant, whose family owned house property in the City of London. His mother, Catherine, was the daughter of Robert Orbell and had inherited some copyhold land near Church Lane (now Kensington Church Street) from her father, who had erected five houses on the land at the end of the seventeenth century.[10] These houses, which were called Orbell's Buildings and later Pitt's Buildings, were approached from a courtyard off Church Lane and appear to have been ranged in a north–south line. In later manorial documents they number only four and by the mid nineteenth century only two houses and their accompanying buildings occupied the site. Even these two houses were sometimes joined together to form one.[11] The names given to these houses at this time were Bullingham House (most confusingly, for a house which had at one time borne that name was then

still standing on a nearby site in Kensington Church Street) and Newton House (see fig. 7). Bullingham House had its main front facing west and from surviving illustrations of the façade appears to have dated from the early to mid eighteenth century, although only a refronting may have taken place at this time. Newton House appears to have been slightly older and it is possible that it basically consisted of two or more of Orbell's five houses joined together. It was named after Sir Isaac Newton, who had lived at Orbell's Buildings for the last two years of his life. Traditionally, however, the claims of Bullingham House as his place of residence and death in 1727 have been more strongly advanced,[12] but all that can be stated with certainty is that Newton lived in one of the houses on Robert Orbell's copyhold land. In 1894 the copyhold was enfranchised and Bullingham House and Newton House were demolished for the building of Bullingham Mansions.

Stephen Pitt died in 1793 and the estate was inherited by his son, also named Stephen. In 1814 this Stephen Pitt sold a narrow piece of land with a short frontage to Kensington High Street to the Vestry in order to provide additional burial ground for St. Mary Abbots Church. This land, which had formerly been occupied by the long carriage-drive to Campden House from Kensington High Street, was part of a field called Paramour's Pingle—a name which might seem to imply that it was a favourite place for clandestine frolics in the hay, but was in fact more prosaically derived from the name of a tenant, Lawrence Paramour. The Vestry paid £2,100 for the land, which is now occupied by the former Vestry Hall and the garden and playground to the north of it (see page 37).[13]

There is evidence that Pitt contemplated some building developments in the 1820's, for the minutes of the Kensington Turnpike Trust for 1826 indicate that Joseph Kay, who was Pitt's surveyor at the time, had entered into an agreement with one Samuel Bickford for building along part of the Kensington Church Street frontage. No houses appear to have been built, however, and it may be that the difficulties which beset the building industry after 1825 prevented the completion of the undertaking.[14]

---

* The fourth Viscount Campden had been created Earl of Gainsborough in 1682.[3]

From 1844 to 1864

The 1840's witnessed a general resurgence in building activity in northern Kensington and the Pitt estate was only one of several areas where large-scale undertakings were begun in that decade. In November 1844 Stephen Pitt entered into an agreement with William Eales, a timber merchant, and Jeremiah Little, a builder, both of St. Marylebone, to develop practically the whole of his estate. Only Newton House and Bullingham House with their large gardens extending to the west were excluded. Campden House and the smaller mansion on its west side, Little Campden House, were included in the area covered by the agreement, and at one time their demolition was contemplated. In the event they were left standing, although with considerably reduced grounds.

The total area involved was approximately fourteen and a half acres, which Eales and Little agreed to take for a ninety-nine-year term at an annual rent of £500 for the first four years and £900 for the remainder. Over a six-year period they were required to build houses to the value of £10,000 (evidently calculated as a multiple of the rack-rental values) and to spend £2,500 in making roads, sewers and pavements. The building materials to be used were specified and the builders were enjoined to observe the provisions of the 1844 Building Act. All houses were to be erected 'under the inspection and to the satisfaction' of Pitt's surveyor, and none were to be of less than £30 annual value. Pitt agreed to grant leases of the houses as soon as they had been covered-in to the developers or their nominees, and undertook that as soon as £900 had been secured in ground rents (equivalent to approximately £63 per acre) any further leases would be granted at ground rents not exceeding five shillings.[10]

The surveyor to the Pitt estate was Thomas Allason, and there is reason to believe that he had a considerable influence on the type of development undertaken by Eales and Little. The layout adopted has no outstanding features but the area was small and of awkward shape, while the street pattern was largely suggested by the presence of already existing roads on the estate, like Pitt Street and Holland Street, and by other roads around its edges. There was certainly no opportunity for the kind of spacious planning with which Allason was associated on the Ladbroke estate. The houses erected on the Pitt estate during the initial years of Eales's and Little's development, however, seem to bear the mark of a supervising architect's influence even though several different builders were involved. They are in the main relatively modest terrace houses consisting of three storeys, usually with basements, and except in the extreme south of the estate— in Holland Street and the southern end of Gordon Place—they are stuccoed. The windows have plain openings, although those on the first floor are surmounted by cornices carried on consoles, and the entrances have simple doorcases with Doric pilasters but are without porches. A continuous balcony with iron railings at first-floor level and a plain or modillioned cornice at roof level form the chief remaining decorative features (Plates 40d, 41b). There are variations, for example at Nos. 10–13 (consec.) Campden Grove, where bay windows rising from the basement through all three main storeys are used to accentuate the centre of the terrace, and subsequent rebuildings coupled with the erosion of many of the mouldings make it difficult to appreciate the original homogeneity. The scale of the houses, however, was well chosen for the somewhat constricted layout and was not disproportionate to already existing buildings around the estate.

While this uniformity could have been imposed by Eales or Little, the fact that it is more likely to have been the result of Allason's influence is suggested by the adoption of the name Allason Terrace for the first houses to be built as part of the development. This terrace, now Nos. 67–81 (odd) Kensington Church Street, consists of four storeys, the ground floor containing shops. The upper storeys are stuccoed and display the architectural features seen elsewhere, although here used in a more elaborate manner. Two houses at each end of the terrace are brought forward and have pedimented cornices above the first-floor windows, while originally a continuous modillioned cornice extended the length of the terrace above the third storey.

Another factor which points to Allason's responsibility for general architectural control is that towards the end of the development the uniformity tends to become less marked. Allason died in 1852[15] and was succeeded as surveyor by John Shaw, architect to Christ's Hospital.[16] Houses completed after this date show far greater variations, although Eales and Little were more directly involved in the building operations than earlier, when they had chiefly relied on other builders. The south side of Gloucester Walk, where building was still in progress in 1855, is less homogeneous than other terraces, and to the west of Hornton Street, where terraces give way to detached and semi-detached villas, the houses reflect the various stylistic predilections of their builders. Nos. 3–9 (odd) Pitt Street provide an instructive example, for these houses, which were first leased in 1853,[17] were built by Jeremiah Little but are more wilful in decorative treatment than his earlier houses in Sheffield Terrace.

All of the leases granted under the agreement of 1844 were calculated to expire in 1943. The device of a short period at a peppercorn rent was not used, but the beginning of the term for each lease was generally fixed at the nearest quarter day to the date on which it was granted. Individual ground rents ranged from £20 per annum for No. 60 Sheffield Terrace, a substantial detached house, to five shillings per annum for houses built towards the end of the speculation when the £900 guaranteed under the agreement had been secured.[18] Although some leases were granted to builders, many lessees were not connected with the building trades. The principal speculators who obtained leases of several houses were John Simpson of St. George's, Hanover Square, and Thomas Simpson of Paddington, licensed victuallers, John Brannan Quick of St. Marylebone, a paper stainer,* Edgar Wright of St. Marylebone, an ironmonger, Thomas Rogers of St. Marylebone, a modeller, and William Philip Beech of Rotherhithe, a ship breaker.[19]† Stephen Pitt died in 1848 and after that date leases were granted by his widow and the trustees appointed under his will.

Several builders did not receive direct leases from the estate and presumably built under contract. Among these was John Salmon of Wiple Place, Kensington Church Street, who was the first to commence building operations in 1845 with the erection of Nos. 67–81 (odd) Kensington Church Street (Allason Terrace). The lessees of this terrace were John and Thomas Simpson.[21] Salmon also appears to have built all the houses

erected in Campden Grove as part of Eales's and Little's development, namely Nos. 1–26 (consec.), as well as Nos. 2–18 (even) Gordon Place, Nos. 70–76 (even) Hornton Street (originally known as Campden House Road north of Holland Street) and Nos. 1, 2, 12, and 13 Gloucester Walk (formerly Gloucester Terrace).[22] Of these houses, Nos. 5–8 Campden Grove have been rebuilt as a result of the construction of the Metropolitan Railway in 1865–8, while No. 22 Campden Grove and No. 76 Hornton Street have been substantially altered.

Another builder employed extensively during the early stages of the development was Thomas Casey of Kensington. He was principally responsible for Nos. 30–42 (even) Holland Street (originally part of a range called Hornton Terrace), Nos. 19–31 (odd) Gordon Place (originally called Vicarage Street at this point) and Gordon Cottages. In Holland Street he was assisted by another local builder, William Potter, who signed documents with a mark.[23]

The attractive cul-de-sac, formerly called Orchard Street, which now forms the south end of Gordon Place, was begun in 1846 (Plate 40c). The main builders were Charles and Frederick Sewell of Paddington, although others were involved, for the lease of No. 46 Gordon Place was granted to Frederick Blucher Dowland of Kensington, builder, and the lessee of No. 39 was George Edward Sewell of Camden Town, builder. The first inhabitants of these houses were generally artisans and there were several instances of multi-occupancy.[24]

The houses on the south side of Pitt Street were also erected during the 1840's, those to the west of Gordon Place originally having ground-floor shops. The builders were Gatehouse and Company of St. Marylebone and a Mr. Watts of Gracechurch Street. Watts built the pleasant terrace formerly called Vassall Terrace, now Nos. 10–18 (even) Pitt Street.[22]

Eales and Little did not apparently take a direct part in the building operations until 1848, the year in which Sheffield Terrace was begun, but notices of the commencement of building for

---

* Henry Brannan Quick, a solicitor, or his clerks, witnessed several deeds.

† Other lessees connected with the building trades, but who took leases of only one or two houses, were: John Birch of St. Pancras, *timber merchant*; George Climpson of St. Marylebone, *carpenter*; John Foot of St. Marylebone, *painter and plumber*; David Little of Paddington, *carpenter*.

An indication of how tradesmen like Climpson, Foot and Little came to acquire leases is contained in an advertisement in 1847 for building work to be done in Campden Grove with 'payment by carcass in exchange'.[20]

all of the houses in that street erected under their agreement were given to the district surveyor by one or other of the partners, principally Little. Of these Nos. 8–14 (even) were rebuilt in 1871 as a result of the construction of the Metropolitan Railway, and the semi-detached villas to the west of Hornton Street, originally called Percy Villas and later Nos. 31–39 (odd) Sheffield Terrace, were demolished after the war of 1939–45. Other surviving houses built by Little are No. 90 Campden Hill Road, Nos. 41, 43, 62 and 64 Hornton Street and Nos. 3–9 (odd) Pitt Street.* Eales gave notice for the building of Nos. 49 and 51 Hornton Street and Nos. 80 and 82 Campden Hill Road.†

Another builder who figured prominently in the later stages of the development was Thomas Bridgewater Richardson of Paddington, who took building leases of Nos. 3–11 and 14–21 (consec.) Gloucester Walk in 1853–5.[27] Four of these houses, Nos. 8–11, were built for him by William Yeo of Paddington.[28] Of the original houses Nos. 5–8 were rebuilt as a consequence of the construction of the Metropolitan Railway. Richardson also built Nos. 66 and 68 Hornton Street.[29]

In Tor Gardens (formerly York Villas) only four houses on the south side, Nos. 1–7 (odd), have survived. The builder of this attractive group of two linked pairs was Thomas Bridges of St. Marylebone in 1851.[30] Bridges also built Nos. 76 and 78 Campden Hill Road.[31]

The last houses to be built under the agreement with Eales and Little were begun in 1855, and with the erection of 185 houses in slightly over a decade the development can be said to have reached a successful conclusion. The houses appear to have been taken as soon as they were finished, generally by people who could afford one or two servants; many of the occupants were annuitants or otherwise living on unearned incomes.[32] For Jeremiah Little this enterprise marked the beginning of a most successful building career in Kensington. He lived at No. 54 Sheffield Terrace (Wilton Villa), a house built by himself (Plate 40a), and conducted building operations on the Sheffield House, Glebe and Phillimore estates as well as elsewhere in Kensington. In 1861 he employed fifty men and ten boys.

At the time of his death in 1873 he owned, leasehold or freehold, over one hundred houses in Kensington and his estate was valued at over £120,000, even after mortgage debts of £50,000 had been taken into account. His property was divided between six of his children, two of whom, Henry Little and Alfred James Little, followed their father's trade. Another son, William, was also a builder, but as he was not included in the settlement he may have died before his father.[33]

Since 1864

The extension of the Metropolitan Railway to Kensington, sanctioned by Act of Parliament in 1864, had an unfortunate effect on the appearance of the Pitt estate. The course chosen for the railway cut across the estate from north to south, and although the line was carried in a tunnel several houses had to be demolished for its construction. When rebuilding took place after the tunnel was completed, the new houses erected were often disproportionate in scale to their neighbours. As compensation for the loss of land which had to be sold to the railway company the trustees of the estate received £6,700.[34]

Perhaps the most glaring example of this unsympathetic rebuilding occurred in Sheffield Terrace, where in 1871 Jeremiah Little erected four new houses, Nos. 8–14 (even), in place of four which he had himself built about twenty years previously and which had had to be demolished. Little in fact purchased the fee simple of the new houses from the Metropolitan Railway Company.[35] They are of three storeys over a semi-basement and are of greater height than the terrace houses on each side, with bay windows and a considerably more lavish use of ornamentation. No doubt they reflect a change over two decades in the type of house which the builder knew would satisfy the needs of middle-class tenants.

Nos. 5–8 (consec.) Campden Grove and Nos. 5–8 (consec.) Gloucester Walk were also rebuilt in 1871 under ninety-year leases granted by the Metropolitan Railway Company. The builders in each case were Igglesden and Myers of Paddington.[36]

The most extensive rebuilding took place in

---

* For several years the site to the east of No. 9 was left undeveloped. Nos. 11 and 13 Pitt Street were eventually built there by Temple and Foster in 1866.[25]

† No. 80 Campden Hill Road (South Lodge) is noteworthy as the former residence of Violet Hunt and Ford Madox Ford.[26]

Gordon Place. The houses on the west side of the street between Pitt Street and Holland Street were demolished, and in 1872 the railway company sold the vacant land to Charles Hall of Lincoln's Inn, a barrister. In the following year Hall engaged the local builder Thomas Hussey to build a new terrace of nine houses, now Nos. 20–38 (even) Gordon Place, under ninety-nine-year leases.[37] Also on the west side of the street, Nos. 40–44 (even) were erected in 1871 by William Cooke of Paddington under eighty-five-year leases granted by the company;[38] these houses replaced a Baptist chapel (see below) and a house on the south-west corner of Holland Street and Gordon Place.

Before the construction of the railway the gardens of Newton House and Bullingham House had extended to the east side of Gordon Place, but the ends of these gardens had to be given up and Nos. 1–17 (odd) Gordon Place were erected in 1872–3 under eighty-five-year leases granted by the company. No. 1, a substantial stuccoed double-fronted house was built by William Cooke; its rear elevation is shaped in a concave curve to accommodate a ventilating shaft for the railway at the rear of the house. Nos. 3–17 were built by Samuel Sawyer of Paddington.[39] Nos. 7, 9 and 11 were rebuilt after the war of 1939–45.

The completion of building on the land taken from the estate for the railway no doubt prompted the trustees to develop the remaining frontage on the south side of Campden Grove. Six houses were erected there in 1877 under an agreement with Thomas Thompson and Thomas Smith of Paddington, builders and contractors, who offered twenty shillings per foot frontage in ground rents.[10] The actual builder was William Ford of Pimlico, who obtained leases of five of the houses, that for the remaining one (No. 27) being granted to Thompson and Smith. An interesting feature of these houses is that while Nos. 27–31 (consec.) Campden Grove are of a typical debased classical variety, faced with white brick and stucco dressings, No. 32 was conceived as a studio-house and is of stock brick with red brick dressings. The same builder was responsible for all six houses and No. 32 appears to have been built as a speculation in the manner of its neighbouring terraced dwellings —perhaps an indication of the catholicity of the work the speculative builder was prepared to undertake at this time of fluctuations in house styles.[40]

The last major building operations to be undertaken under the control of the estate date from 1894. In that year the copyhold of Newton House and Bullingham House was enfranchised and the two houses were demolished. Notice of the intention to build six blocks of flats on the site was given in November 1894 by Joseph Mears of Earl's Court, but he died shortly afterwards and the work was undertaken by Joseph T. Mears, probably his son. Ninety-nine-year leases of Bullingham Mansions, as the flats are called, were granted to Charlotte Mears, the widow of Joseph Mears, senior, at a total ground rent of £220.[41]

Also in 1894, William Adams Daw of the building firm of C. A. Daw and Son of Palace Gate, Kensington, and Percy Frederick Tarbutt of Evelyn Gardens, an engineer, undertook to build on the curtilage of Campden House along the frontages to Gloucester Walk, Kensington Church Street and Sheffield Terrace. Daw and Tarbutt had obtained an assignment of the lease of Campden House from the lessee, Mary Eliza Elder, and surrendered the lease to Thomas Morton Stanhope Pitt, who became tenant-for-life of the estate under Stephen Pitt's will, in order to secure a building agreement. At the same time the strip of land above the Metropolitan Railway, which ran under the grounds of Campden House, was re-purchased by Pitt after having been sold to the railway company which had in turn sold it to Alexander Lang Elder, the late husband of Mary Eliza Elder.[42]

The buildings erected in the former grounds of Campden House are a mixture of blocks of flats and large terraced houses, consisting of at least four main storeys with basements and attics and built predominantly of red brick. Some of the building work was contracted out so that most of the houses and flats on the south side of Sheffield Terrace were built by Hawkins and Company of St. Marylebone, and most of those on the north side of Gloucester Walk by Hailey and Company of Chelsea.[22] Daw and Son built the attractive terrace of studio-houses in Kensington Church Street called Campden House Terrace (Plate 41f). Originally this consisted of six houses, the present No. 7 forming part of No. 1 Sheffield Terrace. Although several builders were involved in the development the head leases were granted to Daw and Tarbutt until June 1897, and after that date to Daw alone. They were for ninety-nine years from 1894 at a total ground rent of £300.[10]

The building which attracted most contemporary notice was the block of flats at the corner of Sheffield Terrace and Hornton Street called Campden House Chambers. The architects were Thackeray Turner and Eustace Balfour. A. E. Street commented that 'Campden House Chambers . . . studiously simple in mass and detail, is, in spite of some obvious affinities with that of Mr. Philip Webb, an original and characteristic work'. Originally the flats had a common dining-room—a large, vaulted room in the basement—in which tenants were served at separate tables.[43]

Little further change took place on the estate until several buildings were destroyed or badly damaged during the war of 1939–45. The most severely affected area was at the northern end of Hornton Street and in 1948 the London County Council decided to acquire two sites with a total area of two and a half acres, one on each side of the street, by compulsory purchase for housing purposes. Building of the housing estate, which was given the name Tor Gardens estate, began in 1953.[44]

Campden House
Plate 39. Demolished

The entry in the court roll of the manor of Abbots Kensington in 1609 admitting Sir Baptist Hicks to a capital messuage and some surrounding land contains a recital of the abuttals of the property and seems to show beyond reasonable doubt that the 'capital messuage' was on the site of Campden House.[1] Moreover, this was almost certainly the house in which (Sir) Walter Cope was living in 1598, at the time of his quarrel with Robert Horseman[45] (see page 25).* The date usually assigned to the building of Campden House is 1612 on the evidence given in Lysons' *Environs* that a window contained the arms of Sir Baptist Hicks and his sons-in-law with that date. In his analysis of the volume of drawings by John Thorpe in Sir John Soane's Museum, however, Sir John Summerson identified two drawings—an elevation and a ground plan of a timber-framed house—with Campden House, but maintained that they were much earlier than 1612.[47] It now appears likely that these drawings (numbers 95 and 96 in Thorpe's book) were of the house which preceded Campden House and which may have been built for Cope towards the end of the sixteenth century. A comparison of Thorpe's drawings with a painting showing Campden House shortly after the Restoration suggests that what took place in *c.* 1612 was perhaps an enlargement and refronting in brick and stone of the earlier house rather than a complete rebuilding (Plate 39).†

The later history of the house can only be recounted briefly here. For a short time during the Civil War it was used by the Committee of Sequestrations for Middlesex,[48] and in the last decade of the seventeenth century it was the residence of Princess Anne of Denmark (later Queen Anne) and her ill-fated son, styled the Duke of Gloucester.[49] Early in the eighteenth century the Countess of Burlington and her son, the third Earl, who became an architect and patron of the arts, lived there.[50] For almost a century after Stephen Pitt purchased the Campden House estate in 1751 the mansion was used as a boarding school, and during this period it underwent considerable alterations including the removal of most of the decorative features from the south front, which was rendered. In 1847 it was rented by William Frederick Wolley, a landowner, who spent considerable sums of money in restoring the house. In 1854 he paid £6,225 for a new ninety-year lease at a nominal annual rent of five shillings.[51] Among the additions made to the house by Wolley was a theatre in which Charles

---

* It has generally been assumed that Cope was then living in West Town, which he purchased in 1591, and where he later had Holland House built, but the available documentary evidence indicates otherwise, West Town being subject to an existing lease when he acquired the freehold.[46]

† The next two Thorpe drawings of the ground- and upper-floor plans of a house (numbers 97 and 98) pose an unresolved problem. They appear to have 'Hix' and 'Mr. Hix' written across them, and from this, their position in the volume and certain features of planning, they have also been tentatively ascribed to Campden House. There are significant differences in the plan of this house from what is known of Campden House, however, and as Hicks was knighted in 1603 the use of the term 'Mr. Hix' after that date would be most unusual.

A further problem is raised by a drawing in Kensington Public Library which purports to be by Hollar and is dated 1647. This shows Campden House without a cupola, but in view of the spate of Hollar forgeries in the nineteenth century its authenticity must be doubted and it may have been taken from the engraving in Lysons' *Environs* showing the house in 1795.

Dickens acted with Wilkie Collins in Collins's play *The Lighthouse* in July 1855.[52]

In March 1862 Campden House was almost totally destroyed by fire. Wolley had insured the house and its contents for nearly £30,000, but the insurance companies refused to pay, alleging that he had started the fire deliberately. He brought an action against one of the companies and won his case.[53] The mansion was rebuilt, presumably out of the insurance money that Wolley was then able to recover, as a reasonable facsimile of the original, although with a somewhat fanciful arrangement of five gables on the south front. In 1872 Wolley sold his lease to the Metropolitan Railway Company, which had taken a strip of land in the middle of the grounds for the construction of its railway. The company in turn assigned the lease to Alexander Lang Elder of the City, esquire.[54]

In 1893 Elder's widow put Campden House up for auction but it failed to fetch the reserve price of £25,000.[55] In the following year two developers, William Adams Daw, builder, and Percy Frederick Tarbutt, engineer, took an assignment of the lease and surrendered it to the freeholder, Thomas Morton Stanhope Pitt, in exchange for an agreement to build in the grounds of the house.[42] At first it was intended to preserve the mansion while building around the periphery of its grounds, and in 1897 Daw asserted that he had no plans to demolish a house which had cost about £25,000 to build.[56] Presumably he also found it impossible to secure a remunerative price, however, and in *c.* 1900 the rebuilt house was demolished and its site added to the communal garden of the new development.

Little Campden House
Also known as The Elms and Lancaster Lodge.
Plate 41a. Demolished

Little Campden House was a long, two-storey building on the west side of Campden House. Lysons thought that it had been built in the 1690's during the residence of Princess Anne of Denmark (later Queen Anne) at Campden House in order to provide accommodation for her household.[57] A photograph of the south front in 1937 (Plate 41a) indicates that the building could well date from the end of the seventeenth century; the modillioned cornice, the roof, the keystones with masks above the first-floor windows, and the narrow windows on each side of the centre are all

suggestive of this period, although the building had undergone considerable alterations and was probably originally brick-fronted. The earliest map showing Kensington on a large scale, dated 1717,[58] shows the building, but it is strange that if it was built for the purpose suggested by Lysons no record of its construction has been discovered.

In 1850 the house was divided and two leases for ninety-three and a quarter years were granted to Jeremiah Little and William Eales respectively.[59] Little's lease was of the eastern part, which was sometimes given the name of The Elms but usually referred to as Little Campden House East or simply Little Campden House. The western part, leased to Eales, acquired the name of Lancaster Lodge and had its main entrance in Campden House Road (now Hornton Street). They were later designated No. 30 Gloucester Walk and No. 80 Hornton Street respectively. Both houses became very popular residences for artists and several alterations and additions were made. In 1944 they were badly damaged by a bomb and were demolished shortly afterwards, their sites now being incorporated in the Tor Gardens housing estate.

In 1869 the Metropolitan Board of Works gave consent for the erection of a studio to the designs of Philip Webb in the garden of Lancaster Lodge, then occupied by Robert Braithwaite Martineau. A studio was built at the north corner of Hornton Street and Gloucester Walk in that year, and presumably this was the building designed by Webb.[60] It was later designated No. 78 Hornton Street but was demolished with Lancaster Lodge and no graphic record has been found.

Bethel Baptist Chapel, Holland Street
Demolished

This short-lived Baptist chapel on the south side of Holland Street, near the south-western corner with Gordon Place, was built in 1847 by Frederick Blucher Dowland of Kensington under a lease granted to Joseph Trigg of Chelsea, a coal merchant, and John Doncaster of Kensington, a builder.[61] It was demolished *c.* 1865 for the building of the Metropolitan Railway.

No. 38 Sheffield Terrace
Plate 40b

This house, which was known as No. 18 Sheffield Terrace until it was renumbered in 1927, was designed in 1876 by Alfred Waterhouse for Edward Coningham Sterling. The builder was W. H. Lascelles and the cost was about £5,500.[62]

The ground on which the house was built had been leased to William Eales in 1850 together with the plot for No. 42 Sheffield Terrace. Eales then sub-let the ground for ninety-nine years from 1844 to Henry Stock, the occupant of the house in Bedford Gardens (now demolished) which stood immediately to the north.[10] Stock used the site for an extension to his garden but the sub-lease contained a provision that two houses could be erected there if they ranged in line with, and were similar in elevation to, the houses on each side in Sheffield Terrace. When Sterling, who had acquired the house in Bedford Gardens, wanted to have a new one built on the Sheffield Terrace frontage, he ignored this provision and the building which Waterhouse designed for him contrasts very sharply in height, materials and style with its neighbours.

It is a tall house of dark brick with some stone dressings, and consists of a basement, three main storeys and a large attic containing a lofty studio with north light. Although the exterior has a marked Gothic appearance, there is little evidence of the Gothic style inside. The rooms are well lit by the large windows, and are generously proportioned, their chief decorative features being arched alcoves, and simple cornices sparingly enriched with paterae, rosettes and dentils. The house is well built and functional, the fenestration providing an accurate reflection of the internal arrangements. The wooden balustrade of the imposing open-well staircase owes little to architectural precedent. Divided into sections by large newels, it consists of widely spaced balusters which are turned in their upper parts, but which are linked in their lower parts by struts and ties producing an effect similar to the iron girders of a bridge.*

---

* In 1877 a visit was made by the Architectural Association to Lascelles's joinery, where the visitors particularly admired the staircase, then being made to Waterhouse's design.[63]

CHAPTER IV

The Phillimore Estate

THE land acquired by the Phillimore family in Kensington in the early eighteenth century, a substantial part of which has remained in the ownership of the family up to the present time, was at one time part of the extensive estate attached to Campden House. In 1708 the third Earl of Gainsborough sold the mansion with its surrounding parks and farmland to Laud D'Oyley of St. Mary le Savoy, a merchant (see page 50). D'Oyley had at least three illegitimate daughters, one of whom, Ann, had married Joseph Phillimore, the younger son of a Gloucestershire clothier,[1] and it was from this somewhat unpromising beginning that the fortune of the Kensington branch of the Phillimore family derived. Joseph Phillimore died in 1704, before his father-in-law purchased Campden House, but not before his wife had borne him three sons and two daughters. She married again, to John Seymour, an upholsterer.

Laud D'Oyley died in 1709, leaving his property to his son Robert.[2] He, in turn, immediately made a will bequeathing the Campden House estate to his half-sister Ann for her lifetime with remainder to the sons of her body in order of birth, i.e. giving precedence to her sons by Joseph Phillimore.[3] In March 1709/10, however, Robert D'Oyley sold Campden House and some land adjoining it (see page 50) so that on his death in c. 1716 Ann Seymour inherited only part of the former estate. What remained consisted principally of about sixty-four acres to the south and west of Campden House, and twenty-five acres to the north. The latter area, known as The Racks, was generally treated as a separate entity and was sold in 1808; its later history is described in Chapter V. This chapter will be primarily concerned with the former area of sixty-four acres to which the term 'Phillimore estate' is generally applied (fig. 8).

Ann Seymour's eldest son, John Phillimore, died, apparently without marrying, either in 1729 or early in 1730,[4] and his brother, Robert Phillimore, became her heir. She herself died in 1741.[1]

From 1741 to 1829

Under the ownership of Robert Phillimore nothing was done to change the essentially rural character of the estate and the land was divided between several tenants engaged in agricultural pursuits. In 1774 he promised the inheritance of The Racks to his younger son Joseph as part of a marriage settlement,[5] but the main part of the estate passed to his eldest surviving son William.

William Phillimore succeeded to the estate in 1779 and within ten years he had decided to venture into the field of speculative building. He began with the turnpike road frontage where roadside development of the kind taking place along many of the major routes leading out of London seemed to offer a good hope of success. In 1788 he entered into agreements with two builders, Samuel Gray, a bricklayer, and John Schofield, a carpenter, who both had addresses in Jewin Street, City, and were acting in association; Samuel Gray's brother Francis Gray was also involved. The agreement with Samuel Gray was for the development of five hundred feet of frontage between the present Argyll Road and Phillimore Gardens, which Gray was to take for ninety-nine years at a rent of a peppercorn for the first two years and £97 per annum thereafter.[6]* The terms of the agreement with Schofield are not known but it covered the much smaller frontage between Phillimore Gardens and the western boundary of the estate at Holland Walk. Although building began immediately on the ground taken by Gray the development of Schofield's section did not begin until about 1795.

---

* It is interesting to compare the return expected by the ground landlord of about four shillings per foot frontage in this case with the return of ten shillings per foot frontage expected for St. Mary Abbots Terrace further to the west some thirty-five years later (see page 107).

Moray Lodge

Thorpe Lodge

Elm Lodge

CAMPDEN HILL

Bedford Lodge

Holly Lodge

Thornwood Lodge

Bute House

DUCHESS OF BEDFORD'S WALK

Observatory House

UPPER PHILLIMORE GARDENS

PHILLIMORE GARDENS

PHILLIMORE PLACE

ARGYLL ROAD

CAMPDEN HILL ROAD

Niddry Lodge

The Red House

HOLLAND ST.

HORNTON STREET

St. Mary's R.C. Chapel

ESSEX VILLAS

Hornton Cottage

STAFFORD TERRACE

UNDERGROUND RAILWAY

PHILLIMORE WALK

HORNTON PL.

Upper Phillimore Place

Lower Phillimore Place

Hornton St. Chapel

KENSINGTON HIGH STREET

100 0 100 200 FT.

0 50 100 M.

Fig. 8. The Phillimore estate. The thick line denotes the extent of the estate inherited by William Phillimore in 1779. The areas within the broken lines were sold in 1827. Based on the Ordnance Survey of 1862–72

In 1788 William Porden exhibited a perspective view of Phillimore Place at the Royal Academy and there is little doubt that he was responsible for the design of these elegant late-Georgian terraces which were a conspicuous feature of the north side of Kensington High Street until well into the twentieth century. Porden, who was later to design several buildings at Brighton and act as surveyor to the Grosvenor estate,[7] was William Phillimore's surveyor. In 1792 he entered into an agreement to develop the remainder of the frontage between Argyll Road and the eastern boundary of the estate, but, with the exception of the short terrace between Argyll Road and Campden Hill Road, the houses erected under this agreement were surprisingly commonplace and showed less influence of an overall design. The terraces to the west of Argyll Road came to be known as Upper Phillimore Place and were numbered 1–32 consecutively from east to west; those to the east of Argyll Road were known as Lower Phillimore Place and were numbered 1–31, also consecutively from east to west.

The completion of the terraces took a long time. The first lease was granted in December 1788 but the last lease was not dated until 1812 and the two houses built under it (Nos. 22 and 23 Lower Phillimore Place) were not occupied until 1816.[8] Building thus spanned the whole period of the French revolutionary and Napoleonic wars.

The first four houses to the west of Argyll Road (Nos. 1–4 Upper Phillimore Place) were completed by 1789 and among the first occupants was the Reverend Joseph Phillimore, William Phillimore's brother (at No. 2).[9] The next five house sites were taken under one lease by Peter Banner of St. Luke's, Old Street, a carpenter,[10] but within two years he had been declared bankrupt. His assignees were Thomas Lett of Lambeth, a timber merchant, and William Hobson of Southwark, a brickmaker.[11] Hobson had also concluded an agreement with Gray under which

he was to be assigned leases[12] and was probably the principal supplier of bricks for the development at this stage. A substantial part of the capital was provided by William Phillimore himself and two leases (each covering two house sites) which he granted directly to Gray were mortgaged back to him for a total sum of £2,000.[13]

Samuel Gray died towards the end of 1791 when fifteen houses had either been completed or were nearing completion. Leases had already been granted for most of them* at ground rents which added up to a little over £90, leaving less than £7 to be secured under Gray's agreement. His widow contracted with George Wightman, a local carpenter, for the assignment of the remaining frontage, amounting to one hundred and seventy-five feet.[14] As well as completing Gray's development in Upper Phillimore Place, Wightman also undertook the leading role in the building of Lower Phillimore Place, which was begun in 1792 under the agreement between Phillimore and William Porden.[15]

Approximately half of the remaining leases for Upper and Lower Phillimore Place were granted to Wightman, and most of the remainder to other people connected with the building trades.† Among the covenants in the leases was a provision that no bow windows or porticoes were to be added to the front elevations of the houses.[17] William Phillimore continued to supply money for the development himself and provided mortgages of between £300 and £400 per house to Wightman, taking assignments of the leases he had granted to the builder as security.[18] Presumably these amounts would have been sufficient to meet the initial building costs, but in 1804 Wightman was forced to mortage several properties for a second time as security for £2,600 which he owed to James Turner of Whitechapel, a timber merchant,[19] perhaps money which had become due for materials obtained on credit. He was unable to meet his commitments, however,

---

* No lease was granted of No. 12 Upper Phillimore Place, the central house of the long terrace between Argyll Road and Phillimore Gardens. It was built for William Phillimore himself although he did not take up residence there until 1801.[9]

† Besides those mentioned in the text above the following persons connected with the building trades were also concerned in the building of Upper and Lower Phillimore Place either as lessees or consenting parties to leases: William Britten of St. George's, Hanover Square, *carpenter*; Thomas Bush of Uxbridge, *surveyor*; William Dickins of St. George's, Hanover Square, *plasterer*; Richard Erlam of St. George's, Hanover Square, *bricklayer*; William Grocock of St. Anne's, Soho, *carpenter*; John Herman and John Anthony Herman of St. James's, *painters and glaziers*; William Howard of Fulham, *lime merchant*; John Lumb of Kensington, *stonemason*; John Miland of St. George's, Hanover Square, *painter and glazier*; John Oldham of St. George's, Hanover Square, *stonemason*; William Pinder of the City, *mason*; Solomon Reeves of St. Pancras, *mason*; Edmund Rogers of St. James's, *surveyor*; James South of Fulham, *plumber*; Thomas Stowers of Finsbury, *painter*; Martin Stuteley of St. Giles in the Fields, *builder*; William Vale of St. George's, Hanover Square, *builder*.[16]

and in 1813 he suffered the fate of so many nine-teenth-century builders by becoming bankrupt.[20] By this time he had ceased operations in Philli-more Place and was building in Hornton Street (see below). Martin Stuteley of St. Giles in the Fields was the builder of the last houses to be completed along the turnpike road frontage (Nos. 22–26 Lower Phillimore Place).[21]*

Although Phillimore Place took over twenty-five years to build the final result was aesthetically satisfactory. The terraces to the west of Campden Hill Road (i.e. Nos. 22–31 Lower Phillimore Place and all of Upper Phillimore Place) were excellent examples of late-Georgian terrace design and survived with relatively little altera-tion† until their demolition in 1931–2. To the east of Campden Hill Road less concern was taken with either symmetry or ornamentation and the majority of the houses were demolished earlier. The only ones remaining, although altered, are Nos. 98 and 100 Kensington High Street (originally Nos. 1 and 2 Lower Phillimore Place), which were built under leases granted in 1803 to George Wightman and John Oldham, a stonemason, respectively.[22] The best illustrations of the terraces as they were built are in the draw-ings presented to the Kensington Turnpike Trust by Joseph Salway in 1811 (Plate 44). Salway must have been guilty of some artistic licence, however, for he shows Nos. 22 and 23 Lower Phillimore Place as completed when they could have been at most in carcase and were probably not even so far advanced at that date.

Whether William Phillimore's original inten-tion was to extend building operations behind the terraces which stretched along the main highway is not known, but it may be that the development of the east side of Hornton Street, which was begun in 1804, was a tentative step in this direc-tion. The conventional terrace of twenty-seven narrow-fronted houses between Hornton Place and Holland Street which was demolished in 1903 (Plate 46a) took almost as long to build, however, as the whole of Phillimore Place. The prime mover in the development, which included building along the south side of Holland Street between Hornton Street and the eastern boundary of the estate, was once again George Wight-man.[23]‡

Approximately twenty houses had been com-pleted in the two streets when Wightman was declared bankrupt in 1813. His assignees in bankruptcy were John Lomas, a butcher, who was the tenant of several acres of pasture land on the estate, John Lumb, the mason who had taken leases of houses in Lower Phillimore Place and Holland Street, and Alexander Millington, a sash-frame manufacturer, who had already taken sub-leases of several houses.[25] They sold a large piece of ground in Hornton Street, on which only two party walls were standing, at auction for £100,[26] but it was left unbuilt on for several years. Eventually, by various assignments, it came into the hands of Richard Wheeler, a victualler turned builder, who erected ten houses to fill the gap. These were begun in 1824 and completed by 1828.[27]

When the leases granted by William Phillimore expired in 1902–3, the opportunity was taken to rebuild the east side of Hornton Street and that part of the south side of Holland Street which was still owned by the estate (see page 66). Of the original houses only the upper part of No. 33 Holland Street (formerly No. 2 Upper Holland Street) survives. This house was one of the properties purchased by the Metropolitan Railway Company for the construction of its railway, but in the event the demolition of the house did not prove necessary.

On the west side of Hornton Street a small house and other buildings including a workshop were built to the south of the mews behind Lower Phillimore Place under a lease of 1792 to George Wightman.[28] To the north of the mews Wight-man built another house for his own occupation in 1812.[29] A small plot to the rear of this house,

---

* Information about some of the notable early inhabitants of Upper and Lower Phillimore Place is contained in W. Gordon Corfield, *The Phillimore Estate, Campden Hill*, a booklet published by the Kensington Society in 1961. This work is par-ticularly useful for its account of the many people of note who have lived on the estate.

† In 1905 the front gardens of Nos. 22–31 Lower Phillimore Place were removed for road widening and shop-fronts inserted into the ground floors of several of the houses.

‡ Besides Wightman other persons connected with the building trades who were granted leases of houses in Hornton Street and Holland Street were: Charles Barber of Kensington, *plumber*; Joseph Coole of St. Marylebone, *smith and fanlight-maker*; James Large of Oxford Street, *paper-hanger*; John Lumb of Kensington, *mason*; John Miland of St. George's, Hanover Square, *painter and glazier*; William Mortlock of St. George's, Hanover Square, *painter and glazier*; George Reynolds of Hammersmith, *plasterer*.[24]

on the north side of the mews, was leased in 1822 to Charles Chesterton, then described as a poulterer.[30] Chesterton, who was living at No. 6 Lower Phillimore Place,[9] was also an agent for the Phoenix Insurance Company, a churchwarden, and a prominent figure in the deliberations of the Kensington Vestry. He also acted as agent for the Phillimore estate,[31] and the family firm of Chesterton and Sons still manages the estate's affairs. Among his great-grandchildren were Gilbert Keith Chesterton, the writer, and Frank Sydney Chesterton, an architect of considerable promise who designed several buildings on the Phillimore estate before his death in action during the war of 1914–18.

Instead of the terrace of houses which might have been expected to match that on the east side of the street, only one house was built on the remainder of the west side of Hornton Street. This was erected in 1817 for Maria Hudson, William Phillimore's housekeeper, who was given a lease for as long as she lived.[32] Later known as Hornton Cottage, the house was demolished in 1972.

While the terraces which were being erected on the southern part of the estate were still uncompleted, a different kind of building enterprise was begun in the north. In 1808 John Tasker of St. Marylebone, an architect and builder, and Thomas Winter of St. James's, a tailor, entered into an agreement with William Phillimore to build on nineteen and a half acres of farmland between the northern boundary of the estate and a footpath which led from the town of Kensington to Holland House (now Duchess of Bedford's Walk).[33] Phillimore was to grant leases for terms which would be equivalent to eighty-one years from Christmas 1808 at aggregate ground rents rising from £116 in the first year to £438 per annum after eight years (equivalent to approximately £22 per acre). It is not known who took the decision to build detached houses in extensive grounds, but by 1817 the development had been completed with the erection of only seven houses. No doubt the proximity of the mansions of Holland House, Notting Hill (Aubrey) House and Campden House exerted an influence, and the fact that there had been virtually no urban development in this part of Kensington away from the main roads may have militated against more intensive building. Whatever the reason, the effect was that this area of Campden Hill retained an atmosphere of rural seclusion for longer than most of Kensington, and it was not until after the war of 1939–45 that its character was changed substantially by the building of Holland Park School and the extension of Queen Elizabeth College.

John Tasker, who designed and built several houses in St. Marylebone and was a regular exhibitor at the Royal Academy,[7] probably designed all seven houses. None were particularly grandiose at first although some were extensively altered by the distinguished occupants attracted to them. As in the case of Phillimore Place part of the capital for the speculation came from William Phillimore himself, for in 1812 when building was only just under way he provided a mortgage of £2,000 and followed this three years later with another loan of an equal amount.[34] The individual history of these houses will be found on pages 68–71. Their locations and the names by which they were generally known are shown on fig. 8.

On William Phillimore's death in 1818 the estate passed to his only surviving son William Robert. He was to outlive his father by only eleven years and during his brief ownership the most significant occurrence for the history of the estate was the sale of about four acres in two plots to (Sir) James South, the astronomer, in 1827.[35] The two areas, the larger of which contained the former family mansion although it had long since ceased to be occupied by the Phillimores, are shown on fig. 8; their history is discussed in more detail at the end of this chapter, pages 73–4.

From 1829 to 1900

When William Robert Phillimore died in 1829 the extensive family property in Hertfordshire, which had been acquired through marriage, passed to his eldest son, also named William Robert. His Kensington estate was left in trust for his younger son Charles, subject to a mortgage debt of £5,400 and a charge to raise £5,000 for each of his two daughters.[36]

Virtually no building took place on the estate for nearly thirty years with the exception of the completion of undertakings begun during William Robert Phillimore's lifetime, such as the building of Niddry Lodge and Hornton Villa (The Red House) by Stephen Bird (see pages 71–2). In April 1855, however, Charles Phillimore entered into a building agreement with Joseph Gordon

Davis, a builder who had been operating in Pimlico for several years.[37] The agreement concerned an area of twenty-one acres now bounded by Holland Walk on the west, Duchess of Bedford's Walk on the north, Campden Hill Road on the east, and Phillimore Walk on the south, with the exception of a small plot at the corner of Campden Hill Road and Phillimore Walk on which a cottage had been built. Davis undertook to build 375 houses and Phillimore agreed to grant leases for terms which would be equivalent to ninety-nine years from 1855 at an ultimate total yearly ground rent after five years of £1,400 (equivalent to approximately £66 per acre). Davis was to provide the necessary roads and sewers and covenanted to complete the development within twelve years. A standard form of lease was attached to the agreement containing the usual covenants including a long list of prohibited uses. These were to be varied in the case of six shops and one public house which Davis was to be allowed to build in or near Phillimore Mews (now Phillimore Walk), apparently the only concession made to commerce in what was otherwise to be a purely residential development.

The agreement of 1855 was amended by two subsequent agreements. By December 1856, when only ten houses had been built, it had become clear that a total of 375 houses would lead to a greater density of housing than was desirable, and that the amenities of the large detached houses on Campden Hill would be likely to be adversely affected by too great a concentration of houses to the south of Duchess of Bedford's Walk. Accordingly the number of houses was reduced to 315 and none were to be built fronting on to Duchess of Bedford's Walk. In 1861, when seventy-eight houses had been built and thirty-nine were in the course of erection, another agreement was made in which the total number of houses was reduced still further to not less than 205 and not more than 225. At this time it was stated that detached and semi-detached villas had been built on some of the land rather than terraces as specified in the original agreement, it having been considered that 'Houses of that Character were better suited to the Locality and more eligible for Letting'. The total value of the houses to be built, including those already completed, was to be £215,000. The original terms on which Davis had taken the land were so favourable—with a total of 375

houses the ground rent per house would have worked out at less than £4 on average—that he could well afford to reduce the number of houses built; in the event 214 were erected.

The details of these agreements are contained in an Act of Parliament passed in 1862.[38] By this time doubts had arisen whether Charles Phillimore had the power under his father's will to enter into certain terms of the agreement with Davis, or whether he had the power to amend that agreement once made. In particular, the variations in ground rents of houses already leased (from £1 to £21), which was quite normal practice in large-scale building speculations, may have contravened a provision in William Robert Phillimore's will that building leases should be granted at 'the best or most improved yearly rent or rents . . . that can be reasonably gotten for the same'.[36] An Act was therefore obtained confirming the leases already granted and authorizing the granting of further leases on similar terms.

Charles Phillimore died in 1863 before the development had been completed. He had remained a bachelor and the estate passed intact to his nephew, William Brough Phillimore.[39]

The tables on pages 75–6 contain a list of the lessees for all of the houses built under the agreements with Davis. The lessee of Nos. 7–13 (odd) Campden Hill Road has been included although these houses were built on the site of the cottage and its garden which had been excluded from the area taken by Davis. Most leases were granted in consideration of the expense incurred in building, the payment of rent and the performance of covenants. Several also specified a monetary consideration which in some cases represented the full value of the house but in other cases was clearly less than this. The highest price for any one house appears to have been £4,109 12s. paid by Lady George Paulet for No. 36 Phillimore Gardens—a spacious detached house with a large garden at the south-east corner of Phillimore Gardens and Duchess of Bedford's Walk—although the lease was executed in the name of her son, St. John Claud Paulet.[40]

Specimen elevations and plans were attached to the original building agreement, but it is clear that each builder in practice supplied his own designs, and by the time of the third agreement of 1861 all that was required was that the elevations should be approved by Charles Phillimore. It is not known who designed the general layout, although Arthur Chesterton, who was Philli-more's surveyor and estate agent, was probably consulted. George C. Handford, a Chelsea architect and surveyor, gave evidence before a committee of the House of Lords that the changes made after the initial building agreement were to the advantage of the estate,[41] but he may only have been brought in as an outside referee at this point.

In May 1856 Davis advertised that building land was available on ninety-nine-year leases,[42] and his first taker was James Jordan the younger, then of Paddington. It was not an auspicious choice. Jordan built eleven houses on the west side of Campden Hill Road—Nos. 15–35 (odd)—and then became bankrupt in 1857.[43] By mid-1858 he was back in business, from an address in St. Ann's Villas, and began building on the east side of Argyll Road at the south end. At least two of his former creditors were prepared to lend him money again.[44] One of them was George Powell, a solicitor, and the other, Powell Warner, may have been related. Powell's firm—Powell, Thompson and Groom of Gray's Inn—also acted as solicitors for Joseph Gordon Davis, and it was no doubt through their help that the indefatigable Jordan was able to persist with his building activities. By 1859 he was back in trouble again, and Nos. 3 and 4 Argyll Road were sold while still in an unfinished state.[45] By March 1860 Nos. 5, 6 and 7 Argyll Road had been taken out of his hands and tenders for completing the houses were invited; the architect was stated to be E. W. Crocker.[46] Presumably Crocker was responsible for the appearance of the complete group of Nos. 2–7 (consec.) Argyll Road. No. 2 occupies two house sites of which Jordan had originally taken separate leases, but they had been joined to-gether by 1861 when the premises were being used for a boarding-house.[47] The rest of the develop-ment appears to have proceeded relatively smoothly.

One builder who played a more extensive role than the table of lessees would indicate was Charles Frederick Phelps. When he took his first lease on the estate in 1860, Phelps was described as an architect and had an address in Furnival's Inn. He seems to have dropped the designation of architect quite quickly, however, for in the following year his name appeared in the Post Office Directory for the first time, as a builder, not an architect, and his address was given as No. 28 Phillimore Gardens.* Besides the houses of which he was the direct lessee, Phelps was granted sub-leases of some houses which had been leased to Davis and was also the builder of several others.[48] He was probably responsible for the whole of Essex Villas (south side now partly demolished), Nos. 24–30 (even) Phillimore Gardens, Nos. 2–4 and 14–18 (even) Phillimore Place and Nos. 7–13 (odd) Campden Hill Road. He went on to build extensively on the Holland estate.

Joseph Gordon Davis was himself responsible for most of the larger houses in Phillimore Gardens and Upper Phillimore Gardens (Plate 47a).[49] Two notable exceptions, both dating from 1859–60, were No. 31 Phillimore Gardens and No. 15 Upper Phillimore Gardens. The first was built for his own residence by George Eugene Magnus, a slate manufacturer who was also 'billiard maker to H.R.H. the Prince Consort'.[50] No. 15 Upper Phillimore Gardens was built by William Brass and Son of the City[51] to the designs of Deane and Woodward for William Shaen, a solicitor. In A History of the Gothic Revival Charles Eastlake described the house as 'A curious example of a suburban villa residence treated to a certain extent in a Medieval spirit. The front is of red brick, with stepped gables. A picturesque staircase turret is on the right hand of the building, and a Venetian-looking balcony projects from one of the windows. It cost 3,000 l.'[52] In 1937 the house was 'reconstructed' by G. Grey Wornum to such an extent that virtually nothing of the original has survived, but a photograph of it is contained in the 1924 edition of Good and Bad Manners in Architecture by A. Trystan Edwards, where the design is described as 'conceived and inspired by Mr. Ruskin himself'.[53]

Most of the houses built as part of Davis's development are of the standard Italianate variety but one group of four houses in Phillimore Place (formerly Durham Villas) provides a con-trasting Tudor Gothic touch (Plate 48a). It con-sists of two detached houses of red brick with blue brick in diaper patterns (Nos. 6 and 12) on each side of a semi-detached pair of similar design although fronted in ragstone (Nos. 8 and 10). The architect of all four was Henry Winnock Hay-ward of Lexden, near Colchester, who was the lessee of Nos. 6 and 12.

* In the Post Office Directory for 1860 an Arthur James Phelps, architect, is listed at No. 8 Furnival's Inn. Perhaps he was Charles Frederick Phelps' father.

The last street to be built to complete the enterprise was Stafford Terrace, for which leases were granted to Davis in March and April 1868 at a yearly ground rent of £1 per house.[54] Each house was occupied by 1874, the year in which Edward Linley Sambourne, the illustrator and cartoonist, took up residence here. The interior and furnishings of his house have been little altered since his lifetime and today it provides an excellent example of High Victorian decorative taste (Plate 49a, b, c).[55]

The enumerators' books for the census of 1861 give an indication of the kind of people who were attracted to the new development. Returns were received from fifty-seven houses, just over a quarter of the number eventually built under the agreements with Davis. The occupants of the new houses were generally members of the substantial Victorian middle class and on average there were between two and three servants to each household. A considerable number of residents belonged to the professions. As might be expected there were several solicitors and barristers, including Charles Clode, the solicitor to the War Office, at No. 47 Phillimore Gardens, as well as surveyors, doctors and one dentist. Perhaps the most remarkable concentration was of artists, seven occupiers describing themselves as such; five lived in Upper Phillimore Gardens, the most noteworthy being Henry Tanworth Wells (at No. 9), Frank Dillon (No. 13) and William Duffield (No. 4). Four men described themselves as clerks, but the size of their households indicated that they were probably in positions of considerable authority. There were a few army and navy officers, mostly retired, including Captain William Hutcheons Hall (later Admiral Sir William Hutcheons Hall) at No. 48 Phillimore Gardens. Few individuals declared that they were living on unearned incomes, and those that did were mostly widows, although two men described their occupation simply as that of 'gentleman'.

As a result of the extension of the Metropolitan Railway to Kensington, some parts of the estate towards its eastern boundary were required by the railway company. The property which changed hands was Nos. 2–5 (consec.) Lower Phillimore Place, Hornton Street Chapel and the schools to the rear in Hornton Mews, some garden ground at the back of houses in Hornton Street, and Nos. 1 and 2 Upper Holland Street.[56]

Not all of the buildings purchased had to be demolished, and after completion of the railway, which was underground at this point, the company embarked on a policy of rebuilding on the surface. Between 1871 and 1875 Nos. 102–106 (even) Kensington High Street were built to replace Nos. 3–5 Lower Phillimore Place, No. 31B Holland Street replaced No. 1 Upper Holland Street, Drayson Mews was laid out, and Nos. 3–6 (consec.) Hornton Place erected. The builder in all these cases was William Cooke of Paddington, who was later to build Airlie Gardens. He was granted building leases by the company for eighty- or eighty-five-year terms.[57]

The last major development undertaken on the estate during the nineteenth century was the building of Airlie Gardens on the curtilage of Elm Lodge. The opportunity was provided in 1878 when the Grand Junction Water Works Company surrendered the lease of Elm Lodge (see page 70).[58] The house stood in extensive grounds and a good deal of open space was preserved by building only on the north and east sides of the plot of land which was made available, leaving the remainder as a communal garden for the inhabitants of the new houses. At first eighteen houses were planned but the number became nineteen when two houses were built on the wedge-shaped site at the angle of the terrace and numbered 10 and 10A. Nos. 15 and 16 were destroyed during the war of 1939–45 and a block of flats has since been built in their place.

Although the houses in Airlie Gardens appear relatively narrow, the majority have frontages of about twenty-three feet and they are exceptionally tall, most containing five storeys plus attic and basement (Plate 47b). They were undoubtedly designed to take full advantage of their situation near the summit of Campden Hill and command extensive views of the surrounding area. They remained in single-family occupation until 1929, when two of the houses were converted into flats.[59] An agreement for the sale of No. 17 before it was actually completed indicates that the house plans had been signed by the architect Spencer Chadwick, but whether he designed these houses or merely approved their design for William Brough Phillimore is not known.[60]

The builder was William Cooke, who was operating from a Hammersmith address when he first gave notice to the district surveyor of his intention to commence building in January

1881.* By January 1882 he had given notice for all nineteen houses, which were completed in carcase by the end of 1883.[61] William Brough Phillimore granted leases for ninety-nine years from Christmas 1880 at annual ground rents of £40 after a short peppercorn term for each house except Nos. 10 and 10A for which the ground rents were only £10 per annum each, no doubt because these houses were not only smaller in area but also did not have access to the communal garden at the rear. All of the leases were taken by Cooke with the exception of that for No. 4, which was granted to the first occupant on Cooke's nomination.[62]

For the most part Cooke financed his building operations by obtaining mortgages on the security of his leases in the usual manner. For instance, Nos. 2 and 3 were mortgaged to Richard Nicholson, William Brough Phillimore's solicitor, for £3,000 each.[63] Sometimes, however, he was able to find a prospective buyer who was willing to put down a substantial payment for a house before it had been completed. In this way the purchaser of No. 17 paid a deposit of £2,000 in August 1881 as part of the sum of £4,550 which he had agreed to pay for the house.[64]†

The leases contained provisions for the upkeep of the communal garden at the rear of the houses. The occupiers of the seventeen houses which backed directly on to it had the right to use the garden together with their families and domestic servants, and a committee of five persons was to be chosen from them with power to levy an annual compulsory rate to cover expenses. For several years the plot of ground immediately to the south of Airlie Gardens which belonged to Bute House was sub-let to the garden committee and was known as the 'Lower Garden'.[66]

In 1891 the owner of No. 1 Airlie Gardens, Douglas William Freshfield, the explorer and geographer,[67] had an addition built on to the south side of his house in a style which has marked affinities with that of Richard Norman Shaw (Plate 47b). Both the corner turret and the gable on the south wall of the extension resemble the latter's then recent work at New Scotland Yard.

No evidence has been found, however, to suggest that Shaw was Freshfield's architect. The builders were S. and S. Dunn of Brewer Street, St. James's.[61]

William Brough Phillimore died in 1887 without issue. He left the estate to his widow for the rest of her lifetime, and, after her death, to Sir Walter George Frank Phillimore. He was the great-grandson of Joseph Phillimore, the younger brother of the William Phillimore who had inherited the estate in 1779.[68]

Since 1900

Sir Walter George Frank Phillimore, who entered into possession of the estate on the death of William Brough Phillimore's widow in 1900, was an international jurist of considerable repute and was created Baron Phillimore in 1918.[67] He quickly set about rebuilding some of the older properties on the estate. The late-Georgian terrace on the east side of Hornton Street was demolished in 1903 as soon as the original leases had expired, and a small block of flats (the present No. 12) and twenty-one houses were built in its place (Plate 46b). Originally Nos. 1–43 (odd), the new terrace was numbered Nos. 12–54 (even) Hornton Street in 1928. The architect was Frank Sydney Chesterton and the building lessees were Messrs. C. A. Daw and Son. Nos. 35–43 (odd) Holland Street were also built as part of this development.[69]

All of these terrace houses are similar in the picturesque massing of elements with a strong vertical emphasis, and consist of three main storeys over a basement with one or, in some cases, two storeys in the roof. Although most of the houses have been much altered internally, a typical arrangement of the accommodation consisted of the kitchen, storage rooms and servants' quarters in the basement, with the dining-room, one other room used as a library, study or morning-room, and a cloakroom on the ground floor, the main living rooms being on the first floor. Stylistically the houses may be divided into three

---

* Corfield, in his history of the Phillimore estate cited earlier, states that Cooke took over from another builder who found himself in difficulties, but no evidence has been found to support this contention and Cooke was the first to give notice to the district surveyor of building operations on the site. Corfield lived at No. 13 Airlie Gardens, and his booklet contains a good deal of information about the houses and, in particular, their inhabitants.

† Other known prices for houses in Airlie Gardens which were sold leasehold shortly after they had been built were £5,200 for No. 1 in 1882 and £4,000 for No. 2 in 1886.[65]

groups. Nos. 35–41 (odd) Holland Street are small in scale and owe much to English vernacular traditions. The basement and ground storeys are faced with red bricks and the first and second storeys have rough-cast rendering. The roofs are of red tiles. Nos. 12–42 (even) Hornton Street are larger, with two attic storeys, dormers and gables, and very steep tiled roofs. The façades are entirely of brick with stone or artificial stone dressings. The tall bays, porches, windows and gables are composed with subtlety, so that although the houses are not identical there is a marked degree of unity, recalling streets of Flemish or North German houses. Nos. 44–52 (even) Hornton Street and No. 43 Holland Street have one attic storey and are based on a freely interpreted Queen Anne style. Throughout, many of the porches have walls lined with brilliant green coloured tiles.

F. S. Chesterton was also the architect, this time in collaboration with J. D. Coleridge, of Hornton Court (Nos. 116–138 Kensington High Street). This block of flats with ground-floor shops and originally an extensive terrace garden at first-floor level (Plate 112e) replaced Nos. 10–21 Lower Phillimore Place in 1905–7. Daw and Son were again the lessees.[70] Chesterton and Coleridge also collaborated in 1908 on the design of Sundial House (Nos. 108–114 Kensington High Street).[71]

The only other rebuilding to take place during the first Lord Phillimore's lifetime occurred when Blundell House (formerly known as Bute House) was pulled down shortly before the war of 1914–18. As the grounds of the house were very extensive its demolition enabled several new buildings to be erected. The southern part of the site, at the junction of Duchess of Bedford's Walk and Campden Hill Road, was let on a 999-year lease for the erection of buildings for King's College for Women (now Queen Elizabeth College, see page 72).[72] No. 1 Campden Hill was built in 1914–15 to the designs of E. P. Warren.[73] The present Blundell House (No. 2 Campden Hill) was built at the same time to the designs of Arthur G. Leighton of the firm of Gale, Gotch and Leighton, and later of Leighton and Higgs. He was also the architect of Little Blundell House (No. 3 Campden Hill), the studio-house built in 1927 for Sir William Llewellyn, who was President of the Royal Academy from 1928 to 1938.[74] A plot of ground

on the north side of the road named Campden Hill also formed part of the original grounds of Bute House and another house was built here in 1914. Officially No. 71 Campden Hill Road, the house was called 'New House' at first but on becoming the residence of the South African High Commissioner in 1946 it was renamed High Veld. The architect was Henry Martineau Fletcher.[75]

Further redevelopment took place shortly after Lord Phillimore's death in 1929. The remainder of Lower Phillimore Place and Upper Phillimore Place were demolished in 1931–2 and replaced by three monumental blocks of shops and flats along Kensington High Street—Phillimore Court, Stafford Court and Troy Court. Of these Troy Court (Nos. 208–222 Kensington High Street), designed by Michael Rosenauer,[76] is the most interesting and stylistically advanced.

Campden Hill Gate, the two large blocks of flats on the north side of Duchess of Bedford's Walk, was also built at this time on land which had been taken from the gardens of Cam House (formerly Bedford Lodge), Holly Lodge and Thornwood Lodge. The architects were Paul Hoffmann, who was responsible for the planning, and J. D. Coleridge, who designed the façades.[77] The gap between the new flats and King's College of Household and Social Science (as Queen Elizabeth College was then called) was filled shortly before the war of 1939–45 by the erection of Duchess of Bedford House, another block of flats.

The war had a serious effect on some of the older properties on the estate, not only through enemy action, but also through the deterioration in the fabric of some of the large houses on Campden Hill which had been requisitioned for wartime use. Both Cam House and Moray Lodge suffered severely in this respect and in 1948 the London County Council decided to purchase these properties together with Thorpe Lodge under a compulsory purchase order for housing purposes. A considerable amount of local opposition greeted this plan and in 1951 the Council decided to use the land for the erection of a school rather than housing.[78] Holland Park School was built on the site, Thorpe Lodge being preserved and used as part of the school premises.

Other parts of the estate which were sold after the war of 1939–45 were the sites of Holly Lodge and Thornwood Lodge, for extensions to Queen

Elizabeth College, and the island site bounded by Hornton Street, Phillimore Walk, Campden Hill Road and Holland Street, which was purchased by the Kensington Borough Council in 1946 to provide a site for new municipal buildings.[79]

Hornton Street Chapel
Demolished

The chapel which formerly stood at the south-east corner of Hornton Street and Hornton Place was erected in 1794–5 under a ninety-nine-year lease granted by William Phillimore in 1794 to William Forsyth, the superintendent of the royal gardens at St. James's and Kensington, John Broadwood, the pianoforte manufacturer, James Gray of Brompton Park, a nurseryman, and James Mackintosh of Kensington, esquire.[80] Although the founders of the chapel included both Presbyterians and Independents, the Congregational form of worship was soon established.[81] In 1845 the building was enlarged to the designs of John Tarring,[82] but it still proved too small for the needs of its congregation and the Horbury Chapel was built in Kensington Park Road. When a further Congregational chapel was opened in Allen Street in 1855, the Hornton Street chapel was no longer needed and its minister moved to Allen Street.[83] In 1858 the building was re-opened as a Baptist chapel.[84] It was demolished c. 1927 for the building of Evelyn House.

Behind the chapel facing Hornton Mews (now Hornton Place) was a small school-house which took up part of the site leased in 1794 but was probably not built until 1815.[85] At first it appears to have been used primarily for a Sunday school in connexion with the chapel but in 1835 a school was established there under the auspices of the British and Foreign School Society.[86] It was demolished c. 1865 for the building of the Metropolitan Railway.

St. Mary's Roman Catholic Chapel, Holland Street
Demolished

St. Mary's chapel in Holland Street was the first church specifically built for the Roman Catholic faith in Kensington since the Reformation. It was built under a ninety-year lease granted by William Phillimore in 1813 to Richard Gillow, who was the first occupant of Bute House (see below), and John Kendall of Kensington, a tallow chandler.[87] By the end of 1813 the first priest, Giles Viel or Gilles Vielle, who was probably a French emigré, had taken up residence.[9] In 1830 a charity school was established in the grounds of the chapel. On the restoration of the Catholic hierarchy in 1850 St. Mary's assumed the status of a parish church, but after the opening of the nearby Pro-Cathedral of Our Lady of Victories in 1869 it was no longer needed as a place of worship and was given over to the needs of the expanded school. The school buildings were demolished c. 1904, shortly after the expiry of the original lease.[88]

Bute House
Also known as Blundell House. Demolished

Bute House appears to have been the first to be completed (in 1812) of the seven houses which were built under the agreement of 1808 between William Phillimore on the one hand and John Tasker and Thomas Winter on the other and which were all probably designed by John Tasker (see page 62). The first occupant was Richard Gillow, who probably belonged to the noted Lancashire Roman Catholic family of Gillow and may have been connected with the furniture firm of that name. His lease included the ground on which Elm Lodge was built to the north slightly later, but he surrendered this lease in 1817 and was granted a new one, excluding the site of Elm Lodge. The addition later of a two-acre field between the house and Campden Hill Road gave Bute House a spacious setting of just under six acres.[89]

The most notable early inhabitant was the second Marquess of Bute, after whom the house was named and who lived there from 1830 until 1842. During his period of residence several embellishments were made to the house. The next occupant was the Honourable William Sebright Lascelles, the brother of the third Earl of Harewood, and after his death in 1851 Lady Lascelles continued to live there until 1856. The aristocratic associations of the house were revived by the sixth Duke of Rutland who lived there from 1865 until his death in 1888. The last owner was Blundell Charles Weld, a Lancashire landowner, who changed his own name to Charles Weld-Blundell and renamed the house Blundell House.

After he left the house in 1912 or 1913 it was demolished.[90]

Thornwood Lodge
Also known as London Lodge. Demolished

Thornwood Lodge was another of the seven houses which can probably be attributed to John Tasker. The first occupant was Thomas Williams, a coachmaker of Oxford Street, who took up residence in 1813.[9] The original leaseholder was Thomas Kitching, a surgeon and apothecary, to whom Williams was indebted for over £3,000. Kitching's lease was of a long strip of land extending to the northern boundary of the estate, but after Thorpe Lodge had been built on the upper part of the plot this lease was surrendered in 1817 and new ones were granted to Williams for each house.[91]

Williams later acquired more property to the north of Thorpe Lodge and in 1827 purchased Notting Hill (Aubrey) House. At the time of his death in 1852 he owned property in Essex, Oxfordshire, Suffolk and Sussex as well as in several parts of London and elsewhere in Middlesex.[92]

After Thorpe Lodge was finished Williams moved there and let Thornwood Lodge. Among the early residents were the Marchioness of Hastings (1817–23) and the fourth Earl of Glasgow (1824–30).[9] In 1833 Williams assigned the lease of the house—at this time called London Lodge—to Henry William Vincent, the Queen's Remembrancer, for £5,000.[93] Sir John Fowler, the eminent railway engineer, lived there from 1867 until his death in 1898.[94] The house was demolished c. 1956 to make way for new buildings for Queen Elizabeth College.

Holly Lodge
Also known as Airlie Lodge. Demolished

The third of the seven houses which can probably be attributed to John Tasker was completed by 1814 and is chiefly noteworthy as the last residence of Lord Macaulay, the historian. He took the house in 1856, partly on the suggestion of the Duke and Duchess of Argyll, who were then living in the house immediately to the west, and he died there in 1859.[95]* The seventh Earl of

Airlie lived there after Macaulay's death and renamed the house Airlie Lodge. The name Holly Lodge was later revived, however. The house was demolished c. 1968 for further extensions to Queen Elizabeth College. The coach-house, built at the same time as the house, was modernized after the war of 1939–45 for occupation by a member of the Phillimore family, and is still standing at present (1972).

Bedford Lodge
Also known as Argyll Lodge and Cam House.
Plate 45. Demolished

This house—the fourth of the seven which were built and probably designed by John Tasker—was occupied in 1815 by Lieutenant-General John Fraser (later General Sir John Fraser).[97] He only lived there until 1819, when a Major Colegrave took over the lease.[9]

In 1823 the sixth Duke of Bedford took an assignment of the lease for £5,250.[98] He had been searching for a house of convenient size near London and the proximity of Holland House was no doubt a factor influencing his choice.[99] He immediately set about enlarging what was basically a simple Regency villa and employed as his architect Jeffry Wyatt (later Sir Jeffry Wyatville), who had previously undertaken work for the Duke at Woburn Abbey. An addition was built on to the east side of the house in 1823 (Plate 45), and six years later Wyatville drew up plans for an extension to the west. These were probably not carried out, as another set of designs was made in 1835 and work began on the new extension in 1836.[100] These alterations made the house one of the most lavish on Campden Hill and for several years it was valued more highly for rating purposes than Holland House.[9] After the Duke's death in 1839 the Dowager Duchess continued to live at Bedford Lodge and made it a famous centre for social gatherings.[101] Shortly after her death in 1853 it was taken by the eighth Duke of Argyll, who renamed the house Argyll Lodge and kept it until his death in 1900.

Sir Walter G. F. Phillimore (later Lord Phillimore), who came into possession of the Phillimore estate in 1900, took the house for his own occupation in January 1901.[102] He renamed it Cam House, after the place in Gloucestershire

* In 1903 the London County Council erected the first of its 'blue plaques' at Holly Lodge to record Macaulay's residence there.[96]

where his remote ancestors had lived. After Lord Phillimore's death it was leased by an American, Mrs. St. George, who carried out several alterations and built another house in the grounds called Plane Tree House.[103]* After being requisitioned for military use during the war of 1939–45 Cam House fell into disrepair. It was demolished in 1955 for the building of Holland Park School.

Elm Lodge
Demolished

Elm Lodge, on the site of Airlie Gardens, was the first to be demolished of the seven houses which were built and probably designed by John Tasker. The first occupant was Sir James McGrigor, who was a noted army surgeon and had been chief of the medical staff of Wellington's army during the Peninsular War.[104] In 1843 he sold the house, together with some freehold land he owned to the north, to the Grand Junction Water Works Company (see page 99). For several years it appears to have been used as the residence of the superintendent of the company's reservoir,† but after the completion of new buildings to the north of the reservoir it was occupied by Alexander Fraser, who was firstly assistant engineer and later engineer to the company.[106] In 1878 the company surrendered the lease and the house was demolished for the building of Airlie Gardens.

Thorpe Lodge
Plate 49d

Thorpe Lodge is the only survivor of the seven houses which were built and probably designed by John Tasker between 1808 and 1817 but it has been substantially altered.

The first leaseholder was Thomas Williams, who moved to the new house in 1816 from Thornwood Lodge to the south.[107] He left the house in 1829 to move to Hillingdon and sub-let it to Edward Stone, a draper, together with a substantial piece of ground to the north of the house which Williams had purchased in 1820 (see page 99).[108] In 1869 Stone surrendered his lease of the additional piece of ground to the Grand Junction Water Works Company, which had purchased the freehold, for £3,000, a sum which was

calculated to include compensation for the adverse effect on Thorpe Lodge of the new reservoir the company was planning to build on the site.[109]

In c. 1875 the house was taken by Henry Tanworth Wells, the painter. He lived there until his death in 1903 and had a studio added to the west side of the house to the designs of John Loughborough Pearson.[110]

In 1904 Thorpe Lodge was occupied by Montagu Collett Norman, later created Baron Norman, who was Governor of the Bank of England from 1920 until 1944. He immediately began to redesign the interior and employed as his architect Walter Knight Shirley (later eleventh Earl Ferrers).[111] Several of the decorative features and items of furniture were based on Norman's own sketches. The principal craftsmen employed were A. J. Shirley for the metalwork and J. H. Wakelin, with his chief joiner Robert King, for the furniture and joinery. Some items of furniture were brought from the Guild of Handicrafts and from Arts and Crafts exhibitions.[112]

When it was announced in 1948 that Thorpe Lodge was included in an area which the London County Council was planning to acquire for housing purposes, there was a considerable local outcry at the proposed demolition of the house. The L.C.C. eventually decided to use the site for a school rather than for housing purposes and agreed to preserve the house as part of the school premises. In 1956 Lady Norman made a gift to the Council of several items of furniture and decoration in the house.[113] Wells's studio, which had been turned into a music room by Norman, is now used as the school's library.

The interior of Thorpe Lodge, despite the addition of desks and bookshelves, still bears testimony to the complete transformation undertaken in a contemporary style between 1904 and 1912. The influence of Ernest Gimson is evident, not only in the plasterwork of the friezes and ceilings, but also in the use of richly figured woods, such as maple. The views of Halsey Ricardo may have prompted the use of hard, rich surfaces for some of the interior walls, especially the entrance hall. Here the walls are lined with tiles made of fractured silicone compounds used in the manufacture of crucibles for smelting, the effect of which, rather similar to mother-of-pearl, was

---

* The site is now occupied by the block of flats of that name.

† It is marked as such on the manuscript map drawn by Joseph Smith for the Metropolitan Commission of Sewers in 1851.[105]

greatly admired by Norman. There are also panels of de Morgan tiles, of basically turquoise and ultramarine colouring, in some of the fireplace surrounds.

Moray Lodge
Also known as West Lodge. Demolished

Formerly known as West Lodge, this was the last to be completed of the seven houses which can all probably be attributed to John Tasker. Tasker himself was the first leaseholder in 1817, and he may have intended to live there but he died later in the same year.[114] According to the ratebooks the first occupant was Patrick King in 1818.

The name Moray Lodge was given to the house by James Malcolmson, a Scotsman, who lived there from 1844 until 1861.[9] For most of the remainder of the nineteenth century it was occupied by Arthur Lewis, of the silk mercers' firm of Lewis and Allenby, and he made it a centre for artistic and literary social events.[115] In 1873–4 the house was extensively altered by Lucas Brothers, builders, of Lambeth,[61] and, externally at least, little was left of the original house.

Moray Lodge was requisitioned during the war of 1939–45 and was used for various official purposes afterwards. It was demolished in 1955 for the building of Holland Park School.

Niddry Lodge
Demolished

This detached house, which was faced with stucco and consisted of two main storeys, was built by Stephen Bird (see below).[116] It was first occupied in 1831 by General Sir John Fraser, who had also been the first occupant of Bedford Lodge, and he lived there until his death in 1843. The next inhabitant was the Dowager Countess of Hopetoun, widow of the fifth Earl. One of the Earl's titles was Baron Niddry and it was no doubt during the Countess's occupation that the name Niddry Lodge was acquired. After her death in 1854, the house was taken by John Francis Campbell, Chief of the Campbells of Islay.[117] In 1972 it was demolished by Kensington and Chelsea Borough Council, which by then owned the freehold of the site, to make way for a new Town Hall.

The Red House
Formerly known as Hornton Villa. Demolished

This house was built by Stephen Bird for his own occupation. He moved in during 1835 and in the following year was granted a lease by Charles Phillimore for ninety-nine years from 1828;[118] he called the house Hornton Villa. Bird was one of the most notable builders and brickmakers of Kensington. He owned a sixteen-acre brick-field to the west of the Potteries and in 1836 gave evidence to the Commissioners of Excise Inquiry as one of the eminent brickmakers in the neighbourhood of London.[119] In 1861, when he was eighty years old, his brickmaking business was still flourishing and employed nearly one hundred hands.[47] At this time he also described himself as a farmer with about forty acres of land. For several years he conducted his building operations in partnership with his son Henry and extended his activities to other areas of London besides Kensington.* In 1838–9 he secured the contract for constructing the new covered part of the Counter's Creek sewer made necessary by the building of the West London Railway, and he was praised by the Westminster Commission of Sewers for the efficient and satisfactory manner in which the work had been carried out. As a result of the precarious financial condition of the railway company he had to take a substantial part of his payment for this work in shares in the enterprise, and after the failure of passenger operations in 1844 he played an increasingly important role in the company's affairs, later becoming its chairman.[120] Bird died in 1865 when nearly eighty-five years old and The Builder described him as a man who was 'well known for his integrity and good sense'.[121] After his death the rates on Hornton Villa were paid by his son William, who was also a builder.[9]

Other occupants included William Martin (later Baron) Conway, the art critic and explorer, and Herbert Hoover, who afterwards became President of the United States. Between 1907 and 1916 Hoover used the house 'as a European lodging place . . . although frequently sublet', and when he left it for the last time it was with some

---

* See Survey of London, volume XXXVI, 1970, page 228.

regret: 'The house with its quaint garden in the middle of a great city was a place of many affections, many happy recollections, and of many stimulating discussions.'[122]

In 1888 W. J. Loftie described the house as having been 'added to in an incongruous fashion; for originally though only a stucco villa it had some architectual pretensions, being in the style described in Vitruvius as Etruscan Doric'.[123] Several alterations appear to have been made in 1885 when a new red-brick stable block was built by Peto Brothers.[61] At the time of the demolition of the house in 1972, however, several features of the Tuscan style were still evident, particularly the eaves-framed pediments and overhanging roofs.

The Abbey
Plate 48b, c. Demolished

The Abbey, which stood at the north-east corner of Phillimore Walk and Campden Hill Road (the site is now occupied by the western part of the Central Library), was built in 1879–80 for William Abbott, a stockbroker. It had no religious associations and owed its name to the humorous caprice of its owner. Abbott, who less than twenty years before had been a draughtsman in the Copyhold, Inclosure and Tithe Commission Office,[124] had acquired a leasehold interest in most of the island site bounded by Phillimore Walk, Campden Hill Road, Holland Street and Hornton Street either through assignments or under-leases. He was thus able to provide one and a half acres of grounds for his new house at the expense of substantially reducing the gardens of The Red House and Hornton Cottage. New stables were built along the north side of Phillimore Walk at the same time as The Abbey, while the house at the north-western corner of Hornton Street and Phillimore Walk, which had been built in 1812, was rebuilt and named The Grey House. Abbott surrendered the leases he had secured and was granted new ones by William Brough Phillimore. He had to pay a ground rent of £270 for The Abbey and its large garden for a term ending in 1954.[125] The house was destroyed by bombing during the war of 1939–45.

The Abbey and its attendant buildings along Phillimore Walk were remarkable structures in the Decorated Gothic style. They were built in Kentish rag with carved stone enrichments and red and black tile roofs. The interior of the house was a sumptuous piece of historical extravaganza dominated by a series of halls on the ground floor and a grand staircase. Statues and wooden panels depicted scenes from English history, stone figures representing England, Scotland and Ireland were placed in niches in the outer hall, and in some of the windows stained glass depicted characters from the Arthurian legends. Abbott's architect was Henry Winnock Hayward, who had designed the house in which Abbott lived (No. 8 Phillimore Place) before moving to The Abbey. The builders were Haward Brothers of St. Marylebone.[126]

Queen Elizabeth College
Formerly Department of Household and Social Science of King's College for Women and later King's College of Household and Social Science

In 1878 a course of lectures for women, held under the auspices of King's College in the Strand, was given in the Vestry Hall at Kensington. They were so well attended that No. 5 Observatory Avenue (now No. 9 Hornton Street) was taken as the venue for the lectures in the following year. In 1885 King's College Women's Department was inaugurated and new premises taken at No. 13 Kensington Square. Under the King's College London Transfer Act of 1908 a semi-autonomous King's College for Women was envisaged, and although Nos. 11 and 12 Kensington Square were taken over it soon became clear that new permanent buildings would be necessary.

The demolition of Blundell (formerly Bute) House provided a convenient site and the University of London took a 999-year lease of the southern part of the grounds of the former mansion, on which new college buildings were erected to the designs of Adams and Holden in 1914–15. The architect who appears to have been principally concerned was Charles Holden and the general contractors were Wallis and Sons of Maidstone.[127] When the new buildings were opened in 1915 they only housed the Household and Social Science Department of the college and a hostel for students, the remaining departments having been moved to the Strand as a result of the recommendations of the Haldane Commission on university education in London. In 1928 the department on Campden Hill was constituted a separate college under the title of King's College of Household and Social Science and in 1953 it was granted a Charter of Incorporation as Queen Elizabeth College.[128]

The college buildings were damaged during the war of 1939–45 and part of the east wing had to be rebuilt. Since then the expansion of its curriculum to cover the sciences generally has necessitated the construction of new buildings on the former sites of Thornwood Lodge and Holly Lodge.

Holland Park School and West London College of Commerce

The planning of Holland Park School was partly dictated by a concern to preserve certain amenities of Campden Hill in deference to the wishes of local residents. The height of the school buildings has been restricted to a maximum of four storeys and care has been taken to preserve as many trees as possible. The footpath at the west end of the roadway named Campden Hill, which follows the line of an ancient footpath, has been preserved even though it passes through the school site; footbridges have been constructed to connect the parts of the school to the south and north of it. The original entrance lodge to the grounds of Wycombe Lodge (see page 99) has been retained and used as the schoolkeeper's house, and, more importantly, Thorpe Lodge has been preserved and adapted for school use. Building began in 1956 and the school took its first pupils in 1958. The London County Council Architect's Department was responsible for the design, the architect-in-charge being D. Rogers Stark.[129]

Central Library, Phillimore Walk

In 1946 the Royal Borough of Kensington purchased land bounded by Campden Hill Road, Holland Street, Hornton Street and Phillimore Walk in order to provide a site for new municipal buildings. The provision of a new central library for the borough was regarded as a matter of some urgency and E. Vincent Harris was retained as architect. As soon as his design was made public there was dissatisfaction in some quarters at its conservative nature and several students from colleges of art and architecture marched in protest. Harris is quoted as saying that the borough council did not want anything modern in style and that 'They wanted a building of good manners. So I designed the Library in a modern

English Renaissance style, which is in keeping with the Royal Borough. . . . It will be a manly type of building, an example of dignified architecture. Architectural good manners are rare today. It will be a durable building and I am sure it will outlast the modern ones.' The Library is faced with red Berkshire bricks and Portland stone dressings over a steel and concrete frame. It was opened in July 1960.[130]

Nos. 1–37 (odd) Hornton Street, Observatory Gardens and Campden Hill Court

The larger of the two plots which were sold by W. R. Phillimore to (Sir) James South in 1827 (fig. 8)[131] included the house which had formerly been the residence of the Phillimore family. Little is known about this house, but it was probably built shortly before 1730 for John and Ann Seymour.[132] When sold the house was no longer used by the Phillimores and had been let to tenants for several years.

James South, who was knighted in 1830, was an astronomer, and he bought the land at Campden Hill as a convenient place for his observations. He lived in the eighteenth-century mansion, which he renamed Observatory House, and had a new observatory built nearby. Among his equipment was a twelve-inch lens, which he had purchased in Paris, and in 1830–1 he had a dome built on to his observatory under the superintendence of Isambard Kingdom Brunel and arranged to have the lens mounted in an instrument made by Troughton and Simms. South, who was an intemperate man, was involved firstly in a dispute over the building of the dome and then in a long lawsuit with the instrument-makers. He claimed that their work had not been executed satisfactorily, but lost the case. He promptly broke up the instrument, selling the metal as scrap in a public auction which was held in his grounds. In 1862 he presented the lens, which had brought him a great deal of trouble, to the observatory of Trinity College, Dublin.[133]

South died in 1867 but a dispute over his will held up the disposal of his property. Eventually in 1870 his land at Campden Hill was sold to Thomas Cawley of Prince of Wales Terrace, South Kensington, a builder, for £19,350.[134] Cawley drew up plans for building on the land, which he called The Observatory estate. According to these plans, two new roads were to be formed, one from east to west (Observatory Gardens), and the other from north to south through the centre of the plot. The latter road was never constructed (the site is now occupied by the blocks of flats called Campden Hill Court) and far fewer houses were built on his estate than Cawley had envisaged. At the start he entrusted operations to other builders with whom he entered into building agreements. Jeremiah Olive Hayward and Josias Stephens of Paddington were to be responsible for Observatory Gardens, while Francis McFarland and Henry Nance of Hackney agreed to build the terrace originally named Observatory Avenue, now Nos. 1–37 (odd) Hornton Street (Plate 47c), and other houses on the southern part of Cawley's land. Building began in 1873 and the capital was largely provided by Cawley himself, partly out of a sum of £12,000 which he had raised by mortgaging the whole plot in 1871, but both building firms were soon in difficulties. Hayward and Stephens were not able to fulfil their agreement and Cawley had to resume possession of the houses which they had built. McFarland and Nance were declared bankrupt in 1875 and apparently did not complete any houses.[135] Cawley then took over most of the building operations himself, although Nos. 31–37 Hornton Street were erected by another builder, William Frayte. The final houses in Observatory Gardens were not begun until 1883 and are somewhat plainer than the rest.[61] Cawley granted long-term leases of some houses to a firm of house agents, but most appear to have been let by him directly on short-term leases at rents ranging between £150 and £200 per annum. In at least one case the lessee was given the option to purchase the freehold for £3,800.[136]

The terraced houses in Hornton Street and Observatory Gardens, which were built as part of Cawley's development, are of basically similar design, each consisting of three main storeys over a semi-basement with a steeply pitched roof containing garrets. They are built of red brick with profuse and florid dressings in painted stone or cement.

The open space which was left facing Campden Hill Road was eventually filled by the building of the large blocks of flats called Campden Hill Court to the designs of Frederick Pilkington (Plate 112c). Building began in 1898, the year of Pilkington's death, and his son, E. C. Pilkington, acted as architect during the period of construction. The builder was Thomas Boyce of Bloomsbury.[137]

Nos. 44–50 (even) Holland Street and No. 56 Hornton Street

The smaller of the two plots purchased by (Sir) James South from W. R. Phillimore in 1827 (fig. 8) was in turn sold by him in 1840 to Lewis Duval of Lincoln's Inn, a barrister.[138] Duval had three pairs of semi-detached houses built, two pairs on the north side of Holland Street known as Hornton Villas, and one pair on the south side of Pitt Street known as Upper Hornton Villas (now demolished). The former were renumbered as Nos. 44–50 (even) Holland Street in 1869. These stucco villas, consisting of two storeys above a basement, were completed by 1845 (Plate 46c). They were not erected under building leases, and the builder was probably Duval's nephew, John Duval.[139] No. 56 Hornton Street was originally built as an addition to No. 50 Holland Street in the late nineteenth century, possibly during the occupation of the house by Sir Charles Stanford, the composer, and it was converted into a separate house in the 1950's.[140]

PHILLIMORE ESTATE LESSEES 1856–68

The names are those of the first lessees of the houses erected under the building agreements made between Charles Phillimore and Joseph Gordon Davis of Pimlico, builder, with the exception of Nos. 7–13 (odd) Campden Hill Road, which were not covered by the agreements. The dates refer to the years in which the leases were granted: these are not always the date of actual building. Leases dated between 1856 and 1863 were granted by Charles Phillimore and those between 1864 and 1868 by William Brough Phillimore. Most were granted in consideration of the expense incurred in building, but where it is known that a monetary consideration other than ground rent was also involved this has been noted. The chief sources are the records of Messrs. Chesterton and Sons at the Phillimore Estate Office, Kensington High Street, and the Middlesex Land Register in the Greater London Record Office at County Hall.

Argyll Road, east side

2–4 consec.	James Jordan the younger of St. Ann's Villas, builder, 1858.
5	John Humphrey Hunter of Paddington, gentleman, at the request of Jordan, 1859. Hunter paid £220 to Jordan.
6 and 7	Jordan, 1859.
9	Caroline Hare of Upper Phillimore Place, spinster, at the request of Jeremiah Little of Wilton Villa, Sheffield Terrace, builder, 1862. Hare paid £1,320 to Little.
11–47 odd	Jeremiah Little, 1861–2.
49	Octavius George Perrott of Norland Place, late captain in H.M. 15th Light Dragoons, at request of Jeremiah Little, 1861. Perrott paid £1,050 to Little.
51	James Beeby of Clarendon Road, gentleman, at request of Jeremiah Little, 1860. Beeby paid £1,000 to Little.
53	Jeremiah Little, 1862.
55	Samuel Read of Paddington, gentleman, at request of Jeremiah Little, 1861. Read paid £990 to Little.

Argyll Road, west side

8	James Furnell of Argyll Road, gentleman, at request of Henry Little of Vicarage Gardens, builder, 1862. Furnell paid £1,100 to Little.
10–38 even	Henry Little, 1861–2.
40	Jane Emma Streatfield of West Ham, widow, at request of Henry Little, 1861. Streatfield paid £1,080 to Little.
42–54 even	Henry Little, 1860–1.

Campden Hill Road, west side

7–13 odd	Charles Frederick Phelps of Russell Road, builder, 1867.
15–35 odd	James Jordan the younger of Paddington, builder, 1856–7.
37–59 odd	Stephen Bird of Hornton Villa, esquire, 1859. Nos. 49 and 51 demolished.

7—S.L. XXXVII

Essex Villas, north side

1	William Hay of St. George's, Hanover Square, baker, at request of Charles Frederick Phelps of Paddington, architect, 1861. Hay paid £300 to Phelps.
3	Hay at request of Phelps, 1861. Hay paid £240 to Joseph Gordon Davis and £60 to Phelps
5–15 odd	Charles Edward Smith of Pimlico, esquire, 1861–2. Smith paid £300 to Davis for each house.
17–21 odd	Davis, 1863.

Essex Villas, south side

2	Charles Edward Smith, 1861. Smith paid £300 to Davis.
4	Smith at request of Charles Frederick Phelps, 1861. Smith paid £300 to Phelps.
6 and 8	Smith, 1862. Smith paid £300 for each house to Davis.
10–20 even	Davis, 1863–4. Nos. 12–20 demolished.

Phillimore Gardens, east side

4–20 even	William Henry Cullingford of Pembridge Villas, builder, 1863.
24	Charles Frederick Phelps of Furnival's Inn, Holborn, architect, 1860.
26	William Henry Ashurst of Old Jewry, gentleman, and Rev. John David Glennie the younger, of St. George's, Hanover Square, 1860. Ashurst and Glennie paid £400 to Davis.
28 and 30	John Thompson of Chelsea, esquire, 1860. Thompson paid £380 for each house to Davis.
32	Henry Burton of Aldersgate Street, City, builder, 1861.
34	Davis, 1863.
36	St. John Claud Paulet, a lieutenant in the 5th Dragoons, 1864. Paulet paid £4,109 12s. to Davis.

PHILLIMORE ESTATE LESSEES 1856–68

Phillimore Gardens, west side

1 and 2	James Wild of Shaftesbury Terrace, Kensington, builder, 1857. Demolished.
3–17 odd	William Henry Cullingford, builder, 1860–1. Nos. 3–7 demolished.
17A and 21	William Yeo of Paddington, builder, 1858.
23–29 odd	George Eugene Magnus of Hammersmith, esquire, 1861–2.
31	Magnus, 1860. Magnus paid £440 to Davis.
33–37 odd	Henry Burton, builder, 1860–1.
39	John Fuller Maitland of St. Marylebone, esquire, 1863. Maitland paid £3,500 to Davis.
43	William Norris Nicholson of Bloomsbury, esquire, 1863.
44	Isaac Solly of Enfield, esquire, and Edward Harrison Solly of Cheshire, esquire, 1862. Lessees paid £2,800 to Davis.
45	James Staats Forbes of Hyde Park Gate South, esquire, 1862. Forbes paid £2,800 to Davis.
46	Louis Edward Engelbach of Brompton Crescent, esquire, 1861. Engelbach paid £2,600 to Davis.
47	Charles Mathew Clode of War Office, Pall Mall, esquire, 1860.
48	William Hutcheons Hall of Lansdowne Road, captain in the Royal Navy, 1860. Hall paid £2,386 to Davis.

Phillimore Place, north side

1	Henry Burton, builder, 1861.
3–17 odd	Davis, 1866.
19	Jeremiah Little, 1862. Little paid £528 to Davis. Demolished and rebuilt as two houses (Nos. 19 and 21).

Phillimore Place, south side

2 and 4	Valentine Holmes of Tottenham, esquire, 1861. Holmes paid £340 for each house to Davis.
6	Henry Winnock Hayward of Essex, architect, 1861. Hayward paid £340 to Davis.
8 and 10	John Kingham Reeves of Berkshire, esquire, 1861. Reeves paid £200 for No. 8 and £320 for No. 10 to Davis.

12	Henry Winnock Hayward, 1861. Hayward paid £430 to Davis.
14	Davis, 1864.
16 and 18	Charles Frederick Phelps, 1864.

Stafford Terrace, north side

1–27 odd	Davis, 1868.

Stafford Terrace, south side

2–28 even	Davis, 1868.

Upper Phillimore Gardens, north side

1	George Augustus Elliott of Campden Hill, esquire, 1859. Elliott paid £1,750 to Davis.
3	Thomas Brooks of Campden Grove, esquire, 1858. Brooks paid £1,309 to Davis.
5	Thomas Allen of Hammersmith, esquire, 1857. Allen paid £380 to Davis.
7	Henry Burton, builder, 1858.
9	Henry Tanworth Wells of St. Marylebone, artist, 1858. Wells paid £1,720 to Davis.
11	Burton, 1859.
13	William Henry Ashurst and Rev. John David Glennie the younger, 1859. Ashurst and Glennie paid £380 to Davis.
15	William Shaen of Holborn, esquire, 1860. Reconstructed.
17	Edward Mansell of Gloucester Road, esquire, 1859. Mansell paid £3,000 to Davis. ?Rebuilt.
19	Hon. William Pitt Lennox, 1859. Lennox paid £1,840 to Davis.
21–25 odd	Davis, 1863.

Upper Phillimore Gardens, south side

2	William Addison Combs of Upper Phillimore Gardens, gentleman, at request of Jeremiah Little, 1860. Combs paid £1,340 to Little.
4	William Duffield at request of Henry Little, 1860. Duffield paid £1,240 to Little.
6	Jeremiah Little, 1862. Little paid £500 to Davis.
8–22 even	Davis, 1865.
24 and 26	Henry Burton, builder, 1861.

CHAPTER V

Bedford Gardens to Uxbridge Street: The Racks

THE area covered by this chapter (fig. 9), which was known by the ancient name of The Racks, was formerly part of the Campden House estate and came into the possession of the Phillimore family during the eighteenth century (see page 58). In 1774 Robert Phillimore appointed the reversion of The Racks to his younger son, Joseph Phillimore, as part of a settlement on the latter's marriage, and confirmed the transaction by his will.[1]

Joseph Phillimore, who became vicar of Orton-on-the-Hill, Leicestershire, sold The Racks, consisting of slightly over twenty-five acres, by auction in 1808 for £6,790 (equivalent to approximately £270 per acre).[2] There were two purchasers. Alexander Ramsay Robinson, who owned other land in Kensington and had at one time been a tenant of The Racks, purchased approximately 14½ acres, while John Jones of Harley Street, esquire, bought the remaining 10½ acres.[3] The dividing line between their respective purchases is shown on fig. 9. In 1810 Jones sold his portion to John Johnson of Horseferry Road, Westminster, a paviour, for £2,660 (approximately £253 per acre).[4]

Robinson also disposed of part of his newly acquired land within a short time when he sold 3½ acres to the West Middlesex Water Works Company (see below). In 1822 he agreed to sell most of the remainder,* or 10¾ acres, for £6,000 (approximately £560 per acre) to Henry Gore Chandless of St. Marylebone. Chandless was the son of a prosperous property owner and brother of a barrister,[6] and, according to the deed of conveyance, he had secured purchasers for part of the land that Robinson had contracted to sell to him before the documents could be drawn up. The new parties to the transaction were two builders from St. Marylebone, John Punter and William Ward, who agreed to pay Chandless £4,300 for

5¾ acres (approximately £750 per acre).[7] Within a few months Chandless had found a buyer for the remaining 5 acres in another builder from St. Marylebone, William Hall;[8] the price paid by Hall is not known, but if it was at a comparable rate to that paid by Punter and Ward, Chandless would have secured a considerable profit on the transactions. He was later found to be under twenty-one years of age at the time of these dealings and had to sign confirmatory deeds when he achieved his majority, but he (or perhaps his father or brother) seems to have shown considerable business acumen.

In 1823 Punter and Ward divided the land which they had jointly purchased, after having agreed to lay out two east–west streets (Campden Street and Peel Street). With minor exceptions, Punter's share consisted of Peel Street and Ward's of Campden Street.[9] Hall also planned to develop his land by constructing an east–west road (Bedford Place, now Bedford Gardens), but he was able to provide house plots of much greater depth (generally about a hundred feet) than those of Punter and Ward. As a result of their decision to make two roads across an area which was of basically the same width as Hall's land, the house plots in Peel Street and Campden Street were in most cases less than fifty feet in depth, and the houses built there were of a different type and catered for a different social group from those in Bedford Gardens.

Bedford Gardens

In 1823 William Hall, who was also building on the Eyre estate in St. Marylebone, secured £9,000 by mortgaging his property in St. Marylebone and Kensington.[10] One of his mortgagees was William Hussey, a solicitor, who had helped to

---

* He retained the small piece of land in the south-east corner of The Racks now occupied by No. 97 Kensington Church Street and Nos. 2–4 (even) Sheffield Terrace. These houses were built under ninety-nine-year leases granted in 1857 by Robinson's descendants to Jeremiah Little, the builder of several houses on Campden Hill.[5]

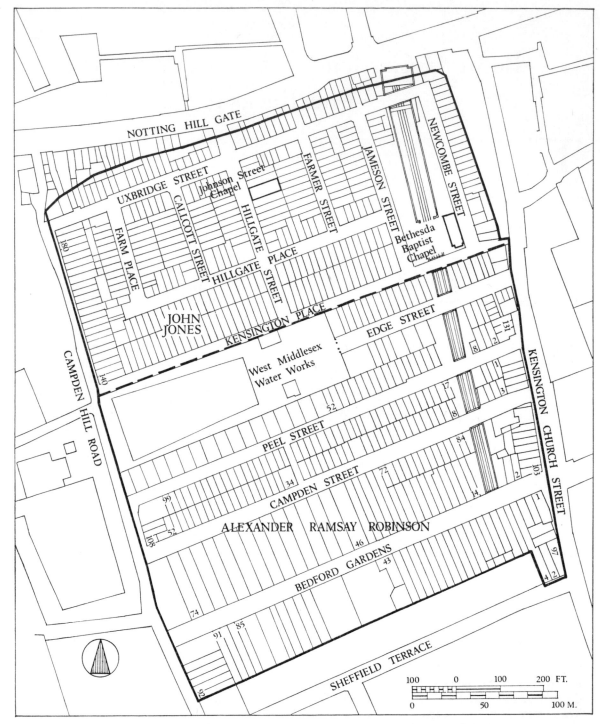

Fig. 9. The Racks area, showing the lands bought by John Jones and Alexander Ramsay Robinson in 1808. Based on the
Ordnance Survey of 1862–72

arrange the sale of Robinson's land in 1822. Of the total amount borrowed, £5,500 was apportioned to Bedford Gardens, and shortly afterwards Hall obtained a further £1,800 on the security of this land. Before the end of the year his mortgagees may have become concerned about Hall's solvency—perhaps because an action was brought against him for the recovery of £5,000 in debts[11]— and Bedford Gardens was put up for sale by auction in ninety-seven lots, providing house plots with seventeen-foot frontages. A number of these plots on the south side of the road towards the western end were bought by various individuals at approximately £70 each,[12] but the whole of the north side and most of the south side became the property of William Bromley, a solicitor of the firm of W. and J. W. Bromley of Gray's Inn.[13] As in the case of Hussey, Bromley's firm had been involved in the transactions which took place in 1822.

Owing to lack of documentary evidence, it is not possible to determine exactly how Bromley came to acquire the freehold of most of Bedford Gardens, but he may have been acting in Hall's interest. In 1824 the two entered into an agreement whereby Hall, by now referred to as William Hall the elder, was to build a terrace consisting of fifty-one houses with seventeen-foot frontages on the north side of the road. The houses were to be built to the satisfaction of William Bromley's surveyor (who was not named) and Bromley agreed to grant ninety-nine-year leases from 1824 to Hall or his nominees.[14] The frontage on the south side of Bedford Gardens, mostly at the eastern end, of which Bromley also owned the freehold, was developed by William Hall the younger, Charles Hall and Caleb Hall, all of St. Marylebone, builders, and probably the sons of William Hall the elder.[15]

The Halls built two late-Georgian terraces of basically identical design at the eastern end of Bedford Gardens, consisting of twenty-three houses on the north side of the street and twenty-two on the south side (fig. 10). Of these Nos. 2–4 (even), 14–46 (even), 3–9 (odd) and 19–43 (odd) survive virtually intact and No. 1 considerably altered. Most of the leases of houses on the

north side were granted directly to William Hall the elder, and of those on the south side to William Hall the younger, Charles Hall and Caleb Hall jointly. Sometimes the Halls nominated other lessees, who were presumably concerned with the development.* The yearly ground rent for each house varied between £8 and £10, and if sold leasehold a house could command a price of approximately £600.[17]

22

Fig. 10. No. 22 Bedford Gardens, elevation

The abrupt termination of the two terraces halfway along Bedford Gardens may be explained by the death of William Hall the younger in 1829 or 1830[18], and by the fact that William Hall the elder appears to have encountered financial difficulties. By 1830 only five houses were occupied on the north side of the street[19] although leases had been granted for seventeen, and in 1831 Nos. 36–46 (even) were leased to another builder, Robert Paten of Paddington, by the direction of two trustees of the estate and effects of William Hall the elder.[20] That a new hand was at work in

* These were: John Bonythorn and Richard Moffatt of Kensington, *carpenters*; George Caton of St. Marylebone, *carpenter and builder*; William and Thomas Cox of St. Luke's, Old Street, *paper-hangers*; James Jannard de Creu of the City, *paper-hanger*; John and George Haynes of Kensington, *carpenters*; William Ifold of St. Marylebone, *surveyor*; John James Kent of Paddington, *surveyor*; Edward May and Aaron Morritt of Oxford Street, *ironmongers*; David Montague and John Turner of Paddington, *cement manufacturers*; Philip Palmer of St. Martin's in the Fields, *glass merchant*.[16]

finishing these houses can be seen by differences in their appearance from other houses in the terrace.

Bromley quickly sold the freeholds of completed houses; in 1827, for instance, he disposed of his interest in twenty houses on the south side of Bedford Gardens and two in Kensington Church Street for £4,580 (a sum equivalent to slightly over twenty years' purchase of the ground rents).[21] In 1831 he sold the remaining ground on the north side of Bedford Gardens, as yet unbuilt on, to Walter Alexander Urquhart, a City merchant. Shortly afterwards Urquhart purchased land on the south side of Campden Street so that he could provide house plots which would extend for the whole distance between the two streets.[22]

Urquhart's solicitors were the firm of Blunt, Roy, Blunt and Duncan, and the developers chosen by Urquhart, probably through his solicitors, were Robert William Jearrad, Charles Jearrad and Charles Stewart Duncan of Oxford Street, architects and surveyors. Charles Stewart Duncan may have been related to John Duncan, a partner in the firm of solicitors, and both were later concerned with developments on the Ladbroke estate. A further connexion is that between Richard Roy, another partner and later a major speculator on the Ladbroke estate, and the Jearrad brothers. All three had considerable interests in Cheltenham, and the Jearrads not only designed several buildings there, but also established a warehouse in London to deal in Cheltenham salt.[23]

The Jearrads and Duncan built seven pairs of semi-detached houses in Bedford Gardens and one detached house facing Campden Hill Road. In 1835 Urquhart granted them ninety-nine-year leases from 1834 at annual ground rents of £12 10s. after a two-year peppercorn term for the semi-detached houses, and £25 for the detached house. Urquhart himself provided £6,000 by way of a mortgage to finance the development.[24] The houses were completed by 1836 and the lessees had no difficulty in finding tenants.[19] Shortly afterwards the semi-detached villas were advertised for sale by auction and were described as follows: 'The property is creditable to the achitectural pretensions of the builder and presents a most refreshing contrast to all the modern school. Substantiality and elegance is combined with an infinity of good taste, and Mr. Jarard* had thus

acquired a new wreath to his well-earned previous fame. The villas are formed on a petite scale, but uniformity prevails throughout. The plan of placing two villas under one roof is here exemplified most successfully. The portico entrée to each gives them a consequence at which their neighbours do not aspire . . . They contain four bedchambers, handsome dining room leading to the drawing-room, dining parlour, small library, cook's room, lots of closets, and a cammodité [sic]; a kitchen, larder, scullery, wine cellars, coal-shed, &c. To each is a large walled garden behind, with plenty of fruit-trees, and a small garden in front. The present low rental is only £50 for each villa, but the time is fast arriving when a considerable addition will be willingly given.'[26] These two-storey brick-faced houses, Nos. 48–74 (even) Bedford Gardens, have since been considerably altered, but sufficient survives to give an indication of their pleasing quality as a group, now enhanced by a number of trees and shrubs.

No. 76 Bedford Gardens, the detached house built by the Jearrads and Duncan, has been demolished and its place taken by The Mount, a block of flats built in 1962–4 to the designs of Douglas Stephen and Partners.[27]

On the south side of the street some of the plots purchased at the auction in 1823 remained unbuilt upon for many years and often changed hands several times before houses were erected. Of the earliest surviving houses, Nos. 85–91 (odd) were built shortly before 1830.[19] Of the later houses, the most interesting is No. 77, which was built in 1882–3 by Perry and Company of Bow to the designs of R. Stark Wilkinson to contain ten studios, some with living quarters attached.[28]

The extension of the Metropolitan Railway (now the Circle Line) to Kensington in the mid-1860's led to the demolition of several houses in the terraces built by the Halls. After the construction of the railway some houses were rebuilt in 1871 by the ubiquitous Campden Hill builder, Jeremiah Little.[29] Of his houses, Nos. 6, 12 and 17 survive.

Campden Street

Campden Street comprised the main part of William Ward's share of the land which he had

---

* Probably Robert William Jearrad, who was the more noted architect of the two brothers.[25]

originally purchased jointly with John Punter in 1822. Little development took place there initially, and by 1844 only twenty houses were listed in the ratebooks, probably mostly built by Ward himself. The rack-rental value of each house was estimated to be approximately £14 and in almost all cases the rates were paid by Ward.[19]

Shortly before 1850 a more concerted attempt to complete building in the street took place. For this Ward relied on other builders, principally Henry Gilbert, who built the Campden Arms public house (now No. 34 Campden Street) and is variously described as a builder and a victualler, and William Wheeler of Portobello Terrace, builder. Gilbert was also responsible for Nos. 72–84 (consec.) on the south side.[30] William Ward died in 1850. In his will[31] he directed his trustees to grant leases of his 'Building Ground' for any term not exceeding seventy-two years, and this became the standard term for the leases granted to Gilbert and Wheeler.

The buildings on the south side of the street to the west of No. 72 were erected piecemeal over several years on land which had been sold by Ward to Walter Alexander Urquhart in 1832 to provide extensive gardens to houses in Bedford Gardens (see above).

The Byam Shaw School of Drawing and Painting Limited (No. 70) was founded by John Byam Shaw and Rex Vicat Cole and opened in 1910. The architect of the building was T. Phillips Figgis.[32]

Peel Street

After John Punter and William Ward had purchased the land on which Peel Street and Campden Street were later laid out, they borrowed £4,800 from Nathaniel Robarts of Covent Garden, a woollen-draper.[33] The firm of solicitors, W. and J. W. Bromley, were probably instrumental in arranging this loan, and when Punter and Ward decided to partition their land, Joseph Warner Bromley acted as their trustee.[9] As in the case of the land purchased by William Hall, for whom the Bromleys also acted, a part of Punter's and Ward's land was put up for auction in 1823. In this instance Peel Street, which Punter had acquired in

the division of the land, was sold in lots corresponding to building plots.

In Peel Street the freeholds were much more widely dispersed than in Bedford Gardens. Most of the purchasers were individuals who were not connected directly with the building trades and their occupations were remarkably diverse, including those of bootmaker, coachman, cowkeeper, grocer, potato salesman, schoolmaster, tailor, victualler and well-digger.[34] Among the gentlemen and esquires was Joshua Flesher Hanson, who was concerned in other developments in Kensington. He bought four plots, only to sell them again almost immediately before houses had been erected on them.[35]

The largest number of plots to be bought by one person was secured by William Humphrey Pilcher, a solicitor, who paid £967 for twenty-one building plots.[36] The amount paid by Pilcher corresponds with the average price of just under £50 for each plot realized at the auction. Punter paid back £3,000 of the £4,800 which he and Ward had owed to Robarts, and the remainder appears to have been charged on Ward's share of the Kensington Church Street frontage.[37]

Punter retained or bought in several plots, principally on the north side of the street to the west of the present No. 52. There he built eight pairs of semi-detached cottages called Claremont Place, which were among the first houses to be erected in the street and were completed by 1826.[19] He also built some houses on the south side of Peel Street and on his share of the frontage to Kensington Church Street, which had not been auctioned. In 1824 he borrowed £2,000 on his own account from Robarts on the security of this property and by 1826 had increased his mortgage debt to £4,000.[38] In 1829 he sold all of his remaining property in The Racks area to John Herapath, the railway journalist. Besides taking over the mortgage debt of £4,000, Herapath paid Punter £2,225.[39]

By 1834 few plots in Peel Street remained undeveloped.[40] Some houses were erected under long-term building leases at annual ground rents of about £5,* but most appear to have been built under contract. Punter and Ward, who was a party to several deeds relating to houses in Peel Street,

* The surviving houses known to have been built under long-term leases and the lessees are as follows: Nos. 25–29 (odd) and 35–37 (odd), William Blenkarn of Kensington, *builder*; Nos. 49 and 51, Samuel Gee of Kensington, *bricklayer*; Nos. 57–65 (odd), Richard Harding of St. Marylebone, *timber merchant*; Nos. 85–91 (odd), John Chandler of Kensington, *joiner*, and George Elwood of Bethnal Green, *carpenter*.[41]

appear to have been involved in the building operations, and other persons connected with the building trades either bought plots directly or were parties in conveyances to others.* Most of the original houses in Peel Street have sixteen-foot frontages, although No. 41 (which had been built by 1834) has a frontage of less than ten feet. The houses are brick-faced and consist in the main of two storeys without basements (Plate 38c). Their rack-rental value was originally as low as £12 per annum.[42] In many cases the parish rate collector only noted the names of house owners, who paid rates for their tenants,[19] and it is possible that some of these small houses were multi-occupied from the time of their erection. In only a few instances did the purchasers of house plots live in the houses built on them. It was not until John Herapath bought Punter's remaining interest in the street that sewers were provided,[43] and in 1856 reports were made to the Vestry that pigs were being kept in a filthy condition at one house in the street, while there were 'foul and offensive' privies at seven other houses.[44]

Several houses at the east end of the street were demolished or rebuilt between 1865 and 1875 as a result of the construction of the Metropolitan Railway, but the most extensive rebuilding took place in 1877–8 when Campden Houses, No. 80 Peel Street and No. 118 Campden Hill Road were built in place of the sixteen semi-detached houses which Punter had sold to John Herapath in 1829. The seven blocks of flats called Campden Houses (Plate 112a) were built as labourers' dwellings for the National Dwellings Society Limited by D. Laing and Company of Westminster, whose tender was for £17,600. The Society's architect was E. Evans Cronk.[45] No. 80 Peel Street was built for Matthew Ridley Corbett, the portrait and landscape painter, who had purchased the site in 1876.[46]

Nos. 92–118 (even) Campden Hill Road

When the building plots in Bedford Gardens were auctioned in 1823 the westernmost plot on the south side, which included a frontage to Campden Hill Road, was bought by Joseph Gardner of St. Marylebone, a butcher. Within a short time he resold it to the solicitor William Bromley, and the terrace comprising Nos. 92–100 (even) Campden Hill Road and No. 95 Bedford Gardens (originally known as Campden Hill Terrace) was built under ninety-nine-year leases granted by Bromley in 1826 to William Jones the elder and William Jones the younger of High Street, Kensington, builders.[47]

Nos. 108–116 (even) Campden Hill Road, including the Windsor Castle public house, stood on land which was allocated to William Ward in the division of his and John Punter's joint purchase in 1823. In 1826 Ward entered into an agreement to grant a ninety-nine-year lease of the site of the Windsor Castle to Douglas and Henry Thompson of Chiswick, brewers, at an annual ground rent of £10, and the public house was built shortly afterwards.[48]

No. 118 Campden Hill Road: West House
Plate 79

In 1876 George Henry Boughton, the artist, purchased a site on the north side of Peel Street at its junction with Campden Hill Road, on which the westernmost pair of the semi-detached cottages built by Punter then stood.[49] These were demolished and Boughton engaged Richard Norman Shaw to design him a house. The builders were Braid and Company of Chelsea.[50]

Although West House, which was named after Benjamin West,[51] has been much altered, several interesting features of Shaw's design can still be discerned. The house is built of stock brick with dressings in both stone and cut and rubbed brick-work, and several of the windows have stone mullions and transoms. There is an extensive use of tile-hanging in the upper of the two main storeys. The smaller of the two gables on the Campden Hill Road façade, now straight-sided, was originally stepped.

The studio was on the first floor at the back. It had a north–south axis, with a gallery at the

---

* These were: Isaac Barber of Kensington, *brickmaker*; George Caton of St. Marylebone, *carpenter*; Abraham Day of St. George's, Hanover Square, *plumber and glazier*; William Dutton of St. Pancras, *paper-hanger*; Joseph Hornsby of St. Marylebone, *builder*; James Whittle Mead of Kensington, *carpenter*; John Miles of St. James's, *painter*; Edward Millwood of Kensington, *builder*; James Moseley of St. Marylebone, *bricklayer*; Isaac Slade of Greenwich, *builder*; Jonathan Slade of St. Marylebone, *carpenter*; Benjamin Toll of Paddington, *brickmaker*.[34]

south end and a large window to let in north light with a small balcony outside at the opposite end.

Nos. 99–135 (odd) Kensington Church Street

The range of houses and shops punctuated by street openings which is now numbered 103–135 (odd) Kensington Church Street was originally called Peel Place. It was built along the valuable frontage to Kensington Church Street (then called Silver Street at this point) which had formed part of the joint purchase of John Punter and William Ward in 1822. The terrace was begun in 1823 and although Punter and Ward divided the frontage between them in the partition of their land in that year, there is evidence that they continued to co-operate in their building work. Among the earliest buildings erected was the original public house on the site of the present Churchill Arms, for which a lease was granted in October 1823.[52] The public house was originally known as the Bedford Arms, but the present name was adopted shortly afterwards and may have been a contraction of 'Church Hill'.

In 1824 Ward sold the freehold of the part of the frontage to the south of Bedford Gardens to William Bromley. Nos. 99 and 101 Kensington Church Street were built under ninety-nine-year leases granted by Bromley in 1826 to William Hall the younger, Charles Hall and Caleb Hall, builders (No. 101), and to Jonathan Turner and Jeremiah White of Soho, timber merchants, by the direction of the Halls (No. 99).[53]

West Middlesex Water Works Company Site

The land bounded on the south by the backs of houses in Peel Street, on the west by Campden Hill Road, on the north by Kensington Place, and on the east by Kensington Church Street was sold in 1809–10 by Alexander Ramsay Robinson to the West Middlesex Water Works Company. Within a month of purchasing a substantial part of The Racks in July 1808 Robinson had offered land to the company. The directors informed the shareholders that the construction of a reservoir on Campden Hill would give the company, which had been incorporated as recently as 1806, a considerable advantage in competing with the older established companies for the supply of water both to Kensington and the parts of St. Marylebone which were becoming increasingly populated. Robinson, whose price was 1,500 guineas for approximately 3½ acres of land (i.e. £450 per acre), was described as a 'Public Spirited Individual'. The sale was concluded, and the reservoir was built in 1809.[54]

Robinson had, however, retained a twenty-foot wide strip of land fronting on to Campden Hill Road, which was then only a footpath at this point, intending to make it into a roadway. After a few months the directors of the company found that they needed this extra land, which adjoined the highest point of their property, in order to construct the works required to enable them to supply water to the upper floors of their customers' houses. In 1810 Robinson sold this strip to the company, but the fact that he had by this time been elected a director did not prevent him from again charging 1,500 guineas, this time for a very much smaller piece of land. He resigned from the board shortly afterwards.[55]

By the 1920's the reservoir was no longer needed by the Metropolitan Water Board, which had taken over the operations of the West Middlesex Water Works Company in 1904. The site of the reservoir itself, which was at the western, or higher, end of the Board's property, was let in 1923 and shortly afterwards sold for use as a garage.[56]

The site of the Board's premises to the east of the reservoir was sold to the London County Council in 1924 and is at present occupied by the buildings of the Fox School and Kensington Institute. The school is named after Caroline Fox, the sister of the third Lord Holland, who had established a charity school on the north side of St. Mary Abbots Mews (now Holland Park Road) in 1842. In 1876 the school was transferred to the School Board for London, which built new premises in Silver Street (now Kensington Church Street). In 1920 the London County Council decided to widen Kensington Church Street where the school buildings stood, and for this reason purchased the present site from the Metropolitan Water Board. The road widening proposals were postponed, however, and it was not until 1935 that work began on the present school buildings.[57]

Edge Street

The eastern, or lowest, part of the land purchased by the water works company in 1809 was not needed for the reservoir or its associated buildings and was let to tenants. In 1825, however, after building developments had begun immediately to the south, the company built a road and sewer and sold the land by auction as building ground. The road, which was originally known as Sheffield Street (the subsidiary names of Edge Terrace, Cousins' Cottages and Reservoir Cottages were used later), is now called Edge Street after one of the purchasers of land fronting it, Andrew Edge of St. Clement Danes, esquire. The other purchasers were William Bartlett of St. George's, Hanover Square, victualler, Samuel and William Cousins of Kensington, builders, and Richard Dartnell of Kensington, gentleman.[58]

Edge Street forms a cul-de-sac and was generally built up with small houses of a similar kind to those in Peel Street. Some of these survive, particularly on the north side, but at the eastern end of the south side there were also groups of tiny cottages arranged around courtyards. These were demolished as a result of the construction of the Metropolitan Railway in *c.* 1865 and the erection of Campden Hill Mansions by the builders E. and H. Harris of Kensington in *c.* 1907.[59] The architect of Campden Hill Mansions was William G. Hunt.[60]

The westernmost building on the south side of Edge Street is the much-altered school established in 1839 as the Kensington Infant National School on land purchased by the Vestry and charity school trustees. In 1865 the school was assigned to the newly established district of St. George's, Campden Hill, and became known as St. George's School. It was closed in 1963 as a result of the reorganization and enlargement of the nearby Fox School, and the building is now used by the Kensington Institute.[61]

Kensington Place to Uxbridge Street

John Johnson, who purchased the northern part of The Racks from John Jones in 1810, was described as a paviour, but this hardly does justice to the extent of his business activities. He quarried stone on Dartmoor and became the contractor for several major projects involving stonework, including the construction of the breakwater at Plymouth. He amassed a considerable fortune and, besides The Racks area, he also owned property in Earl's Court, Westminster, St. Pancras, Ealing and other places outside Middlesex.[62]

Shortly after purchasing the land, Johnson encouraged speculative building around the periphery of the area, while using most of it as a brickfield. The first houses (now demolished) were erected on the north side of Uxbridge Street under eighty-year leases granted in 1814,[63] but relatively little building took place during these early years. The building boom of the early 1820's stimulated development, however, and William Inwood submitted a plan to the Westminster Commissioners of Sewers showing a proposed layout for Johnson's estate.[64] There is no evidence that Inwood acted in any other capacity for Johnson than as a surveyor, and his street pattern was not adhered to. Stephen Bird constructed sewers in Uxbridge Street and New Street (now Newcombe Street),[65] but in the event building was chiefly confined to these streets and parts of the frontage to Plough Lane (now Campden Hill Road). By the late 1820's the pace of activity had slowed considerably—a general trend reflected elsewhere in Kensington and other parts of London.

In 1829 John Johnson transferred the bulk of his property, including his land in Kensington, to his sons, John Johnson the younger and William Johnson, who carried on their father's business.[66] The younger John Johnson became an alderman of the City of London and was Lord Mayor in 1845–6.[67]

In 1839 the Johnsons leased their brickfield, which still occupied by far the largest part of the area, to Benjamin and Joseph Clutterbuck, brickmakers, for fourteen years at an annual rent of £150 plus an extra 2s. 6d. for every 1,000 bricks made above 1,200,000. Benjamin Clutterbuck, who was working a brickfield on the Holland estate (see page 105), shortly afterwards assigned his interest to Joseph Clutterbuck, who became the sole lessee.[68]

John Johnson the younger died in 1848. In his will[69] he left his estates to his brother on trust to sell them to settle his share of their joint debts. The mortgage debts on The Racks and other property amounted to £50,000, and William Johnson immediately began to sell the freeholds of the houses that were then standing in the area. These did not command very high prices, however; for instance, Edward Baker of Stamford Hill, esquire, paid only £1,570 for the freeholds of at least twenty-six houses.[70]

In 1850 Joseph Clutterbuck was granted ninety-nine-year building leases by Johnson of four houses at the east end of Kensington Place.[71] Clutterbuck's lease of the brickfield was shortly due to expire and by 1851 he had entered into an agreement with Johnson to undertake building developments on the land. The agreement itself has not survived, and it is not known who was responsible for determining the layout or for the basic design of the houses themselves, which are markedly similar although erected by a miscellany of builders. Most of the houses consist of two storeys above semi-basements with narrow frontages of approximately sixteen feet, and are brick-faced with stucco dressings in a uniform style (Plate 41e). Clutterbuck himself applied to the Metropolitan Commissioners of Sewers for permission to build over four thousand feet of sewers, partly in continuation of the drainage system begun by Stephen Bird and partly in the new streets about to be laid out, viz: Ernest Street (now Farm Place), William Street (now Callcott Street), Johnson Street (now Hillgate Street), Farm Street (now Farmer Street), St. James or James Street (now Jameson Street) and Dartmoor Street (now Hillgate Place).[72]

Clutterbuck died in 1851 or 1852 and although several leases were granted to builders by the direction of his widow, another developer became involved. He was William Millwood of High Row (Kensington Church Street), who was described variously as a licensed victualler and a builder.[73] The development proceeded with great rapidity and over two hundred houses were erected in a decade. A considerable number of builders were employed, most of them building only a few houses each.* Johnson granted leases at terms equivalent to ninety-nine years from 1850 at very low ground rents, but he disposed of the freeholds shortly after the houses had been completed. In 1855 Edward Baker, who had already purchased several of the older houses, bought the freeholds of over one hundred of the newly erected houses for £8,200.[75]

The evidence of the census of 1861 suggests that the majority of houses were multi-occupied as soon as they were finished.† Several houses contained over twenty people, and in one house in St. James Street thirty-two people seem to have lived, spread among six households. In 1865 Henry Mayhew interviewed several workmen who lived in the vicinity of Silver Street, possibly in these houses, and they extolled the virtues of living in 'the suburbs', where they could enjoy the luxury of two rooms.[76] An observer commented in the 1870's, however, that 'Johnson-street is a dingy, ill-favoured slum',[77] and in 1900 the vicar of St. George's, Campden Hill, made an appeal for the relief of the poverty of the inhabitants of the area, in which he compared their conditions of living to those in the East End of London.[78] The upward social transformation which has taken place in recent years, however, has been remarkable, its most obvious outward manifestation being the liberal application of paint in various pastel shades to the brickwork of the houses.

The most extensive redevelopment has occurred at the eastern end of the area. As a result of the construction of Notting Hill Gate railway station, which was opened in 1868, most of the houses on the east side of St. James Street and the west side of New Street had to be demolished. After the station was completed new houses were erected in 1871–4, the builder responsible being Walter William Wheeler of Victoria Gardens, Notting Hill.[79] The range consisting of Nos. 11–37 (odd) Jameson Street survives as an example of his work.

* The names of the following builders occur either in the district surveyor's returns, or as lessees; only those builders' addresses which were outside Kensington are given: George Arnold of Paddington; Thomas Balls; James Bond; John Bowler; Joseph Clutterbuck; Robert and William Henry Coghill; Daniel Edward Colston; H. Cowley; James Flint; Henry Hardy of Islington; Charles Hawkins; James Hicks; Mark and Noah Holliday of St. Pancras; Thomas Huggett; Messrs. Hurren and Jory; John Charles Lamb; George Langford; Andrew Harvey Langman and Thomas Brooking Langman; William Lapthorne; John MacNolty of Westminster; Charles Maidlow of St. Marylebone; William Garrett May; William James May; William Millwood; James Morgan; Thomas Morgan; James Olding of Lambeth; Thomas Charles Osborne; Edmund Perfect; Robert Raynham; George Robinson; Messrs. Skelton and Chinnock; Benjamin Nicholls Smith; Messrs. Sweet and Buckland; George Torkington of St. Pancras; William Neve Turner; Thomas Webb; William Wheeler.[74]

† A typical list of the occupations of the heads of households in houses in Ernest Street contains: baker, blacksmith, boot and shoe maker, breeches-maker, bricklayer, carman, carpenter, coachman, cordwainer, dressmaker, excavator, gardener, groom, labourer, laundress, mariner, nurse, ostler, painter, plasterer, porter, stonemason, tailor and toll collector.

The whole of New Street (now Newcombe Street), with the exception of the chapel at the corner of Kensington Place, has since been demolished.

No. 23 Kensington Place, built in 1966–7, maintains the scale and frontage line of its neighbouring Victorian houses, although it provides a sharp contrast in design and appearance. The house, which consists of three storeys and has a prominent circular staircase tower on the Hillgate Street front, is faced with blue Staffordshire bricks of a very dark colour. The architect was Tom Kay.[80]

Bethesda Baptist Chapel, Kensington Place
Plate 28a

This chapel was built under a ninety-eight-year lease granted in 1824 by John Johnson the elder to Thomas Worger of Kensington Gravel Pits, a coachmaker. For most of its history, and possibly, indeed, from its establishment, it has been used by various Baptist sects. For several years during the nineteenth century it was known as the Silver Street Baptist Chapel on account of its proximity to the northern part of Kensington Church Street which was then called Silver Street, and on the Ordnance Survey map of 1863–73 it is called The Labourers' Church.[81]

Johnson Street Baptist Chapel

This building, which is now in commercial use, is situated on the east side of Hillgate Street (formerly Johnson Street) and is now known as Hillgate House. It was built in 1851–2 under a lease granted by William Johnson to Peter William Williamson, its first pastor. The builder was James Betts of St. Pancras. The chapel was used by a congregation of Particular Baptists and was described in 1872 as 'one of the plainest of buildings for religious worship, low and uncommanding, . . . a simple meeting-house with a stuccoed front'. A less sympathetic observer commented that it was 'a low, beetle-browed edifice, bearing on its front the outward and visible signs of the strictest sect of Calvinism, as though one should have written thereupon the stern motto, "All hope abandon, ye who enter here".' By 1882 the chapel had ceased to be used for worship, and the building appears to have been refronted shortly afterwards.[82]

CHAPTER VI

Campden Hill Square Area

AMONG the lands which were sold by (Sir) Walter Cope to Robert Horseman in 1599 (see page 25) was a twenty-acre farm known by the name of Stonehills. In 1618 this farm, which was situated on steeply rising ground to the south of the Uxbridge road (now Holland Park Avenue), was conveyed by Horseman's son to James Necton, who appears to have been a cousin, and Thomas Bedingfield, both of Gray's Inn. The transaction was probably in the nature of a mortgage for Necton and Bedingfield entered into a bond to sell back the land on repayment with interest of the stated purchase price of £455, but the bond was later cancelled and Necton retained the property, Bedingfield relinquishing his interest.[1] In 1642 John Halsey of Great Gaddesden, Hertfordshire, purchased the freehold reversion of the farm from Necton, and the land remained in the ownership of the Halsey family until it was bought by (Sir) Edward Lloyd in 1750.[2] Lloyd, who came from Flintshire, was then deputy to the Secretary-at-War.[3] He was created a baronet in 1778. When he died in 1795, he left his property to his wife for her lifetime and then in an entailed line of descent through his great-nephew Sir Edward Pryce Lloyd, who was later created Baron Mostyn.[4]

By 1819 the Lloyds wished to dispose of their property in Kensington, and to enable them to sell it they set aside the entail in a series of transactions whereby the land was conveyed to the joint use of Sir Edward Pryce Lloyd and his son and heir, Edward Mostyn Lloyd.[5] A small piece of copyhold land in the north-east corner of their estate was also freed from entail at the same time,[6] and a further two and a half acres bordering the turnpike road, which had been formerly part of the waste of the manor of Abbots Kensington and were held on lease from Lord Holland, were purchased in fee simple in 1819.[7]*

A substantial part of the land was sold in 1820, but the largest portion, consisting of over thirteen acres which was advertised for sale as building ground in that year,[9] was not disposed of until 1823. It was originally contracted for by Edward Pain, a wax chandler of Soho, but he did not complete the purchase and, with his approval, the land was sold to Joshua Flesher Hanson, a property speculator, in March 1823.[10] The extent of the Lloyd family's holdings and the various purchasers are shown on fig. 11.

Aubrey House

Plate 42a, b

The first building on the site of Aubrey House, and possibly still structurally the core of the present building, was a house attached to a medicinal spring which was discovered in the area and called Kensington Wells. This was completed by 1698 under a fifty-year lease granted to John Wright, a 'Doctor in Physick', John Stone, an apothecary, and two others.[11] Dr. Benjamin Allen's *The Natural History of the Chalybeat and Purging Waters of England*, published in 1699, contained an analysis of the water from the spring on account of its 'being made Illustrious by the Town, in which his Majesty hath been pleased to fix his Mansion Palace'.[12] John Bowack, writing in 1705, said the place was 'much esteem'd and resorted to for its Medicinal Virtues'.[13] The property passed through several hands until in the 1730's it was held by Jeffrey Gillingham the elder of Hammersmith, a pinmaker. By this time it consisted of various ancillary buildings besides the main house, including a 'large room' and a 'Brew House', although whether still resorted to for its health-giving waters is not known. The elder Jeffrey Gillingham assigned the property to Jeffrey Gillingham the younger, also a pinmaker.[14] In 1744 the lease was assigned to (Sir) Edward Lloyd, who six years later purchased the freehold from Frederick Halsey together with the rest of Halsey's property in the area.[15]

* At the same time a thousand-year lease was obtained of these two and a half acres,[8] perhaps because of a dispute over Lord Holland's title to the land (see page 103).

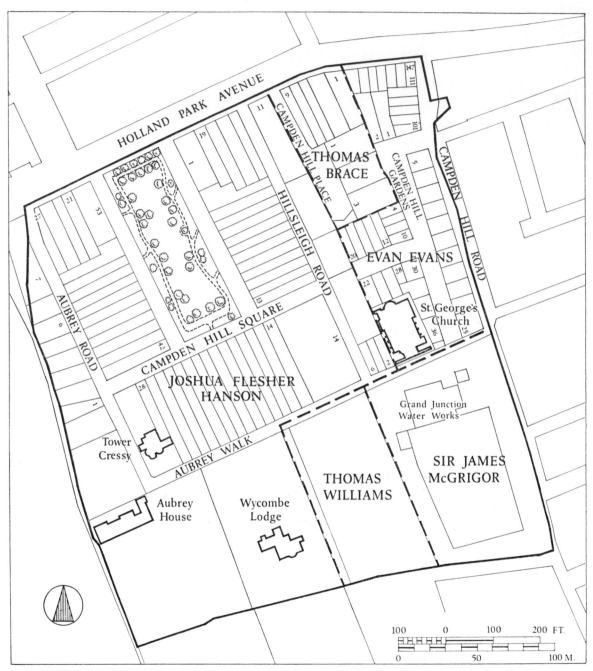

Fig. 11. Campden Hill Square area, showing the land owned by the Lloyd family in 1820 and its later sub-divisions. Based on the Ordnance Survey of 1894–6

It was almost certainly Lloyd who transformed the house into the mansion we recognize today. The evidence of various editions of Rocque's map of the environs of London and his map of Middlesex indicates that wings were added between 1745 and 1754 and the present north front appears to date from about the same period. Although Lloyd was paying rates on the house in 1766[16] he was no longer living there early in 1767, when the mansion was occupied by Richard, Lord Grosvenor, later created first Earl Grosvenor.

In June 1767 the house was taken by Lady Mary Coke, the daughter of the second Duke of Argyll, and she lived there until 1788. During her occupancy several alterations were made, but almost entirely to the interior. In 1767–9 a 'Mr. Phillips', probably John Phillips, the master carpenter, undertook several commissions here and in 1774–5 'Mr. Wyatt', probably James Wyatt, whose Pantheon Lady Mary much admired, remodelled a room in the house.[17]* Little, if anything, has survived of these alterations.

After Lady Mary Coke the house was occupied by a succession of tenants and was used for a time as a school.[18] By 1819 it was empty and appears to have remained so until 1823, when it was included in the property purchased by Joshua Flesher Hanson from the Lloyds. Hanson himself occupied the house, then known as Notting Hill House, for a short while, but by the end of 1824 he was no longer living there.[16] In 1827 he sold the house and grounds to Thomas Williams, a former coachmaker, who already held substantial property on the Phillimore estate on lease and had purchased some land from the Lloyds.[19] Williams paid £3,750 and, in view of Hanson's propensity for building speculation, may have saved the house from demolition. Williams did not live there himself but let the house to Mary and Elizabeth Shepheard, who used it as a boarding-school for young ladies from 1830 until 1854.[20] He retained the kitchen-garden, however, and built a house on it called Wycombe Lodge (see page 99).

Williams died in 1852 and by his will[21] ordered that a large part of his property including Notting Hill House should be sold. His executors carried out his wishes in 1859 when James Malcolmson, who lived in Moray Lodge to the south, bought the house for £5,400.[22] Malcolmson's aim in securing the property seems to have been solely to add part of the garden to that of Moray Lodge and shortly afterwards he let the house, with its grounds somewhat truncated, to Peter Alfred Taylor, M.P.[23] By this time the mansion was known as Aubrey House, no doubt after Aubrey de Vere, who held the manor of Kensington at the time of the Domesday survey. In 1863, Malcolmson having died, Taylor purchased the house from the trustees of his estate with the appropriated pieces of garden restored.[24]

Peter Alfred Taylor was M.P. for Leicester from 1862 until 1884 and was a noted champion of radical causes. His wife Clementia was also famous as a philanthropist and champion of women's rights. They were closely involved in the movement for Italian liberation and Mazzini was a frequent visitor to Aubrey House.[25] In 1873 Taylor sold the house to William Cleverley Alexander, an art collector and patron of Whistler.[26]

During the nineteenth century many alterations were made to the house and the interior was considerably remodelled. The wings were altered and extended and at one time a heavy Victorian doorcase was inserted into the north front, now happily replaced with the more appropriate pedimented doorcase which can be seen today.†

Campden Hill Square

Joshua Flesher Hanson, who purchased the largest share of the former Lloyd estate (see fig. 11), was involved in several developments in Kensington. Besides the Campden Hill Square area, he was also active on the Ladbroke estate, in Peel Street, and at Hyde Park Gate. Before moving to Kensington

---

* A watercolour of 1817 shows the drawing-room decorated in Wyatt's style (Plate 42b).

† Access to Aubrey House was refused during the preparation of this volume. In 1957 Walter Ison made a brief survey of the house for the London County Council and his comments are particularly interesting for the light they shed on the dating of the structure: 'The much altered central block of Aubrey House contains some features suggestive of a nucleus dating from c. 1700. There are the angle chimneys in the first floor rooms, some simple deal wainscot, and the flush-framed windows in flat-arched openings in the south front. Apart from the added attic storey, this south front in its composition and proportions is typical of c. 1700, and refacing might account for the present skin of stock bricks. Incidentally the basement window arches appear to be of red brick. The south front is altogether different in character to the north front, a simple Palladian design of the 1740's, which has been added on to an earlier front, resulting in a wall of unusual thickness.'[27]

he had promoted the building of Regency Square, Brighton, which was begun in 1818.[28] No doubt it was this precedent which prompted him to make a similar square the central feature of his plans for the land he had bought from the Lloyds, and many of the techniques he used in Brighton were repeated.

In 1826 a plan showing the layout of an intended square to be called Notting Hill Square was submitted on behalf of Hanson to the Westminster Commission of Sewers by George Edward Valintine, an architect and surveyor with an address at Furnival's Inn.[29] The basic features of the plan appear to have been derived from Regency Square. In both cases terraced houses were ranged round three sides of a rectangular garden enclosure with a north–south axis, the open side in Brighton being the southern, or sea, end and in Kensington the northern, or turnpike road, end. Similarly, the row of houses on the side opposite to the open end was extended in each case to east and west beyond the building lines of the long north–south sides. These comparable features suggest that the basic concept of Campden Hill Square (its name was changed from Notting Hill Square in 1893) was Hanson's.

Little is known about Valintine besides the fact that he exhibited paintings at the Royal Academy in 1819–21, and the extent of his role in the development of Campden Hill Square is uncertain. He made the application to build the main sewers and submitted the initial requests to lay drains from individual houses in 1826.[30] He may also have provided designs for some of the first houses to be erected, in particular Nos. 2 and 52, the only double-fronted houses in the square (fig. 12). The first occupant of No. 2 was Hanson himself, who lived there from 1828 until 1830 when he sold the house.[31] No. 52 was not tenanted until 1831, when Hanson let it on a twenty-one-year lease at a rack rent of £84, but it was apparently originally intended to be let to Valintine, who as early as 1825 had obtained a mortgage on the security of an agreement for a lease of a house which other transactions suggest was to be No. 52; for some reason the lease was never executed.[32]

Hanson granted some long-term leases, but he also used methods which were less typical of speculations in London. The first houses to be erected were apparently built under contract, and some of these were sold freehold as soon as they had been completed. Many sites were sold before building had commenced, and in these cases the conveyances were accompanied by agreements and covenants binding the purchasers to observe certain stipulations. In this way the sites of Nos. 16–20 were sold in 1826 to Thomas Williams, the coachmaker who was soon to buy Aubrey House, and two years later Williams also purchased the sites of Nos. 15 and 23.[33] In 1830 all of the sites which had not yet been built on (and some finished houses) were sold to Rice Ives of St. Marylebone, a wine merchant.[34] After this date the active prosecution of the development passed to Williams and Ives, and Hanson disposed of his remaining interest in Campden Hill Square in 1839 to settle a mortgage debt of £5,000.[35]

The exact stipulations imposed by Hanson when selling undeveloped parts of the square are not now known, but the gist of them can be deduced from subsequent deeds. An area twenty-five feet deep in front of each house built was to be reserved as a garden, and no shrubs or trees were to be planted there which would grow to a height of more than three feet above the ground floor, nor were any fences to be erected above a similar height. Bow windows were allowed to be built on to the houses provided that they did not project more than three feet beyond the general building line. Above the ground floor the brickwork of the façades was to be left exposed and not covered with stucco or composition. Hanson, on his part, agreed to lay out the garden enclosure, and the owners and occupiers of the houses in the square together with their friends and servants were to have the right to use it on payment of a proportion of the costs of upkeep (see below). There was also reference in several of Ives's subsequent leases to the existence of a 'plan or ground plot' of the square according to which houses were to be built.[36] These stipulations are similar in many respects to those which accompanied conveyances of houses in Regency Square.[28]

Rice Ives died in 1832 and left his property in trust for his infant son, also named Rice Ives.[37] He had taken out a mortgage for £3,000 on his property in Campden Hill Square and by assignment this was vested in John Murdoch and Joseph Venables, hat manufacturers.[38] By his will, Ives's trustees were empowered to sell any part of his property to settle his debts and they proceeded to sell most of the house sites in the square.

The sites for Nos. 9–12 and 42–47 were divided between Murdoch, Venables and their solicitor, Thomas Randall of Holborn. They, in turn, granted conventional long-term building leases of the houses to Christopher Howey, a local builder.[39] Mortgages entered into by Howey[40] show that a substantial part of the money for their construction was provided by Murdoch, Venables and Randall themselves. The site of No. 13 and the ground on the south side to the east of No. 15 were purchased by Thomas Williams,[41] so that when Rice Ives the younger came into his inheritance in 1845 the only parts of the square which remained in his hands were the south side to the west of No. 23, mostly still undeveloped, and two older houses, Nos. 1 and 3, which had also been purchased by his father from Hanson.

The division of the freehold complicated the building history of the square and its development was slow and uneven, spanning a period of twenty-five years from the reign of George IV to that of Victoria. According to the ratebooks fifteen houses (Nos. 1–5, 8, 16–19 and 49–53) had probably been completed by 1830. Five years later Nos. 6–7, 15 and 20–25 had been added. The remaining houses on the east side (Nos. 9–13) were all occupied by 1840 and those on the west side (Nos. 42–47) by 1842. On the south side No. 14 had been finished by 1841. Nos. 26, 27 and 28 were built after 1845, and a lease of No. 28, which was the last house to be completed before later rebuildings, was not granted until 1851.[42] No. 18 was rebuilt in 1887–8 to the designs of J. T. Newman,[43] and Nos. 24–28 were rebuilt after the war of 1939–45 as a result of war damage, at which time Nos. 29 and 30 were added. No. 41, which faces Aubrey Road, although it is numbered in Campden Hill Square, was designed by T. P. Figgis in 1929.[44] Several of the original houses have been substantially altered. The system of numbering employed for the square is puzzling. The high numbers for houses on the west side were settled by 1835[16] but it is difficult to see how a total of fifty-three house sites could have been fitted into the three sides even with the extended south side. In the event, for all of the nineteenth century and part of the twentieth there were no houses to which numbers between 28 and 42 could be assigned.

Although it is not possible to determine the builder of each house in the square, for several were built under contracts which have not survived, the main builder was evidently Christopher Howey. His name can be definitely connected with twenty-one houses (Nos. 5, 6, 9–12, 15, 19, 23–28 and 42–48) and he probably built others; his activity spans the whole building history of the square, for he was involved in the initial building activity in the 1820's and he took a building lease of No. 28 in 1851.[45] Other builders whose names are known were William Jones and Son of High Street, Kensington (Nos. 4 and 7) and John Robert Butler of Uxbridge Street (No. 20).[46]

Even the houses with which Howey was associated show considerable variations in detail, and the present somewhat unsatisfactory appearance of the square as an architectural unit is not entirely the result of subsequent alterations. It is difficult to estimate how far Hanson originally planned a uniform composition, for even in Regency Square, Brighton, which presents superficially a more unified treatment, there are differences in detail between groups of houses. The surviving pilasters on the much altered Nos. 19 and 20 in the centre of the south side of Campden Hill Square suggest that, together with the now rebuilt No. 18, the façades of these houses may have been treated as one architectural unit similar to that in the centre of the north side of Regency Square. The sites for these houses were sold by Hanson before building began, however, and they were not all by the same builder, or, apparently, completed at the same time, which suggests that they may have been built to an existing design. There is also a suggestion of symmetry in the comparison of Nos. 1 and 2 on the east side with Nos. 52 and 53 on the west, but the remaining houses vary widely and reflect the long period over which the square was built and the lack of central control which the dispersal of the freehold made inevitable, despite the covenants insisted on by Hanson. It may be significant that the square was begun at a time of financial depression for the building industry, and the difficulty of securing capital was probably a factor in preventing the rapid completion of the development.

Such homogeneity as does exist is achieved by similar materials, proportions and scale. The houses are generally of three storeys with, in some cases, basements, and have stock-brick façades, mostly rendered on the ground floors, rising to simple stone or stucco copings on the parapets. Some houses have cast-iron balconies set above

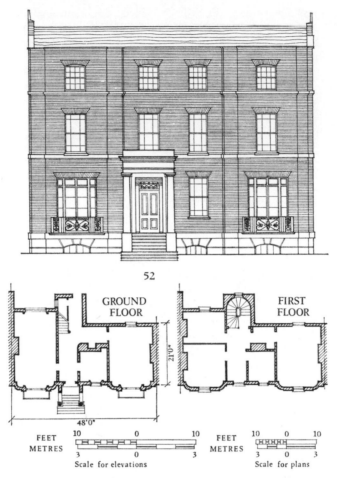

52

Fig. 12. No. 52 Campden Hill Square, elevation and plans

the top string of the rendering, and there are fanlights over the doors, especially elegant in Nos. 2, 4, 5, 6 and 15. On the west side some attempts were made by the introduction of stucco architraves around the window openings to provide fashionable Italianate detail. No. 52 is perhaps the most architecturally distinguished individual house. It is double-fronted with slightly project-ing bays and a Doric porch. The same bay design, an unusual rectangular projection with curved corners set back, is also found at No. 2, the other double-fronted house, and at Nos. 50 and 51, which are single-fronted. Despite the lack of architectural unity in the square, an exceedingly picturesque effect is created by the combination of the mature trees, the mellow brickwork of the house fronts stepping sharply down the hill and

the attractive ironwork in the railings and gates of the central garden (Plate 42c, d).

For the upkeep of the garden enclosure in the centre, Hanson established a five-man committee, consisting of four members who were to be elected by residents of the square and he himself as a life-member. All lessees or purchasers of houses were required to pay a proportionate share of the ex-penses. One of the prominent early members of the committee and for many years its treasurer was Stephen Garrard, a lawyer who lived at No. 18 from 1828 until 1853 and who was professionally involved in several of the property transactions of both Hanson and Thomas Williams. He was subsequently concerned in the development of Pembridge Square and Pembridge Gardens (see page 262). Hanson appears to have taken no part in the committee's proceedings after 1832, and until the 1860's it only consisted of four persons.[47]

Nos. 11–27 (odd) Holland Park Avenue

The site on which No. 11 Holland Park Avenue (Linton House) stands was at the eastern edge of the property Hanson purchased from the Lloyds. In 1830 he sold the plot to the Reverend Hibbert Binney of Paddington,[48] who built a detached house on it known as Mound House. In 1877 a preparatory school called Linton House School was established there, the house itself being used as the headmaster's residence and new school buildings erected in the garden at the rear.[49] The present Linton House, a block of flats designed by T. P. Bennett and Son, replaced the school in *c.* 1936.[50]

The remaining frontage of Hanson's property along the turnpike road was developed in conjunction with Campden Hill Square. Two terraces of four houses each were built, forming in effect short return wings to the square. Both were substantially completed by 1830,[16] although many of the houses have since undergone considerable alterations or possibly rebuildings.

Nos. 23–27 (odd) Holland Park Avenue (Plate 43a) form an architectural group similar to Nos. 2–6 (even) and 24–28 (even) on the north side of the street, which were built as part of Hanson's development on the Ladbroke estate. The main differences are that the group consisting of Nos. 23–27 is nine windows wide rather than seven, the giant unfluted tetrastyle Doric order of the central house (No. 25) is not in antis, and the columns are slightly more slender. There is also a difference in the treatment of the attic storey and the crowning pediment. A ninety-nine-year lease of Nos. 23–27 was granted by Hanson to James Clift, a solicitor, in 1827,[51] and the date 1829 inscribed in Roman letters on the entablature of No. 25 probably indicates the year in which the façades were completed; all three houses were occupied by 1831.[16] Robert Cantwell, who was later surveyor to the Norland estate, is associated with the two groups on the north side of the road (see page 197), and it is significant that

he was living in the house which is now numbered 21 Holland Park Avenue in 1830–1.[16]

Aubrey Road and No. 29 Holland Park Avenue

Aubrey Road (Plate 43c) was laid out primarily as a service road for the houses on the west side of Campden Hill Square and was not given its name until the 1840's. In 1826 Hanson granted a ninety-nine-year lease of a 'cottage' on the west side of the road (now No. 7 Aubrey Road) to Richard Lovekin of Cold Bath Square, a victualler,[52]* but the remaining land between the cottage and Aubrey House (or Notting Hill House as it was then called) remained undeveloped until it was sold by Hanson in 1841 to James Hora, a surgeon.[53] This was the last piece to remain in Hanson's hands of all the property he had purchased from the Lloyd family in 1823.

Hora died shortly afterwards and his wife and eldest son, as trustees under his will,[54] employed Henry Wyatt, an architect,† to develop the property. A plot to the north of the front garden of Notting Hill House was already on lease to Mary and Elizabeth Shepheard, the lessees of the mansion, and could not be used immediately, but on the remaining land Wyatt built six 'Gothic' villas between 1843 and 1847 under ninety-nine-year leases.[56] Now Nos. 1–6 (consec.) Aubrey Road, these were originally called Aubrey Villas. No. 4 is the best preserved, although No. 6 has an ornate bargeboard and No. 2 still has some Perpendicular windows. The rest have been considerably altered and No. 1 was refronted in *c.* 1913.[57] No. 6A was added in the 1960's. Aubrey Lodge was built in 1861–3 by George Drew of Rosedale Villas, Notting Hill,[58] on the piece of ground formerly let to the Shepheard sisters, but it has since been substantially altered and has lost the cornices and stringcourses from the front elevation.

The most remarkable house in Aubrey Road was Tower Cressy, built in 1852–3 for Thomas Page, the engineer who designed Westminster Bridge. The site was part of the property Hanson had sold to Rice Ives in 1830 and was purchased by Page in 1854, after his house had been erected,

---

* Lovekin's lease also included Nos. 50 and 51 Campden Hill Square. No. 7 Aubrey Road has been identified with a cottage built for Lady Mary Coke, but no building is shown on the site in a map of 1822 (Plate 1), and no evidence has been discovered to indicate that the present building is older than the 1820's.

† Probably the youngest son of Mathew Cotes Wyatt, and grandson of James Wyatt.[55]

together with the freeholds of Nos. 24–28 Campden Hill Square, from Rice Ives the younger. The tall structure dominated its surroundings until it was damaged during the war of 1939–45 and demolished shortly afterwards. The builder was John Cowland of Portland Road.[59]

The site on which No. 29 Holland Park Avenue stands had never formed part of the Lloyd family's property but consisted of a small triangular piece of land to the east of Holland Walk which was part of the Holland estate (see fig. 15). This accounts for both the irregular shape of the house and the constricted entrance to Aubrey Road. For several years the ground was let to the occupant of No. 7 Aubrey Road for use as a garden, but in 1851 Lord Holland granted a ninety-year lease to Nathaniel Dando of No. 6 Aubrey Road which allowed him to build a house to the value of £800. The house, which was not, in fact, erected until 1863, is double-fronted with segmental bays that rise from the basement to second-floor level and are enriched with balustrades of stucco. The upper three floors are of brick, with stucco quoins and a modillioned cornice. The builder was George Drew.[60]

Aubrey Walk

Formerly an approach road to Aubrey House, Aubrey Walk was originally called Notting Hill Grove and was given its present name in 1893. When Campden Hill Square was laid out the sites of the houses on the south side of the square extended as far as Aubrey Walk and several coach-houses and stables were built on the north side of the road. Towards the end of the century most of these were converted into, or replaced by, studio residences. Of these, No. 26 is a four-storey composition of eclectic elements having open stairs, arcades of red brick and large studio windows. It was originally built in 1888 to the designs of J. T. Newman[43] as a stable and coach-house combined with a studio at the rear of the rebuilt No 18 Campden Hill Square, but has since undergone some alterations.

Nos. 2–6 (even) Aubrey Walk, which are three-storey Georgian houses of stock brick with stuccoed ground storeys, were built on land purchased by Hanson. No. 6 was the first to be completed under a ninety-nine-year lease granted by Hanson to John Edward Cowmeadow, a coal

merchant, in 1826. Cowmeadow took the house for his own occupation and was living there by 1827. He was also the lessee of Nos. 2 and 4, for which Hanson granted him a similar lease in 1829; they were finished by the following year.[61] Cowmeadow's venture into the field of property was clearly not made from a position of financial security for in 1831 he was excused from paying rates 'on Account of numerous Family and his wife now Lying-in'; later in the year the rate collector noted 'Family in great distress'.[16]

Hillsleigh Road

Hillsleigh Road (known as New Road until 1910) was formed on the east side of Campden Hill Square partly to serve the same function as Aubrey Road on the west, i.e. to provide access to stables and coach-houses at the rear of houses in the square (Plate 43d). A strip of land about fifty-five feet wide was, however, left between the eastern side of the road and the boundary of Hanson's land, and on this three houses were built under leases granted to John Ogle, esquire, in 1829.[62] Two of these, No. 19 (Ness Cottage) and the much-altered No. 20, have survived. The site of the third is now occupied by Nos. 17 and 18, originally built as one house in 1897–8.[63] An addition made to No. 20 in 1902 to the designs of W. Hargreaves Raffles recalls the work of C. F. A. Voysey in its white rendered exterior, low casements, and canopied entrance door in Campden Hill Place.[64]

Although numbered in Hillsleigh Road, Hill Lodge (No. 14) is really situated on the south side of Campden Hill Square. Its site was purchased by Thomas Williams in 1839 (see page 91) and the house was completed by 1842. The builder was John Brunning of Gray's Inn Road.[65] The house has been much altered, but still possesses stucco pilaster strips, at the top of which brackets carry wide eaves. The north front is symmetrical, with a central segmental bow front and moulded architraves.

Campden Hill Place and
Nos. 1–9 (odd) Holland Park Avenue

Thomas Brace, who paid £1,200 for the property which he purchased from the Lloyds in 1820 (see fig. 11),[66] was a partner in the legal firm of

Brace and Selby of Surrey Street, Strand. Two houses were standing on the land, one, which he took for his own occupation, on the site of No. 3 Campden Hill Place, and the other on the site of No. 1 Holland Park Avenue. The latter appears to have been rebuilt in 1820–1 and called Rose Bank, while another house, No. 3 Holland Park Avenue (originally called Ivy Bank), was erected at the same time.[16]*

Brace died in 1836 or 1837 and by his will instructed that his property in Kensington should be sold whenever his trustees 'shall think fit' and the proceeds divided between his four children.[67] His trustees and executors were his two eldest sons, George and Thomas, who carried on their father's business, and Robert Hodson of Oxford Street, gentleman. They decided to develop the property and by 1843 the house Brace had occupied had been demolished and plans drawn up by Mortimore Timpson, a St. Pancras builder, who was also involved in the development of the Norland estate.[68] Three houses facing the Uxbridge road and a terrace of nine houses on the east side of a private cul-de-sac were envisaged. Timpson built the houses facing the Uxbridge road, now Nos. 5–9 (odd) Holland Park Avenue, under leases granted in December 1843,[69] but, apart from the formation of the private road, the rest of the development was not carried out.

Brace's third son, Edward, who was a captain in the service of the East India Company, eventually acquired Campden Hill Place from his father's trustees[70] and had three detached houses built on the east side instead of the nine originally planned. No. 1 (South Bank Lodge) was begun in 1851 for Frederick Wehnert, an architect who was shortly to enter into a flourishing partnership with John Ashdown.[71] Wehnert was granted an eighty-five-year lease by Edward Brace in 1852, and presumably designed his own house,† which is an asymmetrical Gothic villa consisting of two storeys over a basement. The builders were Messrs. Thomas and Son of Bloomsbury.[73] Nos. 2 and 3 Campden Hill Place (Plate 43b), which are two-storeyed double-fronted villas in an Italianate style, were not built until 1862, when Edward Brace granted leases for seventy-five and three-quarter years (to bring

their terms into line with that for No. 1) to the local builder George Drew; Thomas Brace the younger was Drew's mortgagee.[74]

Campden Hill Gardens, Nos. 101–111 (odd) Campden Hill Road and Nos. 147–155 (odd) Notting Hill Gate

Evan Evans, who bought the second largest share of the Lloyd estate (see fig. 11), was formerly a grocer in New Bond Street but had lived for some years in a house standing on copyhold land at the north-west corner of Plough Lane (now Campden Hill Road). His purchase included a large house with extensive grounds called Wycombe House, which appears to have dated back to at least the mid eighteenth century and may have originally been the farmhouse of Stonehills farm.[75]

Evan Evans died in 1825 and left his property in trust for his great-nephew Robert Evans, whose father was carrying on the family grocery business. When Robert Evans came into his inheritance in 1828 he was also described as a grocer of New Bond Street.[76]

Apart from the sale of the site of St. George's Church to the Ecclesiastical Commissioners in 1863 (see below) Robert Evans did not exploit the potential value of his land as a site for speculative building until 1869. What may have prompted him then, besides the existence of the newly built church, was a decision by the Kensington Vestry to widen Plough Lane. This necessitated the demolition of Evan Evans's former house and opened up the opportunity for building along the frontages of the newly widened road and High Street, Notting Hill. By August 1869 plans had also been drawn up for building on the site of Wycombe House‡ and grounds.[77] In May 1870 Evans secured the enfranchisement of his copyhold from Lady Holland[78] and building proceeded rapidly.

The house plot at the corner of Campden Hill Road (the name was changed as soon as road widening had been completed) and High Street, Notting Hill was sold to Richard Swain, the occupant of

---

* This stretch of Holland Park Avenue and the street now named Campden Hill Place were generally known collectively as 'South Bank' until 1875. The present names and numbers were assigned in 1895.

† During 1857 and 1858, when Wehnert was in Wales looking after the partnership's extensive practice there, Ashdown lived in the house.[72]

‡ By this time known as Wickham House, perhaps to distinguish it from Wycombe Lodge which had been built to the east of Aubrey House (see page 99).

the house which had been demolished.* The present building comprising No. 111 Campden Hill Road and No. 147 Notting Hill Gate (the name was changed from High Street, Notting Hill in 1935) was erected there in 1870. Although the firm of Temple and Foster was involved in its construction,[80] the building is similar to Nos. 149–159 (odd) Notting Hill Gate, which were built under ninety-nine-year leases granted by Evans in September 1870 to John Reeves of Kensington Park Road and George Butt of Ladbroke Road, both builders. Reeves was the lessee of Nos. 149–153 and Butt of Nos. 155–159, but the houses were built by them in partnership.[81] At £25 per annum, the ground rent for each house was somewhat high, no doubt reflecting the fact that shops were provided on the ground floors. These were the only houses built under direct lease from Evans. Nos. 157 and 159 have been demolished as a result of war damage.

In 1871, when building was under way both on the west side of Campden Hill Road and in Campden Hill Gardens, Evans sold the freehold of the rest of his property.[82] Reeves and Butt were consenting parties to all of the transactions involved and had probably initially contracted with Evans to undertake the whole speculation. The short terrace on the west side of Campden Hill Road, Nos. 101–109 (odd), was sold to George Butt together with Nos. 1 and 2 Campden Hill Gardens; all seven houses were already under construction. Butt was also the purchaser of the sites of Nos. 22–26 (even) Campden Hill Gardens.

Nos. 4–18 (even) Campden Hill Gardens were sold jointly to William Childerhouse of Paddington, a builder, and Jonathan Pearson of High Street, Notting Hill, a wholesale ironmonger, who were acting in partnership as builders of these houses.[63] The site of No. 20 was originally purchased by Butt, who later conveyed it to Childerhouse and Pearson.[83] They had originally planned to use the site for the erection of the end house of a terraced range of five and had begun building operations there as early as 1870, but they were forced to stop when the owner of Ness Cottage in Hillsleigh Road brought a successful action against them for loss of light and air. Eventually a low building containing two studios was built c. 1895.[84]

The remaining ground in Campden Hill Gardens, as yet unbuilt on, was sold to Jeremiah Little, the builder who had been responsible for several developments in Kensington. Little, who died in 1873, left the actual building operations to his son Alfred James Little, who, between 1871 and 1874, completed Campden Hill Gardens by the erection of sixteen double-fronted houses, Nos. 28–36 (even) and Nos. 5–25 (odd), mostly under ninety-year leases granted by his father.[85] Nos. 32 and 34 have since been demolished as a result of war damage.

The double-fronted houses in Campden Hill Gardens built by Alfred James Little are of three storeys over basements, symmetrically composed, with three-sided bay windows of ornamental stucco. They have dentilled cornices of stucco over what are essentially brick façades, with urns surmounting the party walls above the entablatures. Apart from these houses Campden Hill Gardens consists of tall terraces of stock brick with much stucco enrichment, including richly moulded cornices and stucco bay windows, all somewhat coarsely proportioned and detailed.

The Church of St. George, Aubrey Walk

Plate 17, figs. 13–14

In 1862 Archdeacon Sinclair, the vicar of St. Mary Abbots, sought the general approval of the Ecclesiastical Commissioners and the Bishop of London for a new ecclesiastical district, to be formed partly out of the district assigned to St. Mary Abbots and partly out of that of St. John's, Notting Hill. In this he had the support of the Reverend J. P. Gell, the incumbent of St. John's. One of the principal considerations Sinclair put forward in support of his contention that a new church was needed was that large-scale building operations were being undertaken by William and Francis Radford at the north end of Holland Park. His first choice for a site was close to this development but the Radfords and Lady Holland could not agree on a location, and early in 1863 he entered into negotiations for the purchase of the land on which the church now stands. This was on the property of Robert Evans, whose great-uncle had purchased it from the Lloyd family (see fig.

---

* Swain received £2,000 in compensation from the Vestry, £1,000 of which was to buy the freehold of his new plot.[79]

11), and was then part of the garden of Wycombe (Wickham) House. A formal conveyance of a piece of ground measuring 130 feet by 90 feet was made to the Ecclesiastical Commissioners on 8 December 1863. £455 was paid to Robert Evans for the freehold and £350 for the existing leasehold interest.[86]

The church was built at the expense of John Bennett of Westbourne Park Villas, evidently to provide a living for his son George, who was the first incumbent. The first stone was laid in February 1864. E. Bassett Keeling was the architect, and the general contractors were George Myers and Sons of Lambeth. The extensive ornamental ironwork was made by Hart and Sons of Wych Street. *The Building News* estimated that the total cost, including the fittings and the architect's fee of £500, was about £9,000.[87]

The new church, which had been designed to seat 1,200, was consecrated on 23 November 1864. The consolidated chapelry which was assigned to it in May 1865 stretched from the newly built villas of the Radfords on the west to the artisans' houses on either side of the northern end of Kensington Church Street on the east. The patronage was originally vested in John Bennett and was transferred to the Bishop of London in 1907.[88]

St. George's is orientated north–south, so that the tower is on the south-east corner of the building. The exterior of the church, like that of St. Mark's, Notting Hill, is strange and wilful, in a style which *The Building News* called 'continental Gothic, freely treated'. In the centre of the gabled 'west' front is a large pointed arch. Within this is a circular opening, containing a deeply recessed quatrefoil window, above two lancet arches, each containing two lancet lights surmounted by a small quatrefoil light. The stonework between the openings is embellished with carved capitals and mouldings. This complex central feature is flanked by side windows, partly concealed by the roof of the large cloistered porch which provides the principal entrance to the church. Five steeply pointed arched openings, with massive dwarf columns and carved capitals, pierce the south wall of the porch, entry to which is gained through pointed arches at its east and west ends. The roof was originally of blue slates and red tiles in bands.

The tower, until recently surmounted by a spire, is the sole survivor of the trio which

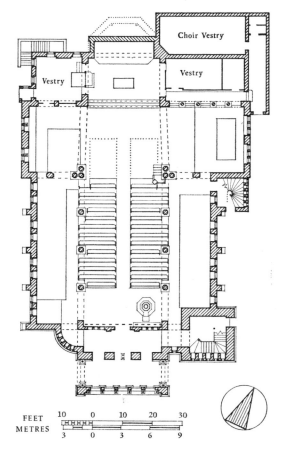

Choir Vestry

Vestry

Vestry

FEET
METRES

Fig. 13. St. George's Church, Aubrey Walk, plan

originally stood on Campden Hill, the other two being the water tower and Tower Cressy, both now demolished. It has no buttresses, and is faced with stone in random courses, Bath stone quoins and dressings, and bands of red sandstone. It is lighted by stepped lancets on the lowest stage which clearly indicate the presence of the gallery stair within the tower—a device much favoured by Bassett Keeling. There are triple lancets with columns and foliated capitals on the second stage, somewhat similar to those of St. Mark's, Notting Hill, and paired lancets on the top stage, again with columns and carved capitals. The original broach spire, which was covered with slate in bands and ornamented with lucarnes, was removed as a result of damage sustained in the war of 1939–45 and replaced by a pyramidal copper cap in 1949 under the direction of Milner and Craze.[89]

The external cloistered porch gives access to three doors that open into the nave. The plan of the church (fig. 13) is cruciform, with nave, aisles, transepts, and originally a doubly recessed apsidal chancel. The chapel on the liturgical south side of the chancel was connected with the transept. The vestry was on the liturgical north side of the chancel with the organ chamber above. The gallery stretched round from the 'south' to the 'north' transept, leaving an open space around the organ and pulpit. There was much contemporary objection to galleries, as they were thought to detract from the architectural effect, so Bassett Keeling gave special consideration to the form of the open framing of the fronts (fig. 14). To the contemporary writer, William Pepperell, who thought the interior of the church was 'exceedingly beautiful and original', the gallery was 'suggestive of a conventional ship's side with the ports complete', not an adverse criticism if we consider the elegance of a nineteenth-century wooden ship. The gallery fronts were regarded as being 'very graceful', and yet 'sufficiently angular to be quite in keeping with the style of the church',[90] but they have been removed except for the portion in the 'west' end of the church. The framing of the ceilings formed by the gallery floors was stained and varnished, dividing the plastering into panels the width of the pews above, so expressing the disposition of seats.

The nave arcading, built with stone springers, keys and corbels, has arches of red and black brick voussoirs, notched at the arrises, carried on cast-iron columns formerly exposed and decorated in strong polychrome. The interior of the church was faced with yellow stocks relieved with blue, red and black bricks, and Bath and red Mansfield stone. The seventeen-foot-high columns rested on brick and stone bases, and the gallery principals were attached to them, about half way up, by wrought-iron bands carried on cast-iron haunches. A group of three columns takes the thrust of the large transept arches, the springing blocks being received in cast-iron dishes forming the now concealed abaci of the capitals. William Pepperell could think of no church where iron was better treated, for the detail was 'sharp and clean', and the columns, somewhat Moorish in appearance, did not seem so slender as to look 'unequal to their task of supporting the brick arches and clerestorey'. He particularly admired the nave roof with its 'saw-tooth cut and intersecting ribs'. His comments show how necessary the gallery was as an aesthetic and structural tie between the columns of the nave.

Contemporary critics noted Bassett Keeling's originality, and some approved of the picturesque effects. *The Building News* pronounced St. George's to be one of the most successful attempts of the 'modern school of Eclectic Gothic, and though perhaps a little free in treatment, evidences an appreciation of . . . continental Gothic which is not too common'.

In 1885 a richly sculptured reredos was erected, occupying three sides of the apse which had been newly decorated. The reredos itself, by Forsyth, was thirteen feet high in the centre, and had three cusped Gothic arches enclosing representations

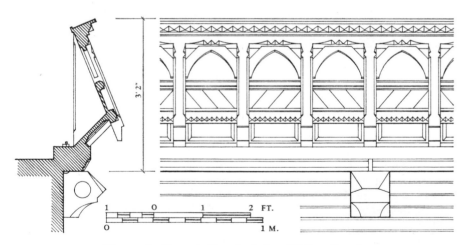

Fig. 14. St. George's Church, Aubrey Walk, gallery front

of the Crucifixion, St. Michael and St. George (Plate 17b).[91]

St. George's, like St. Mark's, Notting Hill, is an expression of that aggressive and somewhat barbarous style which Bassett Keeling evolved. The originality of thought which is very evident in his work is especially apparent in his use of colour, and the bold polychrome must once have been a *tour de force* of interior design.

As a result of a series of alterations beginning in the late nineteenth century, the highly personal character of the church has been lost, although its remains may just be discerned in what is left. The brickwork has been whitened, and the black and blue bricks have been painted over; the cast-iron columns have been cased-in to make them resemble stone piers, and the apse, which had glass by Lavers and Barraud (Plate 17b), has been demolished. The nave arcades, the jagged saw-toothed nave principals, and the west gallery front are the only surviving parts with Bassett Keeling's personal style still discernible.

Grand Junction Water Works Company Site

Thomas Williams and Sir James McGrigor, who in 1820 bought the two adjoining parcels of land indicated on fig. 11,[92] were both living in large houses which had recently been erected on the Phillimore estate immediately to the south (see page 70). In each case the plots which they purchased from the Lloyds were used as extensions to the grounds of those houses. When Williams also acquired Aubrey House in 1827 he separated off its kitchen garden, which lay immediately to the west of the piece of land he had secured from the Lloyds and to the north of part of his leasehold holdings on the Phillimore estate. On the site he built a substantial house called Wycombe Lodge, which was completed by 1829 when the first occupant, the Dowager Marchioness of Lansdowne, took up residence.[16]

In 1843 Sir James McGrigor, who had moved to Harley Street, wanted to sell his property, and the Grand Junction Water Works Company, which was looking for a high-level site for a reservoir, agreed to purchase it for £6,500. Although only the freehold part of McGrigor's land was needed for a reservoir, the company also had to acquire his leasehold house and garden on the Phillimore estate. From 1859 until 1877 this was occupied by Alexander Fraser, who was firstly assistant engineer and later engineer to the company. The reservoir, which was completed by 1845, is no longer in use and its site is now (1972) being built over.[93]

Under the provisions of the Metropolis Water Act of 1852 all reservoirs within five miles of St. Paul's Cathedral had to be covered, and when the company undertook the necessary work at Campden Hill in 1857–8 it also expanded its facilities by building a pumping station and tower (Plate 36a). The contractor for the work was John Aird of Southwark and the designs were provided by Alexander Fraser. Although Joseph Quick, who was consulting engineer to the company, was given the credit for the designs in the journals of the day, his role seems to have been confined to supervising the work of Fraser.[94] The brick-built tower with its spare Italianate ornament was a conspicuous feature of the district for over a century, and even when first built it was well received. *The Companion to the Almanac for 1858* thought that the works of the Grand Junction Water Works Company were especially worthy of notice 'from their having added a conspicuous architectural feature . . . in the shape of a not inelegant tower'. *The Building News* thought that all the buildings 'admirably express the massive solidity of purpose for which they are specially adapted'.[95] The tower was demolished in 1970.

In 1868 the company extended its premises to the west by purchasing the land which Thomas Williams had bought from the Lloyd family and the former kitchen garden of Aubrey House on which Wycombe Lodge then stood. Both plots were owned by Charles Magniac, who had purchased them from Williams's executors in 1866. As in the case of the land which it had secured in 1843, the company had to take an assignment of some leasehold land on the Phillimore estate. This was a plot which had been leased to Williams in 1817 and was used as an extensive garden for Wycombe Lodge. The company paid Magniac £12,000 and also had to pay another £4,500 to buy out the current occupants who held the property under leases granted by Williams. Wycombe Lodge was demolished and additional covered reservoirs were built by John Aird and Sons on the newly acquired freehold land in 1868–9.[96] The covered top of the reservoir is now used as tennis courts and the leasehold property, which the company was unable to use for permanent works, was added to the garden of Moray Lodge and now forms part of the site of Holland Park School.

In 1904 the freehold property of the Grand Junction Water Works Company was acquired by the Metropolitan Water Board when it took over the company's undertakings.

CHAPTER VII

The Holland Estate

THE Holland estate (fig. 15), which consisted of over two hundred acres surrounding Holland House, was purchased in 1768 by Henry Fox, first Baron Holland, from William Edwardes, who was later created Baron Kensington.* Previously the area had formed part of an even larger estate attached to Holland House, consisting of nearly five hundred acres and extending southwards almost to the Fulham Road.

This vast holding had been created by Sir Walter Cope, for whom Holland House had been built, and later came into the possession of the Rich family, the Earls of Warwick and Holland, through the marriage of Sir Henry Rich, first Earl of Holland, to Cope's daughter. When Edward Henry Rich, seventh Earl of Warwick and fourth Earl of Holland, died in 1721, the title to the estate passed to his aunt, Lady Elizabeth Edwardes (née Rich), the sister of the sixth Earl. She had married Francis Edwardes of Pembrokeshire and on her death in 1725 the reversion was inherited by their son, Edward Henry Edwardes.† He died in 1738 and by his will left the estate to his brother William, although encumbered by a lengthy entail.[1]

There is no evidence that any member of the Edwardes family lived at Holland House. In 1746 Henry Fox, then embarked on a successful political career, took up residence at the mansion,[2] and three years later he was granted a lease by William Edwardes of the house and sixty-four acres of land for ninety-nine years or three lives.[3] By the 1760's he had acquired most of that part of the Edwardes estate which lay north of the Hammersmith road (now Kensington High Street) on lease and was anxious to purchase the land outright, no doubt partly out of the profits made from holding the lucrative office of Paymaster General during the Seven Years' War. William Edwardes's estates were subject to heavy mortgages and he was probably not averse to selling in any case, but other factors may have made him accede to Fox's request. Several years later the second Lord Kensington claimed that Fox had secured a commission for a member of the Edwardes family and had thereby placed William Edwardes under an obligation to him.[4]‡ Whatever the circumstances, an agreement was concluded in March 1767 in which Fox, who had recently been created Baron Holland, agreed to pay £17,000 for all of William Edwardes's property north of the Hammersmith road. The conveyance, which was confirmed by Act of Parliament in order to set aside the entail imposed by the will of Edward Henry Edwardes, was completed in 1768.[6]

Lord Holland's accounts for 1767 and 1768 indicate that he paid a further £2,500 as well as the stipulated £17,000.[7] The extra amount was almost certainly a payment to Rowland Edwardes and John Owen Edwardes, who were successors-in-title to the estate under the will of Edward Henry Edwardes, in order to secure their consent to the sale.[4] Besides the land immediately attached to Holland House, the sale included the lordship of the manor of Abbots Kensington and some land on the south side of the highway to Acton and Uxbridge (now Holland Park Avenue) which was held on lease by Sir Edward Lloyd (see page 87). The whole property had yielded a yearly revenue of £470 19s. 11d. to William Edwardes.

---

* Holland House itself is not described in this volume and may form the subject of a separate monograph at a later date. An architectural survey is contained in *Royal Commission on Historical Monuments (England)*. *London Volume II, West London*, 1925, pages 74–7, and accounts of the history of the house and its famous inhabitants in the two volumes by the sixth Earl of Ilchester, *The Home of the Hollands 1605–1820*, 1937, and *Chronicles of Holland House 1820–1900*, 1937.

† The use of the estate was, however, enjoyed by Charlotte, Dowager Countess of Warwick and Holland, the widow of the sixth Earl, as the result of a jointure, until her death in 1731.

‡ As early as 1753 it appears that Fox had tried to procure a favour for Edwardes in order to ingratiate himself with his landlord, 'of whom', he wrote to Henry Pelham, 'I want a bit of a waste, a lease, and 2 or 3 other small favours'.[5]

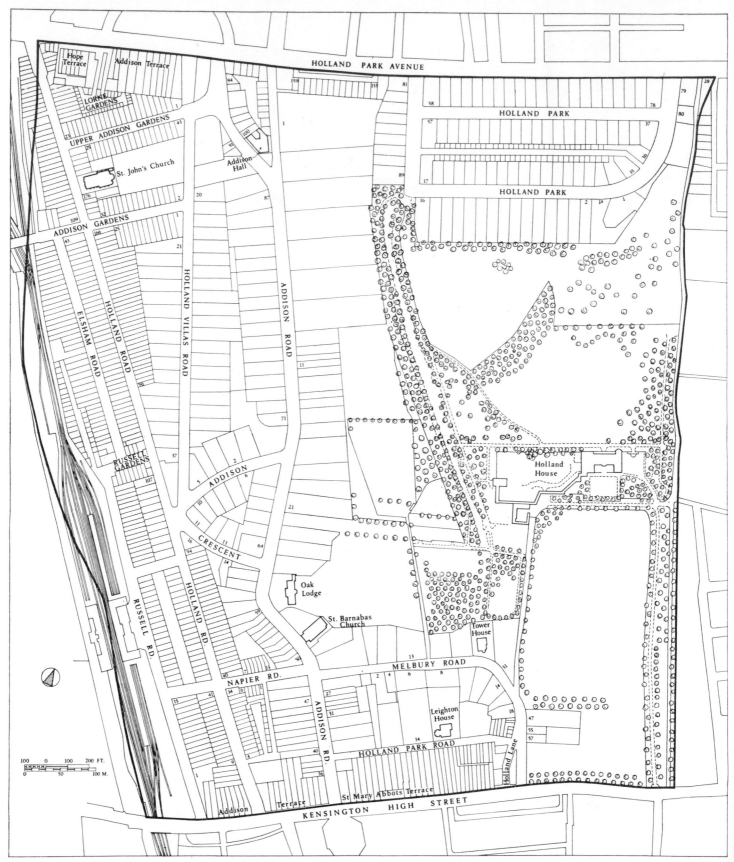

Fig. 15. The Holland estate. The thick line denotes the extent of the estate in Kensington purchased by Lord Holland in 1768. Based on the Ordnance Survey of 1894–6

A survey undertaken in 1770[8] shows that the extent of the Holland estate was 237 acres, including one nine-acre field on the Hammersmith side of the parish boundary. Apart from Holland House itself there were few buildings of note. Little Holland House, an irregular house of some size, approximately on the site of the present No. 14 Melbury Road, was in the hands of a tenant who had taken it on a long repairing lease from William Edwardes in 1758,[9] but the freehold reversion was included in Lord Holland's purchase. Another house, which is referred to in the survey as 'Mr. Machines Mote house', stood near a group of ponds known as The Moats. According to Faulkner this was the ancient manor house of West Town. He claims that it was largely demolished in 1801 although part of it was left standing and converted into a gardener's cottage.* During a large part of the seventeenth century the house had been the home of Thomas Henshaw, the scientific writer and diplomatist.[11] A tavern on the Hammersmith road, which was known successively as the Horse and Groom, the White Horse, and, later, the Holland Arms, and a farmhouse called Weston Farm near Little Holland House were the only other buildings of any significance on the estate.

From 1823 to 1849

The first speculative building on the estate took place during the lifetime of the third Lord Holland. He also held land in Lambeth on lease from the Archbishop of Canterbury and began building there in 1820.† Although anxious to develop part of his Kensington property in a similar manner, he had to await the outcome of a protracted law suit with Lord Kensington. William Edwardes, second Baron Kensington, was the son of the William Edwardes who had sold the estate to the first Lord Holland. He was born in 1777, after the sale had taken place, and, *inter alia*, he disputed whether the entail, under which he would have inherited the land, had been effectually set aside. The matter was finally settled out of court in 1823, when Lord Holland agreed to pay £4,000 for confirmation of his title to the estate.[12] He was now free to deal with the land as he

wished and considered that the price he had paid was 'with a view to immediate improvement by building, in concert with my neighbour L[or]d K[ensington], not more than it is worth'.[13]

An account of the income and expenditure of all the family estates in 1822 shows that the yearly household expenses exceeded the revenue received from rents,[14] and there are indications that Lord Holland thought that letting land for building would bring about a short-term improvement in his income. He referred to the marking out of Addison Road as 'the important profitable but melancholy occupation',[15] and in 1824 he alluded to the 'tremendous and I hope ... profitable works'[16] taking place on his estate. In 1827, when difficulties had beset the building operations, Lady Holland referred to 'our improvident reliance on them as sources of income'.[17] She had always been more pessimistic about their immediate expectations. When Addison Road was being built, but before any houses had been begun, she wrote in a letter to her son, Henry Edward, the future fourth Lord Holland, that 'remote posterity may benefit because for some generations it must be tightly mortgaged', but that she suspected 'none now alive will be much bettered by the undertaking'.[18] Lord Holland and his successors relied heavily on mortgages and the building operations probably facilitated the raising of money by this means. The estate continued to be mortgaged until well into the twentieth century.

The individuals who figured most prominently in the initial stages of development were Benjamin Currey, Henry Harrison and William Woods. Currey, who was the father of Henry Currey, the architect, was the family solicitor, but he acted in effect as the steward of the estate. He handled virtually the whole of its financial affairs including the collection of rents. No doubt as a solicitor he had access to further supplies of capital for builders and developers, and by 1844 he was himself the lessee of several plots although none of these appear to have been leased to him initially.[19]

Henry Harrison was the estate surveyor when building began. The son of a builder and surveyor, he was an architect whose London buildings included Bath House, Piccadilly, and the Guards' Club in Pall Mall, both now demolished, the

---

* One of the manuscript plans prepared by Joseph Smith for the Metropolitan Commission of Sewers in 1851 shows a 'Gardeners House' on this site. It would have been demolished for the building of Oakwood Court, if not before.[10]

† *Survey of London*, volume XXVI, 1956, pages 108–22, contains a history of the Lambeth estate.

Lying-In Hospital in York Road, Lambeth, and Richmond Terrace, Whitehall.[20]* In 1856, when he was about seventy years old, he applied unsuccessfully for the post of Superintending Architect of the Metropolitan Board of Works.[21] Besides practising as an architect, he also engaged in speculative building (including on the Holland estate). In this he did not meet with a uniform degree of success for he was declared bankrupt in 1840,[22] although his bankruptcy does not seem to have greatly affected his architectural practice. From the start his activities on the Holland estate appear to have been less than energetic. He was slow in completing plans for building and at one point Currey remarked sarcastically, 'Harrison has been with me all morning, and is now quite alive'.[23] There is no evidence that he designed individual houses, except perhaps in St. Mary Abbots Terrace, where he was more directly involved (see below).

William Woods was a builder who had taken leases from Lord Holland in Lambeth[24] and had evidently impressed sufficiently to be given virtually the position of clerk of works at Kensington. He built the main sewers along the Hammersmith road and Addison Road which were a necessary preliminary to development and probably supervised the making of Addison Road as well.[25] Several of the first houses to go up on the estate were built by him, many under direct lease from Lord Holland, and even where other builders were the principal parties his name often figures in transactions. Most of the early applications to lay drains from individual houses into the main sewers were made by him, and in one (from another builder) he was referred to as 'Agent for Lord Holland'.[26]

The terms of the settlement of the suit with Lord Kensington were agreed in April 1823 and by May Lord Holland was supervising the marking out of the site of Addison Road, named after Joseph Addison, who had married the widowed Countess of Warwick and Holland in 1716. Little was done during 1823, however, partly owing to Harrison's dilatoriness, but also, according to Lady Holland, through 'the want of means'.[27] By Feburary 1824 she was writing that 'the enterprize is begun ... already 50 or 60 men are employed in making the road which is to join the Uxbridge and Hammersmith great roads'.[18] The course chosen for Addison Road, with a curve where the church of St. Barnabas now stands, was not a concession to the picturesque, but was almost certainly dictated by the presence there of the extensive ponds known as The Moats. The layout plan submitted by Harrison to the Westminster Commission of Sewers, which is dated May 1824,[28] shows a series of roads avoiding the ponds completely, but no doubt in the course of construction it was considered preferable to fill in part of the ponds at this point and make one continuous road with a gentle curve. Permission to construct two main sewers along Addison Road and the Hammersmith road was granted in May[29] and work proceeded on these throughout the year. Lord Holland took a considerable personal interest in the progress of what he called his 'Cloaca Maxima'[30] and Lady Holland commented typically that, 'The Sewer certainly breaks my rest. It swallows up thousands.'[31] An indication of the method of financing these operations is contained in a note in Lord Holland's handwriting on a statement of income and expenditure for his estates in 1826, in which he wrote, 'Woods procured or advanced money for road and sewer—and I have indemnified him therefrom by abating part of his rent and by mortgaging to him or to those who advanced money with him after the same purpose, part of the rent payable to me from others'.[32]

The first leases, dated 1 March 1824, were of sites on the east side of Addison Road and were granted to John Adolphus Snee of Holborn, a coal merchant, and Nicholas Phillips Rothery of Exeter.[33]† As the construction of the road had only just begun, it is likely that Rothery and Snee were providing financial backing for the development. The format of these leases was adopted with only minor variations for all the leases granted during the first stage of the estate's development. They were for eighty years from 24 June 1824, a standard term for all leases granted in the 1820's, and stipulated that no house inferior to the third rate was to be erected, 'or any messuage the external walls of which shall not be at the least two bricks in thickness from the foundations to the surface of the parlour floor and one brick and a half in thickness from thence to the roof'. Later

---

* In Richmond Terrace he adapted a design by Thomas Chawner for the façade and supplied the working drawings, a fact which was not known when the terrace was described in *Survey of London*, volume XIII, 1930, pages 249–56.

† Both Snee and Rothery also took leases in Lambeth.[34]

leases also required houses to be built 'to a plan previously submitted to and approved by ... Lord Holland his heirs or assigns'.

Snee's lease (marked 'No. 1' on the counterpart) was of five adjacent sites, clearly designed for a terrace of five houses, about four hundred feet north of the junction with the Hammersmith road. He sub-let his five plots in May 1824 to William Woods,[35] who proceeded to build a conventional late-Georgian terrace of four-storey houses in stock brick with stuccoed ground storeys. These houses, originally called St. Barnabas Terrace and later Nos. 27–31 (consec.) Addison Road, were among the first to be completed on the estate.[36] They were demolished in 1961.

Rothery's lease was for ten pieces of ground on the east side of Addison Road at its northern end near the junction with the Uxbridge road. These plots, each with a seventy-foot frontage and two hundred feet in depth, were not adjacent but were separated by other plots, also seventy feet in width. This unusual arrangement was perhaps designed to ensure that detached villas of a substantial size would be built. Rothery, who was to pay an annual ground rent of £5 for each plot, also sub-let his plots to Woods in May 1824 at a rent of £45 per annum each.[37] In 1825 Lord Holland leased the intervening pieces of ground, together with some land at the rear of the first seven plots for gardens of greater depth, directly to Woods.[38] The plan on this lease shows the outline of detached houses on the first seven plots and the lease states that these enlarged pieces of ground were already enclosed by brick walls. In the event seven detached houses, Nos. 1–7 (consec.) Addison Road, were built, but the last was not completed until 1838.[36] Although Woods was probably the builder of all seven, the application to lay drains from the last two (Nos. 6 and 7) was made by Edward Bishop of St. Pancras, who was designated 'Clerk of the Works'.[39]

In 1826 Woods assigned his leases and subleases to Randall Gossip of Thorp Arch Hall, Yorkshire,* but by 1844 the leases of Nos. 2–7 Addison Road (the freehold of No. 1 had been sold) were vested in Benjamin Currey.[41]

These seven brick-faced villas, although large, were not outstanding architecturally. No. 1, by far the largest, was taken by Charles Richard Fox, who was the eldest son of Lord and Lady Holland, but as he had been born out of wedlock he could not succeed to the title. He had married Lady Mary Fitzclarence, daughter of the Duke of Clarence (later William IV) and Mrs. Jordan, and pursued a successful military career, rising to the rank of general. He was also a Member of Parliament and at the time of his death was Receiver-General of the Duchy of Lancaster.[42] Fox was probably persuaded to take the house in the hope that other persons of social importance would be attracted to the neighbouring villas and make the speculation a success.[43] The house was ready by April 1827, and it was at first intended to call it 'Spectator House' to maintain the association with Joseph Addison, but it was generally called, most confusingly, 'Little Holland House'.[44] Fox secured the freehold from his father, and large parcels of land to the north, east and west of the house were also granted to him by Lord Holland at various dates up to 1842.[45] In that year the north end of Addison Road was diverted slightly westward at Fox's insistence in order to protect his now extensive grounds from the nuisance of a brickfield which had recently been established on nearby land to the west.[46]† After Fox's death in 1873, the grounds were laid out for building and the house largely demolished, but a small part has survived as the club-house of the Holland Park Tennis Club. The original course of Addison Road was again made into a road and named Holland Park Gardens. Nos. 2–7 Addison Road were demolished in 1966–70 to make way for the Woodsford Square development.

The remaining three plots in Rothery's original lease, together with the intervening pieces of land leased to Woods, were broken up in a series of complex transactions involving Woods, Gossip and several other individuals, some of them mortgagees.[48] Eventually ten houses, Nos. 8–17 (consec.) Addison Road, were built, mostly in the form of semi-detached pairs. They were completed by 1839, except for No. 10, which was not

---

* Randall Gossip was also involved in the development of Lord Holland's Lambeth estate. He was probably related to Wilmer Gossip, who acted as steward of the manor of Abbots Kensington on one occasion and appears to have been associated with Currey in his legal business.[40]

† The brickfield had to be moved on account of the building of the West London Railway (see page 108), and as the estate received a royalty from the brickmaking business, which was owned by Benjamin Clutterbuck, Currey was reluctant to see it brought to an end.[47]

occupied until 1850.[36] Besides William Woods, other builders involved in the construction of these houses were Edward Aslat of Hammersmith and William Wade of Islington.[49] Nos. 8, 9 and 10 were demolished in 1905 to make way for the present No. 8 (see page 135).

No. 11 was originally a double-fronted house, faced with stucco, of two storeys with a basement and attic, but a bay window and other alterations have changed its appearance considerably. Nos. 12 and 13 are large semi-detached houses of three storeys over basements, again faced with stucco, the façades enlivened by elegant porches and canopied balconies at ground-floor level. Nos. 14 and 15 were originally a symmetrically composed pair of semi-detached dwellings of two storeys over basements, but additions have destroyed the balanced design. They have a continuous stucco entablature enriched with rosettes, overhanging eaves carried on brackets, and graceful canopies with trellis work. Nos. 16 and 17 are of basically similar design to Nos. 12 and 13, although without the porches and canopies.

Only six more houses were built in Addison Road during the early years of estate development. Four were erected on the east side to the south of St. Barnabas Terrace. Originally given names like 'Cato Cottage' and 'Homer Villa', they gave rise to the forecast by William Cobbett, who disliked the new building developments taking place in Kensington, that Lord Holland would pay dearly for his taste in the classics.[50] These four houses, later Nos. 32–35 (consec.) Addison Road, were demolished in the 1950's. On the west side of the road, Richard Stanham, a carpenter, took a lease of a piece of ground in 1829 and built two houses, later Nos. 62–63 Addison Road.[51] For several years these were the only buildings on that side of the road. No. 62 was rebuilt in 1852–3.[36]

Apart from Addison Road with its mixture of large and small villas, St. Barnabas' Church (see page 130) and one short terrace, the first stage of estate development consisted primarily of terraces along the turnpike roads. On the south side of the Uxbridge road two terraces were built between Addison Road and the boundary of the parish. The westernmost, called Hope Terrace, consisted originally of seven houses and was built

under the usual eighty-year lease granted in July 1825 to William Woods.[52] It appears to have been largely completed by 1829, but was not fully occupied until 1834, when the second house from the east was taken as a charity school.[36] The easternmost house was a public house named the Duke of Clarence, no doubt after Charles Richard Fox's father-in-law. The other terrace on the Uxbridge road, Addison Terrace, which consisted of eleven houses, was not completed until about 1843. At least three builders were involved, William Woods, Richard Preston of Earl's Court Lane, a bricklayer, and Edmund Gurney of Kentish Town, a carpenter.[53] Both terraces have been demolished, although the rebuilt Duke of Clarence stands on the same site as the original public house of that name.

When Henry Harrison submitted his building plans for the estate, he agreed to take the frontage along the Hammersmith road from Lee's Nursery* in the west to Holland Lane in the east as a speculation.[55] Apart from two houses at the western end of this frontage, which were built on a piece of ground leased by Lord Holland in 1825 to William Goddard of St. James's, a wheelwright[56] (the site is now occupied by the Royal Kensington Hotel), the development for which Harrison was nominally responsible was confined to that part of the Hammersmith road between Addison Road and Holland Lane.

The White Horse, at the corner of Holland Lane, was rebuilt in 1824[57] and named the Holland Arms, and next to it a commonplace terrace of nine houses called Holland Place was erected under leases granted either to Thomas Moore of Long Acre, plumber, or to Thomas Lindsey Holland of St. Marylebone, esquire, who provided much of the necessary capital.[58]

St. Mary Abbots Terrace, which occupied the rest of the frontage westward to Addison Road, was an altogether more ambitious undertaking, and was originally intended to be a symmetrical composition of eight linked pairs of houses. The first leases, for the two westernmost houses, were granted to William Woods in July 1825. The remainder were granted in August 1825 to various persons connected with the building trades and to Henry Harrison, who took leases of three

---

* The Vineyard Nursery, which belonged to the Lee family, was principally situated in Hammersmith, but it included about thirteen acres held on lease from Lord Holland in the south-west corner of his estate. This area was reduced when most of the frontage to the Hammersmith road was given up to Harrison. Further inroads were made subsequently, also for building purposes, and in 1856 the last part of the nursery on the estate was turned into a brickfield.[54]

houses.* The house-sites were not of uniform width and varied from approximately thirty feet for the central two, to about twenty-six feet. The annual rents were calculated precisely at the rate of ten shillings per foot frontage, irrespective of depth. Peppercorn terms were not granted, but although the leases were of the standard term of eighty years from 24 June 1824, the first quarterly payment of rent was not to become due until September 1826. In the leases of those strips which backed on to St. Mary Abbots Mews (now Holland Park Road) the lessees were allowed to erect buildings of not more than twenty feet in height facing that 'back road'.[59]

The terrace consisted of pairs of four-storey houses, brick-built with stuccoed ground storeys and stucco dressings, linked by one- or two-storey connecting wings, except in the centre where the link was carried to full four-storey height. Here a pediment was inscribed 'St. Mary Abbots Terrace', and at ground-floor level there was an Ionic portico in antis similar to that of Harrison's Lying-In Hospital, Lambeth. It is reasonable to assume that Henry Harrison was responsible for the overall design, but it may be significant that William Woods was granted leases before any other builder and that his houses were the first to be finished, by 1826.[36] Woods also made the application to lay drains into the main sewer from all sixteen houses[60] and he may have been acting as clerk of works for Harrison. The surviving graphic evidence,[61] however, shows variations between individual houses, even in such crucial matters as overall height and the size of the window openings, and indicates that close supervision was not maintained over the several years during which the terrace was built. Almost from the start the balance of the composition was upset, for leases of two more houses at the east end were granted in September 1825 to Anthony Unthank of St. Marylebone, gentleman.[62] Finally two more houses were squeezed in between Unthank's and the last house in Holland Place under a lease granted to Thomas Moore in 1837.[63] Apart from these last two houses, the terrace appears to have been finished by about 1830 and each house occupied by 1832.[36]

Holland Place and St. Mary Abbots Terrace, then numbered as 284–342 (even) Kensington High Street, were demolished in about 1960 to make way for the new St. Mary Abbots Terrace and Kenbrook House development.

The layout plan which Harrison submitted to the Commissioners of Sewers in 1824 shows a series of squares and roads to the west of Addison Road,[29] and a contemporary account refers to proposals for building eight hundred houses.[64] What development did take place—along Addison Road and the turnpike roads—was slow in execution. The main problem was that Lord Holland had chosen a very unfortunate time to begin his adventures in building and caught the full force of the economic recession of 1825, which affected the building trades particularly severely.[65] The letters of both Lord and Lady Holland to their son, Henry, the future fourth Lord Holland, were full of tales of financial woe. In December 1825 Lady Holland wrote, 'I wish I were able to say anything agreeable as to finances, but ours are very bad indeed, the failures in England affect the building speculations in that we are at present living upon *borrowed* money'.[66] This last reference was to a loan of £6,000 which Lord Holland had arranged from Coutts' Bank and which was made available to Currey,[67] presumably to support the now sagging speculations. Early in 1826 she wrote, 'the buildings . . . are stopped in consequence of all the failures and panicks, people have no money to spend on villas and keep closely what they have in the bank—It has been unlucky that we have cut up the land for building, as it might otherwise have been productive as pasture grounds'.[68] She continually referred to the possibility that they might have to sell land outright, and justified these thoughts to her son, who would eventually inherit the estate, by the sentiment that, 'in these times one must live from day to day and not like our ancestors think of an unknown posterity'.[69] In December 1826 she remarked, somewhat prematurely, 'the building speculation has failed',[70] and as late as 1833 she still considered that it might be necessary for them to sell land.[71] Lord Holland was somewhat less gloomy, for in October 1826 he was writing that

* A consortium of builders may have been involved, for the lessees, apart from Woods and Harrison, were: John Asquith of St. Martin's in the Fields, *plumber*; Timothy, Francis and Edward Bramah of Pimlico, *engineers*; Richard Cobbett of St. Martin's in the Fields, *glazier*; James Haward and William Thomas Nixon of St. Martin's Lane, *builders*; Philip Palmer of St. Martin's Lane, *glass manufacturer*; George Russell of St. George's, Hanover Square, *surveyor*; John Young of St. George's, Hanover Square, *plumber*.

'In my building speculations I am as well as any of my neighbours and better than most—but that is all that can be said'.[72] Several of his letters, however, refer to the shortage of credit and in the middle of 1827 he did allow himself a *cri de coeur*—'we are all dreadfully poor this year'.[73]

By the mid 1830's very little building was taking place and a lull followed for several years. It was at this time that plans were announced for building a railway to link the Kensington Canal with the London and Birmingham Railway. The course originally proposed for the new line would have carried it across the Holland estate slightly to the west of Addison Road,[74] and Lord Holland's attitude was hostile. He considered that the railway was merely a speculation to revive the moribund fortunes of the canal and remarked, prophetically, that it was likely to prove as signal a failure. 'It will destroy the comfort of all who have recently built on [the Holland] estate and will discourage all further buildings which would otherwise in the natural course of things proceed. The railway is to be raised on arches 23 feet high. It will interrupt the view of the new houses and villas in or near to Addison Road and it is to be apprehended that the noise and smoke and other annoyances will drive the tenants of these houses from their habitations and deter all other persons from building others. There appears to be no real publick object in occasioning all this mischief', he wrote.[75] In the event a compromise was reached whereby the line was to be carried in a cutting at the western edge of the estate near to or along the course of Counter's Creek, which formed the estate boundary. Lord Holland agreed to sell four and a quarter acres of land for the railway at a price of £5,000, while the railway company had to agree to purchase any land that lay between the line and the western boundary of the estate at a rate of £750 per acre.[76] Evidently all parties were reasonably reconciled, for when the enabling Act was passed in June 1836, the proprietors of the railway included Charles Richard Fox and Caroline Fox.[77]*

The railway company did not, however, enjoy Lord Holland's blessings for long. In 1839 he referred in a letter to his eldest son to 'your accursed Railway'[78] and early in 1840 he began an action in Chancery to secure payment of the outstanding part of the purchase money which was still owing to him.[76] At this time, however, the company had no money and had in fact suspended building operations on the line. A further Act had to be passed enabling the company to raise more capital, and the opportunity was taken to change the name from the original Birmingham, Bristol and Thames Junction Railway to the more manageable West London Railway. Eventually the purchase money was paid in full and the land was formally conveyed to the company in July 1844, when, in fact, the railway was already open to the public. A further portion of land along the Hammersmith road was also acquired for a small station. The railway proved initially to be a dismal failure, and the lack of passengers made it the butt of such savage satire from *Punch* that it was known as 'Mr. Punch's railway'. In November 1844, within six months of opening, it suspended passenger operations.[79]

In one respect the estate derived considerable advantage from the railway. Counter's Creek was one of the principal watercourses for the drainage of west London, and the line chosen for the railway involved the diversion of the stream. As a result of pressure from Lord Holland, a new covered sewer was built across his estate in place of the old open ditch. The railway company had to pay most of the cost, but the Westminster Commissioners of Sewers granted £1,500. Currey, on behalf of Lord Holland, agreed to reserve the land over the sewer for roads and to pay five shillings a foot frontage to the Commissioners for the right to use it whenever building should take place. The contract for building the sewer, which also passed through parts of Lord Kensington's estate in the south and the Norland estate in the north, was given to Stephen Bird and the work was finished by the end of 1839 at a cost of £9,547.[80] The Holland estate, of course, benefited immensely from the building of a major covered sewer through the middle of land on which building was planned, as the railway's directors reminded Lord Holland when they were trying to secure more time for the payment of the purchase money due to him.[81] The course taken by the sewer through the estate was, from south to north, along the line of the present Holland Road to Holland Villas Road and then along the line of that road; the last few yards of ground over the sewer, between the end of Holland Villas Road

---

* Presumably the Caroline Fox who was Lord Holland's sister and who lived at Little Holland House.

and Holland Park Avenue, were never, in fact, appropriated for a roadway.

Lord Holland died in 1840. By his will[82] he left Holland House and the Kensington estate to the use of his wife for her lifetime, to revert to his son, Henry Edward, the fourth Lord Holland, on her death. The Dowager Lady Holland gave a succession of elaborate dinner parties (usually at her town house in Mayfair) to maintain her position at the social centre of Whig London, and the fourth Lord Holland, who was British Minister Plenipotentiary in Florence at the time of his father's death, became increasingly concerned over his mother's activities.[83] He was afraid that she cared little for Holland House and its amenities and was anxious to let the grounds on building leases to help pay off debts and maintain her high level of expenditure. There is little doubt from his letters that such plans had been formulated,* but he made it quite clear to Currey that he would not consider any proposals that would lead to the destruction of Holland House or its grounds, 'The preservation of that House being ... my most anxious wish in life'.[85] Although a great deal of land west of Addison Road was still unbuilt upon, the Dowager Lady Holland's advisers no doubt considered that land closer to the mansion would bring in a quicker and surer return, and at one point Lord Holland, when writing of various plans, referred to 'the awful one you have so often spoken of respecting the frontage to the Hammersmith road'.[86] By 1845, however, even he thought that 'dear old H. H. must be sacrificed or at least sadly beset by buildings' but consoled himself with the reflection that it might become 'a fine town house'.[87]

Lady Holland died in 1845 and the fourth Lord Holland succeeded to the estate.

The building that took place during the 1840's was chiefly a continuation of earlier schemes. In 1843 a lease of part of the remaining frontage along the Hammersmith road which had been taken under agreement by Harrison was granted to Charles Bowland Cotton of Kent, who was one of Harrison's creditors, for sixty-two years from Midsummer 1842 (a period equivalent to the eighty-year term of previous leases). The lease was of a terrace of eleven houses, five of which were already built or were in process of construction, between Addison Road and Holland Road, and of two pieces of land at the rear of this terrace. Cotton immediately sub-let the property to a builder, James Mugford Macey of Drury Lane, who had apparently entered into a building agreement with Harrison as long ago as 1830. This part of Addison Terrace, as it was called, was completed by 1846.[88]

The continuation of Addison Terrace to the west of Holland Road was also built by Macey under a direct lease from Lord Holland for eighty years from 29 September 1844,† and was completed by 1847.[89] Of the original houses in Addison Terrace only one, at the Addison Road end, survives as No. 344 Kensington High Street. Four houses on the west side of Holland Road (of which only two, Nos. 5 and 7, remain) were also built under this lease and were finished by 1850.[36]

The only other building activity during these years was in Addison Road. On the west side Nos. 36–39 (consec.) were built by Macey on land at the rear of Addison Terrace which had been included in his sub-lease from Cotton in 1843. Originally called Vassall Cottages, these houses were completed by 1845 (fig. 16).[36] They are linked pairs of stock-brick houses, consisting of two storeys over basements, with pediments over each pair enriched with stucco cornices. To the north of these a terrace of eight 'Gothic' houses, originally called Warwick Villas and now Nos. 40–47 (consec.) Addison Road (fig. 16), was erected under two building leases granted to

---

* A letter in 1841 refers to plans by 'Mr. Hardwick'. The minutes of the Birmingham, Bristol and Thames Junction Railway Company also indicate that 'P. Hardwick' was consulted over matters relating to the estate in 1839 and 1840. Presumably this was Philip Hardwick, who was surveyor to the Portman estate. If he was also acting for the Holland estate during these years, it was probably in an advisory capacity only and there is no evidence that any buildings were erected under his supervision.

Another famous architect whose name was momentarily connected with the estate was Decimus Burton. A report in 1838 by the surveyor to the Westminster Commissioners of Sewers referred to the necessity for consultation with Decimus Burton, 'his Lordship's architect'. Burton may have been undertaking repairs or alterations to Holland House at the time.

The same report refers to Henry Harrison, but only because he held land fronting the Hammersmith road through which the sewer would have to pass, and it is clear that he was no longer acting as estate surveyor by this time. It is possible that a full-time surveyor was not considered necessary during these years of little building activity.[84]

† This was the first lease which was granted for a term other than eighty years from 24 June 1824 or its equivalent.

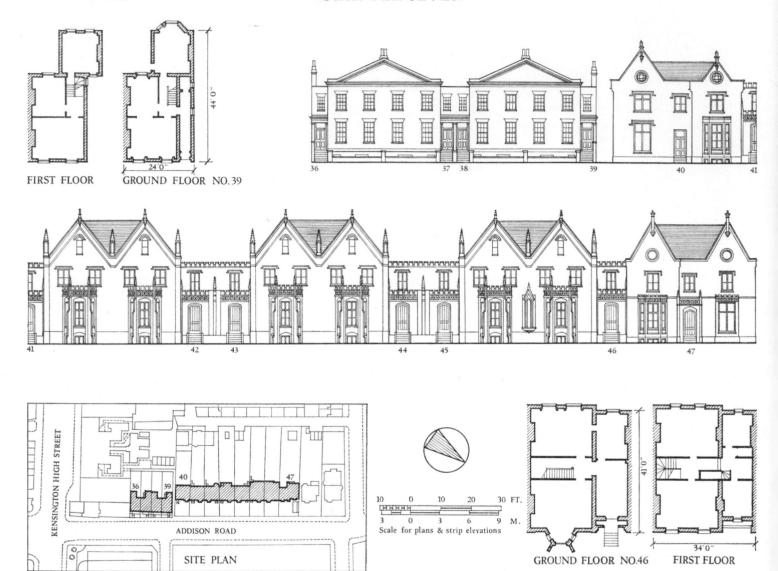

FIRST FLOOR   GROUND FLOOR NO. 39

Fig. 16. Nos. 36–47 consec. Addison Road, plans and elevations

Thomas Moore, the builder of Holland Place. The first lease, granted in 1849 when building was already well under way, was of seven houses and was for eighty years from 1841. These were completed by 1850, and in that year the lease of another house (No. 47) was granted. Moore raised the capital needed to build these houses by selling several which he had built earlier on the estate.[90]

The architect of Nos. 40–47 is not known, although the designs could have originated from one of the architectural publications of the period.* The style did not, however, meet with universal approbation, for it must have been to this terrace that *The Building News* was referring in 1857 when it drew attention to houses on the west side of Addison Road near to 'the ugly pseudo-Gothic church of St. Barnabas'. The houses, it remarked,

* A William Blofield, surveyor, of Clifton Terrace, West Brompton, submitted an application on behalf of Moore to lay drains from No. 47.[91]

'are in the debased Gothic style of the most wretched description, and such has been the badness of the quality of the cement employed in them, that several of the terminations of their gables have already dropped from their giddy eminences'.[92]

The terrace consists of three linked pairs of identical houses in the centre (Nos. 41–46) flanked by two double-fronted houses of somewhat different design (Nos. 40 and 47). Among the attractive features of Nos. 41–46 are the bay windows with angle buttresses and quatrefoil panels crowned by battlements; the similar panels and battlements in the linking wings; and the high gables pierced by lancets and surmounted by octagonal finials, many of which have indeed 'dropped' from their places. Nos. 45 and 46 have a strange niche of the Batty Langley school of Gothic set between them. The porch of No. 47, the double-fronted house at the north end of the terrace, has a festive Regency Gothic flavour.

By 1848 one more house, No. 18, had been built on the east side of Addison Road. This house (now demolished) was leased to John Henry Browne for ninety-nine years at a rent of one shilling per annum.[93] Browne was an architect who had been articled to Rhodes and Chawner and was elected an associate of the (Royal) Institute of British Architects in 1839. He had worked for some time in Pennethorne's office, and in 1847 he was engaged to make extensive alterations to Holland House.[94] This work led to his appointment as estate surveyor, and his house in Addison Road, the first of several on the estate in which he lived, was no doubt intended to serve as both his residence and as the estate office. He may have been responsible for the design of this house, but in general his activity as estate surveyor was confined to drawing up layout plans and approving the house designs submitted by builders or architects; there is no evidence that, except in one or two isolated cases, he was responsible for such designs himself. In 1860 he was granted an annuity of £300 'in consideration of the long and faithful services . . . rendered by the said John Henry Browne as the Steward of the Kensington Estate . . . and of the pecuniary and other advantages derived . . . from such Stewardship and from the skill and ability with which the said John Henry Browne has planned and laid out for Building purposes part of the said Estate and has superintended the erection of Buildings thereon'.[95] For over twenty-five years,

until the estate changed hands in 1874, Browne was its most important officer and wielded much the same influence as Benjamin Currey had exerted under the third Lord Holland.

The returns for the census of 1851 provide useful information about the social structure of the estate after a quarter of a century of development. Most residents were middle class, employing on average two servants per household, but a colony of small tradesmen, artisans and estate workers lived in Holland Lane and at the east end of St. Mary Abbots Mews. Many of the houses here, which were among the smallest on the estate (Plate 51a), were occupied by more than one family, and multi-occupancy also occurred in several houses in Holland Place and Hope Terrace. The vast majority of houses in the middle-class parts of the estate, however, were occupied by single families. Of 155 households of all classes from which returns were received, forty-three householders described their occupations in terms like 'annuitant', 'fundholder' or 'proprietor of houses', often in combination; of these forty-three, fourteen were widows. The other occupations listed were diverse, the most common being merchants of various kinds, of which there were eight instances, and the professions of solicitor or barrister, of which there were seven. Two houses on the Hammersmith road frontage appear to have been used as lodging-houses and there were five schools of various sizes on the estate; the largest boarding-school was at No. 2 Addison Road, where twenty-five pupils between the ages of eleven and eighteen and two governesses were in residence. Of the artisans living in the area, several were employed in the building trades. Shopping facilities were somewhat limited; a grocer and a baker could be found in Holland Place and another baker and a butcher in Hope Terrace, while dairy produce could probably be obtained directly from Holland Farm. A shoemaker, a jeweller, and a carver and gilder with one apprentice provided more specialized services. Over half the heads of families on the estate were born outside London, eight having come from Scotland.

From 1849 to 1874

The second stage of the development of the Holland estate began in 1849 when George Henry Goddard of John Street, Adelphi, who described himself as an architect and surveyor, entered into a building agreement covering all of the area, consisting of about seventy acres of land, between Addison Road and the railway which had not yet been laid out for building. He undertook to build 863 houses and promised to spend various sums on each house, from £800 for those facing Addison Road to £350 at the western edge of the estate. The layout plan accompanying the agreement shows basically the road pattern which was eventually carried out, but more squares and gardens were planned than eventually appeared, including some communal gardens with access from the private gardens of houses, similar to those in slightly earlier layout plans for the Ladbroke estate. The plan also shows that most houses were intended to be terraced or semi-detached, and there were to be very few detached villas. The first twenty houses were to be completed by 1851 and the remainder by 1864. Lord Holland covenanted to grant leases of houses as soon as they were completed in carcase to Goddard or his nominees for ninety-nine years from 1849. The yearly ground rent for each house was to be between £8 maximum and one shilling minimum, and Lord Holland was to receive an ultimate annual ground rent of £1,400 after six years (equivalent to approximately £20 per acre). Lord Holland agreed to construct the new roads and sewers, but the money he spent on doing this was to be repaid by Goddard at 5 per cent interest. As security Goddard was required to build a house facing the Uxbridge road between Addison Road and Addison Terrace on which he would spend at least £1,500. An extensive schedule of the materials which Goddard was to use in building his houses accompanied the agreement.[96]

In June 1849 Lord Holland mortgaged Holland House and its grounds,[97] the first of a series of such transactions during the next few years, and this may have been partly to obtain the money necessary to construct the roads and sewers which he had undertaken to provide. Also in June, Goddard began building in Addison Gardens and at the north end of Addison Road and Holland Villas Road.[98]* He was able to lay the foundations of twelve houses and carry one of them up to second-storey level before he en-

countered financial difficulties. Eventually he found it expedient to remove himself and his family to the Continent, and his creditors were reluctant to press for a declaration of bankruptcy because there was apparently not even enough money left to pay for the fiat.[99]

The completion of the grand scheme begun by Goddard took over twenty-five years, and the projected street pattern was varied slightly as other builders took over. Lord Holland undertook the expense of building the sewers,[100] and hoped to recoup the cost in subsequent building contracts. Several agreements were drawn up, few of which were completely carried out and some not at all, and the estate was beset with constant problems caused by the financial mismanagement which seems to have been endemic among nineteenth-century builders.

The house facing the Uxbridge road which Goddard had been required to build as security was completed as a semi-detached pair and named Addison Villas; the builder was Walter Longhurst of Knightsbridge. A villa at the corner of Addison Road and Holland Villas Road, which was the only house on which Goddard had made substantial progress, was completed by John and Charles I'Anson of St. Marylebone under a ninety-nine-year lease granted to John Henry Browne. The same builders also took a lease themselves of a plot of ground south of the corner house and built another substantial house there in 1851.[101] All four houses have been demolished.

On the east side of Addison Road eight houses were built to fill the gap between No. 18 and the church, including St. Barnabas' vicarage. The largest of these houses (No. 25, later known as Oak Lodge) was built by William Brinkley of St. George's, Hanover Square, for William Reed of Hanworth, to whom a ninety-nine-year lease was granted in 1855. Reed was also the lessee of the house to the north (No. 24), which he assigned to Sir George Barrow, a prominent figure in the Colonial Office. Reed, who figures in many transactions on the estate, was clearly a man of substance and in 1856 he purchased the freehold of No. 25, where he had taken up residence in 1855.[102]

The only one of these eight houses which has

---

* A view of Addison Gardens as designed and proposed to be erected by Goddard was exhibited at the Royal Academy in 1850.

not been demolished is No. 23 (the vicarage of St. Barnabas).* It was built in 1855 by Charles Richard Stanham and, despite extensive alterations including the addition of an extra wing in 1882 to the designs of the architect Arthur Baker, is a picturesque composition in brick and stone with ornate bargeboarding (Plate 10a).[103]

On the west side of Addison Road ten houses were built between 1852 and 1855 by John Parkinson, junior, of Hammersmith, immediately to the north of Napier Road (originally called Warwick Road), which was laid out about this time. These houses, originally called Abbotsford Villas and now Nos. 50–59 (consec.) Addison Road (Plate 51c), are principally in the form of linked pairs, but there is a gap between Nos. 53 and 54, and it may originally have been intended to build only eight houses in two groups of linked pairs. They are brick built, of two storeys over basements, and are enriched by stucco dressings, including pilasters at the corners of each pair of houses and large brackets at the top of the pilasters supporting the overhanging eaves. The first-floor windows have semi-circular heads, while those on the ground floor have segmental heads. Most of the leases were granted directly to Parkinson for ninety-nine years from 1851, although No. 54 was leased for a similar term to Carl Engel, who was its first occupant, and the lessee of Nos. 58 and 59 was William Reed, who was probably providing Parkinson with capital.[104] Nos. 48–49 and 60–61 Addison Road, which were built in 1856–7, were also leased to Reed.† These are, however, detached houses in a different style from Parkinson's; the builders were Nicholson and Son of Wandsworth.[106]

Most of the remaining houses on the west side of Addison Road were erected by James Hall, a builder who had been operating since 1846 in the Pembridge Villas area (see page 261). It is uncertain whether Hall took substantial portions of the estate under agreement from the beginning, but in July 1855, when he had already secured building leases of nine houses in Addison Road, some of which were finished and the rest presumably under construction, he entered into an agreement with Lord Holland to build another 95 houses on the estate. This was followed by two

further agreements in 1857 and 1859 to build 129 more.[107] In the event Hall built approximately 120 houses in Addison Road, Addison Crescent, Addison Gardens, Upper Addison Gardens and Holland Villas Road, which were generally laid out to the plan accompanying the agreement of 1849 with Goddard.

Hall was responsible for building Nos. 64–88 (consec.) Addison Road (Nos. 69, 70 and 88 demolished), although Nos. 79 and 80 were leased to John Watts Elliot of Kensington, builder, probably an associate of Hall in what must have been very extensive building operations, and No. 72 was leased to William Henry Collins and Alfred Horatio Stansbury of Birmingham, wholesale ironmongers, perhaps suppliers of building materials.[108]

The first lease, granted in August 1853, was for No. 65, which was ready for occupation by 1854,[109] and by 1860 all twenty-five houses were occupied. At first Hall's leases of houses in Addison Road were for ninety-nine years from 1852 at annual rents of £10 to £15, usually with a peppercorn term, but after the agreement of 1855 they were generally for ninety-six years from 1855 at £25 per annum, without benefit of a peppercorn term. These were conventional building leases and the covenants were the usual ones requiring the lessees to maintain their houses in good repair and decoration and insured against fire. The houses could not be altered without permission and were not to be used for any trade or business. Built on plots with sixty-foot frontages, they are generally detached, double-fronted, two-storeyed, stuccoed villas with cornices carried on brackets and with crowning balustrades (Plate 50a, fig. 17), and are similar to Hall's earlier houses in Chepstow Villas and Pembridge Place. Some variations in design were introduced, however, particularly in the corner houses with Addison Crescent, of which only No. 64 survives, and in four houses at the north end of Addison Road. The survivors of this latter group, Nos. 85–87, are basically larger houses with more space between them and are faced with brick rather than stucco. All of the houses had substantial gardens, which were originally intended to be supplemented by a communal

---

* Situated immediately to the south of Oak Lodge, the vicarage was originally No. 26 Addison Road until renumbered in 1900 as a result of the demolition of Nos. 22–25 for the building of Oakwood Court.

† Reed was also the lessee of three houses (now demolished) which were built in 1862 on the east side of Addison Road to the south of St. Barnabas' Church.[105]

67
ADDISON ROAD
PLANS AND DETAILS SHOWN BELOW

34
HOLLAND VILLAS ROAD

FT. 10   0   10 FT. 10 0   10   20   30
M. 3   0   3   M. 3   0   3   6   9
Scale for elevations   Scale for plans

31'0"

40'0"

GROUND FLOOR   FIRST FLOOR

INTERNAL CORNICE
Plaster

SKIRTING

No. 67 ADDISON ROAD DETAILS

Fig. 17. Nos. 67 Addison Road and 34 Holland Villas Road, plans, elevations and details

enclosure at the rear, but by 1858 this idea had been abandoned and the private gardens were lengthened instead.[110]

The value to the estate of this flurry of building activity in the 1850's, chiefly in Addison Road, can be calculated from the schedules of ground rents which were attached to a series of mortgage transactions entered into by Lord Holland. In 1849 the total yearly value of ground rents was approximately £750, but by 1858 this had increased to £1,700 (including £88 for a small part of the estate in Hammersmith on which building had begun*).[111] Lord Holland died in December 1859, but his death had no immediate effect on estate development. He had no children and left all his property to his widow.[112]

While Hall was still finishing houses in Addison Road he also began building in Addison

* But excluding £200 rent for Little Holland House and about £250 for Holland Farm.

Crescent, Addison Gardens and Holland Villas Road. Between 1857 and 1859 he was granted leases of Nos. 1–13 (consec.) Addison Crescent,* Nos. 1–38 (consec.) Holland Villas Road, Nos. 2–13 and 30–43 (consec.) Upper Addison Gardens and Nos. 2–18 (even) and 1–13 (odd) Addison Gardens.[114] No. 1 Upper Addison Gardens was leased to John Scott of Addison Road, builder, also associated with Hall in his large-scale enterprise.[115] The leases for houses in Addison Crescent and Holland Villas Road were for ninety-six years from 1855 and so were brought in line with those in Addison Road. Those for houses in Addison Gardens were for ninety-seven years from 1858. Most of the annual ground rents were at the low figure of five shillings, although a few were at higher rates, up to £25, no doubt calculated to provide a yearly sum of ground rents previously agreed with Lord Holland. Very few of these houses were finished by 1860[36] and none were included in the schedule of ground rents in 1858 referred to above.

In Addison Crescent and Holland Villas Road Hall built substantial detached villas, some of two and some of three storeys, similar in design to those he had erected in Addison Road, except that here they are of stock brick, with stucco bays, and the roofs overhang the eaves instead of being set back behind balustrades (Plate 50b, fig. 17). The boundary walls at the fronts of the houses consist of stock-brick plinths and piers, with panels of semi-circular stucco tiles set on top of each other to form screens, or, in some cases, with pierced cast-iron panels. As in Addison Road each plot generally has a sixty-foot frontage and the houses stand in large gardens. No. 1 Addison Crescent and Nos. 7, 19, 20 and 38 Holland Villas Road have been demolished. The first occupant of No. 8 Holland Villas Road was the art collector Constantine Alexander Ionides.†

In Addison Gardens and Upper Addison Gardens Hall erected terraced housing of a more conventional type, of yellow bricks with stucco dressings and an elaborate modillioned cornice.

Each house has a twenty-five-foot frontage and contains three storeys over a semi-basement.

Such extensive undertakings required a large amount of capital, and Hall's general method of securing this was to mortgage each house shortly after he had received the lease from Lord Holland, sometimes even on the same day. Some of these mortgages were for small amounts of money —£200 to £400—but several involved sums of £1,000 or more, and one was for £1,500. Such mortgages were often executed as collateral for money or credit which had been obtained some time previously on the security of promissory notes and bills of exchange, not all of which were subsequently covered by mortgages. His mortgagees were many and varied. Besides the usual solicitors, there were clergymen, several 'gentlemen' from the provinces,‡ a spinster living in Paris and individual tradesmen including a baker and a cowkeeper.[117] In 1858 several mortgages were executed to Samuel and Charles Fields Boydell of Bloomsbury, solicitors. Samuel Boydell, who was at one time Hall's solicitor, advanced money himself and secured further mortgagees in his professional capacity. At the end of 1859 Hall agreed that the leases of nine houses in Addison Gardens and Holland Villas Road should be held by Boydell as security, and that he would finish the houses within two months. This he failed to do, and in 1860 Boydell took a formal mortgage of these houses and a second mortgage of others as security for over £8,000 which was owing to him.[118] At the end of 1859 Hall also mortgaged thirty houses, several of which were already subject to first mortgages, to John Beattie, manager of the Temple Bar branch of the Union Bank of London, for £10,000.[119]

By 1860 Hall had over-reached himself and was in severe financial difficulties, several judgments being recorded against him for recovery of debt. Lady Holland was becoming dissatisfied with his rate of progress and commenced actions for ejectment on account of arrears of rent and non-observance of the time clauses for finishing houses.

* Nos. 14 and 15 Addison Crescent were built c. 1866 by Charles Richard Stanham on land which had been let to William Reed in 1856.[113] No. 16 was built c. 1870 (see page 118).

† He was the brother of Alexander Alexander Ionides, who transformed No. 1 Holland Park into a showpiece of the decorative talents of William Morris and his circle (see page 124n). According to his son, Constantine purchased No. 8 Holland Villas Road because it contained room for a large carpet he had found in the East. He later employed Philip Webb to undertake additions to the house. The Ionides Collection was later bequeathed to the Victoria and Albert Museum.[116]

‡ Including two from the midlands who took mortgages of several houses: Francis Edward Williams of Solihull and Edwin Blackburn of Leamington.

Hall's creditors, concerned that they would lose their securities, urged her to stop the proceedings. This she did, 'having no desire to take any undue advantage of the difficulties or defaults of the said James Hall which defaults if any appeared to have arisen from the too great extent of his undertakings'. The mortgagees paid the arrears of ground rent, and in 1861 Hall assigned his interests in houses for which he held leases to Henry George Robinson, a solicitor, upon trust to apply the rents and profits to settle outstanding liabilities.* Thereafter any money remaining was to be used to make and complete roads or any works necessary to further the development. More complicated financial transactions ensued, however, and one creditor claimed to have advanced 'various sums of money to a large amount' for completing several houses. Finally in 1864 Hall was declared bankrupt, and some of his houses had to be finished by other builders.[121]

During the bankruptcy proceedings, Hall's total liabilities were stated to be £340,000, of which over £100,000 consisted of unsecured debts.[122] He had considerable assets tied up in buildings, but his financial affairs were so tangled that several actions were brought in Chancery to determine the precedence of the claims of his many creditors.[123] In one such case the Master of the Rolls decreed that several houses should be sold and the proceeds allocated to the various creditors according to a schedule of priorities which he ordered to be drawn up, a veritable task of Solomon.[124]†

While Hall was building in Addison Road and the area immediately to the west of it with a greater or lesser degree of success, smaller-scale developments were taking place at the north and south ends of Holland Road. W. Walsham of Bethnal Green gave notice of his intention to build thirty-four houses at both ends of the street in 1853 and 1854, but whether he completed any of them is doubtful, for all except one were returned by the district surveyor as having been 'suspended' towards the end of 1854. Walsham's operations were taken over by John Lines of Hammersmith.[98] Eight houses were built at the north end of the street on the west side under

ninety-nine-year leases granted in 1854 to Frederick Robert Beeston, surveyor, or Gilbert Stephens, gentleman, both of Northumberland Street, Strand.[126] These houses, which were on the Hammersmith side of the parish boundary, have been demolished.

At the south end of Holland Road Lines built two terraces, one on each side of the road, under an agreement concluded in 1851 with William Scott of Hammersmith, a brickmaker. Originally called Holland and Cambridge Terraces, they are now known as Nos. 4–34 (even) and 9–41 (odd) Holland Road. Holland Terrace, on the east side, was the first to be built under ninety-four-year leases granted to Scott in 1856. The annual ground rent for each house was £8 except for the public house at the corner of Napier Road, originally called The Napoleon the Third,‡ but now known as The Crown and Sceptre, for which the ground rent was £30. The leases for Cambridge Terrace were granted to Scott for a similar term in 1858 at an annual ground rent of five shillings for each house. By 1860 only two houses remained unoccupied in the two terraces.[127] Scott was also granted similar leases of Nos. 1–20 (consec.) Napier Place at a total annual ground rent of £40. Originally called Holland Mews, these were built as stables and coach-houses by John Lines and were used partly by himself and James Hall and partly by the residents of Addison Road and Holland Road.[128]

The two short terraces of houses and shops in Napier Road, Nos. 1–6 (consec.) on the south side and Nos. 7–13 (consec.) on the north, were also built under leases granted in 1858 and 1859 to William Scott for ninety-four years from 1856. The leases of those on the north side of the street were granted with the consent of John Parkinson, who may have originally taken the land under agreement when he built Nos. 50–59 Addison Road. The houses in Napier Road, each (with the exception of No. 6) with a seventeen-foot frontage, were among the smallest to be built on the estate. The builders were probably James Randell Thursby of Poplar for the south side and John Palmer of Pimlico for the north.[129] No. 14 was added in 1875.[98]

---

* In 1862 Lady Holland sold the freeholds of several houses in Holland Villas Road and Upper Addison Gardens to George Frederick Robinson, who was a member of the same legal firm, and presumably related to Henry George Robinson.[120]

† At the auction sales which resulted, detached houses built by Hall were sold at prices varying between £1,200 and £2,200, depending partly on the number of storeys in each house and partly on the ground rent.[125]

‡ The Hollands were supporters of the Bonaparte family.

In 1861 Lady Holland sold some land to the London and North Western Railway Company for £7,860 to provide a new station and more track for the West London Railway.[130] Since its suspension of passenger operations in 1844 the West London Railway had been operated on lease by the London and Birmingham (later vested in the London and North Western) and the Great Western companies for carrying freight. The construction of the West London Extension Railway along the course of the Kensington Canal and the opening of the Hammersmith and City Railway, however, gave the West London renewed importance as a passenger line. In 1864 the new station was opened on the west side of Russell Road (although it was called Addison Road station). Its name has now been changed to Kensington (Olympia) and most of the station buildings have been demolished. As a condition of the sale, the railway company was required to construct Russell Road and maintain it until houses were built on the east side, when the costs of maintenance would be borne jointly with the lessees of those houses. The company was also required to build a sewer along the road. In the first, disastrous, phase of its history the West London Railway could hardly have stimulated building developments in the vicinity of the line. After 1864, however, it was a much more important artery of communication and several inter-suburban services passed through Addison Road station.[131]

The area between Addison Road and the railway was virtually completely built up by 1875. By that time houses had been erected on the vacant plots in Holland Road, Upper Addison Gardens and Addison Gardens, and several new streets of terraced housing and stables had appeared, viz Elsham Road, Hansard Mews, Holland Gardens, Lorne Gardens, Russell Gardens, Russell Gardens Mews and Russell Road. This prodigious spate of building activity, involving the erection of over three hundred houses, was undertaken by two pairs of developers, their respective spheres of operation being divided by a line drawn down the middle of Holland Road. The land to the west was taken by Charles Chambers of St. Marylebone, a publican turned builder,

and Henry John Bartley of St. Marylebone, a solicitor, who was his financial backer. The area between Holland Road and Addison Road not yet built up, including the east side of Holland Road, was taken by John Beattie, the manager of the Temple Bar branch of the Union Bank of London,[132] and Harry Dowding of Leicester Square. An agreement was concluded with Chambers in 1862 and he began building in 1863,[133] but Beattie and Dowding's development did not begin until 1870, probably because of the litigation following James Hall's bankruptcy.*

The estate policy towards these developments showed a marked change from earlier building ventures in that the developers were given an option to purchase the freeholds of houses once built. The price of each freehold, as expressed in the agreement with Chambers, was to be thirty years' purchase of the ground rent, amounting to a total of £30,000 for all of the houses built under this agreement.† Generally Lady Holland granted leases of individual houses to the builders in the usual manner and conveyed the freeholds to the developers or their nominees later. This method gave the estate a good deal of control over the type of buildings erected, and John Henry Browne was still responsible for supervising the general layout and plot ratio of the houses. The conveyances contained restrictive covenants which were to apply during the term of the original leases—a useful device to ensure that the general character of the neighbourhood would be maintained. These covenants required the purchasers to paint the outside of the houses every four years; not to allow any trade or business without licence from the Holland estate; not to interfere with the plans, elevations or architectural decorations without licence; and not to erect any new buildings on the site except for re-instatement in case of fire.[135] When it was clear that the speculations were progressing satisfactorily this estate policy was relaxed somewhat and some blocks of land were sold before houses had been built on them, or, therefore, leases granted. In later conveyances the restrictive covenants were not always spelt out in full and purchasers were sometimes simply required to make future lessees enter into covenants similar to those 'usually inserted in Leases

---

* Beattie had been a mortgagee of James Hall (see page 115), and may have undertaken the speculation, which included the completion of streets begun by Hall, as a consequence.

† The option was not taken up in the case of Nos. 21–40 Elsham Road and these houses remained in the possession of the estate until the twentieth century.[134]

granted by the said Vendor [i.e. Lady Holland] of houses . . . built upon her Kensington Estate'.[136] Lady Holland had no children, and her constant need of money to maintain a social life in which she seemed to be trying to outvie even her illustrious mother-in-law[137] was probably the principal reason why she sold so much of the estate after Lord Holland's death.

The results of the speculations of Chambers and Bartley on the one hand and Beattie and Dowding on the other are not architecturally very distinguished. Most of the houses for which they were responsible reflect a number of ingenious permutations of the Italianate idiom but very little originality in design. The majority are three-storey terraced houses with semi-basements and are built of stocks or gault bricks with stucco dressings, except in Russell Gardens, which was begun in 1866, where red facing bricks are used above ground-floor shops. The frontages are generally twenty to twenty-five feet and each house is usually two bays wide. Virtually all have a porch and ground-floor bay window.

Of the builders employed by Chambers and Bartley, Charles Frederick Phelps appears to have had a more considerable influence than most and was probably of great assistance to the inexperienced Chambers. Nos. 1–15 (consec.) Russell Road, which were among the first houses to be built under Chambers's agreement, are of basically the same design as houses in Essex Villas on the Phillimore estate which Phelps had built a few years earlier, although there they are in pairs rather than terraced as in Russell Road. One of Phelps's favourite motifs, an elaborate triple window at first-floor level surmounted by a cornice with a segmental pediment over the wide centre light supported on consoles, reappears several times, even in houses for which he was not nominally responsible.*

An interesting feature of the layout plan adopted by Chambers is that Nos. 1–43 (consec.) Elsham Road back on to Holland Road, with the result that the only gardens of these houses are in the front and that more care than usual has been taken with the rear elevations. This unusual arrangement was necessary if Elsham Road was to be fitted in between Holland Road and the railway land.

The development by Beattie and Dowding shows greater variety than that by Chambers and Bartley, and two groups of houses built as part of their speculation provide a relief from the dominant classical style of house-building on the Holland estate. Nos. 40–94 (even) Holland Road (Plate 50c), together with No. 16 Addison Crescent, mark the somewhat belated introduction of Ruskinian motifs to the area, although expressed in a formal, symmetrical terrace of stock brick, with red brick relieving arches and bands, and stucco decoration. Three pairs of houses, two near the ends and one at the centre, are accentuated, with high gables and façades which project beyond the face of the remainder of the terrace. The result is that the terrace is classical in its proportions, while being Gothic in its ornamentation. No. 16 Addison Crescent, which is attached to No. 94 Holland Road, has attractive ironwork on the roof ridges. The first houses, in the centre of the terrace, were erected by Thomas Snowdon of St. Marylebone, builder, in 1870, but later other builders were involved, namely Walter Lethbridge and John Henry Adams, both of Paddington.[139]

Nos. 170–176 (even) Holland Road, south of the church of St. John the Baptist, have an ecclesiastical flavour with naturalistic carvings enriching the mouldings. No. 176 was built in 1872 as St. John's vicarage, although through lack of money it was not acquired for this purpose until after 1900; the architect was T. Lawrie, and the builder John Henry Adams.[140]

Beattie and Dowding were also the promoters of a different type of development in Lorne Gardens (fig. 18), where thirty-one small 'cottages' without gardens were built between 1870 and 1874 on a plot of ground originally intended for a mews, between the backs of houses in Upper Addison Gardens, Holland Park Avenue and Holland Road. The size of the houses in Lorne Gardens—smaller than most of the stables and coach-houses that were built in the vicinity—contrasts remarkably with the surrounding terraces, but they are of interest in design. An effective use was made of limited interior space by placing the staircases at the back, where in most cases they were originally top-lit because the rear elevations facing the gardens of the larger

---

* Other builders employed by Chambers and Bartley were William Thomas Angel of St. Pancras; Charles Martin Chambers, perhaps Charles Chambers's son; John Perry of Islington; Henry Saunders of Paddington; Samuel Toope Weekes and William Weekes of Kensal Green.[138]

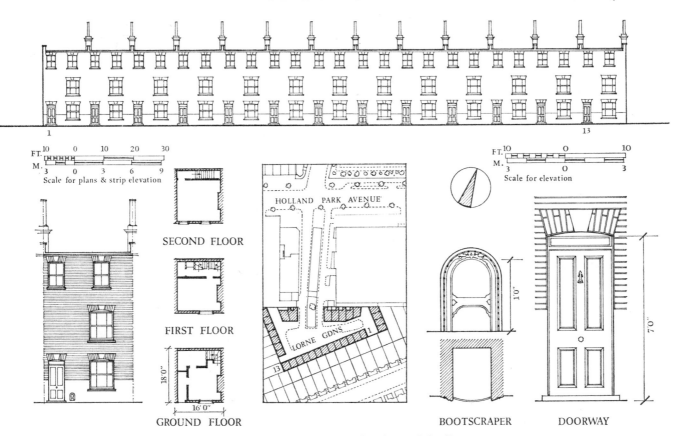

Fig. 18. Lorne Gardens, plans, elevations and details

houses did not have windows. The treatment of the front elevations is also unusual, particularly the positions of the window-openings. The original building leases were granted to William Henry Kingham of Hammersmith, who built most of the houses, but he appears to have encountered difficulties in 1872 and other builders took over.* The freeholds were sold to Beattie and Dowding by Lady Holland in 1871 for a total of £500. In 1954 the Kensington Housing Trust embarked on a programme of modernizing the houses, many of which were then still without bathrooms or electricity, and alterations have been made in the internal arrangement of rooms.[142]

At the same time as these rather humdrum developments were taking shape to the west of

Addison Road, a development which produced houses of much greater distinction was being undertaken further to the east, where Nos. 1–89 (consec.) Holland Park and Nos. 1–67 (consec.) Holland Park Mews were being built (Plate 51d, figs. 19–22). In August 1859, shortly before Lord Holland's death, the brothers William and Francis Radford, who had been engaged in building operations in Pembridge Gardens and Pembridge Square for several years (see page 261), entered into an agreement to build on part of the back park of Holland House next to the Uxbridge road. This agreement was for the erection of seventy-seven detached villas and a terrace of fifty-one houses facing the Uxbridge road. It was modified in December 1859 to exclude the terrace and

* These were F. W. Durrant of Holland Place, Kensington, and W. Turner (probably William Turner of Chelsea).
Other builders employed on houses erected as part of Beattie's and Dowding's development and not mentioned already in the text were: W. Parratt of Clapham Junction; Silas Rowles of Notting Hill; A. H. Tyler of Lambeth; Igglesden and Myers of Paddington. The latter firm built the uniform terrace, Nos. 96–144 (even) Holland Road.[141]

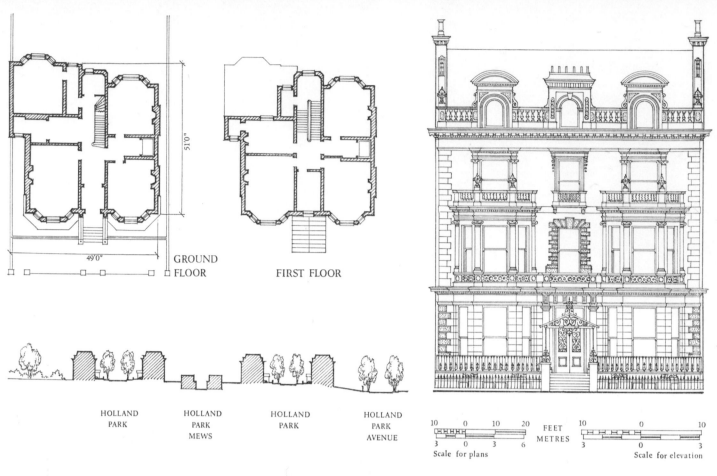

GROUND
FLOOR

FIRST FLOOR

49'0"

51'0"

HOLLAND
PARK

HOLLAND
PARK
MEWS

HOLLAND
PARK

HOLLAND
PARK
AVENUE

10   0   10   20   FEET   10   0   10
                      METRES
3   0   3   6   3   0   3
Scale for plans   Scale for elevation

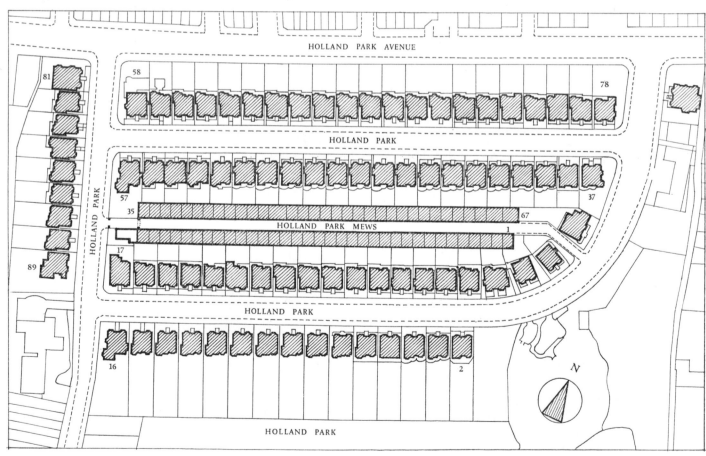

HOLLAND PARK AVENUE

81

58

78

HOLLAND PARK

57

37

35

67

HOLLAND PARK MEWS

1

17

89

HOLLAND PARK

HOLLAND PARK

16

2

N

HOLLAND PARK

Fig. 19. No. 67 Holland Park, plans and elevation

Fig. 20 (facing page). No. 67 Holland Park, details

FEET
METRES

1   0   1   2   3

0   1

CANOPY

2' 10"

2' 11"

STAIRCASE
DETAILS

2' 6"

4' 3"

RAILINGS

EXTERNAL DOOR
IRONWORK

1' 0"

1' 0"

1' 0"

EXTERNAL
DETAILS

1' 4"

2' 10"

10½"

PLASTER CORNICE   GROUND FLOOR DETAILS

3"

DADO

6½"

ARCHITRAVE

1' 2½"

SKIRTING

MARBLE FIREPLACE
Ground Floor Front Rooms

Fig. 21. No. 67 Holland Park, chimneypiece

bring the total number of villas up to eighty. In the event Nos. 1–78 Holland Park were built under this agreement and Nos. 79–89 under a subsequent agreement of February 1864. The decision not to build a terrace on the Uxbridge road has resulted in a long stretch of this major road—now named Holland Park Avenue—being faced by the back elevations and gardens of Nos. 58–78 Holland Park.

The Radfords were to build 'good proper and substantial' private dwelling houses to designs previously submitted to and approved by Lord Holland or his agent, and undertook to spend at least £1,200 on each house (by 1864 this had been increased to £2,000). They also covenanted to build the necessary roads and sewers, and it was expressly agreed that all large trees not on the sites of houses or injurious to them were to be preserved. Leases for ninety-nine years from 1858 were to be granted when the carcases of houses were completed at ground rents which were to be individually not more than one-sixth of the estimated rack rental or less than five shillings, and were to provide a total annual sum of £1,500

after three years. The number of houses to be completed in each year was laid down, and the development was to be finished by 1872. The Radfords also agreed to build seventy coach-houses and stables at a cost of at least £200 each. As was usual in Holland estate agreements, they were to be allowed to build a lesser number of houses and coach-houses, provided the total amount of money which they had agreed to spend remained the same. None of the houses were to be used for trade or business without licence.

The agreement of 1859 did not include any option to purchase the freehold, but in 1861, when Lady Holland agreed to extend the gardens of the southernmost range of houses, a clause was included whereby the Radfords could purchase the fee simple of any of the houses they erected under the earlier agreement on payment of a sum equal to twenty-nine years' purchase of the ground rent.[143]

The first lease was granted in October 1860, and, according to the district surveyor's returns, the last house was begun in 1877 and covered in by 1879, although some of the houses do not

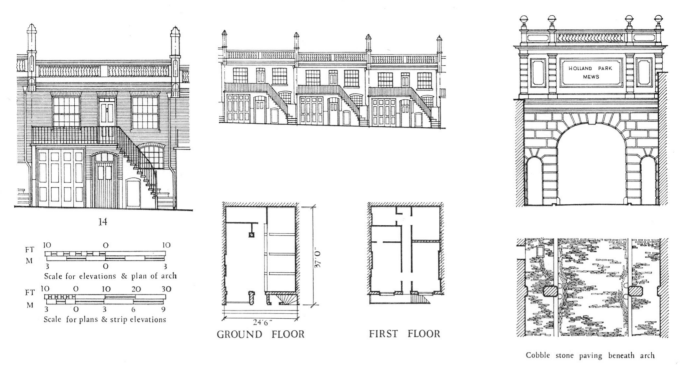

14

FT 10 0 10
M 3 0 3
Scale for elevations & plan of arch

FT 10 0 10 20 30
M 3 0 3 6 9
Scale for plans & strip elevations

37' 0"

24' 6"

GROUND FLOOR   FIRST FLOOR

HOLLAND PARK MEWS

Cobble stone paving beneath arch

Fig. 22. Holland Park Mews, plans and elevations

appear to have been fitted out until several years later.[144] The first conveyances of the freeholds were executed by Lady Holland in 1861 at prices which amounted to exactly twenty-nine times the ground rent of each house, even though sometimes the sum involved was only £7 5s. (29 × 5s.). By 1868 and 1869 the sites of houses not yet begun were being sold, subject to the provision that in each case only a house 'uniform [in] position height elevation and external character' with those already erected by the Radfords should be built on the site. Each conveyance contained covenants that for the period of the original lease (or for a specified period of ninety-nine years from 1858 in the case of a site for which a lease had not been granted) the purchaser would not make any alterations in the plan, elevation or architectural character of the house, erect any buildings in the garden, or permit trade or business to be carried on, without the consent of the vendor. The garden was also to be kept in good order, and a proportionate share paid for the upkeep of roads, sewers and common walls. The conveyances were made to William or Francis Radford individually, or occasionally to their

10—S.L. XXXVII

nominees. The average price for the fee simple of each house was £525 and the total for all houses amounted to over £45,000. The freeholds of the coach-houses in Holland Park Mews were also sold in the same manner for prices ranging from £87 to £147, and probably brought into the estate upwards of £7,500.[145] The value to the purchasers must have been very considerable, for in 1881 the annual rent of a house in Holland Park was stated to be £340, while in 1891 No. 62 Holland Park was sold freehold for £5,100 and No. 54 Holland Park Mews for £1,050.[146]

The Radfords built two long roads parallel to Holland Park Avenue rising from south-west to north-east, with an access road at each end, the eastern one sweeping round in a curve; all the roads are named Holland Park. There are four rows of identical detached villas, apparently designed by Francis Radford himself,[147] facing the longer roads, with more of the same villas by the sides of the shorter roads. The villas, although detached, are generally set so close together that they provide an effect similar to a terrace. They are basically the same as those which the Radfords had previously built in Pembridge Square, and which are described fully on page 266. There are differences, however, in the boundary walls next to the pavements, and the balustrades flanking the entrance steps, those in Holland Park being of stucco and those in Pembridge Square of cast iron. There are many richly ornamented iron and glass entrance canopies in Holland Park, erected at a later date.

Holland Park Mews, situated between the two long roads and entered from its western end through a handsome archway, is noteworthy for the care which has been lavished on the design of its coach-houses and stables (fig. 22). These have widely proportioned windows, external stairs to the living accommodation on the first floor, and crowning cornices, above which are balustrades. The details, such as the stucco mouldings on the chimneys, and the balusters, are similar to those on the villas themselves.

When the census of 1871 was taken thirty-six houses in Holland Park were occupied. In two of them building tradesmen were acting as caretakers and in four more the head of the household was absent. The remaining thirty houses contained 381 people (an average of just under thirteen per household), of whom almost exactly half (190) were servants. Other servants (coachmen and grooms) lived in Holland Park Mews. Twelve householders were merchants or retired merchants, and of these two described themselves as 'West India Merchant', two as 'East India Merchant' and one as 'Australian Merchant'. Two other occupants were listed as Manchester warehousemen. Of the remainder, five lived on income from property or dividends, three were barristers, three 'brokers' (including one who also described himself as a merchant) and two clergymen. There was also a peer, an Italian prince, a brewer and a builder (William Radford, who lived at No. 80 with his wife and daughter and three servants). Of these thirty householders only three

were born in London; five came from Scotland and five from outside the British Isles.

Among the notable early occupants of Holland Park (not all in residence by 1871) were: the fourth Marquess of Londonderry; the second Baron Bloomfield; the Maharajah of Lahore; Prince Louis, Count D'Aquila; Sir William Fairbairn, engineer; Sir William McArthur, M.P., Lord Mayor of London; Sir Michael Roberts Westropp, who served on the Indian judiciary; the Reverend William Henley Jervis, scholar of French church history; Arthur Cohen, lawyer and the first Jew to graduate from Cambridge University; John Humffreys Parry, serjeant-at-law; Benjamin Whitworth, M.P., cotton merchant.[148]

Although some of the houses in Holland Park have been altered, all but three survive. No. 80 was replaced at the beginning of the war of 1939–45 by the block of flats called Duke's Lodge,[149] and Nos. 1 and 1A have since been demolished.*

In 1865, while the Radfords were building their large stucco mansions in the north of the estate and Charles Chambers was erecting terraces of a standard, debased Italianate variety in the west, two houses of highly original design were being built on the north side of Holland Park Road, which had originally been laid out as a mews for St. Mary Abbots Terrace. These houses, now numbered 12 and 14 Holland Park Road (see pages 136–42) were built for two painters, Frederic, later Lord, Leighton and Val Prinsep, their respective architects being George Aitchison and Philip Webb. The principal facing material of both houses is red brick, at that time rarely used for buildings in London, and they were the first of several architecturally outstanding houses erected for artists on the Holland estate. The reasons why Leighton and Prinsep chose adjoining sites on the estate for their new houses can be traced back to a meeting between the fourth Lord

---

* No. 1 was purchased freehold in 1864 for £4,500 by Alexander Constantine Ionides, the Consul-General for Greece, who was also a merchant and financier in the City. He was succeeded in the house by his son, Alexander Alexander Ionides, who also became Greek Consul-General and was an outstanding example of the type of entrepreneur who provided important patronage for artists. The younger Ionides engaged William Morris, Philip Webb, Walter Crane and Thomas Jeckyll to redecorate the interior and the house came to be regarded as a showpiece of their talents. He died in 1898 and ten years later his widow sold the house to trustees for the sixth Earl of Ilchester. It was damaged during the war of 1939–45 and was included in the sale of Holland House and grounds to the London County Council in 1952. When the Council decided to demolish the house in 1953 nothing of value was found to remain in the interior. Of the original furnishings in the house, a piano designed by Burne-Jones, a Morris carpet, and a tapestry designed by Morris, Webb and J. H. Dearle, are in the Victoria and Albert Museum.[150]

Holland and the young painter and sculptor, George Frederic Watts, in Florence in 1843. An immediate rapport was established between the two men, and when one of Watts's friends, Henry Thoby Prinsep, was looking for a new home in 1850, Watts persuaded him to take a lease of Little Holland House, which had fallen vacant. Watts made his home with the Prinsep family and helped to further the artistic career of their son, Val. Leighton, who was rapidly acquiring a considerable reputation as a painter, also became friendly with Watts and was welcomed into the Holland House circle. When Lord Holland died in 1859, Leighton wrote to his mother, 'I was indeed truly sorry to hear of Lord Holland's death ... nothing could exceed their kindness to me, and the House [presumably Holland House] is an irreparable loss to me'. When in 1864 both Val Prinsep and Leighton were looking for building plots it was, therefore, natural that they would gravitate to this part of Kensington.[151]

Despite the considerable sum, amounting to over £100,000, which she received from the sale of parts of her estate, Lady Holland was unable to settle any of the outstanding mortgages on her property or even keep pace with her expenditure. The extent to which at one time she contemplated cutting up even the grounds of Holland House for building is illustrated by a dispute with the Kensington Vestry which was eventually taken to the Court of Queen's Bench.* It was a part of Lady Holland's case that plans had been drawn up for building on the park in front of Holland House, and a map was produced showing virtually all the grounds of the house laid out on a grid pattern. The mansion itself was to survive, but with severely truncated grounds, and with roads passing within a few feet of it. A brief prepared for Lady Holland's counsel claimed that the agreement with the Radfords was part of a plan for building on the whole of the remaining parkland, and it was stated that in 1864 negotiations had begun with James McHenry, a prominent merchant and railway speculator, for the sale to him of the front park for development. 'The Panic which ensued put an end to these negociations which were previously progressing satisfactorily.'[152] If plans were really so far advanced, the financial crisis of 1866 certainly had one beneficial effect in preserving what is now one of London's major open spaces. It is, perhaps, strange that negotiations were not renewed when a more favourable financial climate returned, but wise friends may have dissuaded Lady Holland from a step which would have so disastrously affected the mansion in which she lived.

James McHenry purchased No. 25 Addison Road (Oak Lodge) from William Reed in 1862 for £7,250.[153]† He later acquired considerable land surrounding the house, some by purchase and some by lease,‡ and in 1873 he offered Lady Holland £400,000 for the whole of the Holland estate remaining in her hands.[154] By this time she was in desperate financial straits. Most of the available building land on the western part of the estate had already been sold, and the disastrous effects of living on capital rather than income were becoming increasingly apparent. Edward Cheney, her friend and financial adviser, scolded, 'you never did live on your income, but were always assisted by those windfalls which you received from the buildings at Kensington'. He was in no doubt of the cause of her problem, for in another letter he wrote that, 'When you live at Hd. He. you need not entertain all London'.[155] Perhaps unable to bring herself to sell her late husband's family home, and under pressure not to do so from her friends, Lady Holland eventually sought help from a distant relative, Henry

---

* The dispute was over the ownership of the strips of land on each side of Holland Walk. This was an old right-of-way, but its course was changed on more than one occasion. Its present position was not fixed until 1847, when the fourth Lord Holland entered into an agreement with the Vestry to straighten the southern part of the footpath, which at that time crossed the park in front of Holland House to join Holland Lane. He thereby secured greater privacy for the occupants of Holland House, but he promised that there would be an uninterrupted view over the park until it was laid out for building. In 1869 the Vestry, having decided that this view was being obstructed by the planting of bushes and the erection of fences along the sides of Holland Walk, instructed its officers to remove some of these obstructions as a token gesture. It lost the court case which resulted, however, on the grounds that it had taken the law into its own hands and committed an act of trespass.

† A watercolour drawing by Matthew Digby Wyatt in the collection of the Royal Institute of British Architects is described as a perspective of Oak Lodge, Addison Road, dating from the 1870's. This shows a very elaborate house, which does not, however, appear to fit the ground plan of Oak Lodge shown in Ordnance Survey maps, and it may therefore be an unexecuted design for rebuilding the house.

‡ On the garden wall of No. 13 Melbury Road is a stone tablet inscribed 'J.McH. 1877', no doubt marking the boundary of McHenry's lands.

Edward Fox-Strangways, fifth Earl of Ilchester, who was a direct descendant of Stephen Fox, first Earl of Ilchester, the elder brother of the first Lord Holland. After protracted negotiations he agreed to take the estate, subject as it was to a mortgage debt of £49,000 and a few small annuities (including that of £300 to John Henry Browne), and in return he allowed Lady Holland to live in Holland House for the rest of her life and granted her an annuity for life of £6,000. The formal conveyance took place on 17 January 1874.[156]

Since 1874

When the Earl of Ilchester entered into possession of the Holland estate the total income from rents was £3,227 (of which approximately £130 was for property in Hammersmith). The rate of interest on the mortgage debt of £49,000 was at a stated 5 per cent, reducible to 4 per cent by punctual payment. Lady Holland's annuity had also to be paid, and was, in fact, to be secured by rent charges on the Earl's Dorset property. Holland House and its grounds had to be preserved, at least during Lady Holland's lifetime, and, far from gaining any immediate advantage, the Earl appears to have taken on a financial burden. The reversionary value of the estate was, of course, considerable, but the first building leases were not due to fall in until 1904. For several years little or no gain could be expected, and it appears that the Earl was in part motivated by the desire to preserve Holland House and its grounds from speculators. Owning extensive property in Dorset, he could afford to underwrite the relatively unprofitable Kensington estate until in the twentieth century its potential value could be realized by himself or his heirs. Lady Holland's was a most fortunate choice. After her death in 1889, the Earl and his successors lived in Holland House, and after the mansion had been largely destroyed by bombing during the war of 1939–45 its remains and its park were preserved for the enjoyment of the public.

Some immediate development of the estate was, however, necessary to offset the large outgoings, and had clearly been anticipated in the negotiations for the sale.[157] When more definite plans were announced later in 1874 Lady Holland objected, although it is difficult to see that she had

any real cause for complaint. In the hope of reassuring her the Earl wrote, 'We [the Earl and his agent, Robert Driver] settled not to think of any of the land at present beyond the Little Holland house portion . . . and as we could not touch even that till after Xmas not be in a hurry to dispose of it hoping to get offers for a large class of house; the *only* piece we have offered at all at present is to V. Princeps [*sic*] to build a studio and house for Watts and that is not settled yet. We had *no* dealings with any builders, and as to £70 a year houses, the only plan my Agent drew out simply so as to get to the value of the land was villas with gardens £200 and over, the smallest we should think of but hoping to get offers for larger tenancies.' Lady Holland was not mollified, however, and when building was under way she wrote that 'all the building is a very bitter and sad pill to me'.[158]

The development in question was in Melbury Road, which was named after one of the Earl's properties in Dorset, and consisted of a mixture of houses designed by leading architects for successful artists, and in one case by an architect for his own residence, interspersed with large houses erected by builders as speculative ventures.

Little Holland House, which stood in the way of the new road, was demolished in 1875[159] and the first house to be built was for George Frederic Watts. He had lived at Little Holland House for many years, and he transferred this name to his new house, which was designated No. 6 when numbers were assigned in 1878. The other artists' houses in Melbury Road which were begun in 1875 or 1876 were Nos. 2 and 4, a semi-detached pair, for (Sir) Hamo Thornycroft; No. 8 for Marcus Stone; No. 14 for Colin Hunter; No. 29 (originally No. 9) for William Burges; and No. 31 (originally No. 11) for (Sir) Luke Fildes. These houses are described on pages 142–9. Nos. 6 and 14 have been demolished.

While these important houses were being erected other plots in Melbury Road were taken by speculative builders for equally large, if aesthetically more pedestrian houses. George Martin of Putney built two red brick and stone houses on the north side of the road to the west of William Burges's Tower House. These (originally Nos. 5 and 7) were replaced by the neo-Georgian terrace, Nos. 19–27, in 1968–9. On the south side of the road, between Stone's and Hunter's houses, William Turner of Chelsea built two detached four-storey houses (Nos. 10 and 12). These were demolished *c.* 1964 for the erection of Stavordale Lodge. To the south of Colin Hunter's house, Turner also built the semi-detached pair, Nos. 16 and 18; William Holman Hunt lived in No. 18 from 1903 until his death in 1910. All of these houses were built under ninety-year leases at ground rents of between £70 and £100 with the first two years at half rent.[160]

The initial phase of building in Melbury Road was concluded with the erection of two more houses on the north side at the Addison Road end. George Stephenson of Chelsea gave notice of his intention to build two houses in 1879 and 1880, but apparently only completed one. This was the original No. 1, for which he was granted a ninety-year lease in January 1880.[161] The style of the house appears to have been derived from the work of J. J. Stevenson. In 1935 it was divided and is now known as East House and West House. No. 13 (originally No. 3) was probably completed by Lucas and Son of Kensington Square, and an eighty-seven-year lease was granted to James Stratton Thompson of Cromwell Road in 1882 at an annual ground rent of £100.[162]

The leasing of plots on the south side of Melbury Road necessitated the demolition of some of the farm buildings attached to Holland Farm. This survival of the estate's rural past had inevitably shrunk in area as building activity progressed. In 1854, when a new twenty-one-year lease was granted, the farm consisted of sixty-three acres, chiefly pasture, and was let at an annual rent of £250.[163] This lease, however, contained a provision that Lord Holland could take back any part of the farm for building purposes on granting the lessees an abatement of rent, and by the time the estate was sold in 1874, Holland Farm brought in only £112 in rent.[156] The farmhouse itself was rebuilt in 1859[164] (it was later converted into the present No. 10A Holland Park Road, see page 136). As compensation for the loss of some of their land and buildings in 1875 the farm's tenants, Edmund Charles Tisdall and Elizabeth Tunks, were allowed to build a new dairy with a shop and cow-stalls on the island site bounded by Holland Lane, Melbury Road and Kensington High Street.* William Boutcher of Lancaster Road, Notting Hill, was the architect and Thomas Holland of Newland Terrace, Kensington, was the builder.[166] Boutcher provided a red-brick front with a curved gable to Kensington High Street to harmonize with the nearby lodges at the entrance to Holland Park, and the building survived, latterly in the possession of the United Dairies, until the 1960's, when it was demolished. The parkland of Holland House provided pasture for the cows when all other available land had been built upon, and Sir Luke Fildes's son could remember from his youth the tinkling of the cows' bells as they were brought down Holland Lane by the side of No. 31 Melbury Road.[167]

For a short distance Melbury Road took the course of Holland Lane and, therefore, skirted the front park of Holland House. A lodge had been built on the east side of Holland Lane (on the site of Nos. 41–45 Melbury Road) in 1864,[168] but no more building was undertaken there until after Lady Holland's death, no doubt because she had proved so sensitive about intrusions upon her view from the windows of Holland House. In 1892, however, No. 47 (originally No. 13) Melbury Road was built for Walford Graham Robertson, the artist and playwright, and this was followed shortly afterwards by Nos. 55 and 57 (formerly Nos. 15 and 17). These houses are described on pages 149–50.

The first occupant of No. 57 was (Sir) Ernest Debenham, who in 1900 took a lease of a piece of ground to the south of this house with the intention of having a new house built there. Despite securing a large piece of ground in Addison Road in 1905, on which he had a house built for him by Halsey Ricardo (see page 135), Debenham still retained the lease of this vacant plot in Melbury Road. He was allowed to build a temporary half-timbered studio there in 1910 for the artist G. Spencer Watson, who had taken up residence at No. 57.[169] Finally, in 1925, No. 59 (originally No. 19) Melbury Road was erected to the designs of Williams and Cox of Covent Garden.[170]

* Tisdall was one of the best known dairy farmers in the vicinity of London. In 1847 he married Amelia Tunks, the daughter of a South Kensington dairy farmer, and shortly afterwards entered into partnership with the other daughter, Elizabeth Tunks. As well as Holland Farm, which they took *c.* 1854, they had a larger farm at Epsom. Tisdall helped to found the Metropolitan Dairymen's Association in 1873 and the British Dairy Farmers' Association in 1876. In 1853 he was one of the founding directors of the Temperance Permanent Building Society, and at the time of his death in 1892 he was the Society's President. He was also a prominent member of the Kensington Vestry for many years.[165]

At the corner of Melbury Road and the north side of Holland Park Road stood a group of two-storey cottages built about 1825 by Joseph Guest, a carpenter, and Charles Tomlinson, a bricklayer (Plate 51a).[171] These survived until 1905,* an incongruous and no doubt somewhat displeasing intrusion into the world of the socially successful artists who lived in the expensive houses nearby. They were demolished for the erection of Nos. 20 and 22 Melbury Road and Nos. 2–8 (even) Holland Park Road (Plate 51b) to the designs of Charles J. C. Pawley, architect and surveyor, who built the new houses as a speculation.[173]

The presence in Holland Park Road of the residence of Leighton, the most esteemed of all late Victorian artists and President of the Royal Academy from 1878 until 1896 (see pages 136–41), made that road a Mecca for aspiring artists. The south side consisted of a number of small houses at its eastern end, and the stables and coach-houses of St. Mary Abbots Terrace. Several of these were taken by artists during the last quarter of the nineteenth century and adapted for their own use. Some new studios were also built. All have now been demolished for the recent St. Mary Abbots Terrace development.

On the north side, to the west of the house built for Val Prinsep (see pages 141–2), stood a charity school which had been established in 1842 by Caroline Fox, the sister of the third Lord Holland, for the education of children of the labouring, manufacturing and other poorer classes of Kensington. When the school was taken over by the London School Board in 1876, the Board decided that the premises were no longer satisfactory and resolved to remove the school to a new site in Silver Street (now the northern end of Kensington Church Street).[174] The site in Holland Park Road was sold at auction in 1877 for £2,650, and the school buildings were replaced by the picturesque group of six two-storey studio residences arranged round a courtyard with an arched entrance, originally simply called 'The Studios' and now Nos. 20–30 (even) Holland Park Road. They were probably all built in 1878–9 by Arthur Langdale and Company of Brompton.[175] The house at the end of the courtyard, Court House or No. 24A Holland Park Road, was built in 1929 to the designs of A. M. Cawthorne.[176]

Nos. 32 and 34 Holland Park Road were built in 1900 to the designs of Albert E. Cockerell on a piece of ground which had been the entrance to a riding school situated at the back of Nos. 27–31 Addison Road.[177]

The importance of this small corner of the Holland estate as a centre for the artistic 'establishment' is indicated by the fact that in 1896, the year of Leighton's death, six Academicians were living in Holland Park Road and Melbury Road (Leighton, Prinsep, Thornycroft, Watts, Stone and Fildes) as well as one associate member (Hunter). J. J. Shannon was also to become an associate in the following year and a full Academician later. Of other artists who were not members of the Royal Academy, the most famous was probably Phil May, the cartoonist and illustrator, who lived at No. 20 Holland Park Road, then known as Rowsley House. In that year over twenty residents of these two streets can be identified as artists in the *Post Office Directory*.

In 1873 Charles Richard Fox died and shortly afterwards his house, No. 1 Addison Road, and its extensive grounds were sold for speculative building. As he had been granted the freehold by the third Lord Holland, the land no longer belonged to the Holland estate.† Building began in 1877 along the Uxbridge road frontage, and in 1879 the original northward continuation of Addison Road which had been closed since 1842 was reopened and named Holland Park Gardens.[179] This was also the name first adopted for the terraces built along the main road until they were renamed and renumbered as part of Holland Park Avenue in 1934. Nos. 94–100 (consec.) Addison Road were also built in *c.* 1880 (No. 96 since demolished). Some of the grounds which had formerly belonged to Fox's house were used for the Holland Park Tennis Club, and when the house was demolished a wing survived as the club-house and retained the address No. 1 Addison Road. The blocks of flats to the north of this, Holland Park Court and Carlton Mansions, were erected at the turn of the century to complete building on Fox's former land.[98]

---

* A sketch-book by E. W. Godwin for 1881–2 contains a sketch plan of three houses intended for a corner site in Holland Park Road, almost certainly this site. It is not known whether he submitted proposals to the estate.[172]

† Fox had already sold a small piece of his land which remained on the west side of Addison Road when the course of the roadway was changed in 1842 (see page 105), and three houses, Nos. 90–92 (consec.) Addison Road were built on the site in 1862 by Silas Rowles of Notting Hill.[178] No. 92 has since been demolished.

Most of these buildings are of little architectural merit, but Nos. 133–159 (odd) Holland Park Avenue (originally Nos. 2–15 Holland Park Gardens) form a pleasant terrace of linked pairs of three-storey brick and stucco houses, set back from the main road; they were built between 1878 and 1881 and the builder was probably George H. Gorringe of Chelsea.[98]

Another building on the land which formerly belonged to Fox is the Cardinal Vaughan Memorial School, formerly known as Addison Hall. This terra-cotta-fronted building was erected partly as a school and partly as a hall for public entertainment in 1885. The proprietress of the school, called the Kensington Academy for Girls, was Miss Mary Grant. The architect was named as Hugh McLachlan, but Miss Grant claimed to have provided the specifications herself and had the hall built by direct labour. She had difficulties in securing a licence from the London County Council for public functions to be held in the hall in order to pay for her school, and in 1895 one of her mortgagees secured a foreclosure and took possession of the building. Miss Grant removed her school to No. 96 Addison Road, and the new owners shortly afterwards secured the requisite licence for public use of the hall, which was used for various entertainments, including dances, lectures and, occasionally, theatrical performances, until 1914, when the building was taken over for the newly formed Cardinal Vaughan Memorial School.[180] In 1961–3 additional buildings for the school were erected on the opposite side of Addison Road to the designs of David Stokes and Partners.[181]

The first large blocks of flats were introduced into the Holland Park area at the turn of the century when Oakwood Court was built (Plate 112d). The site of the flats, to the north of St. Barnabas' Church, no longer belonged to the estate, most of the land having been sold to James McHenry after his purchase of Oak Lodge. The Oakwood Court development brought about the final disappearance of the ponds called The Moats, which McHenry had converted into an ornamental lake, and necessitated the demolition of Oak Lodge and the three large houses in Addison Road to the north of it. The builders, who had acquired the freehold of the site, were the brothers William Henry and Edward James Jones of Victoria Street, Westminster. Notice of their intention to build the first blocks was given

to the district surveyor in August 1899. An application made to the London County Council in 1900 by William G. Hunt, architect and surveyor, of Bedford Gardens, Kensington, for approval of the frontage line to Addison Road suggests that he may have been the author of the designs for most of the blocks, although these were built over a period of several years and other architects were involved.[182] The only radical departure from the initial design came in 1928–30 when Nos. 31–62 Oakwood Court were erected to the designs of Richardson and Gill.[183]

In the twentieth century the Holland estate has been further reduced in size by the sale of the few remaining freeholds to the west of Addison Road and several houses on the west side of Addison Road itself. Within the area retained, however, a vigorous policy of development has been pursued. The first new scheme of any size was Ilchester Place, which was completed in 1928 to the designs of Leonard Martin (Plate 50d).[184] Melbury Court was built at approximately the same time on part of the Kensington High Street frontage which had formerly belonged to the front park of Holland House; the design was by Francis Milton Cashmore of the architectural firm of Messrs. Joseph.[185] The southern part of Abbotsbury Road, named from one of the Dorset estates belonging to the Earl of Ilchester, was formed at the same time as Oakwood Court. Only a few houses were, however, built in the road before the war of 1939–45; Nos. 3–9 (odd) date from approximately 1924 and Nos. 8–10 and 24–28 (even) from the 1930's.[186]

The most significant effect of the war of 1939–1945 on the estate was the sale of Holland House. The mansion had been severely damaged by bombing and its restoration as a family residence did not seem feasible. Soon after the end of the war the London County Council began negotiations with the sixth Earl of Ilchester for the purchase of the house and its grounds in order to preserve a vital open space in this part of Kensington. Agreement was reached in 1951 for the sale of the house and fifty-two acres to the Council for £250,000 and the transaction was ratified by Act of Parliament in 1952.[187] A further Act in 1954 allowed the restored east wing of the house and part of the adjoining land to be used for the provision of youth hostel accommodation, and the King George VI Memorial Hostel, built to the designs of Sir Hugh Casson and Neville Conder, was opened by Her Majesty Queen Elizabeth II in 1959.[188]

During the 1950's and 60's building activity on the estate was as extensive as at any time since the 1870's. All of the houses and flats on the west side of Abbotsbury Road to the north of Oakwood Court, namely Nos. 17–137 (odd) Abbotsbury Road, Nos. 1–66 (consec.) Abbotsbury Close and Abbotsbury House, were built during these years by Wates Limited to the designs of Stone, Toms and Partners. The same firm of architects was responsible for the new St. Mary Abbots Terrace development, which, with Abbot's House and Kenbrook House, occupies the whole of the rectangular site bounded by Addison Road, Holland Park Road, Holland Lane and Kensington High Street, and which necessitated the demolition of all the existing buildings on that site.[189] Piecemeal redevelopment of several sites in Melbury Road also took place at this time, and the east side of Addison Road to the south of St. Barnabas' Church was completely rebuilt. Another large-scale development, Woodsford Square, was begun in 1968 on the site of Nos. 2–7 Addison Road, where Wates are at present (1972) building to the designs of Fry, Drew and Partners an intended total of 130 houses on a site formerly occupied by six houses and their grounds.

The Church of St. Barnabas, *Addison Road*
Plates 10, 33d, f; fig. 23

In 1822 the Vestry, concerned that the parish church and the small Brompton Chapel were the only institutions of the established church serving the religious needs of the rapidly growing population of Kensington, appointed a committee to consider what steps should be taken to remedy the situation. When the committee reported in 1823 it recommended that two new places of worship should be built, one at Brompton, and one near Earl's Court Lane. The Vestry resolved that only one was necessary, but changed its mind in 1825 when Lord Kensington offered to donate a site for a chapel at the south end of Warwick Square.[190]* The Commissioners for Building New Churches agreed to grant £10,000 towards the expense of building a church at Brompton and a chapel at the west end of the parish, and Lewis Vulliamy was appointed architect for the

latter. In 1826, however, the site in Warwick Square was given up, possibly because Lord Kensington's development there was running into considerable difficulties which were involving him in litigation, and Lord Holland, a member of the original committee which recommended the building of two new places of worship, provided an alternative site in Addison Road. The vicar of Kensington, Archdeacon Pott, reported to the Commissioners that the new site was an excellent one, particularly as a road and sewer had already been constructed.[191]

Vulliamy had to submit several plans and specifications to the Commissioners before they were satisfied that he had achieved the requisite degree of economy 'consistent with giving to the Building the character of an Ecclesiastical Edifice'.[192] The preparation of the foundations had begun by October 1826,[72] although the formal conveyance of the land to the Commissioners did not take place until January 1827,[193] and building continued until 1829. The contractor for the whole works was William Woods, who received £10,012. His original contract was for £9,332 but the site proved to be not quite so ideal as was first thought and the presence of soft and wet clay and a vein of quicksand made extra foundations necessary. These were provided to specifications by (Sir) Robert Smirke. Perhaps Lord Holland had neglected to inform the parochial authorities that the site had originally been covered by ponds. The clerk of works for most of the period when the church was under construction was George Gattward and the cost, including architect's fees and incidentals, was £10,938.[194] Apart from the Commissioners' grant, the cost of both St. Barnabas' and Holy Trinity, Brompton, which were built simultaneously, was borne by the parish out of a threepenny church rate. £10,000 was raised by a series of securities for £100 each at 4½ per cent. interest, but it was found necessary to raise an extra £3,500 by the same means to fit out the new churches for worship.[195] St. Barnabas', which was designed to seat 1,330 (818 in rented pews and 512 in free seats), was consecrated on 8 June 1829 and was designated a chapel-of-ease to St. Mary Abbots. A district chapelry was assigned to it in 1842 and this became a parish under the Act of 1856 for creating new parishes.[196]

---

* Warwick Square is now the wide north end of Warwick Gardens.

The church is set on a bend in the road and its west façade rises from a sweep of steps directly from the pavement, appearing at an angle when approached from the south. The building is in the Tudor Gothic style, a fashionable choice for 1826, when (Sir) Charles Barry provided designs in the same architectural style for Holy Trinity, Cloudesley Square, Islington. The eight-bay side elevations of the nave, with large windows set between narrow stepped buttresses, were originally surmounted by parapets pierced by trefoil openings similar to those on the west front, while the buttresses were capped by pinnacles, now removed, of 'diminutive and insignificant character'.[197] The present battlements on the north and south elevations were erected towards the end of the nineteenth century. In order to counter the thrust of the broad spreading mass of the building, the tall and narrow buttresses are set close together. The close spacing and the height of the transomed three-light windows add to the effect of loftiness.

As there is no tower, special emphasis was given to the corner turrets and to the prominent façade to the road. The octagonal stone turrets, recalling those of King's College Chapel, Cambridge, have openwork lights and lower panels with shields; that at the north-west corner contains the church's single bell. They are attractive conceits when seen against the dour expanses of white Suffolk bricks beneath. The west front has a wide projecting centre with a large seven-light window beneath an ornamental parapet with blind trefoil panels, central finial and flanking pinnacles. Out of the front projects the western porch, a small-scale tripartite composition with three doorways each framed between buttresses crowned by pinnacles, the central opening being wider and slightly taller than the others, and surmounted by a low-pitched gable. The front has lost much of its original lightness through the replacement in 1957–8 of the original crocketed pinnacles.

The broad proportions so evident in the exterior are equally marked inside, where a flat ceiling borne by nine very long slender transverse ribs crossed by two longitudinal ribs covers a dramatically large space (Plate 10b). The church is planned with a remarkable economy of means, the main consideration clearly being to provide ample space for large congregations at a limited cost without starving the design of ecclesiastical character. With a shallow chancel dominated by an uncommonly wide rectangular nave, it is an

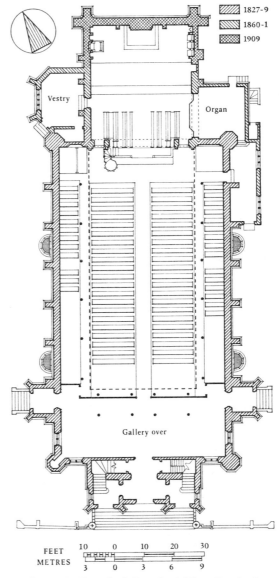

Fig. 23. St. Barnabas' Church, Addison Road, plan

example of a building that follows the Georgian tradition of auditory churches planned rather more for sermons and hymns than for sacramental worship. The long neat panel-fronted side galleries, supported by thin cylindrical cast-iron columns, mask the bases of the windows and were an alteration to Vulliamy's first design, although the panel fronts are very much in sympathy with the original conception. The deep west gallery, enlarged when the side galleries were added, is contemporary with the fabric, and in recent years an entrance lobby has been formed beneath it. Originally, there was a second gallery above, 'containing the organ in a fine case, and seats for the charity children'.[198]

The original chancel was very shallow, being little more than a niche divided from the nave by a triple-arched screen flanked on either side by an identical pulpit and reading desk. The chancel was first reconstructed in 1860–1 to the designs of Thomas Johnson, the Lichfield diocesan architect, the contractors being McLennan and Bird.[199] The alterations enabled 125 more seats to be provided. The screen, pulpit and reading desk were removed at this time, for the very wide arch to Johnson's rearranged chancel was unscreened. The present chancel, dark in contrast to the nave, is essentially of 1909, when the east end of the church was entirely remodelled and extended eastwards by some fifteen feet, an improvement which was made possible by a grant of land from the proprietors of the adjacent blocks of flats known as Oakwood Court in compensation for loss of light and air sustained by the church. The architect for the reconstruction was J. Arthur Reeve, and the contractor was James Carmichael of Wandsworth.[200]

None of Vulliamy's fittings now survive. Some were taken out in 1861, and several more were removed in 1885, when the interior was redecorated in Tudor Gothic style by Dicksee and Dicksee under the architect Arthur Baker.[201] New pews were provided in the nave at this time and the handsome poppy-headed choir stalls were fixed in the still short chancel two years later. Refurnishing continued in the 1890's. The low marble chancel screen, with its beautifully carved seated angels on either side of the steps, and the florid Perpendicular pulpit raised high on an ornate base, were erected in 1895. The organ case was provided in the next year.[202]

The richness of these additions must have emphasized the inadequacy of the old chancel, and encouraged a desire to improve it. The opulently carved stone reredos, with its bold robed and crowned figure of Christ backed by an aureole upon a lush foliate ground and flanked in the lower wings by kneeling angels, was designed by Reeve as a memorial to the Reverend G. R. Thornton, vicar from 1882 to 1905, who, shortly before his death, had been much impressed by Reeve's reredos at St. Saviour's, Westgate, in

Kent. The stone altar, which was based on fifteenth-century tomb designs, was removed at this time, being too small for the new chancel. Enrichment was completed with the erection of the stone canopy to the episcopal throne, while the finely executed piscina and triple sedilia testify to the wealth of the congregation. Messrs. Turner carried out the architectural features of the reredos, and J. E. Taylerson executed the figures.[200]

The glass of the east and west windows was transposed in 1895. The glass now in the east window is by Clayton and Bell, made in 1883. The window was cleaned, reconstructed and raised some feet when the chancel was extended in 1909. The present west window is by O'Connor, and dates from 1851. The canopies and diapered background are rich, but the colour is somewhat garish. Much bright and mostly mid-Victorian stained glass survives in the nave. The two-light window depicting Saints Cecilia and Margaret by the north-west door underneath the west gallery is an interesting Arts and Crafts design, remarkable for its strong drawing and rich gold and yellow colouring, by John Byam Shaw. Opposite the organ in the chancel is a two-light memorial window of 1922 by Geoffrey Webb, a pupil of Sir Ninian Comper. It commemorates parishioners killed in the war of 1914–18, their names being recorded on a stone tablet within a fifteenth-century-style frame in the south-east corner of the nave.[203]

Two mural monuments may be noted. That to George Shaw, the first cousin of John Byam Shaw, in the north-east corner of the nave, was designed in 1901 by Gerald Moira and Francis Derwent Wood (Plate 33d). The pretty monument of wood to John Byam Shaw on the north wall of the nave is a delightful composition in the late fifteenth-century manner, coloured red and dark green with rich gold detail. There is a small painting of Our Lady inset in late fifteenth-century Flemish style, probably by Gilbert Pownall (Plate 33f). [204]

The Church of St. John the Baptist, Holland Road

Plates 20–1; fig. 24

In 1866 the Reverend E. J. May of Nottingham applied to the Ecclesiastical Commissioners for permission to build a church, the patronage of which would be vested in himself. The site which

May proposed was on the west side of Holland Road almost exactly opposite the place where St. John's was eventually built. The principal reason which he advanced for the necessity of a new church was the extensive building operations then taking place on the Holland estate, and he added that, 'had not the monetary panic of last summer taken place,* from 300 to 400 more houses would have been erected by this time ... beyond the large number already erected and mostly inhabited'. The letter implies that his proposal was meeting with the opposition of the incumbent of St. Barnabas', and, although the Ecclesiastical Commissioners were favourably disposed, the assent of the Bishop of London could not be obtained and May's application was rejected. There may well be a hidden story of disputes over doctrine, for within a very short time another clergyman, the Reverend George Booker, had succeeded where May had failed. The dedication to St. John the Baptist had been suggested by May.[205]

The site for Booker's church was made available through the failure of the builder, James Hall, to complete Addison Gardens. A piece of vacant ground lay to the west of the part of the communal garden which had already been laid out and on this a temporary iron church was erected at a cost of £1,700 which was defrayed by Booker; it was opened for divine service on 27 February 1869. The permanent acquisition of the site proved a complicated affair, however. In 1872 John Beattie and Harry Dowding, who undertook to complete James Hall's moribund development, obtained a conveyance of a large piece of land, including the plot on which the temporary church stood.[206] This conveyance made reference to a prior agreement with Booker, who was eventually able to purchase the freehold of the church site for upward of £1,100 in 1875. He conveyed it as a gift to the Ecclesiastical Commissioners in 1884.[207]

Plans for a permanent church to the designs of James Brooks were announced in 1872. The first designs show a tall western tower with a spire and, over the crossing, an octagonal lantern tower topped by a *flèche*.[208] No further progress beyond the laying of the foundation stone was made in that year, however, and a pastoral letter from Booker in 1873 contained a *cri de coeur* about the difficulties being encountered. 'Thus with no gift of a site', he wrote, 'hampered by the special conditions which the circumstances of the land imposed; with no help from Public Church Building Funds, and little from private individuals; having many acquaintances but few friends, and of those none who could call themselves wealthy; ... a wilderness around us, and no decent path through; this church has had to contend with overwhelming difficulties which few others have known'.[209]

Building proper began with the apsidal section of the chancel in 1874; the contractor was Thomas Blake of Gravesend. The remainder of the east end as far as the crossing was not completed until 1885, the builders being Turtle and Appleton. A temporary brick nave was provided and the church was considered sufficiently far advanced to be consecrated on 30 March 1889. The contract for the construction of the nave was taken by Kilby and Gayford in 1890, and in 1892 the church was finished except for the west end. By this time both the lantern tower over the crossing and the western tower had been abandoned, and Brooks provided a new design for the west front in which the principal features were a large rose window and a grand central portal enriched with figure carving flanked by two smaller doorways; three deeply recessed porches were to project in front of these doorways. The rose window and part of the great doorway were completed and encased in rough brickwork, but the remainder of the façade had to await completion until 1909–11, when the work was carried out under the supervision of J. S. Adkins, who had taken over Brooks's practice after the latter's death. He made several alterations to Brooks's design, the most important of which were the substitution of a baptistry for the porch in front of the central doorway and the enclosing of the side porches. The work was carried out by E. A. Roome and Company and the stone carving, including the statue of St. John the Baptist, was by J. E. Taylerson. When finished the façade drew a scathing comment from Maurice B. Adams: 'St. John's, Holland Road, one of Brooks' most noble buildings, has been spoiled by the dismal and incoherent west front . . .; this is to be deplored, as I think his original design, with the western tower, was perhaps the best that he ever conceived'. The total of the accounts submitted for completing the

---

* A reference to the failure of Overend and Gurney in 1866.

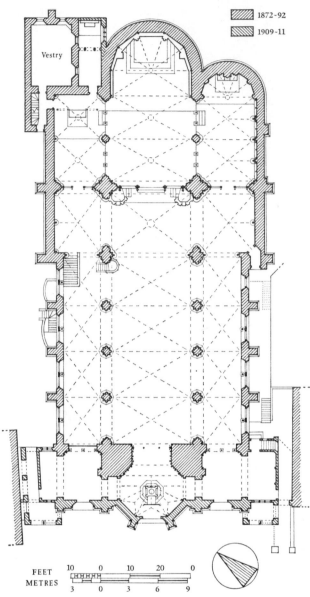

1872-92
1909-11

Vestry

FEET
METRES
10   0   10   20   0
3   0   3   6   9

Fig. 24. Church of St. John The Baptist, Holland Road,
· plan

various parts of the church, including architect's
fees, amounted to approximately £25,000.[210]

Despite the cluster of fussy additions by Adkins,
the west façade of St. John's (Plate 20a) is a
composition of considerable character and emphasis in the context of Holland Road. Behind the
porches, the west front proper is flanked by corner
buttresses gabled in stages and rising to octagonal
pinnacles. It is pierced by a huge rose window set

within a semi-circular-headed arch surmounted by
an open arcade of seven stepped cusped lancets
that suggest a French ancestry. Its tall gable is
pierced by an arcade of trefoil arches on colonnettes which is blind except for the central arch.
Above, under the cross that crowns the apex, is a
quatrefoil light.

The main door to the church from the baptistry porch is richly carved with figures representing the Wise and Foolish Virgins, added by J. E.
Taylerson in 1909–11. This cathedralesque entrance, part of the design by Brooks, is French in
manner, and the architectural origins are even
more apparent in the interior of the church
(Plate 21), except that the vaulting springs from
corbelled brackets and is not continued in ribs
down to the floor as would have been the case in a
true French example.

The church is vaulted and huge, all in stone,
and is dignified and solemn. It consists of a four-
bay clerestoried nave and aisles; short north and
south transepts, so characteristic of Brooks's work,
with a crossing broader than it is long; a poly-
gonally apsed chancel; and north and south
chapels, that to the south being the Lady Chapel.

The French flavour of the church is most
marked in the chancel, the style being Burgundian,
but the nave owes something to English Cistercian
prototypes of the thirteenth century. The lighting
is dim and mysterious, and the overall effect is
suitably medieval. The excellent massing and
control of spaces is typical of Brooks at his best,
but the relationship between the spaces is obscured by the elaborately carved three-arched stone
chancel screen, which he designed in 1895;[211] by
the similar but modified stone screens in the
arches between the chapels and the transepts; and
by the parclose screens in the chancel arcades.
The sculptured detail and figures tend to be out
of character with the architecture of the church
as a whole. In the nave itself, the praying angels,
suspended at right angles to the walls at the apex of
each arch of the arcade, are particularly unsatisfactory, and would only make sense as part of a
timber roof.

There is a lavish stone pulpit, above which is a
richly carved wooden canopy fixed to the north-
west pier of the crossing. On either side of the
chancel screen are ambones of white stone with
coloured marble panels and colonnettes.

The Builder commented favourably on the
solidity and massiveness of Brooks's design, and on

the sparing use of ornament, which in 1885 consisted only of dog-tooth carving on the ribs and capitals. The Architectural Association visited the church in 1891 to view the vaulting of the nave, then in course of completion, a sight which was rare even then.[212]

The richly gilt polychrome reredos is partly the work of Brooks and partly that of Adkins. As first executed in 1892 it was relatively plain and it stood clear of the apse wall. Subsequently the statuary and painting were added and it was moved to the rear of the chancel. In 1909 Adkins gave it extra height by the addition of a blind arcade round the apse wall, and the three sides of the original reredos were separated by projecting piers. Adkins also designed the reredos in the Lady Chapel, the altar of which is brightly painted and has deep relief panels.[213] Other colour is provided by the stained glass, of which some good examples exist in the windows of the apse. Nearly all the glass is by Clayton and Bell, although there is a two-light lancet window of 1895 by C. E. Kempe in the second bay from the east in the south aisle.

No. 8 Addison Road

Plates 90–1

This remarkable house was designed by Halsey Ricardo for (Sir) Ernest Debenham, who had previously lived in another house designed by Ricardo (No. 57 Melbury Road). No. 8 Addison Road occupies the sites of three previous houses (Nos. 8, 9 and 10) and was built under an agreement of March 1905, Debenham being granted a lease in July 1906 for seventy-eight and one half years at an annual rent of £430. By this the lessee was to be allowed at the end of the term of the lease 'to take down and remove all or any glazed tiles wood carving marble and mosaic fastened to or constituting part of the interior', provided that he made good with suitable materials. Among the buildings which Debenham was required to complete within twelve months of securing the lease was a 'Motor House'.[214] The only businesses for which the premises were originally allowed to be used were those of an artist, a physician or a surgeon, but in 1955 permission was given for the house to be used as a training college for teachers of dancing and drama, and in 1965 it was taken as the headquarters and college of the Richmond Fellowship for Mental Welfare and Rehabilitation.[215]

The house is an example of the structural polychromy advocated by Halsey Ricardo in lectures and papers given over several years. It represents an attempt to erect a building immune to the destructive effects of a city atmosphere, and is the expression of an architecture dependent on colour rather than on light and shadow.

The elevations consist of three elements: the basement, forming a podium on which the house rests; the ground and first floors embraced within a giant Florentine motif of pilasters carrying entablatures from which arches spring, and crowned by a richly modillioned cornice; and an attic storey over which is a smaller modillioned cornice. The tall chimneys are decorated with arches and cornices.

The basement is faced with blue-grey semi-vitrified bricks. The pilasters, arches, cornices and main elements of the house above are of Doulton glazed terra-cotta known as Carrara ware, the cream colour being relieved in the upper stages by bands of different colour. In the panels formed by this Carrara ware framework, the walls are faced with glazed Burmantofts bricks, the lower parts coloured green, and the upper a bright blue. The roof is covered with green tiles, semi-circular in section, and imported from Spain. The walls of the long entrance loggia and the corridor connecting the house with the breakfast-room in the garden are lined with De Morgan tiles.

The main feature of the plan is a central domed hall around which is a gallery at first-floor level connecting the upstairs rooms. The dome and pendentives over the hall are covered with mosaics depicting subjects from classical mythology and small portraits of the Debenham family against a background of sinuous plant patterns; the work was executed by Gaetano Meo from designs by Ricardo. The passages, hall and stairs are lined with De Morgan tiles, mostly in plain colour, but sometimes forming elaborate patterns in which the predominant motifs are peacocks and arabesques of Art Nouveau foliage. The colours, mainly turquoises, purples and blues, are rich and glowing. The marble work used in conjunction with the tiles was supplied and worked by Walton, Gooddy and Cripps Limited, and the carving was by W. Aumonier. Marble and tiles are also used in combination in the sumptuous fireplaces throughout the house. The main rooms have ornamental plaster ceilings executed by Messrs.

Priestley from designs by Ernest Gimson. The library is elegantly fitted out in mahogany with delicate inlays of wood and mother-of-pearl in Art Nouveau designs. There is much enriched glass in the house, designed by E. S. Prior. The metalwork throughout, including the electric light switches, was principally designed and made by the Birmingham Guild of Handicraft. The builders were George Trollope and Sons with Colls and Sons.[216]

Nos. 10 and 10A (South House) Holland Park Road

These two houses, substantially dating from 1892–1893, were originally one house, which was known as No. 3 Holland Park Road until 1908 when it was renumbered 10.

The site was formerly occupied by the farm-house of Holland Farm. The laying out of Melbury Road in 1875 necessitated the removal of several of the farm buildings, but the farmhouse, which had been rebuilt in 1859, was not demolished. In 1892 the portrait painter (Sir) James Jebusa Shannon, entered into an agreement with the lessee, Ethel Tisdall, who was probably the daughter of Edmund Charles Tisdall (see page 127), to spend at least £3,500 in rebuilding or altering the farmhouse and erecting a studio adjoining. In return Ethel Tisdall was to grant him a lease for sixty years (the term remaining of a lease granted by Lord Holland in 1859) at an annual rent of £280. The plans, by the architects W. E. and F. Brown, were approved on behalf of the Earl of Ilchester, who had become the ground landlord, and work was begun by the builders, Thomas Gregory and Company, towards the end of 1892.[217]

The house and studio were joined together and remained one unit during Shannon's lifetime. From the plans, it appears that the structural core of the western, or residential, part of the building was provided by the existing farm house, but the exterior was completely altered to match the studio which was built to the east. An addition was made to the north-east of the studio in 1908. After Shannon's death in 1923 the two parts were divided, the eastern becoming No. 10 and the western No. 10A (now called South House).[218]

Leighton House: No. 12 Holland Park Road
Plate 77; figs. 25–7

The factors which led Frederic (later Lord) Leighton to choose a site on the Holland estate when he decided to have a house built for himself are described on page 124. Leighton's letters indicate that he was negotiating for the site in the summer and autumn of 1864. In August he wrote to his father, 'As to the possible expense of the house, my dear Papa, you have taken I assure you false alarm. I shall indeed devote more to the architectural part of the building than *you* would care to do; but in the first place architecture and *much ornament* are not inseparable, and besides, whatever I do I shall undertake *nothing without an estimate*.' In September he complained about the 'preposterous charge' that Lady Holland's surveyor, John Henry Browne, was making for drawing up an agreement and added, 'My architect is Aitchison, an old friend.'[219]

A lease of the house was granted by Lady Holland in April 1866 for ninety-nine years from 1864, an unusual feature of it being a clause allowing Leighton to remove 'any Chimney piece in the nature of a Work of Art' and to substitute a plain marble chimneypiece to the value of £16,[220] presumably if he wished to move to another house. The builders were Messrs. Hack and Son, and the cost was about £4,500.[221] The house, which was ready for occupation by the end of 1866,[36] was originally known as No. 2 Holland Park Road until renumbered in 1908.

The extent to which Leighton influenced his architect, George Aitchison, in the design of the house has been the subject of much speculation. Aitchison had a considerable reputation in his day and was Professor of Architecture at the Royal Academy from 1887 to 1905 and President of the Royal Institute of British Architects from 1896 to 1899, but before receiving his commission from Leighton, whom he had first met in Italy in 1853, he was chiefly concerned with the design of commercial buildings.[222] Leighton himself received the R.I.B.A. gold medal for the knowledge of architecture which he displayed in the backgrounds to his paintings, and no doubt he had definite ideas about the kind of house he wanted, but several of the features of Leighton House reflect Aitchison's ideas about architecture. On more than one occasion Aitchison exhorted his fellow architects to break away from too rigid a

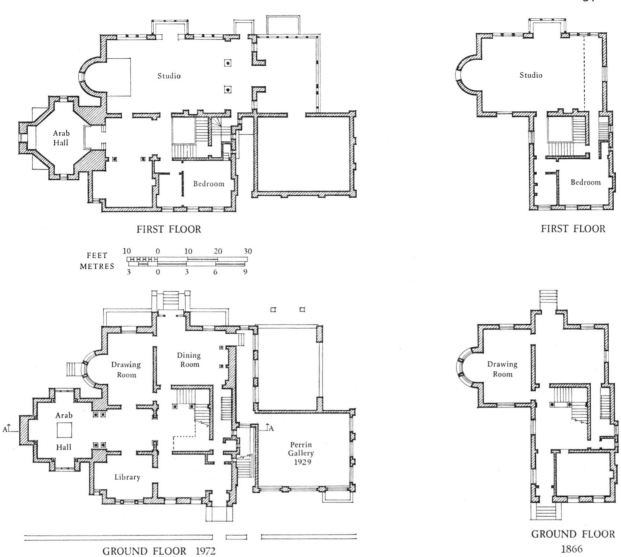

Studio

Arab
Hall

Bedroom

FIRST FLOOR

Studio

Bedroom

FIRST FLOOR

FEET
METRES

10   0   10   20   30

3   0   3   6   9

Drawing
Room

Dining
Room

Arab
Hall

A

A

Perrin
Gallery
1929

Library

GROUND FLOOR 1972

Drawing
Room

GROUND FLOOR
1866

Fig. 25. Leighton House, Holland Park Road, plans

dependence on historical styles, particularly in such matters as the type of mouldings used, and it is perhaps the care taken over both the design and execution of details that is the outstanding feature of the architecture of the house.

The Building News in November 1866 described the newly built house with approval. It commented on the originality of detailing and remarked, 'It is the house of an artist, with a large and lofty studio on the first floor, and it expresses its purpose honestly to the casual passer-by, and no more'.[221] The restrained classical style of the exterior, executed in red Suffolk bricks with Caen stone dressings, did not meet with universal approbation, however, and a few weeks later in the same journal E. W. Godwin gave an altogether different verdict. 'Take Mr. Aitchison's house', he wrote, ' . . . and, allowing for its completion, what can be said of it, except that from one end to the other it is altogether unsatisfactory. . . . Mr. Webb's work, in Mr. Val Prinsep's house next door, comes into close comparison with it, and is chiefly admirable for the very things in which its neighbour is so utterly deficient—viz., in beauty of skyline and pleasing arrangement of gabled mass'.[223]

SOUTH ELEVATION TO HOLLAND PARK ROAD

PERRIN
GALLERY
1929

NORTH ELEVATION TO GARDEN

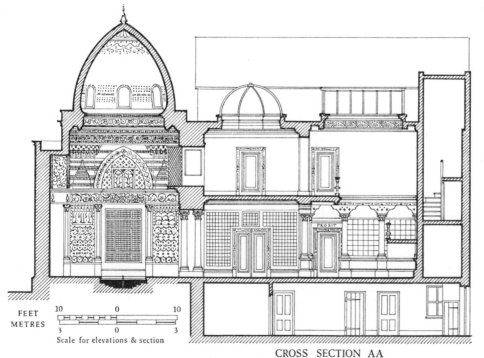

FEET
METRES

10   0   10

3   0   3

Scale for elevations & section

CROSS SECTION AA

TOWER
HOUSE

MELBURY ROAD

LEIGHTON
HOUSE

HOLLAND PARK ROAD

SITE PLAN

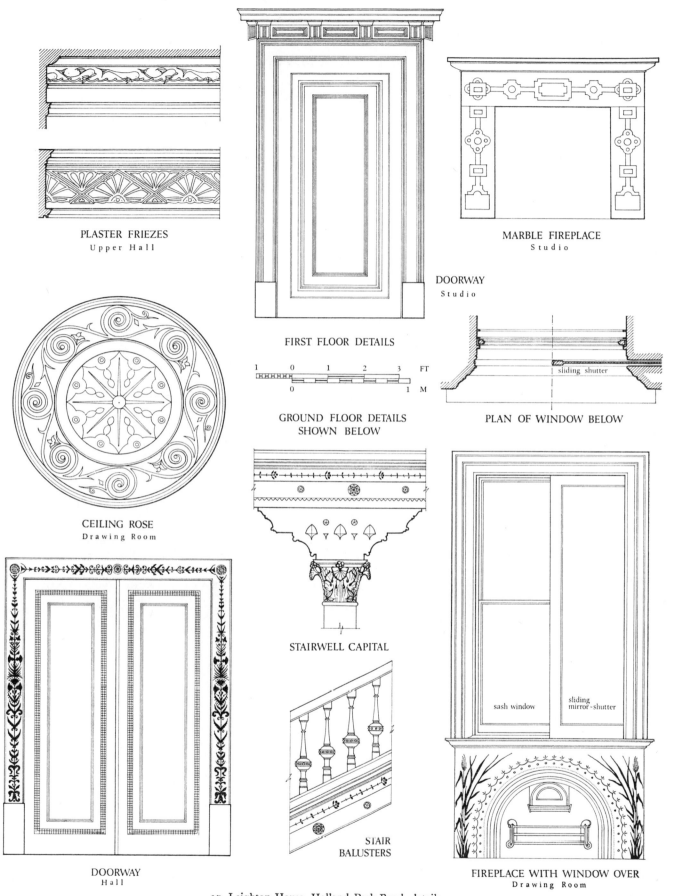

PLASTER FRIEZES
Upper Hall

MARBLE FIREPLACE
Studio

DOORWAY
Studio

FIRST FLOOR DETAILS

1   0   1   2   3   FT
0   1   M

GROUND FLOOR DETAILS
SHOWN BELOW

sliding shutter

PLAN OF WINDOW BELOW

CEILING ROSE
Drawing Room

STAIRWELL CAPITAL

STAIR
BALUSTERS

sash window   sliding
mirror-shutter

DOORWAY
Hall

FIREPLACE WITH WINDOW OVER
Drawing Room

27. Leighton House, Holland Park Road, details
Fig. 26 (facing page). Leighton House, Holland Park Road, elevations and section

As first built the house was much smaller than it is now and the front was only three windows wide, although it was always intended to extend this to five bays. The plan was dominated by the studio on the first floor at the rear, facing north. It originally measured about forty-five by twenty-five feet and had a gallery at the east end. At first the great central window of the studio was stone-framed but this was soon replaced by an iron-framed window to let in more light. A stair led from the east end of the studio to a side entrance which was to be used by models, Leighton clearly having a more conventional Victorian sense of social propriety than his neighbour Val Prinsep, in whose house the models 'usually come up the main staircase'.[224] Apart from the studio the main room was a lofty hall (Plate 77a), lit principally by a large skylight in anticipation of later extensions which were to make it totally enclosed. Only one main bedroom was included in the plan, to discourage long-term guests who might interfere with Leighton's work, although servants' bedrooms were provided over his first-floor apartments and were reached by a back stair. The interior decorations were characterized by a bold use of colour. The woodwork was generally lacquered black with parts of the delicate incised leaf and flower mouldings of the door and window architraves picked out in gold. The beams supported by the stone columns of the entrance hall were painted blue and the sunk ornament above the capitals silvered. The colour of the studio walls was red. Among the surviving original fittings is the drawing-room fireplace, which was placed directly underneath a window. At night the window could be covered by sliding shutters to form a mirror (fig. 27).* Several items of furniture for the house were especially designed by Aitchison.

The first addition to the house was made in 1869–70 when the studio was lengthened to the east. A drawing made by Aitchison in 1870 for the coloured glass of two windows, which were inserted as part of this alteration, indicates that the Arab influence which was later to be so important was already present at this time.[225]

Outstanding among several additions made in 1877–9 was the Arab Hall (Plate 77b), built to house the collection of tiles Leighton had acquired during his visits to the East. According to

Aitchison and Walter Crane, the design of the hall was based on the palace of La Zisa in Palermo. The numerous seventeenth-century tiles are complemented by the carved wooden Damascus lattice-work of the same period in the windows and gallery above. There arc also several single tiles of Turkish origin dating from the previous century, and even earlier examples from Persia. The west wall contains a wooden alcove with inset tiles of the fourteenth century. On each side are brilliantly coloured plaques with floral patterns, and several tiles also depict birds. Apart from the eastern tiles the Arab Hall contains the work of several outstanding Victorian artists. The capitals of the smaller columns were modelled by (Sir) J. Edgar Boehm from Aitchison's designs, and the birds in the gilded caps of the large columns were by Randolph Caldecott. The mosaic frieze was designed by Walter Crane. Many of the tiles in the passage to the Arab Hall and elsewhere in the house are by William De Morgan. The builders were Messrs. Woodward of Finsbury, and among the specialist contractors were George P. White of Vauxhall Bridge Road for the marble work, Burke and Company for the mosaics, and Harland and Fisher for the painted decorations executed from Aitchison's designs.[226]

At the time the Arab Hall was built the ground storey at the front of the house was extended to the west, and the entrance was moved from the western of the original three bays to the eastern. The effect of all these additions was the abandonment of the five-bay symmetrical façade with a central entrance which had been originally envisaged, in favour of an asymmetrical grouping. The cut and moulded brickwork of the new parts reflects an Islamic inspiration. Aitchison also provided a winter studio to the east of the main studio in 1889. Originally it was raised on cast-iron columns, but the ground floor has now been bricked-in. In 1895 he also provided a top-lit picture gallery on the south side of the studio floor above the single-storey extension built in 1877–1879.[227]

After Leighton's death in 1896 several attempts were made to preserve the house for the nation. His two sisters, who were his executrices, assigned the house to representatives of the Leighton House Committee, which had been formed for this

---

* A similar feature exists at No. 2 Palace Green.

purpose, and in 1901 the leasehold interest was offered as a gift to the newly formed Kensington Borough Council, but negotiations broke down over the terms of the transfer. A further approach in 1925 was more successful, and the Council completed the acquisition of the house when it purchased the freehold in 1926 for £2,750.[228]

In 1927 Mrs. Henry Perrin of Holland Villas Road offered to provide additional exhibition galleries and chose Halsey Ricardo as the architect. After several alterations, including a considerable reduction in the amount of window space originally intended, Ricardo's designs were accepted. Approval had to be sought from the Holland estate under the usual provision that no alterations to the architectural character of, or additions to, houses which had been sold could be carried out without licence. It was suggested in favour of the extension that it would hide the cast-iron columns of the winter studio, and permission was secured. The Perrin Galleries were opened in 1929.[229] The interior of the ground-floor gallery was redesigned by Sir Hugh Casson in 1962 to provide a temporary home for the British Theatre Museum.

No. 14 Holland Park Road
Fig. 28

This house, which was known as No. 1 Holland Park Road until it was renumbered in 1908, was designed by Philip Webb for the painter, Valentine Cameron Prinsep. The associations of the Prinsep family with the Holland estate are described on page 125, and the site for Val Prinsep's new house was only a short distance from Little Holland House, where his father lived, and where he had spent much of his youth in the company of his mentor, George Frederic Watts. His choice of Webb as his architect was probably the result of his early association with William Morris and his circle.

Webb was working on plans for the house in 1864.* In January 1865 Prinsep entered into an agreement with Lady Holland to build a house to the value of at least £1,000, and the contract drawings were signed by the builders, Jackson and Shaw, in the same month. A lease for ninety-nine years from 1864 was granted by Lady Holland

in March 1866 and the house was ready for occupation by the middle of that year.[231]

Originally consisting of two storeys and a basement, the house was built of red brick with a sparing use of brick dressings. In its apparent simplicity and absence of ornament, and with its mixture of segmental and pointed arches to the doorway and windows, the house reflected Webb's work at the Red House, Bexley Heath, for William Morris. The original front, or south, elevation, which was completely changed by subsequent alterations by Webb himself (fig. 28), consisted of three bays made up of two short gabled wings projecting on each side of a central recess, the bay to the west, which contained the doorway, being slightly wider. The rear elevation was dominated by two huge studio windows admitting north light, and at the west end of the studio there was a large oriel window making a conspicuous feature on the west side elevation. Several of the windows of the house anticipated the 'Queen Anne' style.

The studio, which measured forty feet by twenty-five feet, took up practically the whole of the first floor. The remaining space was hardly sufficient for domestic requirements, and the dining-room, Prinsep's bedroom and a spare bedroom were all situated on the ground floor. Prinsep was a bachelor at the time the house was built, but the original plan allowed for its extension to the east at a later date.

The first major alterations were made by Webb in 1877[232] when the front was raised by an extra storey (because of the height of the studio the rear part of the house had formerly been higher than the front), and the studio was extended by arching over the central recess at first-floor level. This extension led to the construction of a drawbridge, which could be raised for the passage of large canvases, in the gallery which Webb had originally provided for the studio. In 1892 Webb added the new wing to the east which had been anticipated both in the original planning and the alterations of 1877. This wing, which provided two more bays to the street elevation, extended beyond the line of the original garden front to give the house a reverse L-shape.[233]

During the twentieth century further considerable alterations were made, particularly

* Maurice B. Adams called it 'the first artist's house of its kind erected in London',[224] and Henry-Russell Hitchcock has described it as the first English studio-house.[230] Both these judgments should be qualified by the fact that Aitchison was designing his house for Leighton at almost exactly the same time.

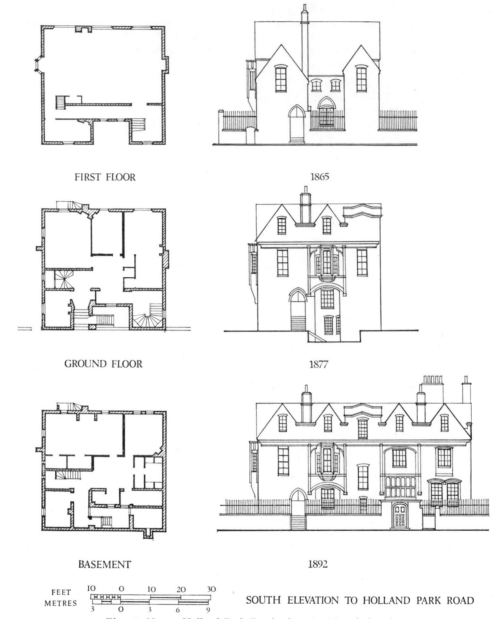

FIRST FLOOR

1865

GROUND FLOOR

1877

BASEMENT

1892

FEET 10 0 10 20 30
METRES 3 0 3 6 9

SOUTH ELEVATION TO HOLLAND PARK ROAD

Fig. 28. No. 14 Holland Park Road, plans (1865) and elevations

to the fenestration, and in 1948 the house was converted into flats.[234]

Nos. 2, 2A, 2B and 4 Melbury Road, Melbury Cottage, and No. 24B Holland Park Road
Plates 82, 84b

In March 1876 Messrs. Adamson and Son of Turnham Green, builders, gave notice to the district surveyor of their intention to build two houses and a studio for 'Mr. Thornicroft'. Although ninety-year leases of these two houses, originally Nos. 2 and 4 Melbury Road, were granted to Thomas Thornycroft, a sculptor,[235] they were built for, and in some measure to the designs of, his more famous sculptor son, (Sir) Hamo Thornycroft. They are of considerable interest in conception as a semi-detached pair,

No. 2 being intended for the Thornycrofts' own residence with a wing containing several studios added to the south-west, while No. 4 was a speculation to let or sell in the normal way. How far Hamo Thornycroft was responsible for the design of these houses is difficult to estimate, but he had 'the advantage of suggestions and technical knowledge afforded by Mr. J. Belcher, architect'.[236] It is perhaps significant that when he wanted another studio built in 1891 he turned to Belcher, who was a lifelong friend,[42] to provide the designs. Certainly this pleasantly asymmetrical pair, with the huge projecting chimney stack accentuating the division between the two houses, shows a careful and sensitive handling.

No. 4 was occupied by Mr. and Mrs. Russell Barrington. Mrs. Barrington, who was the sister-in-law of Walter Bagehot, was a writer who also had some pretensions to being an artist. The house was brought to her attention by Watts and she persuaded her husband to take it. 'I felt this was indeed a delightful opportunity of entering into the highest precincts of art under the most helpful auspices', she wrote later.[237] After Leighton's death she became a leading figure in the movement to preserve Leighton House as a public memorial.

The working quarters of No. 2 were more distinctly separated from the living rooms than in most of the artists' houses of the late Victorian period. The south-west wing contained a large studio for sculpture and several smaller ones for other members of the Thornycroft family. The single-storey entrance porch to the west of the house was set in line with the studios and opened into a small vestibule which led either directly into the house or, via a gallery, into the studios. This plan has enabled the house to be converted into several separate units. In 1931 the present entrance porch was added, and the old entrance way and gallery were converted into a separate dwelling, now known as Melbury Cottage. The alterations were carried out by A. M. Cawthorne, architect.[238] The studios were already subdivided by this date and are now known as No. 2A Melbury Road and No. 24B Holland Park Road. In 1892 a new studio-house (now No. 2B Melbury Road) was built to the west of No. 2 to the designs of John Belcher (Plate 84b); the builders were again Adamson and Sons.[239] After completion of this building, Hamo Thornycroft lived there and No. 2 appears to have been let.[132]

No. 6 Melbury Road
Plate 76. Demolished

This house was built for George Frederic Watts, whose previous home for many years, Little Holland House, had to be demolished for the laying out of Melbury Road. Watts also called his new house Little Holland House.

Watts's architect was a friend, Frederick Pepys Cockerell, the son of Charles Robert Cockerell. Building began early in 1875 and Watts was able to take up residence in February 1876. The Earl of Ilchester granted a lease of the house to Val Prinsep, who gave up part of his garden in order to provide Watts's house with extensive grounds, for a term expiring in 1963 to correspond with that of Prinsep's own house, No. 14 Holland Park Road. Prinsep immediately sub-let No. 6 Melbury Road to Watts.[240]

The eclectic exterior reflected the complex planning of the interior (Plate 76). This included three studios on the ground floor, two of them—for painting and sculpture—rising through the first floor, a small sitting-room on the ground floor and two bedrooms on the first floor. The shortage of living rooms was probably deliberately intended, as in the case of Leighton House, to enable Watts to pursue his work without interruption from too many guests. Several additions were made to the house after Cockerell's death by George Aitchison, including a picture gallery.[241] Watts lived in the house until shortly before his death in 1904. It was demolished c. 1965 and replaced by Kingfisher House, a block of flats.

No. 8 Melbury Road
Plate 78

This house was designed by Richard Norman Shaw for Marcus Stone. The Royal Academy possesses drawings for the house dated September 1875, and the builder, W. H. Lascelles, a contractor often used by Shaw, gave notice to the district surveyor of his intention to begin building in December of that year. Stone was granted a ninety-year lease from 1875 in December 1877 at an annual rent of £90.[242] The house was converted into flats c. 1950.

Built of red brick, with cut and moulded brick dressings characteristic of Norman Shaw's work, and with several of his tall, narrow sash windows, the house originally consisted of two tall storeys over a basement. On the Melbury Road elevation, which has been little altered, Shaw resolved the problem of reconciling a domestic front with the need for ample north light by providing three large oriel windows taking up most of the second storey. Originally these oriels were symmetrical, each one crowned by a tile-hung gable containing a small window, but the central window was extended upwards, no doubt to provide more light, probably shortly after the house was built, and almost certainly to Shaw's design.* The oriels were designed to be executed in wood but the district surveyor refused permission and concrete had to be used. The first floor was taken up with the studio and ancillary rooms, including a winter studio to the east, but the ground floor reflected a greater concern with domestic comfort than was required by some of Stone's fellow artists in the Melbury Road colony. The interior has been much altered but originally it was described as of a 'quiet and homely character', reflecting 'the spirit of an Old English Home'. A back stair was provided for models in a shallow extension which was built on to the south-western corner of the house and crowned with a Dutch gable. The studios were heated by hot-water pipes, but an angle fireplace was also provided 'for the company a cheering fire can afford'.[244]

No. 14 Melbury Road
Plates 81b, 83. Demolished

The last artist to take a plot in Melbury Road during the initial phase of house building there was Colin Hunter. He engaged the architect J. J. Stevenson to provide the designs, and tenders for building were received in August 1876. The lowest, for £4,594 by J. Tyerman of Walworth Road, was accepted and work began at once.[245] The exterior was of red brick with an abundant use of cut and moulded brick dressings. The dominant features of the street front were two large projecting bays crowned by elaborate gables containing the ground-floor dining-room and studio. Between them was a recessed entrance porch, and, to the west, another recessed part contained the kitchen. Above the kitchen was a day-nursery with a two-sided projecting bay supported by a large bracket. A drawing-room was

also provided on the ground floor in another projecting bay to the rear, this combination of kitchen and ancillary rooms with living-rooms and studio on the ground floor being unique in the planning of houses in the Holland estate artists' colony. The first floor was given over to bedrooms, dressing-rooms and nurseries, and there were more bedrooms in the attic. Another entrance, leading directly to the studio, was provided to the east, perhaps for models. The house was damaged during the war of 1939–45 and was demolished shortly afterwards.

Tower House: No. 29 Melbury Road
Plates 81b, 85–9; figs. 29–30

This house, numbered 9 until 1967, was designed by the architect William Burges for his own occupation. Burges began to make drawings for the house in July 1875, but his initial designs differed in some ways from those executed. In particular, the staircase turret, which is the dominant feature of the street front and gives the house its name, did not appear on the first plan. By the end of the year, however, Burges had decided on the present form of the house. No doubt with his designs for Castell Coch still fresh in mind, he placed the stairs in a circular tower crowned by a conical cap of slate. A building agreement was concluded with the Earl of Ilchester in December 1875 and building began in 1876. The contractors were Ashby Brothers of Kingsland Road and the basic cost was estimated to be £6,000. Burges was granted a lease in February 1877 for ninety years from 1875 at an annual ground rent of £50 for the first two years and £100 thereafter.[246]

The design stems from French domestic Gothic of the thirteenth century derived through the influence of Viollet-le-Duc. It makes use of themes explored and developed in Burges's work at Cardiff for the Marquess of Bute. The materials used are a hard red brick with stone dressings and grey slates in diminishing courses for the roof. There are two principal storeys over a basement and a commodious garret in the roof. The three main living-rooms on the ground floor form an L-shaped block with a square entrance hall in the angle, facing south and east. The circular staircase tower, flanked by a small gabled wing, is

* It had been altered by 1896.[243]

placed in front of the hall and approached from it through a pair of pointed arches. A double porch serves both the main entrance and the garden door behind it.

The street front (Plate 85a) is characterized by a striking association of the steep principal gable and the stair turret. The ground and first floors of the house are marked by storey- and sill-bands and in general there are moulded stone dressings to the eaves and gables of the roof, the chimney stacks being finished in moulded brick. The larger windows have stone mullions and transoms with square or cusped heads to the lights but some of the smaller openings are arched in brick or have plain stone lintels. The stone porch has square piers with carved capitals (the first pier was intended to be embellished with further carving) and a deep entablature with an arcaded cornice.

On the garden front (Plate 85b) the western part is again gabled, matching the gable to the street, the centre line of this element being emphasized by a stepped buttress which divides the pair of windows lighting the library. These have finely carved lintels and, like the dining-room windows on the front, emphatically modelled mullions. To the side of the library is a larger range of mullioned and transomed windows belonging to the drawing-room and surmounted by a balcony with a pierced front of brick and stone carried on consoles below the three-windowed width of the armoury on the first floor. An enormous gabled dormer rivalling the main gable breaks into the steep slated roof and carries a shining convex mirror in its apex.*

The interior is decorated in Burges's characteristic manner, every detail having received minute study in a remarkable set of working drawings, some four hundred of which are preserved at the Royal Institute of British Architects. Each room has a unifying decorative theme realized with lavish use of painted decoration, stained glass and carvings, all of a very high quality. On the two main floors the ceilings are beamed, with supporting corbels of stone, and the windows are recessed within broad segmental arches. The chimneypieces have tapered hoods of medieval form and several are treated with great elaboration (Plate 89).

The entrance porch, the inner part of which is enclosed by glazed screens, is incomplete in its decoration but has a mosaic floor depicting Pinkie, Burges's favourite dog. The entrance hall, to which access is gained through a heavy bronze-covered door with figure-subjects in relief panels, rises through two storeys to terminate in a painted ceiling based on the emblems of the constellations arranged according to their positions at the time of the first occupation of the house. The hall has a fine mosaic floor representing a labyrinth in the centre of which Theseus slays the Minotaur. Above plain dados the walls are painted as stone, with scarlet joints in simulation of ashlaring, and over the doorways to each of the major rooms are painted emblems appropriate to their use. Figures representing day and night appear in painted aedicules at gallery level on either side of the hall. The fire-hood opposite to the entrance door is more severely treated than those in other rooms, being simply lined out with scarlet jointing. The garden door into the porch is, like the front door, bronze covered, this time with a relief of the Madonna and Child.

According to Burges's brother-in-law, R. P. Pullan, the decorative scheme in the dining-room at the front of the house (Plate 88a) was 'meant to convey an idea of Chaucer's House of Fame'. But apart from a seated bronze figure of Fame which formerly occupied a position on the marble chimney-hood, none of the decorations appear to have any connexion with Chaucer's poem.† The walls of the room are lined with Devonshire marble below a deep frieze of glazed tiles depicting characters from familiar fairy tales, and the ceiling is covered in enamelled iron and decorated with emblems representing the sun surrounded by the planets and signs of the Zodiac.

The library on the garden side of the house is decorated with themes appropriate to literature and the liberal arts (Plate 86b). The chimneypiece (Plate 89a), one of Burges's most ambitious compositions, has a superstructure of carved and painted Caen stone in the form of a medieval castle. Figures in front of it represent the dispersal of the parts of speech at the time of the Tower of Babel and Nimrod sits in a turreted and gabled niche high in the castle. Below the mantel-shelf a fine plain surround of Mexican onyx is surmounted by a carved frieze in which all of the

---

* The relationship between the plans and elevations of Tower House and an earlier house by Burges at Cardiff is discussed by C. Handley-Read in *Country Life*, 17 March 1966, pp. 600–4.

† The figure of Fame was stolen when the house became derelict between 1962 and 1966.

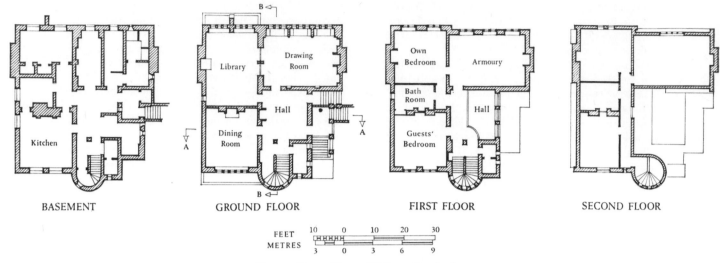

BASEMENT   GROUND FLOOR   FIRST FLOOR   SECOND FLOOR

Fig. 29. Tower House, Melbury Road, plans

letters of the alphabet are incorporated—with the exception of H, which has been 'dropped' on to the onyx below the frieze. In the ceiling the founders of systems of theology and law are seen, and on the doors of the bookcases which surround the room is an illustrated alphabet of architecture and the visual arts with a scene of artists and craftsmen at their work on each lettered door. Pictures of birds by H. Stacy Marks are incorporated into the backs of the bookcase doors. Where visible the walls of the room are painted with a diaper pattern and above the bookcase runs a continuous deep modelled and gilded frieze of formalized foliage.

A wide opening opposite the library fireplace, furnished with sliding doors and a central pair of marble columns, leads into one end of the drawing-room. The execution of the decorative scheme here seems to have been incomplete at the time of Burges's death although drawings had been prepared, and cartoons appear pinned to the walls and ceiling in the photographs taken to illustrate the description of the house by R. P. Pullan in 1885 (Plate 86a). The theme in the drawing-room is 'the tender passion of Love' and the chimney-piece, a fine counterpart to the one in the library, is carved with figures from Chaucer's *Roman de la Rose*. Recently the scheme originally designed for the walls and ceiling has been executed from Burges's drawings. The three windows with their original stained glass are set in deep reveals with

marble linings and ornamented with ball-flower enrichments.

Back in the hall the stair is approached through the two pointed arches divided by a marble column with a carved capital and base. The stained glass in the windows of the stair turret represents 'the Storming of the Castle of Love' and the wall treatment of the entrance hall continues for the whole height of the stair.

Off the first-floor gallery with its turned wood balustrade the two main bedrooms and the armoury are approached. In the guest room on the street front the theme is 'the Earth and its productions' (Plate 87a). The ceiling here is painted with fleur-de-lis and butterfly designs and a convex mirror in a gilded surround is placed at the crossing of the main beams along which are painted frogs and mice. The frieze of flowers growing *au naturel* within a Gothic arcade, once obliterated, has been repainted in the recent renovations.

Burges's own bedroom overlooking the garden is decorated with 'the Sea and its inhabitants' (Plate 87b). The elaborate ceiling (Plate 88b), divided into panels by painted and gilded beams and semi-shafts, is set with tiny convex mirrors within gilt stars. Below the level of the corbels is a deep frieze with fish and eels swimming amongst formalized waves. The frieze to the chimney-piece also depicts fish amongst waves, this time carved in relief, whilst above, on the fire-hood, a

Fig. 30 (facing page). Tower House, Melbury Road, elevations and sections

SOUTH ELEVATION TO MELBURY ROAD

NORTH ELEVATION TO GARDEN

SECTION AA

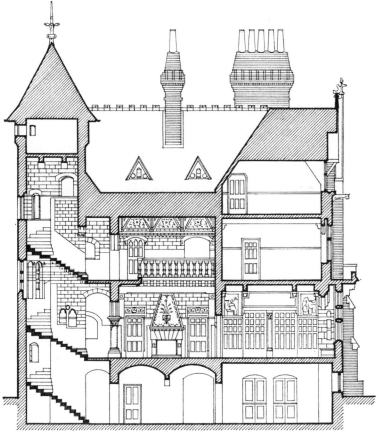

SECTION BB

FEET
METRES

10   0   10
3   0   3

Scale for elevations & sections

vigorously modelled mermaid gazes into a looking-glass (Plate 89b). Sea-shells, coral, seaweed and a mer-baby are also represented.

The large room over the drawing-room originally housed Burges's collection of armour and was known in his time as the armoury. It now contains little of interest beyond the carved chimneypiece with a crocketed gable rising in front of the hood and three roundels carved with medieval versions of Venus, Juno and Minerva.

The storey in the roof, now somewhat altered, contained rooms known as the day and night nurseries (although Burges had no family and remained a bachelor to the end of his life). Two interesting chimneypieces still survive, however. One represents 'Jack and the Beanstalk', with Jack supporting the mantelshelf whilst the giant's head and hands appear to tear through the stone-work above. On the other are three monkeys at play.

The interior decorations were carried out by a small army of artists and craftsmen over several years and were still unfinished at Burges's death in 1881. The names of the specialist firms and individuals who executed the work can be found in the architect's own estimate book for the years 1875 to 1881, which contains over one hundred items relating to Tower House.[247] Burges appears only occasionally to have recorded alternative estimates for the same piece of work, and the craftsmen who worked at Tower House are in the main those who had worked, or were still working, for him on other projects, particularly Cardiff Castle. All of the stone carving, from the elaborate chimneypieces to capitals and corbels, was done by the sculptor Thomas Nicholls. Burke and Company of Regent Street were the principal contractors for the marble and mosaic work, and Simpson and Sons of the Strand supplied and fixed many of the decorative tiles. The bronze work for the great doors was undertaken by John Ayres Hatfield. The carpenter who was apparently responsible for all the woodwork in the house, from the joinery to the new items of furniture made to Burges's specifications, was John Walden

of Maiden Lane, Covent Garden. The figure painting on the library bookcases and elsewhere was by Fred Weekes and Henry Stacy Marks, from whom Burges ordered seventy birds' heads at £1 apiece. Saunders and Company of Endell Street, Long Acre, made the stained glass, several of the cartoons for which were provided by H. W. Lonsdale. Most of the painted decorations were executed by Campbell and Smith of Southampton Row. By 1879, however, other estimates were being taken for decorative work, particularly in the guest room, including from 'Fisher', perhaps of the firm of Harland and Fisher, decorative specialists used by Burges in the past.*

Some of Burges's decorations were painted over in the years following his death, and from 1962 until 1966 the house remained unoccupied and was damaged by vandals. Restoration began in 1966 with the aid of grants from the Greater London Council and the Ministry of Housing and Local Government. In 1969 Mr. Richard Harris acquired the house and further extensively restored the internal decoration. The firm which had largely carried out the original painted decorations, now Campbell, Smith and Company Limited, was the principal specialist contractor employed. It proved possible to restore damaged and obliterated decorations and to finish parts of the scheme which had not been completed at the time of Burges's death from his own drawings.

No. 31 Melbury Road
Plates 80–1

Known as No. 11 until renumbered in 1967, this was the second of two houses in Melbury Road designed by Richard Norman Shaw. It was built for the artist, (Sir) Luke Fildes, and in May 1875 Shaw congratulated Fildes on acquiring 'such a delicious site'. Val Prinsep, who later acted as godfather to one of Fildes's children, had apparently informed him that the site was available, and the position was indeed a commanding one at the bend of Melbury Road, enjoying vistas to the

---

* Other firms and individuals who submitted estimates and may have carried out work at Tower House included Poole and Sons of Johnson Street, Westminster, and George P. White of Vauxhall Bridge Road, stone and marble masons; Barkentin and Krall of Regent Street, goldsmiths; and Hart, Son, Peard and Company, ironmongers. James Moore of Thames Ditton, bronze founder, submitted several estimates for bronze work in 1880 and may well have cast the figure of Fame which was later stolen from the dining-room.

south and west, with Holland Lane (now Il-chester Place) on the east. Shaw had prepared preliminary designs by August 1875, and building began early in 1876. The builder was W. H. Lascelles. Fildes had a friendly—or sometimes not so friendly—rivalry with Marcus Stone, with whom he had shared a studio in Paris in 1874. Each naturally regarded his own house as superior although they were designed by the same architect. In November 1876 Fildes wrote, 'The house is getting on famously and looks stunning . . . It is a long way the most superior house of the whole lot; I consider it knocks Stone's to fits, though of course he wouldn't have that by what I hear he says of his, but my opinion is the universal one.' Fildes took up residence in October 1877 and lived there until his death in 1927.[248]

Although the house has now been converted into flats, the red-brick exterior has been little altered and is one of Shaw's most assured compositions. Of the original interior, Maurice B. Adams com-mented, 'Taking it as a whole, Mr. Fildes' house is more of a residence or dwelling house than some we have illustrated, and although the studio is, perhaps, larger than many, yet it does not over-power the rest of the house'.[249] As the house faced south, the studio was at the rear and was lit by a skylight and six tall windows grouped in three pairs. As with No. 8 Melbury Road, however, these did not apparently provide sufficient light and the central pair were altered in 1881 to provide the present large four-light window rising to the roof parapet.[250] A winter studio was added in the north-east angle of the house in 1885 with a day-nursery underneath,[251] but this has since been completely altered and unsympathetic first-floor windows inserted. The studio was provided with central heating 'by means of hot-water pipe coils worked from a compact vertical boiler placed in a heating chamber in the basement'.[249] It was de-scribed by Edward VII, when he came to sit for a state portrait, as 'one of the finest rooms in London'.[252] The studio was approached by means of a grand staircase leading from an impressive entrance hall. The provision of generous light to the kitchen and other basement rooms neces-sitated the raising of most of the ground floor well above true ground level and resulted in a subtle change of level from the square entrance block, via the angle staircase, to the main rectangular north-west block containing the principal rooms underneath the great studio.

No. 47 Melbury Road

Plate 84a

This building, originally No. 13 Melbury Road until renumbered in 1967, was designed by Robert Dudley Oliver for Walford Graham Robertson, the artist and playwright. Oliver was a little-known architect who devoted most of his early years to painting and exhibited at the Royal Academy, but his obituary in *The Times* described him as 'an architect of skill, artistic feeling, and antiquarian knowledge'. The builder, W. J. Adcock of Dover, began work in 1892 and a ninety-year lease of the house was granted to Robertson in June 1893 at an annual ground rent of £125 for the first two years and £250 there-after. The lease allowed the premises to be used only as a private dwelling or studio.[253]

As first built the front of the house was only four bays wide and two storeys high,[254] but the lease made specific provision for the addition of another wing, not exceeding sixty feet in height. Graham Robertson appears, however, to have used the house as a studio with reception facilities for his clients, while he lived at No. 9 Argyll Road.[255] An extra storey was added, incorporating the existing wooden pediment and cornice, and a new north wing was built to match the existing south wing, to the designs of Basil Procter, in 1912, when Robertson was no longer the owner.[256] The result is a sensitive reproduction of a seventeenth-century façade, which does not give the impression of having been created at different times and by different architects, so excellently have the 1912 additions been matched to the original.

Before these additions the ground floor con-sisted of a grand hallway extending the depth of the house, a staircase, an ante-room, and a billiard-room, while on the first floor there were bedrooms and a large studio. The rear part of the house con-taining the studio was originally much higher than the front and must have presented a some-what strange appearance before the alterations of 1912. It was also built in a contrasting style, and the dominating feature of the garden front is a large Elizabethan-style bay window which rises through the ground and lofty first floors and is flanked by buttresses. The house was converted into flats in 1948.[257]

For several years, from about 1896, Robertson shared his studio in Melbury Road with the brilliant young Scottish 'impressionist' painter, Arthur Melville, until the latter's death in 1904.[258]

Nos. 55 and 57 Melbury Road
Plate 84c

A piece of ground to the south of Graham Robertson's house was taken by Sir Alexander Meadows Rendel, the engineer,[42] who engaged Halsey Ricardo to design this pair of semi-detached houses, originally Nos. 15 and 17 Melbury Road. Plans were drawn up as early as January 1893, but difficulties were encountered in obtaining permission from the London County Council for the erection of covered ways in front of the entrances. Approval was not finally obtained until 1894. Ninety-year leases from 1893 were granted in October 1895 to James Meadows Rendel, a barrister, and presumably the son of Sir Alexander, for No. 55 and to Lady Eliza Rendel, Sir Alexander's wife, for No. 57. The builders were Walter Holt and Sons of Croydon.[259]

An illustration of the two houses appeared in *The Builder* in July 1894, and in a note for the same journal Halsey Ricardo set out his reasons for using the ox-blood-red glazed bricks with which the houses are faced. 'An endeavour has been made', he wrote, 'in building these houses, to recognize and accept the present conditions of house-building in London—more especially as regards the dirt and the impurities of the atmosphere. They are faced externally throughout with salt-glazed bricks, which, being of fire-clay vitrified at a high temperature, may be looked upon as proof against the disintegrating forces of the London air. These bricks, being virtually unchangeable, I have had to renounce the aid that time gives to a building by blunting its edges, softening and blending its colours; but as a *per contra* one has the satisfaction of knowing that the house is built of durable materials, wind-proof and rain-proof; and whatever effect one can manage to secure, that effect is indestructible. In the case of the usual brick house—whilst the brick and stone are ageing and weathering, the woodwork is periodically being renewed (in effect) by repainting—and the acquired harmony of the whole is constantly being dislocated by this renewal; but with these houses, every time the external woodwork is recoloured the bricks can be washed down and the original effect—for what it is worth—maintained.'[260]

An addition was made to the south-east corner of No. 57 in a Ricardo-esque manner by Symonds and Lutyens in 1930. In 1950 the two houses were joined together and converted into flats.[261]

James Meadows Rendel was the first occupant of No. 55, but No. 57 was taken by (Sir) Ernest Debenham[132] and so provided him with that introduction to Ricardo's architecture which was to have such a notable outcome in the building of No. 8 Addison Road.

Commonwealth Institute, Kensington High Street

The Commonwealth Institute is the successor to the Imperial Institute. An Act of 1958 provided for the name to be changed and a new building to be constructed. A site that had originally been part of the front park of Holland House was acquired from the Holland estate on a 999-year lease for £215,000, and Sir Robert Matthew, Johnson-Marshall and Partners were chosen as architects. The main contractors were the John Laing Construction Company, and among several contributions to the new building from Commonwealth countries were twenty-five tons of copper for the roof from the Northern Rhodesia Chamber of Mines. The new institute was opened by Her Majesty Queen Elizabeth II on 6 November 1962.[262]

CHAPTER VIII

The Crown Estate in Kensington Palace Gardens

THE Crown Estate in Kensington consists primarily of Kensington Palace Gardens, a spacious private avenue over a half a mile in length which extends from Kensington High Street on the south to Bayswater Road on the north, and which was laid out in the 1840's, mainly on the site of the former kitchen gardens of Kensington Palace. Large Victorian and Edwardian mansions were subsequently built along the avenue, and are now mostly occupied by the representatives of foreign governments.* The estate also includes the barracks in Kensington Church Street, which occupy a part of the former palace gardens called the old forcing ground, and some properties in Kensington High Street which were purchased by the Crown in the nineteenth and twentieth centuries (fig. 31). Until 1900, when it was all incorporated into the Borough of Kensington, the estate was situated in three separate administrative parishes—those of Kensington, Paddington and St. Margaret's, Westminster.

Most of the area described in this chapter was constituted Crown Estate in 1841, when, by an Act of Parliament, some twenty-eight acres were detached from the grounds of Kensington Palace and handed over to the Commissioners of Woods and Forests, to be laid out for building. Kensington Palace and its grounds had, of course, belonged to the Crown since William III purchased the property (then called Nottingham House) from Daniel Finch, second Earl of Nottingham, in 1689. But as a royal residence it was administered by the Lord Steward's department, whereas since 1810 the Crown Estate (i.e. those lands belonging to the Crown whose revenues had been surrendered by the sovereign in exchange for the Civil List)

was managed by the Commissioners of Woods and Forests (the forerunners of the Crown Estate Commissioners). By the Act of 1841 the revenues from building at Kensington were to be used to pay for improvements to other royal gardens.[1]

The land appropriated included all the palace kitchen gardens. These consisted of the old forcing ground (which appears to have been in continuous use as a kitchen garden since the seventeenth century) and an area to the north (now occupied by Nos. 1–26 consec. Kensington Palace Gardens and Palace Gardens Mews) which was formed in the early nineteenth century. This latter had previously been part of the 'wilderness' which Queen Anne laid out to the north-west of the palace in c. 1705, and before that it was a gravel pit. The rest of the area (now the site of Nos. 1–10 consec. Palace Green) was taken out of some open ground on the west side of the palace called Palace Green.[2]

The plan to build over the kitchen gardens at Kensington Palace had originated in the recommendations of a committee, appointed by the Treasury in January 1838, to inquire into the management of the royal gardens.† In their report, completed in March, the committee proposed, as part of an extensive reorganization, that several gardens, including the kitchen gardens at Kensington, should be abolished, and the ground converted to 'purposes of public utility'. By this the committee seem to have meant development as building land, for although it did not offer any specific suggestions for financing the improvements at the remaining gardens, its account of the funds that would become available for that purpose included a valuation of the gardens at Kensington

---

* The name Kensington Palace Gardens applies to the whole length of the road but the ten houses at the south end are numbered 1–10 Palace Green (see fig. 31).

† The committee was composed of two Members of Parliament and the Treasurer to the Royal Household, who were assisted by Dr. John Lindley, secretary to the Royal Horticultural Society, Joseph Paxton, the Duke of Devonshire's gardener, and John Wilson, the Earl of Surrey's gardener.

which could only be realized if the ground was let for building.[3]

The Treasury received the report with characteristic caution: their Lordships 'were disposed to concur generally in the opinions expressed by the committee', but they wished to be satisfied that the funds that would be thus obtained would be sufficient to finance the general reorganization proposed. They therefore called for a report from the Commissioners of Woods and Forests.[4]

The Commissioners' report was not completed until September 1840, and it contained recommendations based not only on the report of the 1838 committee but also on proposals for improving the management of royal gardens which had been submitted to the Treasury by the Lord Steward in March 1840.[5] These had been forwarded by the Treasury to the Commissioners with the request that they should consider whether immediate measures might not be taken to transfer the kitchen gardens and forcing ground at Kensington from the Lord Steward's department in order to facilitate 'the disposal of the sites of those gardens on building leases'.[6]

The Commissioners accepted that the various improvements recommended by them should be paid for by letting the site of the kitchen gardens at Kensington for building, and a plan of a suggested layout, drawn up by one of their surveyors, Thomas Chawner, accompanied the report. This shows the area of the old garden on the north side of Palace Green divided into plots for ten detached and ten semi-detached houses. The Commissioners were confident that the ground would be let without difficulty and therefore proposed that a sum equal to the total estimated ground rental should be released from Land Revenue funds to enable the proposed improvements at other royal gardens to proceed.[7]

On 6 October 1840 the Treasury authorized the Commissioners to take the necessary steps 'forthwith' to let the site of the kitchen gardens at Kensington on building leases. There was, however, some public opposition to the plan led by J. C. Loudon, who wrote to *The Times* urging 'those who disapprove to employ every means in

their power to prevent Woods and Forests from carrying their intention into effect'.[8]*

Towards the end of October 1840 the Treasury, at the request of the Commissioners, ordered the Lord Steward to start running down the gardens at Kensington. But before the ground could be let for building, control of the gardens had to be formally transferred by Act of Parliament from the Lord Steward's department to the Office of Woods, and in July 1841 the Commissioners' solicitors began to draft the necessary Bill. By this time, however, the Treasury had approved a plan by which the revenue from building at Kensington would be used to lay out a new kitchen garden at Frogmore for the supply of Windsor Castle, and this required additional powers to be drafted into the Bill. Another Bill was also needed to transfer the Frogmore site to the Lord Steward.[10]

In August 1841, before either Bill had been presented to Parliament, Lord Melbourne's Whig administration resigned, and his First Commissioner of Woods, Lord Duncannon, ordered that the work which had already started on the new garden at Frogmore should stop.† Evidently he was anticipating a change in policy for he told the Queen that work had had to be suspended until a new administration took office. The succeeding Conservative Government under Peel did not, however, oppose the proposed improvements and in September Sir Thomas Fremantle introduced both Bills into the House of Commons. Each received the royal assent on 5 October.[11]

Fremantle then asked the Commissioners for a plan of their projected layout at Kensington, and for a report on the conditions proposed by them for letting the ground. The Commissioners' two surveyors, Thomas Chawner and (Sir) James Pennethorne, had been working on this report since October 1840, but did not complete it until November 1841 and it was not submitted to the Treasury until January 1842.[12]

The principal feature of their plan was the broad straight avenue, 70 feet wide, called The Queen's Road (now Kensington Palace Gardens), connecting Kensington High Street with the

---

* It was no doubt Loudon, under the *nom-de-plume* 'an Inhabitant of Bayswater', who had written angrily to *The Times* at the end of August 1838 when it was first rumoured publicly that the kitchen gardens might be used for building. At that time he was trying to promote a scheme of his own for joining Hyde Park and Holland House park in one unbroken open space.[9]

† Until 1851 one of the three Commissioners of Woods was always a member of the Government.

Uxbridge road. A subsidiary road across the site of the forcing ground was to join The Queen's Road to Church Street. As the Crown did not at this date own any property along Kensington High Street, the Commissioners would have to purchase two of the old houses there, including The Grapes public house, in order to make the necessary opening at the southern end of The Queen's Road. At the north end it was proposed to straighten the Uxbridge road frontage and set it back several feet. Two small roads, one to the east of the present No. 4 Kensington Palace Gardens, and the other slightly to the north of the present No. 15, gave access to the palace from the Uxbridge road and the east side of The Queen's Road respectively.[13]

All the ground not laid out for roads, except for the area now occupied by Nos. 1–3 Palace Green, was divided into building plots. Of the total number of thirty-three plots, sixteen were on the west side of The Queen's Road, ten on the east, four along the Uxbridge road (excluding the two corner plots) and three on the forcing ground. The plots in The Queen's Road were intended for detached houses and those along the Uxbridge road for semi-detached pairs.[13] 'There is no intention of making a continuous row of houses', Duncannon had earlier written to the Treasury, 'the Buildings will all be separate like Camden Hill with small plots of ground of near an acre to each'.[14] On the sites now occupied by Nos. 1–3 Palace Green there already stood three houses of late seventeenth- or early eighteenth-century date. The northernmost of these (No. 3), which was usually occupied by the surveyor to the palace, survived until 1969.[15]

The Commissioners proposed to let the plots on ninety-nine-year leases from Lady Day 1842, and for each they had apportioned a minimum annual ground rent, which for those in The Queen's Road worked out at about 16s. per foot of frontage. If all thirty-three plots were let at the minimum rents proposed the estate would have yielded an annual revenue of over £2,300. On all the plots except the three on the forcing ground lessees would have to spend not less than £3,000 per plot on their houses, whose plans and specifications had first to be approved by the Commissioners. Lessees were not obliged to erect the type

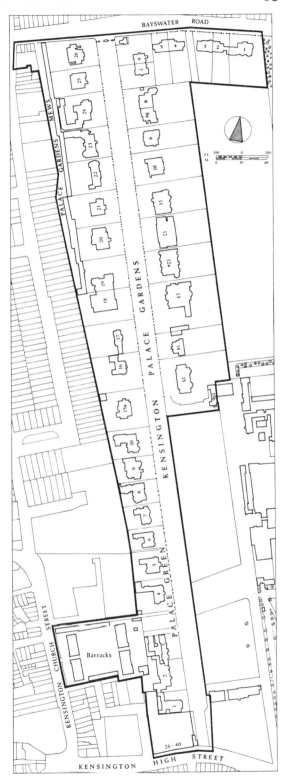

Fig. 31. The Crown Estate in Kensington Palace Gardens. Based on the Ordnance Survey of 1914-22

of house indicated on the plan and would be allowed to build a single house occupying more than one plot provided that the expenditure on that house and the rent payable for the site were not less than the minimum expected if each plot had been let separately. Houses in The Queen's Road were to be built sixty feet from the front of the plot. Leases would be granted when the carcase was completed and roofed over, and each house had to be finished ready for habitation within two years of the lessee taking possession of the ground. Lessees would also have to lay out an ornamental garden to each house, build boundary walls around the plots, and provide carriage entrances and iron gates.[14]

The work of clearing the site, laying out the roads, constructing the sewers, and building a lodge and gates at each end of The Queen's Road to keep the houses 'select and private', was to be undertaken by the Commissioners, but the lessees would reimburse the cost of this work, estimated at £14,185, by payment of a lump sum to be apportioned to each plot in relation to its size and position. The lessees would also have to pay the Commissioners a rate for the maintenance and upkeep of the road and another rate in lieu of land tax, which the Commissioners were to redeem.[14]

On 14 January 1842 the Treasury authorized the Commissioners to proceed with these arrangements for laying out and letting the ground.[16] They began with the construction of the sewers. Early in February six builders of 'known means and stability usually employed in the construction of sewers' were invited to submit tenders. The contract was awarded, at £4,825, to George Bird of the Edgware Road, one of two builders usually engaged by the Commissioners of Sewers in this district. Work began in April and was expected to take five months. The construction of the roadway, which was also undertaken by Bird, was begun in September 1843 but not completed until 1845. Bird's tender amounted to £1,633.[17]

The length of time taken to lay out the road was due mainly to the delay in removing some of the buildings which stood in the way. Chief among these had been the old brick barracks on Palace Green, built in 1689–90 to house the palace guard, which were not vacated until May 1845. At the southern end the two houses in Kensington High Street which did not belong to the Crown and which blocked the opening of The Queen's Road into the High Street were not demolished until late in 1845.[18]

Other old buildings on Palace Green were also demolished including two water towers built to supply the palace, and the little octagonal 'engine-house' near the barracks.[19] One of the water towers was the castellated brick and stone structure, illustrated by Faulkner and others, which stood slightly to the north of the old surveyor's house (now the site of No. 3 Palace Green) and on the line of the proposed road across the forcing ground. This tower had probably been built in 1716–17, and according to an account published in *The Gentleman's Magazine* in 1815 was designed by Vanbrugh, who was Comptroller of Works at Kensington Palace at the probable time of building.[20] Stylistically it has affinities with Vanbrugh's own 'medieval' house at Greenwich, which was also built in about 1717. One modern authority, however, attributes the design to Henry Joynes, the clerk of works at Kensington after 1715 and an associate of Vanbrugh who owed his appointment to the latter's influence.[21] The other water tower stood on the site of No. 6 Palace Green. It was built before 1728, probably to replace the Vanbrughian tower, which is known to have been situated too low to provide a satisfactory supply.[22]

At first the Commissioners proposed to restrict letting to thirteen plots at the north end. These were considered 'the most eligible & likely to be taken by a superior class of tenants', and it was hoped that when these had been let the value of the remaining plots would be increased. Preference was to be given to persons applying to build houses for their own occupation.[14] This condition ruled out most of the applications already received, and in order to encourage others the Treasury allowed the Commissioners to advertise the plots in the daily press.[14]* These advertisements, which appeared in February 1842, invited tenders for plots to be sent to the Commissioners before 8 March.[23] But this method of letting was not, in the Commissioners' own words, 'attended with successes', for, as they later reported to the

---

* Among those who had already applied for plots were Thomas Cubitt (who was willing to undertake the whole or any part of the development); Matthew and Thomas Henry Wyatt, the architects; and William Woods, builder, in association with the architect John Pink.[23]

Treasury, 'in reply to the advertizements issued by us, for Tenders, we did not receive any offer which we felt ourselves at liberty to entertain'.[24]

The main reason why none of the plots were let at this time appears to have been that the minimum prices fixed by the Commissioners for rents and building expenditure were excessively high. One applicant, the architect William Herbert, described the Commissioners' valuation of the ground as being 'very much above what I consider it is likely to produce'.[23]

The first tender to be accepted by the Commissioners was submitted in July 1842 by Samuel West Strickland of Bayswater, a 'land holder'. Strickland applied for the three adjoining plots along the Uxbridge road, for which he offered rents which were somewhat below those of the Commissioners' apportionment. The Commissioners nevertheless decided to accept his offer, and on these three plots Strickland erected one detached and two pairs of semi-detached houses (Nos. 1–5 Kensington Palace Gardens), of which only two (Nos. 4 and 5) now survive.[25]

The Commissioners did not receive another acceptable offer until September 1843, when John Marriott Blashfield of Upper Stamford Street, Blackfriars, submitted a tender to lease no less than twenty plots (the area subsequently occupied by Nos. 6–14 and 16–26 Kensington Palace Gardens, and Palace Gardens Mews), for which he offered a rent rising to a maximum of £1,870 a year. He proposed to complete the whole undertaking within the first three years of the lease and he hoped that the Commissioners would not oblige him to build the houses exactly according to the 'sites & sizes' marked on the plan.[26]

Blashfield, who is described in the Commissioners' files as 'of the firm of Wyatt and Parker' and in the *Post Office Directory* as an 'artist', was probably better known as a manufacturer of inlaid and tessellated pavements. For more than ten years he had been experimenting in the production of tesserae and he had recently been successful in applying a method of compressing porcelain material to their manufacture. It was in order to exploit this discovery 'on an extensive scale' that he associated himself with Wyatt, Parker and Company, the important manufacturers of Roman cement, plaster and scagliola as well as of tessellated pavements.[27]

After the previous difficulties experienced in letting any of the plots it is not surprising that Chawner and Pennethorne should have recommended Blashfield's offer to the Commissioners, for, as they stated in their report, 'were the Board to determine to let the ground to various individuals, it is probable that all the twenty plots would not be disposed of under three years, and that the rents to be derived from them would not exceed the graduated scale proposed'. Moreover the maximum rent offered, which Chawner and Pennethorne described as 'fair and liberal on so large an undertaking', exceeded the minimum rental hoped for from the twenty plots by more than £200. On 25 September the Commissioners informed Blashfield of the terms upon which they would recommend to the Treasury that leases should be granted to him, and two days later Blashfield accepted these conditions.[26]

The preparation of the agreement between Blashfield and the Commissioners occupied the lawyers for several months and it was not signed until July 1844. Under its terms Blashfield contracted to erect twenty-one houses at a cost of not less than £63,000, and to complete them all ready for habitation within the first five years.* Six houses had to be covered in during the first one and a half years and thirteen more within the first three years. The designs for each house had to be submitted to and approved by the Commissioners.[28] In effect this meant that it was Chawner and Pennethorne—or, after Chawner's resignation in October 1843, Pennethorne alone—who decided whether any particular designs would be allowed, for the Commissioners always adopted their recommendations. Pennethorne, however, rarely allowed his own taste to intrude into his reports, which are mainly concerned with

---

* On the plan attached to this agreement Blashfield's twenty plots, originally numbered 4–23 on the published plan, were renumbered 1–21. The extra plot is accounted for by the fact that on the agreement-plan the two plots at the east and west corners of The Queen's Road and the Uxbridge road had been divided in two and one plot in the Uxbridge road suppressed altogether. Apart from this renumbering the boundaries of some of the plots were altered so that there is no exact correlation between the two sets of plot numbers. When the houses were built a third set of numbers was introduced and in addition some of the plot boundaries were adjusted again. Thus, for example, the plot numbered 6 on the published plan was slightly enlarged on the agreement-plan and renumbered 3. When a house was built here the plot was enlarged again and the house numbered 8. Because of this complication, as little reference as possible has been made to the plot numbers in this account.

whether the design would meet the requirements expected of a house that was to cost not less than £3,000 to build.

The outside walls of the houses had to be faced either with cement coloured and jointed to imitate stone, or with best malms or other facing bricks dressed with stone or cement. Blashfield also had to lay out ornamental gardens to the houses, enclose the plots with iron railings on a dwarf wall and set up iron gates at the entrances.[28]

As soon as any house was completed in carcase and covered the Commissioners would grant a lease of the plot to Blashfield or his nominees for a term of ninety-nine years from 10 October 1843. The ground rents for each plot (totalling, of course, £1,870) were specified in a schedule attached to the agreement. The first year of the term was to be at a peppercorn rent.[28]

Blashfield had not, however, waited until July 1844 before starting to build. On 6 October 1843, only a few days after he had written to accept the Commissioners' terms, he submitted for their approval the plans, elevations and specifications of his first house, No. 8 Kensington Palace Gardens, now demolished.[26] This was designed by Owen Jones, whom Blashfield had recently employed to produce a pattern book of designs for mosaic and tessellated pavements.[29]* Jones's designs for No. 8 included a considerable amount of internal and external ornamentation in the 'Moresque' style, to which the Commissioners' architects did not object in principle, though they evidently disliked it. Blashfield himself even suggested stripping away the ornament which Jones intended for the windows: 'The design will then be strictly Italian', he wrote, 'and as I wish.'[26]

Besides designing this house Jones appears to have acted as Blashfield's architect in a more general capacity.[31] But Blashfield was evidently not committed to employing Jones to design all his intended houses, and of a total of six designs approved by the Commissioners for houses built or intended to be built by Blashfield, only two were by Jones.

In March 1844 Blashfield submitted for approval the plans of four more houses, two detached and two semi-detached, which were designed jointly by Thomas Henry Wyatt and David Brandon. The two detached houses were intended for the two large plots at the east and west corners of The Queen's Road and Bayswater Road (subsequently occupied by Nos. 6 and 7 and Nos. 25 and 26 Kensington Palace Gardens respectively), and the semi-detached pair for a site between the north-west corner plot and the western boundary of the estate. The Commissioners approved the designs, but in execution this plan was considerably modified. The plot intended as the site of the two semi-detached houses was divided in two: half of it was appropriated to the adjoining corner plot, where Blashfield built two detached houses (Nos. 25 and 26, both now demolished), and the other half was absorbed into a mews which Blashfield laid out along the western edge of the estate (now Palace Gardens Mews).[26]

This mews was a departure from the original plan, where the stables, arranged in semi-detached pairs, occupy the same plots as the individual houses. Chawner and Pennethorne recommended the change to the Commissioners, as they considered that the great size of Blashfield's houses made it essential for the stables to be as far removed from them as possible. Altogether Blashfield erected twelve stables in the mews, and each was leased to him for a term expiring in 1942. The annual ground rents ranged from £4 to £7 10s.[32]

In addition to the four house plans submitted in March 1844 Blashfield also presented a design by the same architects, Wyatt and Brandon, for a set of gates and a lodge at the north end of the road (Plate 92a). He proposed to erect these (and another set at the south end) at his own expense, provided that the Commissioners would allow him to sell the gravel he excavated while digging the foundations of the houses. The Commissioners agreed to this proposal and approved Wyatt and Brandon's designs.[26] The construction of the lodge and gates at the north end (fig. 32) was undertaken for Blashfield by the well-known building firm of Thomas Grissell and Samuel Morton Peto, whose contract (excluding the ironwork) amounted to £1,200.[33] *The Illustrated London News* praised the 'correct [Italianate] style' of the lodge.[34] Grissell and Peto also erected the decorative iron railings (fig. 32) designed by Wyatt and Brandon, with which Blashfield

* The terrace along the garden front of No. 8 had a 'lively and pleasing' tessellated pavement in different colours designed by Jones.[30]

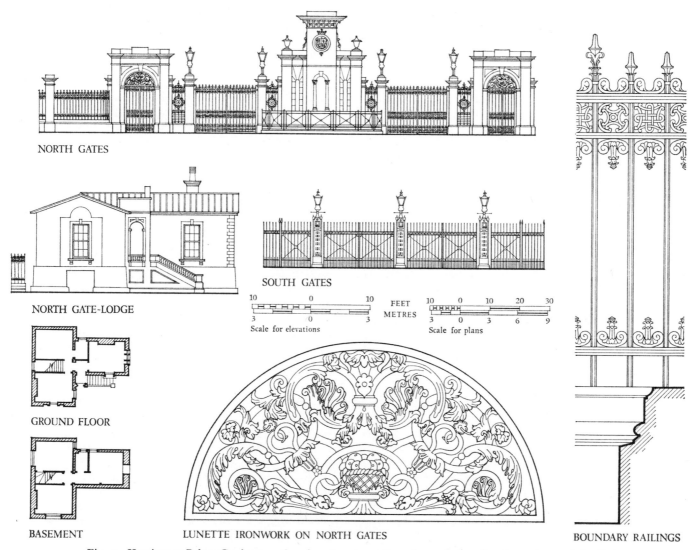

NORTH GATES

NORTH GATE-LODGE

GROUND FLOOR

BASEMENT

SOUTH GATES

FEET
METRES

Scale for elevations

Scale for plans

LUNETTE IRONWORK ON NORTH GATES

BOUNDARY RAILINGS

Fig. 32. Kensington Palace Gardens, north and south gates, and north gate-lodge, elevations, plans and details

enclosed the plots leased to him.[33] Very little of this railing still survives; it is best preserved around No. 11.*

Only one other house was begun by Blashfield in 1844. This was No. 17, an Italianate villa designed by Henry E. Kendall, junior.[35]

Blashfield, however, had never intended to undertake the whole development by himself. As early as December 1843 he had published a prospectus in which he invited offers for his building plots, to be sent to his architect, Owen Jones.[31] Nothing acceptable was evidently received, for by June 1844 he was complaining to the Commissioners that 'There is scarcely a London Builder of any eminence to whom I have not offered plots of ground, at a rent in many instances as low as that which I shall have to pay; but from the uncertain state in which matters stand relative to the opening of the road and the very stringent covenants contained in my

* In October 1843 Blashfield had proposed to erect a 'palisading' designed in 'Moresque' style by Owen Jones, and Chawner and Pennethorne had reported that the design 'cannot fail to produce a rich effect'.[26]

agreement none of them will have anything to do with it.'[33]

The first person to take a plot from Blashfield was Joseph Earle of Brixton, a timber merchant, who in July 1844 agreed to buy the north-east corner plot, where he erected a pair of semi-detached houses (now Nos. 6 and 7) from a design by Wyatt and Brandon.[36]

In 1845 another five plots (two on the east and three on the west side) were taken by Grissell and Peto, who built four houses (one of the plots being laid out as an extra garden) and stables for them in the adjoining mews.[37] The designs for these houses (now Nos. 12, 18, 19 and 20) were obtained from (Sir) Charles Barry, whose new Palace of Westminster Grissell and Peto were then building. Although a large number of drawings for the houses survive in the form of tracings made by Barry's pupils, the contemporary evidence for Barry's personal authorship is equivocal, and the wording of Pennethorne's report to the Commissioners, that the designs for Nos. 12 and 20 'emanate from Mr Barry', would seem to suggest that his office staff may have had a hand in them.[38] Moreover R. R. Banks, who was in charge of the office at this time, was actually named as the architect of No. 12 in a published account.[39] But this evidence must be judged in the light of Barry's almost invariable practice of taking the whole responsibility for the design of his commissions upon himself.[40] In March 1846, while work was in progress, but before any leases had been granted, Grissell and Peto's partnership was dissolved, Peto taking the railway contracts while Grissell retained the building contracts.[41] The leases were therefore granted to Grissell alone.

Only two other houses were begun in 1845: one was No. 24, designed by Owen Jones and built by Blashfield, and the other was No. 21, designed and built by Charles F. Oldfield of Bayswater. The Commissioners also approved plans and elevations submitted by Blashfield for a house designed by T. Hayter Lewis which was never built.[42]

Blashfield's houses were, on the whole, on a much larger scale than those shown on the original layout plan, and they cost considerably more to build than the £3,000 minimum required by the Commissioners, his first house alone having cost nearly five times that sum.[43] It was Blashfield's opinion that houses large enough to attract purchasers willing to pay the heavy ground rents would have had to be 'showily and slightly' built if they were to cost no more than £3,000.[44] But no purchasers could be found,* and in 1846 the mounting mania for railway shares was creating severe financial difficulties for him and many other London building speculators. In May of that year he wrote to the Commissioners claiming to have sustained 'a very serious loss . . . by the outlay I have made on the Queen's Road' and that in consequence he was obliged to suspend payment of the ground rent. Altogether he had spent over £60,500, but not one of his five houses had been sold (although one, No. 26, was occupied, probably on a short lease), and he had contracted a mortgage debt of £42,600 with interest repayments which could not be maintained solely out of the proceeds (less than £4,000) from the sale of plots.[26]†

Blashfield also complained about the Commissioners' long delay in finishing the road, which deterred prospective customers from buying houses there.[26] They found the old barracks particularly offensive, for, as he stated in November 1844, 'the back front faces the Queen's Road. On this back front are places of common convenience for the men—The pavement here is used as a place for the men to wash—These and other circumstances connected with the Barracks are remarked upon by all applicants for residences'.[33] He had also lost money on the building of the lodge and gates at the north end, for they had cost over £2,000 to erect, but the gravel which he had been allowed to excavate in exchange had realized only £1,000.[26]

In spite of these difficulties and the 'unprofitable character of the undertaking up to this period', Blashfield expressed the 'fullest confidence' in its ultimate success, and in consideration of the very large sums which he had invested in it he asked the Commissioners for an extension of the peppercorn term, without which he would be unable to continue, his credit being exhausted.[26] The Commissioners agreed to help and extended the peppercorn term from October 1844 generally to October 1845 and on the unlet plots to 1846. With this concession, equivalent to a remission of rent of £1,500, Blashfield was able to dispose of

---

* Ironically it was the great size of one of the houses (No. 8) which was later considered the reason why it failed to sell.
† This debt included £10,000 owed in part purchase of the cement business of Wyatt, Parker and Company.[26]

two more plots (the sites of Nos. 10 and 16), and he also found purchasers for two of his houses (Nos. 17 and 26).[45]

But these sales were apparently 'effected at a loss . . . compared with the cost of the works', and by April 1847, when the Bank of England reversed its indiscreet policy of cheap money, he was again in financial difficulty. On account of the 'depressed state of the funds' he was unable to raise any more mortgages, and in a desperate attempt to find the money needed to make a large repayment due in early May ('which if not paid will be my ruin'), he asked the Commissioners to buy some of the improved ground rents arising from his unsold houses. 'Nothing short of some such assistance', he wrote, 'can save me from Bankruptcy'.[44] Two days after his letter was written a docket in bankruptcy was issued against him, and on 14 May he was declared bankrupt.[46] In June his entire estate was assigned in trust to two of his principal creditors, Joseph Sutton of Southwark, an 'upright and respectable' sailmaker and ship's chandler, and William Naylor Morrison of Streatham, a brickmaker. Among the creditors who approved the choice of assignees were the architects David Brandon and T. H. Lewis, and the builder Thomas Grissell.[47]

There is insufficient evidence to calculate the extent of Blashfield's loss on his undertaking, but it must have been above £40,000. By April 1847 he had spent £67,300, and at the time of his bankruptcy he and his nominees (who themselves had spent another £69,000) were engaged on work expected to cost about £20,000. On the credit side Blashfield had sold two of his five houses and nine plots: the houses realized probably no more than about £20,000, and the average price of plots appears to have been in the region of £700. He had only been able to sustain these losses by drawing off the profits 'of upwards of £3,000 a year' from his cement-making business, which had also been jeopardized, and without the support of which, so he claimed, he would 'never have embarked on the works' in the first place.[44]

Although Blashfield was unable to continue his speculation at Kensington, his career as a cement manufacturer appears to have been little affected by his bankruptcy. In 1849 he was listed in the *Post Office Directory* as a cement manufac-

turer with an address in Commercial Road, Lambeth, and in the following year he had addresses in Praed Street, Paddington, and Millwall, Poplar, as well.[48] It was at about this time that he took up the manufacture of terra-cotta and in 1858 he moved to Stamford in Lincolnshire, where he soon established himself as the principal terra-cotta manufacturer in the country.[49]

The responsibility for completing the building at Kensington passed to the assignees of Blashfield's bankrupt estate, who inherited his agreement with the Commissioners, five vacant plots (the sites of Nos. 11, 13, 14, 22 and 23), three houses (Nos. 8, 24 and 25), of which one (No. 24) was unfinished, and some stables in Palace Gardens Mews. In August 1847, when the national financial crisis was nearing its peak, they put up the whole property for sale at a public auction, but no bids were received for the vacant plots, and, according to Pennethorne, the prices offered for the houses were much below their estimated value. In fact only one house, No. 24, appears to have been sold, and Nos. 8 and 25 subsequently passed into the hands of Blashfield's original mortgagees. Pennethorne saw little prospect of the assignees being able to dispose of any of the vacant plots while the money market remained generally depressed, and on his advice the Commissioners agreed to relax some of the conditions in the building agreement. Both the time allowed for building the houses and the peppercorn term were extended as required, and the assignees were relieved of the responsibility for erecting the lodge and gates at the south end.[44]

The Commissioners, under pressure from the Treasury to restrict their expenditure, delayed building the southern lodge and gates until 1849, when a modified version of a design by Wyatt and Brandon was used.[33]* The contractor was Robert Hicks of Stangate, whose tender, at £747, was only £1 below the final cost.[51] In 1903–4 the lodge was rebuilt and the gates (fig. 32) set back to allow for the widening of Kensington High Street.[52]

Even with the Commissioners' relaxation of the terms of the building agreement, the assignees were unable to dispose of any more of the vacant plots. The Commissioners' solicitors wanted to

* This design had been submitted by Blashfield in November 1845 and approved by the Commissioners.[33] Wyatt and Brandon's drawing for the gates is preserved in the Public Record Office.[50] The modifications were made by Pennethorne whose own design had been rejected by the Commissioners.[33]

institute proceedings against them, but Penne-thorne advised against this and two months later, in April 1849, the assignees offered to surrender their interest in the estate. This offer was accepted by both the Commissioners and the Treasury, and a deed of surrender was executed on 31 December 1849.[53]

The only plot not surrendered at this time was the site of the present No. 9. Blashfield had mortgaged this plot to Joseph Sutton in 1846 for nearly £2,000, and after the settlement of Blashfield's affairs Sutton had taken full possession and begun to excavate the gravel. By September 1849 Sutton wanted to surrender the plot, which the Commissioners were unwilling to allow. A long-drawn-out dispute ensued, which was finally resolved in 1851 by the Commissioners agreeing to accept a surrender.[44]

By this time the general economic situation had greatly improved, and in the more buoyant market of the early 1850's the Commissioners had little difficulty in disposing of the six surrendered plots. By May 1852 they had received acceptable tenders for all of them, mostly from applicants wishing to build houses for their own occupa-tion.[54] The first was Edmund Antrobus of the Strand, a tea merchant, who built No. 14. He offered a slightly lower rent than Blashfield had paid (equivalent to 15s. a foot instead of 16s.), but Pennethorne advised the Commissioners to accept, 'considering the damp which has been thrown on the whole undertaking and the altered circumstances since Mr Blashfield took the ground'.[55]

All six plots were let for terms expiring in October 1942. The first year was at a peppercorn rent and the second year usually at half the maximum rent offered. In addition to the rent the lessees had also to pay 5s. a year in lieu of land tax. The lessees each undertook to spend not less than a specified sum, still usually £3,000, in building a first-class house which had to be covered in within one year. The date by which the house had to be completed ready for occupation was also laid down. Leases were granted when the carcase of the house was completed. In other respects the conditions on which the plots were let were iden-tical to those in Blashfield's agreement.[56]

During the laying out of Kensington Palace Gardens Pennethorne prepared annual statements of expenditure for the Commissioners and in 1852 his report showed that at the end of March

1851 nearly £25,000 had been expended here and nearly £45,000 on the new kitchen garden at Frogmore. The cost of the new garden at Frog-more exceeded the estimated value of the plots already let for building at Kensington by nearly £3,800, and in order to make up the deficit the Commissioners decided to release more plots. They selected two, one on the east now occupied by No. 15 and its former stable block No. 15B, and one on the west side, now occupied by No. 15A. Both were let on the same terms as the plots surrendered by Blashfield's creditors.[57]

After the completion of Nos. 15 and 15A in 1854 and 1855 respectively no more plots were let for house-building during the nineteenth century. Some further building did, however, take place: No. 12A was erected in the garden of No. 12, and two of the old houses in the south-west corner of Palace Green (now Nos. 1 and 2) were rebuilt. The unlet plots on the west side of the road to the south of No. 15A were leased on a quarterly tenancy to the occupant of that house for use as a paddock, and the forcing ground was let to the War Department as the site for a new barracks (see page 192).

The planting of trees began in 1850. In re-sponse to a request from some of the residents, who had complained of the 'neglected' appearance of the road, the Commissioners planted 'occidental plane trees' on both sides between the southern end and the plots let for building. Unfortunately most of these trees were planted not on the foot-way but further in on grounds then let to a local butcher, for grazing cattle and sheep, and not-withstanding the measures taken to protect them, many of the trees were soon destroyed. In 1862 the Commissioners rejected a suggestion from a resident that trees should be planted along the edge of the footpaths, but when, in 1870, the residents repeated the request ('so as to give an appearance of a Boulevard to the Gardens') the Commissioners consented, provided that the undertaking was organized by the residents them-selves, who were to bear both the initial and the maintenance costs. Altogether the residents planted fifty occidental plane trees in 1870, twenty-five on each side, between the southern end of the road and Nos. 15 and 15A. The trees at the north end, between Nos. 15 and 15A and Bayswater Road, were also planted by the resi-dents, in about 1879.[58]

The final phase in the development of Kensington Palace Gardens took place between 1902 and 1913 when seven substantial houses (Nos. 4–10 Palace Green) were erected on the paddock opposite the palace and hitherto leased with No. 15A.

In spite of the disastrous start in the 1840's all the houses were eventually occupied, and by 1860 Kensington Palace Gardens could be said to have fulfilled the expectations of *The Illustrated London News*, which in 1846 had predicted that from 'its great breadth, imposing aspect, and the correct taste displayed throughout [this road] bids fair to become a most aristocratic neighbourhood'.[34] But in general it was an aristocracy of wealth rather than of birth that was attracted to the road, its social character being aptly summed up in the nickname 'Millionaires' Row'.

By building large and expensive houses Blashfield had virtually excluded anyone who was not very wealthy from living there, but few of the early inhabitants were particularly distinguished. Leigh Hunt wondered 'why anybody should live there, who can afford to live in houses so large', as in his opinion none of them had 'gardens so to speak of'.[59]

Thirteen householders were listed in the census of 1851 and of these five were merchants, two landed proprietors, two builders, one a bookseller and publisher, and one a Member of Parliament. By 1861 the three largest groups were merchants (five), fundholders (five) and landholders (four). The returns of the 1871 census continue to show the predominance of merchants and fundholders.

Prominent among the residents of the first thirty to forty years was the successful industrialist and businessman. Both Grissell, the builder, and Peto, his former partner turned railway contractor and civil engineer, lived there, and so did another civil engineer, James Meadows Rendel, the builder of docks and harbours. Rendel's house (No. 10) was subsequently occupied by Ernest Leopold Benzon, the steel manufacturer, and Peto's first house (No. 12) was bought by Alexander Collie, a cotton merchant, whose firm crashed resoundingly in 1875 with liabilities of £2,000,000. Peto's second house (No. 12A) was taken over after Peto himself had encountered financial difficulties by the builder and contractor

Thomas Lucas. George Moore, the lace manufacturer, lived at No. 15, and Stuart Rendel, the armaments manufacturer, at No. 16.

The census returns of 1851, 1861 and 1871 give some indication of the social composition of the households during this period. In 1851 the average size of each household (including servants) was slightly over ten persons, and the average number of servants per household, six. The largest household, consisting of sixteen persons in all, was John Leech's at No. 18, which included eight servants, and the largest number of servants in any household was nine, at Thomas Grissell's (No. 19). By 1861 the average size of household had risen to slightly over twelve, and the average number of servants to slightly over seven. In that year Sir Morton Peto's household at No. 12 was both the largest in total (twenty-eight), and contained the largest number of servants (sixteen). By 1871 the average size of household had declined to slightly over eleven, while the average number of servants remained at slightly over seven. The largest household then was Lady Harrington's at No. 13, where twenty servants were employed to look after only two people (Lady Harrington and her daughter).* Three other households contained ten or more servants, Don José de Murrietta's (No. 11), Thomas Lucas's (No. 12A) and Isaac M. Marden's (No. 23).

Towards the end of the nineteenth century bankers and financiers were prominent among the residents. In November 1890 *The Metropolitan* commented that although the social composition of the road was less aristocratic than that of Mayfair or Belgravia, Kensington Palace Gardens was second to none in the attractiveness of its surroundings and 'hence it is *facile princeps* in the estimation of our merchant princes, bankers and other leaders of the world of finance'.[60]†

Today Kensington Palace Gardens is better known as a diplomatic enclave than as the haunt of millionaires. Of the countries now represented, Russia was the first to establish an embassy here. In 1930 the Soviet Government approached the solicitors of Lady Richardson, the widow of the lessee of No. 13, to acquire the property for the

---

* In the same year twenty-seven servants and a governess were employed at Argyll Lodge, Campden Hill, to look after the Duke of Argyll's family of eight.

† Eight such inhabitants were listed in *The Metropolitan*: Charles F. Huth (No. 9), Samuel Montagu (No. 12), William L. Winans (No. 15), Baron de Reuter (No. 18), Gustav C. Schwabe (No. 19), Philip Falk (No. 23), Sir James Pearce (No. 24), and Charles Van Raalte (No. 8).

ambassador's residence. As the proposed use of the house 'solely and exclusively' for this purpose did not constitute a breach of covenant, the Commissioners would not intervene to prevent the sale, despite protests from other residents. 'To permit the transfer of a lease to the representatives of a defaulting country', wrote one of them, 'is a disregard of the interest of leaseholders in the vicinity.' The residents' committee foresaw that if the ambassador committed a breach of covenant his diplomatic immunity would protect him from proceedings. One resident complained directly to the Foreign Secretary: 'The Bolshevist Government say that they will have sixteen clerks there . . . this will infringe the covenants but the Crown Estate Office say they can do nothing about it and it is quite clear that these people are not going to observe the covenants. They say they are going to have entertainments five out of seven nights a week—a pleasant outlook for Rothschild who lives just opposite.' The Foreign Secretary declined to intervene and the Russians secured the lease of No. 13.[61] The Russian Government now (1972) occupies five houses in the road. Since the war of 1939–45 most of the houses have been taken over for use as embassies or diplomatic residences and in 1972 only three houses in Kensington Palace Gardens and three in Palace Green are privately occupied.

None of the surviving Victorian houses has been left unaltered, either internally or externally —a natural if perhaps unfortunate result of the great wealth of successive owners. In some houses the alterations have been so extensive that the original design is now hardly distinguishable. Most of these changes are recorded in great detail in the files of the Crown Estate Office, but in the following accounts only the more important have been noticed.*

Nos. 1–5 (consec.) Kensington Palace Gardens

Nos. 1–3 demolished

Of the five houses built by Samuel W. Strickland along Bayswater Road only Nos. 4 and 5 remain. In July 1842 Strickland had applied successfully to the Commissioners for the plot now occupied by Nos. 4 and 5, and in August plans and elevations for a pair of semi-detached villas were ap-

proved. The architect is unknown: the detailed specifications submitted to the Commissioners were signed only by Strickland. By December the carcase of the building was complete,[24] but leases were not executed until March 1843, when, at Strickland's request, that for No. 5 was granted to his sister, Elizabeth Strickland. The annual ground rent for each house was £30.[62] Both were occupied by October 1845, No. 4 by Mrs. H. S. Waring, an elderly annuitant, and No. 5 by Bevis E. Green, a bookseller and publisher. No. 4 is now (1972) occupied by the Institute of Rubber Industry, and No. 5 by the Soviet Consulate.[63]

Nos. 4 and 5 form a pair of semi-detached stucco-faced Italianate houses, consisting of three storeys over a basement. Originally the composition was symmetrical, the central block being flanked by the entrance doors and low wings. Its three-storey façade is five windows wide, with plain pilasters running through the upper storeys to support a dentilled cornice and pediment. Some marble fireplaces dating from the 1840's and a few original cornices survive inside.

In applying for the plot now occupied by Nos. 4 and 5 Strickland also asked that he should be given the first refusal of the two adjoining plots to the east. The Commissioners replied that they did not intend to allow building on these plots 'at present', but that they would bear his application in mind. Five months later Strickland applied again for these two plots as his financial situation did not permit him to 'keep the necessary amount of money unemployed, or invested at a low rate of interest, upon the *doubtful* chance of hereafter becoming the lessee'.[64] Terms were agreed in September and as by then it would not have been possible to roof-over the houses before the winter, the Commissioners allowed Strickland to defer submitting plans and elevations until the following spring.[64]

When the designs were eventually submitted, in August 1844, Strickland proposed to erect only one house on the easternmost plot. The architect of this house (No. 1) was Henry Duesbury, who had to make extensive changes to his designs to satisfy the Commissioners. The architect of Nos. 2 and 3 is not known; in September 1843, however, Strickland had told the Commissioners that he proposed to build houses here of the same

* Facilities granted to the Greater London Council's *Survey of London* staff by occupants for the examination of individual houses were in some cases limited, and in a few others refused.

character as Nos. 4 and 5 and 'only slightly varied in detail'.[64] All three houses were completed in carcase by March 1845[64] and in September the leases were granted to Strickland. The annual ground rents were £20, £40 and £60 for Nos. 2, 3 and 1 respectively.[65] No. 2 was first occupied in 1844 by Strickland himself; No. 3 in 1846 by Samuel Needham, a bank trustee, and No. 1 in 1846 by Charles Lushington, M.P., who was probably responsible for the choice of Duesbury as architect.[66] In 1932 *The Architectural Review* published photographs of the interior of No. 1 as it had existed in 1893 and after remodelling by Wells Coates.[67]

Nos. 6 and 7 Kensington Palace Gardens
Plate 93d

In April 1844 Blashfield had obtained the Commissioners' consent to build one detached house here to designs by T. H. Wyatt and D. Brandon, but this house had evidently not been started when he agreed to sell the site for £750 to Joseph Earle of Brixton, a timber merchant.[36] Subsequently an 'amended plan' for building 'two houses or a double house' on the site, with new designs by Wyatt and Brandon, was submitted by Blashfield, on Earle's behalf, in July 1844 and approved by the Commissioners in August.[68]*

The carcase of the building was completed by February 1845 and in March separate leases were granted to Earle at an annual rent of £40 for each house.[69] While work was in progress a number of alterations to the architects' designs were approved by the Commissioners, including the addition of 'an enriched parapet to surmount the cornice along the whole line of the front'.[26] Both houses were finished by April 1846.[26] Earle himself was the first occupant of No. 6 where he lived from 1846 to 1856. No. 7 was first occupied in 1847 by Anselmo de Arroyave, a Spanish-born merchant.[63]

The front of Nos. 6 and 7 is a pleasant, well-mannered, symmetrical composition in the Italianate style, crowned by the 'enriched parapet' (of unusual star-shaped design), the dies of which were

formerly surmounted by statuary. Both houses are faced with stucco and were originally of three storeys over basements, the fourth storey of No. 7 being added in 1863 from the designs of D. Brandon.[70] The entrances are on the north and south sides, within porches. The interiors have been much altered.

No. 8 Kensington Palace Gardens
Plates 92b, c. Demolished

This house, the first to be built by Blashfield, was erected in 1843–6 to the designs of Owen Jones, whose plans and elevations were submitted for approval in October 1843. The Commissioners' architects reported that 'as regards the Elevations . . . the Design will probably produce an appearance equal to that originally contemplated for this Site and we do not feel we ought to object to the peculiarity of the proposed Moresque enrichments though hitherto not much adopted in this Country'. Blashfield replied that 'The Moresque ornament of the windows might be removed (probably with advantage) by the stroke of a pencil. The design would then be strictly Italian and as *I wish*.' Jones's mildly 'Moresque' details were, however, retained[26]† (Plate 92b). Even without them the design would have been unusual; in particular the fenestration of the upper storeys and the large expanses of plain wall gave No. 8 an exotic quality reminiscent of a Black Sea resort.

When the house was finished *The Illustrated London News* commented that its 'Byzantine character, . . . although novel to this country appears to be more particularly suited to our climate and domestic comforts than most others'.[34] Nevertheless it remained untenanted until March 1852, when a Mrs. Caroline Murray of Maida Vale bought the house for £6,300 from Blashfield's mortgagees, who had provided the £15,000 originally required to build it.[43]

The house as it stood was too large for Mrs Murray, and in the opinion of her architects, F. and H. Francis, it was much too big even for 'the generality of families—a fact proved by the

---

* Wyatt and Brandon's lithograph of the north end of Kensington Palace Gardens in which all the buildings designed by them appear prominently (Plate 92a), presumably shows their original design, as they had presented a copy to the (Royal) Institute of British Architects by May 1844.

† Some of the ornamental motifs on the exterior reappear on Jones's other house for Blashfield, No. 24, where they can still be seen. Jones himself evidently regarded No. 8 as important, for he exhibited the design for the garden front at the International Exhibition of 1862.[71]

length of time it has remained unoccupied'. Mrs. Murray therefore divided it into two, having first built an extension on the south side designed by her architects in a matching style.[72] The southern half, first occupied in 1853 by Mrs. Murray herself, was hereafter called No. 8A, and the northern half No. 8. The latter was first occupied in 1854 by Russell Gurney, barrister and Recorder of London. Subsequently a number of additions, all more or less in a matching style externally, were made to both halves of the building (Plate 92c).[73]

After the war of 1939–45 (when it had been used for the interrogation of spies), the house was in a dilapidated state, and the Crown Estate Commissioners, who were anxious to preserve the building, could find nobody who wanted it either as a private residence, or for conversion to other use. In 1955, however, a developer was found to convert the house into seven 'high class' flats, but before the work could be carried out another developer took over and his architects, Richard Seifert and Partners, advised that the existing structure was unsafe. In 1961 the Commissioners somewhat reluctantly agreed to allow the developer to demolish the house and erect a block of luxury flats.[74]

No. 9 Kensington Palace Gardens
Plate 104c, d

This house was built in 1852–4 for Anselmo de Arroyave, a Spanish-born merchant who had occupied No. 7 Kensington Palace Gardens since 1847. Arroyave offered the Commissioners an annual ground rent of £70 10s. for the site; Pennethorne recommended this offer in April 1852, and in May an agreement was concluded by which Arroyave undertook to spend at least £4,000 in building a first-rate house to be completed by 5 April 1854.[75] The house was designed by Sydney Smirke, whose plans and elevations were submitted to the Commissioners in July 1852 and approved by them, after alterations, in September. Smirke said that he intended to treat all four fronts 'similarly and uniformly', and consequently the Commissioners made it a condition of their approval that no other buildings would be permitted to intrude on the open space around the house.[75] The contractors were Lucas Brothers, who had submitted the lowest tender at £4,280.[76] Building began in about November 1852 and by October 1854 Arroyave was living in the house.[77]

The ground lease was granted to him in June 1855.[78]

It appears from the existence of a few working drawings that Alfred Stevens designed some of the original interior decorations, but none of these survives.[79] The most substantial subsequent alterations have been the addition of an attic (in 1866) and the extensions on the north and south sides. The attic was designed by William Thompson for Charles F. Huth, a 'commission merchant', who occupied the house from 1866 until 1895.[80]

No. 9 is a stucco-faced house consisting of a basement, three storeys, and an attic, the latter largely concealed behind the balustrade. Only the symmetrical west façade survives in basically its original form (Plate 104c). It is three windows wide, and has large plain quoins. The fenestration is unusual: two square windows, flanking the entrance, project from the main façade on the ground floor only. The antae on either side of each window are decorated with pilasters of an amalgamated Tuscan and Roman Doric order, and each window, between the antae, is subdivided by two slender cast-iron columns supported on the sills, the central window being twice as wide as those between the iron columns and the antae. The main entrance is, in effect, distyle in antis, the columns being of the same order as the pilasters. The whole projection on the ground floor is crowned by a plain cornice surmounted by a balustrade at first-floor level. This cornice is continued round the house.

Each of the three identical first-floor windows consists of an aediculated opening, with a segmental pediment over a plain entablature carried on two slender cast-iron columns. The three second-floor windows, above a simple stringcourse that extends round the building, have moulded architraves with crossettes. The façade is surmounted by a dentilled cornice with lions' masks fixed to the cyma recta moulding, the whole being crowned by a stucco balustrade, the dies of which support stucco balls.

The plan was originally symmetrical, the rooms being grouped on either side of the staircase and entrance hall. The walls of the latter are plastered to resemble ashlar work, and four painted panels, depicting cherubic subjects, are set above the doorways right and left. The most important room is the main drawing-room (Plate 104d), to the right of the entrance hall, which extends the full depth of the house. The walls are lined with finely carved and gilded wooden panels of the Louis Quinze period, inserted in 1938, the cartouches depicting varieties of game.[81] There are marble fireplaces surmounted by pier-glasses. Other marble fireplaces of good quality exist in the dining-room, and in the conference-room on the first floor.

The house is now (1972) occupied by the Indian High Commissioner.

No. 10 Kensington Palace Gardens
Plates 100–101

This house, now considerably altered, was designed in the manner of an Italian *palazzo* by Philip Hardwick for Sutherland Hall Sutherland, esquire, of Princes Street, Hanover Square, who bought the site from Blashfield in 1846. Hardwick's plans and elevations (Plate 100) were submitted to the Commissioners on 22 October 1846 and approved by them on 28 October, Pennethorne having reported that the house, 'although only two stories high above the ground & therefore not of the same large scale with other Houses built along this Road ... will in every respect fulfill the Conditions of Mr Blashfield's Agreement'.[82]

Building began at the end of 1846 and because of a misunderstanding over the terms under which Sutherland had taken the plot the Commissioners allowed him an extra year in which to complete the house, provided that the exterior was finished and 'rendered to all appearances habitable' and the gardens laid out by October 1847.[83] The lease was not executed until September 1848, and at Sutherland's nomination it was granted to Charles James Heath of New London Street, Fenchurch Street.[84] But Heath did not occupy the house himself, and it remained untenanted until James Meadows Rendel, the civil engineer, acquired the lease in 1851.[85]

Before Rendel moved into the house, probably early in 1852, it was altered for him by Banks and Barry. These alterations included the insertion of a number of round-headed dormer windows, of which Rendel wrote 'the design has the approval and indeed originated with Mr Barry Junior'. Pennethorne advised the Commissioners to consent but considered that 'the exterior will be somewhat injured'.[86]

Rendel died here in 1856 and in 1862 the house was acquired by Ernest Leopold S. Benzon, a German-born steel magnate, to whose elaborate dinner parties came many of the leading artists, writers and musicians of the day. Benzon began extensive alterations to the house to the designs of Paul Jumelin and Lawrence Harvey, but on his death in 1873 they were discontinued.[87]

In 1896 substantial alterations designed by Leonard Stokes were made for the financier Leopold Hirsch. Stokes had submitted plans for a very elaborate remodelling in December 1895, which were warmly welcomed by the Commissioners' architect, Arthur Cates, who thought they would have 'converted this house into a small palace'. They were, however, replaced by designs for less elaborate, though still extensive, alterations. Their principal features, in so far as they affected the external appearance of the house, were the addition of a mansard roof, square attic windows, a balustrade above the cornice, a one-storey extension on the north side and a new porch. The proportions of some windows were altered and all windows were fitted with small-pane sashes. The walls, which had originally been faced with white bricks and Portland stone dressings, were rendered with stone-coloured Portland cement (Plate 101a, b). Inside, major alterations were made on every floor, including the formation of a round-ended billiard-room on the ground floor, which projects in a semi-circular extension on the south side.[88]

Further alterations were made for Hirsch in 1903–4 by Messrs. Fryer and Company. An extra storey was added to the north side extension and a pedimented attic storey to the centre of the west front (Plate 101a).[89]

The house is now (1972) occupied by the Soviet Diplomatic Mission.

No. 11 Kensington Palace Gardens
Plate 105; fig. 33

This house was built in 1852–4 for Don Cristobal de Murrieta, an elderly Spanish-born merchant who had occupied No. 26 Kensington Palace Gardens since 1845.[90] Murrietta had applied for the plot, for which he offered an annual ground rent of £92, through his son Mariano. Pennethorne recommended his offer, and in May 1852 an agreement was concluded with Mariano who undertook to spend at least £4,000 in building a first-class house, and to complete it by 5 April 1854.[75]

The architect was Sydney Smirke, whose plans and elevations for the house were submitted to the Commissioners in July 1852 and approved by them in September. Smirke proposed to treat all four sides of the building 'similarly and uniformly', and the Commissioners made it a condition of their approval that the ground around the house should be kept free of buildings.[75] The contractors were Lucas Brothers, whose tender, at £5,200, was the lowest submitted.[76] Building began in about November 1852 and by June 1855, when the ground lease was granted to Mariano and his brother José, Don Cristobal was living in the house.[91]

Some of the original interior decorations were designed by Alfred Stevens. In the drawing-room the principal feature of his scheme was a series of canvas panels painted with figures depicting heroines from *The Faerie Queene*. These panels were attached to the wall above eye level within fanciful frames painted on to the wall surface. In the morning-room Stevens designed the ceiling, which was painted with small figures emblematic of the four seasons. None of these decorations now survives. Stevens's biographer, H. Stannus, who must have seen the panels *in situ*, regarded them as among Stevens's most important works, and in 1891 he urged that they 'should be secured for the nation if the present owner should ever part with his interest in the house'.[92]*

The original house has been considerably altered. In 1873 a one-storey ball-room and art gallery was added to the south side for José de Murrietta by the architect Edward Tarver, who had designed a house for the family at Wadhurst in Sussex in 1872. The west elevation of this extension was originally treated in a free Baroque manner which Tarver thought would reduce its apparent width, thereby helping to preserve the detached appearance of the house. In 1874 Tarver designed the present high-pitched château-like roof after the original roof (which was partially hidden behind a balustrade) and top storey were destroyed in a fire. The Commissioners' architect, Arthur Cates, was reluctant to approve Tarver's designs; he would have preferred a mansard roof, but after many modifications Cates eventually recommended the design to the Commissioners, although in his opinion 'it was not free from eccentricity'.[93] In 1894 a one-bay three-

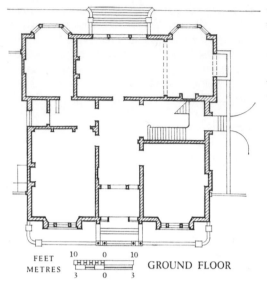

FEET   10   0   10
METRES   GROUND FLOOR
        3   0   3

Fig. 33. No. 11 Kensington Palace Gardens, ground-floor plan in 1855

storey extension was added to the north side for R. W. Perks, M.P., from the designs of Charles Bell.[94]

In 1937 the interior was redecorated for the Duke of Marlborough by Lenygon and Morant, and before the work was carried out the Commissioners ordered a photographic survey.[95] This shows that a number of rooms had elaborate embellishments, although in the drawing-room Stevens's panels (but not his painted ceiling decorations) had already disappeared. In the ball-room the shallow domes of the ceiling (now removed) and the friezes were painted with arab-esque ornaments. The dining-room frieze was painted with panels of figures and animals and the ceiling with floral patterns, and in the first-floor room over the hall the coving was painted with birds and flowers and the ceiling with an oval panel representing the sky. In this room also was a fine carved fireplace and chimneypiece incorporating decorative tiles. Some of this work had been executed by Walter Crane, who in his *Reminiscences* recalled that in about 1873-4 'Mr E. J. Tarver, an architect . . . got me to design and paint a frieze in panels of animals and birds for a house in Palace Gardens'.[96]

Another single-storey extension was added to the north side in 1947-8 for the French Embassy,

---

* Sketches and drawings for Stevens's decorations in this house are preserved in the Victoria and Albert Museum, the Royal Institute of British Architects and the Tate Gallery.

and at the same time considerable alterations were made to the interior.[97] The house is now (1972) the residence of the French Ambassador.

In its elevational treatment this house has certain similarities to No. 9, although the stucco detail is richer. Both the west and east fronts of the original house were symmetrical, but the extensions to the north and south have considerably unbalanced the design.

The house is stucco-faced and consists of three storeys over a basement, with an attic. The front is a composition of some distinction, and has a porch, carried on two pairs of fluted Corinthian columns, surmounted by a balustrade. On either side of this porch, but, unlike No. 9, not attached to it, are two square projections containing windows, their antae enriched by fluted Corinthian pilasters supporting plain entablatures surmounted by balustrades (Plate 105a).

The three widely proportioned first-floor windows of the original house each have two slender cast-iron columns supporting the entablature. The two outer windows have pediments above containing simple cartouches. The second-floor windows are surrounded by moulded architraves with crossettes above a simple string-course. The house has plain quoins and is crowned by a rich entablature, with an anthemion frieze and dentilled cornice. There are dolphins' masks on the cyma. Above the cornice is the attic added by Tarver in 1874, which consists of tall aediculated dormers surmounted by segmental pediments. The dormers in the centre are combined within a Mannerist composition crowned by a pediment. The balustrade between the dormers has open fret patterns instead of balusters, and the dies carry swagged urns. The tall roofs, together with the dormers and urns, give this house a distinctive Parisian appearance.

The garden front has three French windows, opening to a terrace, flanked by two three-sided bay windows (Plate 105b). The first floor has aediculated windows, with cartouches in the pediments. The side windows are widely proportioned, similar to those on the front already described. The second-floor windows have moulded and crossetted architraves, and the entablature and main cornice are carried round from the front. The attic is treated in a similar fashion to that on the front.

The single-storey extensions to the north and south (the latter altered) both have Corinthian pilasters supporting plain entablatures and crowning balustrades.

The interior plan is spacious, and the proportions of the rooms very pleasing. The entrance hall, off which are the library and cloakrooms, leads to a cross-passage containing the stairs. The floor of the hall and passage was laid with black and white marble in 1937[95] (Plate 105c). A large doorway with a cornice carried on large consoles in the Florentine Renaissance manner leads to the main drawing-room, which is decorated in pale cream, with gilded Rococo mouldings featuring feathers, leaves, swags, and flower motifs (Plate 105d). The cove contains figures and swags in low relief. The little drawing-room, to the north of the main room, has more elaborate Rococo décor based on marine motifs. This room gives access to the long dining-room, situated in the most recent extension. The drawing-rooms also extend into what was the ballroom built in 1873. There are now mirrored doors in marble architraves surmounted by pediments, with circular wheel-pattern mirrors over them.

No. 12 Kensington Palace Gardens
Plates 94–5; fig. 34

The building of this handsome house was begun by Thomas Grissell and his partner (Sir) Samuel Morton Peto and completed by Grissell alone after the dissolution of their partnership in March 1846 (see page 158). The plans and elevations were submitted to Pennethorne on 13 February 1845 together with those for No. 20, and in an accompanying letter the builders asked that they should not be 'strictly' bound by the designs, although they had 'no intention of departing from them essentially'. Pennethorne reported that both sets of plans were 'unexceptionable', and, 'considering (as I believe) that they emanate from Mr Barry and are to be built by Messrs Grissell & Peto', he thought the Commissioners would 'probably be willing to allow them to deviate as they request'. On 19 February the Commissioners gave their consent.[37]

The *Companion to the British Almanac for 1846*, which published an illustration as well as a brief description of the finished house, 'understood' that the architect had been Robert Richardson Banks. Banks was a pupil of (Sir) Charles Barry and was at this time the architect in charge of Barry's office.[39] No doubt he was involved in the production of working drawings for the house and he may have supervised the construction.[40]

While building was in progress Grissell and Peto acquired the vacant adjoining plot to the south (now the site of No. 12A), where they proposed to lay out a garden to be leased with No. 12. The Commissioners gave their consent, the builders having spent on No. 12 over £6,000, which was the minimum that they would have been required to spend on building a house on each site, and in May 1847 both plots were granted to Grissell in a single lease at an annual rent of £185. The lease also included a stable in the mews.[98]

Although No. 12 was variously reported as 'finished' in April 1846 and 'nearly ready for habitation' in May, it remained unlet (though probably not unoccupied) until 1853, when Peto took an under-lease from his former partner.[99]* Since the dissolution of their partnership Peto, with his brother-in-law, Edward Ladd Betts, had pursued the career of a railway contractor, and in 1847 he had entered Parliament.[101] At the time of the census of 1861 Peto's household was the largest in Kensington Palace Gardens, comprising twenty-eight occupants, of whom sixteen were servants. Lack of accommodation could not, however, have been the reason why, two years later, he decided to build himself another larger house in the garden alongside No. 12, for his first intention then had been to move to a smaller house in Carlton Gardens.[102]

Before Peto moved into his new house (now No. 12A), No. 12 was sold by his mortgagees for £25,000 to Alexander Collie of Sussex Gardens, Bayswater, a London and Manchester cotton merchant, and in 1864 Collie spent several thousand pounds on alterations designed by Matthew Digby Wyatt. The principal staircase was extended to the second floor, a new breakfast-room was built at the north-east corner, matching the conservatory which Peto had added at the south-east corner, and a new billiard-room, decorated in the 'Moorish' taste, was constructed in the former kitchen. Outside, the chimney-stacks were raised and the second-floor windows at the back were lengthened and fitted with iron and stone balconettes.[103]†

Collie occupied No. 12 from 1865 until the bankruptcy of his business in 1875. He was prosecuted for obtaining £200,000 from a bank by false pretences, broke bail and disappeared. In September 1875 *The Times* reported that hope of recapturing him had not been abandoned, but by 1878 he had still not been re-arrested. In 1875 his creditors had expected the house to realize about £15,000, but ten years elapsed before it was occupied again.[105]

The house is still in private occupation.

No. 12 was aptly described by the writer in the *Companion* as having 'in its general aspect quite as much or even more of the club-house than the usual villa character, it being altogether in that *astylar* Italian palazzo mode which Barry introduced among us in the club-houses built by him'.[106] The design is, indeed, not only similar in its general outlines to Barry's Italianate club-houses in Pall Mall, but also has some close parallels of detail: the unusual relationship of solid and void at the back recalls the garden front of the Travellers' Club, and the sumptuous *cornicione* is very similar to that on the Reform Club.

The house is of three storeys over a basement, five windows wide, with a central doorway, and is flanked by one-storey wings over basements. The front is nobly proportioned, with window openings on the ground and first floors treated in the manner of Michelangelo (Plate 94a). The ground-floor windows are surrounded by architraves and surmounted by segmental pediments on brackets. The main entrance has a round-headed arch with a large keystone, set between engaged Ionic columns which carry an entablature. There is a stringcourse enriched with lattice-work at first-floor level. The north wing contains a niche within an architrave over which is a cornice carried on brackets, while in the south wing the niche has been replaced by a window. The first-floor window-openings have architraves and are surmounted by cornices carried on brackets. The second-floor windows have crossetted architraves only. The house is crowned by a *cornicione* enriched with guilloche carving, dentils, reel-and-bead and egg-and-dart mouldings, brackets, and dolphins' masks on the cymatium (fig. 34).

* In the census of 1851 the house appears to have been occupied by Peter Duval, Grissell's agent and building superintendent, and his wife, who had been living in one or other of Grissell's houses in the road since at least 1849.[100]

† In 1866 Wyatt exhibited a study at the Royal Academy for a painted ceiling executed here, perhaps in the billiard-room.[104]

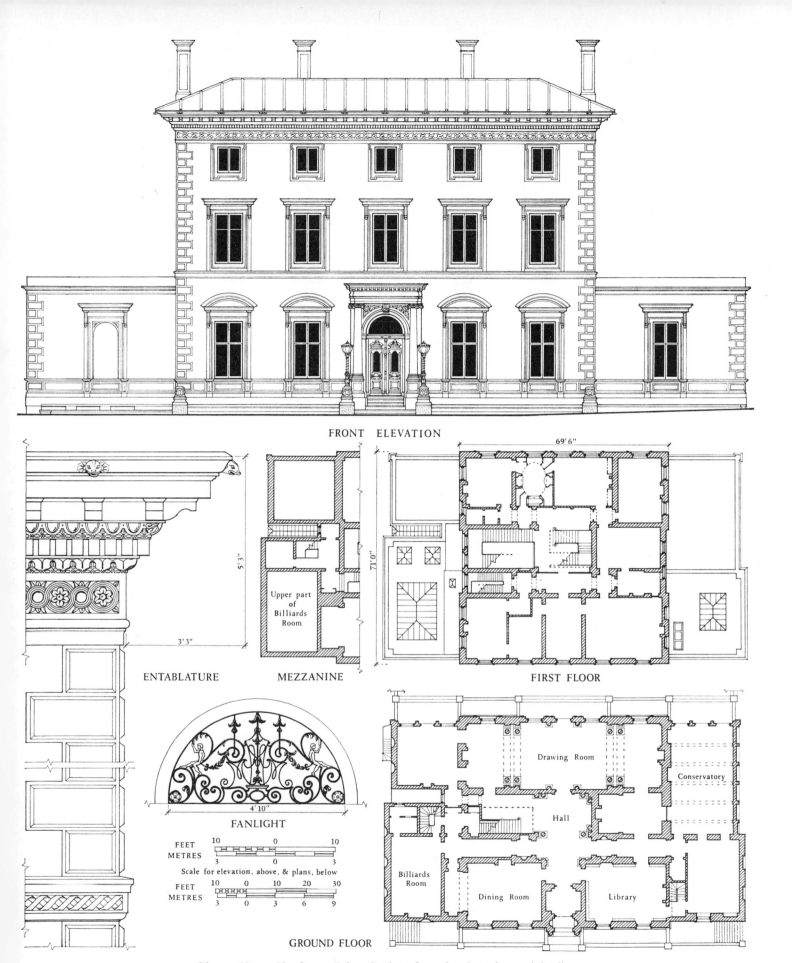

FRONT ELEVATION

ENTABLATURE

MEZZANINE

Upper part of Billiards Room

FIRST FLOOR

69'6"

71'0"

5'3"

3'3"

FANLIGHT

4'10"

FEET 10 0 10
METRES 3 0 3
Scale for elevation, above, & plans, below
FEET 10 0 10 20 30
METRES 3 0 3 6 9

GROUND FLOOR

Drawing Room

Conservatory

Hall

Billiards Room

Dining Room

Library

Fig. 34. No. 12 Kensington Palace Gardens, front elevation, plans and details

At the back, the three middle windows are closely spaced together (Plate 94c). The ground-floor windows and French doors all have round-arched heads, and the architraves and archivolts have rusticated blocks and voussoirs, with large keystones. The first-floor windows rise from the lattice-work stringcourse, each having architraves with three large rusticated blocks, and keystones. They are surmounted by plain cornices carried on brackets. The lengthened second-floor windows, with the iron and stone balconettes of 1864, now give a top-heavy appearance to this façade. The two single-storey wings flanking the house each have three high round-headed windows organized as arcades with moulded archivolts and plain keystones.

The plan of the house is almost symmetrical (fig. 34). The walls of the entrance hall are plastered to simulate ashlar work, and the columns are of the Ionic order (Plate 94b). The corridors to the north and south are vaulted. The floor is of stone, with black marble inlay. There is a stone stair to the first floor, with cast-iron balustrade.

Immediately to the south of the entrance hall is the library (Plate 95c), fitted out with shelves, cupboards, and inlaid doors. There are panels of carved wood over the doors and bookshelves, and the fireplace and overmantel, crowned by a broken segmental pediment, are carved with Florentine and Baroque motifs. The woodwork of this room is markedly similar to that of the staircase from the first to the second floor. The plaster ceiling of the library is ornamented with strapwork in the Jacobean manner. These decorations and fittings probably all date from 1864.

Among the other rooms, pride of place must be given to the billiard- (now flower-)room designed by M. D. Wyatt (Plate 95d). This is a rich and glittering invention in the Moresque style, with a brightly coloured glazed-tile dado above which is a cornice carried on carved brackets. Over this is an arcade on colonnettes of marble, behind which is a series of mirrors. The coved ceiling, decorated with arabesques, is open in the centre and supports a clerestory pierced by eight-pointed star-shaped lights. This clerestory is decorated with intricate geometrical patterns based on Islamic motifs. The colours are varied and strong, and the gilding is lavish.

The drawing-room, which faces the garden to the east and gives access to the terrace, is sub-divided into three parts by unfluted marbled Corinthian columns supporting a modillioned cornice (Plate 95a). In the dining-room (Plate 95b) the original deeply moulded ceiling survives.

No. 12A Kensington Palace Gardens
Plate 107c

This house was erected in 1863–5 for Sir Samuel Morton Peto in the garden of No. 12, the house which he had occupied since 1854. The site, although originally intended as a building plot, had been granted to Peto's former partner, Thomas Grissell, in the lease of No. 12 in May 1847 (see above). But the right of the lessee subsequently to erect a house here had not been extinguished, and in April 1863 Peto, who had agreed to purchase the ground lease from Grissell, informed the Commissioners that his architect, James Murray, would soon be submitting plans and elevations for their approval. Although Peto did not tell the Commissioners his reasons for giving up No. 12 he explained to them that his decision to build a new house here was in deference to his wife's wish to remain in Kensington Palace Gardens; he himself had proposed to move to Carlton Gardens.[107]

Murray's plans and elevations were examined by Pennethorne on 30 April 1863 and approved by the Commissioners on the following day. Subsequently a number of small adjustments were made to the design, apparently at Murray's request.[108] The contractors were Lucas Brothers, an important firm of builders whose two partners, Thomas and Charles Lucas, had been on Peto's staff during his partnership with Grissell.[109] The internal decorations were designed by Owen Jones and executed by Messrs. Jackson and Graham, who were also entrusted with the furnishings. Other decorative work was executed by Messrs. Minton (encaustic and majolica tiles for the conservatory and Roman mosaic pavements in the central hall and vestibules), and Messrs. Elkington (Griotte marble columns with bronze bases and capitals in the hall). The extensive and elaborate stables erected by Lucas's and fitted up by Burton of Oxford Street were in Kensington Mall.* According to *The Builder* the

* When the house was offered for sale in 1903 *The Estates Gazette* described the stables as 'on a scale rarely met with in London . . . something after the style of Tattersalls'. The site is now occupied by Broadwalk Court (see page 40).

total cost was between £45,000 and £50,000.[110]

Peto had moved into his new house by June 1865, but he did not live there long.[111] In May 1866 the financial crisis precipitated by the collapse of the bill discounting firm of Overend, Gurney and Company forced his own firm, Peto and Betts, to suspend payment, and he gave up the house.[112]* In 1867 Peto and Betts were declared bankrupt and although their affairs were finally settled satisfactorily the firm never recovered. No. 12A meanwhile had been acquired by (Sir) Thomas Lucas, one of the partners in the firm which built it, and he lived there from 1866 until his death in 1902.[114] It was for Lucas that the single-storey picture gallery, designed in a matching style by W. J. Green, was erected on the north side in 1876.[115]

The house is now (1972) occupied by the Royal Nepalese Embassy.

No. 12A is a substantial house, faced with stone on the west and east elevations, and consists of three storeys over a basement, with an attic. It is seven windows wide in front, with the single-storey wing of 1876 to the north and a small conservatory to the south. On each side of the three centre windows is a three-sided bay window rising through two storeys.

The restrained treatment of the principal façades is enhanced by the fine quality of the carved stonework. There are quoins, and a principal modillioned cornice with an anthemion frieze, the whole surmounted by a balustrade (Plate 107c). Two other cornices are provided at the first- and second-floor levels, the former being plain, with a Greek-key frieze, and the latter being dentilled, with a guilloche frieze. Elaborately carved stone panels are set above the ground-floor windows. The house has been redecorated several times, and (as far as is known) nothing of Jones's original scheme survives.[116]

The stables in Kensington Mall included living quarters, room for nine coaches, and twelve stalls opening into a central two-storied nave with arched roof on iron columns.[110]

No. 13 Kensington Palace Gardens: Harrington House

Plate 103; fig. 35

In March 1851 the fifth Earl of Harrington, an important landowner in South Kensington who had succeeded to the title only a few weeks previously, applied to the Commissioners for a large vacant plot on the east side of Kensington Palace Gardens where he wished to build a house for his own occupation.† The Commissioners replied that although they could not accommodate the Earl on the terms which he proposed (a ninety-nine-year lease at £120 a year) they would be willing to let the site to him at £147 a year for a period expiring in 1942, subject to his spending not less than £6,000 in building a first-class house to be completed by 5 January 1853. Lord Harrington agreed on condition that he should be allowed to build the house in his favourite style—the Gothic. Pennethorne reported favourably on the designs and on 12 July the Commissioners gave their consent.[117]‡ The contractor was John Baker of Marylebone, who applied for permission to lay the drains in August and began building in October.[118] Lord Harrington was living in the house by July 1853, and in December 1854 he was granted the lease.[119]

The architectural authorship of the design for No. 13 was described by *The Builder* in 1852 as follows: 'The original design for the exterior was made by Mr. Burton, to suit plans sketched by the Earl, but the works are being carried out under the superintendence of Mr. C. J. Richardson.'[120] Another contemporary journal named 'Mr Burton' (i.e. Decimus Burton) as the author of the design but there is no mention of him or any other architect in the Commissioners' records, nor have any of the original drawings been found.[121] Probably both Burton and the Earl made sketches and suggestions, but left the details and working drawings to Richardson, who was surveyor to Lord Harrington's South Kensington estate, and under whose name views of

* J. H. Gurney, one of the directors of Overend, Gurney and Company, had himself lived in Kensington Palace Gardens at No. 24, from 1859 to 1861.[113]

† The site in question consisted of the whole of one of Blashfield's plots and an adjoining part of another, the latter having been left vacant by the builder of No. 14.

‡ That Pennethorne should have recommended without comment a 'Gothic' design for a road where hitherto the houses had all been more or less Italianate is explained by his remark some years later, that the Gothic style was one of many concessions made to the Earl in the discussions which took place before the final plans were approved. No doubt any objections which Pennethorne may have had were overruled by the Commissioners in their determination to acquire so highly desirable a tenant.[107]

the house were exhibited at the Royal Academy in 1852 and 1855.[122] After Lord Harrington's death (in 1862) Richardson did acknowledge that 'The fronts of the building were designed in great measure by his late Lordship', but his account of the house in his book *Picturesque Designs . . .* (1870) seems to imply that he alone was responsible for the design.[123]

In this account Richardson admitted that the exterior of the building had been 'censured on account of the Gothic outline being too flat, the roofs too low, and all the windows having common sash frames'. The windows were, indeed, particularly singled out for criticism. *The Builder* found them 'more eccentric than beautiful'[120] and the *Companion to the British Almanac*, 'by no means elegant'.[121] *The Builder*, which had described the design as 'somewhat German in character', subsequently published a scathing attack by an anonymous correspondent: 'Were I to express my opinion of it without reserve, I should be compelled to make use of language and

epithets which, however justly merited, would be deemed as illiberal as they would be disagreeable. . . . Instead of "repose" we have actual torture—the very thumbscrew of design.'[124] Richardson defended the building on the grounds of 'convenience, comfort, and complete suitability for all domestic purposes', and he quoted letters from Lord Harrington congratulating him on having constructed a house '*without a fault*'. He justified the design of the windows on the ground that 'it may be considered very probable that if the Gothic race of architects had continued with us to the present day, they would have adopted plate glass for their windows, and put aside their lead-lights and small panes of common glass'.[125]

No. 13 is one of the biggest houses in the road, and was said to have cost the Earl about £15,000, although according to Richardson 'as little expense in decoration was gone into as possible'. The original interior was apparently 'very plain', most of the rooms being only ornamented by a

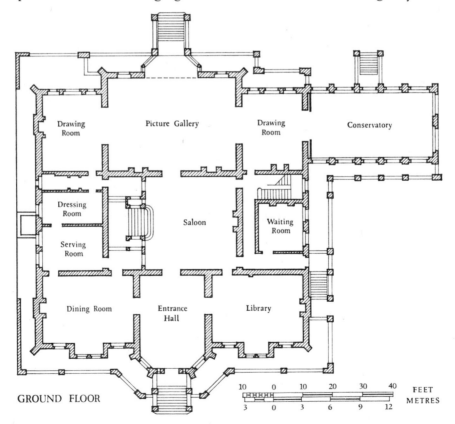

Fig. 35. No. 13 Kensington Palace Gardens, original ground-floor plan

plain cornice of 'running Gothic mouldings'. The saloon (Plate 103b), however, was more elaborately treated, and had a coved ceiling painted with shields, coats of arms, mottoes and monograms.[126]

After Lord Harrington's death his widow continued to occupy the house until her death in 1898.[127] In 1924 it was acquired by Sir Lewis Richardson, a South African merchant, who in that year spent over £25,000 on alterations designed for him by Sidney Parvin. The whimsical bell-turret was removed, new steps were added at both front and back, and a wooden porch was erected in front. The windows of the conservatory were altered and its original sloping roof replaced by the present flat one. Considerable changes were made inside, many of which survive.[128] The house is now (1972) occupied by the Soviet Embassy.

It is constructed of buff-coloured bricks with Bath stone dressings, and consists of two principal storeys over a basement, which is fourteen feet high and of fireproof construction, with a part-storey above, which originally contained the female servants' sleeping quarters.

Despite the loss of its bell-turret the three-storey central tower containing the main entrance still dominates the symmetrical west façade (Plate 103a, c). Above the entrance is a projecting oriel window surmounted by a quatrefoil parapet, and below the central window is a panel now bearing Sir Lewis Richardson's arms. The sash-window openings are rectangular, the only concession to period style being some idiomatic cusping at the corners and the drip moulds over some of the windows. At the corners of the building are diagonal buttresses of stone on brick piers. The house is crowned by an open parapet of crude 'Gothic' design. On the south side of the house is the conservatory, contained in a single-storey extension over a basement.

Inside, a small entrance hall, flanked by the former library and dining-room, leads to the saloon (fig. 35). The latter forms the heart of the house and is two storeys high, illuminated by a skylight in which are the remains of embossed and coloured glass depicting heraldic devices. The present double oak staircase in the saloon, in a late seventeenth-century style, replaced the original stone stair in 1924, when the walls were panelled in oak, and new landings supported on steel cantilevers with oak balustrades were fixed around three sides of the room. None of the original decorations appear to survive in the principal rooms on the ground floor. These were originally warmed with hot-water pipes covered by ornamental iron grilles.

The spacious domestic accommodation originally provided in the basement, which extends under the courtyard on the south side of the house, included a kitchen, scullery, pastry-room, still-room, dairy, wash-houses, laundry, butler's pantry, steward's room, servants' hall, men's sleeping-room, wine cellars, furnace, cart sheds, cowhouse, dung-pit, coach-house, coal cellars, dust-pit and closets.[129]

No. 14 Kensington Palace Gardens
Plate 102; fig. 36

In March 1845 Blashfield submitted plans and elevations for a house designed by T. Hayter Lewis which he proposed to erect on the southernmost of his plots on the east side of the road. In an accompanying letter Blashfield wrote that 'The style here attempted is Venetian and treated much after the manner of Sansovini [sic] the architect for the Library of St. Mark's, Venice'. According to *The Builder* a view of the garden front exhibited at the Royal Academy in 1845 showed that the proposed house had 'an arcade in front of both of the two principal floors'.[130] The Commissioners approved the design, but the plot was still vacant when Blashfield became bankrupt in May 1847.[44]

The present No. 14 occupies a little over half of Blashfield's original plot and was erected in 1850–1 under an agreement between the Commissioners and Edmund Antrobus of the Strand, a tea merchant. In November 1849 Antrobus had applied to lease 100 or 120 feet of the original 170-foot frontage of the plot, for which he offered a rental of 15s. a foot. This was less than Blashfield had paid, but Pennethorne advised the Commissioners to accept Antrobus's offer.[55]

The house was designed and built by Thomas Cubitt. Pennethorne thought the designs (Plate 102a, b) compared unfavourably with other houses in the road; 'the Architecture of the fronts', he wrote, 'would be much inferior to those built by Mr Grissell and other gentlemen'. But Antrobus was unwilling to incur a large expenditure, and as the building would not cost less than the £3,000 which he had agreed to spend,

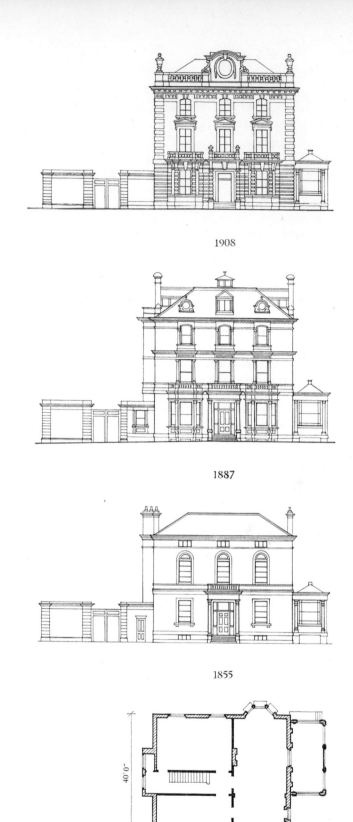

1908

1887

1855

40' 0"

46' 0"

1855

Fig. 36. No. 14 Kensington Palace Gardens, front elevation in
1855, 1887 and 1908, and ground-floor plan in 1855

Pennethorne felt obliged to recommend the design to the Commissioners.[131] Building began in May 1850 and by June 1851 the house was occupied.[132] The lease, for 100 feet of frontage at an annual rent of £75, was granted to Antrobus in January 1852.[133]

Antrobus lived here until his death in 1886, when the ground lease was sold at auction for £8,100 to Henry Solomon of Inverness Terrace, Bayswater. In 1887 substantial alterations were made for Solomon from the designs of N. S. Joseph and Smithem. An extra storey and attic were added, the interior remodelled and the elevations worked over in a French Rennaissance manner (fig. 36). The Commissioners' architect, Arthur Cates, welcomed these changes: 'they will make the house worthy of its position and remove some of its grave defects'. The present front elevation (Plate 102c) was designed by White, Allom and Company in 1908 for Solomon's son.[134] At the back the stucco-dressed white-brick façade of the original design can still be discerned, despite the additions of 1887, and of a bay window designed by Cubitt in 1855 (Plate 102d).

Inside, almost every trace of the original decorations has been removed, except for the cast-iron balusters of the stair. The living-room, which extends from the front of the house to the rear, now has an acanthus-leaf cornice and two Ionic columns that support a beam dividing the room into two compartments. The dining-room, in the north-east of the ground floor, is in the late seventeenth-century manner, the doorways having ornate carved architraves surmounted by broken pediments.

The house is now (1972) occupied by the Finnish Ambassador.

Nos. 15 and 15B Kensington Palace Gardens
Plates 106, 107a; fig. 37

In March 1852 Frederick Chinnock of Regent Street, an auctioneer, applied successfully to the Commissioners for a lease of the southernmost plot on the east side of The Queen's Road, one of two sites which they had made available for building only recently (see page 160). Terms were agreed but in January 1853 Chinnock relinquished his interest: his reasons included 'the greatly increased cost of building within the last few months', and the fact that the site was overlooked by the palace stables. Thereupon Penne-

thorne asked the next applicant to make an offer. This was S. W. Strickland, the builder of Nos. 1–5 Kensington Palace Gardens. He offered a rental of £130 a year for the plot, which was to include an adjoining piece of land to the north, originally intended to be laid out as a roadway, but then let (as was the original building plot itself) to the occupant of No. 14, on a quarterly tenancy. This offer was accepted and by an agreement of February 1853 Strickland undertook to spend not less than £6,000 in building two first-rate houses here, to be completed by 10 October 1855.[135]

Almost immediately Thomas Grissell, the builder who lived at No. 19, made inquiries which led Strickland to believe that he would be willing to take over the agreement. The occupant of No. 14, Edmund Antrobus, was raising difficulties about the termination of his tenancy, and Strickland, who throughout his dealings with the Commissioners adopted an excessively deferential and self-effacing tone, later admitted that he would 'gladly have surrendered to one having a large stake in this property, and being more influential than myself, the task of arranging the difficulties that had arisen with reference to Mr Antrobus'. Grissell, however, eventually declined to take over Strickland's agreement ('I am inclined to think I had better not build more'), but he recommended it to his friend George Moore, the lace manufacturer and philanthropist, who in July 1854 agreed to undertake it provided he should be allowed to build only one house at a cost of about £10,000.[135]

The Commissioners had not been told of these changes when, on 31 July, they received from Moore's architect, James Thomas Knowles senior, the plans and elevations for a large detached house. Pennethorne nevertheless recommended them: 'considering . . . the proximity of this plot in particular to the Palace', he wrote, 'it appears to me that the substitution of a large House for two smaller will be advantageous to the interests of the Crown'. On 8 August the Commissioners approved the plans, but asked to see more detailed drawings, which Knowles submitted in September.[135]

The house was built by Lucas Brothers and Stevens of Lambeth, who began work in December 1854.[136] In June 1855 the house was recorded for the first time in the parish ratebooks but it was not occupied by Moore and his family until the following year.[111] The ground lease was granted to Moore at Strickland's request in November 1855.[137]

George Moore was a typical example of the Victorian self-made man. From an unpromising beginning as a £30-a-year assistant in a draper's in Soho Square he had risen to become the most important lace manufacturer in the country. His biographer was none other than Samuel Smiles, to whom Moore confided his uneasiness at having spent so much on a house: 'Although I had built the house at the solicitation of Mrs. Moore', he said, 'I was mortified at my extravagance, and thought it both wicked and aggrandizing—mere ostentation and vain show—to build such a house.'[138]

No significant alterations were made to No. 15 until 1937–8, when parts of the interior were completely remodelled by Lord Gerald Wellesley and Trenwith Wills for Sir Alfred Beit, the financier and philanthropist.[139] The house is now (1972) occupied by the Iraqi Ambassador.

No. 15 is one of the most architecturally distinguished houses in Kensington Palace Gardens. It consists of three storeys over a basement, although prior to the insertion of the windows in the frieze, the third storey received light only from the roof and from windows in the central recess at the back. The symmetrical west façade is a noble and palatial Italianate astylar composition in the manner of Sir Charles Barry, seven windows wide, with small single-storey wings to the north and south (Plate 106a). The entrance is in the centre, flanked by Roman Doric engaged columns supporting an entablature, and the ground-floor windows have architraves surmounted by bracketed cornices carried on consoles. The ground storey has vermiculated rustication, and is crowned by a large bracketed cornice. The first-floor windows are aediculated, with engaged Corinthian columns supporting entablatures and pediments. The second-floor windows, dating from 1937–8, interrupt the frieze below the rich Roman Corinthian main cornice, and tend to alter the balance of the façade. The southern elevation of the single-storey south wing has an arcade carried on Corinthian columns, and both wings are surmounted by balustrades.

The rear elevation (Plate 106b) is reminiscent of Thomas Allom's contemporary work on the Ladbroke estate. The ground storey, emphasized by vermiculated rustication, has two large bows flanking the centre, and above the windows are Grecian friezes. On the second floor the two terminal façades, each having a pair of aediculated windows, were originally separated by the deep recession of the centre to form a light-well, with two Italianate staircase towers at the inner corners. In 1937–8 this light-well was masked by a screen linking the terminal façades. It consists of two Corinthian columns set in antis and carrying a simplified version of the original entablature. This is surmounted by two draped classical female figures, and the niches in the antae are occupied by large urns.

The plan of the house is symmetrical, the rooms being grouped round a spacious entrance hall, the original fabric of which has survived (fig. 37). This hall has a heavy coffered ceiling, and the entablature, with modillioned cornice, is carried on marbled Ionic columns with gilded capitals (Plate 107a). A stone stair with cast-iron balustrade of Grecian design rises to a first-floor landing of the same area as the hall, and where the architectural treatment is similar. There are low-relief Grecian friezes in the hall and staircase, and on the cream-coloured walls are *grisaille* drapes painted in 1937–8. To the north of the hall are the library and dining-room, both also redecorated in 1937–8. The former is treated as a pastiche of Bavarian Rococo originally designed round J. de Lajoue's painting of an alchemist, but now somewhat unconvincing without the picture (Plate 106c). The colour-scheme is rose-madder, grey, white, and verde antico marbling, with discreet gilding. The parquet floor is inlaid with a star pattern, which echoed that in the painting.

The dining-room is elliptical in shape, but was originally rectangular, with a bow window. It has an order of Corinthian pilasters supporting an entablature with swagged frieze and modillioned cornice. Six rectangular frames in exuberant early eighteenth-century style are set in the panels between the pilasters, and originally contained the six paintings by Murillo depicting the Parable of the Prodigal Son. The colour scheme was turquoise with silver enrichments. The ceiling contains a panoply of arms and armour, designed by Rex Whistler, which concealed the spotlights illuminating the pictures.

South of the hall, and extending the full depth of the house from west to east, is the music-room

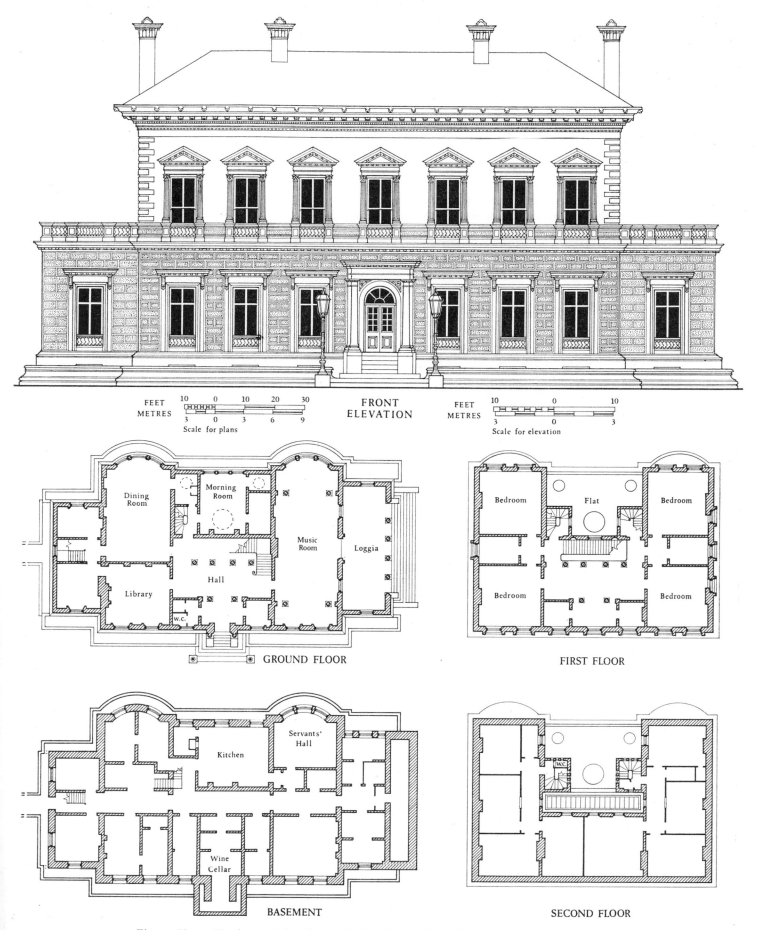

FEET 10 0 10 20 30
METRES 3 0 3 6 9
Scale for plans

FRONT
ELEVATION

FEET 10 0 10
METRES 3 0 3
Scale for elevation

Dining Room

Morning Room

Music Room

Loggia

Hall

Library

w.c.

GROUND FLOOR

Bedroom

Flat

Bedroom

Bedroom

Bedroom

FIRST FLOOR

Servants' Hall

Kitchen

Wine Cellar

BASEMENT

W.C.

SECOND FLOOR

Fig. 37. No. 15 Kensington Palace Gardens before the alterations of 1937–8, front elevation and plans

(Plate 106d), attached to which is the single-storey loggia, formerly a winter-garden. The music-room is spacious and elegant, with *fleur de pêche* marbled Corinthian columns at either end and a modillioned cornice. At the rear of the house is the drawing-room, once a smaller morning-room, but redecorated in mid eighteenth-century style with Ionic marbled columns, modillioned cornice, plaster plaques and swags.

No. 15B, the former stable block of No. 15, was designed by Knowles and built by Lucas Brothers in 1855. It was converted into a house in 1937–8 by J. Fooks and T. Ritchie, architects.[140]

No. 15A *Kensington Palace Gardens*
Plate 107b

The site of this house, like that of No. 15, was made available for building only in March 1852 (see page 160). The Commissioners had, however, already received an offer for it in January from Peter Carthew of Kensington, a 'fundholder', which Pennethorne in April advised them to accept. Terms were agreed and Carthew undertook to spend at least £3,000 in building a first-rate house here, to be completed by 5 April 1854.[141]

The architect was David Brandon (whose partnership with T. H. Wyatt had been dissolved in 1851), and the contractor was John Kelk of South Street, Grosvenor Square, an important and successful builder who subsequently erected the Albert Memorial. Brandon's plans and elevations were approved by the Commissioners in June 1852 and building began in July.[142] By May 1853 the carcase was almost complete but the house was evidently not finished for another two to three years. It was first occupied by Carthew in 1856. The cost was said to have been about £7,000.[143]

The lease of the site, at an annual rent of £73 2s. 6d., was granted to Carthew in July 1855 and at the same time he entered into two agreements with the Commissioners to take a yearly tenancy of all the remaining land to the south on the west side of the road, previously let to a butcher for grazing sheep and cattle. By one of these agreements a strip of land thirty feet in width immediately adjoining the site of the house was to be laid out as an ornamental garden.[144] This piece has now been incorporated into the site of No. 15A. The rest of the area was to be occupied only as a paddock, and a number of rights of way across it were reserved to the Crown. This area was surrendered for building in 1902 (see page 189).

The house is now (1972) occupied by the Nigerian High Commissioner.

It is built of white bricks with stucco dressings and consists of three storeys over a basement, and an attic. From a contemporary description in the Commissioners' files it appears, however, that there were originally no rooms in the roof. The detail is conventional, save for the rusticated surrounds to the ground-floor windows and the plaque set on the single-storey wing. The two tiers of attic storeys on the north side were added in 1934. The interior has been much altered. In the main drawing-room are painted medallions representing classical allegories, set beneath the cornice.

No. 16 *Kensington Palace Gardens*
Plate 99b

This house was designed by T. H. Wyatt and D. Brandon for John Sperling of Norbury Park, Leatherhead, a retired army officer and 'landed proprietor', who purchased the site from Blashfield in 1846. The architects' plans and elevations were approved by the Commissioners in May 1846 and building began soon afterwards.[145] In May 1847 Pennethorne reported that the house was inhabited, although in the parish ratebooks it is recorded as empty until June 1849.[146] When Sperling applied for the lease, in April 1847, he asked for the site to be extended to include part of the adjoining plot to the south.* The Commissioners agreed, and in April 1850 a lease of the enlarged site was granted to him at an annual rent of £105.[147]

Sperling occupied No. 16 until his death in 1877, when the ground lease was purchased by Stuart Rendel, later Baron Rendel of Hatchlands, an armaments manufacturer. In 1877 Rendel engaged Charles Barry, junior, to prepare designs for an extensive remodelling of the house: plans were approved and tenders submitted, but the work was not executed. In 1903 the house was altered both internally and externally by P. Morley Horder, who designed the unusual

---

* This plot was outside the area agreed to be let to Blashfield.

columnar entrance porch and other embellishments.[148]

The house is now (1972) occupied by the Soviet Diplomatic Mission.

It consists of three storeys over a basement, and is three windows wide. The east façade is symmetrical, and the style is Italianate, with undistinguished stucco ornament.

No. 17 Kensington Palace Gardens
Plate 93a, b; fig. 38

This house has been so much altered since it was built by Blashfield in 1844–6 that the original design in the north Italian villa manner is now hardly discernible (Plate 93a). The architect was Henry E. Kendall, junior, whose plans and elevations were approved by the Commissioners in May 1844.[35] The lease of the site, at an annual rent of £82, was granted to Blashfield in October 1844, and in May 1846, when the house was finished, he sold the lease to John Balls of Oxford Street, an upholsterer.[149]* The first occupant, in 1847, was David Laing Burn.[111]

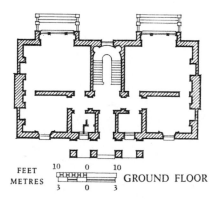

FEET   10   0   10
METRES   3   0   3   GROUND FLOOR

Fig. 38. No. 17 Kensington Palace Gardens, ground-floor plan in 1846

The present front (Plate 93b) is the result of alterations and additions carried out at three different dates. The raised pediment between the two original 'wings' and the third-storey windows below the crowning cornice were inserted in 1884, when the house was altered for S. P. Kennard by J. Kinninmont and Sons, builders and decorators. The three-bay extension on the

south side, designed by Charles E. Sayer, was erected in 1899–1900 for the banker Isaac Seligman, who had bought the lease in 1899. At the same time the original balconies were removed from the first-floor windows. The three-bay extension over a garage on the north side was built for (Sir) Charles Seligman in 1928 from plans prepared by Messrs. Joseph, who also designed the new entrance porch. The interior has also been almost completely remodelled.[150]

This house is still privately occupied.

Nos. 18 and 19 Kensington Palace Gardens
Plate 98; fig. 39

The building of this pair of houses was begun in 1845 by Thomas Grissell and his partner (Sir) Samuel Morton Peto and completed, after the dissolution of their partnership in March 1846, by Grissell alone (see page 158). The designs were submitted to the Commissioners for approval in August 1845 and received an enthusiastic welcome from Pennethorne. 'The Plans and Elevations are in my opinion greatly to be admired', he wrote, 'and the villas if built according thereto will be an Ornament to the place.'[37] The Commissioners' files contain no reference to the name of the architect but there can be no doubt that the houses were designed in (Sir) Charles Barry's office (see page 158). The style of the building is in the Italian *palazzo* manner so favoured by Barry, and is very close to some of the preliminary designs for Bridgwater House, on which he had been working since 1841.

Building began in about September 1845, and by May 1846 Pennethorne was able to report that the carcase of the building was complete except for the slating of the roof, 'which it is not prudent to do for another month until the Towers are built'. In constructing the thick stone-faced walls of the houses the builders used some of the 'small surplus stone' from the new Palace of Westminster.[37] Early in April 1847 both houses were reported built and later in the month the leases were granted to Grissell at an annual rent of £78 (No. 18) and £78 6s. 8d. (No. 19). Each lease included stables in the adjoining mews.[151]

Both houses are first recorded as occupied in 1851: No. 19 by Grissell himself, his wife and nine servants, and No. 18 by John Leech, a

---

* In May 1844 Blashfield had told the Commissioners that the house was to be built for one Charles Bowdler, esquire.[26]

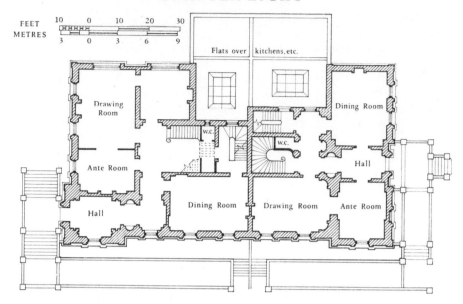

Fig. 39. Nos. 18 and 19 Kensington Palace Gardens, ground-floor plan in 1847

'general merchant', his family of seven, and eight servants.[152]

Both houses have been altered and enlarged, No. 18 rather more extensively than No. 19. In 1870 a two-bay, two-storey extension including a picture-gallery and billiard-room was built at the back of No. 18 for (Baron) Julius (de) Reuter, founder and director of the international news agency, who occupied the house from 1868 until his death in 1899. At the same time (1870) a third tower was erected at the south-west corner, and along the south side a one-storey conservatory and entrance porch were built. The architects for these alterations, designed in a matching style, were F. and H. Francis. In 1904 the middle section of the conservatory was removed and laid out as a terrace.[153]

At No. 19 a one-storey study was built for Grissell at the back in 1857 from the designs of R. R. Banks and Charles Barry, junior, and in 1884 a new porch and a single-storey extension at the north-west corner were erected for Gustav C. Schwabe, a banker, from the designs of F. W. Porter.[154]

Nos. 18 and 19 are unusual in being a semi-detached pair in which the two houses are of different sizes and internal arrangements. The asymmetrical plan (fig. 39) is, however, concealed by a formal stone-faced façade to Kensington Palace Gardens of Palladian design with a central block flanked by two taller towers. The slightly

recessed central block is five windows wide and two storeys high over a basement, and the two flanking towers are each three storeys high, over basements (Plate 98).

Window openings are aediculated: those on the first floor with a Roman Doric order, and those on the second floor with Ionic pilasters supporting segmental pediments. The main cornice is carried on large moulded console brackets, the whole surmounted by a partly balustraded parapet. The towers have quoins and the top stages are decorated with festoons. The elevational treatment is continued on the stone-faced sides, but the back of the houses, in brick, is plain.

Inside there is little left of the original design save for the vaulted entrance halls, and the ceilings in the main reception rooms of No. 19. The dining-room ceiling here has a richly modillioned cornice, guilloche moulding, and a central rose, and there are finely enriched and gilded ceilings in the drawing-room and ante-room.

No. 18 is now (1972) occupied by the Soviet Diplomatic Mission, and No. 19 by the Egyptian Consulate.

No. 20 Kensington Palace Gardens
Plates 96, 97a; fig. 40

This house, like Nos. 12, 18 and 19, was built by Thomas Grissell with (prior to March 1846) his partner (Sir) Samuel Morton Peto (see page

158). The plans and elevations for No. 20 and No. 12 were submitted together to Pennethorne on 13 February 1845 with a request from the builders that they should not be strictly binding. Two days later Pennethorne reported that both sets of designs were 'unexceptionable' and on 19 February the Commissioners gave their consent.[37] In Pennethorne's report both sets of designs were said 'to emanate from Mr Barry' (see page 158).

Although No. 20 was reported to be 'nearly ready for habitation' at the end of May 1846 it appears to have remained unoccupied until 1852, when Louis Blumberg took the house as Grissell's tenant.[155] The ground lease of the site, which included a stable in the adjoining mews, had been granted to Grissell in April 1847, at an annual rent of £78 6s. 8d.[156]

As first built the unusual design of the house, shown in a drawing of 1857 (Plate 96a), was even more reminiscent of the work of Vanbrugh or Hawksmoor than it is today—an effect largely due to the giant order of Roman Doric pilasters standing on pedestals, and to the bold grouping of the chimneys at the corners. The orderly façade was crowned by a large Roman Doric entablature, above which was a balustrade concealing the dormer windows in the roof. The dies of the balustrade were capped by urns, and the corner chimney-stacks decorated with blind arches. The window-openings on the first and second storeys had shouldered and segmental heads with keystones. Between the pilasters the walls were channelled and grooved to resemble ashlar.

In 1857–8 substantial alterations were made by Grissell from the designs of R. R. Banks and Charles Barry, junior (Plate 96b). The roof was raised five feet to provide a full attic storey, the corner chimneys were heightened to correspond, and the triglyphs between the capitals of the pilasters removed. At the back the ground-floor library was extended by the addition of a large four-sided bay. In 1884 a porch was added, and at the back a single-storey billiard-room, both to designs by Robert Sawyer. The present porch, inappropriately decorated with Ionic pilasters, was erected for J. E. Taylor in 1888 and designed by Ernest George and Peto, who also remodelled the principal staircase. In 1890 George and Peto designed the single-storey extension on the north side for Taylor.[157] The façade is now plain rendered and lacks the former keystones over the windows (Plate 97a).

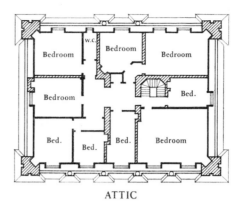
ATTIC

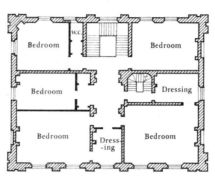
FIRST FLOOR

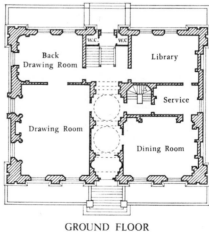
GROUND FLOOR

Fig. 40. No. 20 Kensington Palace Gardens, original plans

The plan creates an effect of symmetry, the main rooms being disposed on either side of the long entrance hall, which is divided into three domed bays (fig. 40). The rooms on the upper floors have been rearranged, and a new staircase has been built out to the rear. On the ground floor, however, many of the original mouldings, cornices and pilasters survive.

The house is now (1972) occupied by the Commission for European Communities.

Nos. 21, 22 and 23 Kensington Palace Gardens

Plates 99a, c, 104a, b

These three houses were all designed and erected by Charles Frederick Oldfield, a builder. The earliest (No. 21) occupies a site which Oldfield had acquired from Blashfield in 1845; the other two were built after Blashfield's bankruptcy on plots surrendered by his assignees.

No. 21 In June 1845 Blashfield, on Oldfield's behalf, submitted the plans and elevations of this house to the Commissioners, and these were approved in July subject to some modifications in the treatment of the chimneys. By December the carcase had been completed, and in April 1846 the house was reported to have been 'nearly finished'. The ground lease, at an annual rent of £90, was granted to Oldfield in June 1846, and by then the house was occupied by Anthony Wilkinson, a 'landed proprietor'.[158] It is now (1972) occupied by the Lebanese Embassy.

This conventional stucco-faced house in the Italianate manner consists of three storeys over a basement, and is five windows wide (Plate 99a). A projecting porch of the Roman Doric order is carried on four columns and is centrally placed in the symmetrical east elevation. The façade is rusticated up to the subsidiary cornice at first-floor level. The first-floor window architraves are surmounted by pediments, and the second-floor windows have plain architraves. The house has quoins and is capped by a modillioned and den- tilled cornice over which is a balustrade.

The interior has been considerably altered. The entrance hall and staircase were remodelled in 1905 by William Flockhart, and are decorated in an early eighteenth-century manner, with richly moulded and garlanded plasterwork. The saloon (Plate 99c) is lined with panels of Rococo design containing cartouches within which are land-

scapes in low relief. The ceiling is coved and moulded, with delicate Rococo enrichments. The panelled dining-room is in the Jacobean style, and has a plaster ceiling with strapwork mouldings.[159]

No. 22 Unlike Nos. 21 and 23, this house was not built as a speculation. It was designed and erected by Oldfield for William Frederick Gostling of Stowell House, Richmond, who in February 1851 had offered the Commissioners a rental of £75 a year for the site. His offer was accepted and an agreement concluded by which Gostling undertook to build and finish the house by 5 July 1853. The plans and elevations were submitted in December 1851 and approved by Pennethorne, who nevertheless suggested that Gostling might like to reconsider some of the details of the upper-floor window-dressings.[160]

Building was reported in progress in December 1851, and by April 1854 Gostling was living in the house. The ground lease was granted to him in April 1853. The principal subsequent alteration to No. 22 has been the building of a two-storey extension, including a ballroom, on the north side in 1883–4. This was designed by Francis Hooper for Alfred Hickman.[161] The house is still privately occupied.

Excluding the extensions the house consists of three storeys over a basement, stuccoed in the Italianate manner, and is five windows wide, the portion containing the centre three windows standing forward (Plate 104a). The house is crowned by a heavy blocked cornice, but there is no balustrade.

No. 23 In April 1852 Pennethorne advised the Commissioners to accept Oldfield's offer of £75 a year for this site, and an agreement was concluded by which Oldfield undertook to finish building a house by 5 April 1854. Oldfield's plans and elevations were approved in May 1852, and in July his clerk of works applied for permission to lay the drains.[162] Building began in September.[163] By December 1853 the house was sufficiently 'advanced towards completion' for Oldfield to be entitled to the lease, which was granted to him in January 1854, and although the house was probably completed soon afterwards it remained empty until 1856. The first occupant was Isaac Moses, a merchant, who bought the lease from Oldfield towards the end of 1855.[164]

Before moving into the house Moses engaged J. D. Hopkins to design two one-storey wings, neither of which appear to have been built, the present one-storey wing on the north side being added in 1970–1. In 1856 the same architect designed for Moses the two-bay three-storey extension at the south-west corner and the bow-fronted ballroom at the back. The elegant conservatory on the south side was erected in 1877–8 to the design of Edward Salomons, who was also the architect of a new billiard-room which was built at the north-west corner in the same year.[165]

This house is now (1972) occupied by the Japanese Embassy.

It consists of three storeys and a basement (Plate 104b). The stuccoed east façade is seven windows wide with the central portion slightly recessed, forming outer pavilions each two windows in width. The coursed ground storey is finished with a plain cornice, and a canopied porch projects from the centre of the façade. The first-floor windows have moulded architraves, the three in the centre having segmental pediments, and the flanking pairs having plain cornices. There are panels of balusters beneath the sills. An enriched stringcourse extends across the front below the second-floor windows, which have crossetted architraves. The façade is finished with a bracketed cornice crowned by a balustrade.

The entrance hall occupies the full depth of the house, and contains a stone stair, with cast-iron balusters, at the rear. The decorations of the hall are plain, the only enrichments being provided by the egg-and-dart moulding of the cornice, and the brackets supporting a beam.

The long dining-room, to the north of the hall, is partly within the original house, and partly in the one-storey wing. It has a fine concave cornice enriched with acanthus leaves. The drawing-room, to the south of the entrance hall, has a modillioned cornice, but is otherwise unremarkable. West of the drawing-room, and approached from it through double doors, is the ballroom, with a large bow projecting into the rear garden. This room is decorated with pilasters, based on Florentine Renaissance originals, supporting a large coved cornice enriched with trellis-work, which has also been copied in the ceiling rose. There is a carved marble fireplace.

The study, a small room adjoining the ballroom, with access from the hall, has plaster walls moulded to resemble linenfold panelling of the Tudor period.

Apart from the cornices above the stairs, and in the hall, dining-room and drawing-room, the internal decorations are not original.

No. 24 Kensington Palace Gardens
Plate 97b; fig. 41

When Blashfield submitted the plans and elevations of this house for approval in August 1845 Pennethorne reported to the Commissioners that 'as the House will be large, handsome & well disposed, I see no reason for objecting to either the plans or Elevation—although the latter is in the Moresque Style, which (though not usually adopted), is admired by some persons & produces a picturesque effect'.[166] Unfortunately these drawings have not survived,* and in the absence of any contemporary picture it is not possible to say how far the present elevation (Plate 97b) represents the intentions of the architect, Owen Jones.[44] The Indian-style domes on the parapet appear to be original, but other 'small cement ornaments' on the parapet and chimney-stacks were removed in 1879.[166]

The Commissioners approved the designs in September 1845, and by December work was sufficiently advanced on the carcase of the house for Blashfield to apply for the lease.[167] This was granted to him on 23 December and on the following day he mortgaged it for an unknown sum to Lewis Vulliamy, the architect, whose pupil Jones had been.[168]

The house had not, however, been completed when Blashfield became bankrupt in May 1847, although the work was reported well advanced, with the exterior 'finished down to the cornice above the ground floor windows'. At first Blashfield's assignees proposed to finish the house themselves, and they obtained from the Commissioners an extension of the time allowed in which to do so. In July, however they decided they did not have the necessary authority to carry out the work, and in August the unfinished house was sold at the auction of Blashfield's estate for £3,400, although Blashfield had spent over £9,000 on the building. The purchaser was James Ponsford, a builder who worked extensively in Bayswater and St. John's Wood as well as on Thomas Cubitt's developments in Belgravia. Ponsford completed the house and lived there with

* In 1878 it was said that Blashfield had borrowed the original plans and failed to return them.[166]

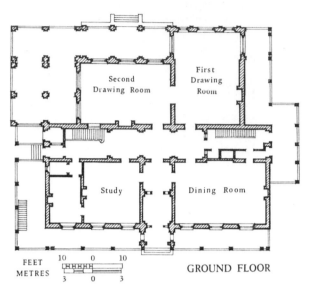

FEET 10 0 10
METRES   GROUND FLOOR
      3   0   3

Fig. 41. No. 24 Kensington Palace Gardens, ground-floor
plan in 1845

his family from 1850 to 1859. In 1851 his household consisted of twelve people of whom five
were servants.[169]

No doubt Ponsford completed the exterior of
the building in accordance with the approved
designs, but there is no evidence that the original
interior decorations were by Jones (as they had
been in his other house for Blashfield, No. 8).
Several additions have been made at the back of
the house, the most important being the picture
gallery designed by Herbert Cescinsky for Chester
Beatty in 1937. Cescinsky had previously converted the adjoining stables in Palace Gardens
Mews into a library for Beatty.[170]

The house is now (1972) occupied by the
Saudi Arabian Ambassador.

It consists of three storeys over a basement,
and is completely faced with stucco. The east
façade is symmetrical, seven windows wide, with
a central projecting porch, and a balcony extending across the full width of the elevation on lotus-
patterned supports (Plate 97b). There is a
crowning cornice and parapet, the latter, like the
balcony, being pierced with geometrical
'Moresque' decoration. The onion-shaped domes
on the parapet give the house a somewhat exotic
appearance, but the eclectic exterior includes
some recognizably contemporary features, and
generally the style of the house owes as much to

English and Italian precedents as to either Moorish or Indian prototypes. The decorative motifs
are used on a basically classical façade, replacing
conventional balusters, consoles, urns and statuary.

On the ground floor the principal rooms have
been remodelled. They include a study with
panelling in the Jacobean style, and a plaster
ceiling and frieze reminiscent of the work of
Ernest Gimson, a first drawing-room in the
Rococo style of the mid eighteenth century, and
a second drawing-room in the Baroque manner.
This has a deep, heavily modelled, cornice of
large acanthus leaves with emblems of geography,
literature, military might and music. Above the
fireplace and over the window opposite are
allegorical cartouches of summer and winter.

Nos. 25 and 26 Kensington Palace Gardens
Plates 92a, 93c. Demolished

In March 1844 Blashfield had proposed to erect
only one house here and he submitted a design
by T. H. Wyatt and D. Brandon which the
Commissioners approved. By the end of the year,
however, two similar, though not identical,
Italianate villas with 'campanile towers' had been
built on the site from the designs of the same
architects.[171] The ground leases, each at an annual
rent of £65, were granted to Blashfield in October
(No. 26) and December (No. 25) 1844.[172] By
June of the following year No. 26 was occupied
by Blashfield's tenant Cristobal de Murrietta, a
Spanish-born merchant and banker.[173]

No. 25, the larger of the two, on which
Blashfield spent over £10,000, was still unoccupied
when he became bankrupt. In August 1847 the
house was put up for auction by his assignees, but
was withdrawn at £6,700. Eventually it came
into the hands of Frederick Dawson of The
Temple, to whom Blashfield had mortgaged the
house for £7,500, and in 1852 he leased it to
Benjamin B. Greene, a 'landowner and merchant',
who was the first occupant.[174]

No. 25 was demolished in 1947 on account of
extensive dry rot, and No. 26 was demolished to
make way for the new Czech Embassy.[175] This
building, erected in 1968–9, was designed by J.
Šrámek, J. Bočan and K. Štěpánský of Prague in
association with Robert Matthew, Johnson-
Marshall and Partners. It occupies all of the site
of No. 26 and part of the site of No. 25, and has a
long frontage to Notting Hill Gate which extends

as far as Palace Gardens Terrace and thus blocks off the old entrance to Palace Gardens Mews.[176]* A new entrance to the mews has now been laid out across part of the site of No. 25.

No. 1 Palace Green
Plates 108–9; fig. 42

In March 1867 George James Howard, the twenty-three-year-old nephew of the eighth Earl of Carlisle, purchased the lease of the old grace-and-favour residence at No. 1 Palace Green for £1,600.[178] This lease, which was for eighty years from 1863, contained a provision that the old house had to be demolished and a new one built at a cost of at least £3,500. Howard, whose 'real devotion was to art', had commissioned Philip Webb to design him a house with a studio, and before buying the lease he had taken the precaution of finding out that a red-brick house by Webb would not be objected to in principle by the Commissioners.[179]

Pennethorne, however, refused to approve Webb's drawings when they were submitted in August 1867. He wrote to Charles Gore, the First Commissioner, that if the house was built according to them it would be '*far inferior* to any one on the Estate—it would look most commonplace—and in my opinion be perfectly hideous'. He made his main objections clear later when he wrote, 'So far as I understand the drawings there would be scarcely any stone visible in the fronts of the house, the whole of the surfaces would be masses of red brickwork without relief from stone or from any important strings or cornices'.[180] He also objected to the steep pitch of the roof and the gable on the east elevation. Webb's original design has not, as far as is known, survived, but Pennethorne's comments and later ones by Webb himself imply that a modicum of stonework may have been intended for the east front, but that on the extensive north and south façades the dressings were to be entirely of brick.

Webb at first refused to compromise and Howard's father, Charles Howard, who was Member of Parliament for East Cumberland, began to put pressure on the Commissioners, beginning a letter, 'George is much annoyed as

well he may be'. Gore replied that 'you must not think me unkind if I do not altogether disregard the interests of the Crown while desirous as far as possible to comply with George's wishes'.[180] Gore disliked the design almost as much as Pennethorne but was prepared to give way. Pennethorne, however, was adamant in his refusal to give his approval, and letters between himself and Webb reveal the irreconcilable differences between an architect in his sixties brought up in the tradition of Nash and a young man in his thirties who wished to reject what he considered to be the artificialities of the stucco age and return to a vernacular tradition of building in brick. To Pennethorne's criticisms Webb replied that, 'I must decidedly disagree with you, that the proper proportioned window openings which I have used, fitted with well divided sashes, is an "unattractive" form . . . I must also beg to differ from your opinion that the materials used would not give the proper relief; a well chosen full coloured red brick, with pure bright red gauged brick mouldings, arches, string courses, cornices &c with the addition of white Portland stone, white sashframes, lead, and grey slates, are in my opinion the very best and most harmoniously coloured materials to be used in London, & more especially in a neighbourhood so happily full of green foliage . . . In conclusion, I must express my great surprise that you should consider it worth your while to hinder the erection of a building, which—whatever may be its demerits—possesses some character and originality, tempered most certainly with reverential attention to the works of acknowledged masters of the art of architecture, and as certainly framed with the wish to avoid adding another insult to this irreparably injured neighbourhood.'[180]†

Anthony Salvin and Thomas Henry Wyatt were called in as referees and endorsed Pennethorne's judgment. Webb commented significantly about one of their criticisms, 'That Messrs. Salvin and Wyatt are "unable to discover what actual style or period of architecture" I have used, I take to be a sincere compliment', for he was attempting to achieve a form of architectural expression which would not be restricted by conformity to one or other of the historic styles. He

---

* The small piece of the Crown Estate at the south-east corner of Notting Hill Gate and Palace Gardens Terrace (to the west of Palace Gardens Mews) was acquired by purchase in 1892.[177]

† 'The greater number of existing houses in Palace Gardens', wrote Webb, 'have their origins clearly written on their faces, though it is a question whether their fathers would be pleased with the likeness.'[181]

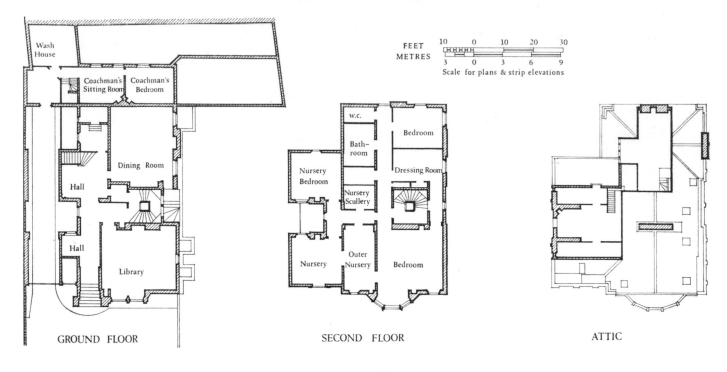

Wash House

Coachman's Sitting Room   Coachman's Bedroom

Dining Room

Hall

Hall

Library

GROUND FLOOR

w.c.

Bath-room

Bedroom

Nursery Bedroom

Dressing Room

Nursery Scullery

Nursery   Outer Nursery   Bedroom

SECOND FLOOR

ATTIC

FEET
METRES

10   0   10   20   30

3   0   3   6   9

Scale for plans & strip elevations

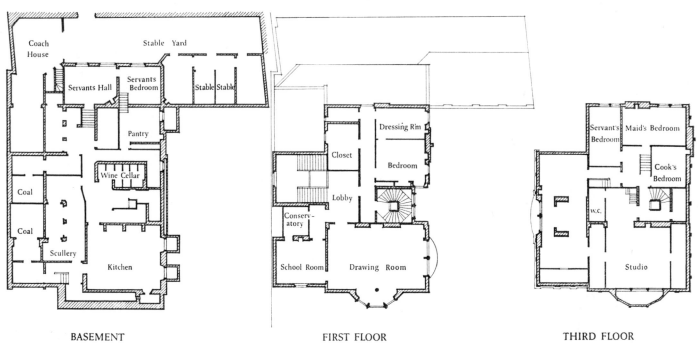

Coach House

Stable Yard

Servants Hall   Servants Bedroom   Stable Stable

Pantry

Wine Cellar

Coal

Coal

Scullery

Kitchen

BASEMENT

Dressing Rm

Closet

Bedroom

Lobby

Conserv-atory

School Room   Drawing Room

FIRST FLOOR

Servant's Bedroom   Maid's Bedroom

Cook's Bedroom

w.c.

Studio

THIRD FLOOR

Fig. 42. No. 1 Palace Green, plans in 1883

agreed finally to modify the design, however, and submitted new elevations in February 1868. In a letter to Howard he explained the main variations from his original design. These consisted principally of the addition of some stonework in the form of a plinth, a broad band of stone at first-floor level with a moulded stringcourse, the substitution of stone for brick and tile sills to most of the windows, and the finishing of the chimney caps in stone. Other alterations included raising and broadening the porch with the addition of 'a considerable amount of carved decoration', redesigning the studio window, which was to be set in 'a more ornamental gable of diapered brick and stone', and the addition of 'a considerable amount of ornamentation' to the drawing-room window on the north elevation. 'Under the circumstances' Pennethorne was prepared to approve the revised drawings, provided that a stone cornice with a projection of at least eighteen inches was substituted for the brick one. Webb refused this point blank, as he considered the construction and proportion of the building to be essentially Gothic and the introduction of a classical cornice to be completely incongruous. Once again there was deadlock and Howard approached William Butterfield to supply another design. Butterfield refused the commission, partly because he considered that Webb had been unfairly treated, but also, according to Howard, because he did not wish to place his work under the control of Pennethorne's taste. T. H. Wyatt was consulted again and advised that a brick cornice was acceptable.[181]

At last the house could be built. It was completed in carcase by June 1869[182] and Howard was in residence by the following summer.[111] With the addition in 1873 of a gable similar to that on the east front to the south elevation[183]—now unfortunately largely obscured—the exterior of the house received the form which survived with little alteration until the 1950's (Plate 108a, c). The interior decoration was carried out over several years, largely to the designs of Webb and fellow artists in the William Morris circle. The *pièce de résistance* was the ground-floor morning-room or dining-room, for which Burne-Jones, assisted by Walter Crane, provided an elaborate frieze painted on canvas panels illustrating the legend of Cupid and Psyche as retold in one of Morris's poems in *The Earthly Paradise* (Plate 109).[184]*

Shortly after Howard, by then ninth Earl of Carlisle, died in 1911, the lease was purchased by John Barker and Company and for a while the house was used as a furniture store. In 1922 Barker's proposed to demolish it and add its site to that on the south, which they had taken under a building agreement with the Commissioners. A strong protest from a group of writers and architects greeted this proposal, and the house was saved.[185] In 1957 permission was granted for its conversion into flats, and the resulting alterations have not only denuded the interior of its original character, but have led to serious changes to the exterior, particularly the addition of several windows in the north elevation (Plate 108b).[186]

No. 2 Palace Green
Fig. 43

This house was built in 1860–2 for William Makepeace Thackeray. It has often been said that Thackeray was himself largely responsible for its design, and that its erection marked a milestone in the history of architectural taste, but there seems to be little evidence for either of these contentions.

In March 1860 Thackeray offered to take the old grace-and-favour house at No. 2 Palace Green on a repairing lease.[187] Pennethorne had suggested that the house should be demolished and a new one built in its place, but the Commissioners, mindful of Queen Victoria's objection to the erection of any new buildings opposite to Kensington Palace, did not immediately act on his suggestion.[188] After negotiation Thackeray's offer was accepted, and on 8 March he wrote, 'I have taken at last the house on Kensington Palace Green in which I hope the history of Queen Anne will be written'.[189]

Thackeray had agreed to spend £1,400 on repairs, but when a careful survey was made of the house its much-dilapidated condition was revealed. In May 1860 Frederick Hering, a sixty-year-old architect with an office in Argyll Street, St. James's, submitted drawings and specifications for a new house to be built of red brick with cement dressings at a cost of at least £4,000.[187] In view of the Commissioners' reluct-

* The panels are now in the City of Birmingham Museum and Art Gallery.

10   0   10   FEET
3   0   3   METRES

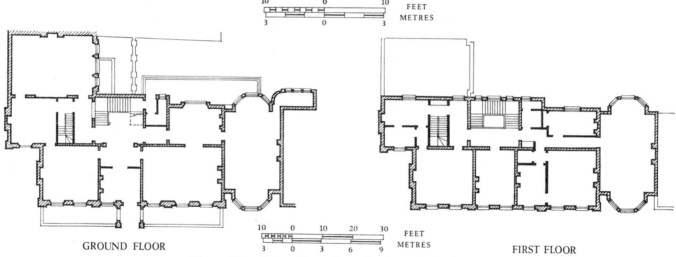

GROUND FLOOR   10   0   10   20   30   FEET   FIRST FLOOR
                     3   0   3   6   9   METRES

Fig. 43. No. 2 Palace Green, front elevation and plans in 1882

ance to sanction a new building on the site, it is likely that discussions had taken place which are not revealed in the correspondence. Pennethorne reported that 'I see no objection to the Design being approved on condition that all the Details be copied from those of Marlborough House*— all the rusticated piers—the Cornices &c . . . to be executed . . . in Stone, or Portland Cement'.[187] In the light of this report the Commissioners' approval, which was sent to Thackeray on 29 June 1860, reads somewhat strangely, for it required all the dressings to be of red brick;[190] in the event both brick and stone or stucco dressings were used. The builders were Jackson and

* Kensington Palace would have been the obvious choice, but Pennethorne may have been thinking of the east elevation of the barracks recently erected on the old forcing ground nearby, which recalls Marlborough House. In fact several of the details of No. 2 Palace Green, such as the raised panels of brickwork and rusticated brick piers, are more suggestive of the palace than of Marlborough House.

Graham, an Oxford Street firm which specialized largely in interior decoration, and the house was ready for occupation by March 1862. The total cost, including fittings, was over £8,000.[191]

The assertion that the design was Thackeray's own appears to have been first made by his biographers shortly after his death in 1863.[192] There is no doubt that he took a close personal interest in the house, and he may have been instrumental in choosing red brick as the facing material, for he undoubtedly endorsed the views of a contributor* to the April 1860 issue of *The Cornhill Magazine*, of which he was the editor, that the ideal house was 'of red brick, not earlier than 1650, not later than 1750'.[193] The choice of red brick, however, also satisfied the Commissioners, who, if they had to sanction a rebuilding at all, wanted the new house to harmonize with Kensington Palace. The relationship between architect and client is not known, but that Hering was more than merely a nominal architect is suggested by the fact that he exhibited a drawing of the projected house under his own name at the Architectural Exhibition held in Conduit Street in 1861. In May 1861 Thackeray wrote about the house, then under construction, to an American friend, calling it 'the reddest house in all the town' and enclosing a sketch from 'fond memory'. This sketch shows several variations from the finished house including seven dormer windows instead of five, the hint of stucco architraves to the windows and the omission of the pilasters from the front elevation. That the pilasters were not a late addition to the design is known from the fact that they were shown in Hering's drawing, which was exhibited before Thackeray wrote his letter.[194] It seems hardly likely that Thackeray would have forgotten about such crucial features in the appearance of the house if he had been so closely involved in its design as has sometimes been stated.

The contention that the house marked a crucial turning point in the history of house-styles may have its origins in a remark by Sir John Millais, who, according to Thackeray's daughter, 'used to laugh, and declared that my father first set the fashion for red brick'.[195] There is no indication, however, that the house received any but the most scant recognition in architectural circles at the time it was built. When Hering exhibited his drawing of the house, *The Builder* ignored it completely and *The Building News*, which made a point of commenting on every entry, described it as 'of red brick, in the Italian style'.[194] In 1869 *The Builder* printed a short obituary of Hering which did not mention No. 2 Palace Green and described him as 'an accomplished and amiable man, [who] seems to have obtained few opportunities to distinguish himself in his profession'.[196]

Several alterations have been made to the house, particularly to the interior. In 1882 Spencer Chadwick added another storey and a canted bay to the single-storey wing on the north side, which had contained Thackeray's library. These alterations necessitated the removal of a Venetian window which faced the road.[197] By 1938 little remained of the original interior decorations, and in that year a further scheme of redecoration was undertaken by Darcy Braddell.[198]

Nos. 4–10 (consec.) Palace Green
Plates 110–11; fig. 44

After the completion of building on the northern part of the land transferred to the Office of Woods and Forests by the Act of 1841, the extensive frontage on the west side of the road between No. 15A Kensington Palace Gardens and the old house at No. 3 Palace Green was left undeveloped for nearly fifty years. Ostensibly, sufficient income had been secured from the leases already granted to cover the cost of laying out the kitchen gardens at Frogmore, but the real reason why building did not take place on this land during the nineteenth century was the wish of Queen Victoria that no new buildings should be erected opposite Kensington Palace.[199] The death of the Queen in 1901, however, changed the situation, and Edward VII was sounded for his views on letting the ground on building leases. The initiative seems to have come from the Office of Woods, and the King, who was anxious to undertake improvements to the gardens at Windsor, at once approved the idea. The Commissioners estimated that a ground rent of at least £600 to £700 per annum could be secured for the land (an underestimate in the event), and that, capitalized at thirty years' purchase, this would provide between £18,000 and £21,000 for the work at Windsor.[200]

Early in 1903 particulars of a scheme for letting the land were made public.[199] The ground was

* According to the *Wellesley Index of Victorian Periodicals* this was John Hollingshead.

divided into seven plots which were to be let for the erection of private houses similar to others in Kensington Palace Gardens. The elevations were to be 'of handsome architectural design, and executed in Portland stone, fine red brick or terra cotta or other material, not inferior thereto, to be approved by the Commissioners', and each house was to consist of not more than three main storeys besides a basement and an attic, with an overall height restriction of forty-five feet. Tenders were invited for the best ground rents for eighty-year leases, and £1,380 was offered by both William Willett* of Chelsea and Holloway Brothers of Lambeth, the latter, however, for ninety-nine-year leases. A compromise was probably reached between the two firms, for, although Willett's tender was accepted, the leasehold term was extended to ninety-nine years and Willett made the three southernmost plots available to Holloway Brothers, who built Nos. 4, 5 and 6.[202]

Although a number of different architects were employed in their design, these houses are very similar in appearance (Plate 110). This similarity results partly from the use of red brick and Portland stone throughout, but may also be partly due to the control exercised by Willett and his architect, Amos Faulkner, on the one hand and the Commissioners' architects—Arthur Green and, after Green's death in 1904, John Murray—on the other. In only one case—No. 8—is the architect not known. He may have been Faulkner himself, who is known to have co-operated on the design of No. 7.[203] Other architects were Read and MacDonald (Nos. 4 and 6), E. P. Warren (No. 5), Horace Field and C. E. Simmons with Faulkner (No. 7), Stevenson and Redfern (No. 9), and E. J. May (No. 10).[204] The first drawings to be submitted by Willett were for No. 9 in July 1903. They were, according to an accompanying letter, by J. J. Stevenson (then in partnership with Harry Redfern), but Green thought that they were 'ill-conceived' and did not show a suitable house. A new set of drawings was submitted and received Green's approval, although he required further details to be sent to him so that he could keep his eye on the work when the house was under construction. Both sets of drawings have been preserved and the rejected designs show a plainer house with less use of Portland stone.[205] The Commissioners' architects continued to pay very close attention to the drawings for the various houses and Willett was careful to try to anticipate their wishes. Thus in 1904 Green wrote with reference to May's design for No. 10, 'The drawings . . . were laid before me on several occasions before being completed and show in my opinion a very good house suitable for the site'.[199]

The last house to be built was No. 7. Willett first submitted drawings for this house in 1909, but later withdrew them as he had not yet been able to find a purchaser for No. 8—a costly house built as a speculation—and did not want to embark on another. In 1910 he wrote, 'Having regard to the depressed condition of the house property market, I think we have not done badly to have built six such fine houses as those which have been erected'. Eventually he found a client who wanted a house especially built for him, and No. 7 was begun in 1912. In the following year No. 8 was sold for the handsome price of £27,750.[206]

Set in modest gardens separated from the road by Portland stone walls, massive gate piers, and iron railings, these houses are similar in style as well as in materials and scale. They fall into two main groups: Nos. 4–7 are symmetrical, with modillioned cornices and pediments, reminiscent of late seventeenth- and early eighteenth-century Dutch examples, while Nos. 8–10 are asymmetrical, also with Dutch influences in the architecture, especially in the gables of No. 9. The latter three houses have two-storey entrance halls with galleries at first-floor level, light being admitted by large windows with stone mullions and transoms. These windows are notable features of the east elevations of Nos. 8 and 9 and the west elevation of No. 10. The entrance halls are panelled, and the gallery balusters are turned and carved.

Apart from these 'Jacobethan' entrance halls (Plate 111b, c), the original interiors seem to have been basically classical in character. That of No. 5 appears to be almost intact and as its builders left

---

* This building firm was established by William Willett senior, who had been joined in the business by his son William Willett junior. They had built up a considerable reputation for soundness of construction and excellence of materials. William Willett junior was also the originator of the idea of British 'daylight saving' time. It has been assumed that the 'William Willett' who corresponded with the Commissioners over this development was William Willett junior, for the leases granted directly to the firm were in his name. William Willett senior died in 1913 and his son in 1915.[201]

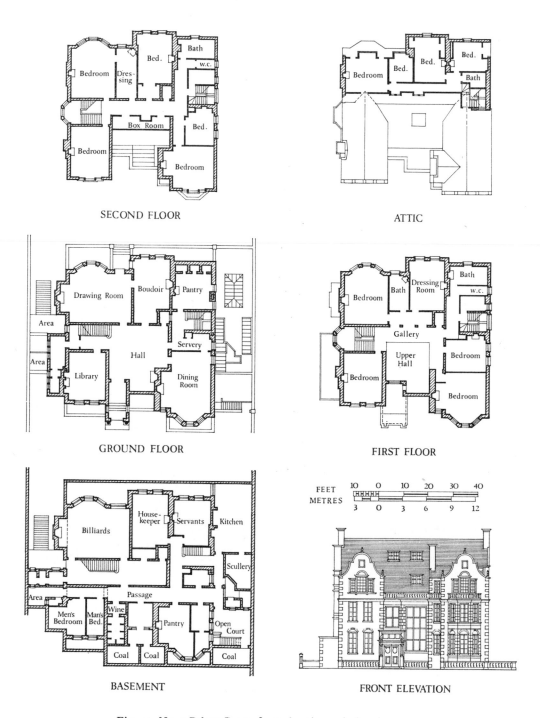

SECOND FLOOR

ATTIC

GROUND FLOOR

FIRST FLOOR

BASEMENT

FRONT ELEVATION

Fig. 44. No. 9 Palace Green, front elevation and plans in 1903

it. The marble staircase with wrought-iron balustrades, symmetrically placed on the main axis of the house, is based on late seventeenth-century examples and is particularly impressive (Plate 111a). The decorations throughout are of plaster, the main rooms having friezes and cornices in the manner of Adam. Of the remaining houses, No. 7 has been completely modernized and others have undergone modifications. Nos. 8, 9 and 10, however, retain their original internal arrangements and character.

The planning was similar in each case, with the kitchen, storage areas and some servants' quarters in the basement, the main living-rooms on the ground floor, and bedrooms on the upper floors, those in the attic being for domestic staff. Electric lifts appear to have been provided for all of the houses.

A high standard of building and finish is evident, the construction being basically of load-bearing brickwork with fire-resistant floors formed of five inches of concrete cast on corrugated iron permanent shuttering carried on rolled-steel joists. The Commissioners had specified that the houses should be 'fire-resisting throughout'.

The Barracks, Kensington Church Street

These barracks, erected in 1856–8, stand on the site of the original kitchen garden of Kensington Palace, which was laid out at the end of the seventeenth century and which was later known as the forcing ground. In the north-east corner of this garden stood the brick conduit, illustrated by Faulkner, which was said to have been built by Henry VIII to supply water to his house at Chelsea Place. At the time of its erection this conduit was on the east side of a four-acre field called 'the More' (and subsequently Conduit Close), comprising the site of the forcing ground and an area to the north, later the sites of Maitland House and York House (see page 29). During the seventeenth century Conduit Close was divided, and by 1672 the forcing ground site had passed into the hands of Sir Heneage Finch, later first Earl of Nottingham, whose son sold it to William III in 1689.[207]

In 1841 the Commissioners' architects, in their plan for building over the kitchen gardens,

had proposed that a short road should be laid out across the forcing ground between Kensington Church Street and The Queen's Road. This plan was approved and in June 1844 a contract for laying a sewer was awarded. By July, however, the Commissioners and the Board of Ordnance were discussing the possibility of building a barracks on the forcing ground to replace the old barracks on Palace Green, which stood on the line of The Queen's Road. An agreement to let part of the site for a barracks was concluded, but in 1854 this was set aside by mutual consent.[208]

Thereupon the Commissioners decided to let the ground for building: a layout plan was selected, which included a row of shops along the Church Street front, a road was constructed across the ground, and in November 1855 terms were arranged to let the whole site to the builder John Kelk. But this development did not take place, for in December the War Department informed the Commissioners that the forcing ground was, after all, required in its entirety for a barracks of large extent.[209]

Under an agreement of 1 July 1856 the site was leased to the Secretary of State for War, who contracted to have the barracks completed within two years.* They were to cost not less than £14,000, and the eastern elevation was to be 'in a plain but good style of architecture of such a character as shall not in the opinion of the . . . Commissioners . . . be unsightly or in any use detrimental to the Houses on each side of the Queen's Road'.[211] The architect was probably Colonel Frederick Chapman, R.E., whose signature appears on the contract drawings; the builders were Benjamin and John Dale of Warwick Square.[212]

The barracks consist principally of two residential blocks, one of two storeys and the other of three storeys, intended originally for the cavalry and infantry respectively. The 'plain but good' style of architecture adopted for the outward-facing façades of each block is a curious mixture of late seventeenth-century English motifs (including brick quoins) and mid-Victorian Italianate.

To compensate the residents of The Queen's Road for the loss of the road laid out in 1855, which they had found useful as a short-cut into Church Street, the War Department constructed

* The old conduit stood on the site but did not itself belong to the Crown. It was acquired by the Commissioners in 1861 and is said to have been demolished in 1871.[210]

a footpath along the north side of the site. This still survives. In 1906 part of the site of the barracks was given up for the widening of Kensington Church Street.[213] The building ceased to be used as a barracks in 1972.

Nos. 26–40 (even) Kensington High Street

This building was designed in 1924 by Sir Reginald Blomfield and H. L. Cabuche for John Barker and Company. Blomfield was responsible for the elevations and Cabuche for the internal planning and construction.[214]

When the London County Council obtained powers to widen Kensington High Street by demolishing most of the existing properties on the north side of the street to the east of Kensington Church Street, the Commissioners of Woods and Forests made it known that they wished to purchase the land to the south of No. 1 Palace Green which the Council planned to acquire.

In 1905, shortly after road widening had taken place, this land was transferred to the Crown, and in 1906 it was advertised as building ground. No tenders were received, and despite re-advertisement several times reasonable offers were still not forthcoming. Proposals to erect a cinema on the site proved abortive, and for a while the ground was used by the Church Army as a 'City Garden'. In 1912 John Barker and Company took a monthly tenancy of part of the site to erect temporary buildings after one of their stores had been damaged by fire. Finally in 1919 the same company submitted an offer for a ninety-nine-year building lease of the plot, which the Commissioners accepted with alacrity. The site made available by the Commissioners under a building agreement concluded in 1921 included some land at the rear of No. 1 Palace Green which they had purchased in 1920. John Murray, the architect to the Office of Woods, insisted on certain amendments to the plans of the proposed building to safeguard the amenities of No. 1 Palace Green.[215]

CHAPTER IX

The Ladbroke Estate

THE estate of the Ladbroke family in Kensington was one of the largest holdings in the whole parish. It consisted of three separate parcels of land, all on the north side of the Uxbridge road (now Notting Hill Gate and Holland Park Avenue): the two smaller parcels, consisting of five acres now occupied by Linden Gardens, Notting Hill Gate, and of twenty-eight acres centred around Pembridge Villas, are described in Chapter X. The third and largest parcel, consisting of some 170 acres bounded on the east by Portobello Lane (now Road), on the west by Portland Road and Pottery Lane, and on the north extending almost as far as Lancaster Road, is the subject of the present chapter (fig. 45).

Large parts of this area became the scene of a layout quite unlike anything previously, or indeed subsequently, to be found in London. Building development was spread over some fifty years, between 1821 and the mid 1870's, but the most intense activity took place between 1840 and c. 1868. Half-a-dozen architects and a rather larger number of major speculators were all involved in the evolution of the layout, and despite exhaustive study of the available evidence, the precise extent of their individual contributions is still not entirely clear.

The estate had probably been acquired in the middle of the eighteenth century by Richard Ladbroke esquire, of Tadworth Court, Surrey,[1] who was a brother of Sir Robert Ladbroke. Sir Robert was a banker in the firm of Ladbroke, Son, Rawlinson and Porker of Lombard Street, and had served as Lord Mayor in 1744–5 and as one of the Members of Parliament for the City from 1754 until his death in 1773. Both he and his brother were extremely wealthy. After Richard Ladbroke's death the estate passed to his son, another Richard, who at the time of his death in 1793 owned four houses, in the City, at Chelsea, at Tadworth and in Reigate, as well as estates in Middlesex, Surrey and Essex. But he

had no children, and he therefore bequeathed life interests in his lands to his mother and his four sisters, with remainder successively to his nephews, and ultimately, in default of issue, to a distant cousin, Robert Ladbroke. By 1819 Richard Ladbroke's mother, sisters and two of his nephews had all died, and the Kensington estates passed to the last surviving nephew, James Weller, who in accordance with the requirements of his uncle's will assumed the name of Ladbroke.[2]

James Weller Ladbroke held the estate until his death without issue in 1847. During his twenty-eight-year ownership a considerable amount of building development took place, and the layout and character of the estate were largely determined. But there is little evidence that he ever took much active part in these processes, beyond the routine signature of leases. He lived at a succession of country houses in West Sussex, the management of the estate at Notting Hill being left to a firm of City solicitors, Smith, Bayley (Bayley and Janson after 1836),[3] acting in conjunction with a 'surveyor', Thomas Allason, who was a distinguished architect. Nor is there anything to suggest that he was personally concerned in the family banking business, which was taken over by Messrs. Glyn and Company in 1842.[4]

Building development in the 1820's and 1830's

Under the terms of his uncle's will James Weller Ladbroke could only grant leases of up to twenty-one years' duration. Encouraged, no doubt, by the tremendous building boom of the early 1820's Ladbroke and his advisers obtained power by a private Act of Parliament of 1821 to grant ninety-nine-year leases,[5] and within a year the first articles of agreement for building had been signed.* This was for the site of Linden Gardens (formerly

* See page 251 for a select list of building lessors and lessees on the Ladbroke estate.

Fig. 45 (facing page). Principal developers on the Ladbroke estate. In the unnamed areas the developer is either unknown or the development too complex for ascription. Based on the Ordnance Surveys of 1863–7 and 1894–6

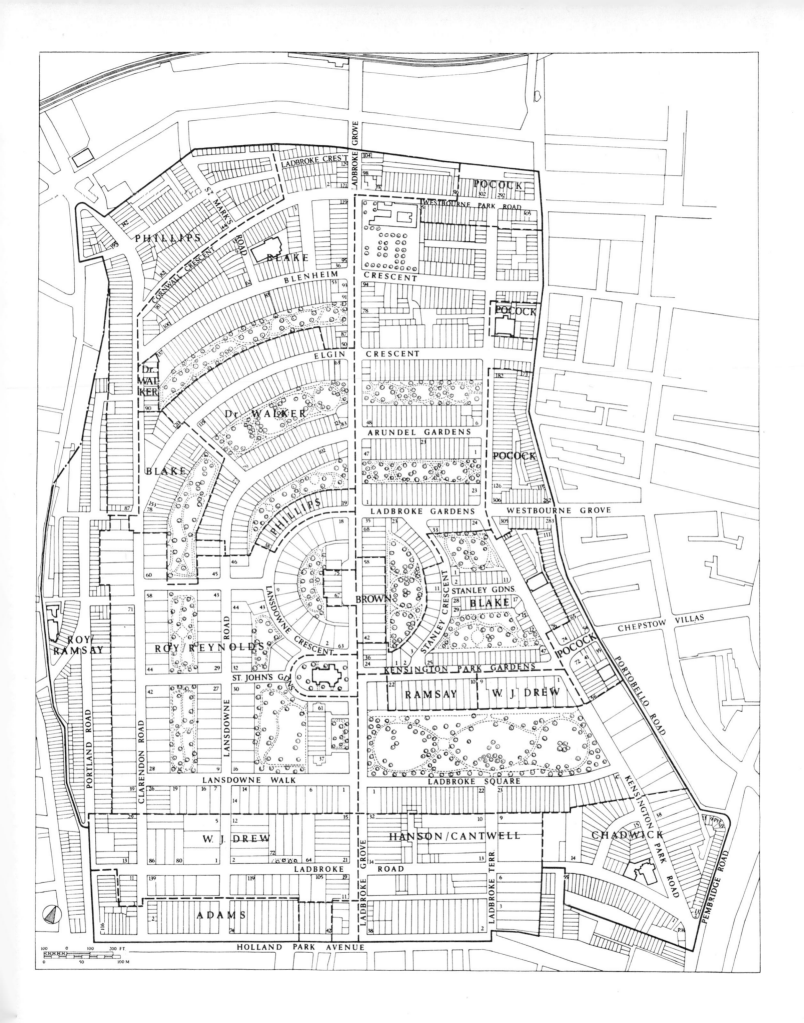

Linden Grove, see page 268) where Ladbroke's own surveyor, Allason, was granted a number of leases in 1824 and 1827.[6]

Allason was born in London in 1790. He became a pupil of William Atkinson, and he won the silver medal of the Royal Academy School in 1809. After a tour of the Continent he published in 1817 his *Picturesque Views of the Antiquities of Pola in Istria*. He was the architect for the Alliance Fire Office in Bartholomew Lane and built a number of country houses. In addition to acting for Ladbroke he was surveyor to the Stock Exchange, the Pollen estate and the Pitt estate in Kensington (see Chapter III), and he also worked for the Earl of Shrewsbury at Alton Towers, where 'He was engaged in laying out the gardens and from this period he was much employed as a landscape gardener.' He lived for some years in Linden Grove, attended the meetings of the Kensington Vestry, and was a member successively of the Westminster and Metropolitan Commissions of Sewers. He remained the surveyor to the Ladbroke family until his death in 1852.[7]

Allason's first task after the passing of the Act of 1821 was to prepare a plan for the layout of the main portion of the estate. At its south-eastern extremity Ladbroke's property occupied the high ground at Notting Hill Gate, which extends north-west for about five hundred yards along a broad flat ridge before the land begins to fall away down a long slope. Due west of Notting Hill Gate the Uxbridge road led down another long slope to Shepherd's Bush. Half way down this slope the ground on the north side of the road rises with increasing steepness to the top of a knoll which forms a level extension of the broad ridge to the east. On the west and north sides of this knoll the ground falls steeply towards Pottery Lane and Notting Dale. As well as being unusually large, the estate thus also possessed unusually varied contours (at least by London standards), and its layout therefore presented an architect such as Allason, a specialist in landscape design, with an unique opportunity.

In his plan of 1823* (Plate 52) Allason provided a broad straight road (originally known as Ladbroke Place and now as Ladbroke Grove)

leading northward off the Uxbridge road for some 700 yards, up over the knoll where St. John's Church now stands and about half way down the further side. Not far from its southern end this thoroughfare was crossed at right angles by an east–west road called Weller Street East and West (now Ladbroke Road). The most striking feature of the design was, however, the enormous circus, some 560 yards in diameter and about one mile in circumference, which was to be laid out to the north of this intersection. All of the ground on the inner side of the circular road, and that on either side of Ladbroke Grove within the circus, extending to a depth of 200 feet, is marked as 'building ground', and a clause in the Act of 1821 provided that up to five acres of land might be appropriated to any one house. Large detached, or possibly semi-detached, houses were therefore evidently envisaged, and the whole scheme must have been heavily influenced by Nash's work at Regent's Park, and also, perhaps, by an unexecuted design exhibited at the Royal Academy in 1802–3 for the layout of a large double circus on the Eyre estate at St. John's Wood. The design for this circus has not survived, but a description of it states that detached houses, each with over an acre of garden, were to be built around the circus, and that the residents of all the houses were to share the use of the large pleasure-ground in the centre.[9]

Whether he knew of this abortive plan or not, Allason made use of this idea for his scheme, for within the two segmentally-shaped areas enclosed by the broad strips of building ground there were to be two large paddocks, plus a third (triangular, and again entirely surrounded by building ground) outside the eastern edge of the circus. The fact that all three of these paddocks were wholly surrounded by land designated for building suggests that they were intended to be private enclosures for the general use of the residents of the adjacent houses. Although the circus was never built, Allason's plan therefore marks the genesis in Notting Hill of this most original and successful idea, which in years to come was to lead to the formation of no less than fifteen such communal gardens on various parts of the Ladbroke estate.

* The plan is not signed, but in the following year, 1824, Allason was concerned in the building of sewers along the Uxbridge road frontage of the estate. In 1831 he was explicitly described as J. W. Ladbroke's surveyor during negotiations for the formation of a watercourse near the western boundary,[8] and it was then that he wrote in pencil on the plan 'I approve this line of open sewer on the part of James Weller Ladbroke'. This is signed T. Allason and dated 22 November 1831. There is therefore no reason to doubt that he was the author of the plan.

Allason's plan remained the basis for building throughout the first stage of the development of the Ladbroke estate, which lasted until about 1833. At least the southern part of the circus was actually staked out,[10] but no houses were built there, and the whole speculation must have suffered a severe set-back through the financial crisis of 1825. Such building as did take place in this period was restricted to the frontage of the Uxbridge road and the land adjacent to it.

In the autumn of 1823 Ladbroke signed two agreements[11] for the disposal of almost all of his land between Ladbroke Terrace on the east and Portland Road on the west, and extending northward from the Uxbridge road to include the southern part of the great circus (fig. 45). The undertaker for the eastern portion, between Ladbroke Terrace and Ladbroke Grove, was Joshua Flesher Hanson, gentleman, the builder of Regency Square, Brighton, and of a number of houses in Hyde Park Gate, who at about this time was also beginning to build Campden Hill Square on the opposite side of the Uxbridge road (see Chapter VI). To the west of Ladbroke Grove the undertaker was Ralph Adams of Gray's Inn Road, brick- and tile-maker, who at about this time established a pottery manufacture in the neighbouring district soon to be known as 'the Potteries'. He took all of the land as far as Portland Road except for an acre and a half on the west corner of Ladbroke Grove, where stood a farmhouse and ancillary buildings. Neither of these agreements has survived, but other sources show that Ladbroke undertook to grant ninety-nine-year leases as houses were completed, and that Hanson covenanted to build twenty houses 'according to such ranges and levels' as Ladbroke's surveyor should approve. The houses along the Uxbridge road were to be ranged at an uniform distance of at least twenty feet from the roadway, while those in the projected circus were to be set back at least thirty feet.[12] Adams covenanted to pay a ground rent of £25 in the first year, rising to £150 in the sixth and all subsequent years.[13]

By December 1824 Hanson had arranged for the erection of eight houses along the Uxbridge road (now Nos. 8–22 even Holland Park Avenue),[14] Thomas Allason having acted on Hanson's behalf in an application to lay a sewer there.[15] But in this same month Hanson agreed to lease all the remainder of his land to Robert Cantwell, who covenanted to build the remaining twelve houses required by Hanson's contract with Ladbroke.[12]

Cantwell is variously described as an architect, a surveyor or a builder, and he was later to act as surveyor for the adjacent Norland estate, where he designed Royal Crescent and a number of other houses. On the Ladbroke estate his financial backer was Major-General Laurence Bradshaw of Harley Street, from whom he was soon obtaining mortgages of over £6,000.[16] At Hanson's nomination Cantwell was in 1826 granted a ninety-seven-year lease from Ladbroke of Nos. 1–4 (consec.) Ladbroke Terrace (Nos. 1 and 2 demolished), and in 1833 a ninety-two-year lease of Nos. 5 and 6.[17] In the Uxbridge road he was the lessee of No. 38 Holland Park Avenue in 1826,[18] and he was also involved in the building of several other houses between Ladbroke Terrace and Ladbroke Grove[19] (Plate 58c). The cost of building varied between £600 and £800 per house.[14]

Almost all of these houses are stucco fronted, and have two or three storeys above basements. In Holland Park Avenue Cantwell was almost certainly the architect for the two identical trios, Nos. 2–6 and 24–28 even (Plate 58a, b). Here each of the central houses has a giant unfluted Doric order of engaged columns, tetrastyle in antis, with pediment above the attic storey. Nos. 24–28 were placed so as to close the vista down the east side of Hanson's Campden Hill Square on the south side of Holland Park Avenue, a little further down which, on the south side, stands a third very similar group, Nos. 23–27 (odd) Holland Park Avenue (Plate 43a), also probably by Cantwell, and dated 1829. By comparison with other houses in Holland Park Avenue, which are relatively unremarkable, all three groups belong clearly to Nash's age of Metropolitan Improvements.

Cantwell's houses in Ladbroke Terrace were more modest. Nos. 1–4 (consec.) were formerly one continuous stucco-faced two-storey range with semi-basements,[20] but (as previously mentioned) Nos. 1 and 2 have been demolished. Nos. 3 and 4 (Plate 58d) each have a centrally placed doorway flanked on either side by a wide and slightly projecting wing containing one window on each floor. The doorways have shallow projecting porches supported on Ionic columns, and the wings have plain pilasters supporting a simple horizontal band of stucco which performs the function of an entablature. A low-pitched slate roof rises above wide eaves carried on brackets set above the pilasters. The entrance to No. 3 is now by way of the semi-basement instead of at the level of the principal floor.

Two drawings in the J. B. Papworth collection in the library of the Royal Institute of British Architects evidently relate to these houses (Plate 59). One of them is inscribed in a later hand 'Villas at Notting Hill. R. Cantwell', and there is no reason to doubt this ascription. They show that as originally conceived these houses were to have formed semi-detached pairs, each house having a width of only two openings including the doorway, which was placed at the outer end. They are indeed shown in this manner on the ground plan attached to Cantwell's lease of 1826, but their alteration to form one continuous range must have taken place either during the course of building or very soon afterwards, for the Kensington tithe map of 1844 shows them all joined together. The drawings are nevertheless of considerable interest for their contemporary evidence about the internal dispositions of houses of this general type.

Each house was originally to be twenty-four feet wide and thirty-two feet deep. The basement contained a front and back kitchen equipped with a stone sink, a copper, a dresser and plate-rack, and a closet-cupboard. The front kitchen, which had a boarded floor, gave access to a covered area off which were a small pantry, a cistern, and a groined coal cellar. The latter was paved with bricks, and the pantry, cistern space and covered area were paved with York stone slabs. The back kitchen, also paved with York stone slabs, had a small area at the rear from which access was gained to a privy and to the steps leading up to the back garden. At the side there were two more cellars, both paved with bricks, one for wine, and the other for beer. On the ground floor, the entrance hall gave access to a stair well, off which were the dining-room, rear drawing-room (smaller than the dining-room), and a small study. On the first floor there were four bedrooms and a water-closet. All rooms except one bedroom had a fireplace, those in the kitchens being presumably furnished with ranges. There was no bathroom. In conclusion it may here be noted that at least two houses were evidently built in accordance with these plans, at Cheltenham, where they may still be seen at Nos. 27 and 29 Tivoli Road. Cantwell is not known to have worked at Cheltenham, but Papworth did so very extensively, and his influence on the Ladbroke estate will be discussed later.

The houses on the east side of Ladbroke Grove to the north of Ladbroke Road, now numbered 14–32 (even) Ladbroke Grove, also stand on part of the land leased by Hanson to Cantwell. Their site was within the area originally intended for the 'great circus', and it was probably for this reason that building did not begin here until the latter part of the 1830's.[21]

To the west of Ladbroke Grove the brick-maker Ralph Adams became the lessee between 1826 and 1831 of the eleven houses now numbered 54–74 (even) Holland Park Avenue (Nos. 62–66 recently rebuilt).[22] These houses, mostly of two or three storeys with stucco fronts, are of less interest than those built under the aegis of Hanson and Cantwell east of Ladbroke Grove, and Adams may therefore have supplied his own designs.* Between Lansdowne Road and Portland Road, where all the first houses have either been demolished or converted into shops with single-storey projections over the original front gardens, Adams was between 1827 and 1831 either the lessee or a party to the lease for most of the houses.[24]

The last portion of the Ladbroke estate fronting the Uxbridge road to be developed was the curtilage of the farmhouse on the west corner of Ladbroke Grove, now partly occupied by the Mitre public house. Here leases of the present Nos. 42–52 (even) Holland Park Avenue were granted in 1833 to John Drew of Pimlico, builder,[25] whose kinsman William John Drew was soon to be active for some years on the Ladbroke estate. John Drew's houses in Holland Park Avenue form a routine range, all stucco fronted except at Nos. 42 and 44, where the stucco is restricted to the ground storey, and all with light iron guard-rails to the first-floor windows. But around the corner, on the west side of Ladbroke Grove and also within the curtilage of the old farmhouse, he and W. J. Drew, beginning in 1833, jointly built the agreeable two-storey stucco-fronted range numbered 11–19 (odd) Ladbroke Grove, the moulded parapet

---

* The records of the Westminster Commissioners of Sewers contain a site plan of these houses, signed Thos. B. Mallam, and dated 16 September 1825. Nothing else is known of Mallam.[23]

of which is surmounted by a central pediment and flanking ornamentation with Greek Revival motifs.[26]

At this point development stopped, and in the five years 1834–8 Ladbroke granted no building leases at all. The Act of 1821 had been badly drawn and doubts had arisen about the validity of Cantwell's title, so in 1832 Ladbroke had had to meet the expense of another Act to put matters right.[12] At about this time the grandiose scheme for a great circus was abandoned.[10] The building boom of the early 1820's had collapsed, and Notting Hill had proved to be still too far west for successful large-scale speculation. Among the very few houses known to have been built in the years 1834–8 were Nos. 12 and 13 Ladbroke Terrace, which at Cantwell's direction were leased in 1838 by the mortgagee, General Bradshaw, respectively to W. J. Drew, variously described as builder or architect, and William Liddard, gentleman, both of Notting Hill.[27]

The Hippodrome racecourse

During the interim before the revival of building activity the Ladbroke estate was used as a race-course, a purpose for which it was in some ways very well suited. There was no course close to London, Epsom Downs being the nearest, and the configuration of the ground, dominated by the hill now surmounted by St. John's Church, enabled spectators to view the races from start to finish as the competitors galloped around the circular course. In August 1836 a Mr. John Whyte took a twenty-one-year lease of 140 acres of ground from Ladbroke.[28] During the winter he laid out courses for steeplechasing and flat racing, the principal entrance being at the modern junction of Kensington Park Road and Pembridge Road (Plate 53a). He secured the fashionable patronage of Count D'Orsay and the Earl of Chesterfield as stewards and the first meeting at the new Hippodrome took place on 3 June 1837.[29]

By this time considerable local opposition had already been raised against the whole project. A public footpath extended across the course, providing the shortest route from Kensington village to Kensal Green and Willesden. The fence with which Whyte had enclosed the course obstructed this path, and in April 1837 over a hundred people had crowded into a meeting of the Kensington Vestry to discuss the matter. The Vestry instructed the parish surveyors of the high-ways to keep the path open, and in May legal proceedings were started against Whyte.[30] When the Hippodrome opened in June large crowds successfully claimed a right of free entry along the path. *The Sunday Times* recorded that 'A more filthy or disgusting crew than that which entered, we have seldom had the misfortune to encounter.' The invaders had not kept to the path, 'but, relying upon their numbers, they spread themselves over the whole of the ground, defiling the atmosphere as they go, and carrying into the neighbourhood of the stands and carriages, where the ladies are most assembled, a coarseness and obscenity of language as repulsive to every feeling of manhood as to every sense of common decency'. Even the racing had not been a success, for the stakes were low and the quality of the horses poor. 'Save Hokey Pokey, there was nothing that could climb, or hobble, much more leap over a hedge, and as to a hurdle, it was absurd to attempt one.' After such an inauspicious start it was perhaps fortunate that the death of King William IV on 20 June put an end to further meetings for some while.[31]

In the two cases heard at Kensington Petty Sessions the magistrates found against Whyte, despite the eloquent pleas of his solicitor, John Duncan, who was later to be involved in the development of the estate. But Whyte was evidently not a man to give up easily. There were counter summonses and an appeal to a higher court, and in January 1838 he was promoting a Bill in Parliament to divert the path. Despite several hostile petitions, including one from the Kensington Vestry, the Bill passed through the Commons, but for some unknown reason was never presented to the House of Lords.[32]

In 1839 the Hippodrome was being directed by a committee of management and a council of titled aristocrats whose avowed intention was to raise a capital sum of £50,000 by dividing the property into five thousand 'proprietorships' of £10 each. The course itself was altered so that it no longer obstructed the footpath. It was extended north-westwards to the neighbourhood of the modern St. Quintin Avenue (far beyond the Ladbroke estate), both the starting and finishing posts being to the west of the hill (Plates 5b, 53b). Besides the racing there were to be livery-stables where horses might be hired for hack riding in the vicinity, and there were also to be facilities for cricket, archery, 'revels, fêtes, balloon ascents, fancy fairs etc. etc.' Perhaps most important of all, the whole park was enclosed by a high wooden fence, thus excluding the rude and licentious populace of the neighbouring Potteries and elsewhere. The opening meeting in May 1839 was attended by a 'brilliant and immense assemblage of the nobility and gentry', and 'not a gambling-booth or table, not a single drunken, riotous, disorderly, or ill-behaved person, or mendicant was to be seen on the grounds'.[31]

The resumption of building, 1841

Yet despite this gratifying improvement in the social tone of the place, the Hippodrome evidently still did not pay, and in October 1840 Whyte assigned his twenty-one-year interest to his solicitor, Duncan, subject to a mortgage for £8,200 to William Chadwick, the builder who had erected the fences and stables for Whyte. The heavy clay soil had proved unsuitable for racing, building in the environs of London was on the upsurge again, and speculators were beginning to look with interest at the land to the east of the Hippodrome, nearest to London. One of these was Jacob Connop, a bill broker in the City of London, who also acted as a commission agent, dealer and chapman, and to whom Duncan had at once assigned his twenty-one-year interest in the land no longer used as part of the race-course.[33] In October 1840 Connop and James Weller Ladbroke signed an agreement whereby Ladbroke undertook, subject to various covenants, to grant Connop ninety-nine-year leases of the land between the Hippodrome and Portobello Lane, comprising some fifty-eight acres; and in February 1841 Ladbroke signed a similar agreement with Duncan, the solicitor, for the granting of long leases of the seventy-seven acres of his land which were then still occupied by the Hippodrome[34] (fig. 46).

Connop and Duncan were business associates, Connop as a bill broker having endorsed bills of exchange for the accommodation of Duncan,[35] and the whole project was probably a joint one, involving the risky combination of racing and building speculation. Connop was evidently to be the dominant partner, for in March 1841 he announced himself to a party of visiting journalists

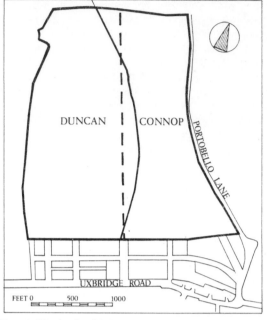

Fig. 46. The lands of John Duncan and Jacob Connop on the Ladbroke estate. Broken line denotes the future course of Ladbroke Grove. Redrawn from a plan of *c.* 1841 in G.L.R.O.(L)

as the new proprietor of the Hippodrome. In the west he was assembling a stud of twenty race-horses to compete at the Hippodrome, which would vie with any course in the Kingdom; while to the east a new town 'or series of Italian villages, with an elegant church' was to arise. With twelve days' racing every year, he estimated that the annual revenue would be £15,000, half of which he would use 'to aid the sports of the succeeding year'.[31]

These dreams proved short-lived, for the last race at the Hippodrome took place only three months later, on 4 June 1841,[29] and it was during the ensuing six or seven hectic years that much of the Ladbroke estate assumed its modern aspect. By the two separate agreements signed with Connop and Duncan, Ladbroke had divided most of his undeveloped property into two parts, and the subsequent history of these two speculations demonstrates that the original undertakers of a large building project often failed, and that success depended largely upon the business capacity of each individual developer, and upon the financial resources which he could command. For both Connop and Duncan the results were disastrous.

The successful development of Connop's lands was postponed for a decade or more, despite the fact that his lands were nearer to London and therefore more likely to prove 'ripe' for building, whereas on Duncan's more westerly lands, Duncan's partner, Richard Roy, was able to organize a dramatic surge of building whose momentum was only halted by the financial crisis of 1847.

In 1826 Connop had taken the benefit of the Insolvent Debtors' Act, and in 1830 he had been declared bankrupt. In addition to 'discounting Bills of Exchange and receiving a commission on such transactions' he also dabbled in patent rights and searching for gold in Australia.[36] Despite these risky activities Ladbroke evidently considered him to be a suitable person to whom to entrust the development of a large part of the estate. By the agreement of 5 October 1840 Connop covenanted that by Christmas 1841 he would spend £2,000 on the building of such roads and sewers as Ladbroke's surveyor (Allason) might approve, and that by Michaelmas 1842 he would spend £5,000 on the building of two or more houses. During the first twenty years of the ninety-nine-year term he undertook to spend the enormous sum of £100,000 on the building of not less than 40 or more than 350 houses, half of which were to be of at least £1,000 in value, and none less than £500. The ground rent during the first year was to be £313, rising to £1,045 in the sixth and all succeeding years, this last figure being equivalent to £18 per acre.

Duncan's agreement contained very similar provisions. He covenanted to spend £80,000 within sixteen years on the building of between 32 and 250 houses, and to pay a ground rent of £405 in the first year, rising to £1,350 in the seventh and succeeding years (equivalent to £17 10s per acre). Either alone or in conjunction with Connop he was also to spend £2,000 on roads and sewers.[34]

Duncan's career as a speculator on the Ladbroke estate was even shorter than Connop's, and extended over little more than two years. He was a partner in the firm of Roy, Blunt, Duncan and Johnstone, solicitors, of Great George Street, Westminster, and Lothbury in the City, whose clients included several railway and insurance companies. He had been drawn into the Ladbroke estate through his client John Whyte, the original promoter of the Hippodrome, whose financial difficulties had prompted Duncan to take over Whyte's interest in the racecourse in October 1840, and (as has already been stated) on the very next day he had assigned his interest in the eastern half to Connop.

In order to raise capital for the fulfilment of his obligation to Ladbroke, Duncan borrowed £6,000 from the London and Westminster Bank (for which Roy, Blunt, Duncan and Johnstone acted as solicitors) upon the security of promissory notes repayable within six months. By an arrangement which he made with his partner, Richard Roy, repayment of these debts was guaranteed by Roy and Pearson Thompson of Cheltenham, esquire, to whom he conditionally assigned all his interest in the estate.[37] In the summer of 1841 his architect, Charles Stewart Duncan (probably a relative) was applying to the Commissioners of Sewers to lay sewers,[38] and he himself agreed to lease twenty building plots to a speculator, Mark Markwick of Worthing, esquire, who contracted with a builder from the City of London, John Jay, for the initial building of a range of ten houses in carcase at a cost of £1,000 each.[39]

Jay laid the foundations for these ten houses, but only completed five of them in carcase. These are Nos. 67–75 (odd) Ladbroke Grove, situated on the summit of the hill. They form a tall dull range of five houses, five storeys in height over basements, stucco-fronted at ground-floor level. Each house has a substantial enclosed projecting porch, also faced with stucco and furnished with sets of paired pilasters.

The whole project was to be financed by Duncan out of borrowed money, and in October 1841 he was obliged to provide Pearson Thompson with further security for his debts. In June 1842 he was able to stave off disaster for a short while by transferring the debt for £6,000 from the bank to Edmund Walker, a Master in the Court of Chancery. But in November 1842 Jay became bankrupt after Duncan and Markwick had failed to pay him the instalments due for his building work, and in December Duncan himself was also declared bankrupt.[40]

The parties possessing interests under Duncan's original agreement with Ladbroke were now the builder William Chadwick (to whom Duncan was liable for debts previously incurred by Whyte for building work at the Hippodrome), Walker, Pearson Thompson, Roy, and the latter's remaining partners, Duncan's own partnership having been dissolved shortly before his bankruptcy,[41] when he owed his former partners over £45,000. In order to extricate the whole speculation from the financial difficulties created by Duncan's collapse, and to get it moving, all these parties agreed in November 1842 to appoint Pearson Thompson as their trustee and Roy as the recipient of all the building leases to be made by Ladbroke for Duncan's lands; and Roy was to hold all such leases upon trust for all parties according to their respective interests.[42]*

In the following year, 1843, Chadwick sold his interest in the westerly lands to Charles Henry Blake, esquire, of Devonshire Place.[45] Blake was one of Roy's clients, and had recently arrived in England from Calcutta.[46] He had lent Roy's firm £10,000[47] (probably in order to help the partners out of the difficulties caused by Duncan's debts to them of over £45,000), and was later to be the largest and most successful building speculator in the whole of North Kensington. At this stage, however, he took no active part in development. The interest which he acquired from Chadwick consisted of a claim for £4,100, or half the original debt of £8,200 incurred by Whyte to Chadwick, the other half having been apportioned to Connop's lands to the east. As the seventy-seven acres still nominally in Duncan's possession provided ample security for the recovery of this sum, Blake agreed to release the southern portion from this encumbrance.[48] This area (fig. 45) consisted of some sixteen acres to the west of Ladbroke Grove and to the south of the site of St. John's Church (later evidently extended to the line of Lansdowne Rise). Control of building development here was now vested in Roy and Pearson Thompson, acting on behalf of Edmund Walker and of Roy's partners as well as of themselves, and it was under their management that this part of the Ladbroke estate acquired its highly distinctive character.

The Cheltenham connexion

At the time of his death in 1872 Pearson Thompson was described as 'the Maker of Cheltenham'. His father, Henry Thompson, after accumulating

an ample fortune as a merchant and underwriter in the City of London, had retired to Cheltenham and bought the Montpellier estate, where medicinal springs were shortly afterwards discovered. His son, Pearson Thompson, had in early life practised as a solicitor in London, but after inheriting Henry Thompson's property in 1820 he removed to Cheltenham to develop the estate. From c. 1824 onwards he employed J. B. Papworth as his architect for both the layout of the Montpellier estate and the design of the Montpellier Pump Room. Papworth also designed a number of large houses in Thompson's wealthy Lansdown district of Cheltenham, including one for Richard Roy. Both Pearson Thompson and Roy were members of the general committee for the provision of fashionable public amusements such as musical promenades and summer balls; in 1836 they were both founder-directors of a local joint-stock bank, and in the same year they were working together in the controversies surrounding the promotion of railway lines to Cheltenham. They were, in fact, experienced and successful estate developers, willing, evidently, to extend their field of operations to the suburbs of London.

We have already seen that when Roy's partner, Duncan, had needed capital in 1841 for his operations on the Ladbroke estate, Roy and Pearson Thompson had acquired a share in the speculation by guaranteeing his promissory notes, and at the time of his bankruptcy they had taken control. Pearson Thompson remained in Cheltenham, his principal role being probably the provision of capital, but Roy, whose residence in the town may always have been restricted to the fashionable 'season', gave up his house there in 1841–2.[49] From 1847 onwards he lived on the Ladbroke estate. He subsequently served as a Poor Law Guardian, as chairman of the commissioners under the Kensington Improvement Act of 1851, and as a vestryman.

The layout and general character of large parts of the Ladbroke estate clearly owe a great deal to the example of the Montpellier estate at Cheltenham. The scale of the layout and the size of most of the houses at Cheltenham are larger than on the Ladbroke estate, but the alternation of curving

---

* Jay's range of five houses was completed in 1844–5 under Roy's auspices by the building of a substantial house at either end, one facing north and the other south, the builder being William Reynolds.[43] Both these end houses were subsequently demolished for the erection of blocks of flats, that at the south end (No. 65) being built in 1938 to designs by E. Maxwell Fry.[44]

crescents with long straight roads, often lined with trees, the large gardens and open spaces, the mixture of house types and architectural styles, and the careful siting of churches and large houses at focal points all provide obvious similarities between the two estates. The use of Lansdowne (which Cheltenham had previously borrowed from Bath) and Montpelier* as street-names in Notting Hill even indicates an element of conscious and deliberate imitation. How the basis of these resemblances was created in the layout plan of the Ladbroke estate must now be described.

The evolution of the layout plan

It is first of all clear that after the failure of his 'great circus' plan of 1823 Ladbroke's own surveyor, Thomas Allason, ceased to be the sole author of later layout plans. His approval of these plans was, however, probably required, and he may well have greatly influenced their preparation; it is also likely that he provided designs for a number of houses. Three features of his abortive 'great circus' plan certainly survived all later vicissitudes. These were, firstly, the large paddocks or private enclosures for the communal use of the residents of adjacent houses; secondly, his crescent, curving round the western slopes of the hill now surmounted by St. John's Church, an idea which in much amplified form provided a basic element in the executed layout of this part of the Ladbroke estate; and thirdly, the straight road (now Ladbroke Grove) which extended northward from the Uxbridge road, up over the hill and down the further side, and thus linked the ends of the crescents.

After Ladbroke's signature of the two building agreements with Connop and Duncan in 1840–1 Allason was, however, evidently no longer able to dictate the layout, and this caused additional complications. The straight course of Ladbroke Grove might with advantage have been taken as the dividing line between Connop's and Duncan's properties, but this was not in fact done, and the common border of their two leasehold properties had followed the gentle curve of the boundary of the Hippodrome (fig. 46). Thus when it was decided to extend Ladbroke Grove straight north

in accordance with Allason's original plan, Duncan had a narrow sliver of land on the east side of the road and Connop an equally awkwardly shaped piece on the west side further north. Arrangements were eventually made to iron out this difficulty by a mutual exchange, in order to make Ladbroke Grove the boundary between Duncan's land on the west and Connop's on the east,[50]† but the legal complications arising from this lack of overall control continued to reverberate until the early 1850's.

The next point to be noted about the layout of the Ladbroke estate is the influence of J. B. Papworth. We have already seen that after Duncan's failure in 1842, control of the land to the west of Ladbroke Grove passed to Pearson Thompson and Richard Roy, who had both previously employed Papworth at Cheltenham. There is no direct evidence that Papworth ever worked on the Ladbroke estate, but there are nevertheless indications, both visual and documentary, that his many-sided genius indirectly affected both the layout and even the design of some of the houses there. Both Allason and Robert Cantwell (whose work on the Ladbroke estate has been mentioned earlier) counted themselves among his admirers, for they were among the group of architects which presented Papworth with a silver inkstand at his retirement in 1847.[52] Allason and Papworth had both worked, either concurrently or consecutively, for the Earl of Shrewsbury in the adornment of the grounds at Alton Towers,[7] while the presence among the Papworth drawings in the library of the Royal Institute of British Architects of the design, referred to earlier and evidently by Cantwell, for a pair of houses in Ladbroke Terrace very similar to a pair in Cheltenham, suggests a professional association of some kind between Papworth and Cantwell.

Most important of all, the influence of Papworth is also revealed by the fact that after the abandonment of Allason's 'great circus' plan, the first revised scheme for the layout of the land to the west of Ladbroke Grove was the work of one of Papworth's pupils, James Thomson. Thomson had entered Papworth's employment in 1812, when he was only twelve years of age, and in a memoir written many years later he referred to his 'long residence' with Papworth.

* Until 1937 Lansdowne Rise was called Montpelier Road.
† This exchange was arranged by Edward Cresy, architect, who in February 1841 was acting on behalf of both Duncan and Connop.[51] This is the only known occasion on which Cresy was concerned with the Ladbroke estate.

Whether his service extended to the years covered by Papworth's work at Cheltenham (*c.* 1824–32) is not clear,[53] for by 1826 he was acting as executant architect under Nash for Cumberland Terrace and Cumberland Place, Regent's Park.[54] But Thomson's sense of personal indebtedness to Papworth was certainly life-long, for he too was one of the architects responsible for the retirement presentation in 1847;[52] and the full extent of Papworth's influence on his work can be seen in Thomson's book, published in 1835 under the title *Retreats: A Series of Designs consisting of Plans and Elevations for Cottages, Villas and Ornamental Buildings.*

Towards the end of 1842, when through Duncan's financial failure Pearson Thompson and Richard Roy were in need of an architect, Papworth was aged sixty-seven and within five years of retirement. After their brilliantly successful previous association with him at Cheltenham, to commission one of his former pupils (perhaps on his recommendation) for a fresh project in London was a natural step. However this may be, there can certainly be no doubt that it was Pearson Thompson and Roy who introduced James Thomson to the Ladbroke estate, for a posthumously published list of Thomson's works includes 'the laying out of Mr. Roy's estate at Notting hill'.[7]

In the autumn of 1842 Thomson was applying on Roy's behalf to the Westminster Commissioners of Sewers for permission to build sewers in Queen's Terrace (later Hanover Terrace, now Lansdowne Walk) and the west side of Ladbroke Grove,[55] and a printed plan, undated but not later than December 1842, is entitled 'Plan of Kensington Park, Notting Hill, as designed and laid out for building, with ornamental grounds, public drives etc. etc. James Thomson, Architect, Devonshire Street, Portland Place' (Plate 54a). Although subsequently much modified, this first plan does include the church (sited near its eventual position), two concentric roads curving round the north-west slopes of the hill to join Ladbroke Grove, and, perhaps at Allason's insistence, several of the 'paddocks' or communal gardens which were to form such important features of this area. All the houses on the southern portion of the estate were to be built in long terrace ranges, but further north there were to be detached and paired houses as well as terraces.

Thomson's plan for the lands to the west of Ladbroke Grove was evidently prepared in consultation with the architect for Jacob Connop's lands to the east, whose layout proposals were shown by Thomson in outline. In July 1841 Connop's 'architect' had been Martin Stuteley,[56] who had previously worked as a builder on the Phillimore estate. He was probably the author of a plan made at about this time for the erection of some 330 houses, almost all in long terraced ranges facing Ladbroke Grove and three streets leading eastward to Portobello Lane, on the west side of which there was to be a church.[57] This undistinguished scheme included a perfunctory attempt to provide a communal paddock, possibly again at Allason's insistence, but by January 1843 Connop was employing a new architect, John Stevens,[58] who was almost certainly the author of the unsigned plan for Connop's lands reproduced on Plate 54b.

Stevens had been a pupil of William Wilkins, and in 1843 he was elected district surveyor for the western part of the City. On the Ladbroke estate he and his partner George Alexander became architects in 1844 for St. John's Church, and he also designed 'many houses' there.[7] His plan for Connop's lands provided three large squares extending eastward from Ladbroke Grove to a new north–south line of communication, now known as Kensington Park Road. The houses in the two southerly squares, to be called Ladbroke Square and Beaufort Square, were to be separated in the traditional manner from the garden enclosure by the roadway, and at the west end of Beaufort Square there was to be a church fronting Ladbroke Grove. But in the northernmost square, to be called Lansdowne Square, the houses were to back directly on to a communal garden— a feature evidently either insisted upon by Allason or borrowed from Thomson. On the northern slope of the hill there were to be fifteen detached houses, each with a large private garden, and long ranges of terraced houses were to line the whole length of the east side of Kensington Park Road, one of whose functions appears to have been to shut off Portobello Lane from contact with the well-to-do inhabitants further west.

This plan must have been prepared in consultation with Thomson, and possibly with Allason also, for the positions of the openings into Ladbroke Grove correspond with those on Thomson's plan for the land to the west. But Stevens lacked

Fig. 47 (facing page). Nos. 2–8 consec. Lansdowne Walk, plans, elevations and details

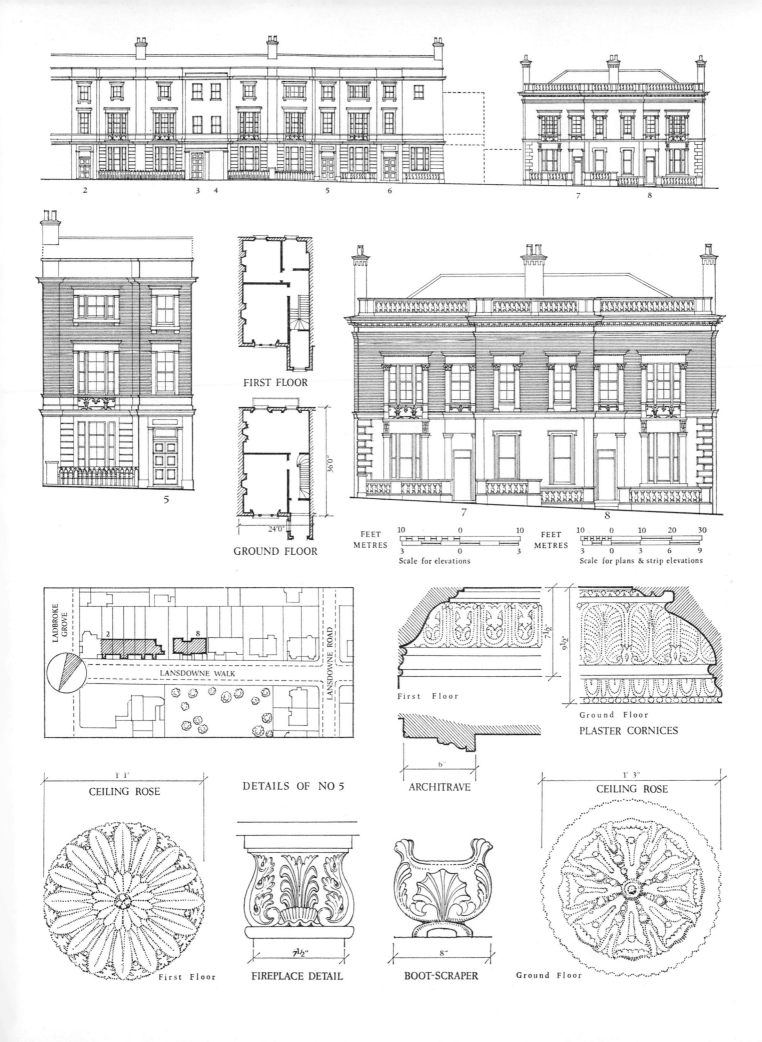

2　3　4　5　6　　7　8

FIRST FLOOR

GROUND FLOOR

36'0"

24'0"

7　8

FEET
METRES

10　0　10
3　0　3

Scale for elevations

FEET
METRES

10　0　10　20　30
3　0　3　6　9

Scale for plans & strip elevations

5

LADBROKE GROVE

2　8

LANSDOWNE WALK

LANSDOWNE ROAD

DETAILS OF NO 5

First Floor

7½"

9½"

Ground Floor

PLASTER CORNICES

6"

ARCHITRAVE

CEILING ROSE

1' 1"

CEILING ROSE

1' 3"

First Floor

FIREPLACE DETAIL

7½"

BOOT-SCRAPER

8"

Ground Floor

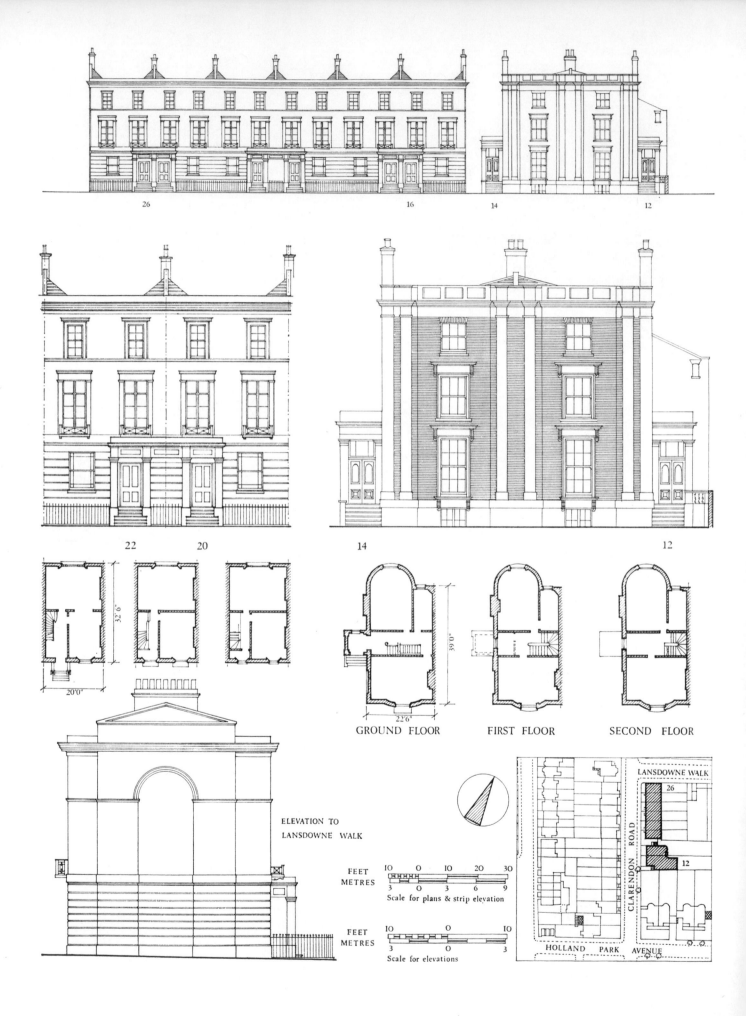

26   16   14   12

22   20   14   12

32' 6"

20' 0"

39' 0"

22' 6"

GROUND FLOOR   FIRST FLOOR   SECOND FLOOR

ELEVATION TO
LANSDOWNE WALK

FEET
METRES
10   0   10   20   30
3   0   3   6   9
Scale for plans & strip elevation

FEET
METRES
10   0   10
3   0   3
Scale for elevations

LANSDOWNE WALK

26

12

CLARENDON ROAD

HOLLAND   PARK   AVENUE

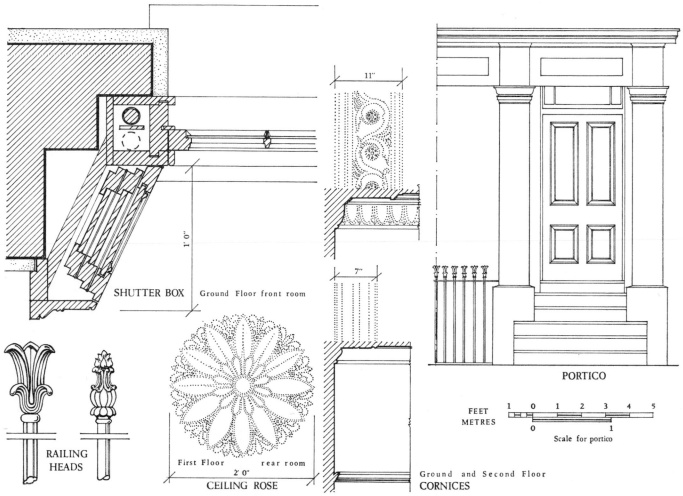

SHUTTER BOX   Ground Floor front room

RAILING
HEADS

CEILING ROSE
First Floor   rear room

CORNICES
Ground and Second Floor

PORTICO

FEET
METRES
Scale for portico

Fig. 49. No. 20 Clarendon Road, details

the experience of landscape and layout which Thomson had acquired in Papworth's office and in Regent's Park, and his scheme seems mean and unimaginative in comparison. Fortunately, little of it ever materialized, the plan being abandoned after Connop's financial collapse in 1845 had resulted in the division of his lands among several speculators, who subsequently employed another architect, Thomas Allom, to prepare a new plan worthy of Thomson's example. Apart from the idea of Ladbroke Square, and the long range of houses along its south side (for the eastern half of which Stevens probably supplied designs), and the layout of Kensington Park Road, the northerly line of which was altered in 1849,[59] little of Stevens's work survives.

His later commission to design St. John's Church was probably the result of a compromise. He and Thomson, presumably on the instructions of their respective clients, had both provided a church at focal points in their plans, the sites being almost opposite to one another on either side of Ladbroke Grove. But in the mid 1840's building development on the west side of Ladbroke Grove was advancing very rapidly under Richard Roy's auspices, whereas on the east side it was bedevilled by Connop's misfortunes (see below). It seems not improbable, therefore, that an agreement was reached whereby the church was built on the west side, on the condition that Stevens should be its architect.

This possibility is supported by the fact that

Fig. 48 (facing page). Nos. 12–26 even Clarendon Road, plans and elevations

by 1844, when the building of St. John's Church begun, Thomson, whose claims to design the church might otherwise have been paramount, had, so far as is known, ceased to have any connexion with the Ladbroke estate. His definitely known connexion extends over a period of only three months, from September to December 1842, during which he prepared the layout plan already referred to (Plate 54a) and on Richard Roy's behalf submitted two applications to the Commissioners of Sewers for permission to lay drains to two ranges of terrace houses. These applications were for Queen's or Hanover Terrace (now Nos. 1–6 consec. Lansdowne Walk) which he is known from another source to have designed,[7] and for Lansdowne Terrace (now Nos. 37–61 odd Ladbroke Grove).* We have already seen that Thomson had had experience of building terraces in Regent's Park, but the failure at the end of 1842 of the twenty-house

range projected by Duncan, Markwick and Jay at the top of the hill may have prompted Roy and Pearson Thomson to decide that the terraces adumbrated on James Thomson's plan were not the appropriate type of house to build on their land. The only terraces in fact built under their auspices were the two certainly designed by Thomson in 1842 (Nos. 37–61 odd Ladbroke Grove and 1–6 consec. Lansdowne Walk) and two small ranges in Clarendon Road (Nos. 16–26 even and 31–39 odd), for which it is likely on stylistic and other grounds that he supplied the designs (Plate 60, figs. 47–9).

All four of these ranges, which were built under leases of 1842–5 to William Reynolds (see below), are of some distinction. Nos. 37–61 Ladbroke Grove have four storeys, but the other three ranges are of three storeys, and all have basements. All four ranges are faced with coursed stucco at ground-floor level, but at Nos. 16–26

* Lansdowne Terrace was originally intended to have consisted of seventeen houses,[60] but when the church-site was finally settled a little later the four northernmost houses were deleted from the plan in order to provide sufficient space for it.

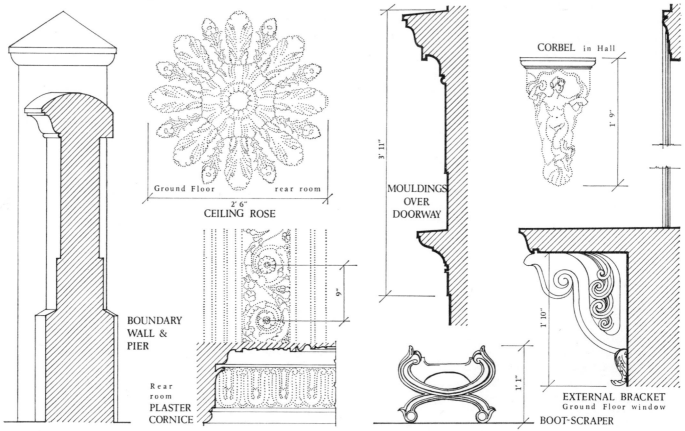

CEILING ROSE

BOUNDARY WALL & PIER

Rear room PLASTER CORNICE

MOULDINGS OVER DOORWAY

CORBEL in Hall

EXTERNAL BRACKET Ground Floor window

BOOT-SCRAPER

Fig. 50. No. 14 Clarendon Road, details

Clarendon Road the stucco extends to the full height. The upper windows of all four ranges have stuccoed architraves and a crowning cornice, also of stucco (now removed at Nos. 31–39 Clarendon Road). Nos. 37–61 Ladbroke Grove (of which Nos. 37, 39 and 51–57 have been re-built in recent years) are set back from the road behind their own shared private enclosure. They are stepped to match the steeply rising ground, and the end houses are set slightly forward to give added emphasis. At Nos. 1–6 Lansdowne Walk, the most sophisticated group in this quartet, the entrances are contained in projections which extend to second-floor level, and the balconies of the first-floor windows have simply detailed Grecian cast-ironwork. The treatment of the return fronts of the ranges in Ladbroke Grove and Clarendon Road must also be mentioned as notable features of Thomson's work. In Ladbroke Grove the central bays at both ends have a double range of plain pilasters surmounted by a pediment, all in stucco, while at the north end of both ranges in Clarendon Road the triumphal arch motif used to link the slightly projecting chimney-stacks recalls something of the scenic display of the terraces in Regent's Park.

Apart from these four ranges, all the other houses erected on Roy and Pearson Thompson's land to the south of Lansdowne Rise were built in pairs, with a few singles and trios. This change in policy required a substantial modification of Thomson's layout if the total number of houses to be built was not to be greatly decreased; and as it also corresponds in date with the end (so far as is known) of Thomson's connexion with the Ladbroke estate, and the appearance by March 1843[61] of William Reynolds, builder or surveyor, regularly acting on Roy's behalf,[62] it seems likely that Reynolds, very probably in conjunction with Allason, was responsible for the substantial modifications which were now to be made to Thomson's original scheme.

The two plans reproduced on Plate 55 show successive stages in the evolution of these modifications. The first is dated 1843, and the second may probably be assigned to c. 1846; neither of them bears the name of its author, although Reynolds's name is mentioned on the second, and an incomplete manuscript version of the latter bears his signature and the date, 1846.[63] The main object of both plans was clearly to introduce more paired houses instead of the long terraced ranges which

had predominated in Thomson's original design. This was achieved by the removal of the site for the church some two hundred feet southward in order to make room at the top of the hill for a new crescent (Lansdowne Crescent), and in the second version, by the introduction of two additional crescents on the lower, northern slopes of the hill. The provision of paddocks or communal gardens was also extended to most of the houses in the area, possibly at Allason's instigation.

The likelihood that Reynolds, in conjunction with Allason, was the author of the final executed layout plan for the Ladbroke estate to the west of Ladbroke Grove does not, however, reduce the significance of Thomson's earlier scheme. It was Thomson who first put Allason's original idea of shared private enclosures into practical form, and it was he who first propounded the idea of concentric crescents skirting round the north-west slopes of the hill. The success of these innovations was later to be attested in the work of other architects, notably Thomas Allom, to the east of Ladbroke Grove, where in the 1850's and 1860's the layout of Stanley Crescent and the formation of five more private enclosures are both derivatives of Thomson's work.

Development by Roy and Reynolds west of Ladbroke Grove, 1842–6

Extensive building development on the lands to the west of Ladbroke Grove began at the end of 1842, with Richard Roy in control as agent for the parties with claims against Duncan. From his office in Lothbury (where his firm also acted as solicitors to the London and Westminster Bank, a life insurance society and two railway companies)[64] Roy was able to command the financial resources needed for large-scale speculation. In November 1842 he signed a building agreement with Ladbroke for an additional three acres of land between Pottery Lane and Portland Road,[65] and within less than four years he had virtually completed the development of a substantial part of the area, extending as far north as Lansdowne Rise and Lansdowne Crescent (fig. 45). Between December 1842 and June 1846 he, as his clients' nominee, was granted 147 building leases by Ladbroke. These yielded a total annual income of £1,127 in ground rents payable to Ladbroke.[66] This revenue was considered to be enough to secure the rent reserved in the original agreement between Ladbroke and Duncan, and entitled Roy to leases from Ladbroke of the remaining lands to the north of Lansdowne Rise, which were granted to him at peppercorn rents on 8 June 1846.[67]

The mechanics of the development which took place to the south of Lansdowne Rise and Lansdowne Crescent between 1842 and 1846 were extremely complicated, and owing to the limitations of the evidence available, are not altogether clear now. The man on the spot was William Reynolds, a builder with a wharf on the Regent's Canal near City Road,[68] who occupied a house or office, first at No. 26 Ladbroke Grove and then at No. 16 Clarendon Road. In 1845 he was also acting in a supervisory capacity as a surveyor in the layout of an estate at Southall.[69] It was he who notified the district surveyor of impending works on Roy's estate and who from March 1843 onwards made application on Roy's behalf to the Commissioners of Sewers for permission to build new sewers in Clarendon Road, Lansdowne Road, Lansdowne Walk, Lansdowne Crescent and St. John's Gardens. Visual evidence suggests that he also supplied the designs for many of the houses which he built in these streets.

Reynolds's relations with Roy are obscure, but basically it was Reynolds's job to organize the building of the roads, sewers and houses, and Roy's to organize a continuous supply of large amounts of capital. The usual procedure was for Roy, as soon as he received a building lease from Ladbroke, to grant a sub-lease to Reynolds for the full extent of his own term less about ten days, but at about double the ground rent reserved to Ladbroke.[70] This was done in at least 112 of Roy's 147 leases from Ladbroke. Roy's profit—or rather, that of his clients—was thus safeguarded, while Reynolds acquired a leasehold interest on the security of which he could raise capital for more building. This he did either by mortgaging his sub-leases (usually for between £500 and £800 per house) or by selling newly completed houses for a lump sum. Occasionally he granted twenty-one-year leases, at rents of about £75 or £90 per year.[71] Reynolds's principal mortgagee and purchaser was Joseph Blunt, one of Roy's partners, whose other clients' need for outlets for surplus capital probably kept him well supplied with resources available for investment in bricks and mortar. In all the deeds giving effect

to these devices, Reynolds's signature was almost always witnessed by members of the staff of Messrs. Roy, Blunt and Johnstone, which indicates that it was through this firm that his financial requirements were met. In at least one case, indeed, that of G. H. Robins, auctioneer of Covent Garden, to whom Reynolds owed £3,500, the firm even undertook to guarantee repayment of the debt.[72]

Many of the houses built by Reynolds have a recognizable 'style' of their own, and may therefore (as previously mentioned) have been designed by him (Plate 63). Most of them are paired, with two or three storeys and a basement, each individual plot having a frontage of about 40 feet and a depth of between 90 and 130 feet. Most houses are faced with stucco at either ground-floor level or throughout their whole height, and all such features as doorways, balconies, window-architraves, cornices and pediments are liberally adorned with coarsely-detailed stucco dressings. A robust coarseness is, indeed, the distinguishing feature of Reynolds's work, as can be seen, for instance, in many of his houses in Lansdowne Road, where his Italianate detail (notably the shell motifs above the first-floor windows at Nos. 15 and 17 and elsewhere) is in marked contrast with the more restrained Grecian treatment practised by Thomson.

There was plenty of variety in Reynolds's work. In Lansdowne Walk, for instance, the pair numbered 7 and 8 (fig. 47) has first-floor windows framed by Corinthian pilasters and dentilled cornices, and a modillioned cornice crowned by a stucco balustrade, while Nos. 11 and 12 have semi-circular headed windows and a bold enriched cornice. All four of these houses, and many others, have suffered by the partial or complete removal of balconies, balustrades, cornices and other ornamentation, or by the insensitive insertion of extra windows, as, for instance, at Nos. 43 and 45 Clarendon Road. This unusual pair of villas has a giant Corinthian order of stucco pilasters carrying an entablature and pediment (now pierced by a window) with a modillioned cornice. Another nearby pair, Nos. 51 and 53 Clarendon Road, has triple-arched windows at first-floor level and ill-proportioned Ionic porches.

A few of the houses leased to Reynolds are, however, markedly different from those described above, and may have been designed by someone else. The quality of the ornamentation of the two pairs numbered 37–43 (odd) Lansdowne Road (Plate 63d), for instance, recalls Thomson's manner rather than that attributed above to Reynolds, while at Nos. 5–8 (consec.) and 13 and 14 Lansdowne Crescent squat Lombardic towers are introduced—an early example of this *genre*, which did not become generally fashionable until the 1850's. The fact previously noted that Reynolds was the lessee for the four ranges designed by Thomson shows that he did not always himself design the houses which he built, and one or two other architects besides Thomson may well therefore have been involved in his building work.

The only other builders to whom Roy granted sub-leases besides Reynolds were Joshua Higgs, senior and junior, of Davies Street, Mayfair, the builders of St. John's Church, for the adjoining Nos. 2–4 (consec.) Lansdowne Crescent and 63 Ladbroke Grove;[73] Frederick Woods and William Wheeler of Notting Hill, for Nos. 16–30 (even) Lansdowne Road;[74] Samuel Clothier of St. Pancras, marble mason, for Nos. 14 Lansdowne Road and 14 Lansdowne Walk;[75] and J. H. Nail, appraiser, for a number of small houses in the vicinity of Pottery Lane.[76] Nos. 2–4 Lansdowne Crescent and 63 Ladbroke Grove, two pairs, one in the Gothic manner appropriate to their situation beside the church, and the other having steeply pitched gables, do not resemble any other houses in the area under discussion, and were probably designed by the Higgs. Four of the eight houses leased to Woods and Wheeler in Lansdowne Road have the same stucco Corinthian pilasters at first- and second-floor level as Reynolds used opposite at No. 9 Lansdowne Road, and were probably designed by Reynolds, as also was the pair at the corner of Lansdowne Road and Walk (Plate 63e, f), where the lease to the marble mason Clothier may have been granted at Reynolds's request in settlement of a debt.

The census of 1851 provides detailed information about the people then living in the houses built under the auspices of Roy and Reynolds. The returns for the forty houses in Lansdowne Road now numbered 2–44 (even) and 9–43 (odd) show that two houses were empty and two others occupied by caretakers. In the remaining thirty-six houses there were 273 residents, of whom 90 were servants. The average number of residents in each house was thus *c.* 7·6, of whom 2·5 were servants. The householders included eleven fund-holders or landed proprietors, five merchants, three

lawyers, two army officers (both in the East India Company's service), two coach-builders, two civil engineers, and one surgeon (with four resident patients), one commercial clerk and one iron and tin manufacturer. Three houses were used as girls' schools, with a total resident staff of nine mistresses.

In Lansdowne Crescent twenty houses were occupied by 133 residents, of whom 53 were servants. The average number of residents in each house was thus 6·6, of whom 2·6 were servants. The householders included three fundholders (all women), three lawyers (one a magistrate), two army officers, two civil servants, and one clergyman, chemist, dealer in stocks and shares, parliamentary agent, wholesale bookseller, warehouseman, varnish maker and merchant.

The most remarkable feature of the development of this area was the creation of five communal gardens, four of them at the rear of the houses on either side of Lansdowne Road, and the fifth at the rear of the houses on the inner side of Lansdowne Crescent. Each house had a small private garden for its occupants' own exclusive use, and these gardens provided access at the rear to a much larger paddock, which was to be shared by all the inhabitants of the houses backing on to it. The five paddocks comprised over five acres of land, and only the houses on the west side of Clarendon Road and the south side of Lansdowne Walk, where the outer boundaries of Roy's land prevented such an extended layout, did not enjoy this precious amenity of suburban living.

Each paddock was leased by Ladbroke to Roy as part of the curtilage of one of the houses abutting on to it. The first to be so leased, in March 1844, was the garden behind the houses in Lansdowne Crescent, and here the paddock was included in the lease of No. 9.[77] When Roy granted sub-leases of the houses (usually to Reynolds), he covenanted to lay out the paddock 'for the convenience and recreation of the tenants and occupiers', and granted them the right to use the garden and 'to walk and demean in and upon the same premises in manner customary in enclosed pleasure or ornamental garden grounds in Squares and other like places in London', provided that 'none of the Livery or other servants . . . save and except the domestic servants in actual attendance on the Children or other members of the family' should be permitted to enter.[77] In his sub-leases Roy reserved to himself an annual garden rent ranging from one to three guineas on each house,[78] and in return he covenanted to maintain the garden at his own cost for the whole of his leasehold term.[77] In later years Roy bought the freehold of many of the houses from the Ladbroke family, and later still, sold many of these freeholds subject to the existing under-leases. These sales included a right to use the appropriate paddock, but the soil itself was excluded. The purchasers, not wishing to under-take the maintenance of the five gardens, con-veyed the garden rents back to Roy, who thus retained his responsibility for maintenance for the remainder of the original leasehold term. In the case of the Lansdowne Crescent paddock, Roy's heirs in 1910 leased the garden rent-charges for one hundred years to trustees acting on behalf of a committee of the inhabitants. The rent-charges are still paid, supplemented by a voluntary additional payment to meet rising costs.[79]

The following table of leases granted by Ladbroke to Roy between December 1842 and June 1846 shows the gathering momentum of building.[66]

1842	8 leases
1843	11
1844	23
1845	52
1846	53
Total	147

Besides the houses there were also the roads and sewers to be built, the total length of sewers for which Reynolds obtained building permission from the Commissioners amounting to some 8,400 feet. The steeply sloping ground presented problems, and in the northern part of Lansdowne Crescent a great mass of clay twenty feet in depth which had been deposited on the turf to make the road slid down the hill, destroying vaults and sewers.[80] And finally there was the church itself (Plate 12), that important adjunct of a successful suburban building speculation, which was built on the summit of the hill on the west side of Ladbroke Grove, but where it could also form a focal point for Connop's estate on the other side of the road. At the time of the consecration of the church, on 29 January 1845, *The Builder* com-mented that 'an entirely new neighbourhood has grown up in this quarter "like an exhalation"'.[81]

During the hectic three and a half years from December 1842 to June 1846 some £120,000 must have been invested in Roy's estate.* Almost all, or perhaps all of this money was channelled to Reynolds through the firm of Roy, Blunt and Johnstone, either directly by Blunt or indirectly by one of the firm's clients with money available for investment. The case of one of these clients, Viscount Canning, was probably typical of a dozen others. In 1843 he had lent £2,000 to the trustees for building St. John's Church.[82] He had also lent to Reynolds, who in 1846 owed him £3,500 (later increased to £8,200) 'for monies lent and advanced or paid for his [Reynolds's] account by the hands of Messieurs Roy, Blunt and Johnstone, the solicitors of the said Viscount Canning'. This loan was at first secured only by the deposit in the firm's custody of six of Roy's sub-leases to Reynolds, but by the end of 1846, when the boom in railway shares was rapidly mounting, money was becoming hard to find and Reynolds agreed that if Lord Canning should require him to do so, he would execute a mortgage which should include 'a power of sale'.[83]

By this time Roy himself had been compelled to make heavy mortgages of his leases from Ladbroke (subject of course to Reynolds's under-leases), probably to his own clients,[84] and some of the existing mortgagees were calling in the money which they had advanced to Reynolds. In May 1846 Reynolds was able to transfer some of these mortgages to the Sovereign Life Assurance Company,[85] but by October he had to sell some of his under-leases to his mortgagees,[86] and even to resort to a loan of £7,000 limited to six months' duration from a group of City magnates. These were the two great bill dealers, Samuel Gurney, of Overend and Gurney, and James Alexander of Alexander and Company, plus Sir Moses Monte-fiore and Lionel Nathan de Rothschild.[87] In December this formidable quartet was willing to take over the mortgages made by the Sovereign Life,[88] but the repayment of the loan in April 1847 evidently exhausted Reynolds's resources and after the Sun Insurance Office had refused his request for a loan of £20,000[89] a judgment for

---

* For this very rough calculation the average cost of the 147 houses built has been assumed to be £750, and the average cost of building 8,400 feet of sewers has been taken as 15 shillings per foot. This gives £116,550, to which must be added an allowance for the cost of road building.

debt was entered against him in May.[90] Throughout the summer of 1847, when there were numerous mercantile failures in the City, he was still able to find purchasers for his under-leases through Roy, Blunt and Johnstone,[91] but in the autumn, when the Bank Charter Act was suspended, there were two more judgments for debt against him.[92] It was at about this time that his connexion with Roy, Blunt and Johnstone came to an end, and the firm itself split. Blunt, who had supplied so much of Reynolds's capital, appropriately became solicitor to the Royal Mint, Johnstone became clerk to the Patent Office, while Roy, who now lived at No. 59 Ladbroke Grove, remained in command in Lothbury.[64] Reynolds himself was not so fortunate, for in February 1848 he was declared bankrupt.[93] But this was not quite the end of him, for within less than eighteen months he was building houses again on the east side of Ladbroke Grove, and sewers in the northern part of Clarendon Road and in Blenheim Crescent.[94] He died intestate in 1850.[95]

For Pearson Thompson, from whom presumably had emanated the original idea of forming a 'little Cheltenham' at Notting Hill, the outcome was different. His investment on the Ladbroke estate had 'so involved his affairs as to compromise the whole of his property', and in 1849 he emigrated to Australia. After practising at the bar in Sydney for a while, he removed to Castlemaine, the centre of a large goldmining district, where he practised very successfully and later became a magistrate. He died there in 1872.[96]

Development by Connop east of Ladbroke Grove, 1841–5

To the east of Ladbroke Grove the progress of building had meanwhile been very much slower. There Connop was deeply involved in Duncan's financial difficulties;[97] like Duncan he was indebted to the builder William Chadwick for work done at the Hippodrome racecourse,[98] and through his activities in the City as a bill broker he also, in March 1842, owed nearly £12,000 on unpaid bills of exchange to William Sloane,[99] a gentleman who had made a fortune in Bengal as an indigo planter.[3] Connop urgently needed capital to get his building speculation moving, and in August 1841 C. H. Blake (see page 221), then still in

Calcutta, agreed to purchase the improved ground rents of nine houses (when completed) for £6,750.[100] Blake seems, however, to have withdrawn from this risky project, and it was Connop's solicitor, William Parkin of Chancery Lane,[101] who persuaded a relative, Henry Parkin, a physician living in Torquay, to provide urgently needed backing. Henry Parkin agreed to buy at fifteen years' purchase the improved ground rents of eleven houses to be erected by Connop, and by February 1842 he had advanced £4,000 to Connop for this purpose, a debt which two years later had risen to £10,000. The security for all these and other debts was Connop's agreement with Ladbroke, but in July 1842 there were still no houses, Connop 'not being able to induce any person to undertake to build'.[102]

In the following month, however, he agreed to grant leases of five plots on the south side of Ladbroke Square (Nos. 23–27 consec.) to William Gribble, a St. Marylebone builder, and building began at last, Gribble's capital being supplied by C. H. Grove, another lawyer of Chancery Lane.[103] By October he had induced another builder, W. J. Wells of Islington, to take four more plots in Ladbroke Square (Nos. 28–31),[104] but misfortune was never far away, for in November he had to execute yet another mortgage of his lands, to his architect, Martin Stuteley, for £7,400 due on unpaid bills of exchange;[105] and in January 1843 some 220 feet of the sewer which he was himself laying in Ladbroke Square collapsed.[106]

By June 1843 building was sufficiently advanced for Ladbroke to grant, at Connop's request, ninety-seven-year leases of twelve houses in Ladbroke Square (Nos. 23–27 and 31–37 consec.), two on the east side of Kensington Park Road (Nos. 44 and 46, now demolished) and five on the east side of Ladbroke Grove at the top of the hill (Nos. 42–50 even), all to William Parkin.[107] John Stevens, who by this time had superseded Stuteley as Connop's architect, was a party in one of the transactions relating to Nos. 31–37 Ladbroke Square,[108] and he may therefore have been the designer of this range. The houses in Ladbroke Grove were certainly not yet finished, for seventeen months later they were still in carcase,[109] and in October 1845 they (Nos. 42–50) together with Nos. 52–58 Ladbroke Grove were re-leased by Ladbroke to John Brown of St. Marylebone, builder.[110] Soon afterwards

Brown mortgaged these houses to Ladbroke's solicitors, Bayley and Janson,[111] which suggests that Ladbroke or his agents were by the provision of capital trying to get development moving.

The houses in the range in Ladbroke Square between Ladbroke Terrace and Kensington Park Road (Plate 61e) are of the conventionally planned terrace type, but have spacious accommodation, being some twenty feet in width on average. Nos. 42–58 (even) Ladbroke Grove, by Brown, are large paired villas, with the exception of No. 50 which is detached, and are built of stock brick with stucco enrichments. The pair numbered 42 and 44 is an eclectic design, having a symmetrical façade of three storeys over a basement, with a small pedimented attic storey in the centre. The front is enlivened with stucco pilasters, architraves, balustrades, porch and large main cornice carried on console brackets.

The grant of leases in June 1843 (referred to above) had probably been an attempt by Connop to provide additional security for his creditors, for he was by then already being closely pressed, and by the end of 1843 two court judgments had been delivered against him for unpaid debts.[112] Soon afterwards Brown was granted leases of Nos. 20–22 (consec.) Ladbroke Square,[113] and William Parkin of three villas, Nos. 48–52 (even) Kensington Park Road (now demolished),[114] Parkin being also nominated as the intended lessee of Nos. 38–46 Ladbroke Square.[115] But the two Parkins were now in their turn in financial difficulty, and in June 1844 they mortgaged their interest in Connop's lands for £8,000.[116] Connop himself was evidently no longer credit-worthy, and in January 1845 a receiver was appointed to administer his estate.[117]

Development by Chadwick in Ladbroke and Kensington Park Roads, 1840–52

By this time doubts had again arisen, as in 1832, about the validity of the leasehold titles created by Ladbroke, and in 1844 a third Act of Parliament had been obtained. In addition to the two contracts of 1840–1 with Connop and Duncan, Ladbroke had also signed three other agreements —one with William Chadwick in 1840 for the development of land around the intersection of Ladbroke Road and Kensington Park Road, one

already mentioned with Richard Roy in 1842 for some three acres between Pottery Lane and Portland Road, and one in 1844 with William Henry Jenkins, a civil engineer, for twenty-eight acres around Pembridge Villas (see Chapter X). All these agreements were now confirmed, and Ladbroke was also empowered to accept surrenders of existing leasehold interests, to grant new leases where necessary, to vary the existing agreements by mutual agreement, particularly as to the maximum numbers of houses to be built, and to sell land for the site of a church.[118] The fact that these and other amendments were needed suggests that Ladbroke and his advisers, Allason (surveyor) and Bayley and Janson (lawyers), had not been very efficient in their management of the estate.

William Chadwick had been active in building on the Trinity House estate in Southwark in the 1820's,[119] and was now in the City, where he described himself as an architect and/or builder.[120] Between 1832 and 1837 he had been the contractor at Kensal Green Cemetery for the building of the two chapels there and the boundary wall. He had been drawn into the Ladbroke estate through his employment by Whyte in the erection of fences and stables at the Hippodrome, and his unpaid account for this work, amounting to some £8,200, had been secured by a lien on the lands contracted by Ladbroke to Connop and Duncan in 1840–1.[121] He was evidently a man of caution and experience, for in his agreement with Ladbroke he only contracted for some seven acres (fig. 45),[122] at an initial rent of £104 rising in the fourth and all succeeding years to £113 (equivalent to £16 per acre), and he only undertook to spend £4,000 in building.[118]

Most of Chadwick's work on the Ladbroke estate consists of well-proportioned and regular terrace houses simply dressed with stucco, and provides a marked contrast with the loosely spreading Italianate façades of his contemporary, William Reynolds. He began, as speculators often did, by building a public house, the Prince Albert, at the junction of Kensington Park Road and Ladbroke Road, of which he was granted a lease by Ladbroke in 1841.[123] By 1848 he had built nine houses in Ladbroke Road—Nos. 1–11 (odd) on the south side (Nos. 9 and 11, Plate 61a, being a large pair of stucco-faced villas with pilasters and a grand cornice supported on huge brackets) and Nos. 14–18 (even) on the north, the latter adjoining Horbury Mews, which was formed many years later (in 1877) on the site of a nurseryman's grounds.[124] No. 14 is a large pedimented three-storey villa with two-storey wings, and has a frontage of seventy-five feet, while Nos. 16 and 18 form a pair of Italianate houses with pediments over the ground-floor windows, a bracketed cornice, and semi-circular headed windows above trabeated doorways (Plate 61b, d). On the east side of Kensington Park Road he had completed another six houses, of which Nos. 32–38 even (four-storey paired villas with stucco fronts) survive,[125] plus twelve small terrace houses on the west side of Pembridge Road (Nos. 13–33 odd Pembridge Road and 2 Kensington Park Road).[126]

The ground rents arising on these houses were enough to secure Ladbroke's interest, and in May 1848 Felix Ladbroke granted Chadwick a lease of most of the remaining land at a peppercorn rent,[127] the plot at the corner of Kensington Park Road and Ladbroke Road being reserved for a Congregational chapel. This was Horbury Chapel (now Kensington Temple, Plate 28b), designed by J. Tarring and built in 1848–9 by T. and W. Piper.[128]

Chadwick's business was large enough for him to employ his own clerk of works,[129] and in 1848 he began to grant leases to other builders, notably to George Stevenson for Nos. 13–19 (odd) Ladbroke Road, a group of houses which avoids the monotony of the terrace which it in fact is by having the entrances set in smaller and lower elements as in St. James's Gardens on the Norland estate and elsewhere. Chadwick's own later building included a range of small houses, models of simple stock-brick terraces, with stucco architraves, and some with shops on the ground floor, at the apex of Kensington Park Road (Nos. 2–30 even), and more similar development in Pembridge Road (Nos. 35–59 odd), the latter extending round into Portobello Lane (the Sun in Splendour public house and Nos. 9–13 odd), all of which was substantially complete by the time of his death in 1852.[130] The building of Horbury Crescent and Nos. 2–10 (even) Ladbroke Road was begun in 1855 by his heir, W. W. Chadwick, for whom a local builder, John D. Cowland, acted as contractor in the building of sewers.[131] The long three-storey range of Nos. 21–55 Ladbroke Road, notable for not having basements, was built by William Wheeler under leases granted by W. W. Chadwick in 1853–4 (Plate 61c).

Development by Drew in Ladbroke Road, 1840–5

One other portion of the Ladbroke estate developed before 1847 remains to be described— the area to the north of Adams's speculation of 1826–31 along the Uxbridge road, extending westward from Ladbroke Grove to Portland Road, and bounded on the north by Roy's holding (fig. 45). The developer here was William John Drew, variously described as builder or architect and doubtless a relative of John Drew of Pimlico, builder, who together had built Nos. 11–19 (odd) Ladbroke Grove (fig. 51), beginning in 1833. No agreement between Ladbroke and W. J. Drew has been found, but between 1839 and 1845 Drew or his nominees were granted leases of all the ground in this area. The fifty or more houses which were built here have a style of their own quite distinct from the work (previously discussed) of Cantwell, Adams, Thomson, Reynolds or Chadwick, and there is some reason to think that Ladbroke's surveyor, Allason, may have been responsible for their design (Plate 62).

After the completion of Nos. 11–19 Ladbroke Grove in about 1838 W. J. Drew had built a similar range of small two-storey stucco-fronted houses in the Grecian manner at Nos. 1–11 (odd) Clarendon Road (now demolished), under leases granted by Ladbroke in 1840–1[132] (Plate 62a). Drew's mortgagee for part of this range was Allason,[133] and in 1843 Drew was mortgaging other houses in the area to Ladbroke's solicitor, R. R. Bayley.[134] It may therefore be that Ladbroke and his agents involved themselves more actively in the development of this part of the estate than was the case elsewhere.

The two characteristic features to be found in most of the houses with which Drew was connected, namely the use, firstly, of vertical strips of stucco, which appear as pilasters with the minimum of mouldings, and extending through two or sometimes even three storeys, and secondly, of semi-circular bowed projections, had both previously been used by Allason in 1827 for his own house. This was Linden Lodge in Linden Grove (now demolished, see page 269), a large two-storey stucco-fronted detached house having simplified pilasters extending through the full height of a central bowed projection (Plate 73a). On the main portion of the Ladbroke estate the first examples of the use of pilasters by Drew are

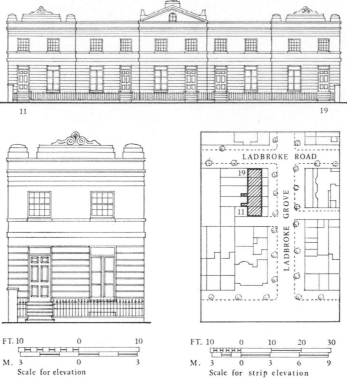

Fig. 51. Nos. 11–19 odd Ladbroke Grove, elevations and site plan

to be seen at Nos. 21 and 23 Ladbroke Grove, leased to him in 1839–40,[135] and at Nos. 25–35 Ladbroke Grove, leased also in 1839–40 to Drew's nominee, Francis Read of Pimlico, builder.[136] This terrace (Plate 62b, fig. 52) is arranged as a series of linked pairs of houses, each of three storeys above a basement, their stucco façades being furnished with slender pilasters. These pilasters unite the ground and first floors beneath a continuous dentil entablature, whilst the upper storey is given an attic order, surmounted in turn by shallow eaves to the low-hipped slate roofs. The façades, each two windows wide in the main face, break back slightly in the linking parts where entrance doors are set within Roman Doric porches.

The houses (mostly paired) in the stretch of Ladbroke Road between Ladbroke Grove and Lansdowne Road, for which Drew was the lessee between 1841 and 1845, have characteristic vertical stucco strips, as well as bowed projections (now often obscured by later additions) at the side or rear. So, too, have Nos. 2–12 (even) Lansdowne Road, of which he was granted leases in

1843[137] (Plate 62d, fig. 53). The latter form three pairs of two-storey houses with basements and attics. Here the giant stucco strips support large consoles which carry wide overhanging eaves. Generally there are three rooms on the main floors, and the bowed projections of the large rear rooms overlook spacious gardens. These houses are faced by Nos. 1–5 (odd) Lansdowne Road, three large detached villas where, exceptionally, neither pilasters nor bows are used. These were leased in 1845 at Drew's direction to his nominee, William Liddard of Notting Hill, gentleman, and have stucco architraves, stringcourses and enriched cornices carried on ornate consoles.[138]

The possibility that Allason may have provided designs for Drew is further supported by the evidence of a group of houses further west. On the west side of Clarendon Road Drew was the lessee in 1840 for Nos. 13 and 15 (a stucco-fronted pair with pilasters)[139] and in 1845 Nos. 17–29 (odd) were leased to his nominees, Liddard for Nos. 17–21 (a plain stuccoed range of three houses) and Allason himself for Nos. 23–29[140] (Plate 62c). The latter form a short

21   23 25   27 29   31 33   35

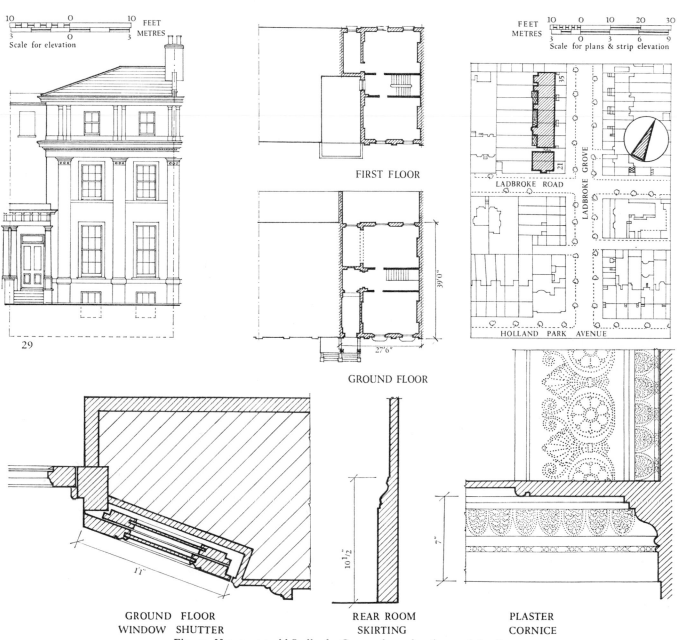

Scale for elevation

FEET
METRES

FIRST FLOOR

GROUND FLOOR

FEET
METRES

Scale for plans & strip elevation

LADBROKE ROAD

LADBROKE GROVE

HOLLAND PARK AVENUE

29

GROUND FLOOR
WINDOW SHUTTER

REAR ROOM
SKIRTING

PLASTER
CORNICE

Fig. 52. Nos. 21–35 odd Ladbroke Grove, plans, elevations and details

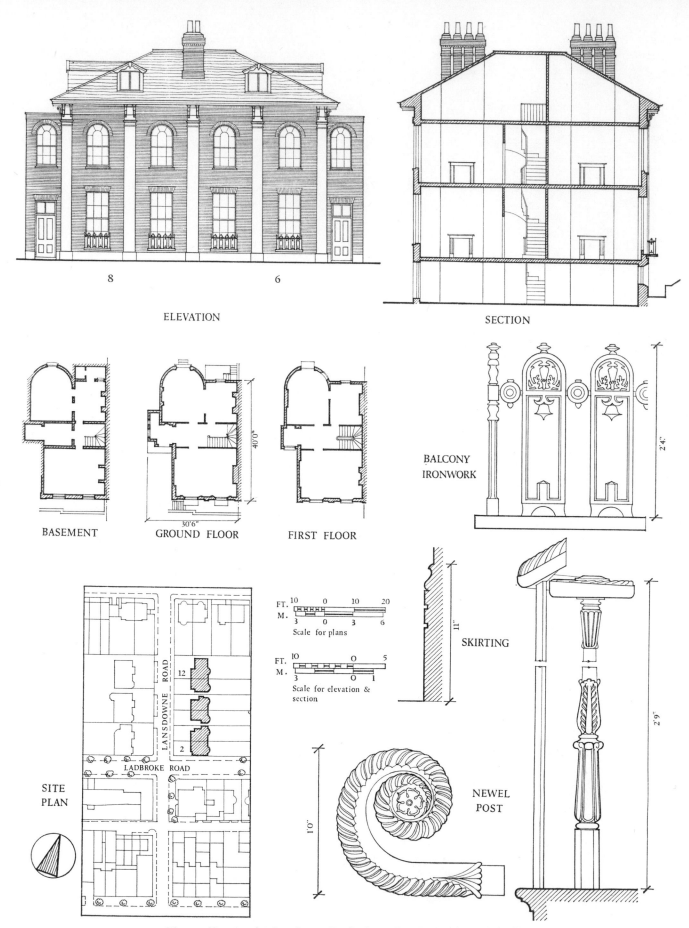

ELEVATION

SECTION

BASEMENT

GROUND FLOOR

FIRST FLOOR

40'0"

30'6"

BALCONY
IRONWORK

2'4"

SITE
PLAN

LANSDOWNE ROAD

12

2

LADBROKE ROAD

FT. 10 0 10 20
M. 3 0 3 6
Scale for plans

FT. 10 0 5
M. 3 0 1
Scale for elevation &
section

SKIRTING

11"

NEWEL
POST

1'0"

2'9"

Fig. 53. Nos. 6 and 8 Lansdowne Road, plans, elevation, section and details

range of narrow terraced houses unique at this period in the development of the Ladbroke estate in having semi-circular projecting bows extending up through the full height of the fronts, three storeys over basements, much in the manner then fashionable at seaside resorts such as Brighton.* At the time of his death in 1852 Allason owned the freehold of all of these nine houses.[141]

Opposite, on the east side of Clarendon Road, Allason was also in 1845, at Drew's nomination, the lessee for Nos. 12 and 14 Clarendon Road (Plate 62e, fig. 50) and for the contiguous Nos. 80–86 (even) Ladbroke Road.[142] These six houses consist of three substantial pairs, all of three storeys over basements, and all with stucco strips rising from the ground floor to support an entablature surmounted by a panelled parapet. Nos. 12 and 14 Clarendon Road have shallow bowed fronts, and the doorways are set back on the flanks. Unmistakably related to this pair is the much larger and slightly later group at Nos. 1–3 (consec.) Kensington Park Gardens, where Allason and Drew were also both involved[143] (Plate 62f). At Nos. 80–86 Ladbroke Road there are paired porches projecting from the centres of the symmetrical fronts. All six houses have bowed projections at the rear. At his death Allason owned the freehold of these six houses,[141] and it may very well be that he had been their architect.

Drew occupied a house at the south-east corner of Ladbroke Grove and Ladbroke Road, where Notting Hill Police Station now stands.[144] Although he lived until 1878, he is not known to have built any houses in Kensington after 1851 (the year before Allason died). After his death his personal estate was valued at around £12,000.[145] His son, George Drew, was an architect, who was responsible for Nos. 95–109 (odd) Ladbroke Grove in 1864, but he had been still a child at the time of the building of the houses discussed above.

Reorganisation east of Ladbroke Grove, and death of J. W. Ladbroke, 1846–7

After Connop's bankruptcy in 1845 it was clear that the development of his lands to the east of Ladbroke Grove would not get under way without the intervention of the ground landlord. In

April 1846, therefore, all the parties having claims on Connop's lands surrendered their various interests to Ladbroke to enable him to enter into new building agreements.[146] Within a week Ladbroke signed new contracts with four of the claimants for some fifty of Connop's original fifty-eight acres, and undertook to grant ninety-four-year leases from Michaelmas 1845. The whole area was divided up substantially in accordance with the plan (probably) prepared for Connop by Stevens (Plate 54b), now modified to harmonize with more recent alterations to the ground plan of the lands west of Ladbroke Grove. Connop's previous architect Martin Stuteley (now also described as a trustee of the Norwich Union Reversionary Interest Company), took twelve acres now the site of Ladbroke Square, at a rent of c. £24 per acre;[147] William Sloane took nine acres of the best land at the top of the hill, now the site of Kensington Park Gardens and Stanley Gardens, at a rent of c. £30 per acre;[148] James Whitchurch, a speculator already heavily engaged outside the Ladbroke estate in the vicinity of Walmer Road, took three acres of the least eligible land at the northern extremity of Ladbroke's estate at a rent of c. £3 per acre;[149] and George Penson, a cheesemonger of Newgate Street, took the remaining twenty-six acres at a rent of c. £10 per acre.[150] The thin sliver of what had originally been Duncan's land on the east side of Ladbroke Grove was excluded from this new division.

The onset of the financial crisis of 1847 prevented these new developers from making any rapid progress in building, and on 16 March 1847 James Weller Ladbroke died at his house at Petworth, Sussex.[3] At the time of his death the Notting Hill estate (excluding the Pembridge Villas portion) yielded an annual revenue of some £3,000 in ground rents.[151] His heir, a distant cousin, Felix Ladbroke of Headley, Surrey, now possessed an absolute title to the estate, and was therefore able to sell the freehold if he so desired. He had been planning against the day of his cousin's death, for he at once transferred the administration of the estate from Bayley and Janson to his own solicitors, Western and Sons,[3] and within a fortnight of James Weller Ladbroke's death, he sold the freehold of ten houses on the south side of Ladbroke Square (Nos. 38–47

---

* It is perhaps worth noting that Allason's own country house was at Ramsgate, where he was surveyor to one of the principal estates.[141]

consec.),[152] and the twenty-nine acres of land which J. W. Ladbroke had agreed in 1846 to lease to Whitchurch and Penson. The purchaser of the houses and three acres of the land was Thomas Pocock, an attorney of Bartholomew Close in the City; the other twenty-six acres of land were bought by Brooke Edward Bridges, a Bedfordshire clergyman, for whom Pocock acted as solicitor.[153]

The next phase in the development of the Ladbroke estate, from 1846–7 onwards, was thus conducted under very different auspices from the earlier phase. With a ground landlord now in possession who was able and often willing to sell in fee simple, the break-up of the estate had begun, and a new generation of developers appeared, the solicitor Roy being the only significant active survivor from the earlier years.

Development by Phillips in Clarendon Road area, 1848–62

It will be recalled that after the great surge of building in the Lansdowne Road area between 1842 and 1846 Roy (still acting on behalf of the creditors of Duncan's estate) became entitled to, and in June 1846 received, leases at peppercorn rents from J. W. Ladbroke of the remaining lands to the north of Lansdowne Rise.[154] He could now raise capital on this undeveloped land, and in April 1848 he disposed of some ten acres of it, in the north-western extremity of the estate (see fig. 45), to the first of the new developers, Stephen Phillips, merchant, of New Broad Street, City, who during the financial crisis of 1847 had lent large sums of money to Messrs. Roy, Blunt and Johnstone.[155]

Phillips was a large-scale speculator with extensive building interests in Islington and on the St. Stephen's estate at Westbourne Park, Paddington; he was also the owner of some sixty leasehold houses in Brompton, and probably had interests in the timber trade.[156] The development of Phillips's ten acres on the Ladbroke estate (of which he acquired the freehold from Felix Ladbroke in 1850)[157] was evidently only a subsidiary part of his activities, and it is worth noting that several of the builders to whom he granted leases were from Islington or Paddington, and had probably already worked with him there. The site was poor—as yet remote, but close to the Potteries

and the adjacent brickfields—and he therefore proceeded cautiously, the houses here being of less pretension than on the adjoining parts of the Ladbroke estate. In 1849 William Reynolds, now apparently credit-worthy again, became the lessee of several paired houses on the west side of Clarendon Road,[158] but on the rest of Phillips's land further north almost all the other houses were built in unremarkable terraced rows. The layout plan of c. 1846 (Plate 55b) was adhered to in the formation of Cornwall Crescent, but Clarendon Road was curved north-westward to join with the adjacent estate of James Whitchurch. H. W. Smith, the surveyor who was acting on Phillips's behalf in 1852, may have been responsible for this diversion.[159]

The principal building lessees working here between 1852 and 1865 were J. V. Scantlebury, who built most of Camelford Road, and Charles Thompson, formerly of Paddington and Islington, who built much of the north side of Cornwall Crescent. Thomas Pocock, a solicitor who has been previously mentioned as active elsewhere on the Ladbroke estate, was the lessee for some thirty houses on the west side of Clarendon Road. Some or all of these houses may have been designed by William King of Canonbury Park, Islington, architect, who acted on Phillips's behalf in the building of sewers in the Talbot Grove area.[160]

By 1861 Phillips had created improved ground rents of £646,[161] and at his death in 1862 his personal estate was valued at around £35,000.[162] The development of the small remaining parts of his Ladbroke estate property was completed soon afterwards by his executors.

Land purchase and development by Blake and Dr. Walker, 1850–3

The straightforward uneventful progress made by such an experienced developer as Phillips was in marked contrast with the feverish activity surrounding the far larger and more risky speculations of Richard Roy and his two principal clients on the Ladbroke estate, C. H. Blake and Edmund Walker's son, the Reverend Dr. Samuel Walker. The ground landlord, Felix Ladbroke, also involved himself in these operations, and the activities of all four speculators were concerted by a fresh plan for the lands east of Ladbroke Grove which was drawn up by Thomas

Allom. The principal building lessee was David Allan Ramsay, a nurseryman of Brompton, who in 1848 had been one of William Reynolds's assignees in bankruptcy[163] and who had himself subsequently turned builder.

The business relationships which existed between the various members of this group are somewhat obscure. Until about 1855 Roy acted as Blake's solicitor, and paid a small part of Allom's professional fees,[3] the rest of which were (so far as is known) paid by Blake; but there is no reason to think that Roy had any share in the profits and losses of Blake's speculation. Roy also acted as Dr. Walker's solicitor, and managed the day-to-day business of his client's estate, but here he may have participated in the profits and losses as well, for their speculation is referred to as a 'joint undertaking'.[164] On behalf of Duncan's creditors he and his firm were concerned for very many years in the administration of the area already developed by Reynolds, the firm itself, to which, it will be recalled, Duncan had owed £45,000, being the principal creditor. Roy was also involved, apparently on his own account, in speculation in Portland Road, Ladbroke Gardens and the northern half of Stanley Crescent. Felix Ladbroke had his own solicitor, Edward Western, and his own surveyor, Allason, and apart from his evident involvement with Allom in the preparation of the layout plan, acted independently of Blake, Roy and Dr. Walker. Ramsay was granted building leases by all four speculators, upon whom he depended for capital; he seems, indeed, to have occupied much the same position as that of Reynolds in earlier years, and eventually he met the same fate.

Blake was (as has already been stated) the largest and ultimately the most successful speculator in the development of Notting Hill and Notting Dale, his activities eventually extending from Lansdowne Road and Kensington Park Gardens on the Ladbroke estate in the south through the St. Quintin and Portobello estates as far as and even beyond the Great Western Railway in the north. He was born in Calcutta in 1794, the son of Benjamin Blake, a master mariner and sea captain who had been plying on the route to India since 1775. Shortly after C. H. Blake's birth his father left the sea, settled in Bengal, and became an indigo planter. At first C. H. Blake followed his father and an older brother into this business. In the 1820's, however, he left India for England, returning at about the time of his brother's death in 1830, under whose will he inherited over £5,000. Later he gave up indigo planting to become a rum and sugar manufacturer, an occupation which he continued to pursue until leaving India for good in either 1842 or 1843, and the profits from which, no doubt, provided the basis for his speculations in Notting Hill.[165] On arrival in England he acquired, in 1843, William Chadwick's interest in the Ladbroke lands to the west of Ladbroke Grove.[166] But when in 1850 he bought twenty acres of land there from Roy (then acting as trustee on behalf of Duncan's creditors),[167] he ceased to be merely an investor and at the age of fifty-five began his twenty-year career as an active speculator.

These lands consisted of all but five acres of the ground to the north of Lansdowne Rise and Crescent which were still in Roy's trusteeship after the sale of the north-western portion to Phillips in 1848. The price for the unencumbered leasehold interest was £22,580 (equivalent to £1,129 per acre), all of which was used to pay some of the existing creditors, including the London and Westminster Bank, a firm of auctioneers and Blake himself.[167] This price included the benefit of six building leases already granted by Roy,[3] but it evidently represented, nevertheless, a substantial increase in land values since 1846, when Roy had signed an abortive agreement to sell the same land, though without the benefit of six building leases, for £800 per acre.[168] In the same year, 1850, Blake also bought the freehold reversion from Felix Ladbroke for £4,200,[3] bringing his total outlay on these twenty acres up to £1,339 per acre. In 1851 he acquired both the leasehold and freehold of the remaining five acres.[169]

By September 1851 Blake had granted building leases of Nos. 49 and 51 Lansdowne Road (fig. 54), Nos. 68–78 (even) Clarendon Road, and Nos. 153–117 (odd) Elgin Crescent, most of these houses being occupied by 1854. Nos. 145–117 were taken by David Allan Ramsay.[170]

In 1851, however, the strategy of land speculation acquired a new form in response to an unexpected turn of events elsewhere on the estate. Martin Stuteley, to whom James Weller Ladbroke had agreed in 1846 to lease twelve acres, now the site of Ladbroke Square and the south side of Kensington Park Gardens, and William Sloane, to whom he had agreed to lease nine acres,

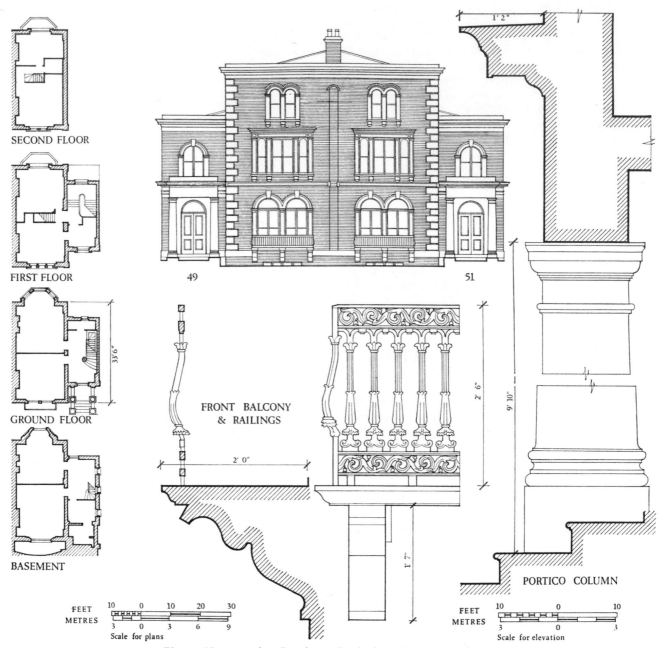

SECOND FLOOR

FIRST FLOOR

49   51

GROUND FLOOR

33' 6"

BASEMENT

FRONT BALCONY & RAILINGS

2' 0"

2' 6"

9' 10"

1' 7"

1' 2"

PORTICO COLUMN

FEET
METRES
10   0   10   20   30
3   0   3   6   9
Scale for plans

FEET
METRES
10   0   10
3   0   3
Scale for elevation

Fig. 54. Nos. 49 and 51 Lansdowne Road, plans, elevation and details

now the site of Stanley Crescent and Gardens and the north side of Kensington Park Gardens, had both failed to fulfil the terms of their agreements, Sloane having died in 1848. By 1852 Felix Ladbroke had recovered possession of all these lands,[171] which from their situation at or near the summit of the hill were among the most valuable on the whole estate, and resolved to develop part of them himself.

It was at this moment that Dr. Walker appeared, hungry for land and able and willing to pay handsomely for it. It has already been mentioned that in 1842 his father, Edmund Walker, a Master in the Court of Chancery, had acquired an interest in Duncan's lands. In marked contrast with his son, Edmund Walker was evidently an extremely wily investor, and by 1845 he had sold his interest in the Ladbroke estate,[172] and thereafter confined his speculations to mortgages in Paddington and Camberwell, acting through the family firm of solicitors, Rickards and Walker of Lincoln's Inn.[173] After his death in 1851 his son, Dr. Samuel Walker, had inherited his 'very large fortune, said to be a quarter of a million'. Since 1841 Dr. Walker had been rector of St. Columb Major in Cornwall, the richest living in the county, worth £1,600 per annum. There he had rebuilt the rectory at considerable personal cost, hoping that it would become the palace of the bishopric of Cornwall which it was his dearest wish to see established. He had even offered his living as an endowment for this great object, but years elapsed without his proposal being definitely accepted, and it was apparently in order to improve the value of his offer that he began to speculate in building, at first successfully at Gravesend, and then on a very large scale at Notting Hill. Here he had thought that his operations would, when completed, earn him £60,000 per annum, but being 'of a most amicable disposition, regardless of all selfish interests, sincere in the views he took, and truly religious in heart and life', he proved ill-equipped for the hurly-burly of suburban speculations. Within four years of his father's death he had lost very large sums of money; his living in Cornwall was sequestered, and after 1863 he lived abroad for several years until shortly before his death in 1869.[174]

Very soon after Edmund Walker's death in July 1851 consultations must have taken place between Felix Ladbroke, Roy, Blake and Dr. Walker about the future development of the remaining parts of the estate. In 1847 Ladbroke had borrowed £25,000 from the Sun Fire Office,[175] and in 1849 his surveyor, Allason, had designed two ranges of houses to be built in the future Kensington Park Gardens (Plate 56). Shortly afterwards Ladbroke had made agreements for the building of Nos. 1–9 (consec.) there with W. J. Drew,[176] to whom he lent £3,000.[177] Allason had previously been associated with Drew in the building of houses in Ladbroke and Clarendon Roads, and his designs for Kensington

Park Gardens would almost certainly have been implemented (though in altered form) had he not died in April 1852. Shortly afterwards Ladbroke completed his arrangements for the repossession of the land to the north of Kensington Park Gardens,[178] and this required the revision of Allason's scheme. Thomas Allom, who had acted as Blake's architect since 1850 in the making of 'surveys and plans' for the lands to the west of Ladbroke Grove,[3] now took Allason's place, and by June 1852 he had, with Ladbroke's concurrence, and probably with that of Roy and Dr. Walker as well, prepared the executed layout plan for Stanley Gardens, Stanley Crescent and the north side of Kensington Park Gardens.[178]

By this time the pattern of land ownership in the area was already being transformed by the arrival of Dr. Walker. In March 1852 he had bought Blake's twenty-five acres of freehold land to the north of Lansdowne Rise.[179] Roy acted as Dr. Walker's solicitor in this purchase, the price being £32,000,[180] equivalent to £1,333 per acre— virtually the same rate as Blake had previously paid in 1850. For this sum Dr. Walker also acquired the benefit of the building leases successively granted there by both Roy (before the sale of 1850 to Blake) and by Blake, and of the roads and sewers which they had built. After having himself paid such a high price, Blake was no doubt relieved to get rid of this expensive investment without loss. Elsewhere in the vicinity Dr. Walker was making other purchases, and between 1852 and 1855 he acquired in all some fifty-six acres of freehold ground in Kensington Park and Notting Dale, besides contracting to buy another thirty-four acres, all in Kensington, and adjacent lands of unknown extent in Paddington (see fig. 55). For his land on the neighbouring Portobello estate, much of which was then still remotely situated, he agreed to pay £1,000 per acre,[181] compared with £828 per acre which Blake was to pay for the same land in 1862, when the impending construction of the Hammersmith and City Railway was no doubt already enhancing land values there.[3] By 1855 Dr. Walker's total contractual liabilities for the purchase of land in Kensington must have amounted to well over £90,000.

In June 1852 Blake bought the unencumbered freehold of part of the land of which Felix Ladbroke had recently repossessed himself. This comprised the sites now occupied by Stanley

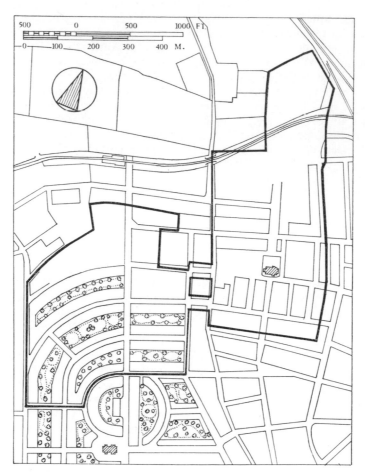

Fig. 55. Lands in Kensington which Dr. Walker bought or contracted to
buy in 1852–5. Based on the Ordnance Survey of 1863–7

Crescent, Stanley Gardens and the south side of
Ladbroke Gardens, some three and a half acres
in all, for which he paid only £1,575, or £450
per acre.[182] This extremely low price can, perhaps, be explained by supposing that Ladbroke
wished to ensure the development of this site in
accordance with the plans prepared by Allom.
In the following year, 1853, Blake also bought
the freehold of the sites of the future No. 24
Kensington Park Gardens and 36–40 (even)
Ladbroke Grove, for which he paid £600.[3]* All
of the rest of the ground on the north and south
sides of Kensington Park Gardens, formerly held
under leasehold agreements by Sloane and Stuteley
respectively, was retained by Felix Ladbroke for
development on his own account.

In all these dealings Roy acted as solicitor for
Blake, and as he had also acted for Walker in the
purchase of Blake's twenty-five acres it is hard
to resist the conclusion that it was he who had
arranged them all. This conjecture is strengthened
by the fact that in August 1852 Roy himself
bought part of Blake's new estate, the land later
to become the northern half of Stanley Crescent
and the south side of Ladbroke Gardens, and in
October he bought the whole of the north side of
Ladbroke Gardens and the south side of Arundel
Gardens from Dr. Walker.[183] Whatever the
relationship between Roy and Blake may have
been, the outcome was that they had each
acquired a small compact estate on the top of the
hill at a very low price, while the unworldly Dr.

* He had previously purchased the leasehold from Martin Stuteley, also for £600.[3]

Walker had burdened himself with a vast sprawling holding on the still remote slopes and dales to the north, and at an enormous cost.

These transactions coincided with and were no doubt prompted by a rapid upsurge in the total volume of building in northern Kensington, the number of houses commenced there having risen from 170 in the crisis year of 1847 to 350 in 1851.[184] As soon as they were able to do so Ladbroke, Roy, Blake and Dr. Walker all started to take advantage of this boom by granting building leases. Roy had started on his leasehold land on the western extremity of the Ladbroke estate, where between 1851 and 1853 he granted over eighty building leases in Portland Road and Heathfield Street to David Allan Ramsay. We have already seen that Ramsay was also at this time Blake's principal building lessee for houses in Elgin Crescent, but he was quite willing to oblige Dr. Walker as well, and of the 120 building leases which Dr. Walker granted in November and December 1852 on his lands to the west of Ladbroke Grove, Ramsay or his relative Henry Malcolm Ramsay took 37, most of them on the north-west side of Elgin Crescent (Nos. 58–120 even).[185]

But it was on the best land at the summit of the hill that Ramsay undertook his largest commitments. Here Blake had decided to develop his freehold estate by direct contract instead of by the normal building lease procedure, and in 1853 he signed a contract with Ramsay for the building of forty houses (Nos. 1–11 consec. Stanley Crescent and 1–29 consec. Stanley Gardens) for some £64,000. Nos. 12 and 13 Stanley Crescent were subsequently included in this contract, at an extra cost of £4,000.[3] Close by on the north side of Kensington Park Gardens, where Ladbroke was the freeholder in possession, Blake took building leases of all twenty-three plots (Nos. 25–47 consec.), and in 1852–3 sub-leased eighteen of them to Ramsay, or to Ramsay's business associates (Nos. 26–31, 36–47).[186] In 1853 Blake also granted building leases to Ramsay for the adjacent Nos. 36–40 (even) Ladbroke Grove.[187] Finally in 1853 Ladbroke himself granted Ramsay the remainder of his land on the south side of Kensington Park Gardens for the erection of thirteen houses, Nos. 10–22 consec. (see fig. 45).[188]

Designs by Thomas Allom, 1850–5

Almost all of the houses which now began to go up in this vicinity were designed by Thomas Allom. Besides having trained as an architect and been a founder member of the Royal Institute of British Architects, he was also famous as an artist, and in 1853 he exhibited at the Royal Academy a picture entitled 'Stanley Crescent,* Kensington Park Terrace etc. now building at Kensington Park Notting Hill for Charles Henry Blake esq from the designs and under the supervision of T. Allom'.[189] This may probably be identified with the very fine lithograph reproduced on Plate 64a. Allom's principal client was certainly Blake, but the incomplete surviving accounts show that he also made 'plans and surveys' for Roy,[3] and Dr. Walker may have been involved as well, for Allom's design for the long range on the north side of Ladbroke Gardens had certainly been settled in October 1852, when Walker sold this land to Roy.[190] Ladbroke, however, is not known to have employed Allom, but a building agreement of 1852 between Ladbroke and Ramsay for Nos. 10–22 (consec.) on the south side of Kensington Park Gardens makes it perfectly clear that Ramsay was required to build in accordance with Allom's designs.[188]

All of Allom's houses still survive (see Frontispiece, Plates 64–6, figs. 56–60 and elevational drawing between pages 234–5). They are Nos. 24–47 (consec.) on the north side of Kensington Park Gardens, No. 24 at the north corner of Ladbroke Grove being Blake's own house (Frontispiece), where he lived from 1854 until 1859; Nos. 10–22 (consec.) on the south side of Kensington Park Gardens; Nos. 1–13 (consec.) Stanley Crescent and 1–29 (consec.) Stanley Gardens, being the forty-two houses built under Blake's contract with Ramsay, for which Allom provided 'surveys, valuations, plans, elevations, sections, specifications'; Nos. 36–40 (even) Ladbroke Grove, and Nos. 1–23 (consec.) Ladbroke Gardens. In 1855 Allom also supplied Blake with drawings for Nos. 14–21 (consec.) Stanley Crescent (Roy having sold this and the land on the south side of Ladbroke Gardens back to Blake),[3] but the houses eventually built here were not by Allom. On the east side of

* Stanley Crescent and Stanley Gardens were probably so named in honour of Edward, Lord Stanley, who succeeded to the Earldom of Derby in 1851 and became Prime Minister in 1852. [The Editor is indebted to Mr. B. R. Curle of Kensington Central Library for this explanation.]

Fig. 56. Kensington Park Gardens, gateway into Ladbroke Square

Kensington Park Road he was the architect for St. Peter's Church (Plate 13), built in 1855–7, Blake having acquired the site of the church and of other adjacent land from Thomas Pocock in 1855.[191]

In addition to designing the houses, Allom was also responsible for the new layout plan for the area between Kensington Park Gardens and Ladbroke Gardens. The idea of a broad straight street (Kensington Park Gardens) leading eastward from St. John's Church to Kensington Park Road was taken from Allason's plan of 1849 (Plate 56), and the idea of communal gardens was, of course, borrowed from earlier precedents to the west of Ladbroke Grove. By the formation of Stanley Crescent and Stanley Gardens he

Section through Cornice above Third Floor Window

Section through Cornice above First Floor

10"

1' 0"

1' 9"

Section through Cornice below Third Floor Window

3' 11"

Section

Part Elevation of Entablature and Pilaster Capitals above First Floor

STUCCO MOULDING DETAILS

2' 5"

2' 10"

3' 0"

First Floor Balcony

Railings on Ground Floor of garden front

IRONWORK DETAILS

Fig. 57. No. 20 Kensington Park Gardens, details

6' 0"

4' 0"

MARBLE FIREPLACE
FIRST FLOOR No. 24

STAIR BALUSTERS
No. 20

PLASTER CORNICE
FIRST FLOOR
No.20

11½"

5' 4"

3' 9"

MARBLE FIREPLACE FIRST FLOOR No. 20

ARCHITRAVE
6"

3' 4"

1' 2"   1' 2½"

SKIRTINGS

5' 10"

3' 10"

MARBLE FIREPLACE FIRST FLOOR No. 20

provided three more such enclosures, and all but two of his 105 houses abutted either directly or via a small private garden on to either one of his three new enclosures or on to Ladbroke Square or the enclosure between Ladbroke and Arundel Gardens.

But while the layout owed much to the example of earlier developments, the architectural forms on this part of the Ladbroke estate changed completely from those previously employed elsewhere. The last threads of the old Georgian traditions, which had been apparent in the terraces of Ladbroke Square, Kensington Park Road and some of the paired villas built by Reynolds and Drew, were now abandoned in favour of a grand display in the latest taste. Allom's early reputation was made as a landscape painter and his compositions appear to have been designed with scenic effect uppermost in his mind. The design of houses, streets, gardens and tree-planting is seen with a painter's eye, so that each turn and every vista is composed in a picturesque manner. Blake's own house (Frontispiece) forms a suitably impressive approach to the splendours of Kensington Park Gardens, and frequent glimpses of grass and trees relieve the stucco façades, which are designed in a freely treated Italianate manner with occasional introductions from Empire and other sources.

It says much for Allom's brilliant scenic display that his strange sort of grandeur is still evident in spite of all the damage that the twentieth century has done. He adopted a more flexible, more romantic approach than the architects of South Kensington or Bayswater. His skill was to make use of the terrace ends, the junctions and the curves in the streets, to introduce special emphasis with great bowed projections, turrets, columnar screens and houses of curious plan forms. His predilection for paired houses placed side by side on the terrace ends, thrusting out bows on all sides, is apparent over and over again.

In the details of the designs, too, the contrast between this work of the 1850's and the traditions surviving in the earlier decades of the century is equally marked. Where the late Georgian buildings had been characterized by restraint, elegance and structural economy, Allom's houses typify the new ideals of grandeur and display. The detail becomes less refined although it is disposed with professional assurance to gain the maximum effect. Not only is the ornament profuse but the use of materials—stucco, timber, iron and stone—is lavish. Where earlier builders had reduced the sections of timber members and mouldings to produce the slenderest and most refined effects, these houses, characteristic of the middle years of the century, employ materials in a manner which reflects the growing material prosperity of the nation as well as a growing tendency towards ostentation. Their construction makes widespread use of stone in hallways, landings and stairs—always to the first floors and sometimes higher. Structural timbers in floors and framed partitions are substantial, there is a free use of cast iron and plaster enrichment internally, and the extensive stucco ornamentation to garden fronts as well as the principal façades must have added considerably to constructional costs as well as subsequent maintenance. Houses in Stanley Gardens at least appear to have been provided with slate damp-proof courses.

Many of the houses display more than usually ambitious interiors for this class of building. For example Nos. 1 and 2 Stanley Crescent and 12 Stanley Gardens all have lavish entrance halls and open-well staircases, whilst No. 24 Kensington Park Gardens has a rich interior in the French taste (Plate 66b). Both inside and out the scale is as large and the enrichment as profuse as the social status of the development could support.

Along the northern side of the great seven-acre garden of Ladbroke Square, which formed the south side of Kensington Park Gardens, were ranged very large houses with frontages in excess of thirty feet (Plates 64c, 66a). They are of four main storeys above a basement, completely stuccoed back and front with great segmental bows to the south, facing the garden. In the principal range (Nos. 10–22 consec.) we find in the façades that all-over richness which the Victorians admired so much. The design is really a study in terrace articulation of the same kind as that to be found in St. James's Gardens on the Norland estate, but far more complicated and now, thanks to later additions and mutilations, extremely difficult to analyse. On careful inspection, however, it resolves itself into the formula:

$$AB^1A - AA - AB^2A - AA - AB^1A$$

The B type house in the centre of each block has a colonnade with paired columns and pilaster responds in the ground storey. The order is Tuscan in the wings and Corinthian in the middle.

Fig. 58 (facing page). Nos. 20 and 24 Kensington Park Gardens, details

6' 0"

1' 2"

EXTERNAL CORNICE

5' 3"

2' 8"

First Floor Balcony railings

IRONWORK DETAILS

Guard railings & stucco pier to
flat roof over billiard room

External Elevation

7' 3"

**CONSERVATORY
DETAILS**
External stucco pilaster &
Internal cast iron column

Section

Plan

Fig. 59. No. 24 Kensington Park Gardens, details

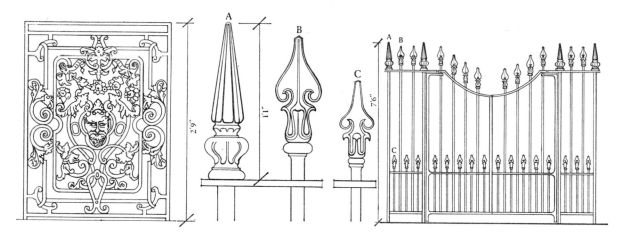

GRILLE   RAILING HEADS   GATEWAY

No 2 Stanley Crescent·   Details of Gateway between Nos 33 & 34 Kensington Park Gardens

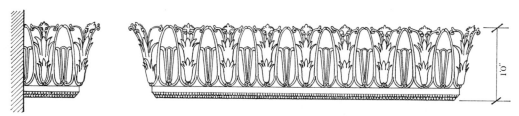

IRONWORK TO WINDOW SILL No 34 Kensington Park Gardens

Fig. 60. Kensington Park Gardens and No. 2 Stanley Crescent, details

The other houses on the south side of Kensington Park Gardens (Nos. 1–9 consec.), are by contrast entirely different, and are not Allom's work. They consist of three four-storey groups, each of three houses, and were all built under building agreements of 1849–50 between Felix Ladbroke and W. J. Drew,[192] whose work elsewhere on the estate has already been discussed. Nos. 1–3 (Plate 62f), which have segmental bowed fronts and a double order of stucco pilasterstrips each rising through two storeys, are amplifications of the smaller design previously executed by Drew, probably in conjunction with Thomas Allason, at Nos. 12 and 14 Clarendon Road. Nos. 4 and 6–9 are more Italianate in manner, but the pilasters favoured by Drew and/or Allason are again used. No. 5 has been completely rebuilt in obtrusive brick and terra-cotta.

On the north side of Kensington Park Gardens (Plate 64b and elevational drawing between pages 234–5) Allom placed two palace façades flanking an arched entry to the communal garden. This entry was set on an axis with the northern gate to Ladbroke Square so that the two gardens were closely related.

The backs of all of Allom's houses facing the gardens were treated with as much care as the fronts. In some cases they were even more ambitious—on the south side of Stanley Gardens, for instance, where the most lavish display is retained for the southern elevations facing the gardens (Plate 66c, d). These façades are enlivened by segmental bow windows of two and three storeys. The stucco of the ground floor is banded and grooved to resemble ashlar work, and a continuous balcony is carried on ornate consoles at first-floor level. The bows and architraves of the windows on the first floor are ornamented with a freely adapted version of the Corinthian order, and the bows are surmounted by stucco balustrades. Where the bay is three storeys high, however, the central window at first-floor level is crowned by a segmented pediment carried on consoles, whilst the Ionic order is introduced on the second floor of the bow only, the window opening normally having plain architraves and cornices.

Allom's connexion with Blake seems to have ended in 1855.[3] An obituary notice published after his death in 1872 refers vaguely to his 'covering the Kensington Park Estate with mansions, for the late Mr. C. H. Blake, at a cost of nearly £200,000'.[193] In his later speculations, which were all in areas of less ambition, both socially and architecturally, Blake contented himself with the professional services of an undistinguished local man, J. C. Hukins of Westbourne Grove, architect and surveyor.[3]

Building boom and collapse in the early 1850's

In 1852 the number of new houses commenced in northern Kensington reached a peak figure of 700,[184] though many of them were not completed until some years later. This great spurt of building involved a large amount of capital, most of which was supplied to the builders by the developers. In Kensington Park Gardens Felix Ladbroke, despite the heavy mortgages which he had himself already made,[194] raised money to enable him to lend £12,000 to D. A. Ramsay for his building on the south side,[195] while on the north side Blake also lent large sums to Ramsay, besides paying for the contract building in Stanley Crescent and Gardens, all apparently out of his own resources, for there is no evidence yet of Blake's having had to borrow.[196]

But by far the largest single source of capital was the unfortunate Dr. Walker. In 1853–4 he advanced over £66,000 to builders on the security of building leases which he had himself granted,[197] Ramsay being the largest borrower. He also lent money to builders working on Roy's land, notably in Portland Road and Arundel Gardens,[198] and in the case of Ramsay he made additional loans on the security of building leases in Kensington Park Gardens which were already mortgaged to Ladbroke.[199] He seems to have had difficulty in converting his own great inherited wealth into ready cash, and in the spring of 1853 he had to assign a number of his own mortgage loans, some to a group of City men, and others to a group in Edinburgh, including one banker.[200] In September Blake, who needed money to pay for the Stanley Crescent building contract with Ramsay, began to press him for payment for the lands to the west of Ladbroke Grove which he had bought from Blake in 1852, a large part of the full price of £32,000 being still outstanding.[3] And in December Dr. Walker in turn began to press Ramsay, who was at that time clamouring for more money to enable him to pay for the timber needed to complete the large number of houses in course of erection on Roy's land in Portland Road. Dr. Walker was now so deeply involved that he had no option but to plunge still further in, and he lent Ramsay another £5,500, secured chiefly by Ramsay's building leases on the north side of Kensington Park Gardens, which had already, of course, been mortgaged to Blake.[3]

In February 1854 the whole of Dr. Walker's short-lived, precarious empire collapsed when Ramsay was declared bankrupt.[3]* Between 1852 and 1856 there was a steep decline in the total volume of house building throughout West London, and in northern Kensington the number of new houses commenced fell from 700 in 1852 to 225 in 1854.[184] Excessive building had far outstripped demand, which in this area continued to be relatively limited until the building of the Hammersmith and City Railway in the mid 1860's.

This collapse gave large parts of Notting Hill a notoriety from which they did not recover for some ten years. The whole of Dr. Walker's property, extending from All Saints' Church on the Portobello estate in the east, to Clarendon Road in the west, was affected. At All Saints' Church, the citadel of the whole disastrous enterprise, building was suspended from about 1855 to 1859, and even in 1861 *The Building News*

---

* The immediate cause of Ramsay's bankruptcy may have been the withdrawal of Ladbroke's support. In February 1854 the Sun Fire Office agreed to renew Ladbroke's mortgage of £25,000 for five years, but by July he had repaid the whole amount.[201]

could still record that throughout the whole area 'The melancholy vestiges of the wreck . . . are not yet wholly cleared away. The naked carcases, crumbling decorations, fractured walls, and slimy cement-work, upon which the summer's heat and winter's rain have left their damaging mark, may still be seen on the estate. Courageous builders have occasionally touched them and lost heart and money by the venture . . . With misfortune came insult, and the opprobrious epithet of "Coffin-row" was fixed upon the dead street, where the windows had that ghastly form [Ladbroke Gardens]. The "Stumps" was a term given to another range of what was intended to be gentlemen's residences. The whole estate was as a graveyard of buried hopes.'[202]

On the north side of Kensington Park Gardens, where Ramsay had been heavily involved, the original leases granted by Ladbroke in 1852 were surrendered, and in the autumn of 1854 new ones were granted to Blake and Dr. Walker as creditors.[203] Blake also acquired the freehold of five houses here,[204] and all his houses were probably completed by contract. Four of Dr. Walker's were evidently finished by J. D. Cowland, a local builder to whom a sub-lease was granted in 1856.[205] The whole street appears to have been completed by about 1858.[144]

In the complicated process of sorting out Ramsay's disordered affairs, which extended over several years, Dr. Walker appears to have been the principal loser, for by 1856 Ramsay himself had changed his rôle once more and set up as an auctioneer in the City.[206] In February 1855 Dr. Walker was still buying land (to the east of Ladbroke Grove, between Elgin Crescent and Westbourne Park Road), but he was unable to pay in cash for it,[207] and he already owed large sums to the London and Westminster Bank for which Blake was (through transactions in bills of exchange) also responsible. He still owed Blake £12,000 for the lands to the west of Ladbroke Grove, which in January 1855 he was obliged to mortgage to Blake subject to repayment within six months,[3] and another £25,000 was due for payment in September on a mortgage of his lands on the Portobello estate.[208] In March 1855, when his total mortgage debts (including the items already mentioned) amounted to some £90,000, he handed over the management of all his estate in Kensington to three trustees, H. M. Kemshead, a West India merchant, E. Robins, an auctioneer,

and the solicitor who had acted for him in all his dealings, Richard Roy.[209] It was only four years since he had inherited his great fortune.

Blake's financial arrangements, 1854–60

If Dr. Walker was the principal loser in the confusions of the mid 1850's, Blake was in the long run the principal beneficiary. But first he had to overcome the immediate problems caused by Ramsay's bankruptcy, and then to weather the threat of total disaster in 1858–60. Under the terms of the contract for building Nos. 1–11 Stanley Crescent and 1–29 Stanley Gardens, he had paid Ramsay rather more than half the total price of £64,000 and was left with forty unfinished houses on his hands. He at once invited builders to tender for completing the work, and the eleven houses on the north side of Stanley Gardens were finished by Messrs. Locke and Nesham. Thomas Allom, the architect, offered to undertake the rest of the work himself, but ultimately Blake allowed himself to be persuaded to employ his own clerk of works, Philip Rainey, on all the other twenty-nine houses, plus Nos. 12 and 13 Stanley Crescent and Nos. 36, 38 and 40 Ladbroke Grove. The result was not a success. It was evidently through Blake's decision to employ Rainey as a contractor that his connexion with Allom came to an end in the autumn of 1855. Rainey submitted extortionate bills to Blake, and when all the work was finally completed in 1858 the total cost amounted to some £11,000 more than the original contract with Ramsay.[3]

These operations were financed by substantial mortgages made from November 1854 onwards by Blake through various firms of solicitors, including the firm employed by J. W. Ladbroke until his death in 1847 to manage the whole Ladbroke estate.[210] With ready money available Blake was therefore able to profit from the complex situation arising from the general slump in building in 1853–4. In January 1855 he extended his operations to the east side of Kensington Park Road, where he bought from the solicitor, Thomas Pocock, all of the freehold land between Westbourne Grove and the backs of the houses on the north side of Chepstow Villas.[211] This acquisition enabled him to present the Ecclesiastical Commissioners (and the inhabitants of his estate) with a site for a church, St. Peter's, designed (as we have already seen) by Thomas Allom,[212] and well placed to close the vista along Stanley Gardens (Plate 64d). The houses to the south of the church, Nos. 76–90 (even) Kensington Park Road, were built in 1859–61 by Philip Rainey to the designs of Edward Habershon, architect.[213] The land to the north of the church was sold by Blake in 1861 to Joseph Offord, gentleman.[214]

By 1856, however, Blake's liabilities were mounting rapidly.[215] Although fourteen of the twenty-three houses on the north side of Kensington Park Gardens were now occupied, only one in the whole of Stanley Crescent and Stanley Gardens was yet inhabited,[144] and money was needed to pay Rainey's bills. The debt of £12,000 due from Dr. Walker for the lands to the west of Ladbroke Grove could no longer be left unpaid, and after allowing him a whole year's grace, Blake foreclosed and in July 1856 some ten of the twenty-five acres which Dr. Walker had bought from Blake in 1852 were put up for sale by auction. But no bidder appeared, and so three months later Blake bought them back himself, for about £795 per acre.[3]

This was no doubt a good bargain if he could afford to wait for the next building boom for a return on his money, but the purpose of the foreclosure had been to obtain ready money, not to extend the scope of his speculations. Through his new solicitors, Messrs. H. and G. Lake and Kendall of Lincoln's Inn, to whom he had recently transferred all his legal business, he was able in June 1856 to add another £6,000 to his mortgage commitments,[3] but by April 1858 he was falling in arrears over payments of interest, some of them now at six per cent. In 1857–8 he sold two newly completed houses in Stanley Gardens,[216] but he was also negotiating more loans through Lake and Kendall,[217] and his affairs were in a very precarious state, with his mortgagees pressing for payment, when the great crisis of his career beset him.

Since its incorporation in 1853 Blake had been a director of the Portsmouth Railway Company, of which Richard Roy was the solicitor. After investing heavily in this company Blake had had a dispute with one of his co-directors, Francis Mowatt, about the purchase of shares, and in 1854 he had filed a bill of complaint in Chancery. Blake also considered that Roy had deceived him in these transactions, and this was evidently the cause for

his removal of his legal business from Roy to Lake and Kendall. The railway did not prove successful, and nor did Blake's lawsuit, for the verdict of the court, given in July 1858, was that Blake must pay Mowatt £20,520, plus interest and costs, by 3 November.[218] After an unsuccessful appeal to a higher court Blake failed to raise the money, and on 1 November Mowatt grudgingly granted him another six months in which to pay.[3]

According to his own calculations, Blake's total assets, including the house in St. Marylebone where he had formerly lived, his furniture and plate and his railway shares, now amounted to £172,000, and his mortgages to £100,000. His attempts to raise more money through a stockbroker and then through the London Assurance Corporation were, however, rejected, and he was therefore compelled to grant an option to sell all his property at Notting Hill to a firm of land surveyors and auctioneers, Messrs. Farebrother, Clark and Lye of Lancaster Place, Strand. According to their surveys, the cost price of his property there amounted to £116,000, and their own valuation of it to £99,090, which they estimated would eventually yield an annual rental of £5,525. They nevertheless agreed to lend him £25,000 at five per cent interest, subject to his selling enough of his property to procure repayment by the end of May 1859. Blake was to execute a mortgage to Clark and Lye of his entire estate, including his railway shares, subject to the existing encumbrances, and if the auction sale did not yield enough to provide for repayment, and if Blake did not within one month thereafter repay all the money due, Clark and Lye were to be at liberty to sell everything without the safeguard of reserve prices.[3]

The debt to Mowatt was quickly paid off with the loan from Clark and Lye, but when the forty-six freehold and five leasehold houses and the building land were offered for sale in individual lots in May 1859, only two lots were bought, Nos. 6 and 7 Stanley Crescent, for prices slightly lower even than Clark and Lye's own valuation. Unexpectedly, the fall in the value of Blake's estate saved him. It was no use for the creditors to press their claims at a time when demand was low. Fifteen of the houses were still unoccupied, and four (Nos. 12–15 Stanley Gardens) were still unfinished; it was clearly more advantageous to wait for better times. During the next few months several more houses were sold privately, and after the railway shares had been sold £13,000 of the debt to Clark and Lye were repaid. To reduce his own personal expenditure Blake removed from his fine house at No. 24 Kensington Park Gardens to the much less eligible No. 21 Stanley Gardens. In September the largest single creditor, Simmonds, to whom Blake owed £23,500, gave notice requiring repayment, but he does not seem to have pressed his claim, and early in 1860 Blake secured another loan of £18,000 at five per cent, by means of which Clark and Lye were paid off and the other creditors for the time being pacified. After being 'in the red' for the previous two years Blake's balance sheet now showed a small surplus, though the £645 excess of income over outgoings only amounted to a yield of about one-half per cent on his total investment.[3]

Blake's new backers were William Honywood of Berkshire, esquire, William Harrison of St. Helen's Place, City, merchant, and Henry Cobb of Lincoln's Inn Fields, land agent and surveyor, who in addition to their loan of £18,000 also immediately accepted a transfer of Simmonds's mortgage.[219] Like Clark and Lye, they took a mortgage of all Blake's property, and they remained his principal source of capital for the rest of his career, a condition of the arrangement being that a member of the firm of Lake and Kendall, Blake's solicitors, should act as receiver of the rents and profits of the estate.[3]

The census of 1861 shows what kind of people lived in Blake's new houses. All of the forty-six houses listed in the census return for Kensington Park Gardens were by then occupied, although the stone-sawyer who lived at No. 1 with his wife and two daughters was probably only a caretaker put in to look after the place until a tenant could be found. The total number of residents was 408, of whom 152 were servants. The average number of inhabitants per house (excluding No. 1) was thus slightly under 9, of whom 3·4 were servants. Two houses were already each divided into two separate households, and there were also two girls' schools, one of which occupied two adjoining houses. The householders included ten 'fundholders' or 'proprietors of houses', plus one 'baronet's widow', who was perhaps too proud of her title to specify the source of her income. There were also five lawyers, five merchants (four in foreign trade), three army officers (all of field rank and above, but in the East India service) and one admiral who was also a Member

of Parliament. Other householders included two warehousemen, two clerks, and one tea-broker, stockbroker, hatter, optician, civil servant, architect, veterinary surgeon and a professor at University College. At the two schools the presence of nine resident mistresses and twenty-seven boarding pupils suggests that day-girls were also taught. The servants' hierarchy included butlers, footmen, ladies' maids, grooms and pages.[220]

In Stanley Crescent all of the thirteen houses built by Blake were occupied by 1861, but of the twenty-nine in Stanley Gardens four were empty. The total number of residents in these thirty-eight occupied houses was 323, of whom 109 were servants. The average number of inhabitants per house was thus 8·5, of whom 2·6 were servants. In Stanley Gardens one house was already divided into two households, and there were no fewer than five girls' schools, plus another two in Stanley Crescent. The householders included six fundholders, six merchants (three in foreign trade), five lawyers, and one army captain, military tailor, coachmaker and club secretary. The residents included seventeen schoolmistresses and governesses, and twelve of the householders were women.[221]

Blake and the revival of building in the 1860's

The involvement of Honywood, Harrison and Cobb as investors in the development of Notting Hill was probably prompted by the growing revival of demand for houses there,[222] several more of Blake's at last finding purchasers. In 1860 he also sold the land on the south side of Ladbroke Gardens and in the northern half of Stanley Crescent, both to Ebenezer Howard, a poultry salesman at Leadenhall Market,[223] and it has already been mentioned that in 1861 the land in Kensington Park Road to the north of St. Peter's Church was also sold. Some of the mortgages were redeemed by Blake with the proceeds of these sales, while several others were transferred to Honywood, Harrison and Cobb, who by 1863 held a portfolio with a nominal value of £52,000, but on which only £33,500 was 'really due'. Other debts amounted to £12,500, bringing the total up to £46,000. By July 1863 he had achieved such a strong financial position that he was able to give all his remaining mortgagees (other than Honywood, Harrison and Cobb) the option of accepting either a reduction in the rate of interest from five per cent to four and a half per cent, or repayment of their loans. The crisis was over,[3] and in this year he was able to vacate No. 21 Stanley Gardens and make his home once more in one of the best houses on his estate, at No. 2 Stanley Crescent.[144]

This dramatic recovery had been made possible by a revival in demand for houses. The total volume of building in Kensington had begun to grow again, very slightly, as early as 1859, and this growth continued almost without interruption until it reached a peak in 1868. This upsurge had enabled Blake to start in 1860 to dispose advantageously of his ground to the west of Ladbroke Grove which he had repurchased from Dr. Walker in 1856. Most of the land was granted on building leases, the principal undertaker being Charles Chambers, variously described as a timber merchant or an engineer, who took all of the south side of Blenheim Crescent and part of the north side as well. Other undeveloped land was sold freehold. As building proceeded on the leased portions Blake bought the improved ground rents from the lessees, and subsequently sold the property outright to investors, usually private individuals, but including the governors of Middlesex Hospital. In 1863 he obtained over £9,000 from such sales, and in 1865–6 almost as much again. After these sales this part of the estate was at midsummer 1867 still yielding him a rental of £670 per annum. By 1868, when building was virtually complete there, he had sold all his remaining interests in this area to the west of Ladbroke Grove, his total receipts from sales between 1863 and 1867 being well over £32,000 (the amounts received were not always recorded). He still retained the bulk of his property in the Stanley Gardens and Crescent area.[3]

Blake's speculations on the Ladbroke estate were now over, for he had already embarked on far more extensive operations on the neighbouring Portobello and St. Quintin estates to the north. In the mid 1860's it was almost impossible to build houses fast enough in Notting Dale, for an entirely new element had been introduced into the situation there by the opening in 1864 of the Hammersmith and City Railway. This was the first of the feeder lines to be connected to the Metropolitan Railway, the first underground railway in the world, which had been opened between Paddington and Farringdon Street in January 1863. The Hammersmith and City line extended from its western terminus at Hammersmith through Shepherd's Bush and Notting Dale (where there was a station at Ladbroke Grove) to its junction with the Great Western Railway at Westbourne Park, and there was also a connexion with the hitherto moribund West London line, built in 1844 from Willesden to West Kensington near the modern Olympia. With a half-hourly service it was now possible for residents in West and North Kensington to reach the City in a matter of minutes.[224]

Blake himself and two other of the largest speculators in Notting Dale (James Whitchurch and Stephen Phillips) had all become members of the provisional committee of the Hammersmith, Paddington and City Junction Railway in 1861, and Blake at any rate was quick to exploit the opportunity of the moment. In November 1862 he contracted with the Misses Talbot to buy some 130 acres of their land for £107,500, and in December 1864 he agreed with Colonel Matthew St. Quintin to take more land on building lease— the first of a series of such agreements. The new railway traversed both these estates, and Blake's speculations there (which are described in Chapter XII) occupied him for the rest of his life. In May 1863 the net annual rental of his property on the Ladbroke estate amounted to £3,535, mostly derived from the Stanley Gardens and Crescent houses, and he was therefore able to borrow freely through Honywood, Harrison and Cobb for the financing of these new operations.[3]

Development by Pocock and Penson in Kensington Park Road area

Blake was indeed the biggest and most successful speculator in nineteenth-century Notting Hill and Dale, and through the survival of a large quantity of his personal papers his career can be traced in some detail. But the normal complexities and confusions of Victorian estate development, and the jerky progress which it made in response to the constantly fluctuating national economic situation, provided endless scope for lesser speculators. Each of these had his own *modus operandi*, suited to his own requirements and to the infinitely various circumstances of time and place. One such was Thomas Pocock, previously mentioned as an attorney of Bartholomew Close in the City, whose activities on the Ladbroke estate (not always very clear, due to limited evidence) extended over more than twenty years. Unlike Blake he evidently had no great financial resources of his own, and he therefore often acted in association with a wealthy backer who wished to invest without being himself actively involved in estate business. But he did also buy and sell land on his own account, take building leases and perhaps build houses by contract—all risky but potentially profitable activities in the hugger-mugger situations created by the failures of Jacob Connop in 1845 and of D. A. Ramsay and Dr. Walker in 1854–5.

Pocock had first become involved on the Ladbroke estate in the latter part of 1846. At that time James Weller Ladbroke was still alive, but his heir, Felix Ladbroke, in confident expectation of his cousin's early demise, was already making arrangements for the sale of part of the estate as soon as circumstances would permit. In December 1846, accordingly, he contracted that as soon as J. W. Ladbroke died he would sell some thirty acres of ground to Pocock for £9,050 (equivalent to approximately £300 per acre). Pocock, of course, did not possess the resources to make this purchase himself, but by the time of J. W. Ladbroke's death on 16 March 1847 he had found a buyer, and on 29 March the freehold of twenty-six of the thirty acres was sold to the Reverend Brooke Edward Bridges, a Bedfordshire parson, for £7,750, subject to the existing leasehold interest already granted by J. W. Ladbroke. The remainder was bought by Pocock himself.[225]

In terms of the modern street names Bridges' ground lay between Ladbroke Grove and Portobello Road, extending from Ladbroke Gardens on the south to Westbourne Park Road on the north. It also included the block of ground between Kensington Park Road, Portobello Road, Westbourne Grove and Chepstow Villas. Pocock's lands consisted of the sites of Nos. 38–47 (consec.) Ladbroke Square (houses then probably in course of erection), the site of the future Nos. 56–72 (even) Kensington Park Road, and three acres on the north side of Westbourne Park Road, still far away from the urban frontier and evidently a long-term investment.[226]

Most of the land bought in fee by the Reverend B. E. Bridges had already been leased in 1846 by J. W. Ladbroke to George Penson, a wholesale cheesemonger of Newgate Street who had outstanding financial claims on the estate arising from Connop's bankruptcy (see page 219). Acting through his architect and surveyor, Benjamin Broadbridge, Penson had at once obtained the approval of the Westminster Commissioners of Sewers for the construction of over a mile of sewers on his leasehold lands,[227] the ground plan being an amplification of that prepared (probably) by John Stevens for Connop in 1842–3, and in June 1846 he was offering plots to be let on building leases.[228]* But probably because of the general decline in building little work was actually done on the sewers, and when in September 1847 the Commissioners demanded an explanation Pocock appeared on behalf of Bridges (the freeholder) and, apparently, of Penson, the leaseholder.[229] Pocock had in fact become the agent for both parties; such sewers as Penson had built were transferred to Pocock,[230] and thereafter neither Bridges nor Penson took an active personal part in the development process. It was probably Pocock who was responsible in 1849 for the modification of the northern end of the projected line of Kensington Park Road, which had been originally intended to curve north-east to a junction with Portobello Road. The line was now straightened, and the intended crescent joining Kensington Park Road and Ladbroke Grove was deleted, the whole alteration being effected by small exchanges of land between Felix Ladbroke, Bridges and Pocock.[231]

In 1852 and 1855 the Reverend B. E. Bridges sold almost all of his land north of Ladbroke Gardens and west of Kensington Park Road to Dr. Walker,[232] while Pocock himself bought most of Bridges' land between Kensington Park Road and Portobello Road. This thin strip of land, extending northward from No. 56 Kensington Park Road as far as Westbourne Park Road, formed the nucleus of Pocock's own estate (fig. 45). On part of it he adopted the usual procedure of granting building leases—at Nos. 115–175 (odd) Portobello Road, for instance—but on parts of the more valuable frontage to Kensington Park Road he seems to have organized the building himself,[233] perhaps by contract, as at Nos.

* The applications were submitted on Penson's behalf by three surveyors, Benjamin, James, and G. Broadbridge, but a plan of June 1846 is signed by Benjamin Broadbridge.[228]

56–74 and 126–182 (even) Kensington Park Road (Plate 67e), and at Nos. 54–62 (even) and 35–41 (odd) Chepstow Villas, all in 1850–3.

This programme was financed in a number of ways, of which outright sale of undeveloped pieces of land to other speculators was probably the simplest. In 1853 Pocock sold two strips of land between Kensington Park Road and Portobello Road (now the eastern extremities of Elgin and Blenheim Crescents) to Dr. Walker[234] to enable Walker to link the street layout of his lands to the west on the Ladbroke estate with those to the east on the Portobello estate. Two years later he sold the ground on the east side of Kensington Park Road between Chepstow Villas and Westbourne Grove to Blake.[235] He also sold improved ground rents in Portobello Road,[236] while Nos. 56–72 Kensington Park Road were built in association with another solicitor, John Day of Red Lion Square. In 1864 he obtained a loan of £4,300 at five per cent from the London Assurance Corporation, on the security of thirteen houses in Lansdowne Road.[237] But his greatest single source of capital was Penson, the City cheesemonger, to whom he had mortgaged some of his houses in Ladbroke Square as early as 1848.[238] Penson himself lived at No. 41 Ladbroke Square from 1851 to 1859, when his increasing prosperity—he now styled himself a provision merchant—enabled him to move to the grander *milieu* first of Westbourne Terrace and then of Connaught Place, both in Paddington. In the 1860's Penson converted his business into a limited liability company, of which he was himself the managing director;[64] he frequently acted as Pocock's mortgagee or business associate,[239] and as his personal estate was valued after his death in 1879 (aged seventy) at around £120,000 he was clearly a valuable ally for a speculator such as Pocock.[240]

In addition to his activities in the area between Kensington Park Road and Portobello Road Pocock also speculated further west. In 1846 he contracted to buy thirty-three acres of leasehold land to the north of Lansdowne Rise from Richard Roy at £800 per acre, but he did in the event only purchase five acres, which he subsequently sold undeveloped to Blake.[241] In the early 1850's he took building leases from Stephen Phillips for some thirty houses on the west side of Clarendon Road, and when Dr. Walker started to grant leases in 1852 on the lands to the west of Ladbroke Grove which (as we have already seen) he had recently acquired from Blake, Pocock was among the lessees (for Nos. 61–75 odd Lansdowne Road).[242]

The aftermath of unsuccessful speculations

The collapse of Dr. Walker's enterprises presented speculators like Pocock or Richard Roy with a wide field of opportunity for many years. For instance, both Pocock and Roy bought half-finished houses in Lansdowne Road and Elgin Crescent from Dr. Walker's trustees. Pocock also lent money on mortgage on property there, financing these activities by transferring the mortgages to clients with money to invest, or to Penson.[243] By 1860, when demand for houses was reviving, Roy was selling or leasing derelict property in Lansdowne Road (the original leases granted by Dr. Walker in 1852 having evidently been cancelled),[244] and in some cases these new building lessees mortgaged to Pocock.[245] In Lansdowne Crescent (Nos. 19–38 consec.) Stephen Phillips was another speculator who profited from Dr. Walker's misfortunes, by buying ground from him cheaply in 1857,[246] and finding a building lessee during the building boom of the early 1860's.

The depressing aspect of this part of the Ladbroke estate was frequently mentioned in *The Building News* at this time. In 1857 it stated that 'On some parts of the Notting-hill estates a large number of houses have been erected; many of them are now fit for occupation, others are in progress, whilst on other portions numerous buildings appear to have remained some time in carcase only, and abandoned in various stages of advancement, apparently for want of funds to complete them.'[247] Two years later there were eighteen first-class houses 'fast hastening to decay for want of being finished' in Ladbroke Gardens, which was popularly known as the 'Goodwin Sands' or (as we have already seen) 'Coffin-row',[248] and where Roy had been heavily involved. By 1860, however, 'Little patches of new work' were beginning to 'appear here and there amidst the desert of dilapidated structures and decaying carcases. When the whole are finished there will be some chance of an adequate return for a portion of the money invested, but till that consummation is arrived at, there are few, we imagine, who would care to dwell in that dreary desolation, with the wind howling and vagrants prowling in the speculative warnings around them.'[249]

In such a confused situation it has often proved impossible to discover the names of the building lessees of many houses, and even when this has been feasible it has often been impossible to assess the amount of work done before building was suspended. The building histories of Ladbroke Gardens, Elgin Crescent and the northern part of Lansdowne Road, all within Dr. Walker's ill-fated estate, are particularly perplexing. In Ladbroke Gardens Richard Roy bought the land on the north side from Dr. Walker and granted building leases in 1852,[250] but little if any work was done for some years, although (as we have already seen) Thomas Allom made designs for the houses here. In 1858 seventeen of the twenty-three sites or carcases in the range were acquired by Ebenezer Howard, the poultry salesman of Leadenhall Market,[251] and under his auspices William Parratt, builder, and John Faulkner of Finchley New Road, surveyor, worked until Parratt's death in 1861.[252] Thereafter William Wheeler, the builder working opposite at Nos. 14–23 (consec.) Stanley Crescent at this time, appears in the many legal transactions affecting the houses,[253] all of which were finished by 1866.[144] With such a complex building history, extending over fourteen years, it is remarkable that Allom's costly designs were never abandoned in favour of something cheaper.

On the south side of Ladbroke Gardens building operations were even more long-delayed. In 1858 Howard leased the site of Nos. 24–33 (consec.) from Blake, removed the carcases of the houses already there (probably the coffins of 'Coffin-row') and after buying the freehold from Blake, sold the property to Penson. A dispute then arose about the southern boundary of the land, and Pocock, to whom Penson had in turn sold, threatened to build a row of workmen's model lodging-houses, the site being (as he claimed) too narrow for the erection of good quality houses.[254] Three of the six-storey houses ultimately built here were still in course of erection in 1873.[255]

In Elgin Crescent William Sim, builder and architect, was probably responsible for the design of many of the houses west of Ladbroke Grove. In 1852 Dr. Walker granted him building leases

for Nos. 69–115 (odd), and in 1855 he exhibited at the Royal Academy 'A view of Elgin Crescent, Kensington Park, from the designs and now in progress of completion under the superintendence of W. Sim'.[256] An undated printed estate plan (Plate 57) advertising 'Family Residences' in Elgin Crescent, to be let at rents from £60 to £80 per annum and requesting potential purchasers to apply to Mr. Sim 'on the Premises' shows that he concerned himself in the sale as well as the design and construction of Nos. 69–115.[3] But he also acted as surveyor to D. A. Ramsay, the building lessee of Nos. 117–145 (odd),[257] and probably also for H. M. Ramsay, the lessee of Nos. 58–120 (even). He was still working in Elgin Crescent as an architect in 1858, when he invited tenders for the completion of ten houses there.[258] To the east of Ladbroke Grove Thomas Pocock seems to have been responsible in the mid 1860's for much of the building in Elgin Crescent on the south side.[259]

Few of the houses built in these confused circumstances call for comment. In the northern, curved, part of Lansdowne Road Nos. 68–102 (even) (Plate 67d) and Nos. 79–123 (odd) (fig. 61) form sequences of three-storeyed stucco houses in which Dutch gables alternating with pierced parapets are employed over groups of round-headed windows set in complicated rhythms. Together with the three-sided bay windows in the ground storey and strangely detailed doorways with shallow hoods on consoles over half round arches, these elements form an amalgam which it is hard to take seriously and which is unlike anything else in Kensington. No. 77 Lansdowne Road, a three-storey stucco-fronted house at the end of a long terrace-range, has a two-storey segmental bay and stucco enrichments reminiscent of Allom's work in Kensington Park Gardens, but the documentary evidence shows that after being leased to Ramsay in 1852, the carcase was sold in 1856 to Thomas Allason, junior, architect.[260] On the outer side of Lansdowne Crescent the four-storey range numbered 19–38 (consec.) was leased to Henry Wyatt in 1860–2,[261] and presents a fine succession of segmental bow fronts of a pattern almost identical with other houses attributed to George Wyatt in Prince's Square, Paddington (Plate 67b).

Further north Elgin Crescent, dating chiefly from the 1850's, has some repose and dignity in its architectural treatment. Semi-circular headed

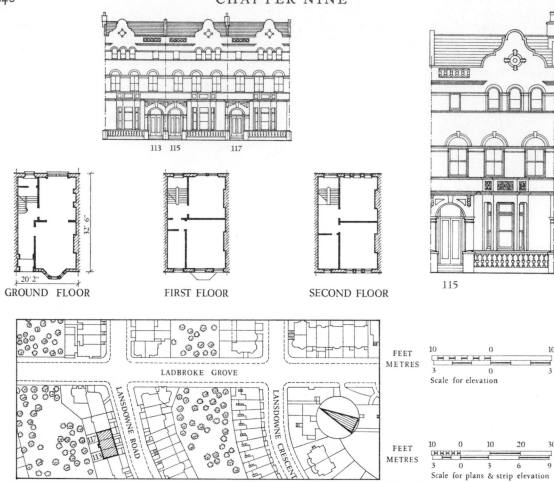

GROUND FLOOR   FIRST FLOOR   SECOND FLOOR   115

Fig. 61. Nos. 113–117 odd Lansdowne Road, plans and elevations

doorways and windows generally prevail, and there is some enrichment of the stucco, especially at Nos. 58–120 (even) (Plate 67c). The modest and well-proportioned houses at Nos. 117–145 (odd) have linked doorways as projecting features, and were probably designed by William Sim. Nos. 149–153 (odd) are also of the very simple terrace type, and again appear to be by Sim, who was also probably responsible for the adjacent Nos. 68–78 (even) Clarendon Road.[262] Blenheim and Cornwall Crescents, built in the early 1860's in a debased classical style, demonstrate the marked degeneration of taste which was then beginning to take place on the remaining parts of the Ladbroke estate.

This decline can also be observed in Ladbroke Grove itself and on the lands to the east, where the houses dating from the 1860's were in general built in long tall terraced ranges. This type of

work may be seen at Nos. 78–94 (even) Ladbroke Grove, probably designed by Edward Habershon in 1861 (Plate 67f), and Nos. 111–119 (odd), by George Drew in 1865, both at the bottom of the north side of St. John's Hill. At the corners of several streets leading off Ladbroke Grove this monotony is relieved by large three- and four-storey houses with stucco ornamentation of some panache. Nos. 81 and 83 Ladbroke Grove, for instance, at the south and north corners of Lansdowne Road, form an almost symmetrical pair, while No. 85, at the south corner of Elgin Crescent, five windows in width, has rusticated and vermiculated stucco at ground-storey level, and a projecting porch extending through two storeys. These three houses appear, however, to date from the 1850's, as also do Nos. 60–64 (even) Ladbroke Grove, a five-storey range begun by H. M. Ramsay in 1854, where the influence of Allom's work is apparent. East of Ladbroke Grove Arundel Gardens consists of dull four-storey ranges, that on the north side being faced with stucco and that on the south side being of stock brick with coarse flamboyant stucco enrichments. Both ranges date from the early 1860's, and represent a marked decline from both Allom's neighbouring houses on the north side of Ladbroke Gardens, and from the long three-storey range built by Thomas Pocock on the east side of Kensington Park Road in 1852, by which the eastward vista along Arundel Gardens is agreeably closed.

Deaths of the principal developers

By the mid 1870's the development of the Ladbroke estate was almost complete, and most of the principal protagonists in the whole complicated process were already dead. Thomas Allason, surveyor to both James Weller Ladbroke and Felix Ladbroke, had died in 1852. Latterly he had lived in Connaught Square, Paddington, and at the time of his death he owned fifteen freehold houses in Clarendon and Ladbroke Roads, plus all the twenty houses which then stood on the site of Linden Gardens, Notting Hill (a small detached part of the Ladbroke estate).[263] Felix Ladbroke died in 1869. By this time he had sold the greater part of his estate at Notting Hill (or very possibly all of it) and also his house at Headley in Surrey, and was living in Belgrave Road near Victoria Station. How he had spent the money which he had raised from his great inheritance has not been discovered, but at the time of his death he was clearly in relatively reduced circumstances, for his 'effects' were valued at under £9,000, and the two small legacies mentioned in his will were not to be paid until after his wife's death.[264]

Dr. Walker and Thomas Pocock also died in the same year, 1869. Dr. Walker, then aged fifty-nine, was living in Hampstead and left a widow and young children. He had by now sold most or all of his lands in Kensington, but as his financial affairs appear to have improved somewhat in the mid 1860's he was able to bequeath his dearest possessions, the advowson of St. Columb Major in Cornwall and the patronage of All Saints', Notting Hill, to his eldest son. His 'effects' were valued at about £70,000, but it

may be recalled that the fortune which he had inherited from his father in 1851 had been estimated at £250,000.[265] Pocock, by contrast, for whom Dr. Walker had unwittingly provided so many opportunities, left 'effects' valued at only about £9,000; but he was probably an entirely self-made man. He was also unlike Dr. Walker in having lived on the scene of his speculations, first at No. 38 Ladbroke Square and latterly at No. 24 Ladbroke Gardens.[266]

Blake and his erstwhile architect both died in 1872, but whereas Allom, living at Barnes, left personal property of around £1,500,[267] that of Blake was valued at about £35,000, and the total value of his residuary real and personal estate was about £120,000. The twenty-four freehold houses which he still owned in the Stanley Crescent and Stanley Gardens area accounted for about one third of this amount, but most of the rest arose from his later speculations on the Portobello and St. Quintin estates (see Chapter XII). His outstanding mortgage debts had fallen to £17,155. He had spent some twenty years in the day-to-day administration of his estates, whose management was now taken over by his son, a barrister, and the solicitor B. G. Lake. For most of this period he had like Pocock lived at the scene of his enterprises, at first at No. 24 Kensington Park Gardens (1854–9) and then at Nos. 21 Stanley Gardens (1860–3) and 2 Stanley Crescent. After 1868 he had lived in semi-retirement at Bournemouth, where he died on 22 March 1872, aged seventy-seven. A monument (which no longer exists) was erected in St. Peter's Church there to record his memory.[268]

Blake's former solicitor, Richard Roy, died in the following year, 1873, aged seventy-six. He too had lived for many years on the Ladbroke estate, at first at No. 59 Ladbroke Grove, and then in the years of his greatest prosperity from 1851 to 1858 at the house (now demolished) at the south corner of Ladbroke Grove and Kensington Park Gardens, facing Blake's house. It was probably financial difficulty which dictated his removal, in 1858–9, down the hill to a less exclusive address, No. 42 Clarendon Road, where he remained for the rest of his life. His personal papers have not survived, and little is known of his financial circumstances. At his death his personal estate was valued at about £16,000, but he almost certainly still owned real property in Notting Hill. His legal practice was continued by his wife's brother, T. B. Cartwright, and as late as 1910 one of her nephews was still concerned in the administration of one of the communal gardens on the estate.[269]

After the death in 1879 of George Penson, the City cheesemonger, who (as we have already seen) left a personal estate of £120,000, there remained only one important survivor, the architect James Thomson, the progenitor of much of the ground plan of one of the finest townscapes in all London. He lived long enough to see the results of his work in the hey-day of its mid-Victorian prosperity, but when he died at a great age in 1883 at his house in Devonshire Street, St. Marylebone, he left a personal fortune of only £789.[270] Suburban building development seems, indeed, to have been at least as fickle in its rewards as gambling had been in earlier days on the races at the Hippodrome, where it may be that some speculators made their first investments on the Ladbroke estate before trying their luck and skill in the more durable field of bricks and mortar.

The Church of St. John the Evangelist, Ladbroke Grove

Plates 12, 33e; fig. 62

St. John's Church is the centrepiece of the Ladbroke estate. It is conspicuously sited at the top of a high knoll, its spire being visible for several miles to the north and west. Built of ragstone in the Early English Gothic manner and set among fine mature trees, it provides a notable contrast with the Italianate stucco and stock-brick fronts of the houses in the surrounding streets.

St. John's was the first church to be built north of the Uxbridge road, and its district, as originally defined in 1845, contained almost the whole of this part of the parish as far north as Kensal Green Cemetery, only the Norland estate (where the building of St. James's was almost contemporaneous) and the Potteries being excluded. The selection of its site and of its architect were evidently the subject of much discussion between the various developers then active on the Ladbroke estate (see page 207), who were all anxious to have the new church on their land. The final decision seems to have been the result of a compromise; Richard Roy, the solicitor in charge of building development to the west of Ladbroke Grove, purchased the site from his clients and presented it to the church's trustees,[271]

while the architects were John Hargrave Stevens and George Alexander, whose client was Jacob Connop, at that time the developer of the lands to the east of Ladbroke Grove.

The foundation stone was laid by Archdeacon John Sinclair, vicar of Kensington and archdeacon of Middlesex, on 8 January 1844, and the church was consecrated by Charles Blomfield, Bishop of London, on 29 January 1845.[272] The builders were Joshua Higgs, senior and junior, who were paid £8,213. The total cost, inclusive of architects' fees, was £10,181. About half of this was paid for by private subscriptions, but two loans, each of £2,000, remained outstanding for some years, the lenders being Viscount Canning and C. H. Blake, both of whom were also investors in the large-scale building developments then proceeding to the west of Ladbroke Grove. The church provided 1,500 sittings, of which 400 were free, and a district parish was assigned in 1845.[273]

St. John's is a solid and substantially built church of ragstone laid in neat courses, with buttresses at the angles of all parts—a structural precaution later found to be fully justified when, in 1955, slight movement of the clay sub-soil required the west front to be strengthened. The exterior is confident and imposing, with consistent Early English Gothic detail. At the time of building the design evoked widespread favourable comment.[274]

The church is cruciform in plan with a tower and broach spire over the crossing. The tower has three lancet openings to each face, square pinnacles enriched with lancet panels, and stepped buttresses at each corner. Two-light gabled lucarnes project from the base of the spire, to which they give added solidity of appearance. The two-bay north and south transepts have polygonal turrets containing staircases to the former galleries and projecting three quarters of the way up the east and west façades, each of which has two lancet lights surmounted by a round window in the gable.

The west front has two tall lancet lights with a small quatrefoil light in the gable above. The western half of the two-bay chancel is flanked by square vestries, now used for other purposes. The east façade of the chancel has three level lancet lights beneath a pair of lancets surmounted by a quatrefoil light in the gable and set within a pointed arch flanked by two blind lancet panels.

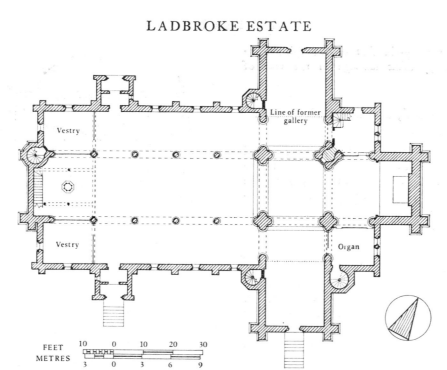

Fig. 62. Church of St. John the Evangelist, Ladbroke Grove, plan

The five-bay nave arcade has cylindrical columns with boldly modelled roll-mouldings and supports a clerestory with groups of three level lancet lights to each bay held within an inner arcade. The lean-to aisles are lit by single lancets on the centre lines of the bays. The spacious interior, now cream-washed, is dominated by the crossing, the capitals of the piers here being carved with naturalistic foliage. The crossing is carried up as a lantern tower, with a wooden ceiling pierced by an octagonal skylight which is fitted with clear glass held by leading in fish-scale patterns.

Across the west bay of the nave and aisles is a gallery, standing at the height of the arcade capitals. Its front is of wood, now painted cream, and is enriched by trefoil arches and little trefoils in the spandrels. The galleries formerly situated in the transepts, access to which was provided within the polygonal corner turrets previously noted, have now been removed.

The chancel is more richly treated than the rest of the church. The east window openings have roll-mouldings and are filled with glass by C. E. Kempe which replaced in 1900 a window of 1860 to the memory of the wife of the first incumbent, the Reverend John Philip Gell. There is other good glass by Kempe in the two-light window above. The rich patterned glass in the single-lancet north and south windows of the sanctuary is nearly contemporary with the building of the church.

The panelling behind the altar was erected under a faculty of 1890; it was later continued round the walls of the sanctuary, and included an elegant sedilia. The panelling, reredos and sedilia are of terra-cotta, in a hard neo-Perpendicular style. The architectural portions of the reredos were designed by (Sir) Aston Webb; the sculptures, by Emmeline Halse, represent the Crucifixion in the centre with seated figures on either side, very much in the *fin de siècle* manner. The panels on either side of the reredos have delicately carved standing angels, probably also by Emmeline Halse, but they are much less lively than the altar composition.[275]

There are two windows by Warrington: one, in the south aisle, was presented by the architect, George Alexander; the other, a small light in the west gable, is a little rose window of pretty foliate design in bright colours.

The whole interior assumed its present appearance when the church was rearranged and redecorated in 1955–6 by Milner and Craze. The altar table was placed beneath the crossing, the walls painted creamy-white, and the rich colour of the terra-cotta fittings obscured by grey paint.

The top twenty-six feet of the spire were rebuilt in 1957 after damage in the war of 1939–45.[276]

St. Peter's Church, Kensington Park Road
Plate 13; fig. 63

This is one of the very few Church of England churches to be built in London after 1837 in the classical style. It was built in 1855–7 to the designs of Thomas Allom, the architect responsible for many of the large Italianate houses then in course of erection in the adjacent Stanley Gardens and Crescent and Kensington Park Gardens, and the site for the church was presented by Allom's client, the speculator C. H. Blake. Situated on the east side of Kensington Park Road and facing west down Stanley Gardens, St. Peter's was, indeed, to be an integral and carefully composed element in the design of Blake's estate, and the classical idiom, however unfashionable, was therefore the natural style to choose.

The church was built at an estimated cost of £5,500 and provided 1,400 sittings. It was consecrated on 7 January 1857, and a district chapelry was assigned in the same year.[277] Its stucco façade has a bold pediment and entablature carried on six engaged Corinthian columns (the outer ones paired), and is flanked at the angles of the building by quadrants behind which rise the semi-circular staircases to the galleries. Each of the three inner bays is pierced by a round-headed doorway leading into the entrance vestibule, and above the central bay rises a square tower, adorned on each side by a clock-face and surmounted by an octagonal copper-roofed belfry.

Originally the church consisted of a seven-bay nave and aisles with no chancel, the east end being composed in a formal design the centrepiece of which was a flattened arch carried on Corinthian columns in the manner of Hawksmoor. In 1879 a one-bay apsidal chancel was added to designs by Edmeston and Barry, the columns which had supported the arch being incorporated into the main arcade.

The columns of the nave arcade have gilded Corinthian capitals and carry an entablature surmounted by a clerestory which is pierced by semi-circular lunettes. At half their height the columns also support the galleries, which are continued across the west end and here occupy the two bays in front of the entrance vestibule. The elegant

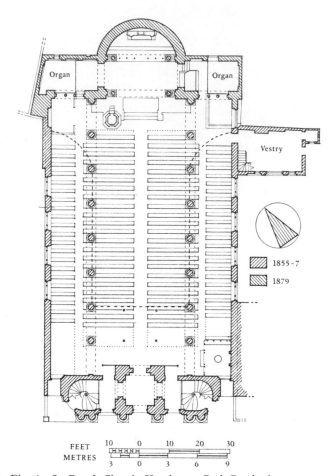

Fig. 63. St. Peter's Church, Kensington Park Road, plan

gallery fronts each contain three panels ornamented with the Keys of St. Peter, floral swags and winged putti. The flat plaster ceilings of both nave and aisles (rebuilt in 1951 under the direction of Milner and Craze) are enriched with framed panels, some of which contain rosettes.

The short chancel has double arches supported on squat Corinthian columns of Torquay red marble, the spandrels of the western arch being ornamented with angels bearing gilded trumpets and garlands. The ceiling has a coffered barrel vault, the panels being also decorated with angels and other motifs. The wall of the apse is covered with a large mosaic version of Leonardo da Vinci's 'Last Supper', erected in 1880. Although it has every appearance of having been added, the change of scale from the nave being somewhat abrupt, the chancel nevertheless provides an effectively rich climax to the interior.

The marble altar is in the sixteenth-century Florentine manner and is supported on graceful columns. This and the marble dado behind were carved in Italy to designs by the Reverend G. F. Tarry. The alabaster and marble pulpit of 1889 has a base of polished grey marble, and its front contains white marble bas-reliefs carved and signed by T. Nelson Maclean.[278] The baptistry, of 1905, in the south-west corner of the south aisle, has a richly wrought iron screen and is ornamented with marble and mosaic. The font is a handsome design with bronze acanthus-leaf rings.

In the centre of the wall of the south aisle is a monument by M. Noble, commemorating Frances Susanna, wife of the Reverend Francis Holland Adams, first incumbent of the church. It is in the Grecian manner reminiscent of the 1830's, but is actually of 1860, and consists of a white marble portrait set on a dark grey marble back-board.

The small semi-circular-headed window which formerly existed within the flattened arch at the east end contained glass which is now in the west window under the tower. The window in the south aisle depicting the Crucifixion is signed by J. Arthur Dix of Berners Street, who also designed the baptistry window erected in 1905.

The internal decoration of the church was said in 1872 to have been 'worked out in Pompeian red', the 'Greek ornament and colouring' being 'at once harmonious and agreeable'.[279]

St. Mark's Church, St. Mark's Road
Plate 16; fig. 64

The Church of St. Mark stands upon a site presented to the Ecclesiastical Commissioners by C. H. Blake, the speculator responsible for the rapid development of this district of the Ladbroke estate during the 1860's. At the time of its building it stood on the edge of the built-up area, but it was very soon surrounded by houses, and is now sandwiched between a short terraced range and a tall, narrow villa.

The architect of St. Mark's was E. Bassett Keeling, and the builders were Dove Brothers, whose contract was for £6,011, including the font, pulpit, and altar fittings. The church was built with funds raised by public subscription (£5,000 of which were given by the first patron, Miss E. F. Kaye), and provided 1,486 sittings. It was consecrated on 27 November 1863 and a district chapelry was assigned in the following year.[280]

St. Mark's is in many ways similar to Bassett Keeling's other surviving church in Kensington, St. George's, Campden Hill, but St. Mark's has no projecting cloistered porch, and the detail is altogether thinner and 'spikier'. The barbaric and emphatic quality of the design aroused both the antagonism of the Ecclesiological Society and the interest of the architectural journals. In November 1862 *The Builder* stated that the church was to be a 'Gothic structure, in coloured bricks and Bath stone, with a Continental touch in it', and that it was to have a spire 130 feet in height.[281] The dark brick exterior with stone dressings certainly owes little to period precedent, and it was this, perhaps, which caused *The Building News* to describe St. Mark's in 1869 as 'an atrocious specimen of coxcombry in architecture'.[282] This verdict appears to have had some effect on subsequent opinion, for by the turn of the century Bassett Keeling's design had already suffered considerable modification, and the church is now only a fragment of the strange and original building which it once was.

The verticality of the asymmetrical west front is emphasized by the steep raked buttresses, by the tall narrow windows, and by the distinctive subdivision of the composition into four clearly defined parts. The first of these is the façade of the nave, an oddly flat Gothic gabled wall pierced by small lancets. The most dominant feature of this element is the huge panel set within a pointed arch with banded voussoirs of black, red and white brick. Three lancets in the panel are set under a large quatrefoil window contained within a circular panel. The staircase which formerly provided access to the galleries is expressed by the windows on the lower stage of the façade.

The second element is the south-west tower with corner buttresses. It has three stages, is very deeply modelled, unlike the façade of the nave, and is surmounted by a tall, purplish-grey slated broach spire. The base of the tower contains a porch, and the church is entered by a double flat-headed doorway, above which is a large quatrefoil light within a circular panel framed by a steeply pointed arch. In the spandrels are carved roundels representing the emblems of the four

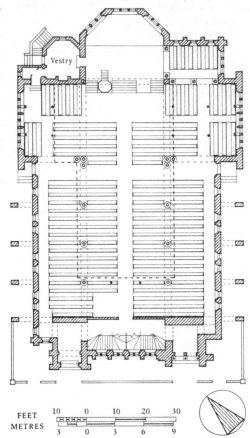

FEET · METRES [scale bar] 10 0 10 20 30 / 3 0 3 6 9

Fig. 64. St. Mark's Church, St. Mark's Road, plan

first stage with strongly profiled buttresses; it has the appearance of a small bell-tower, but was apparently never used as such.

The fourth unit is the gabled porch wedged between the base of the small tower and the main body of the church.

An unusual feature of the original exterior was the series of flying buttresses on either side, all now removed. They were very angular and boney in appearance, their skeletal effect being heightened by the use of black and white bricks for the voussoirs.

The impressive, even perhaps grand, and spacious interior consists of a four-bay nave with tall narrow aisles, wide transepts which have, however, only a token projection beyond the aisles, and an apsidal chancel with a vestry on one side and a small chapel on the other. Cast-iron columns, originally illuminated in strong poly-chromatic designs but now encased in concrete, carry lofty arcades that support a clerestory pierced with quatrefoil lights set in circular openings. The arcades and clerestory, of stock brick, strongly coloured with bands of black, white and red brick and stone, provide a sharpness and rasping individuality which is emphasized by the notched arrises of the brick arches. The principal timbers of the nave roof, also with notched edges, are carried on small marble columns with naturalistic corbels and capitals carved by J. W. Seale of Lambeth.[283] The harsh, jagged and abrasive motifs of the interior were continued outside in the magpie polychromy of the flying buttresses.

The galleries were supported on beams which spanned from the aisle walls to brackets fixed to the iron columns, and originally extended through the transepts, side aisles and west end of the nave. The spacious staircases were placed at the back of the west gallery, and over the staircases was an upper gallery reached from the staircase in the tower which forms an entrance porch on the ground floor. The galleries on the north and south sides were removed in 1896 and those on the west in 1905. The western fenestration was related to the stair to the gallery, and has now lost its *raison d'être*. During these alterations, no account was taken of Bassett Keeling's structural methods, for the building was so weakened that a general strengthening of the fabric had to be organized by Milner and Craze in 1954–5, which included the casing of the iron columns, the tying back of the arcades to the aisle walls by

evangelists. The stair turret to the tower fills in the spaces between the south-west buttresses, and in its upper stage, the second in the tower, be-comes polygonal. Above, the stone base of the belfry stage is battered upwards, this third stage being pierced by three level lancets enriched by trefoil cusping. These open arches, on naturalistic foliate capitals crowning columns behind which are square structural piers, seem deep and sinister. Each face of this belfry stage of the tower is flanked by pilaster buttresses at the corners, and harsh saw-tooth corbelling extends between them in a horizontal band a short distance above the line of lancets. Over this stage, steep gabled dor-mers with single louvred lancets are corbelled out beyond the face of the brickwork below, and cut upwards into the base of the slate-covered spire.

The third element of the façade is the curious little spirelet on an octagonal base set on a square

means of concrete beams, and the demolition of the flying buttresses and their replacement by sturdy stock-brick piers.[276]

In addition to these structural alterations, Bassett Keeling's original design has also suffered considerably from loss of colour and detail. Since the removal of the original altar and reredos the east end of the church has lost its architectural focus, and is now dominated by the huge suspended Rood which was originally at St. Columb's, Notting Hill. The new pulpit, alterations to the chancel, and the new font, all date from 1957. The Stations of the Cross were brought here from St. John's, Holland Road, on the eve of the war of 1914–18.

Monastery of the Poor Clares Colettines, Westbourne Park Road

Plate 24a, b. Demolished

This convent was established in 1857 at the request of Dr. Henry Manning, then Superior of the Oblates of St. Charles. The buildings, which were erected in 1860, are said to have been modelled on those of the Poor Clares' convent at Bruges, which Manning had visited and which supplied the first nuns at Notting Hill.[284] In 1970 the convent removed to Barnet and the buildings were demolished. The site is now (1972) being used for the erection of flats and a day nursery by Kensington and Chelsea Borough Council.

The convent stood at the corner of Ladbroke Grove and Westbourne Park Road. In 1860 the site was described in *The Building News* as being 'in a dreary waste of mud and stunted trees', where the convent shared 'the sole interest' of this desolate district with 'Dr. Walker's melancholy church' of All Saints', then still unfinished, and a lonely public house, now called the Elgin, in Ladbroke Grove. A number of 'low Irish' had settled in the vicinity, and already there had been 'a plentiful crop of Romish conversions there'.[284]

The architect of the new convent was Henry Clutton, and the contractors were Jackson and Shaw.[284] The buildings were economical and austere, being generally two storeys in height, of picked stocks with occasional bands of Staffordshire blue bricks, and with stone dressings to the chapel gables. They were grouped round a central cloistered court and flanked by walled gardens.

The principal entrance was from Westbourne Park Road, and was set in a one-storey linking block beside the chapels, which provided the principal element in the whole group. As the convent was occupied by an enclosed order, it was necessary to have two chapels, one for the nuns and the other for visitors. Clutton arranged the altars back to back, the movements of the celebrant's hands during Mass thus being visible to both the nuns and the visitors.

In 1871–2 John Francis Bentley produced plans for elaborate altars, but only the tabernacle, with its gilt door enriched with enamel and precious stones, and the exposition throne were built to his designs. Both sides of the throne had canopies consisting of hexagonal crocketed spirelets rising from coronas of fleurs-de-lis supported by two angels. The altars were to be made of alabaster and Hopton Wood stone with marble enrichments, and the frontals were to contain painted panels.[285]

Kensington Temple, Kensington Park Road

Formerly Horbury Congregational Chapel
Plate 28b; fig. 65

Horbury Congregational Chapel was an offshoot from the chapel in Hornton Street. It was built in 1848–9 to designs by J. Tarring. The builders were T. and W. Piper of Bishopsgate, whose tender was for £3,592.[286] It continued in Congregational use until 1935, when it became known as Kensington Temple, Church of the Foursquare Gospel. It is now known as Kensington Temple, Elim Pentecostal Church.[64]

The chapel is situated in a prominent position on a wedge-shaped site at the junction of Ladbroke and Kensington Park Roads, the entrance façade being emphasized by the flanking twin towers capped by octagonal spirelets. The style of the body of the chapel is essentially early decorated Gothic, while the towers have elements of Norman and Early English architecture in their details. The principal material is Kentish ragstone, with dressed stone for the quoins and openings.

The chapel is cruciform on plan, with only a vestigial niche to contain the pulpit. The original gallery was erected in 1870,[287] but was subsequently replaced by the present larger one, which is carried on cast-iron columns and is approached by the stairs in the twin towers. The conventional sub-divisions into nave and aisles do not

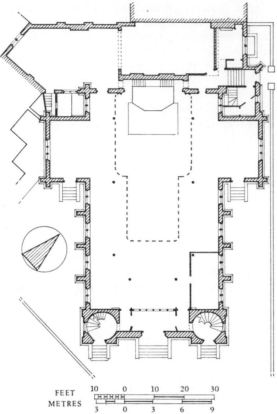

FEET   10   0   10   20   30
METRES |=====|====|=====|
        3   0   3   6   9

Fig. 65. Kensington Temple, Kensington Park Road, plan

exist in this chapel, but the body of the building is four bays long, while the 'transepts' are approximately two bays wide. Architecturally, the medieval styles are very unconvincing, while the plan, designed not for sacramental worship but as a preaching-house, hardly reflects the Gothic at all.

Peniel Chapel, Kensington Park Road
Plate 28c

This chapel stands on the east side of Kensington Park Road between Blenheim and Elgin Crescents. The first chapel here was a proprietary 'iron' church, built in 1862 by the Reverend Henry Marchmont, a clergyman of the Church of England who conducted ritualistic services here.[288] After the destruction of this building by fire in 1867,[289] Marchmont began to build the present church, but in 1871 he was declared bankrupt[290] and the uncompleted carcase was sold

to the congregation of Presbyterians who had hitherto met at a chapel in The Mall, Notting Hill Gate. Under these new owners the church was completed, and until 1919 was known as Trinity Presbyterian Church. It is now in undenominational use.[288] It is a large building, of stock brick with stone dressings. The style is a loosely interpreted Early English Gothic. It consists of a four-bay clerestoried nave with aisles, transepts and a chancel, the latter now being blocked off. There is a gallery in the south transept, which is larger than that to the north. There is also a small gallery at the west end of the church. The west front is tall and gabled, with lean-to aisle walls. There is a gable over the main door, above which are two windows surmounted by a geometrical rose window. A small quatrefoil pierces the gable over the rose.

Notting Hill Synagogue, Nos. 206–208 (even) Kensington Park Road

This building, originally a church meeting hall, was purchased in 1900 by a Jewish congregation and consecrated as a synagogue on 27 May of that year.[291] The exterior, originally Italianate in style, has been much altered, the gable having been removed.

The building is constructed of rendered brickwork, with a five-bay interior. Cast-iron columns support a gallery, which extends round three sides of the hall, and also a modern clerestory and flat roof, replacing the original pitched roof.

The Mercury Theatre, Ladbroke Road

This building was erected in 1851 as a school by the Congregationalists of the adjoining Horbury Chapel. The architect was John Tarring.[292] It was subsequently used as a church hall and then as a sculptor's studio to 1929 before becoming the home of Madame Rambert's Russian School of Dancing. After extensive alterations in 1930–1 it became known as 'Ballet Club' and was subsequently named The Mercury Theatre. It is now occupied by the Rambert School of Ballet,[293] but has not been used for ballet performances since 1965.

It is built of coursed rubble, with dressed stone door and window openings, in a free Gothic style. Although the building has been considerably altered, the original timber roof structure remains. The building presents a main façade to Ladbroke Road, with a large gabled wall placed asymmetrically and containing a large pointed window (now partially blocked up) with a roundel high in the gable.

Twentieth Century Theatre, No. 291 Westbourne Grove

This small theatre seating about 300 was built in 1863, and opened as the Victoria Hall. In 1866 it was renamed the Bijou Theatre, and in 1893 the interior was somewhat altered. From 1911 to 1918 it was used as a cinema, but reverted to a theatre and became the headquarters of first the Lena Ashwell Players, and then the Rudolph Steiner Association, who renamed it the Twentieth Century Theatre. It ceased to be a theatre in 1963, when the fittings were stripped out, and it was converted to use as an antique furniture warehouse. The auditorium still remains substantially as originally built, and is a rare survivor of the early rectangular hall type, with a gallery across one end. The entrance foyer survives, with a good moulded plaster ceiling. Other parts, such as the bar, have been partly reconstructed.

Electric Cinema Club, No. 191 Portobello Road

This was built in 1905 as the Electric Theatre, and is believed to be the second earliest purpose-built theatre in London for the showing of films, and the only one to survive little altered inside. After a short spell as a cinema, it was used as a music hall under the name Imperial Playhouse. After long neglect it is now in use again as the Electric Cinema Club. The interior has remained virtually unaltered since it was built.

No. 14 Lansdowne Road: Hanover Lodge
Plate 63e, f

This house has been occupied by the same family since 1855, and its history can be traced in exceptional detail because one of the family,

Colonel Martin Petrie, compiled a manuscript account of it in c. 1886. This was continued by his descendants, one of whom, Professor Eleanora Carus-Wilson, still lives there, and has kindly given permission to quote from it.

On 7 and 8 March 1844 J. W. Ladbroke leased the pair of houses then known as Nos. 7 and 8 Queen's Villas (now Nos. 14 Lansdowne Walk and 14 Lansdowne Road respectively)* to the solicitor Richard Roy for ninety-six years from Michaelmas 1843 at a ground rent of £7 for each house.[294] On 11 June 1844 Roy under-leased both houses to Samuel Clothier, a marble mason variously described as of Street, Somerset, and of St. Pancras, who was probably a creditor of William Reynolds, the general building undertaker for this part of the Ladbroke estate.[295] Both houses were then still unfinished, and Clothier covenanted to complete them within six months, to complete the roads and footpaths in Queen's Road (now Lansdowne Walk) and Lansdowne Road, to paint the exterior every three and the interior every seven years, and to insure the building for three quarters of its value. In June 1848 Clothier sold his lease of No. 8 Queen's Villas to Thomas Robson, marble merchant, of Abingdon Street, Westminster, for £393, Robson also taking over a mortgage of £550 which Clothier had raised upon the house in 1845. The whole price paid by Robson was thus £943. The first occupant was Colonel Archibald Hyslop, formerly of the Honourable East India Company Service, who in 1851 was living here with his wife, four young children and four servants.[296]

At Michaelmas 1855 Mrs. Louisa Macdowall took Hanover Lodge, then known as 8 Hanover Villas, on a short lease at a rental of £75 per annum from Robson. In the same year Thomas Goudie bought the freehold reversion of the house from Felix Ladbroke.

The watercolour drawing reproduced on Plate 63e gives an extremely romanticized view of the house in its original condition.† It shows that the entrance porch to Lansdowne Road projected from the west front, and did not originally rise above ground-storey level. It was flanked on either side by a small 'cabinet', and in the basement

---

* Lansdowne Walk has at various times been known as Queen's Villas, Queen's Road, Hanover Road, Hanover Villas and latterly as Hanover Terrace. It was renamed Lansdowne Walk in 1938. No. 8 Queen's Villas, the subject of this account, was numbered as 14 Lansdowne Road in 1863, and is also still known as Hanover Lodge.

† It may particularly be noted that the house is incorrectly shown as detached, whereas it has in fact always formed a pair with No. 14 Lansdowne Walk.

below these there was a housemaid's closet and a small scullery. A French window at first-floor level opened on to the flat roof of the porch, which was surrounded by a balustrade, and beneath which was the water-cistern. All the windows had small panes of glass secured by glazing-bars in the traditional Georgian manner.

In January 1861 Captain (later Colonel) Martin Petrie, Mrs. Macdowall's son-in-law, purchased Robson's lease for £925, and at once began to make extensive alterations. He extended the roof, formerly hipped, to make a west gable, replaced the small panes in the windows with plate glass (except in the basement), drained the garden, which had previously been very swampy, and erected an ornamental terra-cotta vase and pedestal. In 1863 he built an extension on the west side, north of the porch, containing the back kitchen in the basement and library on the ground floor, and added label-heads and balconies to the drawing-room windows. In 1874 he built the bowed projection on the south side, which extends up the full height of the house and includes a single-sheet bowed plate-glass window in the drawing-room. On the west side he added a small wing of the same height, which incorporated the original porch and contained a new larder, muniment room, boudoir and dressing-room. The roof was stripped and reslated, the whole of the water system renewed, with a new cistern at the top of the house, and encaustic tiles were laid in the porch and entrance path. The total cost of the works done in this year was £622.

Gas had been supplied to the house since at least 1855, and had certainly lit the garden room, where there was a gaselier. In the late 1870's it was brought up to the corridor of the first floor. The drawing-room, however, continued to be lit by candles until the installation of electricity in the house in 1898. In this year the attics were converted into a spacious nursery floor, with a pantry, bedrooms, and a day-nursery with a French window providing access from it to the flat roof of the west wing.

The freehold of the house was bought by the Petrie family in 1886.[297]

No. 85 Clarendon Road
Plate 75c

This house, known until 1919 as the Clarendon Hotel, was built by William Reynolds under a lease of 1846 from Richard Roy. It is a three-storey stucco-faced building standing at the south corner of Portland Road, the front to Clarendon Road, three windows in width, being ornamented with pilasters. Reynolds established himself here as a licensed victualler and was soon deeply involved in complicated mortgage arrangements similar to those which he made during the course of his building activities in this neighbourhood (see page 210). In February 1848 he was declared bankrupt, and in 1850 his debts (in addition to the mortgages) included some £1,100 to Barclay, Perkins, the brewers, for goods delivered to the hotel.[298] In July of this year he died, and soon afterwards the hotel came into the possession of David Allan Ramsay, a nurseryman who was soon to turn builder, with disastrous results for himself, and who was soon deep in debt to another firm of brewers, William Reid and Company.

One of the mortgages made by Reynolds in 1847 contains a detailed list of the fittings, furniture and equipment in the hotel at that date. On the ground floor there were four public rooms—the tap room, the parlour, the bar parlour and the private parlour. All were heated either by a register stove or an open fire, and none of the floors appears to have been covered. Painted wooden settles extended round forty-five feet of the walls of the tap room, where there were three iron-bound stout deal tables and two forms. In the parlour the settles, hat rails, elbow screens and 'capital strong well made . . . drinking table' were all of mahogany, and there were four Windsor chairs, four iron spittoons and a large chimney-glass in a gilt frame. The bar parlour, evidently a small room, had a mahogany Pembroke table, four cane-seat chairs and scarlet silk curtains protected by a druggett and suspended from brass rods. The private parlour was similar but larger, with four flower-pot stands, six spittoons and thirteen Windsor chairs. The bar itself was described as the 'capital painted and panelled front return counter with stout metal top and gate fitted with twelve brass spirit taps, rinsing basin, five drawers, cupboard shelves etc., metal top to same, double metal drawer and receiver, a handsome seven motion Beer engine with ivory pulls, six metal taps and one brass stop cock, metal drainer, length of waste pipe in carved Spanish mahogany case (by Angliss)'. There were eight one-gallon iron-bound gilt spirit casks with brass taps and a length of pipe to the spirit taps, while the 'return Cabinet' of this splendid *equipage*, in which were stored prodigious numbers of mugs, bottles and miscellaneous requirements such as dice and snuff boxes, was 'finished with a noble cornice, carved plaster etc.'

The kitchen in the basement had an 'oven and boiler range with supply cistern, pull out bar and swing trivet'. The stout deal table in the middle (with eight Windsor chairs) was surrounded by cupboards and dressers accommodating a tremendous iron *batterie de cuisine*. In the beer cellar there were three large store butts, the largest having a capacity of 148 gallons, from which beer was piped up to the engine in the bar above. There was also a spirit cellar and a wash-house, the latter containing a copper and three iron-bound tubs.

On the first floor there was a large club-room and two bedrooms. The second floor contained five more bedrooms and there were also two small attics. The club-room had two register stoves 'with Elizabethan bars', each surmounted by a large chimney-glass. There were ten mahogany drinking tables, each six feet in length, twenty-one Windsor chairs, and twenty-nine iron spittoons.

Most of the bedrooms had a register stove, a painted washstand and dressing table, and a double-rail towel horse. Those on the second floor had Kidderminster carpets. The bedroom next to the club-room was snugly furnished with a drinking table and a 'Loo table on pillar and plinth with painted baize cover'. In the best room the bed was described as a 'Handsome 7ft. carved and turned pillar double screwed mahogany four post bedstead with mahogany cornice rods, brass rings, lath bottom base slip laths'. Beneath the top mattress or 'bed', which was of course of feathers, was a wool mattress and beneath this a straw palliass which rested on the laths.

All the windows throughout the house had either Holland spring roller blinds or green Venetian blinds, and most of the doors had ebony knobs and finger plates. There were altogether eleven register stoves and several open grates, plus the boiler in the kitchen. There seems to have been a piped cold water supply in the bar and the kitchen, but there was none on the first floor. The kitchen and ground-floor rooms and also the club-room on the first floor and part of the staircase were all lit by gas, the meter being in the beer cellar; but none of the bedrooms had gas, fear of accidental asphyxiation being probably the reason. There were two water-closets, one evidently near the lower part of the staircase and the other in the region of the bar. This last was indeed the hub of the whole household, for it was in 'Front of bar' that one or more of the 'eleven spring bells on carriages with brass pendulums, cranks and wires' jangled periodically on the 'painted bell board and eleven painted inscriptions', to summon a servant to one of the public rooms. None of the bedrooms had bell pulls, but in the club-room there were four, of brass and china, 'with cranks and wires'.

At the back of the house there was a skittle ground and a bowling green, equipped with benches, a sacking screen behind the skittle frame, and a movable urinal.[299]

The census returns of 1851 show that the publican then was James Phillips, who conducted the hotel with the assistance of his wife, his daughter aged twelve, one waiter, one servant and a pot boy. There were three resident 'visitors'.[296]

The house ceased to be a hotel in 1919 and has subsequently been used for commercial, social and professional purposes.

SELECT LIST OF BUILDING LESSORS AND LESSEES ON THE LADBROKE ESTATE

Except where otherwise stated, the dates refer to the years in which the leases were granted: these are not always the date of actual building. Lessors' and lessees' addresses are given only for those resident outside Kensington. Many houses are not included owing to lack of evidence. The chief source is the Middlesex Land Register in the Greater London Record Office at County Hall.

Arundel Gardens, north side

2–50 even	Nos. 2–14 built by Edwin Ware, builder, 1862–3. Other houses in this range built by G. W. Simmonds, Leonard Cowling and —Humphreys, 1863.

Arundel Gardens, south side

1–47 odd	21 of these 24 houses built by William Wheeler, builder, 1863. Nos. 43–47 demolished.

Blenheim Crescent, north side

36	C. H. Blake to George Drew, architect, 1864.

SELECT LIST OF BUILDING LESSORS AND LESSEES ON THE LADBROKE ESTATE

62–66 even	Blake, by direction of Charles Chambers, timber merchant, to J. S. C. Small, plasterer, 1863.
68–78, 92–98 even	Blake by direction of Chambers to Thomas Wesson, builder, 1863–4. Nos. 96, 98 demolished.
80, 82	Blake by direction of Chambers to John Burton of Cornhill, builder, 1863.

Blenheim Crescent, south side

53	Chambers to Richard Crowley, builder, 1863.
55–73 odd	Chambers to Thomas May, surveyor, 1863.
75, 77	Chambers by direction of May to Alfred and George Secrett, builders, 1863.
79, 81	Chambers to John Scoley, builder, 1863.
83, 85	Blake to Chambers, 1862.
87–91 odd	Blake by direction of Chambers to Henry Heard, licensed victualler, 1862.
93–115 odd	Blake by direction of Chambers to Wesson, 1861–2.
117–127 odd	Blake by direction of Chambers to Benjamin Reynolds, builder, 1861.
129–135 odd	Blake by direction of Chambers to Wesson, 1861.
137	Sold freehold by Blake to Chambers, 1862.

Camelford Road

	Built under leases from Stephen Phillips, merchant, to J. V. Scantlebury of Paddington, builder, 1864–5. Demolished.

Chepstow Villas, north side

54–62 even	Built by or for Thomas Pocock of Bartholomew Close, City, solicitor, 1851.

Chepstow Villas, south side

35–41 odd	Built by or for Pocock, 1850–1.

Clarendon Road, east side

2–10 even	J. W. Ladbroke by direction of William John Drew, builder, to William Liddard, gentleman, 1845.
12, 14	J. W. Ladbroke by direction of Drew to Thomas Allason, architect, 1845.
16–26 even	J. W. Ladbroke to Richard Roy, solicitor, to William Reynolds, builder, 1844. Probably designed by James Thomson, architect.

28–58 even	J. W. Ladbroke to Roy to Reynolds, 1846.
60–66 even	Roy by direction of Reynolds to H. P. Bruyeres of Junior United Service Club, 1846. Nos. 60, 62 demolished.
68–76 even	C. H. Blake to Thomas Holmes, builder, 1851. Perhaps designed by William Sim, surveyor or architect.
78	Blake to H. W. Smith, builder, 1851. Perhaps designed by Sim.
90–110 even	Dr. Samuel Walker to William C. Gazeley of Camden Town, builder, 1853.
112–120 even	Dr. Walker to Gazeley, 1853. Leased again by Blake to Charles Chambers, timber merchant, 1861. Nos. 114–120 demolished.
122–126 even	Stephen Phillips, merchant, to Gazeley, 1852.
128–142 even	Phillips to William Pilbeam, builder, 1852–5.

Clarendon Road, west side

1–5 odd	J. W. Ladbroke by direction of Drew to Liddard, 1841. Demolished.
7–11 odd	J. W. Ladbroke to Drew, who mortgaged to Allason, 1840. Demolished.
13, 15	J. W. Ladbroke to Drew, 1840.
17–21 odd	J. W. Ladbroke by direction of Drew to Liddard, 1845.
23–29 odd	J. W. Ladbroke by direction of Drew to Allason, 1845.
31–39 odd	J. W. Ladbroke to Roy to Reynolds, 1844. Probably designed by James Thomson, architect.
41–75 odd	J. W. Ladbroke to Roy to Reynolds, 1845.
77, 79, 85	J. W. Ladbroke to Roy to Reynolds, 1846. Nos. 77, 79 demolished.
81, 83	J. W. Ladbroke to Roy to Bruyeres, 1846. Reynolds probably involved. Demolished.
87, 95, 97, 103, 105	Phillips to Reynolds, 1849. Nos. 103, 105 demolished.
99, 101	Phillips to Joseph Helling, plumber, 1852. No. 101 demolished.
107–119 odd	Phillips to Thomas Pocock, solicitor, 1852. Partly demolished. Also, same to same, 1855, of some 24 houses now demolished for Nottingwood House and Allom House.
195–207 odd and most of this island site	Phillips to J. V. Scantlebury of Paddington, builder, 1860–1.

SELECT LIST OF BUILDING LESSORS AND LESSEES ON THE LADBROKE ESTATE

Cornwall Crescent, north side

2–18 even	C. H. Blake to G. and T. Goodwin, builders, 1864. Partly demolished.
44, 46	Stephen Phillips, merchant, to John Calverley, builder, 1862.
48–82 even	Phillips to Charles Thompson of Paddington and/or Islington, builder, 1861–2. Nos. 72–82 demolished.

Cornwall Crescent, south side

3–7, 33–39 odd, 61	Blake to P. R. Baker, builder, 1864–6.
9, 15–31 odd	Blake to C. A. Kellond of Paddington, builder, 1864.
11	Blake to F., E. and B. Bramwell of St. Pancras, stone and marble merchants, 1864.
13	Blake to W. N. Mitchell, 1864.
41, 59	Blake to J. S. C. Small, plasterer, 1864–5.
43–49 odd, 53, 57	Blake to John Scoley, builder, 1864–5.
51	Blake to C. Yates, 1864.
55	Blake to H. Newton, carpenter, 1864.
63	Blake to Thomas Wesson, builder, 1864.
65	Blake to J. Phillips, carpenter, 1864.
67	Blake to W. Scantlebury, builder, 1864.
69	Blake to J. Redman of Duke Street, Mayfair, bootmaker, 1864.
71, 73	Blake to F. Gilder, builder, 1864.
75–81 odd	Blake to Thompson, 1862 (79 and 81 now demolished).

Elgin Crescent, north side

50–56 even	C. H. Blake to Edwin Ware of Paddington, builder, 1862.
58–120 even	Dr. Samuel Walker to Henry Malcolm Ramsay, builder, 1852. Completed 1858.

Elgin Crescent, south side

17–47 odd	Dr. Walker to Robert Russell, builder, 1852.
63–67 odd	Probably built by J. D. Cowland, builder, *c.* 1863.
69–115 odd	Dr. Walker to William Sim, builder or architect, 1852. Completed *c.* 1860.
117–145 odd	Blake to David Allan Ramsay of Brompton, nurseryman, 1851. Perhaps designed by Sim.
147	Blake to Charles Preedy of Islington, builder, 1851. Perhaps designed by Allom or by Sim.

149–153 odd	Blake to H. W. Smith, builder, 1851. Perhaps designed by Allom, or by Sim.

Holland Park Avenue, north side

2–6, 24–28 even	J. W. Ladbroke by direction of Joshua Flesher Hanson to Richard Bescoby, gentleman, 1828. Robert Cantwell, architect or builder, acted on behalf of Bescoby.
8–22 even	J. W. Ladbroke to Hanson, 1823–4. No. 8 demolished.
30	J. W. Ladbroke by direction of Hanson to Francis Bescoby, gentleman, 1826.
32	J. W. Ladbroke by direction of Hanson to Edward May and Aaron Morritt of Oxford Street, ironmongers, 1826.
34, 36	J. W. Ladbroke to William Hammond of Upminster, builder, 1826.
38	J. W. Ladbroke by direction of Hanson to Cantwell, 1826.
42–52 even	J. W. Ladbroke to John Drew of Pimlico, builder, 1833.
54–74 even	J. W. Ladbroke to Ralph Adams of Gray's Inn Road, brick and tile maker, 1826–31. Nos. 62–66 demolished.
80–90 even	J. W. Ladbroke to Adams, 1831.
100–116 even	J. W. Ladbroke to Adams, or Adams a party to leases, 1827–31.

Horbury Crescent

Site leased by F. Ladbroke to William Chadwick of Adelaide Place, City, architect, 1848. Building begun 1855 by J. D. Cowland, contractor. Sixteen houses in course of erection by William Wheeler, builder, 1857.

Kensington Park Gardens, south side

1–9 consec.	F. Ladbroke building agreements with William John Drew, builder, 1849–50. No. 7 was occupied by Sir William Crookes, the scientist, from 1880 to 1919, and is said to have been the first house in England to be lit by electricity. No. 5 demolished.
10–22 consec.	F. Ladbroke to David Allan Ramsay, builder, 1853. Not completed until *c.* 1858. Designed by Thomas Allom.

SELECT LIST OF BUILDING LESSORS AND LESSEES ON THE LADBROKE ESTATE

Kensington Park Gardens, north side

24	Built for C. H. Blake, probably by contract with Ramsay, to designs by Allom, 1853. Blake lived here from 1854 to 1859.
25, 32–35 consec.	F. Ladbroke to Blake, 1852. Allom architect for Blake.
26–31, 36–47 consec.	F. Ladbroke to Blake, 1852. Sub-leased by Blake to Ramsay or his associates, 1852–3. Nos. 26, 28–30 completed by J. D. Cowland, builder, under sub-lease from Dr. Walker's trustees, 1856. Designed by Allom.

Kensington Park Road, east side

2–30 even	Built by William Chadwick of Adelaide Place, City, architect, 1848.
32–38 even	J. W. Ladbroke to Chadwick, 1847.
56–72 even	Built by or for Thomas Pocock of Bartholomew Close, City, solicitor, in association with John Day of Red Lion Square, solicitor, 1850–1.
74	Built by or for Pocock, 1851–2.
76–90 even	Built by Philip Rainey, formerly Blake's clerk of works, under agreement of 1859, to designs of Edward Habershon, architect.
92–112 even	Built under leases of 1861 to Robert Offord of St. Marylebone, coach-builder. Nos. 98–112 demolished.
124	Jane Tringham to Joseph Way, bricklayer, 1853.
126–182 even	Built by or for Pocock, perhaps by contract, 1852.
184	Built by or for Pocock, perhaps by contract, 1853.

Kensington Park Road, west side

1–15 odd	Built by John Wicking Phillips of Paddington, builder, 1860–1.

Ladbroke Crescent

1–24 consec.	C. H. Blake to G. and T. Goodwin, builders, 1864. Partly demolished.

Ladbroke Gardens, north side

1–23 consec.	Richard Roy, solicitor, to G. Wilson, builder (Nos. 1–11) and to James Emmins, builder (Nos. 12–23), 1852. Designed by Thomas Allom, architect. Built *c.* 1858–66, Nos. 7–23 under auspices of Ebenezer Howard, poultry salesman of Leadenhall Market, by W. Parratt, builder, and John Faulkner of Finchley New Road,

surveyor, and probably completed after Parratt's death by W. Wheeler, builder.

Ladbroke Gardens, south side

34, 35	Built by John Wicking Phillips of Paddington, builder, 1858–61.

Ladbroke Grove, east side

14–20 even	Major-General Laurence Bradshaw by direction of Robert Cantwell, surveyor, to George Buckle of Primrose Street, City, architect, 1835. J. R. Butler, builder, also probably involved.
22, 24	Butler and mortgagee to John Sandell of Bread Street, City, gentleman, 1838.
26, 28	Butler and mortgagee to Thomas Barrett of Tottenham Court Road, tradesman, 1838.
30, 32	Butler's mortgagee to William Reynolds, builder, 1843. Built *c.* 1848.
36–40 even	C. H. Blake to David Allan Ramsay, builder, 1853. Designed by Thomas Allom. Completed after Ramsay's bankruptcy in 1854 by Blake's clerk of works, Philip Rainey.
42–50 even	J. W. Ladbroke to William Parkin, solicitor, 1843. Re-leased by Ladbroke to John Brown of St. Marylebone, builder, 1845.
52–58 even	J. W. Ladbroke to Brown, 1845.
60–64 even	Begun by Henry Malcolm Ramsay, builder, for James Lamb of Great Winchester Street, cement manufacturer, 1854. Building suspended 1855.
66, 68	Built by John Wicking Phillips of Paddington, builder, 1858–61.
78–94 even	Probably designed by Edward Habershon, architect, 1861.
98–104 even	Blake to Edmund and Elias Cordery of Bayswater, builders, 1860.

Ladbroke Grove, west side

11–19 odd	J. W. Ladbroke to John Drew of Pimlico, builder, of Nos. 17–19 and site of Nos. 11–15, 1833. Nos. 11–15 leased by John Drew and mortgagees to R. Charsley, gentleman (No. 11) and William John Drew, builder (Nos. 13 and 15), 1838.
21, 23	J. W. Ladbroke to W. J. Drew, 1839–40.

SELECT LIST OF BUILDING LESSORS AND LESSEES ON THE LADBROKE ESTATE

25–35 odd	J. W. Ladbroke by direction of W. J. Drew to Francis Read of Pimlico, builder, 1839–40. Porticoes added 1857 (Nos. 25–33) and 1861 (Nos. 31–35).
37–61 odd	J. W. Ladbroke to Richard Roy, solicitor, to Reynolds, 1842–3. Designed by James Thomson, architect, 1842. Nos. 37, 39, 51–57 recently rebuilt.
63	J. W. Ladbroke to Roy to Joshua Higgs senior and junior of Davies Street, Berkeley Square, builders, 1844.
67–75 odd	Built under contract by John Jay of London Wall, builder, for Mark Markwick of Worthing, esquire, in conjunction with John Duncan, solicitor, 1841–2. Probably designed by either Jay or Charles Stewart Duncan.
83	Dr. Samuel Walker to Kenelm Chandler, builder, 1852.
87	Blake to Edwin Ware of Paddington, builder, 1862.
91, 93	Charles Chambers, timber merchant, to Richard Crowley, builder, 1863.
95–109 odd	Blake to George Drew, architect, 1864.
111–119 odd	Blake by direction of George Drew to C. A. Daw, builder, 1865.
121–129 odd	Blake to G. and T. Goodwin, builders, 1863.

Ladbroke Road, north side

14	J. W. Ladbroke to William Chadwick of Adelaide Place, City, architect, 1843.
16, 18	F. Ladbroke to Chadwick, 1848.
64	J. W. Ladbroke by direction of William John Drew, builder, to Major G. F. Penley, 1844.
66–72 even	J. W. Ladbroke to W. J. Drew, 1845.
80–86 even	J. W. Ladbroke by direction of W. J. Drew to Thomas Allason, architect, 1845.

Ladbroke Road, south side

1–7 odd	F. Ladbroke to Chadwick, 1848.
9, 11	J. W. Ladbroke to Chadwick, 1847.
13–19 odd	Chadwick to George Stevenson, builder, 1848.
21–55 odd	W. W. Chadwick to William Wheeler, builder, 1853–4.
105, 107	Site leased by J. W. Ladbroke to John Drew of Pimlico, builder, 1833.

109–119 odd	J. W. Ladbroke to W. J. Drew, 1841.
137, 139	J. W. Ladbroke to W. J. Drew, 1845. Demolished.

Ladbroke Square

1	Built by W. H. Rowlings of Theobald's Road, 1851.
4–17 consec.	Built by William Wheeler, builder, 1856–60.
20–22 consec.	J. W. Ladbroke to John Brown of St. Marylebone, builder, 1844.
23–27 consec.	Agreement for lease, Jacob Connop, bill broker, to William Gribble of St. Marylebone, builder, 1842. Leased by J. W. Ladbroke to Connop's solicitor, William Parkin, 1843.
28–31 consec.	Agreement for lease, Connop to William Wells of Islington, builder, 1842. Nos. 28–30 leased by J. W. Ladbroke to C. H. Grove, solicitor, 1844.
31 (sic)–37 consec.	J. W. Ladbroke by direction of Connop to W. Parkin, 1843. John Stevens, Connop's architect, a party to mortgages.
38	J. W. Ladbroke to Henry Monson of St. Marylebone, builder, 1846. Rebuilt after damage in war of 1939–45.
39–47 consec.	J. W. Ladbroke to J. T. Crossthwaite of Addiscombe, gentleman, 1846. Probably built by Monson. All except Nos. 41 and 42 finished by Mr. Wilkinson under superintendence of Mr. Brown, 1850. Nos. 39 and 40 rebuilt after damage in war of 1939–45.

Ladbroke Terrace, east side

3, 4	J. W. Ladbroke by direction of Joshua Flesher Hanson to Robert Cantwell, architect or builder, 1826.
5, 6	Same to same, 1833.
7, 8	Probably built by Cantwell and/or William John Drew, builder.

Ladbroke Terrace, west side

10, 11	Probably built by Cantwell and/or Drew.
12, 13	Major-General Laurence Bradshaw by direction of Cantwell to William Liddard, gentleman (No. 13) and to Drew (No. 12), 1838.

SELECT LIST OF BUILDING LESSORS AND LESSEES ON THE LADBROKE ESTATE

Lansdowne Crescent, east side

2–4 consec. J. W. Ladbroke to Richard Roy, solicitor, to Joshua Higgs senior and junior of Davies Street, Berkeley Square, builders, 1844.

5–8 consec. J. W. Ladbroke to Roy to William Reynolds, builder, 1845.

9–12 consec. J. W. Ladbroke to Roy to J. W. Bridger of Chigwell, esquire, 1844.

13–18 consec. J. W. Ladbroke to Roy to Reynolds, 1845. No. 18 demolished.

Lansdowne Crescent, west side

19–38 consec. Stephen Phillips, merchant, to Henry Wyatt of Leinster Square, architect, 1860–2.

42–44 consec. J. W. Ladbroke to Roy to Reynolds, 1846. No. 42 demolished.

Lansdowne Road, east side

Lansdowne House Designed by William Flockhart, 1904.

2–12 even J. W. Ladbroke to William John Drew, builder, 1843.

14 see 14 Lansdowne Walk.

16–30 even J. W. Ladbroke to Richard Roy, solicitor, to Frederick Woods and William Wheeler, builders, 1845.

32–44 even J. W. Ladbroke to Roy to William Reynolds, builder, 1846. Nos. 36–40 demolished.

46 Roy to James Lamb of Hyde Park Square, esquire, 1847. Completed *c.* 1857.

48, 50 Dr. Samuel Walker to James Emmins, builder, 1852. Completed *c.* 1857.

52–66 even Dr. Walker to Henry Wade Smith, builder, 1852. Completed *c.* 1860.

68–102 even Dr. Walker to Jacob Barry, builder, 1852. Completed *c.* 1864, Nos. 78–88 under new leases of 1860–2 from Roy to John Froud of Shepherd's Bush, builder, and Nos. 90–98 under new leases of 1862 to Joseph Lane, carpenter.

Lansdowne Road, west side

1–5 odd J. W. Ladbroke by direction of Drew to W. Liddard, gentleman, 1845.

7 see 16–19 Lansdowne Walk.

9–27 odd J. W. Ladbroke to Roy to Reynolds, 1846. Nos. 11 and 13 were formerly occupied by Sir Edmund Davis, a South African millionaire, for whom several rooms were decorated and furnished by Frank Brangwyn around the year 1900. Charles Conder also painted a number of panels in watercolour on silk. Much of Brangwyn's work still remains. William Flockhart was the architect for the uniting of the two houses.

29–43 odd J. W. Ladbroke to Roy to Reynolds, 1846.

45, 47 J. W. Ladbroke to Roy, 1846. No. 45, Roy to Reynolds, 1847.

49 and 51 C. H. Blake to Michael Longstaff, esquire, 1851.

53–59 odd Dr. Walker to David Allan Ramsay, builder, 1852. Completed *c.* 1855.

61–75 odd Dr. Walker to Thomas Pocock, of Bartholomew Close, City, solicitor, 1852. Completed *c.* 1862.

77 Dr. Walker to Ramsay, 1852. Carcase sold to Thomas Allason, junior, architect, 1856.

79–123 odd Dr. Walker to Kenelm Chandler, builder, 1852. Completed *c.* 1862 under new leases of 1858–60 from Dr. Walker and mortgagees. Lessees include J. D. Cowland, builder (Nos. 89 and 111) and William Reading, builder (Nos. 113–117). Nos. 105–111, 121, 123 demolished.

Lansdowne Walk, south side

1–12 consec. J. W. Ladbroke to Richard Roy, solicitor, to William Reynolds, builder, 1843–5. Nos. 1–6 designed by James Thomson, architect. No. 1 was altered and enlarged in 1900 by (Sir) Aston Webb, who lived there from 1890 until his death in 1930. Nos. 9, 10 demolished.

14, and 14 Lansdowne Road J. W. Ladbroke to Roy to Samuel Clothier of St. Pancras, or of Street, Somerset, marble mason, 1844.

16–19 consec., and 7 Lansdowne Road J. W. Ladbroke to Roy to Reynolds, 1845. No. 16 demolished.

Pembridge Road, west side

Prince Albert public house J. W. Ladbroke to William Chadwick of Southwark, builder, 1841.

13–59 odd Built by Chadwick, now of Adelaide Place, City, architect, 1848–52.

Portobello Road, west side

9–13 odd and Sun in Splendour public house Built by William Chadwick of Adelaide Place, City, architect, 1852.

SELECT LIST OF BUILDING LESSORS AND LESSEES ON THE LADBROKE ESTATE

65–105 odd	Rev. B. E. Bridges and Thomas Pocock of Bartholomew Close, City, solicitor, to numerous local builders, 1848–9.
115–175 odd	Pocock to numerous local builders, 1852–3.
225, Warwick Castle public house	J. Bridges of Red Lion Square, solicitor, by direction of Pocock, and of Paul Felthouse, builder, to Sir Henry Meux, brewer, 1853.

Rosemead Road, south side

1 and 2	C. H. Blake to James Emmins, builder, 1851.

St. John's Gardens, north side

1 and 2	J. W. Ladbroke to Richard Roy, solicitor, to William Reynolds, builder, 1846.

St. Mark's Place, west side

4–10 consec.	C. H. Blake to consortium of local builders, 1864–6.

St. Mark's Road, east side

4	C. H. Blake to C. A. Kellond of Paddington, builder, 1864.

St. Mark's Road, west side

1–9 odd	Blake to Philip Baker, builder, 1865. Demolished.
23–39 odd	Stephen Phillips, merchant, to J. V. Scantlebury of Paddington, builder, 1862. Demolished.

Stanley Crescent, west side

1–11 consec.	Designed by Thomas Allom. Building begun by David Allan Ramsay under contract of 1853 with C. H. Blake for £19,248. Completed after Ramsay's bankruptcy in 1854 by Blake's clerk of works, Philip Rainey.

12 and 13	Designed by Allom. Added to Blake's contract with Ramsay of 1853 for an extra £4,000. Completed after Ramsay's bankruptcy in 1854 by Rainey.
14–23 consec.	Drawings (not used) for eight houses here supplied to Blake by Allom, 1855. Ten houses built here by William Wheeler, builder, under leases of 1862–3 from H. and W. Gardner, brewers.

Stanley Gardens

1–29 consec.	Designed by Thomas Allom. Building begun by David Allan Ramsay under contract of 1853 with C. H. Blake. After Ramsay's bankruptcy in 1854 Nos. 1–11 completed by Locke and Nesham, Nos. 12–15 by J. W. Sanders, builders, and Nos. 16–29 by Blake's clerk of works, Philip Rainey.

Westbourne Grove, north side

282–304 even	Built by or under supervision of Thomas Pocock of Bartholomew Close, solicitor, 1851–2.

Westbourne Grove, south side

283–303 odd	Built by or under supervision of Pocock, 1851–2.

Westbourne Park Road, north side

292–302 even	Thomas Pocock of Bartholomew Close, City, solicitor, to Elias Cordery, builder, 1863. Nos. 304–314 probably also built by Cordery.
316–352 even	C. H. Blake to Edmund and Elias Cordery of Bayswater, builders, 1860.

Westbourne Park Road, south side

305–317 odd	Built by Paul Felthouse, builder, c. 1863.
319–351 odd	Pocock to Cordery, 1863. Nos. 347–351 demolished.

CHAPTER X

Chepstow Villas and Pembridge Square Area

WHEN large-scale building development began here in the late 1840's, the greater part of this area (fig. 66) belonged to three absentee landowners, James Weller Ladbroke, esquire, of Lavington or Petworth, Sussex, Robert Hall, esquire, of Old Bond Street, and G. S. Archer, esquire, of Wingham, Kent.[1] Ladbroke owned some thirty-three acres, consisting of two separate holdings, one of five acres now known as Linden Gardens, and the other of twenty-eight acres. Both these holdings were only relatively small detached portions of his total estate in Kensington, the bulk of which comprised some 170 acres to the west of Portobello Lane (see Chapter IX). Hall's estate, also of twenty-eight acres, formed a buffer separating Ladbroke's three holdings. It was shaped like a Y, the base and left-hand arm extending along the east side of Pembridge and Portobello Roads, and the right-hand arm occupying the modern sites of Dawson Place and Pembridge Square. Archer's land, one field of ten acres, was situated on the east side of Portobello Road to the north of Hall's ground.

The Ladbroke and Hall estates

The earliest building in this area began in the mid 1820's in Linden Gardens (then Linden Grove), but the history of these five acres is quite separate from the rest of the area, and is therefore described separately on page 268. Elsewhere development did not begin until 1844, when, prompted no doubt by the tremendous building boom then in progress in Paddington, James Weller Ladbroke signed an agreement with William Henry Jenkins for the development of his twenty-eight acres.*

W. H. Jenkins was a civil engineer, of 43 Lincoln's Inn Fields. By the agreement he undertook to take Ladbroke's twenty-eight acres, which had hitherto been let at an agricultural rent of £133 per annum (or £4 15s. per acre),[2] for ninety-nine years, paying in the first year a rent of £150, which was to rise in the fifth and all succeeding years to £560 (or £20 per acre). He covenanted that within five years he would spend at least £10,000 on roads, sewers and houses, and that within twelve years he would build at least eighty houses, each of which was to be of at least £500 in value. In return for these undertakings Ladbroke covenanted that he would grant leases to Jenkins or his nominees of all houses as soon as they were covered in. When the ground rent of £560 had been secured by such leases, he would grant the remaining land to Jenkins at a peppercorn rent, and here Jenkins was to be permitted to erect cheaper houses, but of at least £300 in value each.

This agreement was the last of five such contracts made by Ladbroke with building speculators between 1840 and 1844, the other four being all concerned with land on the main portion of his estate further west (see Chapter IX). It was much more precise in its terms than the four previous contracts, and was clearly drawn up in the light of the Metropolitan Building Act passed later in the same year, 1844, which *inter alia* extended public regulation of building to Kensington for the first time. The houses were to be built of sound bricks and Baltic timber conformable to the requirements of the new Act, and the inspection of building work, which elsewhere on the estate had hitherto been done by Ladbroke's own surveyor, Thomas Allason, was, as soon as the new Act had passed, to be done by the new district surveyor for North Kensington.

Ladbroke's own requirements, too, were more precise. All roads were to be at least thirty-five feet in width, including the footways, and Jenkins was to provide brick boundary walls or iron fences between each plot. The lessees of individual houses were to covenant to pay for the upkeep of

---

* See page 272 for a select list of building lessors and lessees in the area described in this chapter.

Fig. 66. Chepstow Villas and Pembridge Square area. Based on the Ordnance Survey of 1863–7

the roads, to insure their houses against fire for three quarters of their value, and to paint the exteriors every four years. They were not to build any additions without Ladbroke's consent, or to practise certain noisome trades. In view of this greater stringency it is, however, remarkable that no control whatever was imposed in matters of elevational treatment, nor was there any reference to a layout plan.[3]

The terms of this agreement were at once confirmed by a private Act of Parliament promoted in 1844 by and at the expense of Ladbroke chiefly for the purpose of clearing up the confusions which the loose wording of the four previous contracts had caused on the main portion of the estate.[3] By August 1844 a layout plan for Jenkins's twenty-eight acres had been prepared; applications were being made to the Westminster Commissioners of Sewers for leave to form new sewers, and building plots were being advertised as to let.[4]

At this point W. H. Jenkins assigned his interest in the estate to his kinsman, William Kinnaird Jenkins of Hyde Park Gardens, esquire.[5] Since at least 1838 W. K. Jenkins had been speculating on adjacent land to the east in Paddington, where Newton, Garway, Monmouth and Hereford Roads were all built under his auspices.[6*] Under his experienced management the development of these twenty-eight acres of the Ladbroke estate went smoothly forward, despite the general slump in building in Kensington in the years 1847–9.

W. K. Jenkins is himself said to have been a well-known lawyer,[7] but whether this was so or not, he certainly employed a lawyer to act for him on the estate. This was T. W. Budd, of the firm of Budd and Hayes of Bedford Row, who had acted in 1835 on behalf of the Bishop of London and the trustees of the Paddington estate in drainage matters in the Westbourne Grove area.[9] On W. K. Jenkins's estate Budd was concerned in 1845 in numerous applications to the Commissioners of Sewers,[10] and it was to him that applicants for building plots were invited to apply.[11] Later, he became a lessee himself, and sub-let to builders.[12] Ultimately he took several

large blocks of land, comprising about one third of the whole twenty-eight-acre estate, on lease from W. K. Jenkins,[13] and developed them himself by the normal procedure of granting building leases. He seems, indeed, to have operated in much the same way as other lawyers, notably Richard Roy and Thomas Pocock, on the main portion of the Ladbroke estate, though on a considerably smaller scale.

The author of the layout plan of the estate is not known, but it may be that Ladbroke's own architect, Thomas Allason, was responsible. The ground was flat, and it was therefore natural to extend Westbourne Grove from its then western extremity in Paddington still further west towards Portobello Lane (now Road), where it would join the main portion of the Ladbroke estate beyond. Another road, Pembridge Villas, curved south-westward towards Notting Hill Gate, where it joined the southern end of Portobello Lane. W. H. Jenkins had originally envisaged rows of paired houses all over the estate,[11] with two straight roads leading due west off Pembridge Villas, but in May 1845 W. K. Jenkins substituted a less rigid layout in which the two straight roads were replaced by Chepstow Villas and Chepstow Crescent, both gently curved.[14]

The originality of the layout of the main portion of the Ladbroke estate to the west is, however, absent. There are no communally shared paddocks abutting directly on to the surrounding houses, each of which here has its own private garden. In Pembridge Square, the only large open space, which is situated on the adjoining estate of Robert Hall, the houses are separated from the central garden by the roadway. The architectural character of the area is, however, more homogeneous than on the other Ladbroke lands—largely due, no doubt, to the leasing of sizeable parcels of land to a few speculators, who adopted a correspondingly small number of house types. Most of the houses are spacious and pleasant detached or semi-detached villas, faced with stucco and set in gardens along broad and often curving streets. There are also a number of smaller houses ranged in terraces. This mixture of house types,

* W. K. Jenkins also owned property in Hereford, and this connexion no doubt explains why he gave names of places in Herefordshire and various parts of Wales to the streets for whose development he was responsible. On his Kensington estate Chepstow, Pembridge, Ledbury and Denbigh were all used for this purpose.[7] Dawson Place, on an adjoining estate, may take its name from J. W. Dawson, an attorney to whom James Hall, an important builder on Jenkins's land, mortgaged several houses in Pembridge Villas.[8] But as James Hall did not build any of the houses in Dawson Place, this explanation is perhaps no more convincing than the traditional theory that the name may commemorate John Sylvester Dawson, who was tenant of Campden Place (now Clanricarde Gardens) at the end of the eighteenth century.

and the mildly Italianate style in which they are generally built, mark a departure from the greater uniformity prevalent in earlier years of the nineteenth century, and give the area its relaxed and informal quality.

Constructional work began soon after August 1844, when the first application to lay sewers was presented to the Westminster Commissioners.[15] Within less than three years permission was granted for W. H. or W. K. Jenkins to lay some 4,840 feet of sewers in Westbourne Grove, Chepstow Villas, Chepstow Place and Chepstow Crescent (the latter then part of Ledbury Road), Pembridge Villas and Pembridge Place. At an estimated fifteen shillings per foot this work represented an investment of some £3,630. The principal contractor was William Judd.[16] At the same time W. K. Jenkins leased several parcels of land to speculators, including Henry Vallance of Campden Hill Square, gentleman (south-east side of Pembridge Villas),[17] James Bennett, builder (north side of Westbourne Grove),[18] and George Treadaway (east side of Chepstow Place),[19] a draper of Harrow Road who is said to have enriched himself by selling clothing to navvies employed on the Great Western Railway.[7]* James Hall, the largest builder on the Jenkins estate, came here from St. Pancras in 1846–7 and took his first block of land at the eastern end of Pembridge Villas. His scale of business was large enough for him to employ his own clerk of works,[20] and between 1846 and 1854 he built some sixty-five houses on Jenkins's land,[21] including most of those in Pembridge Place. Subsequently he moved on to still larger speculations on the Holland estate, where he ultimately overreached himself and became bankrupt (see pages 113–16).

Building proceeded steadily on Jenkins's land, uninterrupted by the frequent bankruptcies and financial failures which had so violently punctuated progress on the main portion of the Ladbroke estate. The building agreement of 1844 with Ladbroke had specified that at least eighty houses should be built within twelve years, but this condition was fulfilled in a quarter of this period, with the full ground rent of £560 secured by the leases already granted on houses covered in. Accordingly

in April 1847 Felix Ladbroke (who had now inherited the freehold) granted W. K. Jenkins a long lease of all the remaining unbuilt land at a peppercorn rent, as had been stipulated in another clause of the agreement of 1844.[22] Immediately afterwards Jenkins assigned about one third of the estate, mostly in the south-eastern part of it, to his lawyer, T. W. Budd,[13] who was no doubt in part responsible for the success of the whole speculation. Two years later, in 1849, Budd bought the freehold of this land from Ladbroke, and W. K. Jenkins acquired that of more than half of the remainder.[23]

Owing to the limitations of the documentary material available no assessment of Jenkins's profit on these operations can be made, but he had evidently been successful, for in January 1846 he had agreed to take a lease of another ten acres of ground to the west from the neighbouring landowner, Robert Hall (fig. 66).[24]† This acquisition enabled him to extend Chepstow Villas westward to Portobello Lane, and to lay out another north–south street, now known as Denbigh Road and Pembridge Crescent, parallel with Ledbury Road and Chepstow Crescent. The principal builders here were James Hall and various members of the Cullingford and Maidlow families. Building progressed more slowly here, and in 1857 *The Building News* reported that in Pembridge Crescent 'several vacant sites yet remain to be filled up'.[25] In 1859, when building in this street was nearly complete, there were several unoccupied houses, and it seems that the supply of this 'run of the mill' type of house had exceeded the demand, at least in this locality.[26]

The remainder of Robert Hall's estate, to the south of Jenkins's land, was developed by the Radford family of builders, and Jenkins was in no way concerned here.‡ Francis Radford (or Francis Radford the younger, as he was often called, although no reference to anyone else of the same name has been found) began to work in the Pembridge area in 1848, when he was aged twenty-seven and was described as of Pickering Place, Bayswater, builder.[27] His first houses were on Jenkins's land, Nos. 37–41 (odd) Pembridge Villas, of which he was granted leases by W. K. Jenkins in 1848. No. 41 was known as Home

---

* Florence Gladstone appears to be mistaken in referring to him as John Treadaway.

† So far as is known Robert Hall was not related to James Hall the builder.

‡ A very detailed account of this area has been written by Irene Scouloudi and A. P. Hands, 'The Ownership and Development of Fifteen Acres at Kensington Gravel Pits', in *London Topographical Record*, vol. XXII, 1965, pp. 77–125.

Cottage, where he lived and/or had his office for some years, and where he was joined in 1849 by his elder brother, William Radford.[28] In 1871 Francis Radford was living in one of the houses which his brother had built, No. 55 Pembridge Villas, and the firm was then employing about sixty men.[29]

Francis and William Radford began the development of the Hall estate in 1849, when the executors of the estate (Robert Hall being now dead) agreed to lease to William Radford of Home Cottage one acre of land on the north side of Dawson Place west of Pembridge Place.[30] During the next fifteen years they built sewers, roads and some 125 houses on the Hall estate, mostly of the large detached variety, including all those in Pembridge Square and Pembridge Gardens,* and many in Dawson Place and on the east side of Pembridge Villas and Pembridge Road. Ninety-nine-year leases of the covered-in houses were granted by Robert Hall's executors to either Francis or William Radford (or sometimes to both of them jointly) or to their nominees. Francis was the dominant partner, however, for on his death in 1900 in his eightieth year an obituary in a local newspaper stated that he was 'both architect and builder of those well-known properties in Holland-park, Pembridge-square, Pembridge-gardens and Dawson-place'. His nephew also later stated that Francis Radford was 'his own architect'. He was originally from Devonshire, but had settled in Kensington, where he was for many years a member of the Vestry.

This speculation was one of the largest and most successful in Victorian Notting Hill. By the time of its completion in about 1864 the Radfords had already moved on to another equally efficiently managed enterprise in Holland Park (see page 119), where they erected some ninety more large detached houses, almost identical in design to the type which had proved so successful in Pembridge Square. Francis Radford's 'effects' were valued in 1900 at some £256,000.[32]

Such little evidence as exists suggests that the Radfords' building work in the Pembridge area was financed by a long series of private mortgages arranged by one of Robert Hall's executors. This was Stephen Garrard, an attorney of the firm of Garrard and James of Suffolk Street, Pall Mall. The mortgagees included a Member of Parlia-

ment, a barrister, a farmer from Southall, a titled Warwickshire clergyman, a publisher (George Bell), a Brentford confectioner and a dealer in patent medicines, as well as James Lock of the famous firm of hatters in St. James's Street, who was related to the Hall family and after becoming one of the executors of the estate was a party with Garrard in the granting of a number of leases to the Radfords.[33] Some of these mortgages were large by the standard of the time—£1,750 for No. 29 Pembridge Gardens in 1858, for instance, or £2,000 for No. 15 Pembridge Square in 1863[34]— but even before the opening of the Metropolitan Railway station at Notting Hill Gate in 1868 there was evidently no shortage of purchasers for the houses, and money was plentiful.

The whole speculation was, indeed, probably successful for all parties concerned. In their leases to the Radfords Hall's executors were able to reserve substantial ground rents, most of those in Pembridge Square being within the range of £34 to £43 per annum. Rack rents in Pembridge Gardens varied from £150 to £210 per annum. In 1860 the executors sold the fee simple of a number of houses, including No. 29 Pembridge Gardens, and in this same year a City gentleman bought both the leasehold and freehold interests in this house for £3,935. This was evidently a good bargain, for only five years later he was able to sell the house, with its back garden now enlarged, for £5,000; and in 1889 the same property changed hands again for £6,500.[35]

Architectural Description

A perambulation of the area shows that there were six well-defined types of house. The first of these is the relatively undistinguished terrace housing in the Ledbury Road district, erected by several different speculators. The second type is the double-fronted and spacious detached villa, faced with stucco, to be found in Chepstow Villas and Pembridge Villas, erected by the builder James Hall. The third type is that of the more ambitious villas of Dawson Place, usually double-fronted, with enriched cornices and other architectural ornament, by the Radfords. The fourth type is the grand monumental villa found in Pembridge Gardens for which the Radfords were also responsible, and which was to be developed to the

---

* The land forming the rear gardens of the houses on the east side of Pembridge Gardens was not part of the Hall estate. It was copyhold of the manor of Abbots Kensington and was leased by the tenant to the Radfords in 1859–60.[31]

even grander fifth variety found in Pembridge Square. The last type of house is that in the Pembridge Crescent area, but it is coarse in comparison with the earlier, gracious proportions of the houses built by Hall and the Radfords.

In Chepstow Crescent, Nos. 2–24 (even) form a curved terrace of stock brick divided vertically by stucco pilasters and with heavy stucco entablatures, an interesting attempt by several speculators to merge their buildings in a single coherent façade. These houses date from 1846–7 and, although some stucco was applied to the façades, the treatment is simple, with no elaborate mouldings or decorative work.

Ledbury Road, of the same period, consists of modest terraces of houses, with frontages of eighteen or nineteen feet, mostly of stock brick with attempts to enrich façades in some cases with stucco Corinthian pilasters and entablatures, and in others with consoles and other Italianate detail. Nos. 32–38 (even), leased to William Cullingford and William Judd, builders, in 1846, are designed as a unified whole, with giant stucco Corinthian pilasters, and rosettes over the architraves of the first-floor windows. Nos. 47–51 (odd), leased to John Snook of Paddington, builder, in 1846, are also of stock brick, with coarse stucco architraves around the window openings. Plans are of the conventional terrace type, with two rooms on each floor, and a staircase to the side.

In Chepstow Villas, Nos. 2–8 (even), leased in 1846 (Plate 68b), are characteristic specimens of the work of their builder, William Reynolds, who was also active on the Ladbroke estate, especially in Clarendon Road and Lansdowne Road. They are semi-detached villas, built of stock brick with stucco-faced ground floor and basement, strings, parapet and architraves of stucco, and poorly proportioned columns, based on the Corinthian order, in the porches.

The restrained fronts of Nos. 25–33 (odd) Chepstow Villas, detached houses built between 1851 and 1853, are by the builder James Hall. They have double-fronted symmetrical stucco façades of two storeys over basements, with widely proportioned windows on either side of the massive central door. The entablatures are enriched, and most of the houses originally had balustrades above, but in many cases these have now been removed. This type of house is markedly similar to J. B. Papworth's design for a house for Captain Capel, and other projects at Cheltenham in 1828.

Similar to houses built by Hall are those in Dawson Place, built by the Radfords in the early 1850's, again mostly of two storeys over basements, double-fronted, with enriched cornices, some having balustrades above. Nos. 6–14 (even) Dawson Place are asymmetrical, while Nos. 18–20 (even) are semi-detached.

The most outstanding houses in Dawson Place are Nos. 13–23 (odd) (Plate 68a). No. 23 is a modification of the standard double-fronted house, for bay windows have been added on either side of the Roman Doric porches forming the centrepieces. The bay windows are sub-divided by pilasters which carry an entablature continuous with that of the porch. Above the main entablature is an attic feature comprising a balustrade between two piers carrying a segmental pediment.

Nos. 25 and 27, probably designed by Thomas Wyatt, surveyor, and built in conjunction with the Radfords in 1851–2, are large houses with dentilled cornices and balustrades over the front porches. No. 29, leased by direction of the Radfords to Wyatt, has an enriched dentilled cornice and balustrades of stucco over the first-floor windows and porch.

These houses in Dawson Place may be considered as models for the larger ones which the Radfords began to build in Pembridge Gardens in 1856–7; and these in turn were the progenitors of the still larger and grander type which they subsequently erected in large numbers in both Pembridge Square and Holland Park. In Pembridge Gardens they built substantial but very closely spaced stucco-fronted detached houses in the Italianate manner, each having three or four storeys over a basement. Nos. 1–15 (odd) and 2–16 (even), with four storeys and frontages of thirty feet, have Roman Doric porches placed asymmetrically, and balconies at first-floor level carried on enriched brackets and with cast-iron balustrades (Plate 68d). The first-floor windows have moulded architraves with cornices above, and there are enriched entablatures above the second-floor windows. At Nos. 17–29 (odd) and 18–34 (even), which are mostly of three storeys with attics and have frontages of around forty feet, the porches are placed centrally, the first-floor windows are aediculated, and there are rich modillioned cornices (fig. 67). All the houses are set back behind shallow front gardens which are enclosed by stucco balustrades and large piers (only a few now survive) supporting high wooden

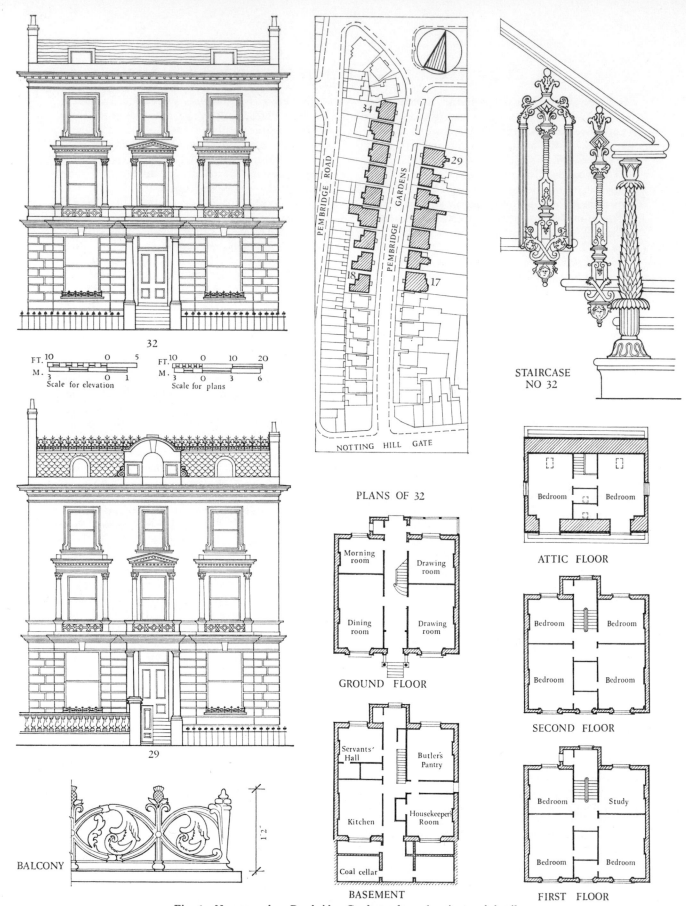

32

FT. 10   0   5
M. 3   0   1
Scale for elevation

FT. 10   0   10   20
M. 3   0   3   6
Scale for plans

34

29

18

17

PEMBRIDGE ROAD

PEMBRIDGE GARDENS

NOTTING HILL GATE

STAIRCASE
NO 32

PLANS OF 32

29

BALCONY

1'2"

GROUND FLOOR

Morning room

Drawing room

Dining room

Drawing room

BASEMENT

Servants' Hall

Butler's Pantry

Kitchen

Housekeeper's Room

Coal cellar

ATTIC FLOOR

Bedroom

Bedroom

SECOND FLOOR

Bedroom

Bedroom

Bedroom

Bedroom

FIRST FLOOR

Bedroom

Study

Bedroom

Bedroom

Fig. 67. Nos. 29 and 32 Pembridge Gardens, plans, elevations and details

gates with cast-iron panels inset. The paths leading up to the projecting porches have coloured tiles. At the rear most of the houses only have small yards, but Nos. 15–29 (odd) have substantial gardens.

The Building News followed the Radfords' work in Pembridge Gardens with interest and on the whole with approval. The houses in building in 1858–9 at the southern end were said to be 'of a very superior description, and of various sizes, to suit large or small families'. On the ground floor of each there was 'a dining-room, library and business-room', and on the half-landing of the staircase, at the rear a small conservatory and cloak-room. The two drawing-rooms were on the first floor, and on the two storeys above there were eight bedrooms and dressing-rooms and one bathroom. 'Every modern convenience' was provided throughout, and in the basement there were 'spacious kitchens, servants' halls, and other domestic arrangements'.[36]

In the larger and wider houses at the north end (Nos. 17–29 odd and 18–34 even) all the reception rooms were on the ground floor. The centrally placed entrance, nine feet in width, led into a hall, on the left of which were the dining- and breakfast-rooms, and on the right 'an elegant suite of drawing-rooms'. On the first floor there were four bedrooms, on the second five, and above were three roomy attics for servants. Another account mentions one bathroom. The basements of 'these desirable residences' were 'all fitted up with every modern improvement for domestic comfort'. Despite its approval for the placing of all the reception rooms on the ground floor, 'which appears to us a very convenient arrangement', *The Building News* nevertheless considered the planning of these houses to be in 'the old-fashioned style, having an entrance in the centre, a staircase opposite, and reception-rooms on each side'.[37]

All of the houses in Pembridge Gardens were very substantially built. The outer walls are three bricks thick in the basements, diminishing to two bricks in the ground floors, and one and a half bricks above. The roofs, covered with Welsh slates, are framed on timbers of considerable sizes. The inner partitions are of brickwork where supporting the stone wall-hung stair that runs from the basement to the first floor, but elsewhere they are of framed and braced studding generally composed of 2″ × 6″ members at 18″

centres with lath and plaster finishes. The staircase balustrades are of cast-iron, with mahogany handrails.

At No. 29 Pembridge Gardens a schedule of fixtures made in 1882 has survived, and was recently published by a later occupant of the house, Miss Irene Scouloudi. Although the house had been considerably altered by 1882, notably by a substantial extension at the rear, the schedule does nevertheless contain valuable information about the internal fittings of a large Victorian dwelling at that time. Miss Scouloudi states that 'hot and cold water were laid on at five points: the housemaid's sink and the bath-room on the second floor, the wash-bowl in the ground-floor cloakroom, the wash-bowl in the basement passage, and the stone sink in the scullery'. The sink in the butler's pantry had a cold tap only, but there was no supply to the best bedrooms on the first floor, to which water was brought in cans by a servant when rung for by means of one of the numerous bell-pulls with which many rooms were equipped. All water was heated by a '5 feet open fire range with open, high pressure boiler' in the kitchen, but there was also a smaller range in the scullery. There was a water-closet on each floor except the topmost, equipped with 'apparatus in mahogany case', that in the basement, however, being of deal. Gas was laid on, but the only light-fittings noted were at the front door and tradesmen's entrance. The mantelpieces were of marble, slate or stone, and many rooms were fitted with register stoves. Doors were in general 'grained', and had brass or black or white porcelain knobs and finger plates. The ground-floor and basement windows had folding shutters, protection being afforded by iron bars on the outside. In addition to the kitchen and scullery the basement also contained the servants' hall, butler's pantry, housekeeper's room, larder, wine cellar and coal cellar, most of these rooms being fitted with shelves, large deal cupboards and/or dressers.[38]

The census of 1861 shows that twenty-eight of the thirty-four houses in Pembridge Gardens were then occupied, and that the total number of residents was 241, of whom 98 were servants. The average number of inhabitants per house was thus 8.5, of whom 3.5 were servants. Foreign connexions, particularly with the East, were common among the householders. Of the seven merchants listed, four were Greek, and two others described themselves as 'East India Merchant' and 'Cape Merchant'. There was also a Major-General in the service of the East India Company, a retired Major-General who had been born in the East Indies, a widowed East India Company pensioner and a 'West India proprietor'. Other householders included three lawyers, and one hosier, chintz printer, bookseller, stockbroker, surveyor, colliery owner and publisher. There were five governesses to look after the children of the numerous large families. The largest single household was that of the East India merchant at No. 32, who employed five servants and a governess to look after himself and his family of ten.

In Pembridge Square the first three houses to be completed, Nos. 1–3 consec. (Plate 69c), stand at the south-west corner between Pembridge Gardens and Pembridge Road, and differ from those built later in the rest of the square. Due to their commanding situation at the principal entrance to the square they have very wide frontages, those of Nos. 2 and 3 measuring over sixty feet. They have stuccoed fronts in the Radfords' Italianate manner, and were originally intended to have three storeys above basements,[39] but at Nos. 1 and 2 one extra storey was added, and No. 3 has five storeys in all, these additions having probably all been made in the 1860's or 1870's. The Doric order is used at ground-floor level but the two original upper storeys are Corinthian, being divided vertically by pilasters with enriched capitals and surmounted by the usual entablature.

Throughout the rest of Pembridge Square (Plate 69a, b), the Radfords produced a standard detached house which they repeated over thirty times there between 1857 and 1864, and about ninety times more in Holland Park. On this design they lavished splendid workmanship, assured detail, and the best of materials. Each house is over forty-five feet in width. They are three windows wide, the central one being narrower, and have a basement, three main storeys, and an attic. The outer bays have three-sided bay windows rising to second-floor level, and are crowned by balustrades ornamented by urns, few of which now survive. The doorways are Roman Doric, with moulded entablatures containing triglyphs and dentils. The quoins are rusticated at ground-floor level and are plain above. The main entablatures of the houses are finely moulded, with fully ornamented stucco-work, modillioned and dentilled, and surmounted by an attic storey treated

with great originality. The two outer windows above the entablature are semi-circular headed with moulded architraves, and are surmounted by dentil cornices and segmental pediments, while the central window has a keystone, moulded archivolts and imposts at the springing, crowned by a bracketed cornice carrying decorative ornament above. These window structures are linked to the balustrades by consoles, as are the tall chimney-stacks on the outer walls, where huge swept brackets with large urns at their feet rise to support the consoles against the stacks.

The internal planning provides a natural development from that of the larger double-fronted houses in Pembridge Gardens which has already been described, but the rooms are bigger and more numerous, and the plasterwork more elaborate.

Iron and glass entrance canopies were added to some houses in the latter part of the nineteenth century, but the substantial cast-iron railings which once surrounded the open space in the centre of the square and enclosed the shallow front gardens of the houses have all been removed. To-day, post and wire fencing, ill-considered alterations involving the destruction of entablatures to accommodate modern windows, and general erosion of detail, have damaged Pembridge Square considerably, yet the grandeur of the mansions is still impressive.

The census of 1871 shows that temporary caretakers still occupied six houses in the square, and that the families normally resident in two others were away on the day of the count. The total number of occupants in the remaining twenty-seven houses was 349, of whom 171 were servants. The average number of inhabitants per house was thus 12·9 of whom 6·3 were servants. In sixteen households the servants equalled or exceeded the number of other residents; usually there was a butler, footman and lady's maid, and often a page. Foreign connexions were common among the householders, as in Pembridge Gardens. Eight of the nine merchants traded abroad (two, both of Scottish origin, with Australia), and there were also two indigo planters and a proprietor of houses in Spain. Other householders included an underwriter, a 'scientific chemist', and a wholesale manufacturing stationer, whose establishment of twenty-one, comprising himself and his wife, their eight children, two governesses and nine servants, was the

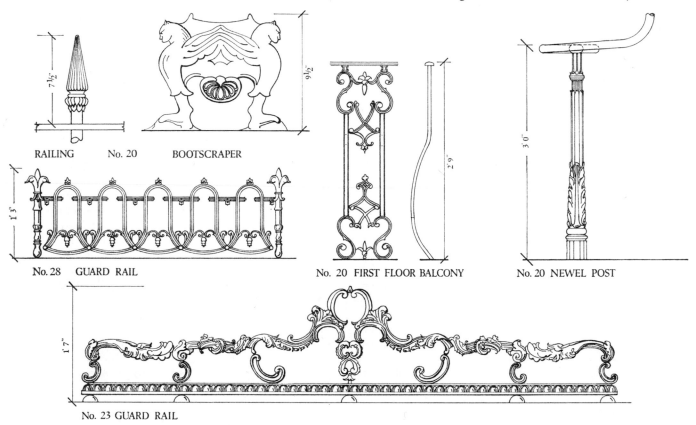

RAILING   No. 20   BOOTSCRAPER

No. 28   GUARD RAIL

No. 20 FIRST FLOOR BALCONY

No. 20 NEWEL POST

No. 23 GUARD RAIL

No. 19 GUARD RAIL

Fig. 68. Pembridge Crescent, details of ironwork

largest in the square. Only four professional men lived in such an opulent *milieu*—three lawyers and one soldier, Field-Marshal Sir John Fox Burgoyne.

Much coarser, smaller, and architecturally less interesting are the houses in Pembridge Crescent, mostly detached or semi-detached, for which two families of builders, the Cullingfords and the Maidlows, were mainly responsible (fig. 68). The Cullingfords favoured an idiosyncratic Romanesque detail whilst the Maidlows inclined to a more correct Italianate style. Typical of the Cullingfords' houses are Nos. 1, 6, 9 and 10

Pembridge Crescent, while the Maidlows' work is best represented by No. 14, a correctly proportioned house with modillioned cornice and aediculated treatment of attic window openings. W. H. Cullingford built similar houses to No. 1 Pembridge Crescent at Nos. 9–15 (odd) and Nos. 14–20 (even) Phillimore Gardens.

The remains of an interesting design of 1857 by the architect W. W. Pocock in what *The Building News* described as the 'Italian Doric' style may be found in Denbigh Road (Nos. 9 and 11), although the stucco detail has been much damaged. These houses, of three storeys and basements, had Venetian windows to the first floors, with pediment heads supported by moulded consoles. The upper lights were surrounded by plainer stucco architraves, and the houses were surmounted by enriched cornices over which were open balustraded parapets. The plans were of the usual terrace type, with two and three rooms to each floor.[40]

The Archer–Bolton estate

The spacious development of Robert Hall's twenty-eight acres, under the auspices of W. K. Jenkins or, after his death in 1850, of his executors,[41] in Pembridge Crescent, and by the Radfords in Dawson Place and Pembridge Square and Gardens, was in marked contrast with the cramped and undistinguished building which took place on the small neighbouring estate to the north. These ten acres, bounded on the north by the Portobello estate, on the east and south by Jenkins's and Hall's lands respectively, and on the west by Portobello Lane, belonged to G. S. Archer, esquire, of Wingham, Kent. He did not actively concern himself with his property, and the effective developer here was T. J. Bolton, a Paddington builder to whose nominees most of the building leases signed by Archer were granted.

Bolton himself was probably responsible for the layout, which provided an extension of Westbourne Grove westward from Jenkins's land to Portobello Lane. This was known as Archer Street until 1938, when it was renamed as part of Westbourne Grove. There were also two subsidiary parallel streets, Lonsdale Road and Bolton Road. The latter has also disappeared from the map, for it ceased to exist when the Royal Borough of Kensington built the group of flats known as the Portobello Court Estate over the site.

Bolton had commenced operations in this area in 1846, when he had taken a lease of a block of land at the north-western corner of Jenkins's estate, to the north of the east end of Lonsdale Road.[42] In December he was applying to lay a thousand feet of sewers here,[43] and in 1847–8 he took leases of two more nearby blocks of land from W. K. Jenkins.[42] By this time he was also working on Archer's land,[44] where he had a brickfield,[45] and had himself built the Earl of Lonsdale public house at the corner of Archer Street (now Westbourne Grove) and Portobello Lane.[46]

Between 1846 and 1854 he built nineteen houses in this area, an average of little more than two a year.[21] He was in fact primarily a promoter of building rather than a builder, by far the largest of whom here were George and Edwin Ingersent. They had a combined total of some 110 houses in progress in the three years 1851–3, chiefly in Bolton and Lonsdale Roads and Archer Street, but by 1854 they seem to have been in financial difficulty, and some of their houses were completed by other builders. In the nine years 1846–54 inclusive no other builder had more than a total of twelve houses each here,[21] but it is worth noting that two 'contractors' from distant parts of London, Nathaniel Levy of Tavistock Square and John Gould of Shoreditch, were both involved in 1848 in building on the north side of Westbourne Grove, where the mortgagee was the Westbourne Gardens Benefit Building Society.[47]

Building on the Archer estate was completed by about 1863. The development had been undistinguished, and Bolton Road soon degenerated into a slum. Relatively few of the original houses now survive, many of them having been demolished in recent years to make way for blocks of flats.

Linden Gardens

The third and last portion of the Ladbroke estate in Kensington consisted of the five acres of ground now occupied by Linden Gardens, Notting Hill Gate. This was in point of time the first part of the estate to be developed, a building agreement being signed in 1822, the year after James Weller Ladbroke had obtained power by a private Act of Parliament (see page 194) to grant ninety-nine-year leases. By this agreement Ladbroke agreed to let the five acres, including the existing mansion known as Hermitage House, to John Dickson of Earl Street, St. John's, Westminster, builder, for ninety-nine years at a rent of £100, rising at Michaelmas 1824 to £160.[48]

Although not a party to the agreement it is virtually certain that Ladbroke's surveyor, Thomas Allason, was responsible for the layout plan attached to it. This provided for a straight road extending from the centre of the frontage to Notting Hill High Street up the length of the ground to its northern boundary. On the east side of this road the land fronting on to the High Street was already occupied by Hermitage House, to the north of which eight paired houses were to be erected. On the west side of the road a terrace of ten houses was to be built fronting the High Street, and all the land to the north was left vacant, evidently for the large house where Allason himself later lived.[48]

All except one of the leases granted by Ladbroke between 1824 and 1827 under the terms of this agreement were made to Dickson's nominees. Dickson was therefore evidently responsible for the building work, but Allason probably designed the houses. In 1824 he was Dickson's nominee for the leases of five of the houses in the High Street, all ten of which (Nos. 26–44 even) still survive, though their fronts are now masked by projecting shop fronts. In 1827 he was again Dickson's nominee for the lease of the eight paired houses on the east side of Linden Grove[49] (as it was known until renamed Linden Gardens in 1877), only four of which (Nos. 38, 38B, 40, 42, Plate 73b) still stand, and in the same year he was also by Dickson's direction the lessee for the capital messuage, stables, gardener's cottage and nearly two acres of ground on the west side.[50]

Allason lived in this house, known as Linden Lodge (Plate 73a), until 1838–9, when he removed to Connaught Square, Paddington.[51] The quietness and sense of enclosure of Linden Grove was emphasized by the erection of gates and a lodge at the entrance from the noisy High Street;[52] the lodge still survives as No. 24B Notting Hill Gate. It was probably this quality of seclusion which attracted two other artists, William Mulready, who lived in the southernmost of the eight paired houses (now demolished) from 1828 until his death in 1863, and Thomas Creswick, who lived at the still surviving No. 42 from 1838 until 1866. In the latter year this house was affected by the building of the Metropolitan Railway. Creswick therefore moved to Mulready's now vacant house, and also, apparently, occupied the adjoining house to the north (with which it formed a pair) until his death in 1869.[53]

In 1849 Felix Ladbroke sold the freehold of all five acres of Linden Grove to Thomas Allason, subject to the existing leases.[54] After Allason's death in 1852 the estate was divided among three of his four daughters,[55] one of whom, Louisa Creswick Allason, subsequently married Arthur Bull, esquire.[56] It was probably the westward

extension of the Metropolitan Railway from Paddington to Notting Hill and thence round to South Kensington in 1864–8 which prompted these new owners to embark upon the redevelopment of the estate. Land values were no doubt rising, the railway passed under part of the curtilage of Linden Lodge, and the possession of a two-acre garden, now overlooked by the houses recently built by the Radfords in Pembridge Gardens and Square, was no longer appropriate to the rapidly changing conditions of Notting Hill Gate in the 1860's.

The redevelopment of all of Linden Grove except the eight paired houses on the east side began in 1871 and was completed by about 1878, all of the new houses being of the tall narrow terraced variety more commonly to be found in South Kensington.[57] Arthur Bull's brother Edwin Bull, who was an architect, designed the seven houses and shops which still stand in Notting Hill Gate (Nos. 14–24A even) to the east of Linden Gardens.[58] He was probably also responsible for the design of the adjoining houses to the north, Nos. 2–32 (even) Linden Gardens,[59] which stand on the former curtilage of Hermitage House, latterly used as a girls' school. On the western half of the estate, hitherto occupied by Linden Lodge and its grounds, the principal builders, with twenty-eight houses plus stables in 1873–4, were Thomas Goodwin and William White, who had previously been working on the adjoining land in Clanricarde Gardens.[21] Their capital was supplied by loans totalling £34,450 at 5 per cent interest from the Hand-in-Hand Insurance Society.[60] The other builders were John Whittlesea (ten houses), George Colls (ten), and G. and G. C. Butt (nine). By 1878 nearly seventy new houses had been built on sites formerly occupied by only ten.[21] The sole survivors to-day of the original development are Nos. 38–42 Linden Gardens and Nos. 24B–44 Notting Hill Gate.

As has already been mentioned, Nos. 38, 38B, 40 and 42 Linden Gardens were probably designed by Thomas Allason. They are modest detached houses of two storeys, built of stock brick with slate roofs and boldly overhanging eaves, very rural in character, and similar to designs found in typical country-villa pattern books of the 1820's. The large terrace houses which date from the 1870's now give Linden Gardens a somewhat cavernous appearance, their tall cliffs of ornate façades being far removed from the bosky rural charm of what was once Linden Grove.

Clanricarde Gardens

The two acres of ground now occupied by Clanricarde Gardens have belonged since 1651 to the Campden Charities, which were established in the seventeenth century by the wills of Baptist Hicks, first Viscount Campden, and Elizabeth his wife, for the benefit of the poor of the parish. The purchase money of £45 needed for the acquisition of this land is said to have been provided by Oliver Cromwell, and this small estate was in consequence sometimes referred to as 'Cromwell's Gift'.[61] The Campden Charities' other two and much larger estates are in Hyde Park Gate, South Kensington, and in Shepherd's Bush.

In 1786 the trustees of the Campden Charities let the two acres by auction to John Sylvester Dawson for eighty-one years at a rent of £38. Dawson spent over £1,500 on building two new houses and on the repair of the existing brewhouse. But the brewery subsequently fell into decay, and after the trustees had agreed to waive certain of the tenant's obligations to repair in exchange for an increase in rent, the whole property became increasingly dilapidated.[61] By the middle of the nineteenth century the narrow lane extending up the length of the estate was lined by some seventy small cottages, whose insanitary conditions in 1856 at once attracted the attention of the newly appointed Medical Officer of Health for Kensington. He informed the Vestry that the houses and their privies were in general filthy, the water supply and drainage defective, and the score of pigs kept in the backyards an intolerable nuisance. The Vestry ordered appropriate remedial measures, but two years later the pigs were still there.[62] Campden Place (as the estate was now known) had, in fact, degenerated into a noisome slum.

When the lease granted in 1786 expired in 1867 the Metropolitan railway line through Notting Hill was in course of construction and the tumbledown cottages of Campden Place had recently acquired grand new neighbours in the adjacent mansions of Pembridge Square and Kensington Palace Gardens. The trustees, who at this time were receiving a rent of £123 per annum, accordingly decided to let the estate again by public auction, and commissioned James Broadbridge, surveyor, to prepare a layout plan. This consisted of one straight street extending from Notting Hill Gate to the backs of the houses in Pembridge Square, to be lined with houses 'of a good Class', and in his report to the trustees Broadbridge recommended that 'it would be very desirable to obtain some builders of position and means who would be prepared to take the whole off the hands of the Trustees and pay a Ground Rent of at least £800 per annum'.[63]

At the auction, held at the Kensington Vestry Hall on 4 February 1869, the highest bidders were Messrs. Thomas Goodwin of Notting Hill Square and William White of Cambridge Gardens, Notting Hill, builders, who proffered a rent of £1,040 per annum for a term of ninety-nine years. By the building agreement signed on the same day they covenanted to build not less than fifty-three houses, as well as six shops on the frontage to Notting Hill. The houses were to cost at least £1,200 each, and the shops at least £1,000, making a total investment of some £70,000, exclusive of expenditure on the road and sewer. The plans and elevations of the houses were to be prepared by Goodwin and White, but were to be subject to the approval of Broadbridge, the trustees' surveyor, and all building work was to be completed by midsummer 1872.[61]

This programme was in fact completed by midsummer 1873, when the last three leases were granted to Goodwin and White,[61] whose building operations were (as previously mentioned) financed in 1872–4 by loans from the Hand-in-Hand Insurance Society.[60] The pigs, the cottages (and of course their inhabitants) and even the very name, Campden Place, were all swept away, and in Clanricarde Gardens there arose fifty-one tall narrow terraced houses (Plate 73c), plus another six with shops fronting on to Notting Hill Gate, all six storeys in height. It must have been a great success, for (as has been previously noted) Goodwin and White at once went on to more work of almost identical character in Linden Gardens.

Convent of Our Lady of Sion, Chepstow Villas

This building, consisting of four storeys over a basement, with an attic storey, is constructed of

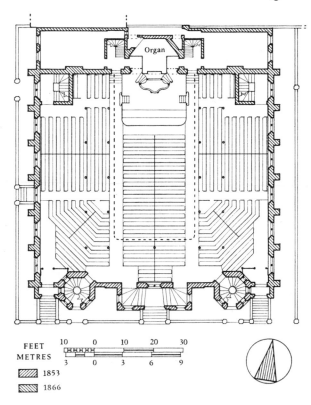

FEET 10 0 10 20 30
METRES 3 0 3 6 9

1853
1866

Fig. 69. Westbourne Grove Baptist Chapel, plan

dark red bricks, and is situated at the corner of Chepstow Villas and Denbigh Road. It was designed by A. Young in 1892–3,[64] and is one of the bulkiest buildings in the area, quite foreign to the adjacent stucco-faced houses. The style owes much to Dutch and North German institutional building of the period, the façade being enlivened by carved, moulded and rubbed brickwork. There is a giant order of Ionic pilasters which rise from the first floor to support a simplified entablature with a large stone cornice carried on brackets. A tower of mildly Italianate appearance stands at the south-west corner of the building.

The chapel is a severe and restrained work in the Italian manner of the late eighteenth century. It consists of a four-bay vaulted nave with three-bay aisles, and a chancel of one bay. There is a gallery at the liturgical west end which contains the organ.

Part of the building is used as a convent school for girls.

Baptist Chapel, Westbourne Grove
Fig. 69

This building stands at the corner of Westbourne Grove and Ledbury Road and was opened on 5 April 1853. It was designed by C. G. Searle[65] in a freely treated version of the Early English Gothic style, and consists of a sub-basement (now sealed off), a semi-basement now used as a warehouse and the chapel above. The aisles were widened in 1866.

The symmetrical south front to Westbourne Grove has three lancet lights over a porch flanked by two octagonal towers which were originally capped by spirelets. Each bay of the side walls is pierced by three lancets (lighting the semi-basement), by a pointed arch containing two lancet windows, and by a quatrefoil light. The gables over the aisles and the spirelets on the south front were destroyed by enemy action during the war of 1939–45.

The interior of the chapel is broad and spacious, three bays long, consisting of a nave and tall aisles. There is no clerestory. The wooden arcades are based on the Marian Tudor style, and are carried on cast-iron columns with foliate capitals, which still retain some of the original colouring. Intermediate columns of cast iron support the gallery, added in 1859, which extends round three sides of the building. The north wall of the nave is pierced by a large pointed arch containing the organ within a delicate wooden Gothic case. The pulpit, placed centrally below, is on a dais with cast-iron balustrades, concealing the baptismal pool.

SELECT LIST OF BUILDING LESSORS AND LESSEES IN THE CHEPSTOW VILLAS AND PEMBRIDGE SQUARE AREA

Except where otherwise stated, the dates refer to the years in which the leases were granted: these are not always the date of actual building. Lessors' and lessees' addresses are given only for those resident outside Kensington. Many houses are not included in this list owing to lack of evidence. The chief source is the Middlesex Land Register in the Greater London Record Office at County Hall.

Chepstow Crescent, east side

2, 4	J. W. Ladbroke to George Stevenson of Paddington, plumber, 1846.
6	Ladbroke to James Swinburn of St. Marylebone, carpenter, 1846.
8	Ladbroke to Thomas Aitchison of St. Marylebone, carpenter, 1846.
10	Ladbroke to Thomas Bryan, 1847.
12, 14	Ladbroke to Stevenson, 1846.
16–20 even	Ladbroke to John Powell, 1846.
22, 24	Ladbroke to Stevenson, 1846.

Chepstow Crescent, west side

1–13 odd	J. W. Ladbroke to Frederick Woods of Paddington and William Wheeler, builders, 1846. Nos. 9–13 now demolished.
15	Ladbroke to Thomas Cole of Hereford Road, Paddington, carpenter, 1846. Now remodelled or rebuilt.
17	Ladbroke to Henry Beedle of Paddington, plasterer, 1846.
19–25 odd	W. K. Jenkins to Woods and Wheeler, 1847.
27	Jenkins to William Nicholls of Paddington, builder, 1847. Demolished.
29–37 odd	Jenkins to Joseph Clutterbuck brickmaker, 1847. Nos. 29–33 now demolished.

Chepstow Place, west side

2–8 even	T. W. Budd, solicitor, of Bedford Row, to James Hall, builder, 1850.
10–44 even	About to be built in 1850 by John Maidlow of St. John's Wood, builder. Nos. 10, 12, 30–34 demolished
46	Executors of Robert Hall to Francis Radford the younger, builder, 1852.

Chepstow Place, east side

15, 17	J. W. Ladbroke to George Treadaway of Paddington, draper, 1847.
21	Budd to John Lawrence of St. Pancras, carpenter, 1847.
23–33 odd	Budd to Treadaway, 1849.
51–69 odd	Built by James Herd of Paddington, builder, 1861

Chepstow Villas, north side

2–8 even	J. W. Ladbroke to William Reynolds, builder, 1846.
10–16 even	Built by John Wadge, builder, 1850.
18, 20	Ladbroke to William Judd, builder, 1846.
22, 24	W. K. Jenkins by direction of William Cullingford, builder, to Judd, 1846.
26–32 even	Jenkins to Cullingford, 1847–8.
34	Robert Hall of Clifford Street by direction of Jenkins to Cullingford, 1847. Demolished.
42–52 even	Built by James Hall, builder, 1851. No. 48 demolished.
54–62 even	See page 252.

Chepstow Villas, south side

1–11 odd	Built 1847–9 by George Passmore of Edgware Road, plumber. Nos. 1–7 leased by F. Ladbroke to W. Allen of Avery Row, Mayfair, ironmonger, 1850.
15	Jenkins to Cullingford.
17–23 odd	Executors of Robert Hall by direction of Jenkins to Cullingford, 1849–50.
25–33 odd	Built by James Hall, builder, 1851–3.
35–41 odd	See page 252.

SELECT LIST OF BUILDING LESSORS AND LESSEES IN THE CHEPSTOW VILLAS AND PEMBRIDGE SQUARE AREA

Clanricarde Gardens

1–51 consec.	Built by Thomas Goodwin and William White, builders, 1869–73.

Dawson Place, north side

6	Executors of Robert Hall to William Radford and Francis Radford the younger, builders, 1852.
8	Execs. of R. Hall to F. Radford the younger, 1851.
10–14 even	Execs. of R. Hall to W. Radford, 1852.
16–24 even	Execs. of R. Hall by direction of W. Radford to H. Pook of Old Kent Road, gentleman, 1850.
26	Execs. of R. Hall by direction of W. Radford to W. Radford of Camden Town, builder, 1850.
28, 30	Execs. of R. Hall to W. Radford, 1850.

Dawson Place, south side

7–11 odd	Built by William Radford and Francis Radford the younger, 1851. Nos. 3 and 5 probably also built at this time.
13–23 odd	Built by W. Radford and F. Radford the younger, 1852.
25, 27	Probably designed by Thomas Wyatt of the Strand, surveyor, 1851–2, and built in conjunction with W. Radford and F. Radford the younger.
29	Execs. of R. Hall by direction of W. Radford and F. Radford the younger to Wyatt, 1851.

Denbigh Road, west side

12–24 even	Execs. of W. K. Jenkins by direction of James Hall, builder, to Henry Cullingford, builder, 1853. William Cullingford, builder, also involved.

Denbigh Road, east side

9, 11	Built in 1856–9 by J. D. Cowland, builder, W. W. Pocock, architect.
17–23 odd	Execs. of Robert Hall to W. Cullingford, 1851.

Denbigh Terrace

13–26 consec.	Execs. of W. K. Jenkins by direction of James Hall, builder, to various local builders, 1852–5.

Ledbury Road, east side

32–36 even	J. W. Ladbroke to William Cullingford, builder, 1846.
38	Ladbroke to William Judd, builder, 1846.

Ledbury Road, west side

39–43 odd	Ladbroke to Cullingford, 1846.
Pembridge Castle public house.	Ladbroke to Cullingford, 1846.
47–51 odd	Ladbroke to John Snook of Paddington, builder, 1846.
53, 55	Ladbroke to John Pilkington of St. Marylebone, gentleman, to Snook, 1846.
57–61 odd	Built by William Turner, builder, 1850.

Linden Gardens

38–42 even	J. W. Ladbroke by direction of John Dickson of Horseferry Road, builder, to Thomas Allason, surveyor, 1827.

Notting Hill Gate, north side

2–12 even	Built by Thomas Goodwin and William White, builders, 1869–73.
14–24A even	Designed by Edwin Bull, and built by J. D. Cowland, builder, 1871.
26–34 even	J. W. Ladbroke by direction of John Dickson of Earl Street, St. John's, Westminster, to Thomas Allason, surveyor, 1824.
36, 38	Ladbroke by direction of Dickson to Archibald Hogg of Edgware Road, flour factor, 1824.
40, 42	Ladbroke to Dickson, 1827.
44	Ladbroke by direction of Dickson to William Allason the elder, gentleman, 1824.
Devonshire Arms public house.	Built by William Radford and Francis Radford the younger, builders, 1853–4. Rebuilt.

Pembridge Crescent, east side

1, 2, 5, 6	Sold by executors of W. K. Jenkins to William Henry Cullingford, builder, in 1859, when in course of building.
3, 4	Execs. of Jenkins by direction of Charles Maidlow, auctioneer, to Jane and Frances Maidlow, 1854.
7, 8	Execs. of Jenkins by direction of C. Maidlow to Christopher Garwood of Paddington, builder, 1854.

SELECT LIST OF BUILDING LESSORS AND LESSEES IN THE CHEPSTOW VILLAS
AND PEMBRIDGE SQUARE AREA

9, 10   Execs. of Jenkins to Cullingford, 1859.

11, 12   Execs. of Jenkins by direction of C. Maidlow to William Maidlow, builder, 1854. No. 12 now demolished.

13, 14   Execs. of Jenkins by direction of C. Maidlow and John Maidlow, builder, to W. Maidlow, 1853. No. 13 now demolished.

Pembridge Crescent, west side

15–19 consec. Execs. of Jenkins to Henry Cullingford, builder, 1854.

20–22 consec. Sold by execs. of Jenkins to William Henry Cullingford in 1858. Completed 1859.

23–25 consec. Execs. of Jenkins to William Cullingford, builder, 1854.

26, 27   Execs. of Jenkins to W. H. Cullingford, 1858.

28, 29   Execs. of Jenkins to James Hall, builder, 1854.

Pembridge Gardens

1–34 consec.   Built by William and Francis Radford, builders, 1857–9. Nos. 31, 33 demolished.

Pembridge Mews Built by William Cullingford, builder, 1849–51.

Pembridge Place, east side

1, 3–9 consec. Built by James Hall, builder, 1849–1851.

2   J. W. Ladbroke to T. W. Budd of Bedford Row, solicitor, to Benjamin Broadbridge of Albany Street, architect, 1846.

10   Built by Francis Radford, builder, 1851.

Pembridge Place, west side

11, 12   Executors of R. Hall by direction of William Radford, builder, to H. Pook of Old Kent Road, gentleman, 1850.

14–18 consec. Built by James Hall, builder, 1849–1851.

Pembridge Road, east side

2–26 even   Built by William Radford and Francis Radford the younger, builders, 1853 onwards.

28–34 even   Built by Henry Gilbert, 1854.

36–48 even   Built by William Yeo, builder, 1854.

Pembridge Square

1–35 consec.   Built by William and Francis Radford, builders, 1856–64. Nos. 4, 5 demolished.

Pembridge Villas, north-west side

2   J. W. Ladbroke to George Stevenson of Queen's Road, Paddington, plumber, 1845.

4   Ladbroke to T. W. Budd of Bedford Row, solicitor, to James Hall of St. Pancras, builder, 1846.

6   Ladbroke to James Hall, now of 4 Pembridge Villas, builder, 1847.

8   Budd to Hall, 1847.

10, 12   Budd at nomination of Hall to C. Hedge of Pimlico, coal merchant, 1848.

14, 16   Budd to Hall, 1848.

18, 20   Budd to Hall, 1848–9.

22   Ladbroke to W. K. Jenkins to Stevenson, 1846.

24, 26   Ladbroke to T. Gurney of Park Street, Grosvenor Square, baker, to Stevenson, 1846–8.

28, 30   Jenkins by direction of Charles Patch of Paddington, builder, to J. D. Bishop of Brewer Street, esquire, and Henry Shirlock of Paddington, plumber, respectively, 1847.

32–40 even   Built by or under aegis of William Weston (or Western), builder, lessee from Felix Ladbroke for Nos. 32 and 34, 1852–3. Lessee of Nos. 36 and 38, Edward Western, Ladbroke's solicitor.

46, 48   Execs. of R. Hall to William Houston of Paddington, plasterer, 1849. The local builder William Henry Cullingford was living at No. 46 in 1861, with his wife and sister-in-law. He was then aged thirty-one, and employed two servants.

50–56 even   Execs. of R. Hall to Charles Maidlow, auctioneer, 1852–3.

58–66 even   Execs. of R. Hall to James Hall, 1851–5.

Pembridge Villas, south-east side

9, 11   Built by James Hall, 1849.

SELECT LIST OF BUILDING LESSORS AND LESSEES IN THE CHEPSTOW VILLAS AND PEMBRIDGE SQUARE AREA

13, 15	J. W. Ladbroke to Budd to Henry Vallance, gentleman, to (respectively) George Trigg of Paddington and William Speller of Berkeley Street, builders, 1846.
17	Jenkins to Trigg, 1847.
19, 21	Built by Trigg, 1849.
23	Built by Trigg, 1852.
25–31 odd	Bay windows added to ground storey, 1865. Date of building not known.
33, 35	Jenkins to Francis Radford the younger, builder, 1849.
37–41 odd	Jenkins to F. Radford the younger, 1848.
43–49 odd	Execs. of R. Hall to William Radford, builder, 1850.
51–55 odd	Built by W. Radford, 1855.

Portobello Road, east side

2–80 even	Most of these houses built under leases from the executors of W. K. Jenkins to William or Henry Cullingford, builders, 1854–8. No. 76 demolished.

Westbourne Grove, north side

122–152 even	W. K. Jenkins to James Bennett, builder, 1847–9.

154–164 even	Built by James Hall, builder, c. 1850. Nos. 158, 160 demolished.
166, 168	J. W. Ladbroke to John Foster of Paddington, 'plumassier', 1847.
170–176 even	Built by John Maidlow, builder, 1852.
178–192 even	Jenkins to T. J. Bolton, contractor, of Paddington, 1848. Nathaniel Levy of Tavistock Square, contractor, John Gould of Shoreditch, contractor, and William Higgs of Buckingham Place, New Road, builder, all also involved.

Westbourne Grove, south side

155–169 odd	Built by James Hall, 1848–1850.
211	Jenkins by direction of Bolton to T. Reed of Lambeth, builder, 1849. Bolton probably responsible for all of Nos. 207–225.
243, 245	Probably built 1856–9 by J. D. Cowland, builder, to the design of W. W. Pocock, architect. See also Nos. 9 and 11 Denbigh Road.
281, Earl of Lonsdale public house.	G. S. Archer, esquire, to T. J. Bolton, builder, 1847.

CHAPTER XI

The Norland Estate

THE Norland estate (fig. 70) consisted of some fifty-two acres of ground, bounded on the east by the streets now known as Portland Road and Pottery Lane, on the south by Holland Park Avenue (formerly the Uxbridge road) and on the west by the boundary of the parishes of Kensington and Hammersmith. Building development began in 1839, and except in the northern extremity of the estate was largely completed within a dozen years, although some houses were not then occupied.* The author of most of the principal components of the layout plan was Robert Cantwell, who also designed several ranges of four-storey terraced houses.

The estate was acquired in the early years of the eighteenth century by Thomas Greene, a wealthy brewer of St. Margaret's, Westminster, after whose death in 1740 it passed to his infant grandson, Edward Burnaby Greene, later to achieve fame as a poet and translator. His inheritance included a fortune of £4,000 per annum, which enabled him to live in some splendour at Norlands, the capital messuage at the south-east corner of the estate, near the site of the modern No. 130 Holland Park Avenue.[1] But he also accumulated large debts, and in 1761 he granted a lease of the house and twelve acres of the adjoining land for an annual rent of £100.[2]

The first tenant was Thomas Marquois, 'Professor of Artillery and Fortification', who used the house as an academy for the civil or military education of sons of the gentry. Board and lodging, plus instruction in Greek, Latin, French, writing and arithmetic could be had for thirty guineas a year, but fortification, mathematics, navigation, drawing, geography, dancing, fencing and riding were all charged as extras. Marquois' prospectus contains a plan of the academy and its grounds, which were indeed very well suited to his purposes. Besides the house itself there were stables, a manege or riding house, a fives court, a cricket ground, gravelled drives for hack riding, and an artificial 'mount' from which the various activities of the pupils could be kept under constant review. The whole twelve-acre area, which extended from Portland Road to the west side of Norland Square and northward roughly as far as Penzance Street, was surrounded on three sides by a brick wall and on the west by a ha-ha.[3]

Despite these advantages, however, Marquois' régime only lasted for four years, and in 1765 the lease of the academy and its grounds, including the horses, the horse furniture and even the four Alderney cows which had supplied the school milk, were put up for sale by auction. The next headmaster, Abraham Elim, appears to have placed much less emphasis on the military side of the school's curriculum, but this tendency was reversed by Lieutenant Bartholomew Reynolds, who succeeded Elim in 1785. He acquired the patronage of the Prince of Wales, which enabled him to give the school the high-sounding new title of 'the Royal Military Academy, Norland-house'. The syllabus was now directed towards preparing boys for the army, and the young gentlemen were taught not only to draw plans of fortifications but even to 'construct works upon the ground belonging to the Academy ... and fit for real service'.[2]

In 1788 the freeholder, Edward Burnaby Greene, died, heavily in debt,[4] and in 1792 all his estates in and near London were sold by auction. The whole of the Norland estate was bought by Benjamin Vulliamy, the watchmaker of Pall Mall, who paid £4,270 for some forty acres of the land (equivalent to £107 per acre), plus an unknown amount for Norland House and its twelve-acre curtilage.[5] Shortly afterwards the Royal Military Academy came to an end, and Vulliamy took up residence at Norlands.[6]

The estate remained in the ownership of the Vulliamy family until 1839. In 1825 Norland House was destroyed by fire. Two years later twenty-five acres of the estate, including the

---

* See page 295 for a select list of building lessors and lessees on the Norland estate.

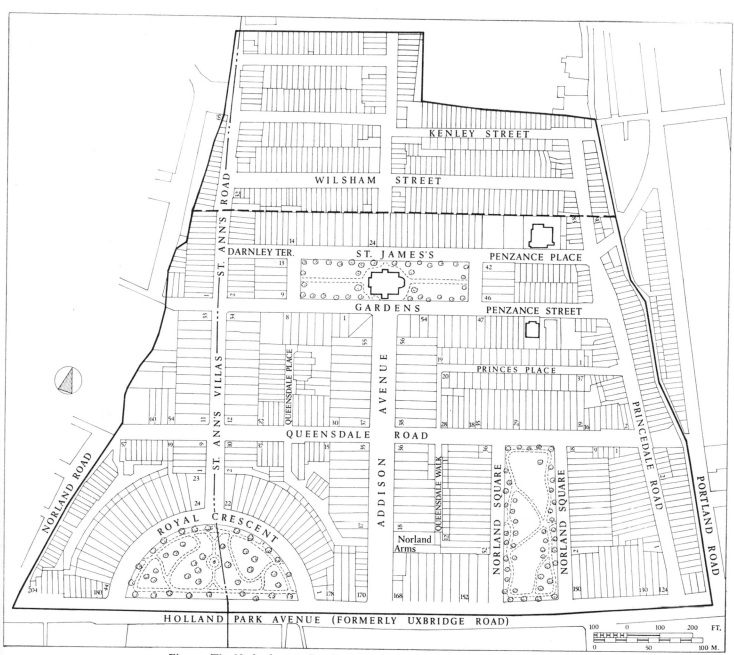

Fig. 70. The Norland estate. Based on the Ordnance Surveys of 1863–7 and 1894–6
————— ––– ––– denotes line of Counter's Creek sewer
––– ––– ––– denotes southern boundary of area sold to Morrison

ruins of the mansion, were offered by the architect, Ambrose Poynter, evidently acting on behalf of the then owner, the clockmaker Benjamin Lewis Vulliamy, to the Justices of the Peace for Middlesex, who were at that time searching for a site for the erection of a county lunatic asylum. The property offered included an ample water supply derived from an artesian well 260 feet in depth which had been sunk at great expense beside the mansion in 1791, but the very high price of £15,875, equivalent to £635 per acre, was probably the reason for the magistrates' rejection of the proposal in favour of a site at Hanwell.[7] The well, now filled up, is commemorated by an inscribed stone in the back yard of No. 130 Holland Park Avenue.

By the mid 1830's, however, the Norland estate was becoming eligible for speculative building. The development of the adjoining estate to the east had been started as early as 1821, when J. W. Ladbroke had promoted an Act of Parliament enabling him to grant ninety-nine-year leases, while to the south the first building leases had been granted on Lord Holland's lands in 1824. Progress on both these estates had been slow after the collapse of the building boom of the early 1820's, but on both the Holland and more particularly on the Norland estate, a new factor was introduced in 1836 by the incorporation of the Birmingham, Bristol and Thames Junction Railway. The object of this ill-fated enterprise was to provide an outlet for the London and Birmingham and the Great Western Railways to the Thames west of London by the construction of a line from the neighbourhood of Willesden to the Kensington Canal. The route authorized by an enabling Act of 1836[8] extended parallel with, but a few yards outside, the western boundary of the Norland estate, across the Uxbridge road at Shepherd's Bush and southward through part of Lord Holland's land.

It was not, however, the prospect of suburban passenger traffic, but the drainage problems posed by the construction of the railway, which provided a fillip to building development on the Norland estate. Between the Uxbridge and Hammersmith roads the railway was to extend along or very close to the course of the Counter's Creek sewer, the natural open ditch or watercourse which discharged surface water from the western parts of Kensington into the Kensington Canal and thence into the Thames. In 1837–8 the Westminster

Commissioners of Sewers insisted that the railway company must divert the Counter's Creek to a new line further east throughout its whole length from Warwick Road in South Kensington to the northern boundary of the Norland estate (a distance of over a mile), and ultimately the company had to submit.[9]

The new sewer, as built by the railway company in 1838–9, extended, from south to north, along the line of the present Holland Road and Holland Villas Road, across the Uxbridge road at the centre of Royal Crescent, and thence up the present St. Ann's Villas and St. Ann's Road (see fig. 70). The contractor was Stephen Bird, a Kensington builder of note and owner of a brickfield to the north of the Norland estate; the total cost was £9,547, of which the Commissioners of Sewers contributed £1,500.[10]

The effect of this diversion was to provide Benjamin Lewis Vulliamy with greatly improved drainage facilities for his estate, at no cost to himself. In September 1838, when discussions between the Commissioners of Sewers and the railway company were still proceeding, he was already celebrating his good fortune by negotiations for the sale of the estate,[11] his prospective purchaser being William Kingdom, a building speculator who was probably already active in the development of Westbourne Terrace and Hyde Park Gardens, Paddington.[12] Kingdom's architect was Robert Cantwell, who besides having been the lessee between 1826 and 1833 for several houses on the Ladbroke estate, was also a member of the Westminster Commission of Sewers.[13] In September 1838, as surveyor to the Norland estate, he approved the proposed line of diversion, insisting, however, that the new sewer should be covered in as far north as the backs of the projected houses in Royal Crescent.[11]

In the event Kingdom did not purchase the Norland estate, for in January 1839 he assigned the benefit of his agreement with Vulliamy to a solicitor, Charles Richardson, for £5,932. The circumstances of the sale are obscure, but it appears that Kingdom's assignment to Richardson was in payment of a mortgage debt, possibly on Kingdom's property in Paddington. Richardson also paid Vulliamy £14,058, making his aggregate recorded outlay £19,990, but it is not clear whether this was the consideration for the purchase of the whole of the Norland estate, which would represent a price of c. £384 per acre, or only for some four-fifths of it.[14] Whatever he may have paid for it, it is, however, certain that Richardson became the freehold owner of all fifty-two acres of the estate.*

Charles Richardson was the son of the Charles Richardson who had kept a well-known coffee house and hotel in the Piazza in Covent Garden in the early years of the nineteenth century. After the father's death in 1827 this business had been continued by another son, Walter Richardson, wine merchant, while Charles junior (later the purchaser of the Norland estate) had entered the legal profession, being admitted as an attorney in 1817. Two years later he was living and practising at No. 28 Golden Square, where he remained with a succession of partners for many years. After his father's death he had inherited the famous lion's head letter-box which had originally been at Button's coffee house in Covent Garden in the days of Addison and Steele, and in 1828 he published a short account of it before selling it to the sixth Duke of Bedford. In 1830 he was Under Sheriff of London and Middlesex, a relative, Sir William Henry Richardson, being Sheriff in that year. By the early 1840's his firm in Golden Square had become parliamentary agents, and were acting as solicitors to the Club Chambers Association of Regent Street and the Medical, Invalid, and General Life Assurance Society.[16] Despite these normal ramifications in the affairs of a busy London solicitor, the development of the Norland estate was to be his main concern for the next dozen or more years until nemesis of somewhat bizarre form overtook him.

With such extensive business experience as this Richardson had no difficulty in raising capital for the development of his estate, and in 1840–1 he borrowed £25,000 from another firm of solicitors, plus £11,500 from the partners of a West End private bank, all at 5 per cent interest. Soon afterwards he transferred the greater part of these mortgages to a retired City merchant, from whom he obtained further advances. By 1844 his total liabilities amounted to about £45,000,[17] much of the money being needed for loans to builders and for the construction of nearly three miles of sewers approved by the Commissioners.[18]

The layout plan of the southern part of the Norland estate, including Royal Crescent, Addison Avenue and Norland Square, was the work of Robert Cantwell.[19] His principal street, Addison Avenue, was originally known as Addison Road North, for when it was laid out it formed an extension of Lord Holland's Addison Road to the south of the Uxbridge road. This wide straight road extends north through the centre of the estate, and is bisected by Queensdale Road (formerly Queen's Road) which extends east–west across its whole width. Within the angles of the cross thus formed Cantwell provided in the south-west quarter a large crescent facing the Uxbridge road and broken in the centre by another north-south road, St. Ann's Villas and St. Ann's Road—an ingenious arrangement evidently occasioned by the need for unobstructed passage for the recently diverted Counter's Creek sewer. In the south-east quarter he provided a square (Norland Square), open to the Uxbridge road at its south end. The other two important elements in the layout as eventually completed, St. James's Church, placed at the northern axis of Addison Avenue, and the square (now St. James's Gardens) in which it stands, may, however, have not been formulated until after Cantwell's connexion with the estate had apparently ended;[20] but they are certainly logical extensions of his work.

The idea of a crescent broken in the centre by a straight road leading northward had emerged during the negotiations over the diversion of the Counter's Creek sewer, the future Royal Crescent and St. Ann's Villas and St. Ann's Road being adumbrated on two sewer plans of 1837–8.[21] At this time Cantwell was acting for William Kingdom, but when Richardson bought the estate in January 1839 he retained Cantwell as surveyor. Cantwell's connexion with the Norland estate appears, however, to have been very short (as in the case of James Thomson on the Ladbroke estate), and the precise extent of his contribution to its development is hard to assess. The Royal Academy exhibition of 1839 contained an item entitled 'Perspective view of Norland [i.e. Royal] Crescent now erecting at Notting Hill from the designs of and under the superintendence of R.

* In 1843 Benjamin Lewis Vulliamy lent £850 on mortgage on the security of each of two houses in Norland Square (Nos. 45 and 46),[15] and in 1844 his son, Lewis Vulliamy, became the architect of St. James's Church. These are the only two known connexions between the Vulliamy family and the estate after its sale in 1839, and there is no reason to suppose that the family retained any residual interest in the property. Nor is there any reason to suppose that Lewis Vulliamy was responsible for the layout of the estate. A detailed list of all his works which he himself compiled shortly before his death in 1871 mentions the church of St. James, but not the estate.

Cantwell'. This probably relates to an undated lithograph showing Royal Crescent and the ranges of houses in the Uxbridge road as far east as the west corner of Norland Square, all of which were described as 'From the designs of Robert Cantwell, Architect'. Another, very slightly different, version of this design is reproduced on Plate 70a. In 1840 Cantwell was applying on Richardson's behalf to the Westminster Commissioners for permission to lay sewers in the Uxbridge road,[22] and in 1842 Richardson granted him a building lease for No. 52 Norland Square.[23] Royal Crescent was therefore clearly built to Cantwell's designs, as also, probably were the terraced ranges of houses in Holland Park Avenue and Norland Square. But there is no evidence that Cantwell was in any way connected with the formation of any of the other streets on the estate, or with the design of any of the houses in them, or that he ever acted on Richardson's behalf after September 1840.

Thereafter most of Richardson's applications to the Commissioners of Sewers for permission to lay sewers in streets to be formed on the estate were presented by another surveyor, Joseph Dunning, the first being in February 1841.[24] At this time Dunning was probably an assistant of Cantwell's, for a plan of the estate presented to the Commissioners in October 1841 (Plate 70c) is signed 'Joseph Dunning for Mr. Cantwell', but by 1843 Dunning had an address of his own, independent of Cantwell.[25] He continued to act on Richardson's behalf until at least 1851,[26] and also from time to time on behalf of two of the principal speculators on the estate,[27] but there is no evidence that he designed any of the houses there. He subsequently built a number of houses nearby in Portland Road,[28] and also in Drayton Gardens, South Kensington.

Building on the Norland estate began on the frontage to the Uxbridge road where Richardson granted the first building leases in October 1839, for the ground between Royal Crescent and Addison Avenue. On an estate so far from the centre of London one way to attract builders was for the ground landlord to build himself, and these first leases were in fact granted by Richardson to his own trustee and man of business, J. C. Bennett.[29] To the east of Addison Avenue a row of four houses which had been built some years earlier was incorporated, probably after renovation and refronting, into a new range of eleven houses extending from Addison Avenue to Norland Square.[30] The westerly six houses here were probably built by William Slark of Gordon Square, esquire, to whom Richardson sold the freehold of the site in 1840.[31]

The principal undertaker on the Uxbridge road frontage, and indeed on the whole estate, was Charles Stewart, a wealthy barrister who had served as Member of Parliament for Penryn in 1831–2.[32] Between 1840 and 1846 he took building leases from Richardson for some 150 houses on the estate, as well as for a number of coach-houses and stables. His principal ventures were in Royal Crescent (where he had 43 houses) and St. Ann's Villas (34), but he also involved himself in Holland Park Avenue, Queensdale Road, Norland Square and Norland Road, in the last of which the Stewart Arms public house (now rebuilt) still commemorates his name.

His first investment was in Holland Park Avenue, where in 1840–1 Richardson granted him ninety-nine-year building leases for all except one of the four-storey stucco-fronted houses in the range (Nos. 124–150 even) between Princedale (formerly Princes) Road and Norland Square; the annual ground rent was £20 per house.[33] The excepted house, No. 130, had a large yard and workshops at the back, and its curtilage included the well which had formerly served Norland House. Here Richardson installed a steam engine to raise water for the supply of the estate, and the house itself was used from 1841 to 1846 as the Norland Estate Office.[34]

In April 1841 Richardson applied to the London Assurance Corporation for a loan of £50,000 at 4 per cent interest on the security of the estate, to enable him 'to assist the builders, and thereby facilitate the letting of the ground'.* In his application Richardson stated that ground rents totalling £1,331 per annum had been formed, secured upon agreements for the building of 150 houses, of which about half had already been built and the remainder would be built in the course of the ensuing summer. Twenty-two acres in the northern part of the estate had been leased to a brickmaker for £1,000 per annum, and the total

---

* It was probably these loans offered by Richardson to prospective building lessees which attracted a number of builders to the Norland estate from such distant parts of the metropolitan area as Deptford, Edmonton, Kingston, Lambeth, Rotherhithe and Wandsworth, as well, of course, as from Kensington and Bayswater.

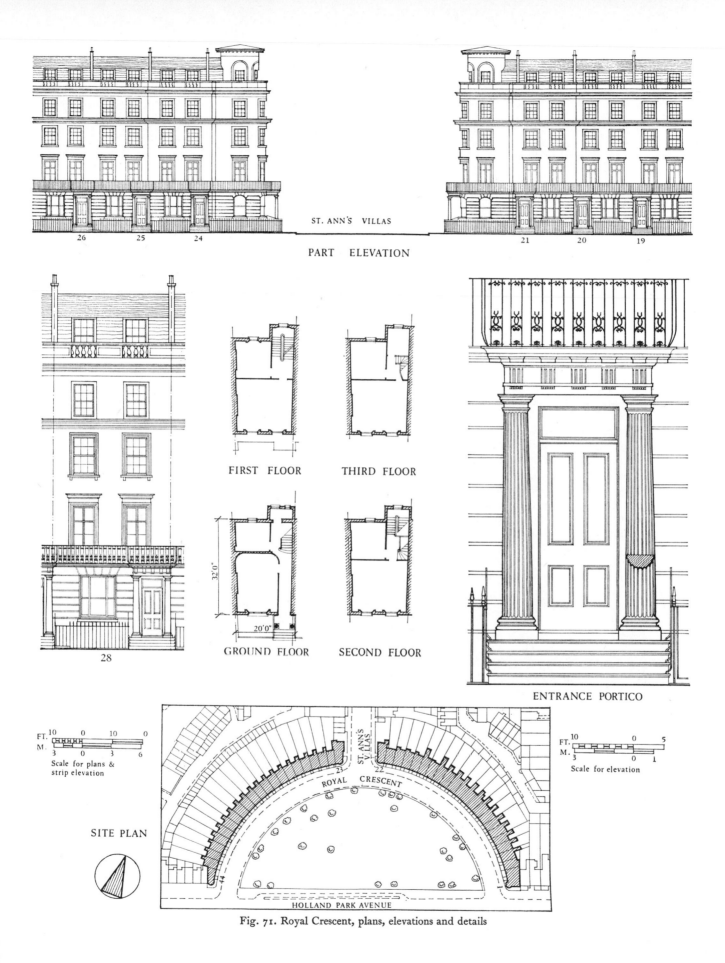

ST. ANN'S VILLAS

PART ELEVATION

FIRST FLOOR   THIRD FLOOR

GROUND FLOOR   SECOND FLOOR

28

ENTRANCE PORTICO

FT.
M.
Scale for plans &
strip elevation

SITE PLAN

ROYAL CRESCENT

ST. ANN'S V. LIAS

HOLLAND PARK AVENUE

FT.
M.
Scale for elevation

Fig. 71. Royal Crescent, plans, elevations and details

value of the estate, he claimed, now amounted to £123,000.

The London Assurance instructed its own surveyor, William Sabine, to inspect the property, and the report which he presented a few days later was not so sanguine. Fifty-five houses were 'in various states of forwardness', but many others for which the ground had been let were not sufficiently advanced to secure the ground rent, and some had not even been started at all; the total value of the estate was considerably lower than Richardson's estimate.[35]

After some hesitation the Corporation decided to offer Richardson a loan of £30,000 at 5 per cent interest, plus an undertaking to make further advances as building development proceeded. But when two months later, in June 1841, Richardson wished to take up this offer, Sabine presented such a gloomy supplementary report that the Corporation demanded additional security—the tenant of the brickfield must be a party to the loan. Richardson refused, however, to accept these terms, and the negotiation ended.[36]

In his second report Sabine had stated that 'Five out of the 6 large houses built by Mr. Richardson [Nos. 1 Royal Crescent and 170–178 even Holland Park Avenue] are still unlet, as are also 6 belonging to Mr. Slark [Nos. 158–168 even], and 12 out of 13 built by Mr. Stewart [Nos. 124–150 even], all on the high road. There is no more ground let, and three of the former holders of ground have given up their interest to other parties ... The premises intended for Mr. R's own occupation [No. 130] are in a very forward state, but on the whole the speculation does not appear to me so favourable as at my last view.'[37]

The main obstacle to development at this stage was, in fact, not so much lack of capital to build as lack of people willing to live in houses still felt to be so far out of London. Stewart's houses in Holland Park Avenue were not all occupied until 1845, while in Royal Crescent, of which he took building leases in 1842–3, the western half was not fully occupied until 1848, nor Nos. 15–22 in the eastern half until as late as 1856.[6]

Royal Crescent (Plate 72a, b, fig. 71) may be seen as part of the vogue for circuses and curved layouts in general, which had been current throughout much of the previous century and which had gained particular favour in the years subsequent to the Napoleonic Wars. It invites comparison with the work of George Basevi in Pelham Crescent, South Kensington, and with Nash's larger and grander composition at Park Crescent, Regent's Park, lacking the delicacy of detail of the former, and the metropolitan assurance of the latter. It consists of tall narrow stucco-faced four-storey houses with basements and attics, with two rooms to each floor. The porches are of the Roman Doric order, and are surmounted by cast-iron balustrades which link with those on the balconies at first-floor level. The ground-floor windows are widely proportioned, and the first- and second-floor windows have moulded architraves. There is a dentilled main cornice above the second floor, above which is a crowning storey with a smaller, less elaborate cornice and balustrade. The houses at each end of the two ranges in the crescent have circular pavilions, somewhat reminiscent of those at the corner of Adelaide Street and Strand, and of those in Victoria Square, Westminster. They are capped by balustrades behind which rise high circular attic lanterns crowned by modillioned cornices. The internal planning is in no way remarkable, being the standard London form, two rooms to a floor.

Richardson did all that he could to attract residents to his estate. He lived there himself, at first at the Estate Office and later (from 1847 to 1855) at No. 29 Norland Square; his brother, Walter Richardson, lived at No. 43 Royal Crescent from 1843 to 1851, and his professional partner, R. R. Sadler, at No. 32 Norland Square.[6] In 1842 he signed an agreement with the Brentford Gas Company for the lighting of the streets,[38] and in the following year a bargain with the Grand Junction Water Works Company provided the estate with a water supply from the mains.[39] In 1843 he also promoted an Act of Parliament whereby the management of the paving, repair, lighting and cleansing of the streets, and the maintenance of the gardens in Royal Crescent, Norland Square and St. James's Square (now St. James's Gardens) were vested in twelve named resident commissioners, who were authorised to raise a rate of up to three shillings in the pound. The original commissioners included Richardson, Cantwell, Slark and Stewart, but they were all obliged to go out of office by rotation, three in each year, the vacancies being filled by election by all residents on the estate rated at over £20 per annum.[38] In 1844 one of the greatest allurements which a ground landlord could provide—a church—was commenced, Richardson presenting the site of St. James's to the Church Building Commissioners.[5]

Despite all these efforts the Norland estate did not, however, progress smoothly. In the southern half of Addison Avenue Richardson was able to grant building leases between 1840 and 1843 for a public house (the Norland Arms) and for twenty two-storey stucco-fronted paired houses (Nos. 18–36 even and 17–35 odd), all the lessees (with one exception) being building tradesmen who evidently supplied their own designs. There seems to have been no difficulty in finding takers for these houses when completed, but in the northern half of Addison Avenue the lessee for the ten houses on the west side (Nos. 37–55 odd) proved unable to keep up the payments to his mortgagee, Frederick Chinnock, an auctioneer, who in 1843 assigned all ten plots back to Richardson's trustee, Bennett.[40] Separate leases were then granted to building tradesmen, but the houses were not all occupied until 1848.[6] On the east side the last leases for the houses were not granted until 1850, when William and Frederick Warburton Stent, surveyors, became the lessees of Nos. 46–52,[41] which were probably built by the Bayswater builder W. G. May.[42]

These twenty houses in the northern half of Addison Avenue (Plate 71a, figs. 72–3) form two ranges of paired two-storey houses with basements and rooms in the roofs, each pair being linked to its neighbours by the principal entrances, which are set back at the sides. The ground-floor windows have architraves surmounted by pediments; the first-floor windows have semi-circular heads, the archivolts springing from stringcourses; the doorways in the linking blocks are large and trabeated with central piers; and the roofs overhang substantial eaves. The houses have stucco façades which are divided by pilasters and plain strings. They have wider frontages than those in Royal Crescent, and are more conveniently planned, with well-proportioned rooms on half the number of floors, thus departing from the traditional central London plan form in favour of a new suburban ideal. Unlike the smaller houses in the southern half of the road, they were clearly all built to one design, which (in default of more

direct evidence) may be tentatively attributed to F. W. Stent.*

Progress in Norland Square was equally unstable. Here leases of all fifty-one plots had been granted by 1844, but three of the principal lessees were involved with Charles Richardson in the whole speculation on the estate, and by taking leases probably hoped to encourage others to commit themselves also. These three were Richardson's trustee again (Bennett, Nos. 7–16 consec. and 51), his brother Walter Richardson, who took the whole of the north range (Nos. 19–35 consec.), and Stewart, who took Nos. 2–4 and 17 and 18. James Emmins, the lessee of Nos. 38–44 (consec.) and the only building tradesman to take more than one lease in the square, proved to be a thoroughly unreliable person. He was declared bankrupt in 1845, and paid his creditors nothing. He repeated this convenient escape in 1848 and again in 1855, when the commissioner in charge of his affairs declared that 'the books of the bankrupt had been so imperfectly kept as to be scarcely worthy of the name of books . . . This is a scandalous case.'[44] In these conditions it is not surprising to find that the houses on the west side of the square were not all occupied until c. 1849, nor those on the north and east sides until 1852–3.[6]

The stucco-faced terrace houses surrounding Norland Square have four storeys over basements, with segmental bays at basement and ground-floor level rising to the underside of a continuous range of balconies with cast-iron balustrading. The Italianate façades, reminiscent of the manner fashionable at seaside resorts in the 1830's and 1840's, have ornate consoles supporting cornices over the first-floor windows, main cornices above the second floor, and a plain cornice over the attic storey. The range of houses on the north side of the square (Plate 71b) has several curious architectural features, including coursed stucco up to the main cornice level, clear demarkation of each house by the introduction of pilasters with vestigial capitals at second-floor level, and framed surrounds to the windows in line with the cornice consoles. The planning of the houses is of the typical London terrace type, with two rooms on each floor.

---

* F. W. Stent had previously served his articles with James Ponsford of the 'Hyde Park and St. John's Wood Estates', where he had 'designed and superintended the erection of more than Four hundred Houses and Buildings'. He had also studied 'the higher branches of architectural design' before setting up in independent practice. He subsequently joined the staff of the military depôt at Woolwich, and in 1856 he was an unsuccessful candidate for the post of Superintending Architect to the Metropolitan Board of Works.[43]

Fig. 72. Nos. 45–55 odd and 54 and 56 Addison Avenue, plans, elevations and section. Original attic fenestration uncertain

PLASTER CORNICE

9"

GROUND FLOOR. DETAILS

STRING COURSE

4¼"

10½"

2' 11"

5¼"

ARCHITRAVES

5½"

SKIRTING

12"

10"

WINDOW DETAIL

4¾"

BALUSTER

2' 6½"

FIREPLACE

3' 9"

DETAILS OF NO. 54

NO. 54

2' 11"

NO. 49 & 51

NO. 39

2' 7½"

NO. 40 Later replacement

1' 11"

NO. 46

1' 11"

BALCONY IRONWORK DETAILS

Fig. 73. Addison Avenue, details

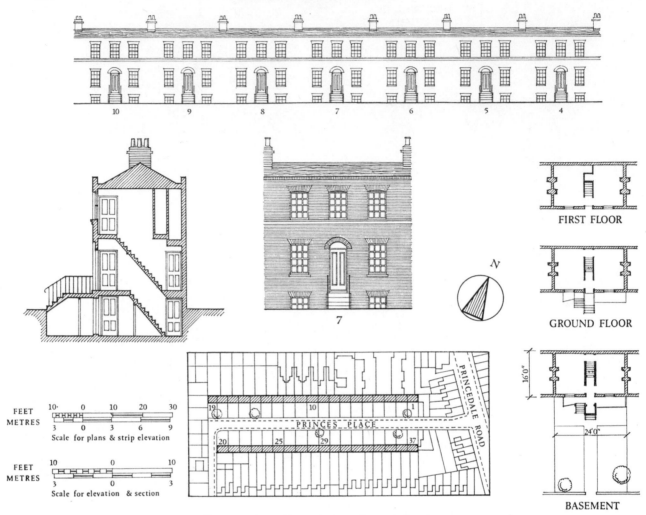

Fig. 74. Princes Place, plans, section and elevation

Behind these houses on the north side of Norland Square stand the two ranges of plain brick artisans' cottages in Princes Place, leased by Richardson in 1844–5 and now (1972) in course of demolition (Plate 72c, fig. 74). These have two storeys and basements, and because they back on to the gardens of the houses in Norland Square and St. James's Gardens they have no rear windows. They are therefore only fourteen feet deep, but they are twenty-four feet wide, and are set back behind substantial front gardens.

On another part of the estate, in the street leading northward out of Royal Crescent and now known as St. Ann's Villas, Stewart or Richardson was experimenting with a quite different type of house. Here Stewart had begun in orthodox

fashion by building two ranges of four-storey terraces, each consisting of five houses (Nos. 2–10 even and 1–9 odd St. Ann's Villas), on plots leased to him by Richardson in 1843. This was a natural continuation of Cantwell's Royal Crescent style, but there was the same difficulty here as in the crescent in finding inhabitants (all ten not being occupied until 1848),[6] and it was probably hoped that the semi-detached villas adumbrated on the layout plan of 1841 (Plate 70c) for the northward continuation of the street might prove more successful. In 1845–6 Richardson granted Stewart building leases for twenty-four paired houses on the land to the north of Queensdale Road, six pairs on either side of the street (Nos. 12–34 even and 11–33 odd St.

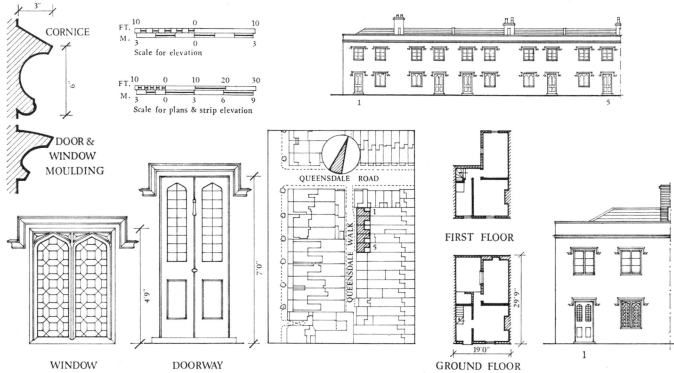

Fig. 75. Queensdale Walk, plans, elevations and details

CORNICE

DOOR & WINDOW MOULDING

FT. 10 0 10
M. 3 0 3
Scale for elevation

FT. 10 0 10 20 30
M. 3 0 3 6 9
Scale for plans & strip elevation

WINDOW

DOORWAY

QUEENSDALE ROAD

QUEENSDALE WALK

FIRST FLOOR

GROUND FLOOR

Ann's Villas). In the leases the houses are described as newly erected, but in 1848 only six of them (Nos. 12–18 even, 11 and 15) were occupied, and the evidence of the ratebooks suggests that only one other (No. 13) had yet in fact been completed. By this time Stewart had assigned some of his leases to Charles Richardson's trustee, or to his brother Walter Richardson,[45] under whose aegis building appears to have been resumed in 1850. But in the following year twelve of the twenty-four houses are listed as empty, and they were not finally all occupied until 1859.[6]

All of these twenty-four houses are in the Tudor-Gothic and Jacobean manner, executed in red and blue brick with Bath stone quoins and window mullions (Plate 72d, e). The documentary evidence associated with their building contains no clue to the identity of the author of the designs. A lithograph in Kensington Central Library entitled 'Elizabethan Villa, Notting Hill' shows Nos. 19 and 21 in reverse, but is unsigned. It may, however, be noted that the architect Charles James Richardson (? a relative of Charles Richardson, the ground landlord)

subsequently published a book entitled *The Englishman's House*, which contains engravings of a design for a double suburban villa 'intended for erection on a leasehold estate at a little distance out of London'. The building illustrated is not dissimilar to the houses in St. Ann's Villas, and the text explains that this was only a preliminary design.[46] But for whoever may have been responsible for the executed design, this experiment in the Tudor manner must have been accounted a failure, if only for the prolonged lack of demand for such houses.

The only other houses on the estate in the Tudor-Gothic style are the stone-faced pair set at an angle at the west corner of Addison Avenue and St. James's Gardens, and the modest stucco-faced mews houses in Queensdale Walk (fig. 75). The latter may have been designed by Richardson's clerk of works, William Carson, who was the lessee of Nos. 1 and 2 in 1844.

There were difficulties, too, in even the building of St. James's Church (Plate 11). Work had started in June 1844, Lewis Vulliamy being the architect. The Church Building Commissioners had promised to contribute £500 towards the cost, and voluntary church building societies had given £2,400. A local committee of residents, in which Walter Richardson (who subsequently became one of the first churchwardens) was active, raised £2,000, but in May 1845, only two months before the consecration was due to take place, the vicar of Kensington had to request the Commissioners to pay their promised grant despite the fact that shortage of money would prevent the building of the intended spire. 'A large number of the new houses at Norland are still unoccupied', he wrote, but he had 'no doubt that when the Houses are occupied the spire will be built'. The church was consecrated on 17 July 1845,[47] but the tower was not completed until 1850.[48] The spire was never built.

To meet his mounting financial difficulties Charles Richardson was obliged to sell the freehold of some twelve acres at the north end of the estate in 1844 (see fig. 70). This area lay to the north of the future St. James's Square (now Gardens), and was already leased as a brickfield. The tenant brickmaker, William Naylor Morrison, now purchased the freehold, for which he paid £7,190, equivalent to approximately £600 per acre.[39] In May of the same year Richardson was able to mortgage ground rents worth £1,945 per annum, the loan being apparently arranged by Charles Stewart's solicitor, Thomas Bothamley, a partner in the firm of Freeman, Bothamley and Benthall of Coleman Street, City.[49] Besides needing capital for himself Richardson also needed it to assist Stewart, whose sagging fortunes he was supporting in November 1844 by the advance of money on the risky security of Stewart's unfinished houses in Royal Crescent.[50] The London Assurance Corporation had already refused to lend to Stewart, and its subsequent refusals, in 1844 and 1846, to lend to Richardson testify to the distrust with which the Norland estate was now viewed by investors.[51]

By this time, however, building societies (mostly still of the terminating variety) were increasing very rapidly in number in London, and this new source of capital was evidently exploited to the full on the Norland estate, where five such societies* were investing between 1847 and 1851. Charles Richardson's brother Walter, who was now deeply involved in the affairs of the estate, was a party in transactions with all five of these societies, one of which was responsible for the building of most of the houses in St. James's Square, the last important remaining part of the estate to be developed.

The plan of the estate presented to the Commissioners of Sewers in 1841 (Plate 70c) shows all the land to the north of Addison Avenue as in lease for brickmaking. We have already seen that in 1844 Charles Richardson sold the freehold of the northern part of this area to W. N. Morrison, and that in the same year he presented the site for the church. He therefore still retained a strip of land some 300 feet wide between the north end of Addison Avenue and the boundary of Morrison's brickfield, and in December 1843 his surveyor, Joseph Dunning, had obtained the permission of the Commissioners to lay sewers in the square now intended to be formed around the church.[57]

Between 1847 and 1851 five ranges, containing a total of thirty-seven houses, were built in the square, to the designs of John Barnett,[58] who had previously designed houses in Clapham and Highbury, and who was in 1856 to be an unsuccessful candidate for the post of Superintending Architect to the Metropolitan Board of Works.[59] All of these thirty-seven three-storey houses (Plates 70b, 71c, d, fig. 76) follow a coherent architectural scheme, the essence of which is the arrangement of the houses in linked pairs, the link taking the form of recessed bays of one or two storeys containing the entrances. The ground and basement storeys are faced with stucco, and the upper storeys are of stock brick. The first-floor windows have stucco architraves and cornices; there are crowning modillioned cornices surmounting each pair of houses; and the doorways and ground-floor windows have semi-circular heads, with moulded archivolts. The frontages are, on average, some eight feet wider than those in the more conventional terraces formed in Norland Square or Royal Crescent. The planning of the interiors is consequently more spacious, and marks a departure from that of the average terrace house of the period. The rooms are well-lit and pleasantly proportioned, sometimes as many as four being provided on one floor, and the

---

* The London and County Benefit Building Society and Economic Investment Association No. 2;[52] the Dissenters' and General Benefit Building Society No. 2;[53] the London and Provincial Building and Investment Society;[54] the Lombardian Benefit Building and Investment Society;[55] and the St. James's Square Benefit Building Society Notting Hill.[56]

Fig. 76 (facing page). Nos. 42–54 consec. St. James's Gardens, plans, elevations and section

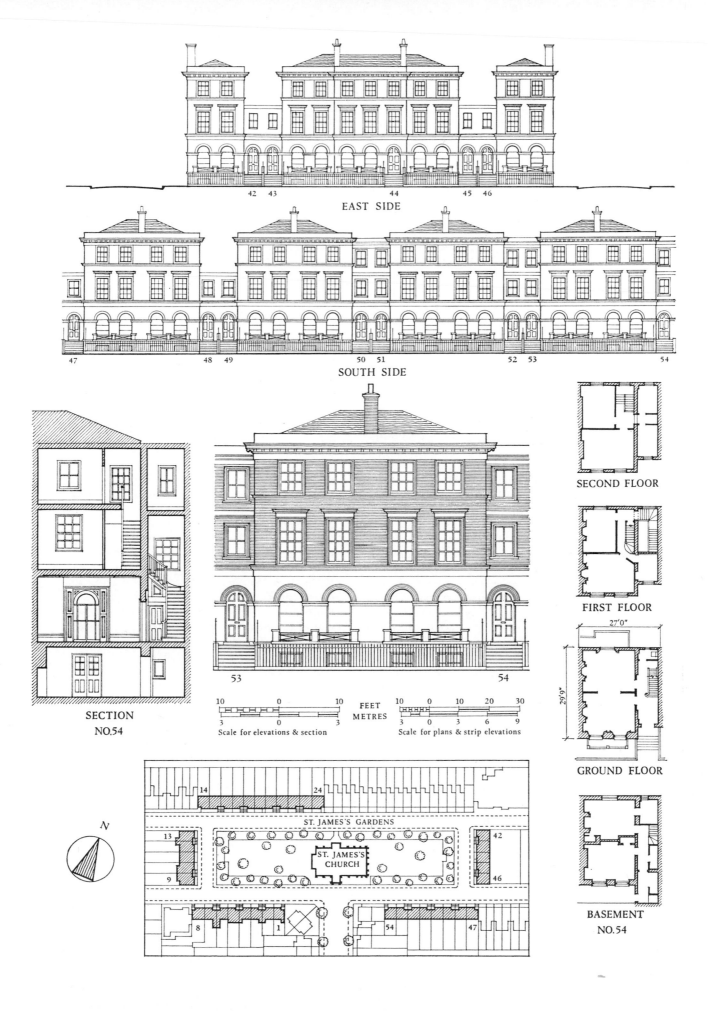

42 43   44   45 46

EAST SIDE

47   48 49   50 51   52 53   54

SOUTH SIDE

SECTION
NO.54

SECOND FLOOR

FIRST FLOOR

53   54

10   0   10   FEET   10   0   10   20   30
                        METRES
3   0   3   3   0   3   6   9

Scale for elevations & section   Scale for plans & strip elevations

27'0"

29'9"

GROUND FLOOR

BASEMENT
NO.54

N

14   24

13

9

ST. JAMES'S GARDENS

ST. JAMES'S
CHURCH

42

46

8   1   54   47

excavations for the basements are only about five feet in depth.

Building began on the south side, where the erection of the present Nos. 1–8 (consec.) St. James's Gardens was notified to the district surveyor in September 1847; a tablet inset in the front wall of Nos. 1 and 2 records that 'The first stone of this Square was laid 1st Novr 1847'. The next houses to be notified were Nos. 9–13 (consec.) at the western end, in March 1848, and then Nos. 14–24 (consec.), on the north side, in November of the following year. In December 1850 came the notification of Nos. 47–54 (consec.) on the south side, and in February 1851 the eastern range, Nos. 42–46 (consec). At this point, with one terrace of the six projected still not commenced, development on the original lines ceased, and building on the still vacant land at the east end of the north side was not resumed until the mid 1860's.*

Nos. 1–24 and 42–54 were built under the aegis of the St. James's Square Benefit Building Society Notting Hill, of which Charles Richardson's partner, R. R. Sadler, and his brother Walter Richardson were trustees and directors.[56] In the late summer of 1847 tenders had been invited for the building of the forty-eight houses which the six terraces, if all built, would have contained, and bills of quantity were supplied by the Society's architect, Barnett. The lowest tender, for £29,830 (equivalent to £621 for each house), was from a local builder, Robert Adkin,[61] who became a shareholder in the Society. He built Nos. 1–8 (consec.),[62] and in February 1848 Charles Richardson granted ninety-nine-year leases of these houses to members of the Society, the leases and lessees' shares in the Society being immediately mortgaged to the Society's trustees.[63] Adkin also started to build Nos. 9–13 on behalf of the Society,[64] but a request to the London Assurance Corporation for a loan of £24,000 was refused, and in July 1848 he was declared bankrupt,[65] his tender (some £10,000 cheaper than the next bid) having been ruinously low. Thereafter a different procedure was followed; no more building leases were granted, all the remaining houses being built, presumably under contract with the Society, by David Nicholson senior and junior, builders, of Wandsworth, who were themselves shareholders

in the Society.[66] Charles Richardson retained possession of the freehold until October 1852, when he was obliged by his mortgagees to sell all thirty-seven houses together with the remaining vacant land on the north side and the sites of the future Nos. 55 and 56 on the south side.[67] Shortly afterwards the purchaser, T. R. Tufnell of Northfleet, Kent, esquire, sold the entire property piecemeal, almost all of the houses (except Nos. 1–8) being acquired by shareholders in the Society, which in October 1852 was described as about to be dissolved.[68] These shareholders included Walter Richardson, who bought Nos. 18 and 19, R. R. Sadler (No. 22), the builders Nicholson and Son (Nos. 36–40 consec.) and John Barnett, the architect (Nos. 15–17 consec.). The latter had been associated with the Society throughout its whole brief existence, having been one of the shareholders to whom Charles Richardson had granted a building lease in February 1848 (of No. 6).[69]

Whether the St. James's Square Building Society was financially successful or not is impossible to assess, the records of its affairs being obscure and very incomplete. The ratebooks indicate that almost all of its thirty-seven houses were occupied within two or three years of the commencement of building (not a very long period compared with other parts of the Norland estate), and its inability to build the sixth and last terrace in the square may well have been caused not by its own financial difficulties but by those of Charles Richardson. As early as 1848 he had been unable to withstand the pressure of his mortgagees any longer, and in May the freehold of the greater part of the estate, comprising five hundred houses yielding £4,000 per annum in ground rents, had been advertised as to be sold by auction.[70] Originally it had been intended to sell the property, divided into 215 lots, at a single sale lasting three days, but in the event the sales seem to have been spread over about fifteen months (probably in order not to swamp the market), and by August 1849 at least 270 houses had been sold. Even so, Richardson's financial position was alarming the partners in his firm, now described as Richardson, Smith and Sadler, for when Smith died in 1849 his will contained the ominous direction that 'I recommend my good friend Mr. Sadler to be

* Work appears to have been resumed in 1864,[60] but Nos. 25–36 (consec.) were not all occupied until 1866–8 and Nos. 37–41 until 1878–9.[6]

adviser in relation to my affairs, he knowing the terms of my partnership and what liabilities thereof attach to Mr. Richardson alone (and they are many)'.[71]

Richardson's expenditure on the estate during the 1840's must indeed have been very considerable. All the sewers, except on the land sold to Morrison in 1844, were built at his expense,[72] and we have already seen that he advanced money of unknown amount to Charles Stewart, the principal lessee on the estate, and to other builders, in order to keep development under way. Although the evidence is not at all clear, he may also have built a number of houses himself by contract with a builder, notably Nos. 170–178 (even) Holland Park Avenue and 1 Royal Crescent, and those in Norland Square and elsewhere with which his agent, Bennett, was concerned. He certainly employed his own clerk of works, William Carson,[73] as well as a surveyor (at first Cantwell and then Dunning). Some idea of the scale of his liabilities may be obtained from his last unsuccessful application in 1846 for a loan from the London Assurance Corporation, when he asked for £120,000.[74]

Despite the sale in 1848–9 of the freehold ground rents arising from a substantial part of the whole estate, Richardson had been obliged in September 1850 to come to an arrangement with Frederick Chinnock, the auctioneer who had conducted these sales.[75] The terms of this bargain are not known, but it may be conjectured that in return for a short-term loan it gave Chinnock a lien on the residue of the estate subject to the existing mortgages, an arrangement similar to that obtained in 1859 by C. H. Blake with another firm of auctioneers at a critical phase in his speculation on the neighbouring Ladbroke estate (see page 234). This device was evidently not successful, however, for in the summer of 1851 the sale by auction of freehold ground rents was resumed,[76] and at about the same time Richardson's principal mortgages were transferred to a new mortgagee, John Davies of Thornbury Park, Gloucestershire.[77] In January 1852 Davies was exercising his right to sell houses in Royal Crescent, Addison Avenue and elsewhere,[78] and we have already seen that in October of the same year the thirty-seven houses in St. James's Gardens and the vacant land there were also sold. What appears to have been virtually the residue of the entire estate was sold in December to Chin-

nock,[79] who in 1860–1 was asserting his rights as freeholder to all the sewers built on the estate by Richardson.[80]

With the exception of the northern land which now belonged to Morrison and of the vacant lands on the north side of St. James's Gardens and nearby in Penzance Street and Penzance Place, the development of the whole of the Norland estate had been completed by the early 1850's. Charles Richardson had been the prime mover in the complex and risky business of promoting the building within a mere dozen years of over five hundred houses on what was still a comparatively remote suburban estate. All his labours seem, however, to have ended only in personal ruin, for in 1854 a silence falls over his affairs until his reappearance in the autumn of 1855 at the rooms of the Glasgow Stock Exchange in the unexpected role of a bankrupt dealer in patent medicines. All his property, both real and personal, was transferred to his creditors by order of the Lord Ordinary of Scotland officiating in the Court of Session at Edinburgh, and in October a trustee of his estate was appointed.[81]

This does not appear, however, to have been quite the end of Richardson's career. We have already seen that James Emmins the builder knew how to make the best use of the bankruptcy laws, and it may be that Richardson's bankruptcy was carefully contrived to enable him to regularize his affairs by shrouding himself for a while in distant Glasgow amidst the decent obscurities of Scottish law. At all events, the Scottish trustee or receiver of the estate got in and sold all Richardson's known available assets, one of the purchasers being Chinnock the auctioneer, who probably bought the mortgage executed by Charles Stewart to Richardson in 1844. To wind up all matters connected with the sequestration Richardson's former partner, R. R. Sadler, purchased all interest in any other assets which Richardson might possess, and by 1858 the case appears to have been settled. The partnership between Richardson and Sadler had been dissolved in April 1855, some six months before the declaration of bankruptcy,[82] but the *Law List* indicates that it was resumed again in 1857, still at the old address in Golden Square, but now with an additional office in the City, at Old Jewry Chambers. From 1860 to 1868 the latter was Richardson's only address, and the final entry in the *Law List* occurs in

1869, when he is given as in Great Knightrider Street, Doctors' Commons.[83]*

Only the northern extremity of the estate, which Richardson had sold in 1844 to the brickmaker Morrison, remains to be described. The plan submitted by Joseph Dunning on Richardson's behalf to the Commissioners of Sewers in December 1843 for the drainage of St. James's Square shows that three streets were then intended to lead out of the north side of the square to the vacant land beyond.[84] One was to be in the centre of the square, and the other two at the two north corners. By 1844, however, when the sale to Morrison had been completed, a plan presented by Dunning on Morrison's behalf shows that the two openings at the corners had been abandoned.[85] The plans of the St. James's Square Benefit Building Society, drawn up in c. 1847, evidently provided for the retention of the centre opening, which was to be flanked on either side by a range of eleven houses. But the projected eastern range was (as we have already seen) not built, and when building on the north side of the square was resumed in 1864 under different auspices, the site of the central opening was built upon, despite a local resident's complaint to the Vestry that a right of way existed there.[86]

There was therefore no access from the main part of the Norland estate to Morrison's land except at the east and west extremities, by way of Princes (now Princedale) Road and St. Ann's Road. Before purchasing the freehold in 1844 Morrison had been Richardson's tenant for the twelve northern acres, which (as previously mentioned) he had used as a brickfield, and when, as the freeholder, he started to build, the unalluring conditions created by his previous brickmaking operations probably compelled him to cater for a socially less ambitious clientèle than that provided for by Richardson on the southern portion of the estate. Morrison and his associates lined the long straight streets which were now to be formed with as many small terrace houses as they could cram in, and the range of houses on the north side of Darnley Terrace and St. James's Gardens provides to this day a social as well as a physical barrier between the two portions of the original estate.

The building processes followed a normal pattern of mortgages (the first to a group of City men and the second to a client of Messrs. Richardson and Sadler), building leases and in 1848 the outright sale of about six acres. After Morrison's death in 1850 his widow sold most of the remainder, and by 1854 she only retained two small pieces. It may be noted that, despite the unpretentious nature of this development, the purchasers were categorically prohibited from making any roads to or from any of the adjoining lands without the written prior consent of Charles Richardson, who had evidently inserted a covenant to this effect into the original sale of 1844 to Morrison; and in particular they were not to permit any gate or way or opening on the east side, leading into that notorious place of ill fame called 'Notting Dale or the Potteries'.[39]

Despite this solicitude for the maintenance of social respectability, development proved slow. The site was still remote and isolated, close only to the stink and disease of the Potteries. By the mid 1860's St. Katherine's Road and William Street (now Wilsham Street and Kenley Street) were nearly complete, but elsewhere there was still more land vacant than built upon.[87] Except in Wilsham Street, little of the original development now survives, many obsolete and decayed houses having been cleared away in recent years by the Borough Council for the erection of blocks of flats.

The census books of 1851 show that in the principal streets of the Norland estate—Royal Crescent, Norland Square, Addison Avenue and St. James's Gardens—virtually none of the inhabited houses were yet sub-divided, and that domestic servants formed nearly one third of the total population here. Among the householders, annuitants or 'fundholders', living on private incomes, were the largest single group, most of them being women. There were six schools in the tall houses of Norland Square and Royal Crescent, three for girls and one for boys in the former (all boarding), and two for girls, one day and one boarding in the latter. In Norland Square there were five lawyers and two doctors, a Russian diplomat, a naval captain and an American author (with seven servants), and trade was represented by *inter alia* a master printer, a master saddler, a wool merchant, a pencil-maker and a quarry-owner.

* The date of his death has not been discovered. It may be noted here that he is not to be confused with another Charles Richardson, of South Wharf, Paddington, and Brunswick Wharf, Vauxhall, a brick, tile, lime and cement merchant, who was active in Hammersmith.

In Royal Crescent, where about a dozen houses were still empty, the mixture was much the same, and included three lawyers, two clergymen without cure, three stockbrokers and three merchants. In Addison Avenue there were three army officers and a surgeon, but most of the other inhabitants were businessmen; they included four clerks, two builders (J. Livesey, plumber, at No. 36 and Arthur Arrowsmith, house decorator, at No. 49), three merchants, a gunmaker, a furrier, and a horse-dealer, as well as at the south end of the street, a victualler (at the Norland Arms), a job-master, an omnibus proprietor and a fruiterer. In St. James's Gardens the pattern was much the same, although the number of servants was noticeably smaller (only about one per house). In Wilsham Street almost all the houses which had been completed by the time of the census of 1861 were occupied by building tradesmen or labourers, and many of them had been subdivided. There were no servants.

Two public houses on the Norland estate call for comment. The Norland Arms in Addison Avenue (leased by Charles Richardson to R. Clements, builder, in 1840) is an interesting three-storey composition, with a boldly detailed ground floor, consisting of a central Doric porch carrying an entablature which extends on either side over the doors and windows of the bar. Over the entablature are piers capped by cast-iron features to which the balcony rails are attached. The stucco architraves of the first-floor windows are surmounted by pediments carried on consoles. The Prince of Wales public house is on the east side of Princedale Road facing down Queensdale Road, and also has a rear court giving on to Pottery Lane (Plate 75a). It possesses an abundance of late nineteenth-century engraved glass on both façades, as well as in the screens inside.

The Church of St. James, Norlands
Plate 11; fig. 77

The Church of St. James, Norlands, occupies a commanding position at the northern end of Addison Avenue, where its tower marks the central north–south axis of the Norland estate. The site was presented by Charles Richardson, the owner of the estate,[5] and the church, designed in 'the Gothic style of the twelfth century' by Lewis Vulliamy, was built in 1844–5 at a cost of £4,941, towards which the Church Building Commissioners made

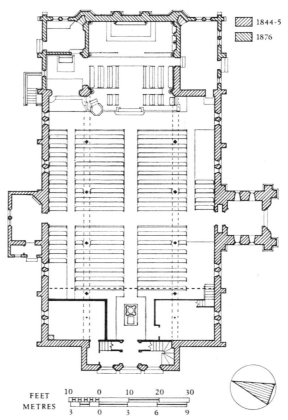

FEET / METRES

Fig. 77. St. James's Church, Norlands, plan

a grant of £500. It provided some 750 sittings, and was consecrated on 17 July 1845. A district parish was assigned in the following year.[88]

The church is built of white Suffolk bricks, with minimal stone cornices, hood moulds, pinnacles and stringcourses. It is orientated east–west, and the tower is positioned south of the central bay, where it projects as the centrepiece of a symmetrically composed south elevation. The entrance is through a cavernous porch of brick set in the base of the tower. A gable containing a trefoil panel extends upwards over the porch into a large light enriched with handsome tracery. The stark simplicity of the body of the church sets off the elegant three-stage tower, which was being 'raised' in 1850.[89] The first stage has gabled buttresses with roll moulded edges, and contains the porch and large traceried window. The very short second stage has a clock-face set in on each side in a shallow circular recess flanked by blind lancet panels. The final belfry stage is lighter and richer, with two deeply-recessed paired lancets flanked by single blind lancet panels set within a panel framed by pilaster-buttresses. A drawing in Kensington Public Library shows that the tower was to have been surmounted by a stone broach spire. This was never built, and with its thin octagonal pinnacles set on each corner, the tower seems somewhat abrupt without it.

The body of the church is broad and barn-like, and consists of a five-bay clerestoried nave with lean-to aisles. Galleries were added in 1850.[90] They rested on supports which spanned from brackets on the cast-iron columns of the nave to the north and south walls, and must have given an appearance of solidity to the interior which has now been dissipated by their removal. The columns, quatrefoil on plan, are widely spaced, and support an elegant arcade above which is the clerestory, pierced by small single lancets, two to each bay. The aisles are lit by two ranges of paired lancets, above and below the former galleries. The roof is carried on simple wooden trusses of meagre design, supported on brackets. Each truss is placed over the top of an arch of the arcade, and the resulting division of each bay into two parts tends to confuse the architectural logic of the design.

Vulliamy's original design provided polygonal apsidal projections at the east and west ends, but these were not built. In 1876 the east end was extended under the direction of the architect, R. J. Withers, to provide the present chancel and vestries and an organ chamber.[91] The east wall of the chancel is a scholarly composition in the Early English style with three stepped lancets set in five stepped-lancet panels. In 1880 a faculty was given for the erection of a reredos, for the reseating of the north and south galleries, and for the opening out of an arch westwards from the organ chamber. The reredos is of wood with a finely carved Last Supper, and has polychromatic decoration. Subsequent to a faculty of 1894, the chancel floor was extended westwards, a dwarf screen wall and ironwork were erected, new stalls were provided, and the walls of the organ chamber were

raised in what is now the Lady Chapel north of the chancel. In 1921 the organ was removed to its present position in the west gallery. Beneath this there is a robustly designed font in which green marble and glazed tiles figure prominently.

Until 1948 the greater part of the interior was coloured, and the whole of the surfaces of columns and arcading up to the stringcourse was covered with printed patterns, with angel motifs in the spandrels. The ceiling surfaces of the nave and aisles were decorated with repeat patterns, that to the nave being an I.H.S. motif. On the wall spaces between each window of the north and south aisles were murals painted on canvas, but these were removed in 1950.[92]

West London Tabernacle, Penzance Place

This building, which has been in commercial use for very many years, was originally erected in the 1860's by Mr. Varley, a Baptist businessman who began to preach in the neighbouring Potteries in about 1863. It was enlarged and 'beautified' in 1871–2 to designs by Habershon and Pite.[93] It is built of yellow stock bricks with stone dressings, the style being a free adaptation of Italian Renaissance. The south front is flanked by two towers, now partially demolished, which contained staircases to the galleries. The centre of this elevation was pierced by a large semi-circular-headed window with a hood moulding in the form of a pointed arch.

Spanish and Portuguese Synagogue, St. James's Gardens

This synagogue was built by Bovis Limited in 1928 to designs by S. B. Pritlove, with M. N. Castello acting as consultant architect. It was consecrated on 9 December of that year.[94] It is built of dark multi-coloured stock bricks, with stucco dressings. The style of the exterior is Byzantine. The interior is one large space approximately square on plan, with a gallery round three sides, and is in the late seventeenth-century manner.

SELECT LIST OF BUILDING LESSORS AND LESSEES
ON THE NORLAND ESTATE

Except where otherwise indicated, the dates refer to the years in which the leases were granted: these are not always the date of actual building. Lessors' and lessees' addresses are given only for those resident outside Kensington. The chief source is the Middlesex Land Register in the Greater London Record Office at County Hall.

Addison Avenue, east side

2–10 even	Probably built by George Langford, *c.* 1860–1.
Norland Arms	Charles Richardson, solicitor, to Robert Clements of Kingston, Surrey, builder, 1840.
18, 20	Richardson to James Wood of Hampstead Road, bricklayer, 1841.
22–28 even	Richardson to Messrs. Thomas and Christopher Gabriel of Lambeth, timber merchants, 1842.
30–36 even	Richardson to James Livesey of Lisson Grove, plumber, 1842–3.
38, 40	Richardson to John Parkes, ironmonger, 1841.
42, 44	Richardson to John and Samuel Peirson of Bishopsgate, ironmongers, 1844.
46–52 even	Richardson to William and Frederick W. Stent of St. Marylebone, surveyors, 1850. Probably built by W. G. May of Bayswater, builder.
54, 56	Richardson to John Buckmaster of Hungerford Market, gentleman, 1847.

Addison Avenue, west side

1–11 odd	Built by John Parkinson, plumber, *c.* 1850–2.
17–19 odd	Richardson to Charles Patch, builder, 1842.
21, 23	Richardson to George Pratt, builder, 1843.
25, 27	Richardson to John Cole Bennett, gentleman, 1843.
29, 31	Richardson to Walter Hawkins and William Strong of Rochester Row, plasterers, 1843.
33, 35	Richardson to Thomas Warwick and Christopher Garwood of Oxford Street, builders, 1843.
37–55 odd	Richardson to John Francis William Brewer of Wyndham Place, St. Marylebone, gentleman (probably identifiable with J. F. W. Brewer of Kennington, wine merchant), 1842. Mortgaged to Frederick Chinnock of

Mayfair, auctioneer, who assigned to J. C. Bennett, gentleman, 1843. Nos. 53 and 55 leased by Bennett to Michael Goodall, carpenter, and John Parkinson, glazier, 1843; Nos. 49 and 51 to John Arrowsmith of New Bond Street, house decorator, 1847.

57 and St. James's Lodge	Richardson to William Naylor Morrison of Streatham, esquire, and of Notting Hill, brickmaker, 1846. Probably built by Stephen Picton.

Darnley Terrace, north side

1–6 consec.	Charles Richardson, solicitor, to W. G. May of Bayswater, builder, 1851.

Holland Park Avenue, north side

118–122 even	Built by W. H. Lovett, *c.* 1862.
124–128, 132–150 even	Charles Richardson, solicitor, to Charles Stewart, barrister, 1840–1841. Robert Cantwell, architect, in charge of building. Not all occupied until 1845.
130	Probably built with Nos. 124–128 and 132–150, but occupied by Richardson and the Norland Estate Office until 1846. The ground at the rear contained a well and steam engine for raising water, and there was a tank on top of the house.
152–156 even	Built before 1827 and sold to Richardson in 1839.
158–168 even	Built 1842–3, probably by William Slark of Gordon Square, esquire.
170–178 even with 1 Royal Crescent	Richardson to John Cole Bennett of Walworth, gentleman (in 1850 described as Richardson's trustee), 1839. Leases assigned back to Richardson, 1840. No. 172 leased by Richardson to Edward May of Oxford Street, ironmonger, 1844.
180–192 even	Richardson to Stewart, 1842. Nos. 188-192 demolished.

LESSORS AND LESSEES ON THE NORLAND ESTATE

Norland Square, east side

2–4 consec.	Charles Richardson, solicitor, to Charles Stewart, barrister, 1842.
5, 6	Richardson to Charles Patch, builder, 1843.
7–16 consec.	Richardson to John Cole Bennett, gentleman, 1843.
17, 18	Richardson to Stewart, 1842.

Norland Square, north side

19–35 consec.	Richardson to Walter Richardson of Regent Street, gentleman, 1843. Not all occupied until 1852–3.

Norland Square, west side

36, 37	Richardson to John Francis William Brewer of Wyndham Place, St. Marylebone (probably identifiable with J. F. W. Brewer of Kennington, wine merchant), 1842.
38–44 consec.	Richardson to James Emmins of Bayswater, builder, 1843–4.
45	Richardson to Frederick Charles Cope of Bloomsbury Square, architect, 1843.
46	Richardson to Frederick Chinnock of Regent Street, auctioneer, 1843.
47	Richardson to Charles Burrows of St. Marylebone, plumber, 1842.
48	Richardson to Thomas Wilkinson of Regent Street, ironmonger, 1843.
49	Richardson to James Dobbins of Chelsea, ironmonger, 1842.
50	Richardson to Thomas Holmes of Belgravia, statuary and mason, 1842.
51	Richardson to Bennett, 1843.
52	Richardson to Robert Cantwell, architect, 1842.

Princedale Road, east side

14 (Prince of Wales public house)—28 even	Charles Richardson, solicitor, to James Emmins of Bayswater, builder, 1844–5. Nos. 26, 28 demolished.
30–36 even	Richardson to Thomas Pool, junior, builder, 1846. No. 36 demolished.
38	Richardson to R. Restall of St. Marylebone, builder, 1848. Demolished.

40	Richardson, by direction of Emmins and his assignees in bankruptcy, to J. Coggins of St. Marylebone, grocer, 1847. Demolished.

Princedale Road, west side

9–13 odd	Richardson to Charles Patch of Edgware Road, builder, 1841.
15–25 odd	Richardson to Thomas Pool of Paddington, builder, 1841.
27–33 odd	Richardson to Patch, 1841.
35	Richardson to George Warren, carpenter, 1844.
37–45 odd	Richardson to Job Way of Shepherd's Bush, carman, 1844.
47–51 odd	Richardson to William Thelwall of St. Marylebone, painter, 1847.
53, 55	Richardson to Thomas Pool, junior, builder, 1851.
Crown public house	Richardson by direction of Pool, junior, to James Watney and partner of the Stag Brewery, Pimlico, brewers, 1851.

Princes Place, north side

1–19 consec.	Charles Richardson, solicitor, to James Jessup of Shepherd's Bush, bricklayer, 1844–5. Nos. 1–10 demolished.

Princes Place, south side

20–25 consec.	Richardson to George Worster of Deptford, bricklayer, 1844.
26–37 consec.	Richardson to Jessup, 1844. Nos. 27–37 demolished.

Queensdale Place

	Lessees from Charles Richardson, solicitor, include Jonathan Gotobed of Edmonton, George Pratt and J. W. Clarke, all builders, and W. T. Roper, surveyor, 1845–9.

Queensdale Road, north side

2–16 even	Charles Richardson, solicitor, to Thomas Pool, senior, of Paddington, builder, or Thomas Pool, junior, bricklayer, 1842–4.
18, 20	Richardson to William Thelwall of St. Marylebone, painter, 1846.

LESSORS AND LESSEES ON THE NORLAND ESTATE

22–28 even	Richardson to George Worster of Deptford, bricklayer, 1844.
32, 34	Richardson to Thomas Wright of 20 Great Marlborough Street, 1845.
36, 38	Richardson to Thelwall, 1845.
40, 42	Richardson to John Christie and James Rodgers of Rotherhithe, masons, 1843–4.
44–52 even	Richardson to George Pratt, builder, 1845. Demolished.

Queensdale Road, south side

3	Charles Richardson to Charles Patch of Edgware Road, builder, 1841.
5–9 odd	Richardson to Charles Stewart, barrister, 1842.
15–23 odd	Richardson to George Pratt, builder, 1844.
25	Richardson to Thomas Byne of Shepherd's Bush, plasterer, 1843.
27	Richardson to Job Way of Shepherd's Bush, carman, 1843.
29–57 odd	Richardson to Stewart, 1843.

Queensdale Walk

1, 2	Charles Richardson, solicitor, to William Carson, surveyor (Richardson's clerk of works), 1844.
3–5 consec.	Richardson to James Emmins of Bayswater, builder, 1844.

Royal Crescent

1	See Nos. 170–178 even Holland Park Avenue.
2–44 consec.	Charles Richardson, solicitor, to Charles Stewart, barrister, 1842–3. Designed by Robert Cantwell, architect. Nos. 23–44 not all occupied until 1848. Nos. 15–22, although covered in in 1844, were in course of completion in 1850 by Mr. Glenn of Islington, and were not all occupied until 1856.

St. Ann's Road, east side

2–26 even	Charles Richardson, solicitor, to W. G. May of Bayswater, builder, 1850–1.

St. Ann's Road, west side

1–19 odd	Richardson to May, 1851. Demolished.
21–31 odd	Richardson to Edward Bifield, builder, 1851. Demolished.

St. Ann's Villas, east side

2–10 even	Charles Richardson, solicitor, to Charles Stewart, barrister, 1843.
12–34 even	Richardson to Stewart, 1845–6.

St. Ann's Villas, west side

1–9 odd	Richardson to Stewart, 1843.
11–33 odd	Richardson to Stewart, 1845–6.

St. James's Gardens, south side

1–8 consec.	Built 1847–8 by Robert Adkin, builder, under contract with St. James's Square Benefit Building Society. Designed by John Barnett, architect.
47–54 consec.	Built by David Nicholson and Son of Wandsworth, builders, for the St. James's Square Benefit Building Society, 1850–1851. Designed by Barnett.
55, 56	Built by George Drew, builder, 1865, and first occupied 1869–1870.

St. James's Gardens, west side

9–13 consec.	Commenced by Adkin on behalf of St. James's Square Benefit Building Society, 1848. Completed after Adkin's bankruptcy by Nicholson and Son, 1849. Designed by Barnett.

St. James's Gardens, north side

14–24 consec.	Built by Nicholson and Son, for the St. James's Square Benefit Building Society, 1849–50. Designed by Barnett, who purchased Nos. 15–17, 1852.

St. James's Gardens, east side

42–46 consec.	Built by Nicholson and Son, for the St. James's Square Benefit Building Society, 1851. Designed by Barnett.

CHAPTER XII

The Portobello and St. Quintin Estates

AT THE BEGINNING of the nineteenth century there were two large farms at the northern extremity of the parish of Kensington. Portobello Farm—so named in honour of the capture of Puerto Bello by Admiral Vernon in 1739—had been purchased in 1755, subject to two life interests, by Charles Henry Talbot, esquire, of the Inner Temple. It was then described as 170 acres of land, 'parcel of the Manor of Notting Barns', and was let to a farmer at an annual rent of £170.[1] Access to it was by way of Portobello Lane (now Road), and the farmhouse (Plate 5d) stood on the east side of the road upon the site now occupied by St. Joseph's Home. By the early 1830's, when a large part of the farm was threatened with inundation by an abortive scheme for the formation of a reservoir by the River Colne Water Works Company, the estate had passed to Sir George Talbot, baronet, and was described as 'a very valuable Grass Farm' of 182 acres, in lease to Mr. Wise at £800 per annum—a more than four-fold increase of rent over the previous seventy-five years. Within a short while, moreover, the property would become eligible for building, when its value was expected to rise to £3,000 per annum.[2] The reservoir was not, of course, built, but Sir George died in 1850, before development could begin, and bequeathed the estate to his two daughters, Mary-Anne and Georgina-Charlotte Talbot.[3]

The other farm was known as 'the Manor or Lordship of Notting Barns', and belonged in 1767 to Thomas Darby of Sunbury, esquire. In that year he conveyed it to William St. Quintin of Scampston Hall, Yorkshire, to whom he was related by marriage.[4] St. Quintin subsequently inherited his father's baronetcy, but after his death in 1795 the title became extinct,[5] and the estate passed to William Thomas Darby, who assumed the name of St. Quintin.[6] He died in 1805, leaving his property to his eldest son, William St. Quintin,[7] upon whose death in 1859 it passed to the latter's brother, Matthew Chitty Downes St. Quintin,[8] formerly colonel of the

17th Lancers.[9] The St. Quintin family owned extensive estates at Scampston and Lowthorpe in Yorkshire, where as landed gentry they played an active part in the affairs of the county; William St. Quintin also had a house in Bruton Street, Mayfair. The 'Manor' of Notting Barns was described in 1767 as consisting of 225 acres, then in lease to Samuel Verry at an annual rental of £150.[4] By 1843 it had been reduced by sales to the Great Western Railway Company and other purchasers to 188 acres.[10] The farmhouse (Plate 5c) stood at the junction of the modern St. Quintin Avenue and Chesterton Road.

Talbot Road Area

Owing to their isolated situation, particularly in the case of Notting Barns, hardly any building development took place on either estate during the first half of the nineteenth century, except at Kensal Green cemetery and the adjacent works of the Western Gas Light Company. In 1852, however, the Misses Talbot attempted to sell the whole of Portobello Farm, now reduced by sales to the Great Western Railway and the gas company to 166 acres. The estate was described as 'admirably adapted for Building ground, Nursery grounds or Market gardens', and was offered either as one lot or in separate lots of not less than ten acres each, the price being £1,000 per acre.[11] But except at its south-eastern extremity the estate was still too far from the suburban frontier for building speculators to be interested at this price, and even for the south-eastern limb there was only one buyer—the unfortunate Dr. Samuel Walker, whose ill-fated speculations on the neighbouring Ladbroke estate have already been described in Chapter IX. He needed the southernmost part of the Portobello estate in order to provide suitable access from Paddington to his sprawling empire further west on the Ladbroke estate, and by a series of agreements which he signed with the Misses Talbot in 1852 he contracted to buy

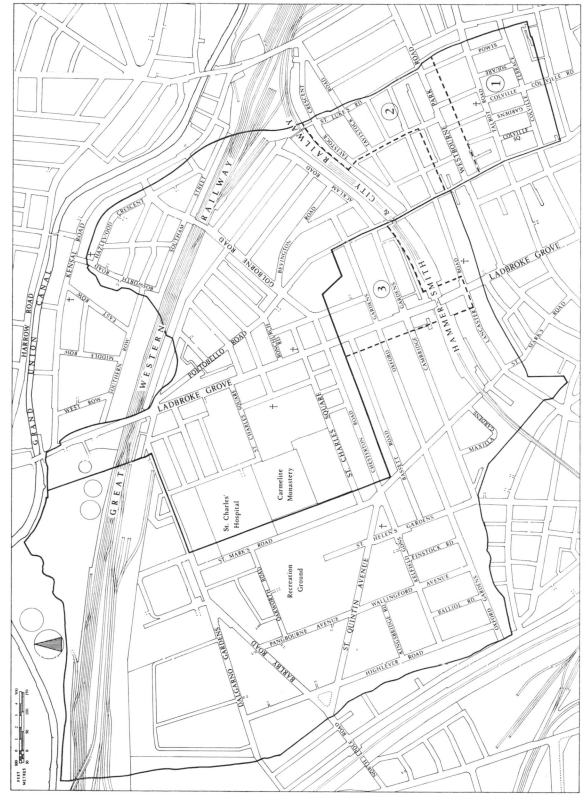

Fig. 78. The Portobello (*right*) and St. Quintin (*left*) estates. Continuous lines denote estate boundaries. Broken lines enclose (1) Tippett's development:
(2) Vigers' and Burbury's development: (3) Blake's leasehold ground on the St. Quintin estate. Based on the Ordnance Survey

fifty-one and a half acres of their land for £51,500. Only the site of the great church (All Saints') which he intended to build on his estate was, however, immediately conveyed to him, and the remainder was left on mortgage at 3½ per cent interest, Dr. Walker undertaking to complete the whole purchase within three years. In May 1853 he paid the Misses Talbot £24,500 and another seventeen acres were conveyed to him.[12] Owing to his subsequent financial misfortunes he was never able to complete the purchase of the rest of the land for which he had contracted.

The building of All Saints' Church began in 1852 (Plates 14, 15). Sewers were laid in Colville Gardens and Terrace[13] but elsewhere on Dr. Walker's seventeen acres hardly any house building took place, the years 1853 to 1856 being a period of steep decline in the total volume of building throughout West London. By 1854 Dr. Walker's financial position was already extremely precarious; the advances which he had made to builders on the security of building leases (mostly on the Ladbroke estate) now amounted to over £66,000,[14] and in March 1855, when his own mortgage debts amounted to some £90,000, he handed over the management of all his property in Kensington to three trustees, H. M. Kemshead, a West India merchant, Edmund Robins, an auctioneer, and Richard Roy, the solicitor who for the previous ten years had dominated the building development on the Ladbroke estate.[15] In October of the same year the trustees sold the northerly ten of Dr. Walker's seventeen acres of the Portobello estate to W. J. Roper of Great Coram Street, gentleman, for an unrecorded sum.[16] The southern portion was, however, retained until 1860, when the upward curve of building activity enabled Dr. Walker (who had by now resumed control of his own affairs) to sell it to a builder, George Frederick John Tippett of Paddington,[17] who later in the same year also bought Roper's land to the north (see fig. 78).[18]

G. F. J. Tippett was thirty-one years of age in 1860.[19] He was a builder of considerable substance who at about this time was building a number of large terrace houses in Prince's Square, Leinster Square and the surrounding vicinity of Paddington.[20] On his Kensington estate two rela-

tives, Thomas Sheade Tippett and John Tippett, assisted him, and another builder, John May, was associated with him as a trustee, a relative of May, Thomas Bassett May, being also concerned. G. F. J. Tippett was, however, the man in charge, combining the roles of ground landlord, developer, builder, and probably architect as well.

The development of his estate took place between 1860 and 1875, when it was virtually complete. Almost all the houses consist of long stucco-faced ranges, four to six storeys in height over deep basements, many having projecting porches supported on columns. None of them has a wider frontage than 22 feet, and the total depth of each plot ranges between 60 and 100 feet. Three ranges—one each in Colville Square (Plate 74b), Colville Gardens and Powis Square—back on to shallow communal gardens,* a feeble imitation of the earlier and more spacious paddocks on the Ladbroke estate, and a device which had already been adopted in Prince's and Leinster Squares. These three ranges are, indeed, very similar to Tippett's slightly earlier work in Paddington, each house on its street front having a doorway projecting across the basement area to the line of the pavement, the projection being carried up through three storeys above the entrance.†

The whole estate presents an unusually homogeneous appearance in marked contrast with the more varied developments in the surrounding streets, the frontiers of Tippett's property being still clearly revealed by the sudden changes of house type in Powis Terrace, Colville Road (between Nos. 21 and 23, for instance) and elsewhere. Tippett evidently intended to cram in as many large houses as he could on his land, and their consistent though undistinguished style suggests a single authorship for their design— very probably (in the absence of any evidence on the point) that of Tippett himself.

Building development proceeded by the normal leasehold method. Through his trustee, May, Tippett was himself the lessee of a large number of plots, and other builders to whom he granted ninety-nine-year leases during the 1860's included T. S. Tippett,[23] Henry Saunders and Walter Blackett (architect and surveyor), all in Colville Terrace; John Wicking Phillips, Edward

---

* Two more such ranges were originally adumbrated, on the north side of Talbot Road flanking All Saints' Church.[21]
† The design of Prince's and Leinster Squares has been attributed to the architect George Wyatt, but there is no evidence that Wyatt was concerned in the design of Tippett's houses there.[22]

Gurling and John May for the whole of Colville Square;[24] John Tippett and Thomas Bassett May for eight plots in Powis Square, and the latter also in Portobello Road.[25] The building of All Saints' Church was resumed after an interval of some years, and at the time of its consecration on 9 April 1861 *The Building News* commented that in recent months 'speculating builders have gradually and timidly approached the church. What has so long been deemed a quicksand has turned out good solid ground, and roads are now being cut, and buildings are rising, north, east, south, and west, around it'.[26] Powis Square, where G. F. J. Tippett himself built thirteen houses, and Powis Terrace, where he built nine, were among the last parts of the estate to be completed, his own work being supplemented in the early 1870's by three builders from a distance—Colls and Sons of Camberwell, J. A. Miller of Upton, Essex, and (prior to his removal to Ladbroke Grove) Walter Lethbridge of Plymouth.[27]

Between 1860 and 1875 some 250 houses were built on Tippett's seventeen acres of land, and if the average cost to the builder of each house is taken to have been £1,000, the total fixed capital invested amounted to some £250,000. Nothing like this sum was, of course, needed as working capital at any one time, but the financial resources required were nevertheless substantial. At first Tippett was able to mortgage the remaining vacant land, the mortgagees including George Penson, the successful City cheesemonger who also invested heavily on the Ladbroke estate, Edmund Robins, the auctioneer who had acted as one of Dr. Walker's trustees in 1855, a solicitor, and a clergyman.[28] Some of these early mortgages were repaid within a few months, to be replaced by larger leasehold mortgages on the security of completed or semi-completed houses, while other houses were sold, either leasehold or freehold.[29] All of these mortgages were arranged through solicitors, Tippett's often being Alexander Copland Hemsley of Albany, Piccadilly, who was doubtless a descendant of Alexander Copland, the speculative builder of Albany, and who was therefore likely to understand the financial requirements of the building business.

But to meet the rapidly growing capital needs for the development of both his Kensington estate and his land in Leinster and Prince's Squares, Paddington, Tippett turned increasingly to insurance companies for his mortgages. As the ground landlord or head lessee he was able to decide with which company all his new houses should be insured against fire; and his undertakings to bring all such new insurance business on a part of his property to a particular company no doubt provided a powerful incentive to its directors to lend him the capital which he needed for the building of the houses. In 1861 he mortgaged six houses in Colville Road to the County Fire Office,[30] and by September 1864 his total loans from this company amounted to £19,000, secured on parts of his property in both Kensington and Paddington.[31] A month later he was able to obtain a loan of £45,000 from the Sun Fire Office on the security of thirty-three houses in Leinster and Prince's Squares, and by April 1865 he had arranged for the insurance of these houses with the Sun for £100,000.[32] In October of the same year he obtained a five-year loan of £6,000 at 5 per cent interest on five houses in Powis Square from the London Assurance Corporation,[33] and in 1866 another £4,500 from the County, plus £3,000 from Ransom, Bouverie and Company, bankers, of Pall Mall.[34] In 1868 he sold thirty-one houses, mostly in Portobello Road, and repaid the mortgage of £45,000 from the Sun.[35] Later in the same year he transferred a number (perhaps all) of his remaining loans from private mortgagees, and those from the London Assurance and Ransom, Bouverie, to the Law Life Assurance Society,[36] which presumably offered better terms, and with which he had assured his life for £10,000. In April 1870 his total mortgage debt to the Law Life amounted to over £125,000.[37]

The builders to whom G. F. J. Tippett granted ninety-nine-year leases seem to have sold their leases for a lump sum when each house was nearing completion. In July 1864, for instance, T. S. Tippett agreed to sell his ground lease of a house which he was then building in Colville Terrace to a lady in Gordon Square, Bloomsbury, for £1,150. She paid a deposit of £150, but before payment of the remainder became due, T.S. Tippett had to meet a debt to a stone merchant, no doubt for building materials, and assigned the benefit of the agreement to him in settlement.[38] We have already seen that G. F. J. Tippett sold some of his houses, but he also retained as many as his overall financial situation would permit, particularly those of the best quality, and let them on short leases of between three and twenty-one years' duration, for rents ranging up to £140 per annum for a single house in Powis Square. By 1869 his total annual receipts for rents amounted to well over £3,800 from his Kensington property, and to over £4,500 from that in Paddington.[39]

The census of 1871 shows the social composition of the inhabitants of Tippett's houses. Forty-six houses, all of four or five storeys over basements, are recorded in the north–south ranges of Colville Square, Colville Gardens and Powis Square. One of these was uninhabited, and the remaining forty-five houses contained 402 residents, of whom 135 were servants. The average number of occupants per house was thus 8·9, of whom 3·0 were servants. Each house was occupied as a single household, but half-a-dozen were used as schools. Three of these were for girls, but the other three, which occupied contiguous houses in Powis Square, evidently consisted of a coaching establishment for young men. In Colville Square a 'classical and mathematical tutor' combined teaching with taking in boarders (who, judging from their advanced ages, were not pupils). Several of the many boarding-houses which were later to become such a feature of this district were already in existence in 1871, for Colville Gardens contained two, in one of which the boarders were of very lowly social status— journeyman printer, 'domestic servant out of employ', and milliner.

Other householders included seven merchants, four stockbrokers and four lawyers, three manufacturers and three retired army officers, two bankers (one the manager of the Hanover Square branch of the London and County Bank) and two physicians, and one jeweller, woollen draper, civil servant and baronet's widow. The largest single household (excluding the girls' schools) was that of a 'wholesale book manufacturer', which consisted of himself, his wife, their eight children and four servants.

This social structure was extremely similar to that of Kensington Park Gardens in 1861 (see page 235), but whereas the houses in the latter street were in large measure to retain their place in the Victorian social hierarchy, Tippett's great tall terraces were soon to prove to have been the wrong sort of buildings for their topographical

situation. In the more prosperous middle-class strongholds of Bayswater and South Kensington houses of such size could retain their social *cachet*, even though much modified internally: but in Tippett's part of North Kensington, at the bottom of the further side of St. John's Hill, with a street market in Portobello Road* growing up on one side and a slum in Bolton Road on another,[41] a gradual decline was inevitable; and once it had set in, it proved irreversible. Tippett had started to build his great solid ranges in the early 1860's at the moment when the future social character of much of North Kensington was about to be transformed by the Hammersmith and City Railway, opened in 1864. Except in the principal street of the locality (Ladbroke Grove), smaller, lower houses, either terraced or paired (in Oxford and Cambridge Gardens, for instance), were now to answer the social requirements of residents who depended mainly on the railway for transport. In the 1880's the carriage-folk for whom Tippett had catered, and for whose equipages he had provided three rows of mews and stables, did not wish to live any longer on a social island surrounded by a sea of predominantly lower middle-class housing. When their twenty-one-year leases expired many of them evidently moved away, and in 1885 Tippett, now describing himself as a house owner and dealer in house property, was declared bankrupt. His total liabilities amounted to some £860,000, on which he claimed that there would be a surplus of some £60,000. He attributed his failure to 'his inability to let a large portion of his property and to the pressure of secured creditors'.[42]

Internal sub-division of houses had begun at least as early as 1881, when two in Powis Terrace had been converted into flats.[43] By 1888 two houses had been sub-divided in each of Colville Gardens, Colville Terrace and Powis Square, while in Colville Houses there were three and in Powis Terrace thirteen sub-divided. Inhabitants of the district included a Member of Parliament, a Major-General, a Baron and (in Colville Terrace) four army officers of field rank.[44] The vicar of All Saints' Church could nevertheless state that 'there is no wealth or even moderate means in the parish to any appreciable extent',[45]

---

* Portobello Market dates back to the late 1860's or early 1870's, when building was still proceeding in part of the street. At first it was held on Saturdays only, principally for food, but since the late 1920's trade has taken place on all weekdays, and the market is now famous for its antiques and bric-à-brac. The stalls extend from Westbourne Grove to Wheatstone Road.[40]

and several houses were already in institutional use; in 1888, for instance, there was a convent, a college of music and dramatic art, a ladies' college, and a home for French governesses. By 1900 seven out of thirteen houses in Colville Houses had been sub-divided, ten plus five boarding-houses out of twenty-five in Colville Gardens, ten out of thirty-five in Colville Square (with several others in institutional use), and thirteen plus three boarding-houses out of forty-eight houses in Powis Square. Three houses here were still occupied by private tutors, who now specialized in coaching for the Indian Civil Service examinations. Most of the divisions were into two or three flats or maisonettes, but in Colville Houses one house had already been divided into six. The number of boarding-houses in these and other streets was, in fact, probably larger than the figures given above, for very many householders in the locality were women, some of whom, it may be conjectured, relied on taking in lodgers for part of their living.[46] In 1911 the vicar stated that 'the neighbourhood grows poorer year by year'.[41]

Soon after the war of 1914–18 the Kensington Borough Council bought twelve houses in Powis Square and converted them into a total of sixty-eight flats. By 1922 only five of the forty-eight houses in the square were listed as still in single occupancy, and except in Colville Square and Terrace, where only about half the houses had been divided, the pattern was much the same in the surrounding streets. The tenants housed by the Council in Powis Square probably accelerated (or were thought to have accelerated) the continuing social decline, and internal sub-division into ever smaller units continued.[47] In 1928 the locality was described as 'rapidly becoming poorer and more Jewish', and in 1935 as a 'largely slum area: and partly large houses turned into one-room tenements and small flats'.[41] By the 1950's and 1960's, some hundred years after Tippett had created it for a very different clientèle, the district had become a profitable field for the exploitation of poor tenants, and Nos. 1–9 Colville Gardens provides a case in point. 'The entire terrace, let off a floor at a time to [rent-]controlled tenants, was bought in 1954 for £8,000. Between this date and 1962, it produced an estimated gross income of £78,000. But between 1962 and 1966,

only four years later, the income was again £78,000: the result of easing out the former tenants and reletting by the room.'[48]

The building of the Hammersmith and City Railway

In the layout of the remainder of the Portobello estate the developers were catering for a new clientèle for whom suburban living had for the first time become possible by the building in the early 1860's of the Metropolitan Railway and the branch line from Paddington to Hammersmith. The large, or at any rate spacious houses, some of them paired and all of them with either their own gardens or with access to a large communal open space, which had hitherto been built in such large numbers on the Ladbroke and Norland estates, did not answer the social needs of North Kensington in the 1860's. On the Portobello estate the speculators were also the ground landlords and therefore had a free hand in determining the type of building development to be undertaken, subject only to the general supervision of the Kensington Vestry, the Metropolitan Board of Works and the district surveyors. Their object was to cover the ground with as many modestly-sized dwellings as possible. Narrow three-storey terraced houses, mostly with basements and only a small back yard, are therefore the predominant type here. In marked contrast with the earlier layout of the Ladbroke and Norland estates, there were no squares,* crescents or communal gardens, and even that other characteristic feature of Georgian and early Victorian suburban layouts, the mews, was noticeably less frequently to be found, for few of the residents could afford a carriage, and the railway was nearby to supply their travelling requirements.

On the St. Quintin estate, rather more remotely situated, the developers were subject to a measure of control by the ground landlord. The streets were wider than on the Portobello estate, the house-plots (which provided both a front and back garden) were larger, and in the first phase of building during the 1860's and 1870's in Cambridge Gardens and Oxford Gardens west of Ladbroke Grove, and in Bassett Road, the houses were detached or paired, and substantial

* St. Charles Square was merely a group of religious and educational buildings occupying a large rectangular space and surrounded by houses.

in size. Even here, however, the almost complete lack of mews accommodation demonstrates that this, too, was from the first a suburb primarily intended for frequent or even daily users of the railway.

The building of such a suburb in North Kensington had been made possible by the construction of the Metropolitan Railway from Paddington to Farringdon Street, on the outskirts of the City—the first underground railway in the world. The first building contract had been awarded in December 1859, but formidable constructional difficulties were still being encountered in June 1862, and the line was not opened to the public until 10 January 1863. During the first six months of its operation the railway carried a daily average of 26,500 passengers, trains running at fifteen-minute intervals throughout most of the day, with a ten-minute service at the rush hours. The third-class return fare was five pence, and in May 1864 a workmen's fare of threepence return was introduced.[49]

This first stretch of the Metropolitan Railway provided quick, cheap access to the City from the northern and western suburbs of London, and in order to extend its catchment area still further afield several new feeder lines were within a few years connected to it. The first of these (and the only one to serve North Kensington) was the Hammersmith and City Railway, an independent company incorporated by Act of Parliament in 1861 and supported by both the Great Western and the Metropolitan Railway. It extended from the Great Western main line at Green Bridge—about a mile west of Paddington Station—southwestward across North Kensington and into Hammersmith, where it terminated near the Broadway. A branch line from Latimer Road provided a connexion with the hitherto moribund West London Railway, opened in 1844 from Willesden to West Kensington near the modern Olympia. Throughout almost its whole course the new line passed across the fields adjoining the suburban frontier, and when it was inaugurated in 1864 its half-hourly service through Paddington Station on to the Metropolitan and thence to Farringdon Street, for a third-class return fare of sixpence, opened almost all the remaining undeveloped parts of North Kensington to the building speculators.[50]

Three of the original directors of the Hammersmith and City Railway Company had, indeed,

been already engaged in building speculation in the area for some years. These were Stephen Phillips, a City merchant, who in addition to extensive building interests in Islington and at Westbourne Park, Paddington, also owned some ten acres of the Ladbroke estate around Camelford Road (see page 220); James Whitchurch, an attorney of Southampton origin who owned a large quantity of partially developed land in the vicinity of Bramley Road (see page 344); and much the most important, Charles Henry Blake, esquire, whose extensive speculations on the Ladbroke estate, largely completed by 1860, have been described in Chapter IX. His contribution to the direction of the new company, and those of his co-director, John Parson, are worth examining in some detail for the murky light which they cast upon the ethics of mid-Victorian business behaviour.

Blake had probably been the principal promoter of the Hammersmith line. In 1861 he had recently completed the development of Kensington Park Gardens, Stanley Crescent and Stanley Gardens, and was beginning to exploit land in the vicinity of Blenheim Crescent which had formerly belonged to Dr. Walker. In March of that year, when he had been the principal witness for the embryo company's Bill during its passage through Parliament, he had stated that the proposed railway was 'very much wanted', and that it would double the value of property adjoining his own.[51]

By this time the Misses Talbot, who owned about two thirds of the land in Kensington needed for the construction of the railway, were once more finding buyers for their Portobello estate, and had in December 1860 sold seven acres on either side of Westbourne Park Road to Edward Vigers, a timber merchant, and his associate, Samuel Burbury of Leamington, the latter having probably been drawn into metropolitan land speculation through a relative who was a lawyer of Lincoln's Inn. The price was £1,000 per acre—the same as that paid for adjoining land by Dr. Walker in 1853—and the conveyance also granted to the purchasers a five-year right of pre-emption over any ten other acres of the estate which they might select.[52]

Blake was not the man to let a profitable opportunity slip by, and in or before November 1862 he took the greatest risk of his life when he agreed with the Misses Talbot to buy the whole of the remainder of their estate, which was then estimated as 130 acres in extent, subject to Burbury's and Vigers' right of pre-emption. The purchase price was to be £107,500, equivalent to about £828 per acre, the reduction from £1,000 per acre being no doubt due to the right of pre-emption and to Blake's willingness to take the whole property.[53]

In order to finance this colossal investment Blake immediately offered a one-fifth share to Rummins, the contractor for the building of the railway, who refused, and then to the chairman of the company, John Parson, who accepted. Blake's own solicitors, Benjamin Green Lake and John Kendall, each took a one-tenth share, and Blake himself retained the remaining three fifths.[53*]

When Blake signed the agreement to purchase the whole estate, the Hammersmith Railway Company had already given notice to the Misses Talbot of its intention, pursuant to the powers conferred by its Act of 1861, to buy two acres.[53] The land now had to be acquired from one of the company's own directors, acting in association with the chairman, and in December 1862 Lake and Kendall demanded £7,500—a figure subsequently raised, after Burbury and Vigers had filed a bill in Chancery against Blake to enforce their right of pre-emption, to no less than £20,000, i.e. £10,000 per acre.[54] The directors of the company, with Parson in the chair, made no objection, and the purchase price was referred to the Board of Trade for arbitration in the usual way.[55]

Parson, who besides being chairman of the Hammersmith and City was also deputy chairman of the Metropolitan and a director of the Great Western,[54] had already had experience of situations of this kind. He was a solicitor by profession, specializing in railway business. In 1850 he had become (to quote Professor T. C. Barker) 'legal adviser and virtual dictator' of the Oxford, Worcester and Wolverhampton Railway, but his reign there had ended in 1856 'after he had been openly accused of jobbing in shares and bringing a vast amount of lucrative business' to his own firm.[56] He was not, therefore, likely to have any qualms about involving himself in an attempt to sell land at an extortionate price to a company of which he was himself chairman.

For Rummins, the contractor, however, the claim put forward by Lake and Kendall on behalf of Blake and Parson meant ruin. In addition to contracting to build the railway for £150,000, he had also bound himself to acquire all the land needed, in both Kensington and Hammersmith, for £46,000. Faced with the formidable competition of two of the directors of the company, he now demanded (successfully) that the latter part of the contract should be cancelled. By March 1863 rumours of misconduct were circulating, and in July one of the shareholders, a stockbroker named Cornelius Surgey, convened a meeting of the proprietors at which he revealed the whole situation. A resolution was then unanimously carried that 'the conduct of the two Directors in purchasing land, part of which they knew at the time would be required by the Company, and the subsequent demand from the Company of an enormously enhanced price for it, was in the judgment of this meeting, inconsistent with their position as Directors of the Hammersmith and City Railway Company ... and with the reten- of their offices as such Directors ...'.[57]

Blake, who had been the prime mover in the purchase of the Portobello estate, offered no defence and at the half-yearly meeting of the company held in February 1864 he did not seek re-election to the board.[58] His long delay in disassociating himself from the company was no doubt due to his wish to await the outcome of the action for defamation which Parson brought against Surgey. At the hearing it was asserted that Blake, with Parson's consent, had instructed his solicitors, Lake and Kendall, to make a claim for the land needed by the company, 'but giving express directions not to refer to themselves'. Lake and Kendall (each of whom, it will be recalled, also had a one-tenth share in Blake's purchase) were, in fact, to make whatever claim they thought fit without further reference to their clients; and the price claimed was in any case only intended to be a starting-point for negotiations. Parson successfully asserted that the claim for £20,000 had been made without his knowledge, and he therefore gained the verdict of the court, but the damages awarded were only for the nominal sum of £25.[54] Despite the un-favourable remarks made by the Lord Chief Justice about 'the impropriety of Directors speculating in land through which their railway

---

* These proportions were subsequently modified (see page 306).

is intended to pass', Parson claimed this result as a vindication of his personal reputation. But he nevertheless resigned from the board immediately afterwards, and the shareholders passed a resolution congratulating Mr. Surgey for his 'essential service not only to this Company but to the public at large'.[58]

Apart from the damage to their personal reputations, neither Blake nor Parson suffered by the severance of their connexion with the company. The dispute over the price of the land required was in due course settled at £2,105 per acre,[54] substantially less than the claim for £10,000 per acre, but nevertheless representing a handsome profit over the figure of £828 per acre to which Blake had induced the Misses Talbot to agree less than two years earlier. This was, moreover, only the first of a series of profitable bargains for Blake and Parson, for the railway (opened from Hammersmith on 13 June and from West Kensington on 1 July 1864) proved an instant commercial success, the total number of passengers exclusive of season ticket holders for the half year ending in March 1865 being over 1,270,000.[59]

Development by C. H. Blake on the Portobello and St. Quintin estates

Blake's agreement of November 1862 with the Misses Talbot to buy the whole of their estate had been subject to Burbury's and Vigers' right of pre-emption over ten acres. This right was exercised in 1862 and 1864, when the ten acres bounded on the north by the Hammersmith and City Railway, on the east by St. Luke's Road, on the south by St. Luke's Mews and on the west by All Saints Road were conveyed to Burbury and Vigers, who were already developing the adjoining land further east in Paddington. The price was £1,000 per acre.[60] The whole of their estate, including the land which they had purchased in 1860, is shown on fig. 78. Two acres had also been sold by the Misses Talbot in April 1862 to the Franciscan nuns for the establishment of the convent (now Dominican) on the west side of Portobello Road.[61]

The whole of the remainder of the Portobello estate (fig. 78), now consisting of 130 acres, was sold to Blake in three stages. In July 1863 the south and east part of the estate, consisting of forty-eight acres and including a few acres on the

north side of the Great Western main line in Kensal Green, was conveyed to him for £40,000, of which he subscribed £24,000 ($\frac{3}{5}$), Parson £8,000 ($\frac{1}{5}$), and Lake and Kendall £4,000 each ($\frac{1}{10}$ each).[62] A year later he bought another forty-one acres to the north of the Franciscan convent between Ladbroke Grove on the west and the Great Western Railway on the north-east, plus another small piece in Kensal Green. The price was £33,750, of which he himself subscribed £22,500 ($\frac{2}{3}$) and Parson £11,250 ($\frac{1}{3}$).[63] Lastly, in 1868, he bought the remaining forty-one acres, all to the west of Ladbroke Grove, for £34,000, of which his share was again two-thirds and Parson's one-third.[53] The total price actually paid for the whole 130 acres was thus £107,750, equivalent to £829 per acre, Blake's own personal outlay being £69,166.

He was able to finance this enormous investment because the total volume of house building in Kensington had begun to grow again, very slightly, as early as 1859, and continued to grow almost without interruption until 1868. This renewed activity had enabled him to find new backers in 1860 in the persons of William Honywood of Berkshire, esquire, William Harrison of St. Helen's Place, City, merchant, and Henry Cobb of Lincoln's Inn Fields, land agent and surveyor. They had lent him £18,000 at 5 per cent interest, and accepted transfers of many of his existing mortgages, all on the security of his property on the Ladbroke estate (see page 235). Other mortgages had been paid off with the proceeds of sales, principally of land and improved ground rents to the west of Ladbroke Grove, and by 1863 his total debts had been reduced to £46,000, of which Honywood, Harrison and Cobb held £33,500 (representing a nominal value of £52,000). The interest payments on these liabilities, some at the rate of $4\frac{1}{2}$ per cent interest and others at $4\frac{3}{4}$ per cent, amounted to about £2,153 per annum, but the net rental from his property on the Ladbroke estate now stood at £3,535, and would increase in 1864 to £3,988.[53] His overall financial position was therefore strong enough for him to obtain another loan, and in July 1863 Honywood, Harrison and Cobb advanced him an additional £25,000 at $4\frac{3}{4}$ per cent interest, with which he paid his £24,000 share of the first purchase from the Misses Talbot,[64] this land being added to the Ladbroke lands as an additional security for the mortgagees. His total debts now amounted to £71,000, mostly at 4¾ per cent interest, which represented annual outgoings of £3,339. With the rental income of £3,535, the surplus income from his whole property was only about £196 in 1863, which on his investment of £71,000 represented a return of less than one per cent.

In July 1864, when Blake bought the second portion of the Portobello estate from the Misses Talbot, he was able to secure another loan of £20,663 (at 5 per cent interest) from Honywood, Harrison and Cobb, this new land being added to their overall list of securities covering the whole of Blake's property. His total debts to them now stood at £79,000, but Honywood's own personal share amounted to only about one eighth of this amount, and Harrison and Cobb appear not to have directly involved their personal fortunes at all. They acted as City money dealers, the greater part of the money being subscribed by their clients, about a dozen private individuals with money to lend, of whom the Lake family, relatives of Blake's solicitors, Lake and Kendall, were the most substantial. The whole arrangement, which provided Blake with a reliable source of capital for the continuation of his speculations, was rounded off by the appointment of Henry Lake, and, after his death, of his partner Benjamin Green Lake, solicitor, as receiver of all the revenues of the estate, with power to pay the mortgage interest to Honywood, Harrison and Cobb, and the surplus, if any, to Blake.[53]

In addition to buying 130 acres of freehold land from the Misses Talbot, Blake was also the lessee for some twelve acres of ground on the adjoining St. Quintin estate (see fig. 78). He evidently took this land because in order to provide satisfactory access to the northern part of his Portobello estate, it was necessary to extend Ladbroke Grove due north from the northern boundary of the Ladbroke estate. This involved traversing land belonging to Colonel Matthew Chitty Downes St. Quintin, with whom in December 1864 Blake signed a building contract. He agreed, *inter alia*, to take a ninety-nine-year lease of all the frontage land, amounting to about four acres in all, on both sides of the intended extension of Ladbroke Grove between Lancaster Road and a point half-way between the modern Bassett and Chesterton Roads, where Ladbroke Grove entered Blake's Portobello lands. He covenanted that within nine months he would build

the road, sixty feet wide, and lay sewers along it, and that within two years he would continue it across his own freehold land to the Admiral Blake public house beside the Great Western Railway, access to it from St. Quintin's lands further west being also guaranteed. At the same time he also took an option (which he subsequently exercised) on another eight acres of St. Quintin's land to the east of the land fronting the east side of Ladbroke Grove, and bounded on the south by the Hammersmith Railway and on its east side by Portobello Road and the Franciscan convent.[53]

In order to provide advantageous access and lines of communication the general layout plans of the two estates were drawn up in mutual conjunction. But in many other respects building development diverged at once, and the results of this may still be seen in the social character of the area to-day. Colonel St. Quintin was an absentee ground landlord who lived in Yorkshire and employed a well-known London architect to supervise his estate in Kensington. This was Henry Currey, whose father had acted as solicitor on the Holland estate, and whose large practice included the design of St. Thomas's Hospital. His layout plan provided long straight parallel streets (now Cambridge and Oxford Gardens and Bassett Road) leading westward from Ladbroke Grove, and extending via St. Mark's Road to St. Quintin Avenue, which provided access to the more distant parts of the estate. The streets were fifty feet wide, and (except in Blake's eight-acre leasehold property east of Ladbroke Grove) lined with substantial detached or paired houses, each with its own front and back garden. Those in Cambridge and Oxford Gardens and Bassett Road were probably designed by Currey. All development (at any rate in the 1860's and 70's) proceeded under leasehold building agreements, the lessees being closely controlled by the terms of their agreements with St. Quintin. Blake, for instance, in his agreement with St. Quintin for the land fronting Ladbroke Grove (where terraced houses were permitted), had to covenant to build at least seven shops, each to be worth not less than £700, and at least fifty-four houses, each of £1,200 in value. He was to submit all plans and elevations for Currey's approval, to comply with a detailed constructional specification, and to complete the whole programme within four years. In return, St. Quintin was to grant him ninety-nine-year leases at a peppercorn rent for the first twenty-one months and then at £610 per annum, equivalent to a ground rental of about £152 per acre.[53]

On his own freehold lands on the Portobello estate Blake, by contrast with St. Quintin, was both ground landlord and speculator in personal charge of operations. Although he frequently consulted his principal partner, Parson, on business matters, it was Blake who always initiated and decided. He lived in one of his houses on the Ladbroke estate, within half a mile of his Portobello lands, and in addition to his almost daily visits to his solicitors, Lake and Kendall, in Lincoln's Inn, he evidently exercised close personal supervision on site as well. His sole object was to exploit his land as rapidly as possible, either by granting building leases or by outright sales, in order that he might free both his Ladbroke and Portobello lands from his enormous mortgages. For his layout plans he was therefore satisfied with the services of a local surveyor, J. C. Hukins of Westbourne Grove, assisted by a clerk of works to supervise building lessees. The building agreements which he granted stipulated the minimum value of the houses to be built, but they do not seem to have contained any constructional specification or requirements of design. Most of the houses erected here were of the three-storey terraced variety with basements. The plots were usually only some 18 to 20 feet wide and 60 feet deep, compared with some 30 to 35 feet by 100 feet on the St. Quintin estate, and there was therefore only room for a yard at the back. Some of the streets developed by these means have in the twentieth century achieved nationwide notoriety as the scene of some of the worst housing conditions in all London; and it is therefore worth noting that even as early as 1868, Colonel St. Quintin's agent was so perturbed by the type of housing in course of erection on Blake's lands that he threatened, during negotiations over an adjustment of boundaries, to prevent all access to them from the St. Quintin estate 'unless arrangements were come to regulating the class of houses to be built by Mr. Blake'. And in the following year he 'declined to enter into any arrangements as to roads until he knew what class of property would be erected' on an adjoining section of Blake's property.[53]

Blake seems not to have repeated his previous unhappy experiment in Stanley Gardens of building houses on his own account by contract with a builder, and the development of his Portobello and St. Quintin lands was mainly by the traditional procedure of building agreements followed by the grant of building leases. In the autumn of 1864, for instance (to take one example, probably typical of hundreds of others) he agreed with William and James Rickett of Paddington, builders, to lease one acre of ground on the north side of Lancaster Road between Basing Street and All Saints Road. The term was to be for ninety-nine years from Michaelmas 1864, but payment of the ground rent of £143 per annum was not to commence until December 1867. Building was to commence by Christmas 1864, and in October Blake's surveyor, Hukins, was applying to the Kensington Vestry to lay a sewer along Lancaster Road. W. and J. Ricketts were to spend over £12,000 on the building of at least twenty houses plus stables, and fifteen of the houses were to be completed by September 1866. Each house was to have three storeys and a basement, and a frontage of eighteen or nineteen feet. Until September 1866 the Ricketts were to have the option of buying the land for £2,388, but if they did not exercise this option Blake covenanted that as soon as the ground rent of £143 had been secured by the building of houses, he would grant them the remaining land in fee.[65]

Most of Blake's building agreements with individual builders were for a score of houses or less, but the field of operations of the Land and House Investment Society Limited was very much larger, ultimately comprising the greater part of the land bounded by Portobello Road, the Great Western main line, and Acklam Road. The directors of the company included Alexander Fraser, a civil engineer of Campden Hill,[66] who on his own account also bought some two acres from Blake in the vicinity of Tavistock Crescent and Road,[67] and its solicitor was Frank Richardson of 28 Golden Square, doubtless a relative of the Charles Richardson of the same address who had organized the development of the Norland estate in the 1840's. In the winter of 1864–5 the company's architect and surveyor, Joseph Houle, was supervising the building of the roads and sewers in the area between Golborne and Acklam Roads,[68] and in 1866 Blake and the company granted thirty-three building leases of individual houses in this vicinity, almost all of them to builders. In 1868–9 they granted a total of nearly four hundred leases there, nearly all of the houses in these long monotonous streets being of the narrow three-storey terraced type, mostly with basements and projecting bay windows at ground-floor level (Plate 74a, e). The paving of the roads as well as the building of the sewers was paid for by the company.[69] By 1870 vacant land and a number of completed houses south of Golborne Road were sold to the company. By 1875 this pattern had been repeated in the area to the north of Golborne Road, and in 1878 the company was wound up voluntarily.[70]

An important function of the developer was to keep up the momentum of building once it had started. Blake, with an ample supply of capital at his disposal, was able to do this by lending money to the builders with whom he had made building agreements, usually at 6 per cent interest reducible to 5 per cent for prompt payment. A large proportion of these loans was to builders working in Ladbroke Grove, where it was particularly important to maintain the progress of building (see also page 331). This was the principal line of north–south communication across Blake's property, and speculators would be more likely to take land in the side streets if building in Ladbroke Grove were already well advanced. Blake's partner, Parson, who also made loans of this kind, did so, for instance, to F. and J. Gait when they were building in Ladbroke Grove in 1873, and some of the building agreements even contained a schedule of the loans to be made to the builder by Blake and Parson as work progressed. By this means the builders were protected from unforeseen fluctuations in the money market, and development proceeded smoothly, even during the financial crisis of 1866. There is no record of any of these loans being dishonoured, and in 1873 (the year after Blake's death) loans outstanding to builders amounted to over £10,000, most of which were to the executors of J. W. Phillips for houses in Ladbroke Grove, and to Messrs. McFarland and Nance for work in St. Lawrence Terrace. Loans to builders continued to be made in diminishing amounts by Blake's executors throughout the 1870's; they were all repaid by 1884.[53]

Another way in which Blake assisted the builders while at the same time making a profit for himself was by the purchase and sale of improved ground rents. By purchasing the improved ground rents of newly completed houses from the builders to whom he had granted building leases, he provided them with a quick return of their capital and thus enabled them to enter into fresh building agreements elsewhere on the estate. In 1872, for instance, he bought improved ground rents in Bonchurch Road from the builder John Howell at a price equivalent to eighteen times the annual ground rent (i.e. 'eighteen years' purchase'). Two years later his executors granted fresh building leases to the same builder, to whom they were also making mortgage loans, for houses in St. Charles Square.[71] Blake's own large capital resources allowed him to wait for the profit which he could hardly fail to make by selling investments of this kind a few years later, for the value of both land and houses was constantly rising in the 1860's and 1870's. In the five years 1874–8 his executors spent an average of some £920 per annum on the purchase of newly improved ground rents, while at the same time selling others; and sometimes (as in the case of Howell, who bought the freehold ground rents which he had himself created in St. Charles Square) they sold the freehold interest for rates as high as twenty-four years' purchase. The buyers included builders and other private investors (particularly spinsters and clergymen), and corporate owners such as the Tallow Chandlers' Company and the Prudential Assurance Company.[72]

The financial assistance which Blake was able to provide for the builders on his estate was probably partly responsible for the infrequency of bankruptcies there during the 1860's and 70's. The majority of the builders cannot, however, have been assisted by Blake, either by loans or by the purchase of improved ground rents, for in 1871, for instance, there were no less than thirty-seven different builders at work on the Portobello and St. Quintin estates. The total number of houses and stables in course of erection was 172, the average number for each builder being therefore between 4 and 5. The largest number of houses undertaken by any one builder in that year was 13—by J. W. Phillips, and 13 also by Messrs. Pargeter.[73]

The outright sale of vacant land was another profitable means by which Blake and later his executors maintained the progress of building, the receipts being used either to reduce the mortgage debt or to finance fresh capital outlay. As early as 1865 he considered selling the greater part of the Portobello estate (a hundred acres) to the West London Freehold Ground Rent Association (Limited), at a price of £1,350 per acre—a useful profit on the £828 per acre which he had agreed in 1862 to pay to the Misses Talbot. In its public announcement of its provisional agreement to purchase, the Association stated that it expected to make a profit of some £150,000 within ten years by the formation and ultimate sale of improved ground rents.[74] This bargain did not, however, materialize, and no large sales of vacant land took place until 1868, when the purchase of the third and last part of the estate, consisting of forty-one acres, from the Misses Talbot required the payment of £34,000, of which Blake's two-thirds share was £22,666. His mortgagees, Honywood, Harrison and Cobb, evidently refused to increase their loans to him, which then stood at about £55,000, and so too did the Scottish Union Insurance Company, to whom he applied for an advance of £9,000. Honywood, Harrison and Cobb did, however, agree to the sale of parts of the property comprised in Blake's first and second purchases from the Misses Talbot (1863 and 1864), in exchange for the third portion being included in their list of securities. In October 1868, when payment of the £34,000 was already four months overdue, the lawyers acting for the Misses Talbot were 'very pressing', and the matter was not completed until December, by which time Blake had become 'unwell'.[53]

This crisis was surmounted by large sales of land between 1868 and 1870 at very high prices. The Land and House Investment Society bought 19 acres in the area between Golborne and Acklam Roads at c. £1,816 per acre and contracted to buy another 15 acres north of Acklam Road and east of Portobello Road for c. £1,787 per acre. Messrs. Pargeter, builders, paid £2,062 per acre for 1½ acres probably in Bonchurch Road, and there were other sales in this price range. By 1870 all of the 48 acres of Blake's first purchase (1863) from the Misses Talbot had been sold or contracted for, either as vacant land or in the form of improved ground rents, plus 24 of the 41 acres of the second purchase (1864).[53]

On the third portion of 41 acres, only acquired in 1868, Blake also made two large sales by 1870, but at slightly lower prices, probably due to the more remote situation of the area. The Freehold Securities Company Limited (which was closely associated with the Land and House Investment Society, having the same solicitor, Frank Richardson, and which had previously participated in development in Golborne Road), bought eight acres in the vicinity of the present St. Charles Hospital for prices ranging between £1,400 and £1,600 per acre.[75] The other purchaser, who had also previously worked elsewhere on the Portobello estate, was a builder, Gaius Foskett. In 1866 he had been granted leases by Blake of plots in Portobello Road and in Edenham Street (north of the Great Western main line)[76] before buying freehold land in Bevington Road in the following year.[77] He subsequently built houses on the south side of Chesterton Road,[78] and in 1884 blocks of artisans' dwellings in Charing Cross Road, Westminster.[79] In 1869 he paid £1,700 per acre for eight acres of land to the north and east of the present St. Charles Hospital. This hospital was originally built in 1878–81 by the Guardians of the Poor Law Union of St. Marylebone as an infirmary for their sick poor, and in 1876 both Foskett and the Freehold Securities Company sold part of their lands to the Guardians for the site.[80]

In almost all these sales Blake obtained double the price of £829 per acre which he had himself paid to the Misses Talbot and sometimes he obtained substantially more than double. With the proceeds, and the proceeds of sales of his property on the Ladbroke estate to the west of Ladbroke Grove, he was able to repay much of his mortgage debt, and when he died at the age of seventy-seven on 22 March 1872 at Bournemouth (where he had been living for several years owing to ill health), his total mortgage liability had been reduced from £79,000 in 1864 to £17,155. In May 1873 the value of the estate stood as follows:[81]

Assets

	£
1. Personal property	35,000
2. Freehold houses	
24 on former Ladbroke estate in Stanley Gardens and Crescent, Kensington Park Road and Ladbroke Grove	
1 on Portobello estate (later valued at £1,050)	40,530
3. Leasehold houses	
2 on former Ladbroke estate in Kensington Park Gardens	
13 on St. Quintin estate in Ladbroke Grove	
1 in St. John's Wood	
1 in Bournemouth	20,465
4. Freehold ground rents in Blake's sole possession arising from two houses on Portobello estate in Golborne Road	500
5. Freehold land and ground rents on Portobello estates, Blake's ⅔ share amounting to	40,000

6. Leasehold land and ground rents on St. Quintin estate, Blake's ⅔ share amounting to   8,134
7. Loans on mortgage to builders   10,411
8. In hand, approximately   1,994

       157,034

Liabilities

Mortgages on real property   17,155
Family charges (marriage settlements for Blake's four children, small annuities)   19,000

       36,155

There was therefore a surplus of assets over liabilities of some £120,879, which yielded a gross income of £3,905.[53]

This last figure represents a return of only about 3¼ per cent on the capital invested—not a very high rate for Blake's twenty-two years' assiduous attention to his property, for the imminence of ruin in 1859 on the Kensington Park estate and for the acquisition, perhaps, of a reputation for unscrupulousness through his dealings with the Hammersmith and City Railway Company in 1862–4.

By his will Blake bequeathed one third of his residuary estate to each of his two sons and one sixth to each of his two daughters, all subject to his widow's life interest.[82] His two executors—his elder son, also named Charles Henry Blake, who was a barrister and had assisted his father in the management of the estate for some years, and the solicitor B. G. Lake, continued to lease freehold and leasehold ground for building, make loans to builders, and buy improved ground rents. Other ground rents were sold in order to reduce the mortgage. After John Parson's death in December 1874 they bought his one-third share in the Portobello and St. Quintin estates for £20,000, temporary accommodation being provided by a loan of the full amount from the London and County Banking Company. The money was later raised by the sale of land, the largest purchaser being Cardinal Manning. In 1872 he had bought two acres for St. Charles Roman Catholic College at £1,800 per acre (an unusually high price for land so far north),[83] and in 1875 he bought another seven-and-a-half acres of adjoining land for the same purpose at £1,763 per acre.[84] At about the same time five acres of contiguous land were sold for £1,735 per acre to the Duke of Norfolk for the building of a Carmelite monastery, a Roman Catholic enclave of nearly fifteen acres at St. Charles Square being

thus formed. Other smaller sales included one of a single acre for £2,000. These prices exceeded the executors' expectations, and in 1876 the rents of house property were also still rising.[53]

By 1876, when Blake's widow died, all the outstanding charges on the estate had been paid off, and the value of the residuary estate was £75,890. This produced a net income of £5,000 per annum, which was equivalent to a return of over 6½ per cent on the capital. Blake's four children were now entitled to possession of their residuary interest, and they were, indeed, the chief beneficiaries from their father's long labours, one of them having a house in Scotland at Blairgowrie as well as a London residence on the Kensington Park estate. In 1877–8 they received £14,000 of capital, and between 1879 and 1882 an average annual income of £4,007, the latter representing an average annual return of 6½ per cent on the total value of the estate.[53]

In 1883 the net rental yielded £5,072, of which £4,097 was in respect of the Kensington Park estate and only £974 of the Portobello and St. Quintin properties. In the following year, however, there was a substantial fall in the amount available for distribution as income. The cost of repairs was rising, a number of houses were unlet, and when a taker could be found a lower rent had to be accepted. The area was, in fact, already beginning to decline, and it was probably for this reason that the executors decided to divide the estate among the four beneficiaries, who could then individually decide whether to sell or keep their respective shares. This was done in 1886, and in the following year C. H. Blake junior, who was probably the most knowledgeable of the beneficiaries, sold twenty-three of his leasehold houses in St. Lawrence Terrace.[53]

At the time of the division in 1886 the estates consisted of:[53]

Property		Rental £
1. Freehold houses		
23 on former Ladbroke estate in Stanley Gardens and Crescent, Kensington Park Road and Ladbroke Grove		2,862
2. Leasehold houses		
2 on former Ladbroke estate in Kensington Park Gardens		
12 on St. Quintin estate in Ladbroke Grove		
1 in St. John's Wood		
Annual rental	£1,135	
less ground rent	210	925

3. Freehold ground rents on 76 houses in Chesterton Road and 28 in St. Charles Square, all on Portobello estate   870

4. Leasehold ground rents on 23 houses in St. Lawrence Terrace, 1 in Bassett Road and 2 in Lancaster Road, all on St. Quintin estate

     Annual rental   £168

     less ground rent   5   163

               Total rental   4,820

Small samples taken from the census returns of 1871—the most recent at present open to public inspection—illustrate the social status of the inhabitants of some of the houses built on the Portobello and St. Quintin estates. In Acklam Road (Plate 74e) there were sixty-four occupied houses, most of them having three storeys with basements. Twenty-seven of them were already in divided occupation (although none of them had been built more than eight years previously), and in fifteen of these there were three or more households. The average number of inhabitants per house was 8·1, but in one case there were as many as 23 occupants. Only 22 of the 518 residents in the street were servants, but there were at least 40 lodgers. In St. Ervan's Road (Plate 74a), where the houses were very similar to those in Acklam Road, thirteen of the nineteen inhabited houses were in divided occupation, and ten of these contained three or more households. The average number of inhabitants per house was 10·8, but one house contained 27 people. Only two of the 206 residents in the street were servants, and there were only five lodgers.

The occupations of the householders in the two streets were in general similar, workers in the building trades (21 in Acklam Road and 7 in St. Ervan's Road) and on the railways (6 in Acklam Road and 16 in St. Ervan's Road) predominating in both cases. But the residents of Acklam Road were evidently marginally higher in the social scale than those of St. Ervan's Road; they included nine widows, eight clerks, three accountants, two secretaries, two army officers (both only lieutenants), two surgeons and two publishers, as well as two cooks, two bakers, two tailors, and one laundryman, toll collector, pawnbroker, cheesemonger, butler, groom, sailor and messenger. In St. Ervan's Road there were three widows and three clerks, and other householders included four policemen and four labourers.

The houses in both these streets were built

under the aegis of the Land and House Investment Society Limited. Nearby, however, in Cambridge and Oxford Gardens east of Ladbroke Grove, the situation was strikingly different. The houses here were built under Blake's aegis on land which he had leased from Colonel Matthew Chitty Downes St. Quintin. Here he had had to covenant to build houses of at least £800 in value, whereas a house in Acklam Road sold leasehold a few years later fetched only £365. In Cambridge and Oxford Gardens the houses were therefore larger, having four storeys over basements, and the small front gardens, the columns flanking the doorways, and the liberally applied coarse stucco enrichment all expressed aspirations to gentility. Here in 1871 there were fifty-five inhabited houses, of which only five were in divided occupation. The average number of residents per house was only 6·0, and 84 of the 332 inhabitants were servants, two households in Cambridge Gardens containing as many as four each, and only four having none. The householders included seven widows, five merchants, five clerks, four 'independents', three lawyers, two builders, and one naval captain, lieutenant-colonel, minister, architect, corn broker, fish factor and draper. Here, in fact, the social structure was analogous to that of the southern part of the Norland estate in 1851 (see page 292), but whereas the latter district was able (despite the presence of the adjacent Potteries) to retain its position in the social hierarchy, the eastern portions of Cambridge and Oxford Gardens were within a generation to be engulfed in the generally deteriorating conditions prevalent on the Portobello estate—a matter discussed in more detail in Chapter XIV.

Later development of the St. Quintin estate

We have already seen that effective development of the St. Quintin estate had begun in 1864, when Blake had acquired leasehold rights from Colonel Matthew Chitty Downes St. Quintin over some twelve acres of land in the south-east corner of the estate to the north of the Hammersmith Railway. At about the same time Colonel St. Quintin started to grant ninety-nine-year leases to builders of his land to the south of the railway in Lancaster Road. Some three or four years later the same process began in Cambridge and Oxford

Gardens, followed by Bassett Road in 1876.[85] These were the three long parallel streets planned by St. Quintin's architect, Henry Currey, to provide access from Ladbroke Grove to the main portion of the estate to the north-west. They were all to be intersected diagonally by St. Mark's Road, which extended north-westward from the Ladbroke estate across Lancaster Road and under the railway to the western extremity of Chesterton Road (which marks the site of Notting Barns farmhouse). From there it turned due north, parallel with the boundary of Blake's Portobello property, to the remoter parts of the estate, while another arm—St. Quintin Avenue—continued north-westward to the point known as the North Pole.

The houses to the west of Ladbroke Grove in Cambridge Gardens, Oxford Gardens as far as St. Helen's Gardens, and in Bassett Road were all built between about 1867 and 1890,[73] building proceeding from east to west under leases granted by the St. Quintins. By 1890, when building came to a halt, a few houses had also been built in St. Mark's Road to the north of Chesterton Road, in St. Quintin Avenue and in the northern part of Highlever Road.[86]

The house plots in Oxford Gardens and the north side of Cambridge Gardens are about 45 feet in width. Those in Bassett Road and the south side of Cambridge Gardens are slightly narrower, but the latter have a greater depth, some 170 feet compared with 100 feet in the other ranges. On the north side of Cambridge Gardens Nos. 60–68 (even) are large three-storey detached houses, raised on shallow basements and with centrally placed doorways flanked by columns and projecting bay windows. They are of stock brick, stuccoed at basement and ground-floor level. Westward from No. 70 the houses were built in pairs in order to reduce cost, but the fronts remain as before. On the south side there are three-storey paired houses, again with shallow basements, each house being two windows wide and the projecting bay beside the columned entrance extending up to first-floor level. All have front gardens with enough space for mature trees.

East of St. Mark's Road the pattern is very similar in Oxford Gardens and Bassett Road, most of the houses in the former being detached (figs. 79–81) while in the latter many are paired; some have projecting porches supported on columns, the entablature being surmounted by a

balustrade which extends across the full width of the house at first-floor level. Some of the stucco-work at ground-floor level is grooved and partly rusticated. Between St. Mark's Road and St. Helen's Gardens the houses in Oxford Gardens are built of red brick, paired but without basements. They have projecting wooden porches with gabled roofs, and wooden balustrades extend across the full width of each house at first-floor level.

The building over a period of more than twenty years of some two hundred houses of this nature indicates that there were plenty of buyers for them; and indeed their complacent air of quality and substance even recalls the equally repetitious grandeurs of the somewhat earlier mansions in Pembridge Square and Holland Park. The close common affinity which these two hundred houses possess also suggests that they were all designed by one architect—probably Henry Currey—and this conjecture is strengthened by the fact that they were built by a dozen or more different builders.

Between 1871 and 1890 some four hundred houses were built on the whole of the St. Quintin estate, some eighteen different building firms being involved. The largest of these builders was John Gimbrett, who built 74 houses in Cambridge and Oxford Gardens, St. Mark's Road and St. Quintin Avenue between 1871 and 1886; John Bennett, with 69 in the same streets between 1872 and 1885; J. E. Mortimer, with 54 in Maxilla Gardens (now almost totally demolished for the elevated motorway), Bassett Road and St. Quintin Avenue in 1878–90; James Rutter, with 50 in Highlever Road and St. Quintin Avenue in 1880–3; Edward Bennett, with 34 in Bassett Road and St. Quintin Avenue in 1876–1885; and Walter William Wheeler with 25 in Cambridge and Oxford Gardens in 1877–88. The other dozen firms built an average of between 7 and 8 houses each. The peak years of activity, when over 30 houses were commenced on the estate, were 1873, 1876, 1878–80, and 1883; the low years, when less than 10 were commenced, were 1871, 1875, 1884–5 and 1889–90.[73]

When Colonel St. Quintin died in 1876 his 'effects' were valued at £60,000,[87] compared with the £25,000 of the previous owner, his elder brother, who had died in 1859.[88] Colonel St. Quintin was succeeded by his son, William Herbert St. Quintin. At the time of his marriage

GROUND FLOOR 72   FEET METRES   FIRST FLOOR 72

38' 6"

39' 0"

10 0 10 20 30
3 0 3 6 9

72   OXFORD GARDENS   50

55

CAMBRIDGE GARDENS

LADBROKE GROVE

FEET METRES

10 0 10
3 0 3

ARCHITRAVE
Ground Floor

6"

1' 2½"

SKIRTING

1' 3"

EXTERNAL BRACKET

6"

ARCHITRAVE

3' 3⅝"

2' 8"

2' 10"

STAIR BALUSTER

Ground Floor FIREPLACE Front Room
marble and tiles

RAILINGS

CEILING ROSE

1' 9"

PLASTER CORNICE
Ground Floor

CEILING ROSE
Front Room

3' 10"

PLASTER CORNICE
Hall

8½"

White

Yellow

Light
Red

Black

Blue

Dark
Red

2' 2"

FLOOR DETAIL
Hall

Fig. 80. No. 72 Oxford Gardens, details of plasterwork and floor tiling

Fig. 79 (facing page). No. 72 Oxford Gardens, plans, elevation and details

STAIRCASE DETAILS

DECORATED GLASS DETAILS

Coloured Green and Brown

INCHES 12   6   0   12
MM   100   0   100   200   300   400   500

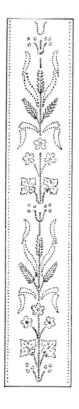

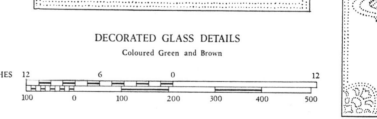

in 1885 the ground rental of his Kensington estate amounted to £3,510 per annum.[85]

Between 1891 and 1904 virtually no building took place on the estate,[73] and in 1902 St. Quintin was probably glad to sell three acres of land freehold at the northern extremity to the Great Western Railway Company.[89] Development was resumed, however, in 1905, under the auspices of Trant, Brown and Humphreys, a firm of civil engineers acting on St. Quintin's behalf. A building agreement was signed with the building firm of E. T. Daley and A. S. Franklin, and between 1905 and 1914 several hundred two-storey red brick houses with projecting bay windows were built in terraces (or occasionally in pairs) in the south-west corner of the estate (Plate 74f). They stand in the streets now known as Oxford Gardens (west of St. Helen's Gardens), Finstock Road, Wallingford Avenue, Balliol Road, Highlever Road, Kingsbridge Road, Kelfield Gardens and St. Quintin Avenue, for the layout of which Trant, Brown and Humphreys were responsible, their plans superseding those prepared by Henry Currey in 1878. Almost all the houses here have frontages of only about twenty feet, but their plots extend to a depth of about a hundred feet. They have no basements. Most of them were built by Daley and Franklin, but other builders included Thorning and Son, W. H. Eyeles and Company, and H. G. Gates.[90]

After the war of 1914–18 most of the remaining land on the St. Quintin estate was used for the provision of working-class housing, either by the Kensington Borough Council or by the numerous housing trusts then active in the Borough. In 1919 the Council bought nine acres in the vicinity of Methwold and Oakworth Roads, and by 1926 had built 202 cottages or cottage flats, to designs by the architect A. S. Soutar. The total price paid for the land was £13,500, equivalent to an average of £1,500 per acre, though the price for one part of it was £2,000 per acre.[91] In 1929–30 the Sutton Dwellings Trust built 540 flats on land to the north of Dalgarno Gardens,[92] and in 1932 the Council bought some nine-and-a-half acres of land to the east for more housing—the last remaining vacant building site of any size in the Borough. The price here was £3,100 per acre.[93] One acre was sold to the Sutton Trustees, another acre was leased at a nominal rent to the Kensington Housing Trust, and the Peabody Donation Fund took some five acres of the re-mainder on similar terms. By 1938 some 545 flats had been built here by these three bodies.[94]

A playground was provided to the east of the adjoining premises of the Clement Talbot Motor Company. The land for another, consisting of some six acres on the west side of St. Mark's Road, had been bought in 1923 with funds provided by the Kensington War Memorial Committee. This was presented to the London County Council and was officially opened as the Kensington Memorial Recreation Ground on 24 June 1926.[95] In the same year the foundation stone of the Princess Louise Kensington Hospital for Children (hitherto the Kensington Dispensary and Children's Hospital in Kensington Church Street) was laid on a site on the east side of Pangbourne Avenue. The hospital was opened by King George V on 21 May 1928. The architects were George A. Lansdown and J. T. Saunders.[96]

In 1933 the ground landlord of the estate, William Herbert St. Quintin, still of Scampston Hall, Yorkshire, died, leaving 'effects' valued at some £380,000,[97] compared with the £60,000 of his predecessor in 1876. By this time the freehold of large parts of the estate had been sold, and the process of dispersal has continued in more recent years.[98]

The social evolution of the Portobello and St. Quintin estates is described on pages 348–51.

All Saints' Church, Talbot Road
Plates 14, 15; fig. 82

In the minds of many of the developers of London's Victorian suburbs the provision of a church was often thought to be essential for the success of their speculations, and the motives which underlay their gifts of sites and their contributions to the building funds were not, perhaps, always entirely disinterested. But here at least, at All Saints', the motives of the ground landlord, the Reverend Dr. Samuel Walker, were evidently entirely unworldly, and the unfinished state of his great and beautiful church provides a sad monument to his financial innocence.

In 1851 Dr. Walker had inherited a very large fortune from his father, Edmund Walker, a Master in the Court of Chancery. As rector of St. Columb Major in Cornwall, the richest living in the county, to which his father had presented him some years previously, he had rebuilt the rectory

Fig. 81 (facing page). No. 72 Oxford Gardens, decorated glass and staircase details

there at great cost, hoping that it might become the palace of the bishopric of Cornwall which it was his dearest wish to see established. He had even offered his living as an endowment for this great object, and it was apparently in order to improve the value of his offer that he had started to speculate in building at Notting Hill. Between 1852 and 1855 he bought or contracted to buy some ninety acres of land on the Ladbroke and Portobello estates (see page 223), and on 17 July 1852, within a year of his inheriting his father's fortune, the corner stone of the 'free and open church' which was to be the spiritual centre of his new estate, had been laid.[99]

The architect was William White, who had worked in (Sir) George Gilbert Scott's office before setting up in independent practice at Truro, where Dr. Walker had put him in charge of the rebuilding of St. Columb's rectory.[100] The designs for All Saints' Church, which included a group of collegiate buildings in addition to the church itself, at once attracted attention, and in August 1852 *The Ecclesiologist* noted that the 'internal arrangements are . . . very correct; and an effect of great internal breadth will be produced, especially in the choir'.[101] All the outer walls and the spire were to be built of Bath stone, while the columns of the arcade were to be of marble.[102] No expense was, in fact, to be spared, but in March 1855 the collapse of Dr. Walker's building speculations obliged him to hand over control of all his estate to trustees (see page 233), and work at All Saints' stopped. By this time the church had been covered in and glazed, but the interior was undecorated and unfurnished, neither the tower buttresses nor the spire had been commenced,[103] and a debt of £2,000 remained due to the builder, Myers of Lambeth.[104]

Dr. Walker was never able to provide funds for the completion of the church, and in this semi-derelict state, with Myers in possession, and surrounded by the equally derelict carcases of numerous half-completed houses, it remained for some four or five years, being commonly referred to as All Sinners' in the Mud. In about 1859, however, the Reverend John Light, who had been nominated to the incumbency by Dr. Walker as patron, organized a committee to raise funds, and after some £4,000 had been spent on decorations, the purchase of an organ and the discharge of the debt to Myers, the church was at last consecrated, still without its spire, on 9 April

1861.[104] It provided 880 sittings, of which only 200 were free, and a district chapelry was assigned later in the same year.[105] The total cost is said to have been about £25,000.[106]

William White, the original architect, was not concerned in the works of completion of 1859–60. According to *The Ecclesiologist* these were 'entrusted to another hand, (hitherto, we believe, only conversant with civil engineering), to whom are due the strange painting, and the feeble reredos of sham materials'.[107] This 'other hand' is said to have been a brother of the incumbent, John Light. The decorations and fittings in general were regarded as 'deficient in taste'.[108]

As built, in the Gothic style of the fourteenth century, the church consists of a four-bay nave and aisles with short transepts gabled out from the nave roof, and a two-bay chancel with half-aisles on either side. The two principal entrances are at the base of the great tower at the west end, and through a gabled porch projecting from the south aisle. The exterior is of pale honey-coloured Bath stone, with bands and voussoirs of red, grey and buff stone.

The tower is in the Flemish manner, and provides a conspicuous landmark throughout Notting Dale. Its three lower stages are severely plain, but the belfry stage has pairs of traceried lights, and the octagonal top stage, pierced with traceried lights in continuous sequence, contains much constructional colour, both in bands and shafts. The elegant angle buttresses become free-standing at the octagonal stage, to which they are joined by discreetly detailed short flying arches.

The main body of the church is unusually lofty, the clerestory on each side containing three pairs of large plate-traceried windows, each of four lights, surmounted by trefoil windows. The aisles are of considerable height, but owing to the need to accommodate the clerestory the pitch of their roofs is too low in relation to that of the nave. The transepts, although not of great projection, possess a nobility of scale emphasized by their height and the confines of the site. Each is pierced by a rose window, that to the south having a tall traceried light set under the rose.

All Saints' is not large, but White nevertheless obtained an appearance of great size for the interior. He boldly carried the nave arcades (the pillars of which are of Devonshire marble) across the transepts, filling in the space above with stone arcading, and formed a continuation of the cleres-

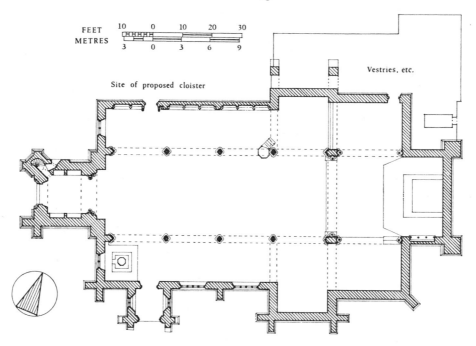

Fig. 82. All Saints' Church, Talbot Road, plan

tory, an arrangement frequently found in medieval Italian churches. The spandrels between the heads of the side and middle lights of the clerestory are inlaid with mosaics by Steven of Pimlico, while the walls were lined all round below stringcourse level with black, red and buff tiles, and bricks in courses, graduated so as to increase the lightness upwards.[103]

The sills of the north aisle windows are raised to allow for the incorporation of the cloister which it was intended should connect the church with the collegiate buildings to be erected on the north side. In the north transept the space below the rose window was designed by White for the organ, but was unaccountably not used for this purpose, Light placing it in the south transept instead, where it obscured the windows. After the war of 1939–45 the organ was moved to a new gallery at the west end of the church.

Few of the original fittings survive. The original reredos, carved by J. F. Redfern in 1878, was replaced in 1933 by the present one, which was designed by G. F. Bodley's partner, Cecil G. Hare, in the fifteenth-century Flemish Gothic manner. The marble and alabaster pulpit has been replaced by a wooden pulpit, designed by Romilly B. Craze in 1951. The hanging rood was erected in 1934,

and a new reredos was put into the Lady Chapel to the south of the chancel in 1936. Canopies over the shrines of Our Lady and St. Joseph were supplied by Beyaert of Bruges, and the statues of St. Joseph, St. Anthony and St. Mary Magdalene were made by Dupont of Bruges.[109]

The interior of the church was painted during the 1930's, obliterating the rich colours of the stone and much of its Victorian character. It was perhaps at this time that the mural painting of the Annunciation, executed by Henry Holiday in the chancel and highly praised by Charles Eastlake in 1872, was lost.[110]

All Saints' was severely damaged during the war of 1939–45. On 29 September 1940 an incendiary bomb closely followed by a high explosive bomb destroyed the Lady Chapel and the chapel in the south transept. Further damage occurred in 1944, when the glass (by Alexander Gibbs)[111] and the tracery of the east window were shattered, the roof was damaged, and the high altar was wrecked.

Restoration was completed in 1951 under the direction of Milner and Craze. The roof now differs considerably from White's design, and much of the richness was lost in the rebuilding. Some of the fixtures from St. Columb's, Lancaster

Road, which had served as the parish church while All Saints' was derelict, were moved to the restored church, including the altar of St. George and its reredos by Martin Travers, now in the south transept, and the Lady altar, now the altar of St. Columb in the north transept.

Sir J. Ninian Comper designed the sounding board above Romilly B. Craze's new pulpit, and also restored the Lady Chapel, which contains a reredos of 1953 and windows of 1955 typical of Comper's later manner. All the glass existing today, apart from that by Comper, was designed and executed by Gerald E. R. Smith of the A. K. Nicholson Studios.

The vicarage, in Clydesdale Road, was designed by Edgar P. Loftus Brock in 1891.[112]

The Church of St. Andrew and St. Philip, Golborne Road
Demolished

This church was erected in 1869–70 upon a site purchased by the trustees of the Bishop of London's Church Building Fund, a large part of the building cost of £12,000 being contributed by an anonymous 'Christian lady in Bayswater'. The architect was E. Bassett Keeling. The church provided 820 sittings and was consecrated on 8 January 1870. A consolidated chapelry was assigned in the following year.[113]

St. Andrew and St. Philip's was in the 'Early Gothic and Italian' style,[114] and was built of red brick with Bath stone mouldings. It was cruciform on plan, and consisted of nave, aisles, transepts and chancel, with a belfry at the south-east end. There were no galleries. According to William Pepperell, writing in 1872, the church was 'a credit to the architect'. He had here been 'forbidden the versatility of device' which he had displayed at St. Mark's, Notting Hill and St. George's, Campden Hill, and had proved unusually restrained. The church was said to be 'admirably adapted for the free passage both of light and sound, and the plain but variously stained glass windows ...' contributed to the 'beautiful effect of the whole structure'.[115]

In 1951 the benefice was united with that of St. Thomas, Kensal Road, and the church was subsequently demolished. Its site now forms part of the eleven acres recently redeveloped for housing by the Borough Council.

The Church of St. Michael and All Angels, Ladbroke Grove
Plate 18a, b; fig. 83

The site for this church was given by C. H. Blake and John Parson, the two principal developers of the Portobello estate, on condition that building was completed within two years from 30 December 1869. The funds were provided by J. E. Gray, who was the first patron of the living and the father of the first incumbent, the Reverend Edward Ker Gray, and the foundation stone was laid on 1 November 1870 by a cousin of the Grays, J. R. Mowbray, M.P. (afterwards Sir John Mowbray, baronet). The architect was James Edmeston, in partnership with J. S. Edmeston, and the builder was J. D. Cowland, a local man who became one of the first churchwardens. His contract was for £4,300 exclusive of the fittings and the upper part of the tower. The church originally provided some 700 sittings. It was consecrated on 17 May 1871 and a district chapelry was assigned later in the same year.[116]

The style chosen—Rhineland Romanesque in brick with terra-cotta, red Mansfield and Forest of Dean stone dressings—was a curious one for the time, when architects were tending to favour late Gothic for ecclesiastical buildings. The exterior is gritty, bare and uncompromising, the main points of interest being the apsidal projections containing the east sanctuary, the west baptistry and the south chapel, and the tower, which was to have had a gabled spire. The details of the richer parts, notably of the south wall of the nave and of the western baptistry with the picturesque stair turret to the tower and western gallery, are strong and boldly modelled. The western apse, the polygonal turret between it and the middle of the tower, and the tower itself, of which only the first two stages were built, combine to form one of the few notable architectural features at the northern end of Ladbroke Grove.

The building is basically one large almost barn-like space with no aisles, and is lit by semi-circular headed windows set within shallow recesses. It has an apse at both the east and west ends, an apsidal south chapel, and a rectangular Lady Chapel to the north. The steeply pitched wooden roof is carried on large double trusses spanning the full width of the church. These trusses rest directly on the walls, extra support being provided by semi-circular wooden arches

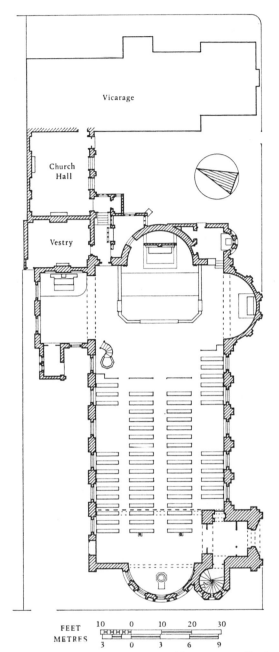

FEET
METRES

Fig. 83. St. Michael and All Angels' Church, Ladbroke
Grove, plan

cylindrical columns, and cuts off the apsidal west baptistry from the main body of the church.

The chancel is defined by a dwarf screen of alabaster, formerly bearing eagle lecterns, erected in the late 1880's, while the sanctuary occupies the eastern apse, which is approached through a semi-circular headed arch without capitals. On the north side of the nave a similar though smaller arch leads into the Lady Chapel, which was added in 1882 to Edmeston's designs, and a marble mural tablet records that the opening of what was then the 'North Transept' was performed by the Duke and Duchess of Edinburgh.[117] In the east wall of the nave a door on the north side of the sanctuary arch opens to the sacristy and vestry, while on the south side a broader segmental-headed archway leads to a chapel used for the reservation of the sacrament—a beautifully furnished little room, almost domestic in character, which is approached through wrought-iron gates painted amber red.

The finest object in the church is the Baroque reredos, an opulent Flemish design of indeterminate date, but probably of the late seventeenth or early eighteenth century, which was presented to the church during the incumbency of Prebendary H. P. Denison in about 1914.[118] The winged plaster putti, now on the wall of the south chapel, were originally seated on scrolls above the entablature of the reredos, and were replaced there by two figures in Franciscan habits which formerly flanked the large painted panel in the centre. The reredos is shown, shortly after its installation, in the frontispiece of Denison's book, *Seventy-Two Years' Church Recollections.* The painted panel which forms the centrepiece of the reredos was given by the widow of the second incumbent in his memory.[119]

The wooden pulpit, approached by a curving stair, is in the Gothic manner of the early nineteenth century. The font, of quatrefoil section on plan, is of two different marbles on a stone base, and has an octagonal spire-shaped cover. The Jacobean reredos in the Lady Chapel was erected in the late 1880's.[119]

By the 1890's the church had been richly decorated with mural paintings and diaper-work, and further murals were added during the incumbency of Prebendary Denison. These have all now been obliterated by a general redecoration carried out in 1955 under the direction of Milner and Craze, when the walls were painted a creamy grey.

which spring from brackets set into the walls. The trusses are tied by iron bars, which contribute to the utilitarian character of the church. The west gallery, erected in or soon after 1877, is supported on cast-iron volute brackets and

The vicarage was built by Cowland in 1876 to designs by J. and J. S. Edmeston, the first stone being laid by the Duchess of Teck.[120] The short cloister which joins the adjacent parish hall to the church has been obscured by later additions.

During E. K. Gray's incumbency (1871–86) St. Michael's was a fashionable church, famous for its music and frequented by members of the Royal Family. Its services were advertised on the front page of *The Times*, and the Duke of Edinburgh was known to play the violin in the orchestra. By the latter part of the 1880's, however, the social character of the area was changing, and with Gray's departure for the Curzon Street Chapel in Mayfair, St. Michael's fashionable hey-day was over.[119]

Christ Church, Telford Road
Plate 18d. Demolished

This church was built in 1880–1 by Messrs. Hook and Oldrey to designs by J. E. K. Cutts. It provided seats for 744 people and cost £5,103. It was consecrated on 14 May 1881.[121]

It was built in the French Gothic style of the thirteenth century in stock brick with bands of black and red brick, and consisted of a clerestoried nave with aisles of five bays, a chancel, and a narthex containing the baptistry. Vestigial transepts gabled out from the nave walls contained the organ chamber and part of the clergy vestry. The steeply pitched roof of slate was crowned by a tall *flèche* sited over the chancel arch.

In 1940 the benefice of Christ Church was united with that of St. Michael and All Angels, and the church was subsequently demolished. The site is now occupied by the Notting Hill Adventure Playground.

St. Helen's Church, St. Quintin Avenue

Between 1867 and 1884 the area served by this church had formed part of the consolidated chapelry of St. Clement (see page 352), whose indomitable incumbent, the Reverend Arthur Dalgarno Robinson, mindful of the rapid progress of building development on the St. Quintin estate in the latter part of the 1860's, had built the parsonage of the cure in North Pole Road in 1874–6. Until its demolition some years ago this enormous house, consisting of sixteen rooms besides 'various offices, bathroom and dressing rooms',[122] stood on the sites now occupied by Nos. 1A–4A North Pole Road and Coronation Court. Its building was soon followed by the building of a church, upon a triangular island site presented by the ground landlord of the surrounding estate, W. H. St. Quintin, who also gave £1,000 towards the building costs on condition that work began forthwith. The architect was Henry Currey, who was also acting for St. Quintin in the layout of his property, and most of the remainder of the costs was met by private benefactions and by funds accruing from the recent union of the benefices of two churches in the City. The builders were Perry and Company, whose contract was for £9,374. The new church, which provided some 900 sittings (all free), was dedicated to St. Helen and consecrated on 15 January 1884. In that year it became the parish church of the cure, but the name of the cure itself continued (very confusingly) to be St. Clement's, Kensington.[123]

St. Helen's Church was destroyed by enemy action in the war of 1939–45, and in 1951 the benefice was united with that of Holy Trinity, Latimer Road, Hammersmith.[124] The present Church of St. Helen, which was designed by J. B. Sebastian Comper, was completed in 1956 at a contract cost of £44,440. It is the principal component in an ingeniously planned group of pale pinkish-red brick buildings intended for church purposes. The ancillary buildings—vicarage, church hall, parish room and stores—are clustered round the church, which is in a freely treated late Gothic style, with elements of Perpendicular and of North European sixteenth-century architecture. It is approached through a forecourt, an attractive paved space flanked by the vicarage and the hall. The west front is of brick, pierced by the stone-dressed west door and two flanking rectangular windows, above which is a canopied niche and a small rose window high up. A bellcote surmounted by a thin spirelet caps the composition.

The church consists of a five-bay clerestoried nave with aisles and a much lower Lady Chapel which projects to the east, allowing a window above the high altar to be inserted. Dominating the west end of the church is the organ case, a handsome design by the architect's father, Sir J. Ninian Comper. It is this organ case that contributes to the Netherlandish character of the interior, with its whitewashed, Calvinistic appearance and the sparse use of colour and elaborate fittings.

The five-light east window above the high altar and the three-light east window of the Lady Chapel contain glass by Sir J. Ninian Comper in the flat manner of his later period, with much use of clear or uncoloured glass.

There is a fine brass lectern which was saved from the former church, and some robustly designed pews by R. Norman Shaw, brought here from Holy Trinity, Latimer Road.

Besides building the churches of St. Clement and St. Helen, several schools and a parsonage, Dalgarno Robinson also had a hand in the building of Bracewell Road and Brewster Gardens, in the parish of Hammersmith. In 1868 he had persuaded the Bishop of London, as lord of the manor of Fulham, to grant five acres of ground here as glebe land for the endowment of the chapelry of St. Clement, and part of this ground had subsequently been used as a site for the parsonage. In 1883 he signed a building agreement with James Rutter, a builder then active in Highlever Road and St. Quintin Avenue, for the development of the remainder of the glebe. But while he was impatiently awaiting the approval of the Ecclesiastical Commissioners the pace of building slackened and Rutter filed a petition in liquidation. Much to Dalgarno Robinson's annoyance, the terms offered in 1884 by Peter Tinckham, the builder ultimately responsible for the development of Bracewell Road and Brewster Gardens, were substantially less advantageous.[125]

Dalgarno Robinson died at his parsonage in 1899, after some forty years' work in North Kensington. [122] Dalgarno Gardens, a street-name approved by the Metropolitan Board of Works in 1887, commemorates his connexion with the area, as also does Dalgarno Way, approved by the London County Council in 1936.

Serbian Orthodox Church of St. Sava, Lancaster Road. Formerly the Church of St. Columb

A mission church dedicated to St. Columb was built here in 1888, the dedication being doubtless intended to commemorate the Cornish connexions of Dr. Samuel Walker, the founder of All Saints' Church, in whose parish the new church was situated. It was designed by Edgar P. Loftus Brock and built at a cost of some £1,400[126]

upon a site which had had to be purchased.[127] After the erection of the present church in 1900–1 it was used as a parish hall until its demolition in 1970 to make way for the social centre of the Serbian community in London.

In 1898 W. A. Pite prepared plans for an impressive new church,[128] but probably for reasons of cost they were not executed, and the architect of the present church was C. Hodgson Fowler of Durham. Building began in 1900, and St. Columb's was consecrated on 15 June 1901. It provided 668 sittings, and a district chapelry was assigned in 1902.[127]

The church, which is orientated north-south, is in the manner of the early Christian basilicas of Italy and is very broad in relation to its length. It is built of stock brick and has a low-pitched roof. The plain north front has a lean-to narthex and is pierced by a range of seven narrow round-headed lights beneath a large circular window.

The interior walls are of bare unplastered brick. The four-bay nave is flanked by three-bay lean-to aisles, and at the south end by short galleried transepts which do not project beyond the walls of the aisles. The one-bay sanctuary extends across the full width of the nave. The aisles are separated from the nave by arcades carried on stout stone columns and large brick piers. The clerestory is lit by two tall lights to each bay, and the west transept by three large windows. The east transept has no lights. The wooden roof is carried on simple trusses with semi-circular arches between the struts.

In 1951 the benefice of St. Columb was united with that of All Saints',[127] and since 1952 the building has been used as the Serbian Orthodox Church of St. Sava. Byzantine paintings and other ornaments have been introduced, but the low arcaded sanctuary screen with ambones of alabaster and marble has been retained. In the baptistry there are three windows with glass by Martin Travers. Other fittings include a bronze memorial tablet to the Serbian guerrilla leader, Drazha Mihailovich (1893–1946), by Dora Gordine.

Dominican Convent, Portobello Road
Plate 25a, b; figs. 84–5

This group of buildings on the west side of Portobello Road was originally occupied by nuns of the Third Order of St. Francis, whose convent had been founded in 1857 at the instance of Dr.

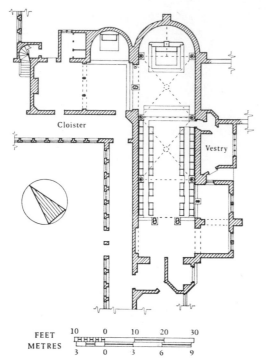

Cloister

Vestry

FEET
METRES

Fig. 84. Dominican Convent, Portobello Road, plan

Henry Manning, then Superior of the Oblates of St. Charles. The first abbess, Mother Mary Elizabeth Lockhart, was a daughter of Mrs. Lockhart, a friend of Manning during his Anglican years, who had entered the Roman Catholic Church in 1846. The young community occupied three houses in Elgin Road from 1857 to 1862, when it removed to the newly-erected buildings in Portobello Road. In 1897 it migrated to Essex, and the premises were sold to the Dominican order.[129]

The convent buildings are constructed of plain stock brick enlivened by bands of dark blue bricks, and are visible above the high wall along Portobello Road, the principal elements of the design being the little spirelet and the projecting apses of the chapels. The convent is entered through an archway which leads to a long corridor terminating in the cloister. The buildings are grouped round a central cloistered court, and there are gardens to the south and east, surrounded by brick walls.

The architect for the original buildings of 1862 was Henry Clutton, but some additions were made in 1870 to house a girls' orphanage which existed here until 1896. John Francis

Bentley, who had been Clutton's assistant, became architect to the convent in 1883, when he built a new chapter room with eight cells above facing the garden, the corridor linking the cloister with the garden to the south, the new infirmary overlooking the high altar, and the octagonal bell turret.[129] The latter is of brick with stone dressings, capped by a brick spirelet, and is very similar to the belfries at the church and school of St. Francis of Assisi, Pottery Lane, and at the church of Our Lady of the Holy Souls, Kensal New Town.

The most important part of the fabric is the chapel. It is a boldly-handled essay in simplified French Gothic of the early thirteenth century, and originally consisted of nuns' choir, sanctuary, and transept (the latter reserved for the orphans and for visitors). It is of three bays and an apse, and is vaulted, the ribs being carried on columns with simplified foliate capitals attached to the walls. The westernmost bay has a pointed barrel roof with a central transverse rib carried on rich portrait corbels. The transept is also vaulted, with an apse in which is the altar originally dedicated to St. Francis of Assisi but now to the Sacred Heart.

Bentley had designed a brass sanctuary lamp for Clutton's chapel in 1863, and in 1870 he was commissioned to design a high altar and a votive altar to St. Francis. The high altar has a deeply recessed frontal with pilasters inlaid with arabesques, animals and birds. The alabaster tabernacle is aediculated, with a trefoil arched centrepiece inlaid with gold mosaic, and a door of brass depicting the *vesica piscis*, the chalice, and the alpha and omega motifs. The chapel was enlarged by Bentley by the addition of an ante-chapel at the west end with a flat ceiling supported by coupled columns on high pedestals, and by an extension south of the ante-chapel into an organ chamber open to the nave, the wall being removed and replaced by coupled columns.[130] The chapel is lit by clerestory windows, that in the south wall overlooking the altar now being sealed, and by borrowed light from the former organ chamber. Three windows open from the infirmary above the flat ceiling of Bentley's ante-chapel so that patients may see the altar. There is also an opening from the priest's room at high level in the transept.

New fronts and backs to the choir stalls have changed the scale of the chapel, and the

Fig. 85 (facing page). Dominican Convent, Portobello Road, high altar

SECTION OF TABERNACLE

6"

4¼"

ENCAUSTIC TILE

SECTION a-a

6'3"

a

a

PLAN above and~ below Altar Table

obliteration of the original colour scheme has further altered its character. Recent changes to the conventual buildings have included additional storeys to parts of the residential wings and the insertion of metal windows.

St. Joseph's Home, Portobello Road
Plate 25c

This home for the aged and infirm is managed by the Little Sisters of the Poor, who came to North Kensington from Brittany in 1865.[131] It occupies the site of Portobello Farm, and while the old buildings were being demolished and part of the present ones erected, the Sisters appear to have lived nearby. They first occupied the new building in 1869.[132] Three years later this was described as 'a large brick edifice, giving the impression of a workhouse hospital', in which over two hundred residents were accommodated.[133] It was considerably enlarged in 1882 to designs by F. W. Tasker, who may also have designed the original building.[134] The home now consists of a large group of outwardly utilitarian three-storey buildings with semi-basements and attics, built of yellow stock bricks with bands of blue-black brick and stone, and stone dressings.

St. Charles College, St. Charles Square
Demolished

This college was founded in 1863 by 'command' of Dr. Henry Manning, then Superior of the Oblates of St. Charles. It provided a Roman Catholic education for boys of the upper classes on the system of 'our English public schools', and Manning's nephew, the Reverend William Manning, was its first principal. When its first home in Sutherland Place, Paddington, became too small, it removed to premises adjoining the Church of St. Mary of the Angels (the mother church of the Oblates of St. Charles), where boarders could be accommodated. In 1874 it moved to a new site in St. Charles Square which had been bought at the instigation of Dr. Manning, now Cardinal Archbishop of Westminster. Here 'a fine building of noble dimensions' 300 feet in length with a tower 140 feet in height surmounted by the Papal Tiara and Crossed Keys, had been erected in 1873 to the designs of F. W. Tasker. The fifteenth Duke of Norfolk was one of the principal benefactors, and the total cost was

£40,000. The college was conducted by the Oblates of St. Charles and in 1876 there were 130 students, several of whom were studying for the priesthood.[135] In 1878 Manning's abortive Kensington University College was amalgamated with St. Charles College as a higher department.[136]

In 1903 the college was discontinued, and in 1905 the buildings in St. Charles Square were taken over by the nuns of the Sacred Heart for use as a Catholic teacher-training college. The latter had been established by Reverend Mother Digby in 1874 in a wing of the Sacred Heart Convent at Roehampton, and had shortly afterwards removed to separate premises at West Hill, Wandsworth. From there it moved in 1905, under Reverend Mother Stuart, to the buildings in St. Charles Square, where it assumed the name of St. Charles's Training College for Catholic Women Teachers. In 1908 a chapel (now the Church of St. Pius X) was built to the designs of P. A. Lamb and R. O'B. North. The college remained here until its evacuation to the country on the outbreak of war in 1939. During the war the original buildings were extensively damaged by enemy action, and in 1946 the college returned to its original birthplace at Roehampton, where it took the name of Digby-Stuart College.[137]

The site and curtilage of the original college in St. Charles Square were subsequently acquired by the Archdiocese of Westminster, and with the help of substantial grants from the London County Council two Catholic secondary schools have subsequently been erected there—Cardinal Manning School for Boys, opened in 1954–5, and Sion-Manning Girls' School, opened in 1957. St. Charles Primary School, which had occupied an adjoining site and had been demolished during the war, was also rebuilt and re-opened in 1953.[138] The western extremity of St. Charles Square is now occupied by the Catholic Crusade of Rescue, and the Paddington College of Further Education also has premises adjoining the boys' secondary school.

Roman Catholic Church of St. Pius X, St. Charles Square
Plate 23c; fig. 86

This church was built in 1908 to the designs of P. A. Lamb and R. O'B. North as the chapel of St. Charles's Training College (see above). The inward-facing stalls which were originally ranged along both sides in the usual collegiate manner were removed when the chapel was converted into a parish church in 1955.[139]

The church is built of red Essex bricks, with a Staffordshire blue brick plinth. It consists of a six-bay nave with a low passage-aisle on the ritual south side, a one-bay square chancel, and a transept to the ritual south of the chancel. The long Italianate nave, lit by semi-circular-headed windows, has a barrel-vaulted ceiling, with wide transverse arches springing from brackets marking each bay. There are recessed panels with lush borders of fruit and foliage in the centres of each bay of the plaster ceiling, flanked by garlanded swags.

The short chancel, lit by lunette clerestory windows, is divided from the nave by a semi-circular coffered arch carried on deeply fluted Ionic pilasters. Filling the ritual east wall of the chancel is a large reredos in florid Italian Baroque that stands behind the simple marble altar. The tabernacle is domed, as is the exposition throne, above which is a crowned statue of the Madonna carrying the infant Jesus set within a shell-headed niche. On either side are columns of the Corinthian order supporting a segmental arch surmounted by a crown. Above the niche trumpeting angels look down, while behind them a cartouche with papal emblems is linked to the crown above. The rest of the reredos is smaller in scale, and consists of an order of debased Renaissance Ionic pilasters carrying an entablature in low relief crowned by garlanded obelisks. The dies on which the pilasters stand are enriched with entwined serpentine forms, and between them are ornate balusters. Two kneeling angels above panels in low relief depicting the Annunciation flank a central figure of the Madonna, the aediculated treatment and the positioning of the figures recalling the box-fronts of an Italian theatre.

Carmelite Monastery of The Most Holy Trinity, St. Charles Square

Plate 26; fig. 87

This convent was established by the French Carmelite nuns, nine of whom came here in 1878. One of them was a sister of the fifteenth Duke of Norfolk, who appears to have bought the site from the freeholders,[53] and who was certainly

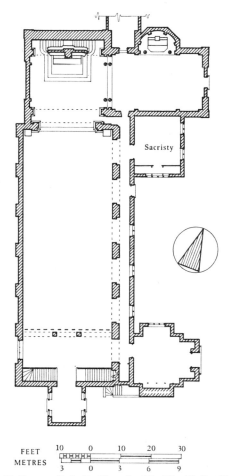

for many years a very generous benefactor of the new community. Building began in the spring of 1877 to the designs of F. H. Pownall, and the first stone of the chapel was laid by Cardinal Manning on 16 July of that year. The nuns entered the convent on 28 September 1878. Substantial additions were made to the buildings in 1893–4.[140]

The convent consists of a large irregular group of stock brick buildings, roofed with slate and enclosed by high walls. The domestic buildings are austere and plain, but well detailed and proportioned. The chapel is in the High Victorian Gothic manner, and is very little changed from its original condition. It dominates the small entrance courtyard, and is reached by a flight of steps within a vestibule leading directly from the court. On the wall of the staircase is a tablet

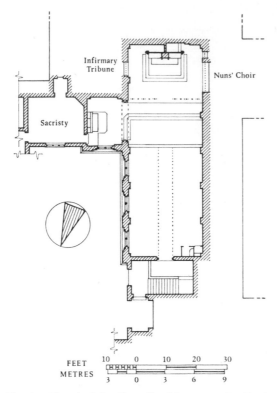

Fig. 87. Chapel of the Carmelite Monastery, St. Charles
Square, plan

commemorating Mother Mary of Jesus, who
came to England in the year of the convent's
foundation and who as prioress subsequently
founded thirty-three Carmels in Great Britain.
The exposed brick walls of the staircase anticipate
those of the chapel itself, which are strongly
polychromatic in dark red brick with bands of
dark blue and white bricks. They are further
enlivened by a deep patterned frieze, and enclose
a space six bays long with a varnished wooden
roof, lit on the liturgical north side by three
windows of two lights each with cinquefoil
tracery heads. Above the large white stone reredos,
which is raised on steps in a tile-floored sanctuary,
is a wheel window in the manner of the French
Gothic style of the thirteenth century. The projecting bay on the 'north' side contains the Lady
altar, and is reached through a segmentally-
headed arch supported on brick walls flanked by
cylindrical stone columns. The nuns' choir and
infirmary tribune, also faced with brick, are
situated on either side of the sanctuary, and are
protected by iron grilles.

Roman Catholic Church of Our Lady of the Holy Souls, Bosworth Road
Plate 23d; fig. 88

The Church of Our Lady of the Holy Souls is
one of four churches established in West London
by the Oblates of St. Charles during the second
half of the nineteenth century. It is the furthest
north of these, and is in the vicinity of the Roman
Catholic cemetery of St. Mary at Kensal Green,
which explains the dedication of the church.

The Oblates' first mission in Kensal New
Town was established in two small cottages which
were used as a school. In 1872 a two-storey red
brick building was erected in Bosworth Road to
the design of S. J. Nicholl, the upper storey being
used as a school and the lower as a church.[141]
This building quickly became too small to meet
the demands of a growing number of parishioners,
and in 1873 John Francis Bentley was asked to
provide a temporary iron church on adjoining
vacant land. This was used for several years, but
in 1880 the Oblates invited Bentley to design a
permanent church providing in the plainest manner possible at least five hundred sittings. The site
was limited, occupying an irregular parallelogram
at the corner of Bosworth Road and Hazlewood
Crescent, and Bentley was instructed to provide
a design in the 'Roman' (i.e. Italian) style, without pointed arches or stained windows, the
materials to be used being stock bricks without
stone facings or carvings. The contract for the
first stage of this work was not to exceed £1,200.[142]

By the time that Cardinal Manning laid the
foundation stone on 24 May 1881, Bentley had
succeeded in entirely diverting the Oblates from
their original intentions, departing from them
over both style and detail. His design, which he
estimated would cost over £4,000 to realize, is
not at all 'Roman', being an idiosyncratic version
of Early English Gothic, and comprising a six-
bay nave with narrow aisles, and a three-bay
chancel flanked by a sacristy and side chapel. The
exterior is of plain red brick with Bath stone
dressings. The main roof, continuous over both
nave and chancel, was originally covered with
green slates.[142]

The western façade in Bosworth Road has an
entrance opening into what was to be only a
temporary porch. Over this the wall is pierced by
triple lancets set between tall slender buttresses,
and in the top stage, between the two central

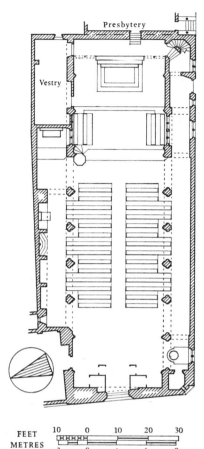

FEET
METRES

Fig. 88. Roman Catholic Church of Our Lady of the Holy Souls, Bosworth Road, plan

the cinquefoil cusping, coupled clerestory lancets, and the tracery of the screen between the sacristy and the chancel. The east end of the church abuts directly upon the presbytery, and there is therefore no east window, but the carved and painted wooden reredos, in the Tudor style, designed by the Reverend Arnold S. Baker, which formerly adorned the whole expanse of the east wall, is now masked from view. There is now no division between the chancel and the nave, a handsome chancel screen in the fifteenth-century style, surmounted by a Rood, having recently been removed. This screen was also designed by Father Baker, painted by Haslop and constructed by Clark. In the north aisle is a wooden altar designed by Bentley and painted by Stacey. The inner side of the wooden entrance porch at the west end was covered with a profusion of painted subjects, both figures and arabesques, arranged in panels, the work of the Marquis d'Oisy.[143] At some time after George Bodley's death, in 1907, the walls were painted by a former member of his staff, the whole *De Profundis* being inscribed in Gothic letters beneath the clerestory windows.

In recent years the church has been much altered. The walls are now painted in pale washes, and, as the church was always well lit, the effect is one of glare. The floor is now covered with tiles of the vinyl type, while the sanctuary floor is partly covered by a light-veined simulated marble. The description of the church, written in 1905 by Father Francis Kirk, the founder of the mission in Kensal Green, as 'graceful and pleasing to the eye', now seems sadly inappropriate.

Former Congregational Chapel, Lancaster Road

This pleasant chapel, now used for commercial purposes, is situated at the corner of Lancaster Road and Basing Street. It is in the Romanesque style, and was built in 1865–6 by James Rankin of St. Marylebone in white bricks and rubbed yellow stocks, with stone dressings sparingly used.[144]

The front to Lancaster Road is symmetrical, with a central gabled section pierced by a door and two small flanking lights, above which are three linked semi-circular-headed lights. In the upper portion is a round window with plate tracery. The wings of the façade contain the gallery

buttresses, the gable is pierced by three more small lancets. At the corner of Bosworth Road and Hazlewood Crescent is a bell turret crowned by a spirelet. The southern elevation to Hazlewood Crescent consists of a plain brick aisle wall pierced at either end by small paired cusped lancets, above which rises the high clerestory pierced by seven pairs of cusped lancets. The projection containing the organ loft forms a transeptal block which is flush with the aisle wall, relieving and terminating the long line of clerestory windows. At street level the transeptal projection contains an entrance to the church and sacristy, while its gable is decorated with stone bands, alternating with brick courses, a favourite device of Bentley's.[142]

The detailing of the interior of the church is sparse and conventional, with the exceptions of

stairs, and are each pierced by a door and a window. All the openings have semi-circular heads.

The elevation to Basing Street is plain, with round-headed windows now bricked up. The interior has been completely remodelled.

The Talbot Tabernacle, Talbot Road
Plate 28d

In 1869 an iron church was erected by Gordon Furlong near All Saints' Church, Talbot Road, to serve as a 'non-sectarian Church of Christ'. Furlong, who had formerly been a barrister, made his reputation as a preacher in Victoria Hall, Archer Street, and he was able to raise funds to build a temporary church within two years of commencing his meetings.[145]

The iron church was larger than most similar buildings in Kensington, and had an end gallery, the total capacity being for over a thousand people.[146] In 1887, during the ministry of Frank Henry White, the present chapel with its Romanesque façade of red brick and terra-cotta was built. The architects were W. G. Habershon and Fawckner.[147]

Jubilee Hall, Latimer Road

Jubilee Hall (now the Pentecostal Church) was established by the London City Mission, the foundation stone being laid on 17 June 1884. The architect was J. C. Hukins.

The building consists of a five-bay clerestoried nave with aisles, and is constructed of stock brick with red brick voussoirs to the windows and doors. Slender cast-iron columns carry the thin roof trusses. Both the clerestory and aisle windows consist of continuous bands of glazing sub-divided by vertical timber bars, similar to the glazing of industrial buildings of the period.

St. Charles Hospital, Exmoor Street
Plate 36c

This hospital was built by the Board of Guardians of the Poor Law Union of St. Marylebone as an infirmary for the sick poor of that parish, no site being then available in St. Marylebone itself. Until 1922 it was known as St. Marylebone Infirmary. In 1923 it was renamed St. Marylebone Hospital, and when it was taken over in 1930 by the London County Council under the Local Government Act of the previous year it was given its present name of St. Charles Hospital.

The foundation stone was laid by the chairman of the Guardians in 1879, and the infirmary, which provided accommodation for 760 inmates, was opened by the Prince and Princess of Wales on 29 June 1881. The contractors were Wall Brothers, whose contract sum of £109,000 included all fittings and engineering works.[148]

The architect was H. Saxon Snell, a specialist in the design of hospitals, who practised with his sons, Henry and Alfred Saxon Snell, and was one of the first members of the Architectural Association. During his career he was much involved in the harnessing of new inventions to serve functional buildings, and as a specialist in hospital design, he was the author of *Charitable and Parochial Institutions* and, with Dr. F. J. Mouatt, of *Hospital Construction and Management*. He had been an assistant of Sir Joseph Paxton and of Sir William Tite, and in 1851 had won the Royal Academy's Silver Medal for measured drawings of St. Mary-le-Bow. He was later chief draughtsman in the Science and Art Department, South Kensington, assisting Captain Fowke in the Dublin Exhibition, and in 1866 was appointed architect to the St. Marylebone Board of Guardians. He died in 1904. A week before his death he was much occupied 'with his scheme for solving the problem of hospital sites in London by building in the public parks'.[149]

The excellent plain brickwork, strong self-confident design, and assured functional planning and detail make St. Charles Hospital a most significant building for its period. It occupies a rectangular site of three and a half acres near the north-west end of Ladbroke Grove, which was purchased from C. H. Blake's executors. The buildings are planned on the pavilion principle, each block being, as far as compatible with facility of communication, isolated from the others. There are five parallel pavilions, the central administrative block being flanked on either side by two blocks of wards. The central block is surmounted by a massive tower, 182 feet in height, which forms a prominent landmark when viewed from the north and west. The chimney-shaft from the boilers below is carried up inside this tower, the upper part of which has a corbelled stage derived from northern Italian work of the Middle Ages. The tower contains a number of large tanks, providing storage for 25,000 gallons of water pumped from a well 500 feet in depth.[150]

The pavilions on either side of the tower are linked to each other by cast-iron galleries and canopied walks. A block of buildings situated at the entrance contained the residences of the medical officers, and over the spacious arched gateway in the centre there was a chapel 60 feet long by 30 feet wide, with a boarded wagon-roof of trefoil section.

In a report on the infirmary written by Snell, he described the elaborate systems of heating and ventilation. Open fires heated coils of pipes containing water which then circulated, humidity also being contrived so that air would not be dried, a great advance for the time. The lighting was by gas, and fumes were carefully vented away.[151] This 'Thermhydric' system, patented by the architect, included upright flues in the external walls, inlets being provided for fresh air which was warmed as it entered, and air was also admitted directly through the walls into skirting-boxes between the beds, while flues carried off the foul air and the products of gas combustion.

Nos. 152–168 (even) and 177–193 (odd) Ladbroke Grove

Plate 74c, d

The unusually plentiful documentary evidence available for these two facing ranges of four-storey terrace houses illustrates in detail a number of important aspects of building development in the area. They stand on part of the four acres of ground fronting Ladbroke Grove which Colonel Matthew Chitty Downes St. Quintin agreed in 1864 to lease for building to Charles Henry Blake.[53] In 1868 Blake nominated a firm of builders from Canning Town, Essex, George Heritage, senior and junior, for the grant of a building lease from St. Quintin for six houses in the easterly range of nine (Nos. 152–168).[152] The agreement of 1864 with St. Quintin stipulated that each house was to be worth at least £1,200, and the Heritages' capital outlay therefore amounted to over £7,000. Blake himself lent them £1,000 for each house, but in February 1869 they applied to him for a further advance of £750, offering as security two other houses in Cambridge Gardens.[53] This request was evidently refused, and in November 1869 the

Heritages' creditors instituted proceedings in the Court of Bankruptcy. In March 1870, when the building of the houses was probably complete, Blake bought both the creditors' interest and the Heritages' lease, the latter subject to the mortgages to himself.[153]

Thomas Goodwin and William White, who built the range on the opposite side of Ladbroke Grove (Nos. 177–193) and some thirty-eight houses in Cambridge Gardens, were, in contrast with the Heritages, able to command other financial resources and did not resort to Blake. They were about to invest some £70,000 in the building of fifty-one large houses in Clanricarde Gardens, Notting Hill Gate (see page 270), and in 1872–4 they were able to borrow over £34,000 from the Hand-in-Hand Insurance Society.[154] In Ladbroke Grove they were granted building leases (at Blake's nomination) by St. Quintin in 1868, and then mortgaged (through a solicitor), firstly to a private gentleman at Newark-upon-Trent and secondly to two London solicitors. In November 1869, when the houses were probably complete, Blake bought both Goodwin and White's lease and the second mortgage; but the first mortgage remained outstanding.[155]

Blake was now able to sell both ranges of houses and in 1870 he offered thirteen of them at auction, all except one (already let at £90 per annum) with vacant possession. In the case of those built by Goodwin and White, where the first mortgagee was willing to leave his money on loan, he was able, without using any of his own capital, to offer prospective purchasers the extra inducement of mortgages of up to £855 per house.[53]

The sale particulars were addressed 'To Investors in First Class Leasehold House Property, and Gentlemen desirous of purchasing for present occupation.' The houses were described as 'most conveniently situate, and are especially deserving of the attention of Gentlemen engaged in business in the City, the facilities afforded by the Hammersmith and City Railway, in connection with the whole Metropolitan system, affording the means of speedy access to all parts of London. The Ladbroke Road Station is within a few seconds' walk of the Property. There are excellent Shops close at hand. For their size it would be difficult to find Residences more perfectly planned or finished in better taste, every presumed requirement of their future occupants having been specially studied.' They were held for ninety-nine years from Christmas 1864 at ground rents of £14 per house, and were estimated to let at rents ranging from £98 to £110 per annum.

Before the auction sale Blake fixed the reserve price for the houses built by the Heritages at £1,200 each and for those by Goodwin and White at £1,300. Bidding did not, however, reach these figures, despite the offer of mortgages for purchasers of the houses in the westerly range, and all of the houses were bought in.

In 1884 Blake's executors offered the houses (by this time all occupied) for auction again, but sold only one, and for only £1,000. They regarded this as unsatisfactory, 'but having regard to the wasting nature of the leasehold property, the heavy outlay constantly required for repairs, and the diminishing rents obtained for any of these houses falling vacant', they had considered that this portion of the estate ought to be sold.[53]

Each house has a frontage of some twenty feet (or twenty-five in the case of those at the corners), and the total depth of each plot is about one hundred feet. The two ranges contain four storeys with basements, and (according to the sale particulars of 1870)[53] present 'a noble and harmonious elevation, rendered in Suffolk brick, with cement dressings, mouldings and balcony, surmounted by balustrade, relieved at intervals by ornamental vases'.

Except in the four corner houses, where there were minor variations, the accommodation provided in each house was almost uniform. The entrance hall (with tessellated pavement) was approached by a flight of half-a-dozen steps leading over the basement area from the roadway. It was divided by a glass panelled door from the inner hall and a passage, which led to the garden, 'Water Closet and Lavatory', and the stone staircase to the first floor. There were two rooms on the ground floor—at the front the dining-room, with a projecting window, measuring twenty-two feet by fourteen feet, and at the back a 'library'. Both of these rooms had polished slate chimney-pieces, and were 'suitably papered and grained light oak, with pollard oak panels'.

On the first floor was 'An elegant front Drawing Room, 18 feet 6 by 17 feet, chastely decorated in mauve and white, the panels described by gilt mouldings, the wood work grained maple, statuary marble chimney piece and French casement, opening to Balcony'. The back room had a veined marble chimneypiece and could be used as either a drawing-room or bedroom.

On the half-landing above there was an enclosed cupboard, and on the second floor were the two best bedrooms, each fitted with 'wardrobe cupboards' and that at the front having a veined marble chimneypiece. On the next half-landing was the bathroom, which was fitted with a bath, sink (both having hot and cold water service), water-closet and a fireplace. The third floor contained four bedrooms, the two larger having 'wardrobe cupboards'. Gas was laid on to the second floor—a fact which was given some prominence in the sale particulars and was evidently thought to provide a considerable attraction.

The basement contained a 'Capital Kitchen', furnished with cupboards, a dresser, and a range supplying 'bath and hot water service'; a scullery, with a sink and a washing copper; a housekeeper's room, larder, wine cellar, water-closet, three vaults and a paved area for the tradesmen's entrance. The corner houses also contained a butler's pantry.

At the time of the census taken in April 1871 only three houses were in permanent occupation, the householders being a stockbroker, a jeweller and an independent gentleman. Caretakers and their families had been installed in another four, all of whom worked in the building industry.

Both ranges of houses were first listed in the Post Office Directories in 1873, when the inhabitants included a clergyman, an army captain and a surgeon. In 1880 No. 183 was occupied by a lieutenant-general, and in 1890 a colonel still lived at No. 181. By 1900 five of the southernmost houses (Nos. 177–181 odd and 152 and 154) were being used as shops, and four others were in professional occupancy (solicitor, doctor, veterinary surgeon). In 1914 seven of the eighteen houses were in divided occupancy, and by 1920 at least eleven of them were in professional or commercial use.

CHAPTER XIII

Kensal Green

DESPITE its favourable topographical situation, on high, well-drained ground overlooking most of North Kensington, the area now known as Kensal Green and Kensal Town has suffered from a long series of misfortunes. Until 1900 some 144 acres of it formed a detached portion of the parish of St. Luke's, Chelsea, from whose distant Vestry Hall it had hitherto been administered. When the London Government Act of 1899 provided that this locality should be annexed in part to the new Borough of Kensington and in part to that of Paddington, the Kensington Vestry, in the last weeks of its life, offered strenuous, though unsuccessful, opposition to this sensible rationalization of boundaries.[1] The area then known as Kensal New Town, bounded on the north by the canal, was incorporated into the Borough of Kensington, to be administered from the Town Hall in Kensington, High Street, which was not much nearer than that of Chelsea.

By this time the isolation of this remote district had been greatly increased by the construction of the Paddington branch of the Grand Junction Canal, opened in 1801, and of the Great Western Railway, opened in 1838. These two barriers, each for many years traversed from north to south by only one public bridge,* extended in approximately parallel courses across the neighbourhood of Kensal Green, and effectively segregated the area between them. Both the landowners of the detached portion of Chelsea—All Souls College, Oxford, and William Kinnaird Jenkins, esquire[2]— were in 1845 absentees, who took no direct personal interest in their properties, and so too were the owners of the adjoining lands in the parish of Kensington, the Talbot and St. Quintin families. Further west the General Cemetery Company had in 1831 bought fifty-four acres of land[3] for use as a burial ground, which had not increased Kensal Green's social *cachet* as a place of residence; and in 1845 the Western Gas Company had opened a

gasworks on land (previously the property of Sir George Talbot) with frontages to both the canal and the railway. When building development on a significant scale began in the early 1840's, several of the ingredients for the making of a slum were, in fact, already present.

The earliest building was on Jenkins's land. Since at least 1838 W. K. Jenkins had been speculating in Paddington in the vicinity of Hereford and Garway Roads, and in 1844 he acquired the interest of his kinsman, W. H. Jenkins, in twenty-eight acres of the Ladbroke estate in Kensington around Pembridge Villas (see page 260). In all these speculations Jenkins acted through his solicitors, Budd and Hayes of Bedford Row, and under their aegis West Row, Middle Row, East Row and part of Southern Row were laid out between 1841 and 1851 with small two-storey cottages, many with small front gardens.[4] The sole survivors of this phase of development are a few workshops in Southern Row, whose pantiled roofs can still be seen from the railway line, and the small chapel in Middle Row, which was built by Michael Puddefoot in 1852.[5] Laundry work provided the principal source of employment for the inhabitants, many of the men being comfortably supported by the labours of their wives, while others worked at the gasworks. Rustic pursuits and disorders still prevailed in the 1850's and 1860's, and gipsies sometimes wintered here.[6]

Except in the case of the gasworks, whose premises were gradually expanded westward until they eventually occupied all of the land to the west of Ladbroke Grove between the railway and the canal, little more building took place until the mid 1860's, when C. H. Blake's purchase of the Portobello estate from the Misses Talbot (see page 306) included some sixteen acres to the north of the railway. This was in the vicinity of Bosworth Road, Hazlewood Crescent, Edenham Street and Southam Street, where the building of

---

* In the 1840's there were two other bridges across the railway, but they only served the needs of the local farms.

tightly-packed ranges of small narrow houses proceeded rapidly in the 1860's and 1870's, every room being occupied as fast as the houses were completed. Access to this new quarter was greatly improved by the extension of Golborne Road north-eastward over the railway by another bridge,* and by the early 1880's building development had been substantially finished. Many of the residents were railwaymen, while others were migrants whose previous homes in the central districts of London had been demolished. There were no front gardens here, and the social climate of this area was evidently always wholly urban in character.[9]

With the establishment of schools, mission halls, chapels and churches (St. Andrew and St. Philip in 1870, Our Lady of the Holy Souls in 1882 and St. Thomas in 1889) Kensal Green gradually acquired the usual adjuncts of a Victorian suburb. In 1903, however, Charles Booth, evidently referring only to the area developed by Jenkins, could still state that Kensal New Town 'retains yet something of the appearance of a village, trampled under foot by the advance of London, but still able to show cottages and gardens; and gateways between houses in its streets leading back to open spaces, suggestive of the paddock and pony of days gone by'. Over 55 per cent of the inhabitants were, nevertheless, classified as 'in poverty',[10] and when Emslie J. Horniman presented an acre of ground between East Row and Bosworth Road to the London County Council in 1911 for recreational purposes he stated that there was then 'no place within a mile or more where children could play, except in the streets, nor anywhere for the mothers and old people to rest'.[11]†

Severe overcrowding had long prevailed in and around Southam Street, where in 1923 some 140 houses contained 2,500 inhabitants.[12] In 1925 the Kensington Borough Council acquired two derelict houses in Bosworth Road and converted them into twelve flats,[13] and in 1928–9 the com-

mon lodging house for men in Kensal Road was renovated and reopened as a refuge for women under the auspices of Mrs. Cecil Chesterton. Large-scale redevelopment did not, however, get under way until 1933, when the Borough Council, acting in response to a circular issued by the Minister of Health, adopted a five-year programme of clearance and improvement.[14] Five clearance areas were declared in Kensal Town,[15] and by 1938 ninety-nine new flats had been built or were in course of building (thirty of them by the Kensington Housing Trust)[16] plus another sixty-eight by the Gas Light and Coke Company on land fronting Ladbroke Grove.[17]‡ Fifteen acres in and around Southam Street had also been declared an improvement area. Here 5,818 people lived at a density of 390 to the acre, mostly in the four-storey terrace houses built under C. H. Blake's auspices in the 1860's and 1870's. By 1935 all of the 778 basement rooms had been closed and vacated, and 1,802 of the inhabitants of the area had been removed, many of them to the new flats in course of building at this time in Dalgarno Gardens. The population of the Southam Street area was thus reduced by 29 per cent, and the houses were thoroughly renovated.[19]

During the war of 1939–45, however, housing conditions in the Southam Street area again deteriorated very rapidly, and after slum clearance work had been resumed in 1950, some twenty acres bounded by Bosworth Road, Kensal Road and the railway were scheduled for clearance. The eleven acres between Bosworth Road and Golborne Road were redeveloped by the Borough Council to the designs of Sir William (now Lord) Holford,[20] the last of the 549 flats provided there being opened in 1969.[21] To the east of Golborne Road the remainder of the twenty scheduled acres is now (1972) in course of redevelopment by the Greater London Council to the designs of Erno Goldfinger and Associates. The only parts of Kensal Town which are still of recognizably

---

* The old bridge over the canal at Ladbroke Grove was also widened in 1881–3, to the designs of H. Vignoles, the contractors being Messrs. Nowell and Robson of Kensington.[7] It may be noted that the iron founders who supplied the materials were J. M. Bartle and Company, a local firm with premises in Lancaster Road.[8]

† This recreation ground has been enlarged in later years and is now known as the Emslie Horniman Pleasance.

‡ This was Kensal House, built in 1936–7 through the agency of The Capitol Housing Association Limited for the Gas Light and Coke Company, and 'intended as a practical experiment in mass automatic fuel service to low-rental flats'. Besides the flats there were also club-rooms for adult tenants and a nursery school for children. Kensal House was designed by a committee consisting of Robert Atkinson, C. H. James, G. Grey Wornum, and E. Maxwell Fry, the latter being the 'executant' architect.[18]

nineteenth-century origin are the area between Bosworth Road and Ladbroke Grove and the thin strip between Kensal Road and the canal.

The Cemetery of All Souls, Kensal Green
Plates 29–32; fig. 89

During the 1820's, when the population of the whole of London increased by some 20 per cent, the insanitary and indecent conditions which prevailed in the already grossly overcrowded graveyards of the metropolis first began to attract public attention. Some of these ancient burial grounds contained over 3,000 bodies per acre, and the average number of new burials sometimes exceeded 200 per acre per year. Often the rate of new interments exceeded the rate of decay, the level of the ground rose, and hideous means were employed by the grave-diggers to provide space for new intakes.[22] It was in order to alleviate this situation that Parliament, between 1832 and 1847, authorized the establishment of eight commercial cemetery companies in the vicinity of London. The first of these new cemeteries was that of the General Cemetery Company at Kensal Green.

The leader in the public demand for reform was George Frederick Carden, a barrister, who first concerned himself in the matter in 1824.[23] In the following year he issued a prospectus for the General Burial Grounds Association, in which he advocated the establishment of a cemetery on the lines of that of Père-Lachaise in Paris, and stated that a suitable site (at Primrose Hill) was available. Although the public meeting which he had intended to hold was cancelled owing to the financial crisis of 1825,[24] Carden was doubtless soon encouraged by the growing interest displayed by architects and men of business. In 1824 Thomas Willson had exhibited at the Royal Academy designs for a 'Pyramid Cemetery for the Metropolis', a multi-storey affair very economical in its use of land,[25] which Carden did not support, and in 1827 A. C. Pugin (in association, it is said, with Marc Isambard Brunel) exhibited more orthodox plans in the Gothic manner.[26] At about this time, too, a new cemetery was established in Liverpool, which within two years was paying a dividend of 8 per cent.[27]

In February 1830 Carden convened a meeting at his chambers at which a provisional committee was formed.[24] In April an exhibition (almost certainly prompted by Carden) was held in Parliament Street, conveniently close to the House of Commons, of plans by Francis Goodwin for a cemetery equipped with temples, mausolea, cloisters and catacombs, 'a very magnificent display of architecture' all set within forty-two acres of garden;[28] and in May one of Carden's supporters, Andrew Spottiswoode, M.P., presented a petition to the Commons on Carden's behalf praying for the removal of the metropolitan graveyards 'to places where they would be less prejudicial to the health of the inhabitants'.[29] This was immediately followed up by the issue of another prospectus, this one being for an intended General Cemetery Company.[24]

In the following two months, June and July 1830, Carden held two public meetings at the Freemasons' Tavern. Resolutions were passed by which the intended General Cemetery Company was established and officers and a provisional committee appointed; aristocratic patronage for the project was also secured by the election of a bevy of titled vice-presidents. Subscriptions were invited at £25 per share, and in order to prevent unseemly speculation in a matter concerned with Christian burial, it was decided that the shares should not be transferable until three fifths of their value had been paid up by the original subscriber. Carden himself was elected treasurer.[30]

One of the members of the provisional committee was Sir John Dean Paul, partner in the firm of Strahan, Paul, Paul and Bates, bankers of the Strand, who was soon to come into collision with Carden.[31] It was he who found and conditionally purchased fifty-four acres of land at Kensal Green for the 'moderate' price of £9,500 (i.e. £174 per acre), and at the proprietors' meeting held in July 1831 this initiative was confirmed. It was also decided to apply to Parliament for an Act of incorporation for the company.[32]

This was an unusually propitious moment to make such an application, for in October 1831 England began to experience its first cholera epidemic, and many people thought that cholera was propagated by the evil miasmas which arose from the decaying matter present, among other places, in overcrowded graveyards. In July 1832 the Bill 'for establishing a General Cemetery for the Interment of the Dead in the Neighbourhood of the Metropolis' received the royal assent. It incorporated the General Cemetery Company, authorized it to raise up to £45,000 in shares of

£25, buy up to eighty acres of land and build a cemetery and a Church of England chapel. To obviate the opposition of the metropolitan clergy, many of whom depended in substantial measure for their incomes upon the revenues from burial fees, the Act also provided that for each burial in the cemetery a fee ranging from 1s. 6d. to 5s. (depending on the type of grave) should be paid to the incumbent of the parish in which each body originated.[33]

By this time the infant company was already deeply involved in the architectural squabbles which eventually culminated in the triumph of Sir John Dean Paul and the dismissal of G. F. Carden. Their quarrel seems to have centred round the rival merits of the Grecian style, advocated by Paul, and the Gothic, championed by Carden; but no doubt there was also a conflict of personalities, as well as an *embarras de richesse* in the sheer number of architects anxious to design the cemetery.

To start with, at least three of the shareholders were architects—A. C. Pugin and Thomas Willson, whose interest in this field has already been mentioned, and John William Griffith, surveyor to the parish of St. Botolph, Aldersgate, and to the London estates of St. John's College, Cambridge,[25] who was probably supported by Paul and who was ultimately to be the author of the executed designs for the two chapels and the principal entrance gateway. At the time of its formation in February 1830 the provisional committee had nevertheless invited Benjamin Wyatt to act as architect, but he had declined, and recommended Charles Fowler instead. This proposal was not taken up, however, and in June both Francis Goodwin and Thomas Willson were drawing the committee's attention to their respective designs. It was at this time that the committee accepted Carden's view that the cemetery should follow the example of that of Père-Lachaise, and that the public should be 'at liberty to erect what description of monuments they please'.[34]

Thereafter the committee was for some months engaged in finding and provisionally purchasing a site. The land ultimately acquired was, indeed, extremely suitable. It enjoyed a high, well-drained situation, 'surrounded by beautiful scenery', and with good access to London both by road along the Harrow Road and by water along the Grand Junction Canal, which extended across the site.[32]*

The next problem before the committee was the layout of its new property. In September 1831 it was resolved to consult John Nash, and shortly afterwards Sir John Dean Paul presented a sketch 'drawn under the eye of Mr Nash' by Mr. Liddell, who had worked in the office of the Commissioners of Woods and Forests under Nash. J. W. Griffith was, however, instructed to prepare plans and sections of the ground, and shortly afterwards Liddell withdrew. In October Griffith produced working drawings for a boundary wall, and building tenders were invited. Later in the year he, Paul and Pugin were all concerning themselves in the planting of trees, and it might therefore be conjectured that Griffith had become responsible for the general layout. But in August 1832 (?John) Hanson, architect, was reporting to the directors about the execution of Liddell's plan, which was then adopted. The precise authorship of the design for the layout therefore remains in doubt.[35]

In the meantime the committee had decided that for the design of the buildings a competition should be held, and in November 1831 a premium of one hundred guineas was offered for the best plans for a chapel with ample vaults and for an entrance gateway with lodges. The total cost was not to exceed £10,000 for the chapel and £3,000 for the gateway.[36]

Griffith did not enter the competition, for he was appointed one of the judges, but he was nevertheless constantly strengthening his position with the company. In January 1832 he was negotiating on its behalf with Robert Stephenson, engineer of the London and Birmingham Railway, over that company's intention to build a tunnel under the northern extremity of the site of the cemetery; and in March he was instructed to proceed with the erection of the brick wall to enclose the cemetery. William Chadwick of Southwark was the builder of this wall, and Sir John Soane, for whom he had previously worked, was asked to supply a testimonial as to his capability.[37]

There were forty-six entrants for the competition, and in March 1832 the judges (Griffith, Paul, Pugin, Carden and two others) awarded the premium to H. E. Kendall, senior, for his Gothic

---

* The land to the south of the canal was never used for burial and was subsequently acquired for the extension of the adjoining gasworks.

design, which included a water-gate from the canal.[38] This verdict was, however, contested at the next meeting of the committee, when one member (probably supported by Paul) stated that he would press for it to be rescinded. Eventually it was decided to leave the matter to the directors who would be appointed shortly after the Bill (then still in progress through Parliament) had received the royal assent.[39]

At the shareholders' meeting held immediately after the incorporation of the company in July, Paul was elected treasurer in place of Carden, who was reduced to the position of registrar.[40] Prolonged architectural discussions evidently ensued among the directors, and in October the views of Cockerell, Pennethorne, Smirke and Wyatville were all solicited,[41] Kendall meanwhile busying himself with the publication of his Gothic designs.[38] The Gothic faction was, however, probably greatly weakened by the death of Pugin in December 1832, and the matter was finally decided in February 1833 when Carden was suspended from the board of directors for making statements prejudicial to the company. In June he was also deprived of his position as registrar.[42]

After Carden's suspension the victory of the Grecian faction, led by Paul, was at once celebrated by the adoption of Griffith's plans (prepared some months previously) for a nonconformist chapel.[43] By this time the cemetery had been consecrated, on 24 January 1833, by the Bishop of London, and a small temporary Anglican chapel had been erected. The first burial took place on 31 January.[44]

By March 1834 the building of the nonconformist chapel, the entrance gateway and lodges, and the great enclosing wall had all been completed to Griffith's designs, Chadwick being the builder.* The idea for the colonnaded 'catacombs' which were built along part of the north wall was apparently borrowed from a new cemetery at Frankfurt.[45]

In June 1834 Francis Bedford exhibited at the Royal Academy a model for a chapel for the General Cemetery Company,[46] but it was Griffith who in 1836 received the directors' request to design the cemetery's principal monument, the Church of England chapel and its catacombs. This he did, again in the Grecian style beloved by Paul, and by June 1837 the building had been

completed, Chadwick again being the contractor. The temporary chapel was demolished in the following year.[47]

Cemetery companies had by now become generally accepted, and Griffith's precocious son, William Pettit Griffith, also an architect, was anxious to set himself up as an expert in this new and doubtless lucrative field of professional practice. In 1836 he published a design for a cemetery chapel (very similar indeed to that of his father), accompanied by a knowledgeable commentary which concluded with the advice that, in cemeteries where two chapels were required, 'each chapel should be constructed in a different style of architecture: it would gratify the tastes of all parties, and, at the same time, add to the ornament of the cemeteries'.[48]

The two chapels are, however, both distinguished essays in the manner of the Greek Revival, and are built mainly of Portland stone (Plates 29b, c, 30). They are prostyle tetrastyle, the Anglican chapel being Doric, while that of the nonconformists is Ionic. Both porticoes have flanking colonnades, those on the nonconformist chapel being curved, and both have brick vaulted catacombs underneath, with stone coffin racks and cast-iron protective grilles of similar detail to balconies of the period (Plate 30b, c, d). In the dark vaults, hundreds of coffins, many once clothed in rich-hued velvets secured to the wood by brass studs, lie in their loculi. An interesting innovation in the Anglican chapel was the hydraulic lowering device by which coffins were taken down into the catacombs at the end of the committal service. This chapel was damaged by enemy action in 1940, and restored by E. R. Bingham Harriss in 1954.

The gateway, flanked by single-storey lodges and an office, is on the Harrow Road, and is basically a triumphal arch with a giant Doric order applied to its two storeys (Plate 29a). An attic storey rises above the central arched entrance.

During the first nineteen years of its existence over 18,000 burials took place in the cemetery,[49] and in the latter part of the nineteenth century it was enlarged by the acquisition of more ground to the west. A crematorium was built here in 1938.

The monuments erected at Kensal Green

---

* Chadwick's name appears on a set of drawings for the nonconformist chapel in the possession of the company.

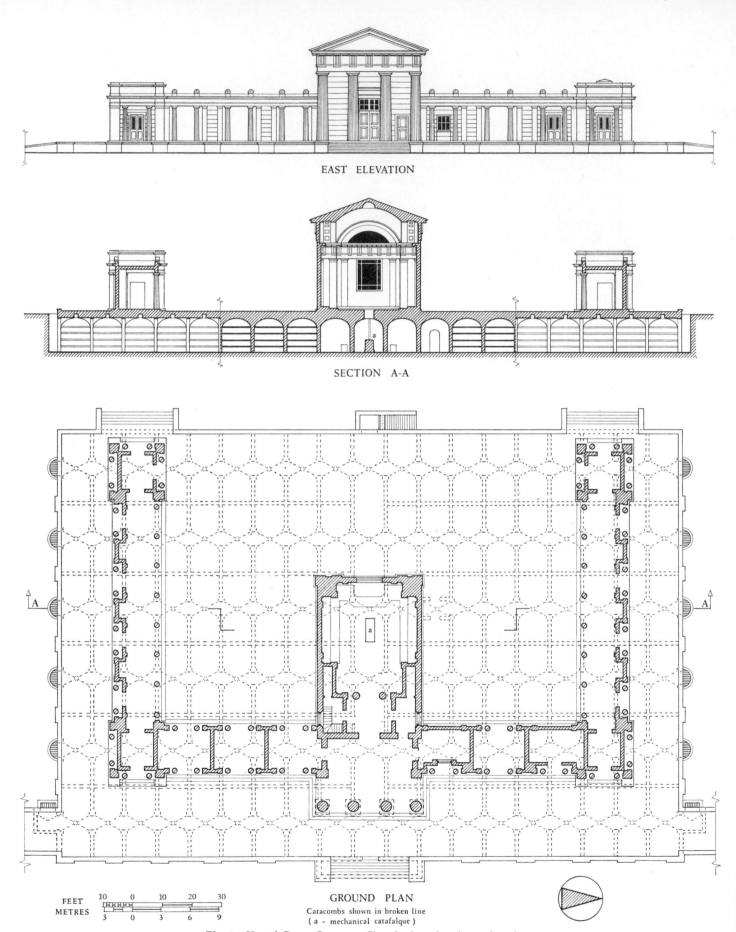

EAST ELEVATION

SECTION A-A

FEET 10 0 10 20 30
METRES 3 0 3 6 9

GROUND PLAN

Catacombs shown in broken line
(a - mechanical catafalque)

Fig. 89. Kensal Green Cemetery Chapel, plan, elevation and section

cemetery display the whole range of Victorian taste, from early classical tombstones to the strangest eclecticism of the latter part of the century (Plates 31–2). Contemporary opinion of most of them was in general very low—'What a *rendezvous* of dreary inanities it is!' exclaimed *The Builder* in 1854, and Ducrow's Egyptian mausoleum of 1837 was singled out in particular as an example of 'ponderous coxcombry'.[50] A few monuments were, however, approved, including those to Thomas Hood, the poet, by Matthew Noble, to James Ward, the painter and engraver, by J. H. Foley, and to General Forester Walker by Edward Blore.[51]

Immediately in front of the Anglican chapel are several tombs of distinguished design, among them that of Princess Sophia (*d.* 1848), daughter of George III, which consists of a beautiful *quattrocento* sarcophagus set on a podium (Plate 32a). The design was by L. Grüner of Dresden, and the sarcophagus was carved in Carrara marble by the Signori Bardi, the podium being by Edward Pearce. Nearby is the simple slab covering the grave of the Duke of Sussex, who was so shocked at the confusion at the funeral of King William IV that he declared that he would not be buried at Windsor. His nephew, the second Duke of Cambridge (*d.* 1904), lies in a tomb of a simplified Egyptian style. Mention may also be made of the octagonal monument of 1866 to the Molyneux family (Plate 31d), by John Gibson, a spectacular example of High Victorian Gothic, very much in the style of Scott, with rich polished granites and finely carved detail, and having a somewhat French appearance when seen among the surrounding leafy arbours. The original squat spire has been removed.

St. Mary's Roman Catholic Cemetery, Harrow Road

This cemetery, which is entirely separate from that of All Souls, Kensal Green, and is outside the parish of Kensington, was opened on 10 May 1858. The chapel and the lodge were both erected in 1860 to the designs of S. J. Nicholl. During the first eight years of its existence some 12,500 burials took place, many of the Irish migrants of the Great Famine years finding their last resting place here. The surplus revenues from the burial fees are used for the support of invalid priests.[52]

The Church of St. Thomas, Kensal Road

The original church here was built in 1889 to the designs of Demaine and Brierley of York, J. Demaine being described as 'Diocesan Surveyor'. The site was purchased by the trustees of the Bishop of London's Church Building Fund for £800, and a large part of the building expenses was provided from funds which had accrued from the amalgamation in 1886 of the benefice of St. Thomas in the Liberty of the Rolls with that of St. Dunstan in the West. The builders were Thomas Gregory and Company of Clapham, and the total cost about £5,500. The church was consecrated on 28 October 1889.[53]

During the war of 1939–45 it was severely damaged by enemy action. In 1951 the benefice was united with that of St. Andrew and St. Philip, Golborne Road, and in 1967 St. Thomas's was completely rebuilt to the designs of Romilly B. Craze.

The Potteries, Bramley Road Area, and the Rise of the Housing Problem in North Kensington

ETWEEN the Ladbroke and Norland estates there extended northward from the Uxbridge road a lane which provided access to the half-dozen fields between the northern boundary of the Norland estate and the southern boundary of Notting Barns Farm (later the St. Quintin estate). In the eighteenth century this lane was known as Green's Lane, perhaps from the Greene family, then the owners of the Norland estate, but after the establishment of tile and pottery kilns near the northern part of the lane in the first half of the nineteenth century, it became known as Pottery Lane. The site of the southern part of the lane is now occupied by the southern part of Portland Road. From the mid 1830's onwards the south-eastern part of the district served by the lane was commonly referred to as the Potteries (fig. 90), and after the cholera epidemic of 1848–9 the conditions of filth, disease and insanitation in which its inhabitants were found to be living and dying gave the area a notoriety perhaps unsurpassed by any other district in London.

The Potteries are situated on the flat, low-lying, stiff clay ground at the bottom of the hill now surmounted by St. John's Church. According to Mary Bayly, authoress of *Ragged Homes and How to Mend Them* (1859), the first migrant to this desolate place was Samuel Lake, whose noxious trades of scavenging and chimney-sweeping compelled him, in the early years of the nineteenth century, to remove from his premises in Tottenham Court Road to a more solitary spot. He took a lease of land off Green's Lane, and there he was soon joined by one Stephens, a bow-string maker, who was compelled to remove for the same reason as Lake. When building development began on the Bishop of London's estates in Paddington in the 1820's the pig-keepers of Tyburnia also had to find a new home. Stephens himself changed over

to this trade, and soon a little colony of pig-keepers had established itself in the district. Meanwhile some sixteen acres of adjoining land to the west were being dug for brick earth by Stephen Bird, one of the principal brickmakers in London and also a builder active in Kensington; and with the arrival of the potters several of the principal ingredients for the making of the hideous future of the district were already present.[1]

The manufacture of pottery appears to have been established here before 1827 by Ralph Adams[2] of Gray's Inn Road, brick- and tile-maker, who between 1826 and 1831 was the building lessee for most of the houses in Holland Park Avenue between Ladbroke Grove and Portland Road, the earth for the bricks having been no doubt dug from the Potteries area. The ratebooks first refer to this locality as 'the Potteries' in 1833. The tithe map of 1844 shows what appears to be a kiln on the east side of Pottery Lane near the present No. 34. The only kiln shown on the Ordnance Survey map surveyed in 1863 is that which still stands on the east side of Walmer Road opposite to Avondale Park (Plate 36b).* The Adams family's business was chiefly concerned with the production of drain-pipes, tiles and flower-pots, and in 1856 it was said that 'there seems to be no other manufactory of the kind in the neighbourhood'.[4]

Until the establishment of the Office of Metropolitan Buildings in 1844 there was no public control whatever over standards of building in Kensington, and in the absence of any private supervision by the ground landlord either, sheds and shanties of the most deplorable kind could be erected with impunity. As early as 1838 conditions at the Potteries had already attracted the vigilant eye of the Poor Law Commissioners, who stated that some of the cottages there were actually built over stagnant pools of water. 'In

* The kiln was rebuilt by Charles Adams in 1879.[3]

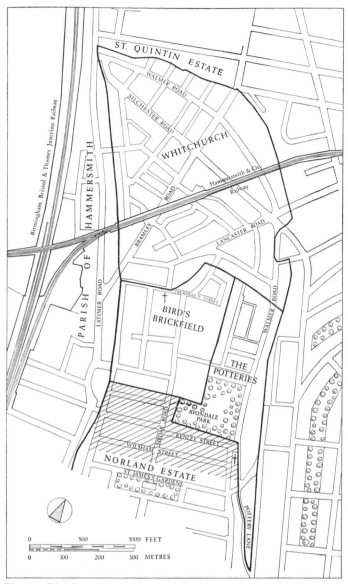

Fig. 90. The Potteries and Bramley Road area. Hatching denotes the 'Avernus' or Notting Dale Special Area. Based on the Ordnance Survey

some instances the floors have given way, and rest at one end of the room in the stagnant pool, while the other end, being still dry, contains the bed or straw mattress on which the family sleep.'[5] The formidable combination of large quantities of semi-liquid pig manure and other organic matter with the great cavities dug by the potters and the brickmakers, all in an area anyway difficult to drain, provided problems which the Westminster Commissioners of Sewers were incapable of solv-

ing. To the complaints which they received from 1834 onwards from the parish poor law authorities and adjoining property owners they replied that the drainage channel at the Potteries 'was a private Ditch and not under the control of the Commissioners', and when Richard Roy, the principal building promoter on the adjoining part of the Ladbroke estate, who also owned a small piece of land in the Potteries, called their attention in 1845 'to the disgraceful and neglected state' of the district, he was curtly told that 'he must himself take measures for the proper drainage of his property'.[6]

In December 1847, when fear of an outbreak of cholera in England was giving sanitary reform fresh urgency, all the ancient district commissions of sewers throughout London (except that of the City) were superseded by a single new authority, the Metropolitan Commission of Sewers, upon which extensive new powers were conferred in the autumn of 1848. During the three years 1846–8 living conditions at the Potteries had become so appalling that the average age at the time of death among the 1,056 inhabitants was only 11 years and 7 months, compared with an average age at death throughout the whole of London of 37 years.[7] Under Edwin Chadwick's aegis the new Metropolitan Commissioners immediately ordered their surveyors to investigate the drainage of the locality, and in March 1849 a preliminary report was presented, which was followed in September by an engineering survey.

The inhabitants of the Potteries were found to be living at a density of about 130 to the acre, and the number of pigs was 'upwards of 3000'. The whole district was skirted by open ditches, 'some of them of the most foul and pestilential character, filled with the accumulations from the extensive piggeries attached to most of the houses. Intersecting in various parts, and discharging into the ditches on the north and west, are many smaller but still more offensive ditches, some skirting houses, the bedroom windows of which open over them; some running in the rear and fronts of houses, others at the sides and through the middle of the streets and alleys, loading the atmosphere throughout their course with their pestilential exhalations.' The streets themselves were unpaved and full of ruts, their surface was strewn with refuse and often they were wholly impassable. Most of the houses were 'of a most wretched class, many being mere hovels in a ruinous condition', filthy in the extreme, and containing vast accumulations of garbage and offal. The water provided by the wells in many yards was 'so contaminated by the percolation of the foul drainage as to be wholly unfit for domestic use, the inhabitants being compelled to fetch water from a pump at some distance, belonging to Mr. Bird, paying a yearly rent for the privilege'. Much of the surrounding locality was pockmarked by the excava-

tions made for brick-earth, which were now filled with stinking stagnant water. The largest of these pools, an acre in extent, occupied part of the present Avondale Park, and was known as 'the Ocean'. Several adjacent houses discharged their drainage direct into this slimy sea, upon whose western shore stood the National Schools of St. James, Norland, attended by some 150 pupils.[8]

The only covered sewer in the area extended along the modern Kenley Street and Walmer Road, but at too high a level to provide drainage for the houses there. The only possible outfall was to the main Counter's Creek sewer, some 1,300 feet to the westward, and by September 1849 the building of this line was in progress.[9] In the winter of 1850–1, when this work had evidently been completed, the Metropolitan Commissioners began to build over 3,000 feet of sewers in the streets of the locality.[10]

By this time cholera had broken out in the Potteries, and in the first ten months of 1849 there were 21 deaths there from either cholera or diarrhoea. With 29 other deaths from typhus and other causes during the same period the mortality rate reached the enormous figure of 60 per 1,000 living, compared with the average for all London of 25·4 per 1,000 in the years 1846–50.[11] Goaded by their medical officers, and by those of the General Board of Health, who insisted that efficient drainage alone would never remove the evils connected with the piggeries, the Kensington Board of Guardians of the Poor at last agreed to prosecute a number of the pig-keepers. At a case brought before the magistrates at Hammersmith Police Court in September 1849, the court ordered the immediate removal of the pigs from one particularly offensive spot, and it was also announced that orders would be issued for the gradual removal of all the pigs in the locality. But the presiding magistrate stated that 'he wished the Orders to be executed in such a way as would be attended with the least injury to the Poor People to whom the Pigs belonged'. With this encouragement the inhabitants of the Potteries promptly presented a petition to the Guardians protesting against the intended removal of the pigs, and in October the Guardians (one of whom owned property in the Potteries) decided that no further penalties would be enforced, provided that the premises in question were kept clean.[12]

When another case was brought in 1853 the 'Islanders', as the pig-keepers now regarded themselves, were defended by their own lawyer, who (according to an account published in *The Builder*) asserted that his clients had a prescriptive right to their piggeries, and that they had settled in the district before the surrounding streets had been built. 'If a pig was a nuisance, why we should have no more pork. It was a nuisance to the pig-dealer to have a respectable neighbourhood, and the best thing the complainants could do would be to remove.'[13] The magistrates' order was evidently not rigorously enforced, and although the total number of pigs declined by about half between 1849 and 1856, the mortality rate of the Potteries showed no corresponding fall. Deaths from cholera during the outbreak of 1854 totalled 25 (compared with 21 in 1849), and in 1856 the general death rate there was said to fluctuate between 40 and 60 per 1,000 living, 87 per cent of deaths being among children under five years of age.[14] The statement made in 1850 by one of the medical officers of the General Board of Health, that the 'amount of sickness and death' in the Potteries 'may be equalled, but can scarcely be exceeded by any part of England' was probably still true six years later.[11]

In 1855 the administration of London was re-organized by the Metropolis Management Act[15] and the reconstituted vestries and new district boards became responsible, under the overall supervision of the Metropolitan Board of Works, for local sewers. They could compel owners of existing houses to construct drains into the common sewer, and no new houses were to be built without proper drains. They were to be responsible for street paving, lighting and cleansing, for the regulation of underground vaults and cellars and for the enforcement of the cleansing of houses. It was also their duty to enforce an important new Nuisances Removal Act,[16] and they were to appoint their own medical officer of health and inspectors of nuisances.

The Potteries at once became the principal target of the Kensington Vestry's first medical officer, Dr. Francis Godrich. In his first reports to the Vestry and its Sewers Committee he stated that the inhabitants in general looked 'sallow and aged, the children pale and flabby, their eyes glistening as if stimulated by ammonia'. Many of them lived in converted railway carriages and vans, the water supply was exiguous, and small-pox was ten times more fatal than in the surrounding districts. The principal sources of livelihood were the rearing and fattening of pigs, which in April 1856 numbered 1,041 beasts, and the preparation of pig wash. This consisted of refuse and offal ('blood, sheeps' entrails, liver and vegetable matter, all undergoing decomposition and often in a state of putrefaction'), which was collected from the hotels and club-houses of the West End as well as from local slaughter houses, and boiled down in huge coppers which emitted the 'most sickening' odours over the adjacent locality.[17]

Dr. Godrich recommended to the Vestry that the pigs should gradually be removed, that a water supply should be laid to each house and the open privies converted into closets properly drained, and that 'the Ocean' should be filled in. These policies were accepted, but the Vestry was impressed by the dependence of the inhabitants upon the pig industry, and therefore decided that the removal of the beasts 'should be dealt with cautiously under the circumstances'. Proceedings were, however, at once taken against four pig owners,[18] and during the four years 1856–9 a series of legal contests ensued. The result appears to have been inconclusive,[19] for although large numbers of animals were annually removed at the behest of the Vestry, pigs breed fast, and by 1869 the total number of beasts (which was no doubt constantly fluctuating) had actually increased to 1,190.[20]

There was, however, some improvement in other directions. As early as 1853 Mary Bayly, who lived in Lansdowne Crescent, had formed a Mothers' Society in the Potteries, *inter alia* for the education of its members in the elements of hygiene, and between 1858 and 1863 the first makeshift schools in the area were replaced by permanent buildings—a ragged school, built under Lord Shaftesbury's auspices, in Penzance Street in 1858, and St. James's National Schools in Penzance Place in 1863.[21] St. John's Church was building a school on the west side of Walmer Road in 1861,[22] while the Roman Catholics catered for the Irish element of the population with the Church of St. Francis (1859–60), followed by a school (1862–3), both in Pottery Lane.[23] In 1865 a school was built beside the intended new church of St. Clement's, Treadgold Street (consecrated in 1867), and several non-conformist congregations were also active in the area. These civilizing influences were accompanied by improvements in the drainage of the locality, which were effected during the 1860's by the

Vestry and, indirectly, by the completion of the system of main sewers by the Metropolitan Board of Works. The streets, too, were paved and taken over by the Vestry, and by 1863 even 'the Ocean' had at last been filled in. Despite the continued presence of the pigs Dr. Godrich felt able in 1869 to report that 'the Potteries are in a more cleanly and healthy condition, principally owing to the improved drainage afforded by the Metropolitan Board of Works'.[24]

In 1871 Godrich was succeeded as medical officer by Dr. Thomas Orme Dudfield, who held the post until his death in 1908. Despite the improvements made in the 1860's, Dudfield was clearly aghast at the state of the Potteries. He found that the population was rising, probably due to an influx of people displaced from more central parts of London by the extensive railway demolitions of the 1860's, and that 'there were probably as many pigs as human beings in the place'. The density of population had risen to 180 per acre, compared with an average of 71 for the whole parish, and the death rate in 1870 was 31 per 1,000 living (21 for the parish), 63 per cent of these deaths being among children under five years of age.

Dudfield brought a new energy to the redress of the conditions which these figures represented. He at once persuaded the Vestry to appoint a third sanitary inspector to his staff, and in 1873 he touched on the heart of the problem when he used the Artisans' and Labourers' Dwellings Act of 1868 to certify a number of houses in the Potteries as unfit for human habitation. Some of these houses were repaired, and some were demolished, but others remained in the same condition, and little improvement in housing took place for many years. But with the pigs he was more successful. Seven hundred animals were removed during his first year in office, despite the insults and even violence to which the local sanitary inspector was subjected. Three years later 'nearly all' the pigs had been removed, though many of them had merely been taken a few hundred yards westward into the parish of Hammersmith, and prosecutions were being brought against the dealers in 'wash', the noxious effluvia of which now constituted the principal nuisance.[25] The keeping of pigs in the Potteries as a regular business finally ceased in 1878, although short-lived attempts to revive it were made in later years, the last being in 1894.[26]

By this time extensive new building was taking place on the ground to the west and north-west of the Potteries. Shortly before his death in 1865[27] Stephen Bird had started to build on the sixteen acres of his brick-field, and new houses were also springing up in great numbers on the land further north.[28] Here the principal developer was James Whitchurch, an attorney from Southampton,[29] whose Hampshire origins are still commemorated by Silchester and Bramley Roads (fig. 90). Under its Act of 1836 the Birmingham, Bristol and Thames Junction Railway Company had been required to buy intact some 130 acres of land belonging to the Bishop of London, and to sell those parts not required for the line.[30] In 1841 Whitchurch, in association with two other gentlemen, one from Southampton and one from Banbury, had bought some forty-seven acres of this land in Hammersmith from the company, of which he had been appointed a director in the previous year, for c. £138 per acre.[31] Four years later he bought forty-nine acres in Kensington, to the north of Bird's brick-field, from G. Archer Shee of Manchester, esquire, for approximately £240 per acre.[32] During the building boom of the mid 1840's Whitchurch was making arrangements, on behalf of his associates as well as of himself, with the Westminster Commissioners of Sewers for the drainage of the whole of these lands. By the end of 1847 he had built over a mile of sewers in and around Latimer, Bramley, Silchester and Walmer Roads,[33] the bow-shaped course of the latter extending along the northern extremity of his land, parallel with the adjacent boundary of the St. Quintin estate. A few of the small detached or paired houses built at this time still survive, in sadly dilapidated condition, but this first phase in the development of the area was halted by the financial crisis of 1847, and when building began to revive a year or two later it appears to have been under the auspices of the Frugality Building and Investment Society, with offices in the City.[34]

Whitchurch was, however, still concerned in the development of the area, and the impetus of the building boom of the early 1860's was no doubt greatly strengthened by the construction of the Hammersmith and City Railway line, of which he was a director. This railway, opened in 1864, was the first of the feeder lines to be connected to the Metropolitan Railway, which had been opened between Paddington and Farringdon Street in

January 1863. It extended from its western terminus at Hammersmith through Shepherd's Bush and Notting Dale (where there was a station at Ladbroke Grove) to its junction with the Great Western Railway at Westbourne Park, and there was also a connexion with the Birmingham, Bristol and Thames Junction (now renamed the West London Railway). With a half-hourly service it was now possible for residents in even such hitherto inaccessible parts of North Kensington as Whitchurch's estate to reach the City in a matter of minutes.[35]

But the construction of the great high arches upon which the railway strode across the half-completed streets of Whitchurch's carefully contrived layout had an impact upon the existing social fabric of the locality exceeded only by that of the elevated motorway which was opened along much the same course in 1970. With Bird's worked-out brick-field and the Potteries to the south, and the noise and dirt of frequent steam trains traversing the estate, the area had no attraction for middle-class residents. After the introduction of cheap workmen's fares in the early 1860's working-class suburbs were beginning to be a practicable proposition, and in the ensuing decades Bird's and Whitchurch's remaining vacant lands were covered with densely packed rows of three- or four-storey houses and artisans' cottages.*

The southern part of this area quickly became an overspill for the Potteries, to which, it was stated in 1865, many working men were being driven 'from other parts of Kensington, Paddington, etc., by the inroads of railways'.[36] Migrants also came here after displacement by clearances at St. Giles in the Fields, Campden Place at Notting Hill (now Clanricarde Gardens) and Jennings's Buildings in Kensington High Street.[37] Hemmed in on the west by the West London Railway, and cut off from the more well-to-do parts of the Norland estate on the south by the houses in Darnley Terrace and St. James's Gardens, it became an isolated backwater whose social problems could easily be forgotten at the

Vestry Hall in far-away Kensington High Street. As early as 1872 Dr. Dudfield informed the Vestry of the high rates of mortality prevalent in the area now occupied by Henry Dickens Court, and in 1878 he referred in general terms to the existence of overcrowding.[38] But after the elimination of the pigs from the Potteries in 1878, the Vestry's concern seems to have declined. It had not bothered to use its powers conferred by an Act of 1846 for the provision of baths and wash-houses until 1878 (when the neighbouring parishes, Paddington, Hammersmith and Chelsea, had all built such establishments), and subsequent progress was slow. The purchase of a suitable site proved troublesome, a special Act had to be obtained, and Kensington's baths and wash-houses, built at the junction of Silchester and Lancaster Roads to designs by Thomas Verity, were not finally opened until 1888.[39]† Nor did the Vestry trouble to exercise its powers under an Act of 1866 for the regulation of the number of persons who might occupy a house let in lodgings, or inhabited by members of more than one family. When the Local Government Board at last compelled the Vestry to act in 1883, the staff of the sanitary inspectorate was not increased, and progress was extremely slow.[41] Even in the one major public improvement made in the locality during these years—the purchase of four and a half acres of derelict ground known as Adams' Brickfield, for recreational purposes—the Vestry was prompted by the vicar of St. Clement's Church (who by means of a letter to *The Times* collected £637) and assisted by substantial contributions from the Metropolitan Board of Works and the Charity Commissioners. The Vestry's original intention to install a refuse destructor was abandoned, the site was purchased from the Adams family in 1889, and after the excavations, seven feet in depth, had been filled in, the park was formally opened on 2 June 1892. It was called Avondale Park in memory of the recently deceased Duke of Clarence and Avondale.[42]

Private agencies and the churches were,

---

* With the building of the elevated motorway in the late 1960's the greater part of Whitchurch's former property has been designated as an area of comprehensive redevelopment. Kensington and Chelsea Borough Council is now (1972) in course of building some 1,200 flats on twenty-seven acres of land bounded on the north by the railway, on the west and south by Bramley and Lancaster Roads respectively, and on the east (on the former Ladbroke estate) by St. Mark's Road. The Greater London Council is engaged on a similar scheme for the Silchester Road area to the north of the railway.

† Likewise the Public Libraries Act of 1855 was not adopted by the Vestry until 1887. The public library built in 1890–1 at the corner of Ladbroke Grove and Lancaster Road to designs by T. Phillips Figgis and H. Wilson (Plate 37c) was, until the opening of Kensington Central Library, Hornton Street, in 1960, the only public library building in Kensington specially designed for the purpose.[40]

however, a good deal more active. The London City Mission and a rescue society were both working in the area, the latter being a temperance organization with its own 'workmen's hall', opened in 1861. The Latymer Road Mission opened a ragged school two years later,[43] and the West London Tabernacle in Penzance Place was built in 1864. At the corner of Queensdale and Norland Roads there was a Baptist chapel, later taken over by the Salvation Army, while at the diagonally opposite extremity of the area, an 'iron' church, St. Andrew's, was built at the corner of Walmer and Lancaster Roads in 1862,[44] followed by schools in 1865.[36] After the destruction of this church by fire in 1867[45] a Methodist chapel was built on the site in 1878–9,[46] but another church, St. Clement's, had in the meantime been built in 1867 in Treadgold Street, within the site of Bird's former brick-field,[47] also two London School Board schools (Latimer Road, 1879, and St. Clement's Road, 1880), a district relieving office and dispensary (later a workhouse) in Mary Place, and a police station (1878).[48]

Yet despite all these efforts the social problems of the area were soon to be publicly shown to be far from resolved. By the early 1890's the principal causes for the original establishment of a slum here—grossly inadequate drainage, water supply and control of building, plus the presence of the piggeries and the brick-fields—had all been removed, but new forces ensuring its continued existence were already exerting their influence. We have previously seen that in the 1860's and 1870's migrants displaced from their dwellings elsewhere by the building of railways and by clearances in other parts of Kensington had found refuge here. In the 1880's and 1890's this process was continued, the fall in demand for casual unskilled labour in the central areas of London (caused by the decline of some industries there and the removal of others to the outskirts), and the demolition of more of the remaining slums there, being probably the principal reasons for more migrations into the Potteries.[49]

The social situation thus created was first brought to the public notice in January 1893 through the publication in the *Daily News* of an article entitled 'A West-End Avernus'. In this article the author denounced in the lurid language appropriate to the popular press the social conditions in St. Katherine's Road (now Wilsham Street), William (now Kenley) Street, Bangor

and Crescent Streets (sites now occupied by Henry Dickens Court) and part of St. Clement's (now Sirdar) Road, and concluded that he had never seen 'anything in London more hopelessly degraded and abandoned than life in these wretched places'. The incumbents of St. James and St. Clement and the chairman of the Kensington Vestry's Works and Sanitary Committee all wrote letters to the editor, the clergy in support of the article and the chairman in bitter resentment at the 'assumption that the Vestry of Kensington are indifferent to the state of the poor people inhabiting what is known as the "Potteries" district, Notting Dale'. In face of continued public interest the Works Committee held a special meeting on 2 March, to which a number of local inhabitants were invited, and the whole party subsequently made an inspection of the area.[37]

Almost all the houses within the five streets in question (fig. 90) had already been registered by the Vestry as let in lodgings or occupied by more than one family, and were therefore liable to periodic inspection. There were also eleven common lodging-houses, providing accommodation for 723 persons, which were regularly inspected twice a week by the police. The population was in fact extremely migratory in character, and the Vestry felt able to claim that most of the houses were in fair structural and sanitary condition, the streets clean and the sewerage satisfactory; but that such defects as did exist were 'of constant recurrence in houses occupied by the lowest classes, and are largely brought about by the dirty and careless or mischievous habits of the people themselves'. The remedy must therefore be increased house-to-house inspection, and a temporary extra sanitary inspector was accordingly appointed.[37]

It is clear, however, that Dr. Dudfield, the medical officer, was taken aback by the extent of the problems which had been revealed. He admitted cautiously that there was 'possibly a good deal of overcrowding',[37] and by the summer of 1893 he was making extensive use of his powers (which he had apparently only used once before, in 1873) to certify a number of houses as unfit for human habitation. (Most of these houses were subsequently repaired by the landlords under the Vestry's superintendence.)[50] He seems to have been unaware of the incidence of mortality within the 'Avernus' area, and in 1893 he could only report that the death rate in Notting Dale was probably 'considerably in excess of the average for the whole Parish'.[37] But he now began to make new calculations, and in 1895 it was found that in the whole of the sanitary district in which the 'Avernus' was situated, the death rate (33·3 per 1,000 living) was more than double that for the whole of the parish (16·4), while in the 'Avernus' itself the number was no less than 42·6 per 1,000.[51] This last figure showed that the incidence of death in the 'Avernus' in the 1890's was comparable with the rates which had prevailed in the pig- and disease-ridden Potteries in the 1850's. Nor was this all, for in 1896 Dr. Dudfield published the first figures for infantile mortality within the 'Avernus', which showed that no less than 432 out of every 1,000 children born there died before reaching the age of one year, compared with only 176 per 1,000 births in the whole parish and 161 in all London.[52] These figures must have come as a terrible shock to Dudfield, for as recently as 1888 he had been congratulating himself on the steady fall in the death rate of the parish taken as a whole. In his annual report for that year he had pointed out that whereas the death rate for all Kensington in the years 1866–1870 had been 20·2 per 1,000 living, 'In 1871, upon my appointment, a more vigorous sanitary administration' had been organized, 'which soon began to produce good results', culminating in the years 1881–7 in a fall to 16·1 per 1,000.[53] He, at all events, was now determined to do everything possible to eradicate the shame of the 'Avernus'.

But the sanitary record of the Kensington Vestry was marred in its closing years by indifference to the urgency of the problem. In 1896 a special committee of the Vestry was set up to inquire into what steps might be taken to remedy the deplorable mortal statistics revealed by Dr. Dudfield. In its report the committee, like its predecessor in 1893, 'attributed the bad condition of the houses, and the evil state in which the inhabitants were found, or represented, to be, to the vicious proclivities and evil habits of the people themselves', who were 'largely made up of loafers, cab-runners, beggars, tramps, thieves, and prostitutes'. Again as in 1893, the committee 'concluded that the necessity for frequent sanitary inspection can hardly be over-stated'. In fact, however, the Vestry reduced the sanitary staff from seven inspectors to six,[52] thereby making each inspector responsible for the sanitary welfare of over 28,000 inhabitants—almost the highest ratio

in all London. The yards and streets were paved with asphalt and minor improvements were made to the drainage,[54] but all of Dr. Dudfield's pleas for an increased inspectorate were resolutely rejected.[55] His other remedy, that the Vestry should buy houses in the area and let them in lodgings itself, could not be achieved without a change in the law, for which he vigorously campaigned.[54] Meanwhile the population of the Notting Dale Special Area, as Dudfield now termed the 'Avernus' district, was increasing at the rapid rate of 4 per cent per annum, many of the new immigrants being employed in the building of the Central Tube Railway,[56] and the death rate was actually rising, to an average of 53·4 per 1,000 living for the years 1897–9.[57]

In May 1898 the Local Government Board announced its intention to inquire into the sanitary administration of the parish, but before the inquiry could begin the London County Council instructed one of its medical officers to investigate.[54] In his report, which was published by the L.C.C. in December 1899, he stated that 'whereas in former years the Vestry of Kensington compared favourably with other London sanitary authorities in the exercise of the powers which they then possessed, they have not at the present time the staff necessary for the proper exercise of the additional powers which Parliament has in recent years conferred upon London sanitary authorities'. In Notting Dale it was impossible even to make a single thorough inspection in the course of a year of the houses let in lodgings, whereas the common lodging houses (now under the L.C.C.'s supervision) were inspected weekly. He flatly contradicted the Vestry's views when he stated that 'the condition of rooms such as those found in large numbers in Kensington can by no means be excused on the ground of the uncleanly habits of the occupants', and concluded unequivocally that at least four additional sanitary inspectors were required.[58]

Shortly afterwards the Vestry was superseded, under the terms of the London Government Act of 1899, by the Kensington Borough Council. The new authority quickly called for an inquiry into the nature and extent of overcrowding,[59] and in 1901 four extra sanitary inspectors were appointed.[60] Later in the same year the Council accepted Dudfield's recommendation that it should adopt the powers conferred by Part III of the Housing of the Working Classes Act of 1890, which the Vestry had been precluded from using. These empowered the Council to buy and renovate existing lodging-houses and also to build new ones itself. The Council decided to do both, in Kenley Street, within the Notting Dale Special Area, where the houses on the north side abutting on Avondale Park were deemed suitable for renovation, while those on the south side, on shallow sites with basements and inadequate ventilation, were to be totally rebuilt. The difficulties encountered in buying all the interests in a large number of properties were overcome by Sir Henry Seymour King, the first Mayor of Kensington, who made a large interest-free loan to the Council and accepted personal liability for all the purchases. On the north side of Kenley Street 26 houses were remodelled as 52 dwellings, with new sculleries, lavatories, stoves, dressers and larders, while on the south side 17 houses were demolished and replaced by six blocks arranged in 36 self-contained two-room flats. Nearby in Hesketh Place and Thomas (now Runcorn) Place 26 one-room tenements were also built, and by the end of 1906 120 tenements containing 245 rooms had been provided in the area, at weekly rents ranging from 3s. 6d. up to 8s. At a density of two per room there was accommodation for some 490 people,[59] and the total charge to the rates was £1,231 per annum until 1929, decreasing annually by £28.[61] The general level of the rents seems, however, to have been too high for the casually-employed, unskilled poor, for only one fifth of the families housed in Kenley Street after the Council's building works had lived in the street before,[59] and in 1912 it was generally acknowledged that the Kenley Street scheme had led to an extension of the furnished room trade to other parts of the Borough.[62]

The Kenley Street scheme and the greatly improved system of house-to-house inspection which he was able to provide under the Borough Council's aegis marked the culmination of Dr. Dudfield's long career, and by 1907 (the year before his death) the number of deaths per 1,000 living had fallen in the Notting Dale Special Area from an average of 50·4 in 1896–8 to 30·2. The labours of the clergy, of the district nurses and district visitors and a number of other philanthropic agencies, coupled with those of the Board of Guardians and the sanitary department, had all contributed to produce what was in 1907 considered to be a 'very marked improvement in the moral aspect of the place'[63]—a verdict endorsed by Octavia Hill, who since 1899 had been responsible for the management of a number of houses in the locality.[64]

After the completion of the Kenley Street scheme in 1906, no more rehousing was undertaken by the Borough Council until after the war of 1914–18, but during these intervening years the problems of North Kensington were becoming increasingly complex. In 1901 the population of Golborne Ward (fig. 91), in the north-eastern extremity of the Borough,* reached its virtual peak figure of 26,307, equivalent to a density of 233 persons per acre, or nearly double that of Norland Ward (120 per acre), in which the Notting Dale Special Area was situated.[62] At that time the Registrar General regarded two as the standard number of persons who might occupy a single room without overcrowding it, and, despite

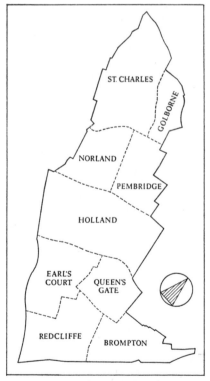

Fig. 91. Ward areas in Kensington

* The building history of the area comprised in Golborne Ward is described in Chapters XII and XIII.

the very high density, there was, by this standard, relatively little overcrowding in Golborne Ward —only 84 cases in single rooms compared with 343 in the Norland Ward. According to the Borough Council's by-laws, which required 400 cubic feet of space for each adult, there were few cases of overcrowding anywhere, for many of the three- or four-storey terrace houses common in North Kensington contained rooms adequate by this standard for six persons.[65] The population of Golborne Ward was evidently at this time more evenly distributed than that of Norland Ward, and the death rate there was still substantially lower (in the years 1905–7 17·5 per 1,000 living compared with 19·3). In his survey of social conditions published in 1902 Charles Booth only referred to one small part of Golborne Ward, Kensal New Town, and even here he found that there were only comparatively few 'very poor' inhabitants; whereas in Sirdar Road in Notting Dale he found extensive poverty 'of as deep and dark a type as anywhere in London'.[66]

Fresh pockets of poverty and overcrowding were nevertheless forming in areas away from Notting Dale during the first decade of the twentieth century—in Barlby Road and Treverton Street, near the Great Western Railway,[67] and in Bolton Road, off Westbourne Grove, for instance—and this seems to have been directly related to a *fall* in the overall population. In the decade 1901–11 this fall amounted to 2·9 per cent in Golborne Ward and to 10·7 per cent in Norland Ward, many well-to-do people having evidently emigrated to better accommodation in the new houses being built on the St. Quintin estate and further afield.[68]

The effect of this fall in population upon the social character of Golborne Ward was clearly stated by the medical officer in 1911. 'As the difficulty of finding tenants for the lodgings in such Wards as Golborne increases, the housing problem becomes more and more perplexing. Landlords find themselves in a dilemma where the choice lies between receiving the lowest class of tenant and leaving their houses unoccupied. If they elect to take lodgers of doubtful character, their property is knocked about and the rent is not paid. On the other hand if no more than half the tenements in a lodging-house are let to persons who pay regularly, and the rest of the house stands empty, legitimate returns on the capital outlay are eaten up by the cost of necessary repairs. It will

accordingly be understood that the task which is set the Council of securing satisfactory lodgings for the less fortunate of the working population in the Ward of Golborne and similar districts is one of the utmost difficulty, and further that no small part of the difficulty experienced has been directly due to an exodus from Kensington to districts where better accommodation can be obtained at lower rents.'[69] By 1914 there were over one thousand vacant rooms in North Kensington available for the working classes. Areas of extreme poverty prevailed in all four of the wards there, and in Golborne, where the whole population was now of the working classes, there were 'large numbers of semi-destitute persons who have no regular employment'.[70]

During and immediately after the war of 1914–1918 the decline of population was reversed, and the census of 1921 showed that the number of inhabitants in each of the four wards of North Kensington had risen since 1911—in Golborne to its absolute peak of 26,329. By this time there were over 5,000 houses in the Borough which were let in lodgings and occupied by some 55,000 of the working classes without having been adapted to this new use. Houses of this kind had been built for occupation by a single family but were now occupied by up to seven. Often they had eight or nine large living-rooms spread over three or more floors, but with only one water-closet and one water tap, both in the basement. There were no sinks upstairs, and clean water had to be carried up and dirty water down. An important part of the Borough Council's housing effort was accordingly directed towards the unspectacular work of remedying conditions of this kind. This was done by continuing the registration of all houses let in lodgings (after 1923 at the rate of at least four hundred per annum), by the improvement of all registered houses, if necessary by compulsion, by closing underground rooms and by closing houses deemed unfit for human habitation. In 1923 the Council decided that landlords should be required to provide one water-closet for every twelve people, and a proper water supply.[71] By 1926, when the Council promulgated new by-laws for the control of houses let in lodgings, over 3,600 such houses had been registered.[72]

In the provision of new housing the Council decided in 1920 that 314 dwellings would be required within the next three years to meet the needs of the Borough, and by 1927 it had built

317 new flats or houses, most of them in the Notting Dale area or on the St. Quintin estate. As a matter of urgency it had also provided in 1919 another 102 flats or maisonettes by the conversion of a number of large old houses, of which twelve were in Powis Square.[73] But in general the Council considered that 'there are many objections to the local authority of any area becoming property owners on a large scale, and they have not felt disposed to acquire neglected and dilapidated houses except in cases where the dwellings could not be placed in good ownership by any other plan'.[74]

Houses in bad repair were therefore often brought to the attention of the housing associations which became active in North Kensington in the 1920's. The Improved Tenements Association Limited (now the Rowe Housing Trust Limited) had been founded in 1900 for the acquisition and improvement of poor house property, while the Wilsham Housing Trust had been established in 1923 to continue the work begun by Dr. Silvester in 1914 in both the building of new houses and flats and the improvement of existing tenements.[74] This dual function was also performed by the Kensington Housing Trust Limited, founded in 1926 under the aegis of Lord Balfour of Burleigh,[75] and a number of other similar bodies. Beween 1914 and 1927 they provided a total of 422 new or renovated dwellings in North Kensington, almost exactly equalling the 419 provided in the same period by the Council.[76] When the Sutton Dwellings Trust (established in 1900 under the will of W. R. Sutton, the carrier) bought some eight and a half acres of land on the north side of Dalgarno Gardens and built 540 flats there in 1929–30, the total stock of housing provided by these private agencies (1,054) amounted to almost double the number (558) provided by the Council, even including the pre-war Kenley Street dwellings.[77]

In 1932 the Council acquired the last remaining building site of any size in the Borough, some nine and a half acres on the north side of Dalgarno Gardens to the east of the Sutton Trust's flats. One acre of this land was sold to the Sutton Trustees, another acre was leased at a nominal rent to the Kensington Housing Trust, and the

Peabody Donation Fund took some five acres of the remainder on similar terms.[78] By 1938 some 545 flats had been built here by these three bodies.[79]* By the same year the total number of houses or flats provided by all housing associations amounted to 1,989, while that provided by the Council amounted to 708 (plus 16 houses acquired in 1938 in connexion with the redevelopment of the Becher Street area).[81]

The close co-operation which existed between the Borough Council and the housing associations also extended to the complex rehousing processes involved in the Council's slum-clearance and improvement schemes. In the eight years following the Housing Act of 1930 the Council dealt with thirteen clearance areas (mostly in Notting Dale and Kensal Green) in which 219 premises occupied by 1,117 people were demolished. In the three improvement areas, at Southam Street (Kensal Green), Treverton Street (on the west side of the north end of Ladbroke Grove) and Crescent Street (Notting Dale), unsatisfactory basements were closed, overcrowding abated and the houses thoroughly reconditioned. In the fifteen-acre Southam Street area, for instance, where there were no less than 390 persons to the acre, 778 basement rooms were closed, sinks, drains and water-closets etc. renewed, and the total population reduced by 29 per cent by the rehousing of overcrowded families, many of them in accommodation provided by the housing associations.† At Crescent Street the Council decided in 1938 to redevelop the whole area, and the blocks of flats now known as Henry Dickens Court were built here after the war of 1939–45. Between 1922 and 1938 some 1,790 individual houses deemed to be unfit but capable of repair were also renovated at the Council's instigation.[82]

More stringent overcrowding standards were introduced by an Act of 1936, when a survey showed that in the whole of Kensington there were 2,529 families living in overcrowded conditions, of which 2,342 were in North Kensington. By the end of 1938, 740 overcrowded families had been rehoused, but meanwhile 138 new cases had been discovered.[82] The census of 1931 had shown that Kensington was one of only four among the twenty-eight metropolitan

---

* The whole scheme was severely criticized in *The Architectural Review* for lack of co-ordination and for the inadequate size of the playground—half an acre for the children of a population estimated at about 6,000.[80]

† The complete redevelopment of the Southam Street area in more recent years is described on page 334.

boroughs where an overall increase in population had taken place during the previous decade. But whereas the other three boroughs were all on the peripheries of London and still possessed room for new migrants, in Kensington there was hardly any open space left. The principal cause of this inward migration was thought to be the relatively central situation of the Borough, attractive for different reasons for both rich and poor, and a factor likely always to aggravate the problem of overcrowding there.[83]

This was to be particularly the case in the north-eastern part of the Borough, in Golborne Ward. Between the war of 1914–18 and that of 1939–45 a large proportion of the joint housing efforts of the Council and the housing associations had been concentrated upon Notting Dale, which with the Potteries had been the original centre of Kensington's social problems, while many of the new dwellings built in this period had of necessity been erected in St. Charles Ward, on the St. Quintin estate and around Dalgarno Gardens, where the only remaining vacant land was situated. Except at Kensal Green, and in Wornington Road on the south side of the Great Western Railway, where the Kensington Housing Trust had soon after its foundation in 1926 bought and renovated forty-eight dilapidated houses,[84] relatively little building or general improvement had yet been carried out in Golborne Ward. The censuses of both 1921 and 1931 had shown that both the density of population per acre and the average number of persons per room were far higher in Golborne than in Norland Ward. At the census of 1931, indeed, the density of population in Golborne (209·6 per acre) was the third highest of all the wards throughout London, and the Borough Council's survey of overcrowding, made in 1935, had shown that one in every thirty-one families were overcrowded in Golborne, compared with one in every thirty-eight in Norland.[85] From about 1934 onwards the average death rate in Golborne began to exceed that of Norland for the first time (in 1934–8, 14·8 per 1,000 living compared with 13·2). After the war of 1939–45 the erection of the Henry Dickens Court cluster of blocks of flats in Notting Dale completed the almost total rebuilding of the streets first exposed to the public gaze by the 'Avernus' disclosures of 1893, and the centre of gravity of the Borough's social problems shifted north-eastward to Golborne

Ward, which has become the principal field of more recent effort.

St. Clement's Church, Treadgold Street
Plate 18c

This church is the principal surviving memorial to the formidable energy of its first incumbent, the Reverend Arthur Dalgarno Robinson, who laboured in North Kensington for some forty years. After serving as curate of St. Stephen's, Shepherd's Bush, he came to Notting Dale in 1860, where he found large numbers of artisans' dwellings already in course of erection, and many more in prospect after the building of the Hammersmith and City Railway. He quickly persuaded James Whitchurch, the principal landowner in the district, to promise to give a site for a church, but this was lost (according to Robinson by 'delay') and in 1862 he erected a temporary iron church at the junction of Lancaster and Walmer Roads, to which a short-lived 'conventional district' known as St. Andrew's was assigned.[86] Three years later he was building a school for the children of the Potteries,[36] and shortly afterwards he purchased a site for a permanent church out of his own personal resources. Here the present Church of St. Clement was built and consecrated by the Archbishop of Armagh on 7 May 1867.[87] Throughout the whole of the previous seven years he had worked without any personal remuneration whatever.[88]

The architect of St. Clement's was J. P. St. Aubyn. It was an inexpensive building costing only about £4,000 and although there were no galleries it provided some 900 sittings, all free.[89] It is a wide, low church, built of yellow brick with red bands and stone dressings, and has a large expanse of slated roof, from which rises a slate-hung belfry turret containing a clock, and crowned by a steep pyramidal spire. As with many village churches, St. Clement's is small in scale and very much part of its surroundings. It consists of a broad nave flanked by three-bay, cross-gabled aisles, and by projecting transepts of two bays each. The chancel is narrow and low, with lean-to aisles on either side, the southern of which contains the Lady Chapel. There is a small porch at the north-west corner, and an eastern range of vestries extends across the full width of the chancel and its aisles.

The most striking feature of St. Clement's is

its roof, supported by cast-iron columns which are so light and elegant as to suggest the subdivision of nave and aisles with practically no physical interruption of the unity of the interior. Throughout, the corbels which support the roof are carved, but they lost much of their distinctiveness when the strongly coloured brick interior was painted white. The columns are now painted a pale powder blue, and little of the former warmth and richness remains. The chancel arch and the lateral arches of the chancel arcade have notched edges and hood mouldings of splayed brickwork. There are carved naturalistic capitals on the columns in the chancel.

The windows are generally lancets with sexfoil roundels contained within the gables. The three-bay chancel has stepped triple lancets at the east end. There are four lancets in the south aisle with glass by Walter Tower of C. E. Kempe's firm. Tower also designed the window in the Lady Chapel. The west window of the north aisle is by Martin Travers.

The principal treasure of the church is the large cartoon of 'Jesus at the well of Samaria' by Sir Edward Burne-Jones, which was presented by Lord Leverhulme. It is drawn in pencil on paper, and is a design for stained glass. In the north transept is an oil painting of the Annunciation by Alonzo Cano, which is said to have formed part of an altarpiece formerly in Seville Cathedral.

The Crucifixus and richly ornamented candlesticks on the high altar are by Omar Ramsden, the cross being signed by him. The altar itself replaces that destroyed by enemy action in 1944, and is backed by a florid Renaissance-style reredos. The gates of the finely-wrought iron dwarf screen to the chancel have been removed, as also has the iron enclosure around the font. The open benches, by St. Aubyn, are simple designs in wood, with the construction clearly expressed by wedges and tenons.

Few structural alterations have been made to the church, and later additions have not detracted from its character. The removal of detail, however, has contributed to the gradual erosion of St. Aubyn's realized conception, and the painting of the interior, a common fate of Victorian polychrome brickwork, has greatly weakened the original design.

Dalgarno Robinson's original iron church of St. Andrew's had been destroyed by fire some six weeks before the consecration of St. Clement's,[90]

and a Methodist chapel was built on its site in 1878–9. A consolidated chapelry was assigned to St. Clement's in 1867,[87] and in 1875 Dalgarno Robinson began the building of a second set of schools.[91] By this time he was also concerning himself with the northern part of his district, where building development had been rapidly progressing on the St. Quintin estate, and it was here, in North Pole Road, that in 1874–6 he built himself an enormous parsonage house, followed in 1882–1884 by another church, dedicated to St. Helen. In the latter year this became the parish church of the cure, and Dalgarno Robinson's headquarters for the remaining fifteen years of his ministry[88] (see page 322).

Roman Catholic Church and Schools of St. Francis of Assisi, Pottery Lane
Plates 22, 23a, b, 33c; fig. 92

The main body of the Church of St. Francis of Assisi, Pottery Lane, was built by Jackson and Shaw in 1859–60 to the designs of Henry Clutton, but the building work was supervised by John Francis Bentley, then aged twenty, an assistant in Clutton's office. In 1861 Bentley became sole architect for the additions then in progress, and he also designed many of the fittings still to be seen in the church.[92]

The church, presbytery and school form a close-knit irregular group on a tight wedge-shaped site bounded on the east by the backs of houses in Portland Road, on the west by Pottery Lane, and on the north by Hippodrome Place. The buildings stand in the Potteries, an area which in the mid nineteenth century was notorious for its insanitary conditions of living and for the extreme poverty of its inhabitants, many of whom were Irish immigrants or of Irish extraction. The site for the new church was acquired by the English branch of the Oblates of St. Charles Borromeo, a small community of priests founded at Bayswater in 1857 by Dr. Henry Manning (later Cardinal Archbishop of Westminster) at the behest of Cardinal Wiseman for the purpose of missionary and educational work in north-west London. One of the Oblates, the Reverend Henry Augustus Rawes, was sent to the Potteries very soon after the opening of the Oblates' Church in Bayswater. The Church of St. Francis of Assisi was built at Father Rawes' own personal expense, and was opened on 2 February 1860.[93]

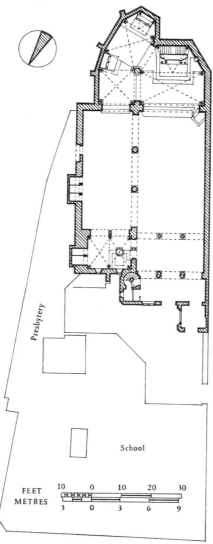

Fig. 92. Roman Catholic Church of St. Francis of Assisi, Pottery Lane, plan

St. Francis's is built of stock brick relieved by bands of black bricks, and is outwardly very simple and austere. It is orientated north–south, and is approached through a little courtyard (Plate 23a) bounded by the gabled wall of the church on the south, by the presbytery on the east, by the schools on the north, and by a pierced wall on the west. It originally consisted of a three-bay nave, divided from a liturgical north aisle by octagonal piers carrying an arcade; a Lady Chapel; and a chancel. The nave and aisle have a pitched timber roof with exposed tie beams and braces resting

directly on the walls (Plate 22a). Light is admitted by lancets in the nave, by cinquefoil lights cut in plate tracery of stone, with pierced spandrels, set in circular reveals in the chancel, and by lancets and a rose window in the gable of the liturgical west end. The style is a severely simple French provincial Gothic based on thirteenth-century examples. The church was subsequently enlarged and enriched, but the original fabric remains relatively untouched.

The Chapel of Our Lady of the Seven Dolours extends 'eastwards' in a curve by cants nearly half of the way round the apsidal chancel. It consists of two bays and a three-sided apse, with groined vaulting that springs from marble colonnettes and from a pair of corbels. The liturgical north side is pierced by two pairs of coupled lancet windows, and on the 'south' side, an archway opens into the chancel. The walls of the chapel are lined with tiles above which are paintings, those of the reredos being framed by carved alabaster.[94]

Very soon after its opening, it became apparent that the church was too small, and Bentley was asked to design additions. Some adjoining land was acquired in 1861, and a start was made with the addition of a baptistry at the 'west' end of the existing aisle. By 1863 the structural enlargements had been completed, the porch at the north-west (or ritual west) end, and the presbytery and school having also been built.

The baptistry (Plate 22c), at the 'west' end of the aisle, was enthusiastically described in *The Building News* in 1863 as promising to be one of the 'most complete little chapels in England'. The materials with which it is constructed are of excellent quality, and the design was declared to be 'very effective'.[95] It is a rectangular room the width of the aisle, the stone vault, two bays wide, being carried on marble columns with richly carved capitals. Certain details of the masonry were finished by Hardman in 1907 under the direction of Bentley's son, Osmond, who also designed the iron gates and screens dividing the baptistry from the rest of the church.[96] The granite font is an integral part of the design, and is set on a pedestal of marble and alabaster. Its canopy of oak was given by Bentley in 1865 as a thank-offering for his conversion to Roman Catholicism in 1862, his being one of the first baptisms to take place in the church from whose patron saint he took his middle name of Francis.

While still Clutton's assistant, Bentley had also

designed a number of small accessories for the church, including an alabaster offertory box, an oak chancel seat, and a bracket for a statue of the patron saint by the 'west' door. The altar of St. John, however, on the 'north' wall of the Lady Chapel, was designed by Bentley in March 1861 and marks an important development of his powers (Plate 33c). It consists of an altar and reredos, the latter with a moulded cusped frame of alabaster, made by Earp of Lambeth, surrounding a painting by N. H. J. Westlake. This was Westlake's first work in collaboration with Bentley. The frontal below has two paintings by Westlake completed at the same time, one to each arch, representing Daniel and St. John.[96] The architecture of this altar embodies many of the elements of Bentley's creative genius. The miniature columns, huge capitals, and intricate inlays of marble are indicative of what was to come later. *The Building News* noted that Westlake's pictures were 'interesting in a technical view, having been painted in encaustic on slate, the effect being thoroughly ecclesiastical'.[95]

Bentley also designed the altar and piscina of the Lady Chapel. The former is of alabaster, its frontal incorporating miniature paintings, and its table carried on four marble columns, each surmounted by capitals and elongated blocks that contain panels in which an angel is depicted. The central panel of the frontal consists of a quatrefoil panel within which is a lozenge-shaped smaller panel framing a painting of Our Lady of Dolours. On either side are circular panels containing paintings of female saints. The super-altar is decorated with square foliate paterae and bosses of coloured marble.[94]

Westlake executed the seven paintings on slate representing the Seven Dolours of Our Lady, three on the 'north' wall, three on the reredos, and one on the 'south' side which forms the 'north-east' pier of the sanctuary. The designs were exhibited at the Architectural Exhibition in Conduit Street in 1861, Westlake's address being given as 8 Gloucester Terrace, Clarendon Road, Notting Hill.

The sumptuous high altar and reredos were constructed in 1863 (Plate 22b).[96] They are of alabaster, richly inlaid with marble and glass mosaic. The brass door of the tabernacle is set with enamels and precious stones, and is of exquisite workmanship. The altar frontal consists of four marble columns with ornate capitals and richly carved cushions that support the table. Recessed behind the columns is a painted panel representing the dead Christ, while the lateral panels, set back farther, are enriched with mosaics in the early thirteenth-century style. The first super-altar is inset with triangular patterns of dark and light marbles, while the second is ornamented by circular recessed panels, each with its inlay, and divided vertically by inlays of black foliate patterns remarkably Art Nouveau in appearance.

The reredos is of alabaster, and is set beneath a strongly carved leaf cornice. It has four recessed panels in the form of eight-pointed stars, containing painted figures. A corbel is projected from this cornice over the reredos, and carries a throne on high with a *vesica piscis* panel in which mosaics are set in an early thirteenth-century pattern. The gilded canopy over the throne is surmounted by the Pelican in Piety.

During 1863 Bentley designed reliquaries and a confessional, and in the following year several other items for Father Rawes, including metal work, a monstrance, an iron offering-stand, a processional cross, a music-stand, candlesticks, vestments and frontals.[97] In 1864 the unfinished stonework in the porch was carved, the chancel was further enriched with marble, and the sanctuary was completed with painted decoration. Between 1865 and 1870 new Stations of the Cross were painted by Westlake, in a style described as 'a kind of modification of the German School of the sixteenth century'.[98]

In 1870 Bentley designed a canopied niche for the statue of Our Lady, obtaining, in the words of his biographer, a 'very precious and refined effect by the juxtaposition of various coloured marbles and crystals'.[97] The elaborate bracket-pedestal is carried on a richly carved capital and corbel bracket. The statue itself was carved by Theodore Phyffers, who had been brought from Antwerp by A. W. N. Pugin to work at the Palace of Westminster. It is surmounted by a crown decorated with fleur-de-lis motifs and carried by two angels bearing palm fronds, a very similar design to that of the exposition throne in the chapel of the convent of the Poor Clares Colettines in Ladbroke Grove. Phyffers also carved a crucifix, which was 'executed in a bold and masterly manner', to stand at the 'west' end of the church.[95]

In 1882 the church and presbytery were altered when a tribune was constructed over the baptistry, and a new room was added in the presbytery with accommodation for three priests. The tribune is reached from inside the presbytery, the door being in the dining-room on the first floor.

The crucifix on the altar of St. John was given to the church in 1909. Until 1871 it had stood for many years on the high altar of the chapel of the Tuileries Palace in Paris.

Osmond Bentley redecorated the Lady Chapel in 1913, and Westlake's paintings were restored. In 1917 a piscina designed by Walters was erected in the sanctuary, and the statues of St. John and St. Joseph, both the work of the Belgian sculptor Blanchard, of the Guild of St. Luke, were presented to the church.

The interior of St. Francis's was painted and cleaned by G. N. Watts in 1926, and it was restored and redecorated in 1960 under the direction of A. J. Sparrow.[99]

The schools and presbytery are in the same thirteenth-century French Gothic style as the church, and are built of stock brick enlivened with bands of black brick. They are grouped around the small courtyard previously mentioned, a playground for the children being provided on the flat roof of the school-house. The silhouette of the whole group of buildings, with gables, pinnacles, metal finials and school bell-turret, adds a welcome liveliness to this corner of Notting Dale.

Notting Hill Methodist Church, Lancaster Road

Plate 28e, f; fig. 93

This church, built of white Suffolk bricks with yellow stock brick voussoirs and bands, stone dressings, and a grey slate roof, is conspicuously sited at the junction of Walmer and Lancaster Roads. It was erected in 1878–9 by Jesse Chessum of Shoreditch;[100] the architect is not known. It is a two-storey building, the church halls being situated in the semi-basement, while the church proper and several small meeting-rooms are on the first floor. The style is eclectic Gothic.

No. 235 Lancaster Road

This house was designed in 1863 by John Francis Bentley, and was his 'first essay in purely domestic architecture'. It was commissioned by the artist N. H. J. Westlake.[101]

The house is situated at the corner of Lancaster Road and Treadgold Street. It has three

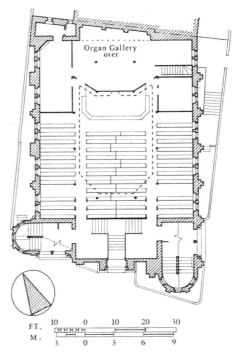

Fig. 93. Methodist Church, Lancaster Road, plan

storeys over a basement and is built of brick with stone dressings. The main entrance, on the corner of the house, is approached through an arched opening and a flight of steps. The arched motif appears again on the third storey, where a pair of windows enlivens the façade to Lancaster Road. Bentley intended a painted frieze to add further interest to the exterior, but this was not carried out.[101]

There is a niche at the corner of the house which is filled by a cylindrical colonette, a curious device, and quite unlike any recognizable model. Indeed, the style of the house and its ancestry are impossible to define, for there are elements from Italian and Spanish medieval architecture applied to an almost dourly plain exterior.

The house has been much altered since Westlake's day; modern windows have been inserted and other changes have obscured the original design.

The single-storey Roman Catholic Primary School of St. Francis, south of No. 235 Lancaster Road, is entered from Treadgold Street. It has similar fenestration to that of St. Francis's School, Pottery Lane, and the detail evidently derives from Bentley's work.

References

ABBREVIATIONS

A.P.S.D.	*Architectural Publication Society Dictionary*, 1852–92.
B.	*The Builder.*
B.A.	Building Act case, Greater London Council.
B.M.	British Museum.
B.N.	*The Building News.*
Boase	Frederick Boase, *Modern English Biography*, 6 vols., 1965 ed.
B.R.	Building Regulation case, Greater London Council.
C.C.	Records of the Church Commissioners, Millbank.
C.E.O.	Crown Estate Office, Carlton House Terrace.
Colvin	H. M. Colvin, *A Biographical Dictionary of English Architects, 1660–1840*, 1954.
D.N.B.	*Dictionary of National Biography.*
D.S.R.	District Surveyors' Returns for northern Kensington in Greater London Record Office, County Hall and Dartmouth Street.
E/HOL	Holland estate records in Greater London Record Office, County Hall.
Faulkner	Thomas Faulkner, *History and Antiquities of Kensington*, 1820.
G.E.C.	*The Complete Peerage*, ed. G.E.C., 1910–59.
Gladstone	Florence M. Gladstone, *Notting Hill in Bygone Days*, with additional material by Ashley Barker, 1969.
G.L.C.	Greater London Council.
G.L.R.O.(L)	Greater London Record Office, County Hall.
G.L.R.O.(M)	Greater London Record Office (Middlesex), Dartmouth Street.
H.L.R.O.	House of Lords Record Office.
I.L.N.	*The Illustrated London News.*
K.P.L.	Kensington Central Public Library, Hornton Street.
L.C.C.	London County Council.
M.B.W.	Records of the Metropolitan Board of Works in Greater London Record Office, County Hall.
M.C.S.	Records of the Metropolitan Commissioners of Sewers in Greater London Record Office, County Hall.
M.L.R.	Middlesex Land Register in Greater London Record Office, County Hall.
M.O.H. Reports	*Reports of the Kensington Medical Officer of Health*
Pepperell	Rev. William Pepperell, *The Church Index: A Book of Metropolitan Churches and Church Enterprise. Part I. Kensington*, [1872].
P.O.D.	*Post Office Directories.*
P.P.	*Parliamentary Papers.*
P.R.O.	Public Record Office.
R.B.	Ratebooks in Kensington Central Public Library, Hornton Street.
R.I.B.A.	Royal Institute of British Architects.
W.C.S.	Records of the Westminster Commissioners of Sewers in Greater London Record Office, County Hall.

General Introduction

(pp. 1–24)

1. E. Ffooks, 'The Kensington Turnpike Trust' in *Annual Report of the Kensington Society*, 1969–70, pp. 34–45.
2. *M.O.H. Reports, passim*; see especially for 1887, pp. 113–14.
3. H. A. Shannon, 'Migration and the Growth of London, 1841–91', in *The Economic History Review*, vol. v, 1935, pp. 79–86.
4. Migration figures for the 1860's calculated from the tables of births and deaths in *33rd Annual Report of the Registrar General* (*P.P.*, 1872, vol. xvii, pp. 280–1); those for the 1870's calculated from the figures contained in *35th–43rd Annual Reports of the Registrar General* (*P.P.*, 1873, vol. xx, p. 41; 1875, vol. xviii, pt. 1, p. 41; 1876, vol. xviii, p. 41; 1877, vol. xxv, p. 41; 1878, vol. xxii, p. 41; 1878–9, vol. xix, p. 41; 1880, vol. xvi, p. 41; 1881, vol. xxvii, p. 41; 1882, vol. xix, p. 41).
5. H. J. Dyos, 'The Slums of Victorian London', in *Victorian Studies*, vol. xi, 1967, p. 30.

6. P.R.O., census returns of 1851; *P.O.D.*
7. P.R.O., census returns of 1871.
8. J. H. Clapham, *An Economic History of Modern Britain*, vol. ii, 1932, pp. 362–3.
9. *B.N.* 3 April 1857, pp. 322–3.
10. E. W. Cooney, 'Capital Exports, and Investment in Building in Britain and the U.S.A. 1856–1914', in *Economica*, new series, vol. xvi, 1949, pp. 347–54.
11. *Kensington News*, 12 January 1900.
12. P.R.O., census returns of 1851.
13. Guildhall Library, MS. 8733/15, p. 34.
14. *P.P.*, 1886, vol. xii, *Select Committee on Town Holdings*, p. 356.
15. *The Railway Times*, 13 February 1864, pp. 192–5.
16. Hermione Hobhouse, *Thomas Cubitt Master Builder*, 1971, pp. 173–84.
17. 14 and 15 Vict., c. 116, local and personal.
18. Charles Marriott, *Now!*, 1910, p. 28.
19. *The Kensington, Notting Hill, Brompton and Knightsbridge Directory for 1876*, pp. 267–314 (copy in B.M., pressmark PP 2505 ye/23).
20. *P.P.*, 1883, vol. lxi, *Major Mandarin's Report to Board of Trade on Workmen's Trains on the Metropolitan Lines*, pp. 445–54.

CHAPTER I (pp. 25–41)

The Village Centres around St. Mary Abbots Church and Notting Hill Gate

1. K.P.L., Millington's Book, p. 1.
2. P.R.O., C66/1513, mm. 24–7.
3. Faulkner, pp. 51–2, 63.
4. P.R.O., C54/1393, Barker to Cope; Faulkner, pp. 59–60.
5. P.R.O., C54/1653, Cecil to Cope.
6. *Ibid.*, C54/1693, Cope to Anderson.
7. K.P.L., Millington's Book, pp. 21–7.
8. P.R.O., C54/1062, Cornwallis and Wingfield; C66/1851, no. 19.
9. *Ibid.*, C2/Eliz/C.24/33 (reference kindly supplied by Dr. Stephen Pasmore).
10. K.P.L., Millington's Book, pp. 5–6; P.R.O., C54/1666, Chamberlain *et al.* to Horseman.
11. Documents in the possession of Messrs. Gregory, Rowcliffe and Co.
12. *Harleian Society, Registers*, vol. xvi (Kensington 1539–1675), 1890, p. 95.
13. P.R.O., C54/2313, no. 22.
14. *Ibid.*, C54/3905, no. 5.
15. *Ibid.*, PROB 11/290, f. 204.
16. M.L.R. 1722/1/72–4; 1722/6/327–30; P.R.O., C11/65/12.
17. M.L.R. 1718/4/243–4; 1723/4/77–9.
18. K.P.L., MS. 1433; tablet in wall of building.
19. R.B.
20. M.L.R. 1727/2/125; documents in possession of Messrs. Gregory, Rowcliffe and Co.
21. P.R.O., MPH 258.
22. M.L.R. 1724/2/344.
23. *Ibid.*, 1723/2/411; 1723/6/367; 1725/1/365.
24. *Ibid.*, 1729/5/348; documents in the possession of Messrs. Gregory, Rowcliffe and Co.; *B.* 14 May 1870, p. 395.
25. M.L.R. 1725/2/503.
26. D.S.R. 1882.
27. P.R.O., PROB 11/614, f. 65.
28. M.L.R. 1727/2/366.
29. *Ibid.*, 1728/6/38.
30. *Ibid.*, 1728/1/266, 425; 1728/3/339; 1728/6/38; 1729/2/11; 1729/5/348.
31. *Ibid.*, 1736/4/550–1.
32. *Ibid.*, 1747/1/49–50; 1758/3/287–8.
33. *Ibid.*, 1736/2/218–19.
34. R.B.; plan attached to deed in possession of Messrs. Witham, Weld and Co.
35. M.L.R. 1841/3/189; R.B.
36. G.L.C. Members' Library, file 992; K.P.L., unidentified article, 'Mistress Walter Crane at 13 Holland Street' in N1801.
37. K.P.L., Vestry Minutes, 13 April 1763; K.P.L., MSS. 1478–9.
38. M.L.R. 1764/4/154–7; deed in possession of Messrs. Witham, Weld and Co.
39. Deed in possession of Kensington and Chelsea Borough Council; M.L.R. 1834/6/418.
40. R.B.; deeds in possession of Kensington and Chelsea Borough Council.
41. K.P.L., index of notable inhabitants.
42. *Ibid.*, Vestry Minutes, 4 Nov. 1767.
43. *B.* 19 June 1875, p. 561; D.S.R. 1875.
44. P.R.O., C54/3905, nos. 5, 9.
45. *Ibid.*, C54/4433, no. 6; PROB 11/340, f. 121.
46. K.P.L., Millington's Book, pp. 22, 24; C.E.O., file 11119.
47. P.R.O., PROB 11/340, f. 121; K.P.L., MS. 63/1379 (Great Church Book), pp. 157, 169.
48. K.P.L., MS. 63/1379 (Great Church Book), rate assessments; deeds in M.L.R.; *D.N.B.*; *G.E.C.*
49. P.R.O., C105/5, Bowman *v.* Reynell.
50. *Ibid.*, C54/4433, no. 6; K.P.L., MS. 63/1379 (Great Church Book), pp. 157, 169; P.R.O., PROB 11/487, f. 63.
51. M.L.R. 1764/4/116, 316; R.B.
52. M.L.R. 1781/3/321, 569; G.L.R.O.(M), MR/PLT 4890–2.
53. C.E.O., file 15348.

54. *Ibid.*, file 16017; *The Architectural Review*, vol. LIX, p. 133, vol. LXX, pp. 231–5.
55. *B.* 13 Jan. 1928, pp. 84, 86, 96.
56. L.C.C. Improvements Committee Minutes and Papers, 1912–16 *passim*.
57. D.S.R.; *P.O.D.*
58. *The Architect and Building News*, 13 Dec. 1935, pp. 314–16.
59. G.L.R.O.(L), Q/SHR/122, 127.
60. K.P.L., Court Books of Abbots Kensington, vol. 1, pp. 16, 31.
61. B. R. Curle, 'Some Aspects of Public Health in Kensington in the Nineteenth Century' (typescript in K.P.L.), p. 44; *Annual Reports of the Princess Louise Kensington Hospital for Children*, 1925, 1927; B.A. 41380.
62. L.C.C. Minutes, 1902–5 *passim*.
63. *The British Architect*, 30 April 1909, p. 309.
64. B.R. 8907; *The Kensington Post*, 15 Nov. 1963.
65. K.P.L., K66/57.
66. *B.* 4 Jan. 1902, p. 10.
67. [John Bowack], *The Antiquities of Middlesex*, part 1, 1705, p. 15; K.P.L., MS. 1456.
68. K.P.L., MSS. 1784–5 and 63/1379 (Great Church Book), pp. 13, 153f.; Vestry Minutes, 3 Feb. 1705/6, 9 Dec. 1706.
69. *Ibid.*, MSS. 1795–6.
70. *Ibid.*, Vestry Minutes, 11 Oct. 1769 and 1769–1772 *passim*.
71. *Ibid.*, MSS. 24, 1454, 1795–6, 1811–12.
72. *Ibid.*, MS. 1826; *St. Mary Abbots Parish Magazine*, 1882, pp. 47–65, 95–109, 132–144; *The Kensington News*, 22 Nov. 1879.
73. *St. Mary Abbots Parish Magazine*, 1890, p. 126, 1893, p. 202; *B.N.* 5 Sept. 1890, p. 346.
74. Alexander Rottmann, *London Catholic Churches*, 1926, pp. 100–7; Pepperell, p. 41; *B.N.* 20 July 1866, p. 488; R.B.; K.P.L., typescript history, and Court Books of Abbots Kensington, vol. 5, pp. 158–63.
75. Information kindly supplied by Sir Giles Scott, Son and Partner.
76. K.P.L., Court Books of Abbots Kensington, vol. 6, pp. 121–2, 256–7; *B.* 10 July 1886, p. 54; D.S.R.
77. Pepperell, p. 21; *P.O.D.*; K.P.L., Kensington Valuation Book, 1911, and entry in information index.
78. K.P.L., Charity School Accounts, vol. 1, pp. 1–3.
79. *Ibid.*, MSS. 2143–5.
80. *Ibid.*, MS. 79.
81. *Ibid.*, Charity School Minutes, 7, 9, 14, 21 May, 4 July 1711, 25 June 1712; Charity School Accounts, vol. 1, pp. 77, 88–9.
82. *Ibid.*, Charity School Minutes, 16 Sept. 1818.
83. *The Gentleman's Magazine*, vol. LXXXV, May 1815, p. 423.

84. K.P.L., MS. 2133; Charity School Minutes, 8 March, 12 April, 3 July 1804.
85. *Ibid.*, Charity School Minutes, 15 Nov. 1815, 3, 27 April, 11 June 1817, 10 Feb. 1818.
86. *Ibid.*, MSS. 1944, 2205; D.S.R.
87. K.P.L., Charity School Accounts, vol. 1, p. 119.
88. Playbills and newspaper cuttings in K.P.L.; playbills in possession of Dr. Stephen Pasmore; M.L.R. 1839/6/444; G.L.R.O.(L), C/84/101–5; M.C.S. 290, ff. 510a–12; N. M. Bligh, 'The Royal Kent Theatre, Kensington' in *Theatre Notebook*, vol. XIII, no. 4, 1959, pp. 124–8.
89. K.P.L., Vestry Minutes, 6 March 1851, and contract drawings for Vestry Hall; G.L.R.O. (L), M.B.O. 27, p. 267f, case 1,426; D.S.R.
90. K.P.L., 2446 (020/B.31), 2486c (020/B.40).
91. *Kensington Vestry Annual Report*, 1879–80, p. 30.
92. *Ibid.*, 1877–8, pp. 46–7; K.P.L., MS. 1936.
93. *B.N.* 1877 *passim*; *B.* 1876–7 *passim*; *The Architect*, 28 April 1877, p. 268.
94. *Kensington Vestry Annual Reports*, 1878–9, p. 27, 1879–80, pp. 30–1; *B.* 14 Aug. 1880, p. 201.
95. *The Municipal Journal and London*, 14 April 1899, p. 452.
96. K.P.L., Court Books of Abbots Kensington, vol. 1, *passim*.
97. G.L.R.O.(L), BRA 329/6; P.R.O., MPH 258; *G.E.C.*; *D.N.B.*
98. *G.E.C.*; P.R.O., C7/99/85.
99. M.L.R. 1736/5/231–2, 340–1; Dulwich College, Kensington deeds.
100. *Survey of London*, vol. XXXVI, 1970, p. 264.
101. Dulwich College, Kensington deeds.
102. M.L.R. 1737/3/535–6; *Survey of London*, vol. XXXIII, 1966, p. 61.
103. M.L.R. 1741/1/303–4.
104. *Ibid.*, 1747/1/1.
105. Colvin.
106. Dulwich College, Kensington deeds; G.L.C. Members' Library, file 1259; *Mendelssohn and his Friends in Kensington*, ed. R. B. Gotch, 1934.
107. P.R.O., PROB 11/1810, f. 10, will of George Barker.
108. M.L.R. 1859/9/107–8; 1859/12/943.
109. *Ibid.*, 1856/10/937–8; 1857/4/852–3; D.S.R.
110. M.L.R. 1863/14/929.
111. *B.* 23 Sept. 1865, p. 678.
112. B.A. 75180.
113. K.P.L., Vestry Works Committee, 15 Sept., 13 Oct., 10 Nov. 1865; M.L.R. 1867/2/365; 1869/26/720.
114. *B.N.* 31 Jan., 26 June 1868, pp. 85, 427.
115. P.R.O., census returns of 1871.
116. L.C.C. Minutes, 1953–62 *passim*.

117. *D.N.B.*
118. M.L.R. 1873/9/191; C.E.O., file 10504; D.S.R.; John C. Ballantyne, *Origins of the Essex Church, Notting Hill Gate, London*, [n.d.], (copy in K.P.L.).
119. M.L.R. 1863/2/722; K.P.L., Vestry Works Committee, 13 Sept. 1861; Pepperell, p. 44; *P.O.D.*
120. C.E.O., file 10504; *The Architectural Review*, vol. LX, pp. 66–73.
121. L.C.C. Theatres Committee Papers, Coronet Theatre, and Theatres and Music Halls Committee, 15 Nov. 1916; *The Era*, 26 Nov. 1898, p. 11, 3 Dec. 1898, p. 10; *B.* 15 Jan. 1898, pp. 61, 62; *The Official Guide to the Royal Borough of Kensington* [1917].

CHAPTER II (pp. 42–8)

The Sheffield House and Glebe Estates

1. P.R.O., C54/1791, Cope to Coppin, and Chamberlain *et al.* to Coppin.
2. *Ibid.*, C54/2165, no. 12.
3. *Ibid.*, PROB 11/131, f. 24, 11/197, f. 141; Faulkner, p. 142.
4. M.L.R. 1723/1/333.
5. G.L.C. Print Collection, cuttings relating to the Sheffield family of Kensington.
6. M.L.R. 1744/3/245; K.P.L., Vestry Minutes, 3 Aug. 1759, 27 May 1767.
7. K.P.L., Vestry Minutes, 21 July 1791.
8. Faulkner, p. 298.
9. Dulwich College, Kensington deeds, surveyor's letter of 1 Sept. 1798; R.B.
10. P.R.O., PROB 11/1511, f. 268.
11. *Ibid.*, PROB 11/1693, f. 685.
12. Guildhall Library, MS. 9531/11, f. 147.
13. K.P.L., Millington's Book, p. 21.
14. *Ibid.*, MS. 1550.
15. Faulkner, p. 298; W. J. Loftie, *Kensington Picturesque and Historical*, 1888, pp. 174–5.
16. *B.* 13 April, 11 May 1872, pp. 281–2, 362, 20 Oct. 1877, p. 1052; *B.N.* 3 Aug. 1877, p. 100.
17. Tablet on building.
18. C.C., file 3583, pt. 1.
19. M.C.S. 298, ff. 398–9.
20. K.P.L., Vestry Sewers Committee, 10 July 1860.
21. *Ibid.*, 14 Oct. 1856.
22. *Ibid.*, MS. 2583.
23. P.R.O., census returns of 1861.
24. M.L.R. 1850/4/574; 1858/3/697.
25. *Ibid.*, 1858/3/441–6.
26. *Ibid.*, 1881/30/22; D.S.R.
27. M.L.R. 1850/4/574; 1858/11/301; 1858/15/342; 1869/28/596.
28. K.P.L., Vestry Works Committee, 1868–70 *passim*.
29. C.C., file 51854, pt. 5.
30. M.L.R. 1861/8/691–5; 1861/15/40–4.
31. C.C., file 51854, pt. 1.
32. *Ibid.*, file P.G. 124.
33. *Ibid.*, files 51854, pt. 5, 95766, pt. 2.
34. *I.L.N.* 29 Sept. 1855, p. 375.
35. C.E.O., file 10067.
36. *St. Mary Abbots Parish Magazine*, 1885–9 *passim*; *B.* 24 July 1886, p. 118; *B.N.* 23 July 1886, pp. 119–20, 11 March 1887, p. 353, 2 Nov. 1888, p. 591; *R.I.B.A. Journal*, third series, vol. IV, 1896–7, p. 360.
37. C.C., file 95770.

CHAPTER III (pp. 49–57)

The Pitt Estate

1. B.M., Add. Roll 59150.
2. P.R.O., C54/2313, no. 22.
3. *G.E.C.*
4. *Ibid.*; *Journals of the House of Lords*, vol. XI, p. 623.
5. P.R.O., SP 23/G. 183, pp. 79–80.
6. 14 Ch. II, c. 38, private.
7. K.P.L., MS. 3663; documents in the possession of Messrs. Gregory, Rowcliffe and Co.
8. K.P.L., MSS. 3663–8; M.L.R. 1712/5/26.
9. K.P.L., MSS. 3673–5, 3678–83.
10. Documents in the possession of Messrs. Gregory, Rowcliffe and Co.
11. K.P.L., Court Books of Abbots Kensington, vol. 5, pp. 136–40.
12. *Ibid.*, Bullingham House, cuttings (F. 740).
13. P.R.O., K.B. 122/927, no. 73; M.L.R. 1712/5/26.
14. K.P.L., Kensington Turnpike Trust Minutes, 13 Feb. 1826.
15. *A.P.S.D.*
16. Documents in the possession of Messrs. Gregory, Rowcliffe and Co.; Colvin.
17. M.L.R. 1853/6/471; 1853/12/381.
18. *Ibid.*, 1864/7/866.
19. *Ibid.*, 1846–55 *sub* Pitt.
20. *B.* 21 Aug. 1847, p. 403.
21. M.L.R. 1846/4/541–8.
22. D.S.R.
23. *Ibid.*; M.L.R. 1850/9/119–24.
24. D.S.R.; M.L.R. 1847/3/73; 1847/7/319; P.R.O., census returns of 1851.
25. K.P.L., Vestry Works Committee, 3 Aug. 1866.

26. Douglas Goldring, *South Lodge*, 1943.
27. M.L.R. 1853/13/688; 1854/9/793; 1855/13/185.
28. M.C.S. 294, f. 783.
29. M.L.R. 1855/2/179.
30. M.C.S. 291, f. 451a; 292, f. 246.
31. M.L.R. 1850/11/869-70.
32. P.R.O., census returns of 1851.
33. K.P.L., MS. 4463; P.R.O., census returns of 1851 and 1861.
34. K.P.L., Court Books of Abbots Kensington, vol. 6, pp. 68-70.
35. M.L.R. 1873/5/709; D.S.R.
36. M.L.R. 1871/23/1242-5; 1872/10/69-72; D.S.R.
37. M.L.R. 1872/15/790; 1873/6/682-3; 1873/7/59-62; 1873/11/4-6; 1873/14/432; D.S.R.
38. M.L.R. 1872/4/9-11; D.S.R.
39. M.L.R. 1873/17/278; 1873/23/168-9; D.S.R.
40. M.L.R. 1877/26/107-9; 1877/36/331-2; 1878/16/103; D.S.R.
41. K.P.L., Court Books of Abbots Kensington, vol. 7, pp. 52-4; D.S.R.; documents in the possession of Messrs. Gregory, Rowcliffe and Co.
42. M.L.R. 1894/36/737-9, 752.
43. *The Architectural Review*, vol. XIX, 1906, pp. 207-8; K.P.L., K 66/102; *Flats, Urban Houses and Cottage Homes*, ed. W. Shaw Sparrow, [1907], p. 53.
44. L.C.C. Minutes, 2 Nov. 1948, p. 647, 14 May 1952, pp. 287-8, 3 Feb. 1953, p. 16.
45. P.R.O., C2/Eliz/C.24/33 (reference kindly supplied by Dr. Stephen Pasmore); K.P.L., Millington's Book, p. 22.
46. P.R.O., C54/1393, Barker to Cope.
47. *Walpole Society*, vol. 40, 1966 (The Book of Architecture of John Thorpe in Sir John Soane's Museum), p. 72, and further information kindly supplied by Sir John Summerson.
48. Faulkner, p. 308.
49. *Notes and Queries*, fifteenth series, vol. CXCII, 1947, pp. 244-8, 267-72.
50. [John Bowack], *The Antiquities of Middlesex*, part 1, 1705, p. 21.
51. M.L.R. 1854/10/517; Guildhall Library, MS. 8733/17; K.P.L., K 66/439.
52. *I.L.N.* 14 July 1855, p. 43.
53. *Ibid.*, 29 March 1862, p. 309, 5 Sept. 1863, p. 234.
54. M.L.R. 1872/7/282; 1872/9/502.
55. G.L.R.O.(L), Acc. 64. 72; cutting in possession of G.L.C. Survey of London section.
56. B.A. 8794.
57. Daniel Lysons, *The Environs of London*, vol. III, 1795, p. 179.
58. P.R.O., MPH 258.
59. M.L.R. 1850/9/379; 1850/11/781.
60. K.P.L., Vestry Works Committee, 2 Dec. 1868, 24 Feb., 16 June 1869; *P.O.D.*
61. M.L.R. 1847/6/147; G.L.R.O.(L), M.B.O. 68, p. 272f.
62. Stuart Allen Smith, 'Alfred Waterhouse', unpublished Ph.D. dissertation, University of London, 1970, pp. 72-4, 453-4; D.S.R.
63. *B.N.* 23 March 1877, p. 286.

CHAPTER IV (pp. 58-76)

The Phillimore Estate

1. W.P.W. Phillimore and Lord Phillimore, *The Genealogy of the Family of Phillimore*, 1922, p. 201.
2. P.R.O., PROB 11/509, f. 140.
3. *Ibid.*, PROB 11/554, f. 204.
4. *Ibid.*, PROB 6/107.
5. M.L.R. 1775/1/69-71; P.R.O., PROB 11/1056, f. 355.
6. M.L.R. 1798/2/821; K.P.L., Kensington Turnpike Trust Minutes, 12 May 1788.
7. Colvin.
8. M.L.R. 1789/1/287; 1812/8/424; R.B.
9. R.B.
10. M.L.R. 1789/4/421.
11. *Ibid.*, 1791/9/217.
12. *Ibid.*, 1789/2/194.
13. *Ibid.*, 1789/9/219-20, 421-2; 1790/1/144; 1790/4/143.
14. *Ibid.*, 1798/2/281.
15. *Ibid.*, 1792/7/734.
16. *Ibid.*, 1789-1812 *sub* William Phillimore.
17. K.P.L., MS. 127.
18. E.g. M.L.R. 1800/4/442; 1801/5/295, 598; 1802/2/247; 1803/6/516.
19. M.L.R. 1804/3/468.
20. *The London Gazette*, 11 Dec. 1813, p. 2503.
21. M.L.R. 1811/8/435; 1811/9/413-14; 1812/8/424.
22. *Ibid.*, 1803/2/228-9.
23. *Ibid.*, 1804/3/306; 1814/6/309.
24. *Ibid.*, 1807/7/337-8; 1810/9/380-1; 1811/5/558; 1812/2/218-19, 318; 1814/6/309; 1815/4/597.
25. *Ibid.*, 1797/4/964; 1814/5/503.
26. *Ibid.*, 1818/4/510.
27. W.C.S. 179, p. 135; M.L.R. 1823/9/342; 1829/2/257.
28. M.L.R. 1792/8/189.
29. *Ibid.*, 1812/3/818.
30. *Ibid.*, 1822/6/677.
31. H.L.R.O., H.L. Committee Book, vol. 208, p. 2.
32. M.L.R. 1817/3/718.
33. *Ibid.*, 1809/1/238.

34. *Ibid.*, 1812/6/602; 1815/4/556.
35. *Ibid.*, 1827/3/387; 1827/6/410.
36. P.R.O., PROB 11/1756, f. 309.
37. Hermione Hobhouse, *Thomas Cubitt Master Builder*, 1971, pp. 213, 216, 228; *P.O.D.*
38. 25 and 26 Vict., c. 1, private.
39. Phillimore, *Genealogy . . .*, p. 215.
40. K.P.L., MS. 579.
41. H.L.R.O., H.L. Committee Book, vol. 208, p. 15; *B.* 17 July 1858, p. 492.
42. *I.L.N.* 31 May 1856, p. 607.
43. M.L.R. 1857/13/873.
44. *Ibid.*, 1856/9/778; 1856/10/102; 1858/2/914; 1858/10/529–30.
45. *B.N.* 15 July 1859, p. 659.
46. *B.* 3 March 1860, p. 144.
47. P.R.O., census returns of 1861.
48. M.L.R. 1864/14/161–3; K.P.L., MSS. 631–632, and Vestry Works Committee, 26 April 1861.
49. K.P.L., Vestry Sewers Committee, 20 April 1858, 25 Jan., 9 Aug., 20 Sept. 1859; Vestry Works Committee, 15 March 1861, 20 June, 12 Dec. 1862, 29 May 1863, 5 Feb. 1864.
50. *P.O.D.*
51. K.P.L., Vestry Sewers Committee, 14 June 1859.
52. Charles L. Eastlake, *A History of the Gothic Revival*, 1872, p. 395.
53. K.P.L., estate agent's prospectus of No. 15 Upper Phillimore Gardens; A. Trystan Edwards, *Good and Bad Manners in Architecture*, 1924, p. 138 and Figure 31 opposite.
54. M.L.R. 1869/11/685–712; K.P.L., MS. 639.
55. Elizabeth Aslin, *The Aesthetic Movement*, 1969, p. 114, and 'Luxury and Refinement' in *The Sphere*, 6 Jan. 1962, pp. 28–30; Christopher Hussey, '18 Stafford Terrace, Kensington' in *Country Life*, 4 April 1952, pp. 996–9.
56. M.L.R. 1870/23/857.
57. *Ibid.*, 1872/7/26; 1873/23/256–7; 1874/2/323–8; D.S.R.
58. M.L.R. 1878/8/417.
59. W. Gordon Corfield, *The Phillimore Estate, Campden Hill*, 1961, p. 29.
60. M.L.R. 1881/33/121.
61. D.S.R.
62. M.L.R. 1881/25/893–6; 1881/35/439–41; 1882/7/324–7; 1882/26/115; 1882/35/591–596; 1882/40/613.
63. *Ibid.*, 1882/11/120–1; 1883/31/889–90.
64. *Ibid.*, 1881/33/121.
65. Documents in the possession of Messrs. Frere, Cholmeley and Co.
66. Documents in the possession of Messrs. Chesterton and Sons; Corfield, *op. cit.*, pp. 36–7.
67. *D.N.B.*
68. Phillimore, *Genealogy . . .*, p. 216.
69. K.P.L., K 64/246; Royal Borough of Kensington Council Minutes, 17 Feb. 1903, p. 162, 2 Aug. 1904, p. 393.
70. *B.* 23 March 1907, between pp. 368 and 369.
71. B.R. 34950.
72. M.L.R. 1930/57/163.
73. *Recent English Domestic Architecture*, ed. Ernest and W. G. Newton, [n.d.], vol. VI, pp. 96–7.
74. B.A. 41058; *D.N.B.*
75. B.A. 40435.
76. *The Architect and Building News*, 28 Sept. 1934, pp. 375–9.
77. *The Morning Post*, 5 May 1932.
78. L.C.C. Minutes, 2 Nov. 1948, p. 647, 4 Dec. 1951, p. 733.
79. Royal Borough of Kensington Council Minutes, 12 Feb. 1946, pp. 70–2, 80.
80. M.L.R. 1794/5/622; *D.N.B.*
81. Pepperell, pp. 42–3.
82. G.L.R.O.(L), M.B.O. 16, p. 403f., case 107.
83. John Stoughton, *Congregationalism in the Old Court Suburb*, 1883, pp. 80, 84–5.
84. W. T. Whitley, *The Baptists of London, 1612–1928*, [n.d.], p. 184.
85. Faulkner, p. 319; R.B.
86. *Reports of the British and Foreign School Society*, 1835, p. 53, 1837, pp. 62–3.
87. M.L.R. 1813/3/651.
88. *Souvenir Brochure of the Solemn Opening of Our Lady of Victories*, 1959; Catholic directories in Archbishop's House, Westminster.
89. R.B.; M.L.R. 1814/7/104; 1817/1/589, 612; 1817/8/215.
90. R.B.; *Burke's Peerage*; *The Aristocracy of London, Part I, Kensington*, 1863 (B.M. pressmark P.P.2505.ae); *P.O.D.*
91. M.L.R. 1813/4/181–2; 1817/1/587–8, 650–1.
92. P.R.O., PROB 11/2146, f. 85.
93. M.L.R. 1833/7/34.
94. T. Mackay, *The Life of Sir John Fowler*, 1900, p. 321.
95. Sir George Otto Trevelyan, *The Life and Letters of Lord Macaulay*, 1876, vol. II, pp. 332, 334, 405–6.
96. G.L.C. Members' Library, file 332.
97. R.B.; *D.N.B.*
98. Bedford Estate Office, abstract book no. 3, Middlesex bundle 16, no. 3.
99. B.M., Add. MS. 51748, letter of 28 May 1823.
100. Bedford Estate Office, volume of designs for Bedford Lodge by (Sir) Jeffry Wyatt (Wyatville).
101. *I.L.N.* 25 July 1846, p. 60.
102. Phillimore, *Genealogy . . .*, p. 261.
103. B.A. 69888.
104. M.L.R. 1817/4/251; *D.N.B.*
105. G.L.C. Map Collection.

106. Information kindly supplied by Mr. G. C. Berry, archivist to the Metropolitan Water Board.
107. M.L.R. 1817/1/651; R.B.
108. M.L.R. 1829/7/745; P.R.O., census returns of 1861.
109. Metropolitan Water Board, assignment of 25 Jan. 1869 from E. Stone to Grand Junction Water Works Co.
110. *P.O.D.*; *D.N.B.*; *The Architectural Review*, vol. i, 1897, p. 82.
111. *Burke's Peerage.*
112. Ian Colquhoun, 'Montagu Norman designer' in *Design*, No. 71, Nov. 1954; Sir Henry Clay, *Lord Norman*, 1957, pp. 60–2.
113. L.C.C. Minutes, 6 Nov. 1956, p. 629.
114. M.L.R. 1817/1/613; R.B.; P.R.O., PROB 11/1600, f. 48.
115. Corfield, *op. cit.*, pp. 21–2.
116. M.L.R. 1836/7/29.
117. R.B.; *D.N.B.*; *G.E.C.*; *The Aristocracy of London* (see ref. 90 above).
118. R.B.; M.L.R. 1836/7/27.
119. *P.P.*, *Eighteenth Report of the Commissioners of Inquiry into the Excise Establishment*, 1836, vol. xxvi, p. 158.
120. British Transport Historical Records, WLR 1/11, pp. 132, 160; *The Aristocracy of London* (see ref. 90 above).
121. *B.* 29 April 1865, p. 303.
122. *D.N.B.*; *P.O.D.*; *The Memoirs of Herbert Hoover: Years of Adventure 1874–1920*, 1952, pp. 76–7, 122, 128–9, 212.
123. W. J. Loftie, *Kensington Picturesque and Historical*, 1888, p. 263.
124. *The Aristocracy of London* (see ref. 90 above).
125. M.L.R. 1880/25/1111–15; 1885/9/964–70; G.L.C. Members' Library, sale prospectus of The Abbey, 1889.
126. G.L.C. Members' Library, The Abbey, *ut supra*, p. 3; *P.O.D.*; D.S.R.
127. M.L.R. 1930/57/163; B.A. 40815; *The Architectural Review*, vol. xl, 1916, pp. 13–17.
128. F. J. C. Hearnshaw, *The Centenary History of King's College London 1828–1928*, 1929, pp. 312–18, 438–42, 455–7, 489–509; *Victoria County History of Middlesex*, vol. i, 1969, p. 353; *St. Mary Abbots Parish Magazine*, 1882, p. 113.
129. L.C.C. Minutes, 30 March 1954, p. 159; *The Architect and Building News*, 2 Dec. 1959, pp. 553–61.
130. Information in K.P.L.; *The Daily Telegraph*, 26 Jan. 1959.
131. M.L.R. 1827/3/387.
132. *Ibid.*, 1729/6/318; 1730/1/186.

133. *D.N.B.*; K.P.L., MS. 2226; E. Walford, *Old and New London*, 1897, vol. v, pp. 130–2; *The Times*, 22 Dec. 1842.
134. M.L.R. 1871/5/212; 1871/10/624–5.
135. *Ibid.*, 1874/10/228; 1875/4/911–14; 1875/5/211–13; 1876/2/453; 1876/6/946–7; 1876/24/247–8; 1877/2/911; 1879/28/130; D.S.R.
136. M.L.R. 1877/30/592; 1880/6/67–8, 233–4; 1880/20/75–6; 1880/23/248; 1886/19/507.
137. *B.* 4 Jan. 1902, p. 12; D.S.R.
138. M.L.R. 1827/6/410; 1840/9/134; *P.O.D.*
139. M.L.R. 1845/7/354; P.R.O., PROB 11/2004, f. 697; *P.O.D.*
140. G.L.C. Members' Library, file 1301.

CHAPTER V (pp. 77–86)

Bedford Gardens to Uxbridge Street: The Racks

1. M.L.R. 1775/1/69–71; P.R.O., PROB 11/1056, f. 355.
2. W. P. W. Phillimore and Lord Phillimore, *The Genealogy of the Family of Phillimore*, 1922, pp. 221–2.
3. M.L.R. 1809/3/349–50; 1809/4/192–7.
4. *Ibid.*, 1811/6/21–6.
5. *Ibid.*, 1857/8/130–2.
6. P.R.O., PROB 11/1670, f. 267; Boase.
7. G.L.R.O.(M), Acc. 891/2/6/1716–17.
8. M.L.R. 1823/1/301.
9. G.L.R.O.(M), Acc. 891/2/6/1719–20.
10. M.L.R. 1823/1/302.
11. *Ibid.*, 1824/2/413.
12. K.P.L., MSS. 182–4, 190, 277–8.
13. *P.O.D.*
14. M.L.R. 1831/5/278.
15. *Ibid.*, 1824/9/733–8.
16. *Ibid.*, 1824–8 *sub* Bromley.
17. *Ibid.*, 1830/7/442.
18. P.R.O., PROB 11/1765, f. 34.
19. R.B.
20. M.L.R. 1832/1/37–8.
21. *Ibid.*, 1827/2/122.
22. *Ibid.*, 1833/1/47–50; *P.O.D.*
23. Gwen Hart, *A History of Cheltenham*, 1965, pp. 182, 185, 191, 199, 274, 309; Colvin; *Robson's London Directory*, 1835, 1836.
24. M.L.R. 1835/4/317–30; 1835/5/493; 1835/8/542.
25. Colvin.
26. K.P.L., 2204f (KE 70/300).

27. B.R. 124720.
28. *B.N.* 4 May 1883, p. 588; D.S.R.
29. M.L.R. 1872/19/686; D.S.R.
30. M.L.R. 1849/10/883–4; 1851/3/874; 1851/10/450–1; D.S.R.; M.C.S. 292, f. 297, and 293, f. 5.
31. P.R.O., PROB 11/2123, f. 864.
32. B.A. 41421; *B.* 7 May 1948, p. 564; K.P.L., prospectus of the Byam Shaw School.
33. M.L.R. 1824/10/422; *P.O.D.*
34. M.L.R. 1823–5 *sub* Punter.
35. *Ibid.*, 1823/10/824; 1824/6/73, 309; 1825/1/666; 1827/9/686.
36. *Ibid.*, 1823/10/823; *P.O.D.*
37. M.L.R. 1824/10/422.
38. *Ibid.*, 1824/4/366; 1826/10/596
39. *Ibid.*, 1828/4/474.
40. W.C.S. P/31/985.
41. M.L.R. 1824/3/163; 1825/2/331–2; 1825/7/319; 1825/13/782; 1829/2/578.
42. *Ibid.*, 1835/2/254.
43. W.C.S. 74, pp. 421–4.
44. K.P.L., Vestry Sewers Committee, 16 Dec. 1856.
45. M.L.R. 1876/2/556; 1876/21/171; 1879/20/154; *B.* 11, 25 Aug. 1877, pp. 822, 868; D.S.R.
46. M.L.R. 1876/2/556; 1876/20/946; 1877/22/23; *D.N.B.*
47. M.L.R. 1824/2/73; 1824/7/677; 1826/1/378–380; 1826/8/69–72; 1827/1/263.
48. *Ibid.*, 1826/8/410.
49. *Ibid.*, 1876/13/295–6.
50. *B.N.* 28 June 1878, p. 648.
51. M. D. Conway, *Travels in South Kensington*, 1882, p. 182.
52. G.L.R.O.(M), Acc. 891/2/3/235 and 891/2/6/1718.
53. M.L.R. 1824/11/717; 1826/6/8–9.
54. Metropolitan Water Board, Minutes of West Middlesex Water Works Co., 9 Aug., 6 Dec. 1808, 7 Nov. 1809.
55. *Ibid.*, 2 Aug., 28 Sept., 6 Nov. 1810; M.L.R. 1810/8/107.
56. Metropolitan Water Board, conveyance of 15 May 1928 to F. and P. Vandervell, Ltd.
57. *Ibid.*, conveyance of 7 Nov. 1924 to L.C.C.; M.L.R. 1842/6/595; *Endowed Charities* (*London*), vol. IV, 1901, pp. 471–2; L.C.C. Education Committee Minutes, 18 July 1934, 6 Nov. 1935, and *Education Services Information*, 1939.
58. Metropolitan Water Board, Minutes of W.M. W.W.C., 1 July, 2, 23 Aug., 20 Nov. 1825, 19 Sept. 1826; M.L.R. 1825/13/416, 525; 1830/7/573; 1835/5/245–6.
59. K.P.L., K 66/72.
60. B.R. 53476.

61. *Endowed Charities* (*London*), vol. IV, 1901, pp. 473–4; K.P.L., MS. 1764; Charity School Minutes, 5, 23 Nov., 4 Dec. 1838, 3 Jan., 7 Nov. 1839; *L.C.C. Education Bulletin*, No. 536, 5 Dec. 1962, item 13.
62. *The Times*, 1 Jan. 1849; M.L.R. 1829/5/621.
63. M.L.R. 1824/1/512.
64. W.C.S. P/21/681.
65. *Ibid.*, 180, pp. 231, 254.
66. M.L.R. 1829/5/621.
67. *I.L.N.* 15 Nov. 1845, p. 320.
68. M.L.R. 1840/3/414; 1840/8/848.
69. P.R.O., PROB 11/2089, f. 199.
70. M.L.R. 1851/9/668.
71. *Ibid.*, 1850/8/938; 1850/9/858–60.
72. M.C.S. 291, ff. 588–90; 292, ff. 164–5, 204, 206.
73. M.L.R. 1852/15/81–6; M.C.S. 298, ff. 5–6a.
74. M.L.R. 1850–9 *sub* William Johnson; D.S.R.
75. M.L.R. 1855/13/1.
76. Henry Mayhew, *The Shops and Companies of London*, 1865 (B.M. pressmark 1802.a.18), pp. 152–3.
77. K.P.L., K 62/431 (286 HIL/A).
78. *The Kensington News*, 26 Jan. 1900.
79. D.S.R.
80. Maurice Webb, *Architecture in Britain Today*, 1969, pp. 113–14, 251; B.A. 106187.
81. M.L.R. 1825/6/722; Pepperell, p. 54.
82. M.L.R. 1852/4/508; G.L.R.O.(L), M.B.O. 28, p. 206; Pepperell, p. 54; K.P.L., K 62/431 (286 HIL/A); W. T. Whitley, *The Baptists of London*, *1612–1928*, [n.d.], p. 172; *P.O.D.*

CHAPTER VI (pp. 87–100)

Campden Hill Square Area

1. Hertfordshire Record Office, records 12335–7, 14474.
2. *Ibid.*, 12340, 14474; M.L.R. 1750/2/206–7.
3. *The Gentleman's Magazine*, vol. XIV, Feb. 1744, p. 109.
4. P.R.O., PROB 11/1263, f. 460; *G.E.C.*
5. M.L.R. 1819/4/418.
6. K.P.L., Court Books of Abbots Kensington, vol. 3, pp. 93–8.
7. *Ibid.*, vol. 1, pp. 246–7; M.L.R. 1830/7/1.
8. M.L.R. 1821/1/469.
9. Faulkner, p. 428.
10. M.L.R. 1823/5/292–3.
11. *Ibid.*, 1736/4/513; K.P.L., Local 58/5630, Assessment Book 1683–1728.

12. Benjamin Allen, *The Natural History of the Chalybeat and Purging Waters of England*, 1699, pp. 129–32.
13. [John Bowack], *The Antiquities of Middlesex*, part 1, 1705, p. 20.
14. M.L.R. 1736/4/513.
15. *Ibid.*, 1744/2/241; 1750/2/206–7.
16. R.B.
17. *The Letters and Journals of Lady Mary Coke*, [ed. James A. Home], 1889–96, vol. 11, pp. 45, 188, 221, 284, 294, 399, 111, pp. 11, 114, 118, 439, 1v, pp. 439–40; Colvin.
18. Florence M. Gladstone, *Aubrey House Kensington 1698–1920*, 1922, pp. 28–34.
19. M.L.R. 1827/6/2.
20. Gladstone, *Aubrey House* . . ., pp. 36–8; R.B.
21. P.R.O., PROB 11/2146, f. 85.
22. M.L.R. 1859/10/601.
23. *Ibid.*, 1860/7/324; Gladstone, *Aubrey House* . . ., p. 44.
24. M.L.R. 1863/19/221.
25. *D.N.B.*; Louisa M. Alcott, *Shawl-Straps*, 1873, pp. 281–2; Gladstone, *Aubrey House* . . ., pp. 45–8.
26. M.L.R. 1873/18/880.
27. G.L.C. Members' Library, file 1303.
28. Antony Dale, *Fashionable Brighton, 1820–1860*, 1947, pp. 41–4.
29. W.C.S. P/20/665.
30. *Ibid.*, 180, pp. 130, 243–5.
31. R.B.; M.L.R. 1830/8/162.
32. K.P.L., MS. 655; M.L.R. 1826/8/46; 1834/3/409; W.C.S. 180, p. 243.
33. M.L.R. 1827/6/1; 1828/6/665.
34. *Ibid.*, 1830/8/162; P.R.O., PROB 11/1804, f. 516.
35. M.L.R. 1839/8/778, 1839/9/158–9, 827; title deeds of No. 52 Campden Hill Square inspected by kind permission of Rt. Hon. Hugh and Lady Antonia Fraser.
36. E.g. M.L.R. 1845/8/520.
37. P.R.O., PROB 11/1804, f. 516.
38. M.L.R. 1831/4/701; 1833/3/288.
39. *Ibid.*, 1838/1/35; 1838/3/214; 1840/4/100–1; 1841/3/266–9; 1849/8/720.
40. E.g. M.L.R. 1841/3/270–1; 1841/7/879; 1849/8/720.
41. M.L.R. 1837/6/756; 1839/7/258; 1839/9/338.
42. *Ibid.*, 1851/6/386.
43. *B.* 1 Oct. 1887, p. 482; D.S.R.
44. B.A. 13415.
45. M.L.R. 1827/7/541; 1830/2/487; 1832/6/644; 1834/2/217–18; 1838/1/35; 1838/3/214; 1841/3/266–9; 1849/8/720; 1851/6/386; W.C.S. 181, p. 298.
46. M.L.R. 1827/7/541; 1830/1/773; 1830/2/487.
47. K.P.L., MS. 413; Campden Hill Square Garden Committee, Minute books.
48. M.L.R. 1830/1/807.
49. K.P.L., prospectus of Linton House School, 1922; D.S.R.
50. B.R. 10836.
51. M.L.R. 1830/9/253.
52. *Ibid.*, 1826/8/46.
53. *Ibid.*, 1841/8/457.
54. P.R.O., PROB 11/6986, f. 699.
55. R.I.B.A. Library, Wyatt papers.
56. M.L.R. 1843/9/411–12; 1844/4/631–2; 1844/6/342–3; W.C.S. P/43/1399; R.B.
57. B.A. 40325.
58. K.P.L., Vestry Works Committee, 7 June 1861; M.L.R. 1863/9/651.
59. M.L.R. 1854/14/362; D.S.R.; *D.N.B.*
60. E/HOL, first lease book, pp. 240–1; K.P.L., Vestry Works Committee, 1 May 1863.
61. M.L.R. 1826/11/349; 1829/7/445; R.B.
62. M.L.R. 1829/7/177–8.
63. D.S.R.
64. *The British Architect*, 28 Nov. 1902, pp. 381, 385.
65. M.L.R. 1839/7/258; R.B.; W.C.S. 78, p. 275, P/38/1194.
66. M.L.R. 1821/2/401.
67. P.R.O., PROB 11/1881, f. 516.
68. W.C.S. P/41/1339.
69. M.L.R. 1844/2/210–12.
70. *Ibid.*, 1847/8/21; 1849/2/744; 1854/2/645.
71. *A.P.S.D.*; *B.N.* 10 Nov. 1871, pp. 347–8.
72. *P.O.D.*
73. M.L.R. 1852/14/869; D.S.R.; M.C.S. 293, f. 108.
74. M.L.R. 1862/14/131–4.
75. *Ibid.*, 1821/1/336–7; K.P.L., Court Books of Abbots Kensington, vol. 3, pp. 115–17; R.B.
76. M.L.R. 1828/6/711–12.
77. K.P.L., Vestry Works Committee, 3 Aug. 1869.
78. M.L.R. 1870/13/185.
79. K.P.L., Vestry Minutes, 19 Jan., 16, 30 March 1870.
80. M.L.R. 1870/17/41; K.P.L., Vestry Works Committee, 18 July 1870.
81. M.L.R. 1870/21/488–90; 1870/23/952–4; K.P.L., Vestry Works Committee, 13 July, 5 Oct. 1870.
82. M.L.R. 1871/10/676–9; 1871/14/262–5, 921–2.
83. *Ibid.*, 1874/12/536.
84. *B.* 1 April 1871, p. 252; *P.O.D.*
85. M.L.R. 1872/5/293–6; 1872/6/60; 1872/17/837–9; 1872/23/1021–3; D.S.R.
86. M.L.R. 1863/22/764; C.C., files 26966, 28273.
87. *B.N.* 29 Jan., 22 July, 30 Sept. 1864, pp. 85, 560, 726.
88. *I.L.N.* 26 Nov. 1864, p. 527; C.C., file 26966.

89. C.C., file 28273; information kindly supplied by Mr. R. B. Craze.
90. Pepperell, pp. 33–4.
91. *B.* 4 April 1885, p. 499.
92. M.L.R. 1820/3/590, 683; 1820/7/686.
93. *Ibid.*, 1843/6/904; Metropolitan Water Board, Minutes of Grand Junction Water Works Co., 10 May, 7 June 1843, 23 April 1845; information kindly supplied by Mr. G. C. Berry.
94. *Minutes of the Proceedings of the Institution of Civil Engineers*, vol. CXXIII, p. 434.
95. *The British Almanac for 1858. Companion*, p. 129; *B.N.* 26 June 1857, p. 665, 5 Feb. 1858, p. 124.
96. M.L.R. 1866/19/12; Metropolitan Water Board, Minutes of G.J.W.W.C., 19 Feb., 1 April, 20 May 1868, 1 Dec. 1869, conveyance of 25 April 1868 from C. Magniac to G.J. W.W.C.

CHAPTER VII (pp. 101–50)

The Holland Estate

1. 8 Geo. III, c. 32, local; *G.E.C.*; K.P.L., MS. 2804.
2. B.M., Add. MS. 51418, letter of 17 June 1746.
3. M.L.R. 1749/1/449.
4. P.R.O., C13/1619/27.
5. *The History of Parliament. The House of Commons 1715–1754*, 1970, vol. II, p. 5.
6. 8 Geo. III, c. 32, local; E/HOL, documents relating to sale of Holland estate, 1767–8.
7. B.M., Add. MS. 51409, accounts for 1767–8.
8. *Ibid.*, Crace Collection, Views portfolio XXXVI, sheet 45.
9. E/HOL, lease of 1 June 1758 to W. Bowles.
10. G.L.C. Map Collection.
11. P.R.O., E214/322 and 796; *D.N.B.*
12. *G.E.C.*; P.R.O., C13/1619/27; E/HOL, bargain and sale of 6 May 1823.
13. B.M., Add. MS. 51748, letter of 11 April 1823.
14. *Ibid.*, Add. MS. 51815, accounts for 1822.
15. *Ibid.*, Add. MS. 51748, letter of 13 May 1823.
16. *Ibid.*, Add. MS. 51749, letter of 27 Aug. 1824.
17. *Ibid.*, Add. MS. 51766, letter of 5 Jan. [1827].
18. *Ibid.*, Add. MS. 51763, letter of 7 Feb. 1824.
19. Boase; Coutts' Bank, accounts of Lord Holland, 1829–30; G.L.R.O.(L), T.A.9.
20. M.L.R. 1828/1/794; Colvin; *Survey of London*, vol. XXIII, 1951, p. 42, vol. XXIX, 1960, pp. 380–1; *P.P.*, *Report from the Select Committee on the Office of Works and Public Buildings*, 1828, vol. IV, p. 400.
21. M.B.W. 213.
22. P.R.O., B4/48, H.251.
23. B.M., Add. MS. 51812, letter of 18 March 1824.
24. *Survey of London*, vol. XXVI, 1956, pp. 112, 113.
25. W.C.S. 180, pp. 93–4; B.M., Add. MS. 51815, accounts for 1826.
26. W.C.S. 179, pp. 105–6, 108, 219; 180, pp. 93–94, 214–15; 182, pp. 20, 190–1; 185, p. 76.
27. B.M., Add. MS. 51763, letter of 7 Oct. [1823].
28. W.C.S. P/18/598.
29. *Ibid.*, 68, pp. 143–5.
30. B.M., Add. MS. 51749, letter of 24 Sept. 1824.
31. *Ibid.*, Add. MS. 51764, letter of [? 23 July 1824].
32. *Ibid.*, Add. MS. 51815, accounts for 1826.
33. E/HOL, leases of 1 March 1824 to J. A. Snee and N. P. Rothery; *P.O.D.*
34. *Survey of London*, vol. XXVI, 1956, pp. 113, 114.
35. M.L.R. 1852/3/746.
36. R.B.
37. M.L.R. 1852/3/747.
38. E/HOL, lease of 5 July 1825 to W. Woods.
39. W.C.S. 191, pp. 131–2.
40. *Survey of London*, vol. XXVI, 1956, p. 109; K.P.L., Court Books of Abbots Kensington, vol. 3, p. 210.
41. M.L.R. 1852/3/750; G.L.R.O.(L), T.A.9.
42. *D.N.B.*
43. B.M., Add. MS. 51749, letter of 18 Sept. 1826.
44. *Ibid.*, Add. MS. 52058, letters of 30 March, 13 April 1827.
45. M.L.R. 1842/2/215–20.
46. *Ibid.*, 1842/5/683; W.C.S. P/39/1243; B.M., Add. MS. 51788, letters of Aug.-Sept. 1839.
47. B.M., Add. MS. 51812, letter of 30 Sept. 1839.
48. M.L.R. 1832/1/351–3, 366–8; 1835/4/301–2; 1836/2/333; 1836/4/400; 1838/3/312; 1846/10/715; 1847/3/368.
49. W.C.S. 188, p. 128; 191, p. 57.
50. G.L.C. Historic Buildings Division, file 445; R.B.
51. M.L.R. 1829/10/402; W.C.S. 185, p. 27.
52. M.L.R. 1852/3/749.
53. M.L.R. 1826/1/693; 1829/2/483; 1835/5/598–9; R.B.
54. E. J. Willson, *James Lee and the Vineyard Nursery Hammersmith*, 1961; E/HOL, lease of 6 Jan. 1816 to J. Lee and J. Kennedy; G.L.R.O.(M), MR/UP/73D; R.B.
55. B.M., Add. MSS. 51812, letter of 25 Nov. 1823, 51815, Harrison's proposals [1823].
56. M.L.R. 1826/4/109.
57. B.M., Add. MS. 51749, letter of 24 Sept. 1824; M.L.R. 1824/12/668.
58. M.L.R. 1825/13/814; 1827/3/352; 1829/3/676; E/HOL, leases of houses in Holland Place.

59. E/HOL, leases of houses in St. Mary Abbots Terrace.
60. W.C.S. 179, p. 219.
61. K.P.L., postcards nos. 221 and 258, portfolio C(37).
62. E/HOL, leases of 1 Sept. 1825 to A. Unthank.
63. M.L.R. 1837/5/94.
64. K.P.L., 1423e (KE 70/273).
65. J. Parry Lewis, *Building Cycles and Britain's Growth*, 1965, pp. 32–8.
66. B.M., Add. MS 51765, letter of 16 Dec. [1825].
67. Coutts' Bank, accounts of Lord Holland, 1825–1826.
68. B.M., Add. MS. 51766, letter of 5 Jan. [1826].
69. *Ibid.*, letter of 18 Jan. [1826].
70. *Ibid.*, letter of 19 Dec. [1826].
71. *Ibid.*, Add. MS. 51771, letter of 4 Jan. 1833.
72. *Ibid.*, Add. MS. 51749, letter of 3 Oct. 1826.
73. *Ibid.*, Add. MS. 51750, letter of 31 July [1827].
74. G.L.R.O.(M), MR/UP/149.
75. B.M., Add. MS. 51815, draft memorandum on railway by Lord Holland.
76. P.R.O., C13/1582, Holland v. Birmingham, Bristol and Thames Junction Railway Co.
77. 6 Wm. IV, c. 79, local.
78. B.M., Add. MS. 51793, p. 122.
79. British Transport Historical Records, GEN 3/97 and WLR 1/7, p. 192; 1/9, pp. 99, 166; 1/10, pp. 85, 179; 1/11, pp. 7, 143; M.L.R. 1845/4/229; 1846/9/683–4; 3 and 4 Vict., c. 105, local.
80. W.C.S. 77, pp. 168–73, 338–40, 472; 190, pp. 168–76, 237–46; 192, p. 36; P/36/1121; P/37/1165.
81. British Transport Historical Records, WLR 1/7, p. 82.
82. P.R.O., PROB 11/1941, f. 108.
83. *D.N.B.*; Earl of Ilchester, *Chronicles of Holland House 1820–1900*, 1937, p. 248.
84. B.M., Add. MS. 51775, letter of 5 April 1841; British Transport Historical Records, WLR 1/7, pp. 180, 203; W.C.S. 77, p. 339; Colvin.
85. B.M., Add. MS. 52064, draft letter of [April 1841].
86. *Ibid.*, Add. MS 51775, letter of 5 April 1841.
87. *Ibid.*, Add. MS. 52034, letter of 8 July 1845.
88. M.L.R. 1840/2/422; 1843/5/286–7; R.B.
89. M.L.R. 1846/5/15; R.B.
90. E/HOL, leases of 21 Dec. 1849 and 27 Dec. 1850 to T. Moore; R.B.; M.L.R. 1845/7/821; 1846/4/17.
91. M.C.S. 290, f. 534.
92. *B.N.* 4 Sept. 1857, p. 931.
93. M.L.R. 1849/1/622.
94. *R.I.B.A. Transactions*, first series, vol. XXXII, 1881–2, p. 59; Ilchester, *Chronicles ...*, pp. 368–70.
95. E/HOL, grant of annuity dated 22 Aug. 1860 to J. H. Browne.
96. *Ibid.*, agreement of 7 Feb. 1849 with G. H. Goddard.
97. M.L.R. 1849/6/943.
98. D.S.R.
99. E/HOL, folio volume containing miscellaneous items, pp. 3–7.
100. M.C.S. 292, f. 475; 293, ff. 164–7.
101. *Ibid.*, 292, f. 352; M.L.R. 1850/6/785; 1851/8/6; D.S.R.
102. M.L.R. 1855/15/504–5; 1856/8/455; 1856/13/24–5; 1857/2/69; M.C.S. 298, ff. 591, 647; *D.N.B.*
103. M.L.R. 1855/14/22–5; M.C.S. 298, f. 636; *B.* 4 Feb. 1882, p. 149; C.C., file 29182.
104. M.L.R. 1852/12/33–4; 1852/15/180–1; 1853/11/523–4; 1854/7/673–4; 1856/9/681–2; D.S.R.; R.B.
105. E/HOL, leases of 1 March 1862 to W. Reed.
106. M.L.R. 1856/9/683–4; 1857/3/800–1; K.P.L., Vestry Sewers Committee, 14 Oct. 1856; R.B.
107. P.R.O., C16/392/69, answer of H. S. Stephens, pp. 2–9.
108. M.L.R. 1853/3/376; 1856/10/459–60.
109. *Ibid.*, 1853/11/1047; R.B.
110. M.L.R. 1853–8, Lord Holland to Hall; E/HOL, leases of houses in Addison Road.
111. M.L.R. 1852/1/578; 1855/6/151; 1858/13/950.
112. *Ibid.*, 1860/4/392.
113. *Ibid.*, 1857/3/798–9; K.P.L., Vestry Works Committee, 28 Sept. 1866.
114. M.L.R. 1857–9, Lord Holland to Hall.
115. *Ibid.*, 1858/15/849.
116. R.B.; *D.N.B.*; Alexander C. Ionides Jnr., *Ion. A Grandfather's Tale*, 1927, p. 15; Victoria and Albert Museum, Dept. of Prints and Drawings, E. 104–5 (pressmark A.166).
117. M.L.R. 1853–60 *sub* Hall; P.R.O., C16/392/69, answer of H. S. Stephens, p. 16; C31/2072/2405, pp. 5, 12–13; E/HOL, mortgage of 8 Oct. 1858, Hall to W. J. Dawson.
118. P.R.O., C31/2072/2405, pp. 18–20; C16/392/69, bill of complaint of S. Boydell, pp. 5–15.
119. M.L.R. 1860/16/641; *P.O.D.*
120. Documents in the possession of Messrs. Fladgate and Co.; *P.O.D.*
121. M.L.R. 1860/16/796, 988–9; 1860/17/4–6, 77, 427; P.R.O., C16/392/69, bill of complaint, pp. 16, 18, answer, pp. 10–15.
122. *The Times*, 30 June 1865.
123. P.R.O., C16/373/91; C16/392/69; C16/557/243; C16/579/92.
124. *Ibid.*, C33/1138, pp. 853–4.
125. K.P.L., MSS. 692–707; *B.N.* 16 April 1869, p. VII, 21 May 1869, p. 472.

126. M.L.R. 1855/6/922–4; 1855/7/376–80.
127. E/HOL, agreement of 1 July 1851 with W. Scott; M.L.R. 1856/11/727–42; 1858/10/289–305; R.B.
128. M.L.R. 1854/11/743–5; D.S.R.; R.B.
129. M.L.R. 1858/10/45–50; 1858/13/697–9; 1858/14/444–6, 551–3; 1859/8/412–15, 607–10.
130. E/HOL, conveyance of 27 July 1861 to London and North Western Railway Co.
131. British Transport Historical Records, GEN 3/97, pp. 44–5, 48, 52–3; T. C. Barker and Michael Robbins, *A History of London Transport*, vol. I, 1963, p. 205.
132. *P.O.D.*
133. E/HOL, agreement of 13 Nov. 1862 with C. Chambers; K.P.L., Vestry Works Committee, 30 Oct. 1863.
134. E/HOL, second lease book, pp. 316–95; estate map of 1910.
135. K.P.L., MS. 269.
136. E/HOL, conveyance of 1 Sept. 1870, to C. Chambers and H. J. Bartley.
137. Ilchester, *Chronicles . . .*, p. 431.
138. K.P.L., Vestry Works Committee, 1863–70 *passim*; M.L.R. 1872/1/667–8.
139. E/HOL, leases of 1870 and 1871 to T. Snowdon, W. Lethbridge and J. H. Adams; M.B.W. 1788, nos. 1995, 2015, 2277; D.S.R.
140. St. John's Building Committee Minute Book; C.C., file 36133; *B.* 18 May 1872, p. 394.
141. E/HOL, conveyance of 14 Dec. 1871 to J. Beattie and H. Dowding; D.S.R.
142. E/HOL, conveyance of 31 Dec. 1871 to Beattie and Dowding; D.S.R.; K.P.L., K 64/153.
143. E/HOL, agreements of 22 Aug., 8 Dec. 1859, 12 Sept. 1861 and 11 Feb. 1864 with W. and F. Radford.
144. M.L.R. 1860/16/732; D.S.R.; *P.O.D.*
145. Conveyances of houses in Holland Park and Holland Park Mews in the possession of Messrs. Fladgate and Co.
146. [W. S. Clarke], *The Suburban Homes of London*, 1881, pp. 286–7; *B.* 13 June 1891, p. 479.
147. *The Kensington News*, 12 Jan. 1900.
148. *P.O.D.*; *D.N.B.*; Boase.
149. *B.* 29 May 1942, p. 467.
150. G.L.C., Legal and Parliamentary Dept. deeds, docket nos. 10528–9, Historic Buildings Division, file 869; *P.O.D.*; *Ionides Family Tree*, compiled by D. B. [Dorothea, Lady Butterworth] (B.M. pressmark 9920.d.30); Alexander C. Ionides Jnr., *op. cit.*, *passim*; Gleeson White, 'An Epoch-Making House' in *The Studio*, vol. XII, 1898, pp. 102–21; Elizabeth Aslin, *The Aesthetic Movement*, 1969, pp. 93–4.

151. M. S. Watts, *George Frederic Watts*, 1912, vol. I, pp. 47–8, 198–200; Mrs. Russell Barrington, *The Life, Letters and Work of Frederic Leighton*, 1906, vol. II, p. 67.
152. E/HOL, documents relating to dispute over Holland Walk; *The Times*, 1 June 1891; K.P.L., Vestry Minutes, 7 June 1871.
153. M.L.R. 1862/18/360.
154. B.M., Add. MS. 52152, letter of 10 April [1873] with enclosure.
155. *Ibid.*, Add. MS. 52120, letters of 27 Feb. and 18 May 1873.
156. Conveyance of 17 Jan. 1874 to Earl of Ilchester in the possession of Messrs. Fladgate and Co.
157. B.M., Add. MS. 52120, letter of 18 April 1873.
158. *Ibid.*, Add. MS. 52152, letters of [18 Oct. 1874] and 16 June [? 1876].
159. M. S. Watts, *op. cit.*, vol. I, pp. 281, 290.
160. E/HOL, leases of 20 July 1876, 31 Jan. 1877 to G. Martin; leases of 7 Nov., 26 Dec. 1876, 21–22 Aug. 1877 to W. Turner; D.S.R.; G.L.C. Members' Library, file 286.
161. E/HOL, lease cited in licence of 20 June 1935 to C. J. Harman; D.S.R.
162. E/HOL, second lease book, pp. 428–33; D.S.R.
163. E/HOL, lease of 18 March 1854 to E. C. Tisdall and E. Tunks.
164. *Ibid.*, lease of 20 Aug. 1859 to Tisdall and Tunks.
165. *Journal of the British Dairy Farmers' Association*, vol. VII, 1892, pp. 96–9; Seymour J. Price, *From Queen to Queen. The Centenary Story of the Temperance Permanent Building Society, 1854–1954*, [1954], pp. 12–13, 23–24; P.R.O., census returns of 1861.
166. *B.N.* 12 April 1878, p. 366.
167. L. V. Fildes, *Luke Fildes, R.A. A Victorian Painter*, 1968, p. 46.
168. E/HOL, documents relating to dispute over Holland Walk.
169. Lease of 27 Nov. 1900 and licence of 4 Aug. 1910 to E. R. Debenham in possession of Messrs. Fladgate and Co.
170. B.A. 34557.
171. M.L.R. 1826/10/53; 1849/3/726.
172. Victoria and Albert Museum, Dept. of Prints and Drawings, E.225, pp. 52–4 (pressmark A.123.b).
173. B.A. 27398, 29394.
174. *Endowed Charities (London)*, vol. IV, 1901, pp. 471–2; M.L.R. 1841/3/832.
175. Minutes of School Board for London, 1 Aug. 1877, p. 1066; D.S.R.
176. B.A. 61016.
177. *Ibid.*, 16825.
178. K.P.L., Vestry Works Committee, 28 March 1862.

179. B.A. 10140.
180. *B.* 26 July 1884, p. 150; L.C.C. Theatres Committee Papers, Addison Hall; D.S.R.; K.P.L., K 64/241 (373 VAU/L).
181. B.A. 47753.
182. *Ibid.*, 16645, 22395; D.S.R.
183. B.A. 62951; *B.* 20 Sept. 1929, p. 469, 2 May 1930, pp. 857–8.
184. *B.* 20 July 1928, pp. 93–4, 99.
185. Information kindly supplied by Mrs. Josephine Cashmore.
186. K.P.L., K 66/154; E/HOL, agreements of 30 Sept. 1936 with C. Wright, 29 July 1938 with C. Wright and H. D. Sugden.
187. 15 and 16 Geo. VI and 1 Eliz. II, c. 5, local.
188. 2 and 3 Eliz. II, c. 41, local; *B.* 11 Sept. 1959, pp. 184–6; photographs and cuttings in K.P.L.
189. K.P.L., estate agents' brochures.
190. K.P.L., Vestry Minutes, 16 Dec. 1822, 5 March 1823, 22 Feb. 1825; C.C., file 20637.
191. C.C., H.M. Commissioners for Building New Churches, Minute Books no. 16, p. 138, no. 20, p. 422.
192. *Ibid.*, Minute Books no. 19, p. 261, no. 21, pp. 99–101, 127–8, 130; file 20636.
193. Guildhall Library, MS. 9531/24, ff. 630–1.
194. C.C., file 20636; Commissioners' Minute Book no. 22, pp. 164–7.
195. K.P.L., MSS. 1507–24; Vestry Minutes, 14 May 1826, 14 Nov. 1828, 11, 13 June 1830.
196. Guildhall Library, MS. 9531/24, f. 627; C.C., file 35433.
197. *The Gentleman's Magazine*, vol. ci, July 1831, p. 10.
198. *Ibid.*, pp. 10–11.
199. *B.* 16 March 1861, p. 182.
200. *Notes Descriptive of the Chancel and Its Principal Features*, 1910.
201. *B.* 8 Aug. 1885, p. 209.
202. Information from tablet at west end of church.
203. *B.* 24 Jan. 1852, p. 63; British Society of Master Glass Painters, *A Directory of Stained Glass Windows*, 1939, p. 84.
204. Information kindly supplied by James Byam Shaw.
205. C.C., files 36133, N.B. 23/244.
206. E/HOL, conveyance of 10 July 1872 to J. Beattie and H. Dowding.
207. C.C., file 36133.
208. *B.N.* 29 Nov. 1872, p. 422, 4 April 1873, p. 390.
209. *Church of St. John the Baptist, Kensington: A Pastoral Address by Rev. George Booker, M.A.*, 1873, p. 18 (copy in K.P.L.).
210. St. John's Building Committee Minute Book; D.S.R.; C.C., file 36133; *B.* 23 April 1892, p. 323, 27 Oct. 1911, p. 480; Maurice B. Adams, *Architects from George IV to George V*, 1912, p. 10.

211. *B.* 29 June 1895, p. 488.
212. *Ibid.*, 23 May 1885, p. 724, 18 April 1891, p. 316.
213. *The Architect and Contract Reporter*, 5 March 1909, p. 160.
214. Lease of 2 July 1906 to E. R. Debenham in possession of Messrs. Fladgate and Co.
215. Licences of 24 Jan. 1955 and 12 Dec. 1966 in possession of Messrs. Fladgate and Co.
216. *The Architectural Review*, vol. xxi, 1907, pp. 159–73; William Gaunt and M. D. E. Clayton-Stamm, *William De Morgan*, 1971, p. 47.
217. E/HOL, lease of 20 Aug. 1859 to E. C. Tisdall and E. Tunks; licence of 6 Nov. 1892 to E. Tisdall; agreement of 16 Nov. 1892, E. Tisdall with J. J. Shannon; D.S.R.
218. E/HOL, licence of 21 May 1908 to E. Hamilton; deed of 9 May 1925, E. Hamilton to Dame Florence Shannon.
219. Mrs. Russell Barrington, *op. cit.*, vol. ii, pp. 115–16.
220. E/HOL, lease of 30 April 1866 to F. Leighton.
221. *B.N.* 9 Nov. 1866, p. 747.
222. Sydney C. Hutchison, *The History of the Royal Academy 1768–1968*, 1968, p. 234; *R.I.B.A. Journal*, third series, vol. v, 1898, pp. 409–11.
223. *B.N.* 30 Nov. 1866, p. 800.
224. *Ibid.*, 29 Oct. 1880, p. 511.
225. *Leighton House. A Collection of Essays on Lord Leighton and his Works*, [n.d.], p. 48 (copy in K.P.L.); R.I.B.A. Library, Aitchison's drawings (U.1/5).
226. *Leighton House, ut supra*, pp. 48, 159n.; Walter Crane, *An Artist's Reminiscences*, 1907, pp. 215–16; *B.N.* 1 Oct. 1880, p. 384.
227. E/HOL, licence of 27 July 1889 to E. C. Tisdall; *B.* 9 Nov. 1895, p. 336.
228. Royal Borough of Kensington Council Minutes, 26 Nov. 1901, pp. 34–6; 21 Jan. 1902, pp. 102–4; 7 April 1925, pp. 225–9; 11 May 1926, p. 282.
229. *Ibid.*, 26 July 1927, pp. 373–4; 28 May 1929, p. 284; 23 July 1929, p. 354; K.P.L., drawings KQ 33–41 and 439.
230. Henry-Russell Hitchcock, *Architecture: Nineteenth and Twentieth Centuries*, 1963 ed., p. 263.
231. K.P.L., Vestry Works Committee, 25 Nov. 1864; E/HOL, agreement of 21 Jan. 1865 with, and lease of 8 March 1866 to V. C. Prinsep; R.I.B.A. Library, Webb's drawings (V.16/65–8); R.B.
232. R.I.B.A. Library, Webb's drawings (V. 16/70–76).
233. *Ibid.* (V. 16/77–131).
234. Lease of 6 July 1948 to R. Parr (Builders) Ltd. in possession of Messrs. Fladgate and Co.

235. E/HOL, second lease book, pp. 416–21, 434–9.

236. *B.N.* 27 May 1881, p. 610.

237. Mrs. Russell Barrington, *Reminiscences of G. F. Watts*, 1905, pp. 6–7.

238. B.A. 68796.

239. E/HOL, drawings of studio by J. Belcher dated 14 Oct. 1891; D.S.R.

240. M. S. Watts, *op. cit.*, vol. 1, pp. 279, 304; E/HOL, agreement of 15 Feb. 1875 with, and lease of 9 Nov. 1876 to V. C. Prinsep; lease of 6 July 1948 to R. Parr (Builders) Ltd. in possession of Messrs. Fladgate and Co.; D.S.R.

241. *B.N.* 7 Oct. 1881, p. 460; Mrs. Russell Barrington, *Reminiscences of G. F. Watts*, 1905, p. 8.

242. E/HOL, lease of 24 Dec. 1877 to M. C. Stone; D.S.R.

243. A. L. Baldry, *The Life and Work of Marcus Stone, R.A.* (*The Art Annual*, 1896), p. 28.

244. *B.N.* 30 April 1880, p. 527.

245. *B.* 12 Aug. 1876, p. 796; D.S.R.

246. E/HOL, draft lease of 7 Feb. 1877 to W. Burges; *B.* 14 April 1877, p. 385; Charles Handley-Read, 'Aladdin's Palace in Kensington: William Burges's Tower House' in *Country Life*, 17 March 1966, p. 601; D.S.R.; R.I.B.A. Library, Burges's drawings.

247. Victoria and Albert Museum Library, William Burges's estimate book (pressmark RC.JJ.40).

248. L. V. Fildes, *op. cit.*, pp. 33, 35, 43, 45, 56; R.I.B.A. Library, drawing by R. Norman Shaw (V.10/97); D.S.R.

249. *B.N.* 17 Dec. 1880, p. 702.

250. L. V. Fildes, *op. cit.*, p. 74.

251. *Ibid.*, p. 197.

252. *Ibid.*, p. 46.

253. G.L.C. Historic Buildings Division, file 516; *The Times*, 23 Feb. 1923; lease of 13 June 1893 to W. G. Robertson in possession of Messrs. Fladgate and Co.; D.S.R.

254. K.P.L., J.1441.

255. *Letters From Graham Robertson*, ed. Kerrison Preston, 1953, pp. xiii, xxvii.

256. E/HOL, licence of 12 April 1912 to J. E. Mounsey.

257. Licence of 5 April 1948 to Parr Properties Ltd. in possession of Messrs. Fladgate and Co.

258. *Letters From Graham Robertson*, pp. xviii, xix; Agnes Ethel Mackay, *Arthur Melville: Scottish Impressionist*, 1951, p. 107.

259. B.A. 4928; D.S.R.; leases of 21 and 22 Oct. 1895 to J. M. and Lady E. Rendel respectively in possession of Messrs. Fladgate and Co.

260. *B.* 7 July 1894, p. 12.

261. Licences of 14 April 1930 and 19 April 1950 in possession of Messrs. Fladgate and Co.

262. Commonwealth Institute, *Annual Reports*, 1958, 1962.

CHAPTER VIII (pp. 151–93)

The Crown Estate in Kensington Palace Gardens

1. 5 Vict. c. 1, public general; C.E.O., file 11119; John Hayes, *Kensington Palace a history and guide*, 1969, p. 3; R. B. Pugh, *The Crown Estate*, 1960, pp. 16–18.

2. 5 Vict. c. 1, public general; Hayes, *op. cit.*, pp. 7, 15; G.L.C. Map Collection; P.R.O., T90/190.

3. P.R.O., T29/397, pp. 333–4, 513; T90/189, 190.

4. *Ibid.*, T29/400, pp. 480–1.

5. *Ibid.*, T1/3903.

6. *Ibid.*, T29/423, pp. 531–3.

7. *Ibid.*, T1/3903; B.M., Crace Collection, Maps portfolio x, no. 8.

8. P.R.O., T29/430, p. 108; K.P.L., extra-illustrated copy of Faulkner, vol. 3, ff. 209, 210; *The Times*, 4 Nov. 1840.

9. *The Times*, 1 Sept. 1838 (reference kindly supplied by Mr. Derek Hudson); *The Architectural Magazine*, vol. v, 1838, pp. 620–1.

10. P.R.O., CREST 25/47, nos. 3619, 3797; 25/48, 27 July 1841; T1/4664, file 26346; C.E.O., file 11170.

11. P.R.O., T1/4664, file 26346; *Journals of the House of Commons*, vol. 96, pp. 568, 571, 599; 5 Vict. c. 1 and c. 2, public general.

12. C.E.O., file 11170; P.R.O., T1/4664, file 26346; T29/445, p. 261.

13. P.R.O., MPE 758, nos. 4, 5.

14. *Ibid.*, T1/4664, file 26346.

15. Hayes, *op. cit.*, p. 5; information supplied by the Crown Estate Office.

16. P.R.O., T29/445, p. 261.

17. C.E.O., files 10715, 11170.

18. *Ibid.*, files 11157, 11118, 11122; *Wren Society*, vol. vii, 1930, pp. 145–7, 169; *I.L.N.* 31 Jan. 1846, p. 78.

19. P.R.O., MPE 758, no. 1.

20. *Wren Society*, *op. cit.*, p. 189; *The Gentleman's Magazine*, vol. LXXXV, May 1815, p. 423; Colvin.

21. Sir John Summerson, *Architecture in Britain 1530–1830*, 1970 ed., p. 277; Kerry Downes, *Hawksmoor*, 1969, p. 56; Colvin.

22. P.R.O., MPE 758, no. 1; Faulkner, p. 40; Hayes, *op. cit.*, p. 13, Pl. 15.

23. C.E.O., file 11170.

24. *Ibid.*, file 11169.

25. *Ibid.*, files 11151, 11169; P.R.O., census returns of 1851.

26. C.E.O., file 11157.

27. *Ibid.*, file 11157; *P.O.D.*; *Designs for Mosaic and Tessellated Pavements: by Owen Jones, architect, with an essay on their Materials and Structure by F. O. Ward, published for J. M. Blashfield*, 1842, pp. 3, 4.
28. C.E.O., London lease book 57, pp. 467–98.
29. *Ibid.*, file 11157; *Designs, ut supra.*
30. *The British Almanac for 1846. Companion*, p. 245.
31. K.P.L., Kensington Palace Gardens, C. Pict. 472.
32. P.R.O., MPE 758, no. 5; C.E.O., file 11157; London lease book 58, pp. 149–203, 453–516; 59, pp. 1–12.
33. C.E.O., file 11154.
34. *I.L.N.* 31 Jan. 1846, p. 78.
35. C.E.O., file 11157; lithograph in K.P.L. and R.I.B.A.; *B.* 11 May, 1844, p. 239.
36. C.E.O., files 11150, 11157; P.R.O., census returns of 1851.
37. C.E.O., file 11142.
38. R.I.B.A., Murray (Italian) tracings and Moulton Barrett Collection (Sir Charles Barry's drawings); C.E.O., file 11142.
39. *The British Almanac for 1846. Companion*, pp. 243–5; A. Barry, *The Life and Works of Sir Charles Barry*, 1867, p. 327n.; H.-R. Hitchcock, *Early Victorian Architecture in Britain*, 1954, p. 180.
40. *Country Life*, 16 Dec. 1971, p. 1733 (letter from P. Hodson), and information kindly supplied by Mr. Hodson.
41. Boase; [Sir H. Peto], *Sir Morton Peto, A Memorial Sketch*, 1893, p. 16.
42. C.E.O., files 11101, 11105, 11141, 11158.
43. *Ibid.*, file 11317.
44. *Ibid.*, file 11158.
45. *Ibid.*, files 11157, 11158.
46. P.R.O., B4/51, B. 170; B5/106, p. 217; *The Times*, 19 May 1847.
47. P.R.O., B5/106, pp. 217–18; C.E.O., file 11158.
48. *P.O.D.*
49. *B.N.* 1 April 1864, p. 249, 20 Nov. 1868, p. 787; R. Gunnis, *Dictionary of British Sculptors, 1660–1851*, rev. ed., [n.d.], p. 56.
50. P.R.O., MPE 1181.
51. C.E.O., files 11154, 11318.
52. *Ibid.*, files 14986, 15117.
53. *Ibid.*, file 11158; London lease book 60, pp. 369–78.
54. *Ibid.*, file 11103.
55. *Ibid.*, file 11101; P.R.O., census returns of 1861.
56. C.E.O., files 10473, 10476, 11101, 11106, 11108, 11110, 11130.
57. *Ibid.*, files 11103, 11318.
58. *Ibid.*, file 11152.
59. Leigh Hunt, *The Old Court Suburb*, 2nd ed., 1855, vol. 1, p. 130.
60. *The Metropolitan*, 22 Nov. 1890.
61. C.E.O., file 13956.
62. *Ibid.*, London lease book 57, pp. 374–408.
63. Ratebooks of St. Mary, Paddington; P.R.O., census returns of 1851.
64. C.E.O., file 11151.
65. *Ibid.*, London lease book 58, pp. 217–57.
66. Ratebooks of St. Mary, Paddington; P.R.O., census returns of 1851; *D.N.B.*
67. *The Architectural Review*, vol. LXXII, July 1932, pp. 29, 35–8.
68. C.E.O., file 11157; R.I.B.A., MS. 72.036(42).
69. C.E.O., file 11150; London lease book 58, pp. 279–308.
70. *Ibid.*, file 11150; P.R.O., LRRO 1/2207.
71. International Exhibition of 1862, *Official Catalogue*, Fine Art Dept., p. 88.
72. C.E.O., file 11317; P.R.O., LRRO 1/2048.
73. Ratebooks of St. Mary, Paddington; P.R.O., census returns of 1861; *D.N.B.*
74. C.E.O., files 18338, 18338A, 18891.
75. *Ibid.*, files 11103, 11108.
76. *B.* 17 July 1852, p. 462.
77. M.C.S. 294, f. 673, Nov. 1852; ratebooks of St. Mary, Paddington.
78. C.E.O., London lease book 63, pp. 277–92.
79. Victoria and Albert Museum, Dept. of Prints and Drawings, D1220.1908, D1245.1908.
80. C.E.O., file 11103; P.R.O., census returns of 1871; *P.O.D.*
81. C.E.O., file 15701.
82. *Ibid.*, file 11137; P.R.O., MPE 832.
83. C.E.O., file 11137.
84. *Ibid.*, London lease book 60, pp. 68–80.
85. Ratebooks of St. Mary, Paddington; Boase; C.E.O., London lease book 60, p. 68.
86. C.E.O., file 11137; R.I.B.A., MS. 72.036(42)-92B, vol. 4.
87. Boase; ratebooks of St. Mary, Paddington; C.E.O., file 11137; *The Times Literary Supplement*, 2 Aug. 1971, p. 784.
88. C.E.O., file 11137; *Architecture. A Monthly Magazine*, ed. J. P. Morgan, vol. 1, 1896, p. 209.
89. C.E.O., file 15293.
90. Ratebooks of St. Margaret's, Westminster; P.R.O., census returns of 1851.
91. M.C.S. 294, f. 673, Nov. 1852; ratebooks of St. Margaret's, Westminster; C.E.O., London lease book 63, pp. 293–308.
92. H. Stannus, *Alfred Stevens and his Work*, 1891, p. 13.
93. C.E.O., file 11108; M. Girouard, 'Gilded Preserves for the Rich' in *Country Life*, 18 Nov. 1971, p. 1363.
94. C.E.O., file 14361; P.R.O., LRRO 1/2493.
95. C.E.O., file 14361.

96. Walter Crane, *An Artist's Reminiscences*, 1907, p. 156.
97. C.E.O., plans in map-rack.
98. *Ibid.*, file 11142; London lease book 59, pp. 243–286.
99. *Ibid.*, files 11157, 11142.
100. P.R.O., census returns of 1851; C.E.O., file 11158.
101. Boase.
102. P.R.O., census returns of 1861; C.E.O., file 10475.
103. C.E.O., London lease book 69, pp. 330–40; file 10475; *B.N.* 25 May 1877, p. 507.
104. *Royal Academy Catalogue*, 1866, no. 793.
105. Ratebooks of St. Margaret's, Westminster; *The Times*, 22, 24, 29 July, 5, 10 Aug., 7 Sept. 1875.
106. *The British Almanac for 1846. Companion*, pp. 243.
107. C.E.O., file 10475.
108. *Ibid.*, file 10475; P.R.O., LRRO 1/2340, nos. 1–10.
109. *B.* 23 Sept. 1865, p. 678; *I.L.N.* 10 May 1862, p. 481.
110. *B.* 23 Sept. 1865, pp. 676, 678.
111. Ratebooks of St. Margaret's, Westminster.
112. [Sir H. Peto], *op. cit.*, pp. 46, 47, 101; *The Times*, 12 May 1866.
113. Boase; ratebooks of St. Margaret's, Westminster.
114. *The Times*, 10 Oct. 1867, 18 Jan. 1868; [Sir H. Peto], *op. cit.*, pp. 47, 48; C.E.O., London lease book 69, p. 341; file 12881; ratebooks of St. Margaret's, Westminster; *P.O.D.*; *Burke's Peerage*.
115. C.E.O., file 12881; P.R.O., LRRO 1/2340, nos. 11–15.
116. C.E.O., files, 12881, 12881[1].
117. *Ibid.*, file 10476; C. J. Richardson, *Picturesque Designs for Mansions, Villas, Lodges ...*, 1870, p. 382; *B.N.* 1 April 1870, p. 242.
118. M.C.S. 292, f. 223, 27 Aug. 1851; D.S.R. 1851, no. 601.
119. Ratebooks of St. Margaret's, Westminster; C.E.O., London lease book 63, pp. 194–208.
120. *B.* 5 June 1852, p. 360.
121. *The British Almanac for 1853. Companion*, p. 251.
122. *Royal Academy Catalogue*, 1852, no. 1181; 1855, no. 1183.
123. Notes on MSS. formerly in possession of the late Rupert Gunnis; C. J. Richardson, *op. cit.*, pp. 378–97.
124. *B.* 5, 12 June 1852, pp. 360, 374.
125. C. J. Richardson, *op. cit.*, pp. 379–80, 392–3, 396.
126. Notes on MSS., *ut supra*; C. J. Richardson, *op. cit.*, pp. 386–7.
127. *P.O.D.*; *Burke's Peerage*.
128. C.E.O., file 13956; P.R.O., LRRO 1/4453.
129. C. J. Richardson, *op. cit.*, pp. 378–97; P.R.O., LRRO 1/4453.
130. C.E.O., file 11101; *B.* 17 May 1845, p. 229.
131. C.E.O., file 11101; Hermione Hobhouse, *Thomas Cubitt Master Builder*, 1971, pp. 464–5.
132. M.C.S. 290, f. 510, 12 June 1850; D.S.R. 1850, no. 151; ratebooks of St. Margaret's, Westminster.
133. C.E.O., London lease book 61, pp. 224–37.
134. *Ibid.*, file 11101; *B.* 13 Nov. 1886, p. 719; ratebooks of St. Margaret's, Westminster.
135. C.E.O., file 11110.
136. *Ibid.*, file 11110; M.C.S. 298, f. 532, 4 Dec. 1854; D.S.R. 1855, no. 196.
137. C.E.O., London lease book 63, pp. 375–91.
138. *D.N.B.*; Samuel Smiles, *George Moore Merchant and Philanthropist*, 2nd ed., 1878, pp. 55, 102, 109, 165, 173.
139. Christopher Hussey, '15, Kensington Palace Gardens, its redecoration for Sir Alfred Beit, Bt., M.P.' in *Country Life*, 25 Feb. 1939, pp. 198–202; P.R.O., LRRO 1/4458; *D.N.B.*
140. P.R.O., LRRO 1/4457–8; D.S.R. 1855, no. 197.
141. C.E.O., files 10473, 11103; P.R.O., census returns of 1861.
142. C.E.O., file 10473; R.I.B.A., MS. 72.036(42); D.S.R. 1852, nos. 560, 1232.
143. C.E.O., file 10473; ratebooks of St. Margaret's, Westminster.
144. C.E.O., London lease book 63, pp. 309–34; file 10473.
145. *Ibid.*, file 11143; R.I.B.A., MS. 72.036(42); *D.N.B.*; P.R.O., census returns of 1851.
146. C.E.O., file 11158; ratebooks of St. Margaret's, Westminster.
147. C.E.O., file 11143.
148. *Ibid.*, file 11143; *Men and Women of Our Time*, 1899; *B.* 28 July 1877, p. 772.
149. C.E.O., file 11157; London lease book 58, pp. 66–80; M.L.R. 1846/6/332.
150. C.E.O., file 11136; P.R.O., LRRO 1/4455.
151. C.E.O., file 11158; London lease book 59, pp. 202–28.
152. Ratebooks of St. Margaret's, Westminster; P.R.O., census returns of 1851.
153. C.E.O., file 11135; *Who Was Who ... 1897–1916*; ratebooks of St. Margaret's, Westminster; *P.O.D.*; P.R.O., LRRO 1/2300.
154. C.E.O., file 11699.
155. *Ibid.*, file 11142; ratebooks of St. Margaret's, Westminster.
156. C.E.O., London lease book 59, pp. 229–42.
157. *Ibid.*, files 11142, 11132; P.R.O., LRRO 1/2109, nos. 3–8.

158. C.E.O., file 11105, London lease book 58, pp. 439–52; P.R.O., LRRO 1/2031 and census returns of 1851; ratebooks of St. Margaret's, Westminster.

159. C.E.O., file 11105.

160. *Ibid.*, file 11130; P.R.O., MPE 835.

161. D.S.R. 1851, no. 769; R.B.; C.E.O., London lease book 62, pp. 72–84, file 11130.

162. C.E.O., files 11103, 11106; M.C.S. 294, f. 19, 19 July 1852.

163. D.S.R. 1852, no. 933.

164. C.E.O., file 11106; London lease book 62, pp. 402–12; R.B.; P.R.O., census returns of 1861, LRRO 1/2160.

165. C.E.O., file 11106; *B.* 9, 16 June 1877, pp. 596, 622.

166. C.E.O., file 11141.

167. D.S.R. 1845, no. 292; C.E.O., file 11141.

168. C.E.O., London lease book 58, pp. 372–85; M.L.R. 1846/1/871; Colvin.

169. C.E.O., files 11141, 11158; Hermione Hobhouse, *op. cit.*, p. 322; M.B.W. 213, 4 Feb. 1856; R.B.; P.R.O., census returns of 1851.

170. C.E.O., file 17074A; *The Architect and Building News*, 24 Dec. 1937, pp. 369–71.

171. C.E.O., file 11157; R.I.B.A., MS. 72.036(42); *The British Almanac for 1846. Companion*, p. 243.

172. C.E.O., London lease book 58, pp. 52–65, 134–48.

173. *Ibid.*, file 11157; R.B.; P.R.O., census returns of 1851.

174. C.E.O., files 11133, 11158; P.R.O., census returns of 1861.

175. C.E.O., file 11133.

176. *Ibid.*, file 11133; plans in map-rack; information supplied by the Czech Embassy.

177. C.E.O., London lease book 83, pp. 426–8.

178. *Ibid.*, file 13434; *D.N.B.*

179. *D.N.B.*; C.E.O., file 10525.

180. C.E.O., file 10525.

181. *Ibid.*, file 13434.

182. P.R.O., CREST 19/55, p. 81.

183. Drawings in the possession of Mr. John Brandon-Jones.

184. *The Studio*, vol. xv, no. 67, Oct. 1889, pp. 3–13; Walter Crane, *op. cit.* (ref. 96), pp. 167–9.

185. C.E.O., file 15838.

186. G.L.C. Historic Buildings Division, file 406.

187. C.E.O., file 10225.

188. *Ibid.*, file 10224.

189. *The Letters and Papers of William Makepeace Thackeray*, ed. Gordon N. Ray, vol. IV, 1946, p. 180.

190. P.R.O., CREST 19/48, p. 272.

191. P. Metcalf, 'Postscript on Thackeray's House' in *Journal of the Society of Architectural Historians*, vol. XXVIII, no. 2, May 1969, pp. 118 n., 122; C.E.O., file 10229.

192. Theodore Taylor, *Thackeray The Humourist and The Man of Letters*, 1864, p. 175.

193. *The Cornhill Magazine*, vol. I, Jan.–June 1860, p. 478.

194. *B.N.* 17 May 1861, p. 419.

195. *The Works of William Makepeace Thackeray with Biographical Introduction by his Daughter, Anne Ritchie*, vol. XI, 1899, p. xxxv.

196. *B.* 8 May 1869, p. 373.

197. C.E.O., file 10227.

198. 'Thackeray's Kensington House, 2, Palace Green, and its Redecoration by Mr. Darcy Braddell' in *Country Life*, 13 May 1939, pp. 510–11.

199. C.E.O., file 15231.

200. *Ibid.*, file 15344.

201. Information kindly supplied by Willett Estates Ltd.; *D.N.B.*

202. C.E.O., files 11652, 15323–4, 15552.

203. B.A. 36840, 33367.

204. P.R.O., LRRO 1/2581, 2591–2, 2625, 2658; C.E.O., files 15321–4, 15461, 15552, 15566; *Recent English Domestic Architecture*, ed. Mervyn E. Macartney, 1908, pp. 31–2, 183, 184, 185; *Flats, Urban Houses and Cottage Homes*, ed. W. Shaw Sparrow, [1907], pp. 121–2; *B.N.* 13 June 1913, p. 821; *B.* 15 Dec. 1906, p. 694, 25 May 1907, p. 639.

205. C.E.O., file 15322; P.R.O., LRRO 1/2581.

206. C.E.O., files 15461, 15566.

207. *Ibid.*, file 11119; P.R.O., C54/1666, Chamberlain *et al.* to Horseman, C54/2313, no. 22; K.P.L., Millington's Book, pp. 22, 24; *D.N.B.*

208. C.E.O., files 10067, 11118, 11144.

209. *Ibid.*, files 11119, 11120, 11155.

210. *Ibid.*, file 11119, London lease book 67, pp. 380–384; W. J. Loftie, *Kensington Picturesque and Historical*, 1888, p. 147.

211. C.E.O., London lease book 66, pp. 25–9.

212. P.R.O., Works 43/59–71; K.P.L., Vestry Sewers Committee, 23 Sept. 1856, 3 March 1857.

213. C.E.O., files 10410, 15296, London lease book 90, pp. 428–9.

214. *B.* 1 Aug. 1924, p. 164.

215. C.E.O., files 14986, 15188, 15412, 15453, 15641, 16284; L.C.C. Minutes, 1 Aug. 1905, p. 995.

CHAPTER IX (pp. 194–257)

The Ladbroke Estate

1. M.L.R. 1763/4/12–13.
2. *Ibid., loc. cit.*; P.R.O., PROB 11/992, f. 435; 11/1243, f. 148; 1 and 2 Geo. IV, c. 26, private; F. G. Hilton Price, *A Handbook of London Bankers*, 1890–1, p. 99.
3. G.L.R.O.(L), Blake papers in Ac.61.39.
4. Hilton Price, *op. cit.*, p. 99.
5. 1 and 2 Geo. IV, c. 26, private.
6. M.L.R. 1823/10/3; 1824/12/1227; 1828/2/29–30.
7. *A.P.S.D.*
8. W.C.S. 68, pp. 69, 296; 72, pp. 344–6.
9. Sir John Summerson, *Georgian London*, 1945, p. 158.
10. M.L.R. 1833/8/218.
11. *Ibid.*, 1825/2/115; 1833/8/219.
12. 2 and 3 Wm. IV, c. 27, private.
13. M.L.R. 1825/2/115.
14. *Ibid.*, 1825/3/390.
15. W.C.S. 68, p. 296.
16. M.L.R. 1825/3/91; 1827/10/457.
17. *Ibid.*, 1827/2/587; 1833/8/220.
18. *Ibid.*, 1827/2/586.
19. W.C.S. 70, pp. 241, 252–3.
20. Ordnance Survey map, 1863.
21. W.C.S. 78, pp. 275–6; 79, p. 69; 83, p. 218.
22. M.L.R. 1826/9/406; 1828/6/289; 1829/7/335; 1831/6/45.
23. W.C.S. P/19/646.
24. M.L.R. 1827/5/480; 1827/9/671; 1828/6/422; 1829/7/336; 1831/6/44; 1831/8/63.
25. *Ibid.*, 1833/6/244–5.
26. *Ibid.*, 1833/6/246; 1838/5/109.
27. *Ibid.*, 1838/4/138–9; W.C.S. 192, p. 105.
28. W.C.S. 77, pp. 9–15.
29. B. R. Curle, 'The Hippodrome Race-Course, Notting Hill', in K.P.L. *Local History Occasional Notes No. 2*, 1969.
30. K.P.L., Vestry Minutes, 12 April, 19 May 1837.
31. *Ibid.*, 798.4 Hip.
32. *Ibid.*, Vestry Minutes, 15 March 1838; *Journals of the House of Commons*, vol. 93, pp. 236–420, *passim*; *Hansard's Parliamentary Debates, Third Series*, vol. XLII, 2 April 1838, cols. 269–74.
33. K.P.L., MS. 4574; P.R.O., B9/122.
34. 7 and 8 Vict., c. 33, private; K.P.L., MSS. 4546, 4836.
35. H.L.R.O., Main Papers, 30 May 1844, Judge's Report on Ladbroke's estate Bill, deed of 10 Nov. 1841.
36. P.R.O., B9/122.
37. K.P.L., MSS. 4637, 4684.
38. W.C.S. 80, p. 356.
39. M.L.R. 1841/8/163.
40. K.P.L., MSS. 4532–3, 4550, 4613, 4615, 4684.
41. M.L.R. 1841/8/872.
42. K.P.L., MSS. 4532, 4575.
43. M.L.R. 1844/7/765; 1845/10/658.
44. *The Architect and Building News*, 25 Nov. 1938, pp. 210–13.
45. K.P.L., MS. 4540.
46. *Ibid.*, MSS. 4540, 4683.
47. *Ibid.*, MS. 4550.
48. *Ibid.*, MS. 4544.
49. Gwen Hart, *A History of Cheltenham*, 1965, *passim*; Colvin; Cheltenham Reference Library, Alfred Miles, 'History of Cheltenham', vols. IV and VI; *Cheltenham Annuaires*, 1837–50, *passim*.
50. M.L.R. 1842/8/852.
51. K.P.L., MS. 4543.
52. Wyatt Papworth, *John B. Papworth, Architect to the King of Wurtemburg*, 1879, p. 94.
53. *Ibid.*, pp. 23, 73.
54. Colvin.
55. W.C.S. 82, pp. 16, 169.
56. *Ibid.*, 80, p. 504.
57. M.L.R. 1842/2/714.
58. W.C.S. 82, pp. 235–6, 248.
59. M.L.R. 1855/3/92.
60. W.C.S. P/40/1309.
61. *Ibid.*, 82, p. 271.
62. *Ibid.*, 83, p. 135.
63. *Ibid.*, P/46/1512.
64. *P.O.D.*
65. 7 and 8 Vict., c. 33, private; M.L.R. 1844/5/450.
66. M.L.R. 1847/7/279.
67. *Ibid.*, 1846/6/396–403.
68. *Ibid.*, 1848/3/931.
69. *B.* 30 Aug. 1845, p. 419.
70. M.L.R. 1845/7/590.
71. K.P.L., MSS. 4602, 4871.
72. *Ibid.*, MS. 4572.
73. M.L.R. 1844/9/71.
74. *Ibid.*, 1845/9/41–4; 1845/11/269–72.
75. *Ibid.*, 1844/5/356, 370.
76. *Ibid.*, 1845/8/447–9.
77. *Ibid.*, 1844/6/877.
78. *Ibid.*, 1845/7/590.
79. Deeds in the possession of Mr. Michael White.
80. W.C.S. 85, pp. 455, 472.
81. *B.* 1 Feb. 1845, pp. 54–5.
82. C.C., file 18218.
83. M.L.R. 1847/11/836.
84. *Ibid.*, 1845/7/590; 1845/10/659.
85. *Ibid.*, 1847/5/473.
86. *Ibid.*, 1846/10/675.
87. *Ibid.*, 1846/10/162–4.

88. *Ibid.*, 1846/12/495.
89. Guildhall Library, MS. 11931/13, p. 176.
90. M.L.R. 1847/7/498.
91. *Ibid.*, 1847/5/568, 758; 1848/1/149.
92. *Ibid.*, 1847/9/375, 905.
93. *Ibid.*, 1848/3/931.
94. M.C.S. 288/727; 289/234, 263, 265.
95. K.P.L., MS. 4886.
96. Cheltenham Reference Library, Alfred Miles, 'History of Cheltenham', vol. v, p. 116; vol. vi, pp. 165, 216–20.
97. M.L.R. 1842/8/838; H.L.R.O., Main Papers, 30 May 1844, Judge's Report on Ladbroke's estate Bill, deed of 10 Nov. 1841.
98. M.L.R. 1841/5/248.
99. *Ibid.*, 1842/2/714.
100. K.P.L., MS. 4683.
101. *Ibid.*, MS. 4834.
102. *Ibid.*, 798.4 Hip, deed of 1 Nov. 1842; M.L.R. 1842/6/287; 1844/5/883.
103. K.P.L., 798.4 Hip, deed of 1 Nov. 1842; M.L.R. 1842/6/574.
104. M.L.R. 1842/8/474.
105. K.P.L., 798.4 Hip, deed of 1 Nov. 1842.
106. W.C.S. 82, pp. 230, 280–3.
107. M.L.R. 1843/8/311–29.
108. *Ibid.*, 1843/8/420.
109. *Ibid.*, 1845/2/85.
110. *Ibid.*, 1846/2/462–70.
111. *Ibid.*, 1846/2/471.
112. *Ibid.*, 1844/1/728; 1844/7/734.
113. *Ibid.*, 1844/3/115–17.
114. *Ibid.*, 1844/5/754–6.
115. *Ibid.*, 1844/3/378.
116. *Ibid.*, 1844/5/757.
117. *Ibid.*, 1846/4/842.
118. 7 and 8 Vict., c. 33, private.
119. *Survey of London*, vol. xxv, 1955, pp. 105–16.
120. M.L.R. 1842/6/574.
121. *Ibid.*, 1841/5/248.
122. W.C.S. P/40/1312.
123. M.L.R. 1842/1/804.
124. *Ibid.*, 1843/8/228; 1847/4/510; 1848/5/960; 1848/6/849; B. 15 Sept. 1877, p. 943.
125. M.L.R. 1847/4/508–9; 1847/7/279.
126. *Ibid.*, 1848/5/13–14; 1848/6/850–1.
127. *Ibid.*, 1848/5/416, 960.
128. *I.L.N.* 15 Sept. 1849, p. 181; B. 5 Aug. 1848, p. 382.
129. M.C.S. 289/229.
130. *Ibid.*, 288/671, 786; 293/274; *Survey of London*, vol. xxv, 1955, p. 110.
131. M.C.S. 298/629.
132. M.L.R. 1840/4/505; 1842/1/292.
133. *Ibid.*, 1840/4/506.
134. *Ibid.*, 1843/8/336.
135. *Ibid.*, 1839/9/195.

136. *Ibid.*, 1839/9/196–7; 1840/3/485–8; 1840/6/412–13.
137. *Ibid.*, 1843/8/333–5.
138. *Ibid.*, 1846/1/428–9.
139. *Ibid.*, 1840/7/689.
140. *Ibid.*, 1846/1/304, 424–6.
141. P.R.O., PROB 11/2150, f. 277.
142. M.L.R. 1846/1/304.
143. *Ibid.*, 1850/1/798; 1850/5/221; plan in R.I.B.A. Library reproduced on Plate 56.
144. R.B.
145. Principal Probate Registry, 1878, f. 212, will of W. J. Drew.
146. M.L.R. 1846/4/843.
147. *Ibid.*, 1846/8/762; 1847/7/279; 1847/8/705.
148. *Ibid.*, 1846/5/158; 1847/7/279.
149. *Ibid.*, 1846/4/829; 1847/9/61.
150. *Ibid.*, 1847/4/28.
151. *Ibid.*, 1847/7/279; 1848/5/241.
152. *Ibid.*, 1847/9/62.
153. *Ibid.*, 1847/4/28; 1847/9/61–2.
154. *Ibid.*, 1846/6/396–403.
155. *Ibid.*, 1848/4/710–12; 1848/5/415; K.P.L., MS. 4884.
156. Principal Probate Registry, 1862, f. 622; *P.O.D.*
157. M.L.R. 1850/5/746.
158. *Ibid.*, 1850/1/209–15.
159. M.C.S. 294/788.
160. B. 17 Aug. 1867, p. 616.
161. M.L.R. 1861/1/418.
162. Principal Probate Registry, 1862, f. 622.
163. M.L.R. 1848/3/931.
164. K.P.L., MS. 4905.
165. India Office Library, N/1/1/4; O/5/26–28 *passim*; Bengal wills 1820, pp. 629–33; 1830 part 4, pp. 229–34; Bengal inventories 1832 part 1, pp. 446–8; directories.
166. M.L.R. 1843/3/871.
167. K.P.L., MSS. 4583, 4900.
168. M.L.R. 1847/7/470.
169. *Ibid.*, 1851/9/943–4.
170. *Ibid.*, 1851/11/300–7; 1852/6/801–2; 1852/10/36–55; 1852/15/317; R.B.
171. G.L.R.O.(L), Blake papers, Ac.61.39; M.L.R. 1852/13/126.
172. M.L.R. 1844/1/335; 1845/7/168.
173. *Ibid.*, 1845/5/871; 1849/9/886–90.
174. P.R.O., PROB 11/2144, f. 973; Principal Probate Registry, 1869, f. 375; *Royal Cornwall Gazette*, 25 March 1869; *Western Morning News*, 22 March 1869; *The Register and Magazine of Biography*, 1869, vol. i, p. 40; Boase.
175. Guildhall Library, MSS. 11931/13, 11932/27–8.
176. M.L.R. 1850/1/798; 1850/5/221.
177. Guildhall Library, MS. 11932/29.

178. M.L.R. 1852/13/126.
179. *Ibid.*, 1852/10/56–61.
180. *Ibid.*, 1854/17/544.
181. K.P.L., MS. 2259.
182. M.L.R. 1852/10/708–9; G.L.R.O.(L), Blake papers, Ac.61.39.
183. M.L.R. 1852/13/742–86; G.L.R.O.(L), Blake papers, Ac.61.39.
184. D.S.R.
185. M.L.R. 1851–3 *passim.*
186. *Ibid.*, 1852/13/389–410; 1854/15/502.
187. *Ibid.*, 1853/10/845–7.
188. K.P.L., MS. 4594.
189. *Royal Academy Catalogue*, 1853, no. 1138.
190. M.L.R. 1852/13/741, 762–3, site plans.
191. *Ibid.*, 1855/4/444–7; C.C., file 20646.
192. M.L.R. 1850/1/798; 1850/5/221.
193. *B.* 26 Oct. 1872, p. 840.
194. M.L.R. 1847/6/626; 1848/5/241.
195. *Ibid.*, 1853/2/373; 1856/11/562.
196. *Ibid.*, 1853/4/726–39.
197. *Ibid.*, 1856/4/432.
198. *Ibid.*, 1853/17/963–85; G.L.R.O.(L), Blake papers, Ac.61.39.
199. M.L.R. 1856/11/562.
200. *Ibid.*, 1853/7/685–716; 1853/17/987–1014.
201. Guildhall Library, MS. 11932/30, pp. 138, 166, 198.
202. *B.N.* 12 April 1861, pp. 300–1.
203. M.L.R. 1854/15/502, 554–60; 1854/16/744–5; 1854/17/363–7.
204. *Ibid.*, 1854/15/731–5.
205. *Ibid.*, 1856/13/632.
206. *Ibid.*, 1857/4/154.
207. *Ibid.*, 1855/3/90.
208. K.P.L., MS. 2259.
209. M.L.R. 1855/14/576.
210. *Ibid.*, 1854/16/107–8; 1855/1/497.
211. *Ibid.*, 1855/4/444–7.
212. C.C., file 20646.
213. G.L.R.O.(L), Blake papers, Ac.61.39; M.L.R. 1859/10/962.
214. M.L.R. 1861/16/794.
215. *Ibid.*, 1856/6/490; 1856/7/569; 1856/10/93; 1856/15/1055 etc.
216. *Ibid.*, 1857/13/1000; 1858/9/980.
217. *Ibid.*, 1857/8/922; 1858/6/169.
218. P.R.O., C15/95, no. 213; C34/67, f. 612.
219. M.L.R. 1860/3/157.
220. P.R.O., RG 9/13, pp. 29–33, 82–6.
221. *Ibid.*, RG 9/13, pp. 33–6, 86–91, 100.
222. *B.N.* 27 July 1860, pp. 593–4.
223. M.L.R. 1860/13/213–14.
224. T. C. Barker and Michael Robbins, *A History of London Transport*, vol. 1, 1963, pp. 126–7.
225. P.R.O., C54/13512, no. 3; C54/13514, no. 14; C54/13572, nos. 12 and 13.
226. M.L.R. 1847/4/233; 1847/9/61–2.
227. W.C.S. 85, pp. 154–5, 324.
228. *Ibid.*, P/46/1541.
229. *Ibid.*, 86, pp. 270, 307.
230. M.C.S. 290, no. 419; 291, no. 175.
231. M.L.R. 1855/3/92.
232. *Ibid.*, 1852/1/576; 1855/3/90.
233. K.P.L., Vestry Sewers Committee, 19 Oct. 1858.
234. M.L.R. 1853/2/795.
235. *Ibid.*, 1855/4/444–7.
236. *Ibid.*, 1852/16/228–9; 1853/5/71.
237. Guildhall Library, MS. 8733/21–2.
238. M.L.R. 1848/6/583; 1850/8/188.
239. *Ibid.*, 1851/10/253; 1856/7/379; 1863/16/388.
240. Principal Probate Registry, 1879, f. 367.
241. M.L.R. 1847/7/470; 1851/9/943.
242. *Ibid.*, 1854/7/462–4; 1854/12/560–2.
243. *Ibid.*, 1856/4/591–2; 1856/6/165–6; 1856/7/379–80.
244. *Ibid.*, 1860/13/367, 444, 481, 504, 549; 1862/7/68–9, 72.
245. *Ibid.*, 1862/18/265–9.
246. *Ibid.*, 1859/1/962.
247. *B.N.* 19 June 1857, p. 635.
248. *Ibid.*, 27 July 1860, pp. 593–4; 22 July 1859, p. 662.
249. *Ibid.*, 27 July 1860, pp. 593–4.
250. M.L.R. 1853/17/911–33.
251. *Ibid.*, 1861/12/205.
252. *Ibid.*, 1861/4/44.
253. *Ibid.*, 1863/1/194–5, 332, 494.
254. P.R.O., C16/82/29; C16/83/55.
255. D.S.R. 1873, nos. 81–3.
256. *Royal Academy Catalogue*, 1855, no. 1259.
257. M.C.S. 291, no. 176.
258. *B.N.* 5 March 1858, p. 254.
259. K.P.L., Vestry Works Committee, 6 March 1863; M.L.R. 1862/8/287; 1863/1/441.
260. M.L.R. 1856/13/919; 1857/4/154.
261. *Ibid.*, 1860/12/632–5; 1860/15/475–8; 1860/17/684–5 etc.
262. M.C.S. 291, no. 176.
263. P.R.O., PROB 11/2150, f. 277; *A.P.S.D.*
264. Principal Probate Registry, 1869, f. 715.
265. *Ibid.*, 1869, f. 375.
266. *Ibid.*, 1869, f. 284; M.C.S. 291, no. 453.
267. Principal Probate Registry, 1873, f. 1.
268. *Ibid.*, 1872, f. 221; G.L.R.O.(L), Blake papers, Ac.61.39.
269. Principal Probate Registry, 1873, f. 376; *P.O.D.*; deeds in the possession of Mr. Michael White.
270. Principal Probate Registry, 1883, f. 643; *A.P.S.D.*
271. *B.* 1 Feb. 1845, pp. 54–5; see also K.P.L., 283/St. Joh.
272. *B.* 13 Jan. 1844, p. 24; 1 Feb. 1845, p. 54.
273. C.C., files 18218, 20647.

274. *I.L.N.* 22 Feb. 1845, p. 124; *B.* 14 Oct. 1843, p. 440; 13 Jan. 1844, p. 24; 1 Feb. 1845, p. 54; 8 Feb. 1845, p. 66.

275. *B.* 23 Aug. 1890, p. 142; 20 Dec. 1890, p. 480.

276. Information kindly supplied by Mr. Romilly B. Craze.

277. C.C., file 20646; *B.* 24 Nov. 1855, p. 571.

278. N. C. Wallace, *The First Hundred Years of the Church and Parish of St. Peter*, 1957, p. 21.

279. Pepperell, p. 35.

280. C.C., file 29827; *B.* 1 Nov. 1862, p. 790; *B.N.* 18 Sept. 1863, p. 716.

281. *B.* 1 Nov. 1862, p. 790.

282. *B.N.* 13 Aug. 1869, p. 121.

283. *Ibid.*, 18 Sept. 1863, p. 716.

284. *Ibid.*, 20 Jan. 1860, p. 43.

285. Winefride de L'Hôpital, *Westminster Cathedral and Its Architect, c.* 1920, vol. II, p. 589.

286. *I.L.N.* 15 Sept. 1849, p. 181; *B.* 5 Aug. 1848, p. 382.

287. *B.N.* 1 July 1870, p. vii.

288. George Ronald Bryce, *History of Trinity Presbyterian Church, Notting Hill*, 1913.

289. *West London Observer*, 1 June 1867.

290. K.P.L., MS. 575.

291. Henry Shaw, *Notting Hill Synagogue Diamond Jubilee 1900–1960*, p. 9.

292. G.L.R.O.(L), M.B.O.27, p. 40.

293. Mary Clarke, *Dancers of Mercury. The Story of Ballet Rambert*, 1962, pp. 55–6, 70, 73.

294. M.L.R. 1845/7/79–80.

295. *Ibid.*, 1844/5/356, 570.

296. P.R.O., HO 107/1468.

297. MS. history of Hanover Lodge, compiled by Colonel Martin Petrie, *c.* 1886, with additions by his daughter, Mrs. Ashley Carus-Wilson, after his death in 1892, and kindly made available by Professor E. M. Carus-Wilson.

298. K.P.L., MS. 4886.

299. *Ibid.*, MS. 4883.

CHAPTER X (pp. 258–75)

Chepstow Villas and Pembridge Square Area

1. M.L.R. 1848/6/277.

2. *Ibid.*, 1824/3/636.

3. 7 and 8 Vict., c. 33, private.

4. W.C.S. P/44/1439; 83, p. 549; 84, p. 32.

5. M.L.R. 1845/3/147.

6. W.C.S. 79, pp. 82–3.

7. Gladstone, p. 167.

8. M.L.R. 1846/11/279; 1847/2/121; 1847/6/602.

9. W.C.S. 75, p. 32.

10. *Ibid.*, 84, pp. 278, 360.

11. *Ibid.*, P/44/1439.

12. M.L.R. 1846/7/734; 1846/8/79.

13. *Ibid.*, 1847/5/600.

14. W.C.S. P/44/1470.

15. *Ibid.*, 83, p. 549.

16. *Ibid.*, 83–4, *passim.*

17. M.L.R. 1849/7/690.

18. *Ibid.*, 1850/4/828.

19. *Ibid.*, 1849/9/172.

20. M.C.S. 291, 14 May 1851, no. 5.

21. D.S.R.

22. M.L.R. 1847/5/519.

23. *Ibid.*, 1849/7/217, 600.

24. *Ibid.*, 1846/2/118.

25. *B.N.* 19 June 1857, p. 635.

26. *Ibid.*, 22 July 1859, p. 662; G.L.C. Street Naming Section, plan 22.

27. M.C.S. 288, 11 Feb. 1848, no. 6.

28. *Ibid.*, 289, 2 March 1849, no. 8.

29. P.R.O., RG 10/36.

30. M.L.R. 1849/5/687.

31. Irene Scouloudi and A. P. Hands, 'The Ownership and Development of Fifteen Acres at Kensington Gravel Pits' in *London Topographical Record*, vol. XXII, 1965, pp. 111, 118.

32. *The Kensington News*, 12 Jan. 1900; undated typescript in the possession of Mrs. G. Christiansen of a lecture entitled 'Kensington', given by Alfred Moor Radford to the London Society and the Kensington Chamber of Commerce; Principal Probate Registry, 1900, f. 492.

33. M.L.R. 1849–63 *passim sub* Radford.

34. Scouloudi and Hands, *op. cit.*, p. 105n.

35. *Ibid.*, pp. 105–6, 118.

36. *B.N.* 5 Feb. 1858, p. 124; 14 Jan. 1859, p. 36.

37. *Ibid.*, 5 Feb. 1858, p. 124; 22 July 1859, p. 662.

38. Scouloudi and Hands, *op. cit.*, pp. 77–125.

39. *B.N.* 6 March 1857, p. 236.

40. *Ibid.*, 6 March 1857, pp. 236, 239.

41. P.R.O., PROB 11/2123, f. 900.

42. M.L.R. 1849/7/690.

43. W.C.S. 85, p. 32.

44. M.L.R. 1849/1/151, 555–6.

45. Gladstone, p. 168.

46. M.L.R. 1847/9/624.

47. *Ibid.*, 1849/4/180, 182.

48. *Ibid.*, 1823/10/3.

49. *Ibid.*, 1828/2/30.

50. *Ibid.*, 1828/2/29.

51. R.B.; P.R.O., PROB 11/2150, f. 277.

52. Ordnance Survey map, 1867 ed., 5 feet to mile scale.

53. R.B.

54. M.L.R. 1849/8/981.

55. P.R.O., PROB 11/2150, f. 277.
56. Gladstone, p. 95.
57. R.B.; *P.O.D.*; D.S.R.
58. K.P.L., plan by Edwin Bull.
59. M.B.W. Minutes, 25 Oct. 1872, p. 467.
60. Guildhall Library, MS. 10687.
61. Deeds in the possession of the Campden Charity Trustees.
62. K.P.L., Vestry Sewers Committee, 17 June, 12 Aug., 14 Oct. 1856, 29 June 1858.
63. Campden Charity Trustees' Minutes, 10 Dec. 1868, pp. 366–7.
64. L.C.C. Minutes, 29 Sept. 1891, p. 928; 2 Feb. 1892, p. 78.
65. *B.* 10 April 1852, p. 237.

CHAPTER XI (pp. 276–97)

The Norland Estate

1. R.B.; *D.N.B.*; Gladstone, p. 39.
2. R.B.; K.P.L., 373.24, Nor/A.
3. B.M., Maps K 30.11.1.
4. *D.N.B.*
5. C.C., file 20639.
6. R.B.
7. G.L.R.O.(M), MA/AJ3/10; inscribed stone at No. 130 Holland Park Avenue.
8. 6 Wm. IV, c. 79, local and personal.
9. W.C.S. 77, pp. 168, 338, 372; 190, pp. 237–46; 191, pp. 136, 264.
10. *Ibid.*, 77, p. 473.
11. *Ibid.*, 77, p. 338.
12. Barry Supple, *The Royal Exchange Assurance. A History of British Insurance 1720–1970*, 1970, p. 322.
13. W.C.S. 93, p. 90.
14. C.C., file 20639; M.L.R. 1839/2/201.
15. M.L.R. 1844/1/424; P.R.O., PROB 11/2188, f. 250.
16. Information kindly supplied by the librarian of The Law Society; Charles Richardson, *Notices and Extracts Relating to the Lion's Head which was erected at Button's Coffee-House in the year 1713*, 1828; *Survey of London*, vol. XXXVI, 1970, pp. 84, 90, 168, 192.
17. K.P.L., KQ 213, abstract of title of Mortimore Timpson to land at Notting Hill; C.C., file 20639.
18. W.C.S. 78–83 *passim*.
19. *Ibid.*, P/36/1121; P/37/1165; P/38/1193, 1218, 1221.
20. *Ibid.*, P/39/1268.
21. *Ibid.*, P/36/1121; P/37/1165.
22. *Ibid.*, 79, p. 289.
23. M.L.R. 1842/1/984.
24. W.C.S. 80, p. 39.
25. *Ibid.*, 80, pp. 503–4.
26. M.C.S. 291, 5 Feb. 1851, nos. 35–8.
27. W.C.S. 83, p. 339; 84, p. 211.
28. D.S.R. 1855, nos. 433–59.
29. M.L.R. 1839/8/417–21.
30. *Ibid.*, 1840/9/593; R.B.; G.L.R.O.(M), MA/A/J3/10b, plan of 1827.
31. M.L.R. 1840/5/741.
32. Boase.
33. M.L.R. 1841/1/185–96; 1841/2/60–72.
34. *Ibid.*, 1842/7/579; R.B.
35. Guildhall Library, MS. 8733/10, 7 April 1841.
36. *Ibid.*, MS. 8728/28, 14 April 1841; 8733/10, 13 April, 18 June 1841.
37. *Ibid.*, MS. 8733/10, 18 June 1841.
38. 6 and 7 Vict., c. 33, local and personal.
39. K.P.L., KQ 213, abstract of title of Mortimore Timpson etc.
40. M.L.R. 1843/2/68.
41. *Ibid.*, 1850/2/684–5.
42. D.S.R. 1850, nos. 24–7.
43. M.B.W. 213, 4 Feb. 1856.
44. *West London Observer*, 20 Oct. 1855.
45. M.L.R. 1846/2/403; 1847/4/571–4; 1847/6/299; 1848/3/24.
46. C. J. Richardson, *The Englishman's House from A Cottage to A Mansion*, [1871], p. 192.
47. C.C., file 18217.
48. D.S.R. 1850, no. 53.
49. M.L.R. 1844/5/181–2.
50. *Ibid.*, 1844/9/436.
51. Guildhall Library, MS. 8733/11, 8 June 1842, 28 Feb. 1844; 8733/12, 4 March 1846.
52. M.L.R. 1849/9/366.
53. *Ibid.*, 1847/6/299.
54. *Ibid.*, 1851/2/69.
55. *Ibid.*, 1851/4/812.
56. *Ibid.*, 1848/2/949.
57. W.C.S. 83, p. 214.
58. Guildhall Library, K/Jam, coloured lithograph.
59. *B.* 23 Nov. 1844, p. 588; 2 Aug. 1845, p. 371; 9 Feb. 1856, p. 78; 15 Sept. 1866, p. 692.
60. K.P.L., Vestry Works Committee 1864, *passim*.
61. *B.* 4 Sept. 1847, p. 427.
62. M.C.S. 288, 21 Jan. 1848, no. 5; D.S.R. 1847, nos. 310–17.
63. M.L.R. 1848/2/942–55; 1848/3/77–9; 1853/2/779.
64. M.C.S. 288, 7 April 1848, no. 5; D.S.R. 1848, nos. 52–6.
65. *The Times*, 12 July 1848.
66. D.S.R. 1849, nos. 212–16, 301–11; 1850, nos. 367–74; 1851, nos. 85–9.
67. M.L.R. 1852/16/793; 1853/2/780.
68. *Ibid.*, 1852–3 *passim sub* Tufnell.
69. *Ibid.*, 1848/2/946.

70. *The Times*, 30 May 1848; G.L.R.O.(L), BRA 747/18.
71. P.R.O., PROB 11/2090, f. 228.
72. W.C.S. Minutes, *passim*.
73. *Ibid.*, 82, p. 493.
74. Guildhall Library, MS. 8733/12, 4 March 1846.
75. M.L.R. 1852/16/793; K.P.L., Vestry Works Committee, 23 Nov. 1860, 15 March 1861, 25 April 1862.
76. *B.* 7 June 1851, p. 368.
77. M.L.R. 1852/16/154; 1851/6/995.
78. *Ibid.*, 1852/1/804.
79. *Ibid.*, 1853/9/851.
80. K.P.L., Vestry Works Committee, 23 Nov. 1860, 15 March 1861, 25 April 1862.
81. M.L.R. 1858/4/374–5.
82. *Ibid.*, 1858/4/375–6; Scottish Record Office, B.C. Seqs, sec.v, R1/1.
83. Information kindly supplied by the librarian of The Law Society.
84. W.C.S. P/43/1388.
85. *Ibid.*, P/43/1394; 83, p. 339.
86. K.P.L., Vestry Works Committee, 15, 29 April 1864.
87. Ordnance Survey map, 1863.
88. C.C., file 18217; *B.* 26 July 1845, p. 356.
89. D.S.R. 1850, no. 53.
90. *Ibid.*, 1850, no. 184.
91. *B.* 29 Jan. 1876, p. 110.
92. Information kindly supplied by Mr. Romilly B. Craze.
93. Pepperell, pp. 49–50; *B.* 18 Nov. 1871, p. 915.
94. *Spanish and Portuguese Synagogue, Holland Park. History, 1928–1953*, pp. 13, 16; foundation stone.

CHAPTER XII (pp. 298–332)

The Portobello and St. Quintin Estates

1. M.L.R. 1755/2/221.
2. K.P.L., *The River Colne Water Works. Proposed Aqueduct. Objections on the Part of Sir George Talbot.*
3. *Burke's Dictionary of the Peerage*, 1869 ed., *sub* Earldom of Shrewsbury.
4. M.L.R. 1767/5/70–1.
5. *D.N.B.*
6. M.L.R. 1802/2/663.
7. P.R.O., PROB 11/1426, f. 384.
8. Principal Probate Registry, 1859, f. 687.
9. *Walford's County Families of the United Kingdom*, 1909 ed.
10. G.L.R.O.(L), Kensington Tithe Apportionment.
11. K.P.L., Portobello Farm sale particulars.
12. *Ibid.*, MS. 2259; M.L.R. 1852/9/917; 1853/10/826–44.
13. M.C.S. 298, 29 April 1853, no. 77a; 27 Aug. 1853, no. 144.
14. M.L.R. 1856/4/432.
15. *Ibid.*, 1855/14/576.
16. *Ibid.*, 1855/14/655.
17. *Ibid.*, 1860/7/983–4; 1860/15/591–2, 913; 1860/17/768.
18. *Ibid.*, 1861/1/383.
19. Phoenix Assurance Co. Ltd., Minutes of the Law Life Assurance Society, 22 July 1868.
20. M.L.R. 1860/15/608; 1869/28/521.
21. *Ibid.*, 1863/21/829.
22. G.L.C. Historic Buildings Division, file 512.
23. M.L.R. 1864/3/487–91.
24. *Ibid.*, 1864/9/331.
25. *Ibid.*, 1864/10/855–6; 1868/3/302.
26. *B.N.* 12 April 1861, pp. 300–1.
27. D.S.R. 1871–3.
28. M.L.R. 1860/15/607; 1860/17/769; 1861/10/271, 311.
29. *Ibid.*, 1861/1/746, 748; 1861/6/1021; 1861/7/897–902; 1861/10/272.
30. *Ibid.*, 1861/7/768.
31. *Ibid.*, 1863/21/829–30; 1864/18/245–6; Sun Alliance and London Insurance Group, Minutes of the County Fire Office, 1863–9 *passim*.
32. Guildhall Library, MS. 11932/34, p. 367; 11932/35, pp. 10, 97.
33. *Ibid.*, MS. 8733/22, pp. 36, 53.
34. M.L.R. 1868/3/302.
35. Guildhall Library, MS. 11932/36, p. 231.
36. M.L.R. 1868/27/214; 1868/28/453, 871–3; 1868/30/387.
37. Phoenix Assurance Co. Ltd., Minutes of the Law Life Assurance Society, July 1868–April 1870.
38. M.L.R. 1864/19/37.
39. *Ibid.*, 1868/27/214; 1868/28/453; 1869/28/521; Guildhall Library, MS. 11932/34, p. 367; 8733/22, p. 36.
40. B. R. Curle, 'Portobello Market', K.P.L. *Local History Occasional Notes No. 1*, 1969.
41. C.C., file 11898.
42. *The Times*, 11 Feb. 1885.
43. *B.* 14 May 1881, p. 624.
44. K.P.L., *Kensington Directories*.
45. C.C., file 39469.
46. K.P.L., *Kensington Directories*; Gladstone, p. 183.
47. *M.O.H. Report* for 1920; K.P.L., *Kensington Directories*.

48. Jane Morton, 'New Hope for Notting Hill', in *New Society*, 21 March 1968, p. 416. The editor is indebted to Mrs. Patricia Malcolmson for this reference.

49. T. C. Barker and Michael Robbins, *A History of London Transport*, vol. 1, 1963, pp. 113–17, 121–2.

50. 24 and 25 Vict., c. 164, local and personal; *Herapath's Railway Journal*, 18 June, 9 July 1864.

51. H.L.R.O., Minutes of Select Committee of House of Lords on Hammersmith, Paddington and City Junction Railway Bill, 14 March 1861.

52. M.L.R. 1861/1/105, 444; G.L.R.O.(L), Blake papers, Ac.61.39.

53. G.L.R.O.(L), Blake papers, Ac.61.39.

54. *The Railway Times*, 13 Feb. 1864, pp. 192–5.

55. *Herapath's Railway Journal*, 25 July 1863.

56. Barker and Robbins, *op. cit.*, vol. 1, pp. 105, 112.

57. *Herapath's Railway Journal*, 25 July 1863; *The Railway Times*, 13 Feb. 1864, pp. 192–5.

58. *Herapath's Railway Journal*, 16 April 1864.

59. *Ibid.*, 18 June, 9 July 1864; 25 March 1865.

60. M.L.R. 1863/4/429; G.L.R.O.(L), Ac.61.39.

61. M.L.R. 1862/4/624.

62. *Ibid.*, 1863/13/611; G.L.R.O.(L), Ac.61.39.

63. M.L.R. 1864/14/682; G.L.R.O.(L), Ac.61.39.

64. M.L.R. 1863/13/616; G.L.R.O.(L), Ac.61.39.

65. G.L.R.O.(L), Ac.61.39; K.P.L., Vestry Works Committee, 28 Oct. 1864.

66. *P.O.D.*

67. M.L.R. 1865/26/541.

68. K.P.L., Vestry Works Committee, 17 Feb. 1865.

69. *B.N.* 15 April 1870, p. 292.

70. M.L.R. 1870/5/849; 1875/27/115; 1878/21/171–3.

71. *Ibid.*, 1874/23/93; 1874/24/234; G.L.R.O.(L), Ac.61.39.

72. M.L.R. 1875/28/610; G.L.R.O.(L), Ac.61.39.

73. D.S.R.

74. *B.N.* 5 May 1865, pp. vii, 327.

75. M.L.R. 1869/29/375; M.L.R. index *sub* Freehold Securities Co., 1868–70, *passim*.

76. *Ibid.*, 1866/3/855; K.P.L., Vestry Works Committee, 16 Feb. 1866.

77. M.L.R. 1867/7/275.

78. *Ibid.*, 1875/6/86–7.

79. *Survey of London*, vol. XXXIII, 1966, p. 299.

80. M.L.R. 1876/26/99–100; G.L.R.O.(L), Ac.61.39.

81. G.L.R.O.(L), Ac.61.39; Principal Probate Registry, 1872, f. 221.

82. Principal Probate Registry, 1872, f. 221.

83. M.L.R. 1872/16/691; G.L.R.O.(L), Ac.61.39.

84. M.L.R. 1875/17/889; G.L.R.O.(L), Ac.61.39.

85. M.L.R. 1885/21/513.

86. Ordnance Survey map, 1891–3.

87. Principal Probate Registry, 1876, f. 604.

88. *Ibid.*, 1859, f. 687.

89. M.L.R. 1902/16/543.

90. B.A. 25840; L.C.C. Minutes, 1904–14, *passim*; G.L.R.O.(L), L.C.C. Building Act Committee, Presented Papers, 23 Jan. 1905, item 51.

91. B.A. 46117; *M.O.H. Report* for 1922.

92. *M.O.H. Report* for 1931.

93. Kensington Borough Council Minutes, 1 Nov. 1932, p. 406.

94. *M.O.H. Reports* for 1933, 1935, 1938.

95. Kensington Borough Council Minutes, 13 Feb. 1923, p. 154; L.C.C. Minutes, 15 June 1926, p. 886.

96. K.P.L., 362.78 Pri; *Annual Reports of the Princess Louise Kensington Hospital for Children*, 1927, 1928.

97. Principal Probate Registry, 1933, folio unnumbered.

98. Information kindly supplied by Mr. W. W. Males.

99. *B.N.* 15 Sept. 1876, p. 256.

100. *R.I.B.A. Journal*, third series, vol. VII, 1900, pp. 145–6.

101. *The Ecclesiologist*, Aug. 1852, vol. XIII, p. 299.

102. G.L.R.O.(L), M.B.O. 30, p. 215, no. 1693.

103. *B.* 13 Oct. 1855, pp. 486–7.

104. *B.N.* 12 April 1861, p. 301.

105. C.C., file 24857.

106. K.P.L., 283/All.

107. *The Ecclesiologist*, Oct. 1861, vol. XIX, p. 328.

108. *I.L.N.* 22 June 1861, p. 586.

109. Rev. J. H. C. Twisaday, *Thirty Years at All Saints Notting Hill London W.11*, 1964, pp. 7–9.

110. Charles L. Eastlake, *A History of the Gothic Revival*, 1872, p. 291.

111. *B.N.* 22 Nov. 1872, p. 406.

112. *B.* 10 Jan. 1891, p. 40.

113. C.C., file 41861; Pepperell, pp. 3–4.

114. *B.* 22 Jan. 1870, p. 73.

115. Pepperell, pp. 3–4.

116. C.C., file 42587; Edward Ker Gray, *Thirty Years of the Lights and Shades of Clerical Life in the Diocese of London*, 1902, pp. 10–11; Pepperell, pp. 55–6; *B.* 12 Nov. 1870, p. 909.

117. *B.* 21 Jan. 1882, p. 90.

118. Henry Phipps Denison, *Seventy-Two Years' Church Recollections*, 1925, p. 91.

119. Denison, *Short History of St. Michael's, North Kensington* (in parts, undated).

120. Gray, *op. cit.*, p. 13.

121. C.C., file NB23/321; *B.* 12 Jan. 1884, p. 75.

122. C.C., file 24076.

123. *Ibid.*, file 63671.

124. *Ibid.*, file NB23/242.

125. *Ibid.*, file 64027.
126. *B.* 29 Sept. 1888, p. 239.
127. C.C., file 73881.
128. *B.* 3 Dec. 1898, p. 508.
129. Winefride de L'Hôpital, *Westminster Cathedral and Its Architect*, c. 1920, vol. II, pp. 380, 463–5.
130. *Ibid.*, vol. II, p. 464.
131. Information kindly supplied by the Little Sisters of the Poor.
132. R.B.; information kindly supplied by the archivist, Archbishop's House, Westminster.
133. Pepperell, pp. 63–4.
134. *B.* 22 April 1882, p. 503.
135. Francis J. Kirk, *Reminiscences of an Oblate of St. Charles*, 1905, pp. 72–9.
136. E. S. Purcell, *Life of Cardinal Manning, Archbishop of Westminster*, 1896, vol. II, p. 504.
137. G.L.R.O.(L), EO/TRA/3/43; *B.* 27 June 1908, p. 748.
138. L.C.C. Minutes, 1951–7, *passim*.
139. *B.* 27 June 1908, pp. 748–9.
140. *In the Silence of Mary. The Life of Mother Mary of Jesus, Carmelite Prioress and Foundress, 1851–1942*, 1964, *passim*.
141. Kirk, *op. cit.*, pp. 29–33; *B.* 14 Sept. 1872, p. 732.
142. de L'Hôpital, *op. cit.*, vol. II, pp. 402–5.
143. Alexander Rottmann, *London Catholic Churches*, 1926, p. 123.
144. K.P.L., Vestry Works Committee, 1 Sept., 8 Dec. 1865.
145. Gladstone, pp. 183–4.
146. Pepperell, p. 58.
147. Gladstone, *loc. cit.*; *B.* 23 April 1887, p. 627.
148. *B.* 12 July 1879, p. 785; 25 June 1881, p. 792.
149. *Ibid.*, 16 Jan. 1904, p. 64.
150. *Ibid.*, 19 March 1881, pp. 354–5.
151. *Ibid.*, 25 June 1881, p. 792.
152. M.L.R. 1868/17/481.
153. *Ibid.*, 1870/6/820.
154. Guildhall Library, MS. 10687.
155. M.L.R. 1868/28/786–94; 1869/27/148.

CHAPTER XIII (pp. 333–9)

Kensal Green

1. *Kensington Vestry Annual Report*, 1899–1900.
2. G.L.R.O.(L), Chelsea Tithe apportionment; W.C.S. 81, *passim*.
3. M.L.R. 1832/3/169.
4. W.C.S. 81 *et seq.*, *passim*.
5. G.L.R.O.(L), M.B.O. 30, p. 107.
6. Francis Kirk, *Reminiscences of an Oblate of St. Charles*, 1905, p. 30; Gladstone, pp. 197–201, 207.
7. *Kensington Vestry Annual Reports*, 1881–2, 1883–4.
8. Inscription on bridge.
9. Kirk, *op. cit.*, p. 32; Gladstone, p. 202.
10. Charles Booth, *Life and Labour of the People in London*, first series, vol. I, 1902, pp. 243, 246.
11. L.C.C. Minutes, 14 March 1911, p. 565.
12. Gladstone, p. 202.
13. *M.O.H. Report* for 1925, p. 90.
14. *Ibid.*, for 1933, p. 36.
15. *Ibid.*, for 1935, p. 36.
16. *Ibid.*, for 1936, p. 38; 1938, p. 41.
17. *Ibid.*, for 1936, p. 47.
18. *The Architectural Review*, vol. LXXXI, 1937, pp. 207–10.
19. *M.O.H. Report* for 1936, pp. 39, 40, 47.
20. *Ibid.*, for 1955–64, *passim*.
21. K.P.L., *Local Affairs*, no. 12, Sept. 1970.
22. *P.P.*, 1843(509), vol. XII, *Report on the Practice of Interment in Towns*, pp. 27, 133.
23. *The Penny Magazine*, 2 Aug. 1834, p. 299.
24. Papers in the possession of the General Cemetery Company.
25. Colvin.
26. *D.N.B.*; *Royal Academy Catalogue*, 1827, no. 958.
27. *The Morning Chronicle*, 6 July 1830.
28. *The Gentleman's Magazine*, vol. C, 1830, p. 351.
29. *The Morning Advertiser*, 14 May 1830 (reference supplied by Mr. J. S. Curl).
30. *The Times*, 10 June, 6 July 1830; *The Morning Chronicle*, 6 July 1830; *The Gentleman's Magazine*, vol. C, 1830, p. 552.
31. Boase.
32. *The Times*, 13 July 1831.
33. 2 and 3 Wm. IV, c. 110, local and personal.
34. Minutes in the possession of the Company, 8 Feb., 9 June 1830.
35. *Ibid.*, Sept. 1831–Aug. 1832.
36. *Ibid.*, 1 Nov. 1831.
37. *Ibid.*, Jan.–March 1832.
38. *The Gentleman's Magazine*, 1832, vol. CII, p. 245.
39. Company Minutes, March 1832.
40. *The Gentleman's Magazine*, 1832, vol. CII, p. 171.
41. Company Minutes, Oct. 1832.
42. *Ibid.*, Feb.–June 1833.
43. *Ibid.*, 20 Feb. 1833.
44. *The Times*, 25 Jan. 1833; *The Gentleman's Magazine*, 1833, vol. CIII, p. 169.
45. Company Minutes, 1833–4 *passim*.
46. *Royal Academy Catalogue*, 1834.
47. Company Minutes, 1836–8.
48. *The Architectural Magazine*, vol. III, Dec. 1836, pp. 562 *et seq.*

49. *P.P.*, 1867, vol. LVIII, *Returns relating to Metropolitan Cemeteries*, p. 728.
50. *B.* 2 Sept. 1854, p. 460; 27 Dec. 1856, p. 700.
51. *Ibid.*, 7 Nov. 1863, p. 789; 8 April 1866, pp. 305–6.
52. *Ibid.*, 21 April 1860, p. 251; Kirk, *op. cit.*, p. 36; *Catalogue of the Architectural Exhibition at Conduit Street*, 1860, nos. 224, 325.
53. C.C., file 68965.

CHAPTER XIV (pp. 340–55)

The Potteries, Bramley Road Area, and the Rise of the Housing Problem in North Kensington

1. Mary Bayly, *Ragged Homes and How to Mend Them*, 1859, pp. 22–4; *P.P.*, 1836, vol. XXVI, *Eighteenth Report of the Commissioners of Inquiry into the Excise Establishment*, p. 149; K.P.L., Court Books of Abbots Kensington, vol. 3, pp. 210–12.
2. K.P.L., Court Books, *loc. cit.*
3. D.S.R. 1879, no. 57.
4. *B.* 26 Jan. 1856, p. 43.
5. *Fourth Annual Report of the Poor Law Commissioners*, 1838, *Appendix A, Supplement no. 1*, p. 109.
6. W.C.S. 74, p. 311; 84, pp. 54, 104, 327.
7. G.L.R.O.(L), Kensington Board of Guardians' Minutes, 11 Oct. 1849.
8. M.C.S. 477/27.
9. *Ibid.*, 477/73.
10. *Ibid.*, 12, 6 Dec. 1850, 3 Jan. 1851.
11. *P.P.*, 1850, vol. XXI, *Report of the General Board of Health on the Epidemic Cholera of 1848 and 1849*, pp. 48–50.
12. G.L.R.O.(L), Kensington Board of Guardians' Minutes, 13, 20 Sept., 11 Oct. 1849.
13. *B.* 6, 13 Aug. 1853, pp. 506, 522.
14. *M.O.H. Report* for 1856.
15. 18 and 19 Vict., c. 120, public.
16. 18 and 19 Vict., c. 121, public.
17. K.P.L., Vestry Sewers Committee, 1 April 1856; *M.O.H. Report* for 1856.
18. K.P.L., Vestry Sewers Committee, 1 April 1856.
19. *B.* 9 April 1859, p. 245.
20. K.P.L., Vestry Works Committee, 25 Aug. 1869.
21. *B.* 26 June 1858, p. 446; 17 Jan. 1863, p. 50.
22. K.P.L., Vestry Works Committee, 6 Dec. 1861.
23. *B.N.* 16 Jan. 1863, pp. 44–7.
24. *M.O.H. Report* for 1869.
25. *Ibid.*, for 1871–4.
26. *Ibid.*, for 1878, 1894.
27. M.L.R. 1865/17/1046.
28. K.P.L., Vestry Works Committee, 1860–6 *passim*.
29. British Transport Historical Records, WLR 1/5, p. 113; 1/9, p. 6; Gladstone, p. 141.
30. 6 Wm. IV, c. 79, local and personal.
31. British Transport Historical Records, WLR 1/8, p. 258; 1/7, p. 251; W.C.S. 85, p. 246.
32. K.P.L., MS. 4908.
33. W.C.S. 85, p. 123; 86, p. 402.
34. M.C.S. 289, 16 March 1849, no. 2; Misc. sewer plans, P/1/33.
35. T. C. Barker and Michael Robbins, *A History of London Transport*, vol. 1, 1963, p. 127.
36. *I.L.N.* 5 Aug. 1865, p. 107.
37. *M.O.H. Report* for 1892.
38. *Ibid.*, for 1878.
39. *Kensington Vestry Annual Reports*, 1878–9, 1885–6, 1888–9.
40. K.P.L., K67/174.
41. *M.O.H. Reports* for 1883–5.
42. *The Times*, 29 Oct. 1888; *Kensington Vestry Annual Reports*, 1888–9, 1891–2, 1892–3.
43. K.P.L., *Latymer Road Mission Centenary Leaflet*, 1963.
44. K.P.L., Vestry Works Committee, 10 Sept. 1862.
45. *B.* 30 March 1867, p. 232.
46. D.S.R. 1878–9.
47. *I.L.N.* 29 June 1867, p. 649.
48. *P.O.D.*
49. Gareth Stedman Jones, *Outcast London*, 1971, pp. 324–6.
50. *M.O.H. Report* for 1893.
51. *Ibid.*, for 1895.
52. *Ibid.*, for 1896.
53. *Ibid.*, for 1888.
54. *Ibid.*, for 1899.
55. *Ibid.*, for 1898.
56. *Ibid.*, for 1897.
57. *Ibid.*, for 1902.
58. L.C.C. Minutes, 19 Dec. 1899, pp. 1842–3.
59. K.P.L., *Record of the Work of the Borough Council under the Housing of the Working Classes Act, 1890 (Part III), Dec. 1900–June 1906*.
60. *Ibid.*, Mayoral Minute for 1900–1.
61. *Ibid.*, Mayoral Minute for 1905–6.
62. *M.O.H. Report* for 1912.
63. *Ibid.*, for 1907.
64. *Life of Octavia Hill as Told in her Letters*, ed. C. Edmund Maurice, 1913, pp. 560, 579; E. Moberly Bell, *Octavia Hill. A Biography*, 1942, pp. 253–5.
65. *M.O.H. Report* for 1901.

66. Charles Booth, *Life and Labour of the People in London*, first series, vol. I, 1902, pp. 243, 246.
67. Agnes Mary Alexander, *Some Kensington Problems*, 1904, p. 4.
68. *M.O.H. Reports* for 1910–12.
69. *Ibid.*, for 1911.
70. *Ibid.*, for 1914.
71. *Ibid.*, for 1923 and 1924.
72. *Ibid.*, for 1926.
73. *Ibid.*, for 1920 and 1927.
74. *Ibid.*, for 1923.
75. K.P.L., *Kensington Housing Association Annual Reports*.
76. *M.O.H. Report* for 1927.
77. *Ibid.*, for 1930; K.P.L., *The Sutton Dwellings Trust*, Annual Report, 1950, p. 7.
78. *M.O.H. Report* for 1933.
79. *Ibid.*, for 1935 and 1938.
80. J. Fletcher, 'Kensington Builds for the Poor', in *The Architectural Review*, vol. LXXV, 1934, pp. 81–6.
81. *M.O.H. Report* for 1938.
82. *Ibid.*, for 1936 and 1938.
83. *Ibid.*, for 1932.
84. *Ibid.*, for 1930.
85. *Ibid.*, for 1936.
86. C.C., file 24076; *B.N.* 29 March 1867, p. 230; K.P.L., Vestry Works Committee, 10 Sept. 1862.
87. C.C., file 34709.
88. *Ibid.*, file 24076.
89. *Ibid.*, file 34709; *I.L.N.* 18 May 1867, p. 491; 29 June 1867, p. 649.
90. *B.N.* 29 March 1867, p. 230.
91. *B.* 21 Aug. 1875, p. 763.
92. Winefride de L'Hôpital, *Westminster Cathedral and Its Architect*, c. 1920, vol. II, p. 369; *B.N.* 20 Jan. 1860, p. 43.
93. MS. diary in possession of the church, kindly lent by the Rev. Cyril Wilson; de L'Hôpital, *loc. cit.*
94. de L'Hôpital, *op. cit.*, vol. II, p. 375.
95. *B.N.* 16 Jan. 1863, pp. 44–7.
96. MS. diary; de L'Hôpital, *op. cit.*, vol. II, pp. 370–4.
97. de L'Hôpital, *op. cit.*, vol. II, pp. 376–7.
98. *B.N.* 14 Oct. 1870, p. 285.
99. MS. diary.
100. D.S.R. 1879, no. 68.
101. de L'Hôpital, *op. cit.*, vol. II, p. 473.

Index

NOTE

The symbols in the left-hand margin distinguish those persons who have worked on the fabric of the area, including the architects of unexecuted designs:

    a   Architects and surveyors
    b   Builders and allied tradesmen
    c   Artists, craftsmen and decorators

PLATES

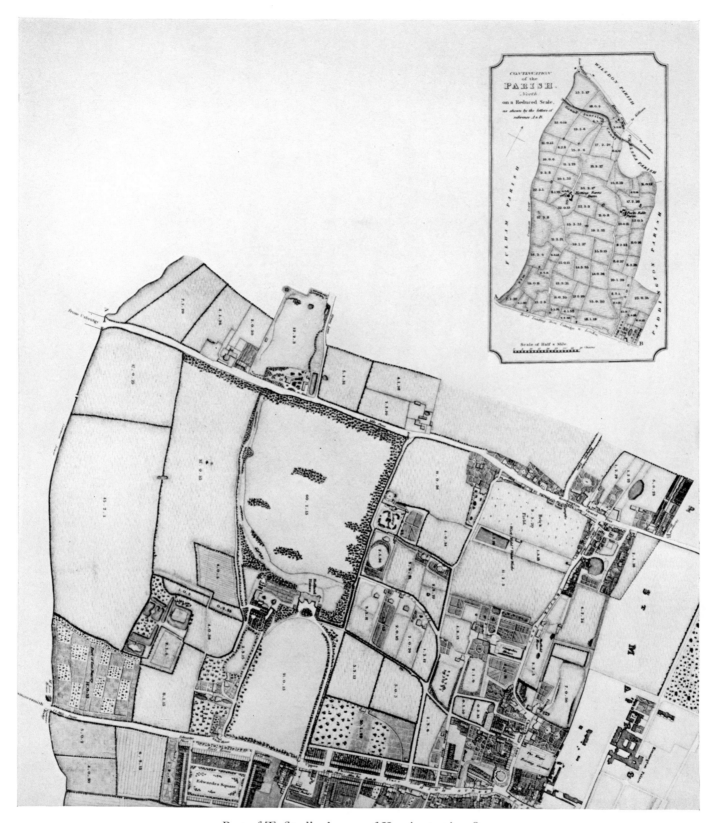

Part of T. Starling's map of Kensington in 1822

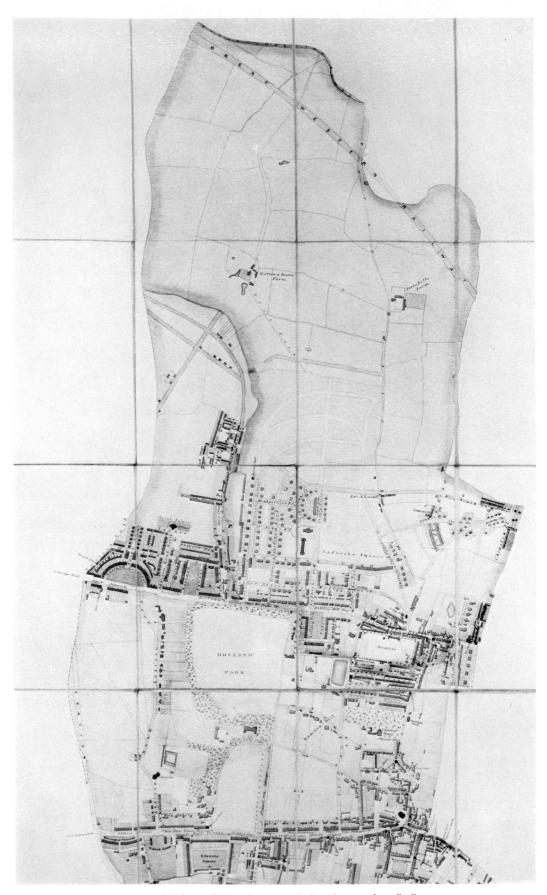

Part of Edmund Daw's map of Kensington in 1848

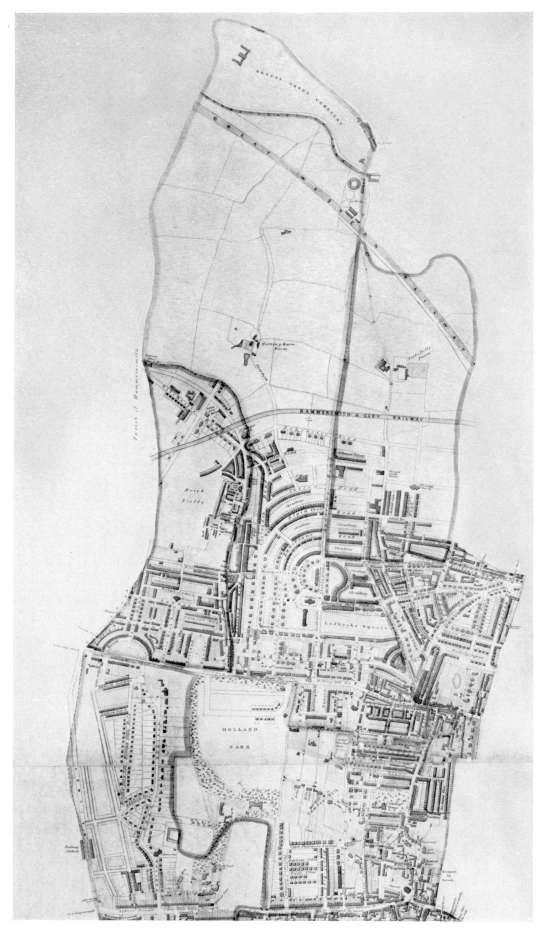

Part of Edmund Daw's map of Kensington in 1863

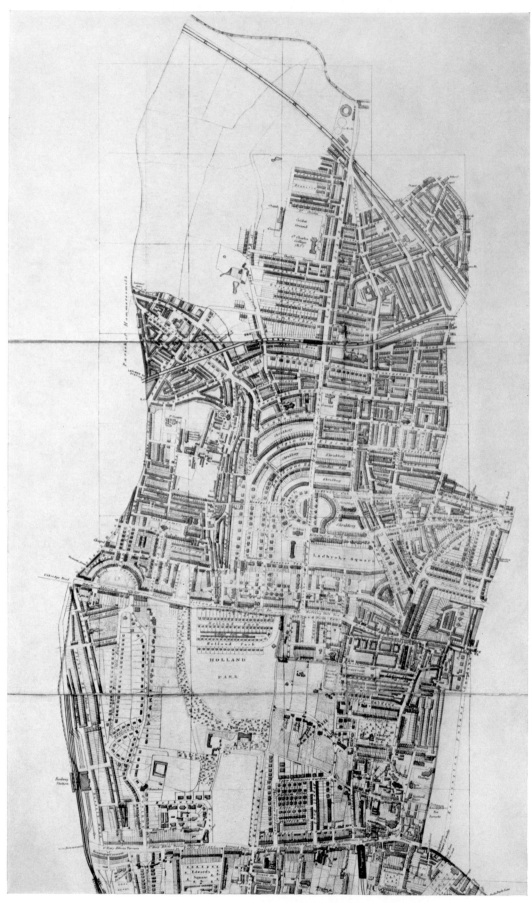

Part of Edmund Daw's map of Kensington in 1879

a. Kensington Gravel Pits, Notting Hill, in 1811–12

b. The Hippodrome Racecourse in 1841, looking north to Notting Barns Farm (*right*)

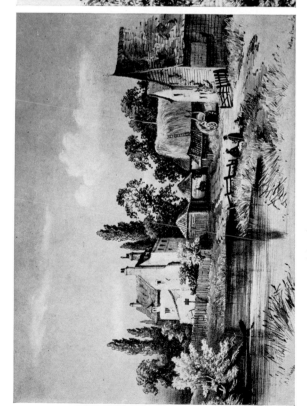

c. Notting Barns Farm

d. Portobello Farm in 1864, looking south to All Saints' Church

6

a. South and east fronts in *c.* 1810

c. Interior in 1869

b. South and east fronts in *c.* 1868

St. Mary Abbots, the old church (p. 32)
Demolished 1869

b. Tower and spire

a. West front

St. Mary Abbots Church, 1869–79. Sir George Gilbert Scott, architect (p. 32)

8

b. Chancel

a. Nave

St. Mary Abbots Church, 1869–79. Sir George Gilbert Scott, architect (p. 32)

9

a. Nave, west end

b. Cloister, 1889–93. John Oldrid Scott, architect

St. Mary Abbots Church (p. 32)

a. Exterior in *c.* 1860

b. Interior

ST. BARNABAS' CHURCH, ADDISON ROAD, 1826–9. Lewis Vulliamy, architect (p. 130)

a. South front with intended spire

b. Interior

c. South front

ST. JAMES'S CHURCH, NORLANDS, 1844–5. Lewis Vulliamy, architect (p. 293)

b. Interior looking west

a. South and east fronts in 1844–5

St. John's Church, Ladbroke Grove, 1844–5. J. H. Stevens and G. Alexander, architects (p. 242)

13

b. Interior

a. West front

St. Peter's Church, Kensington Park Road, 1855–7. T. Allom, architect (p. 244)

14

b. Exterior

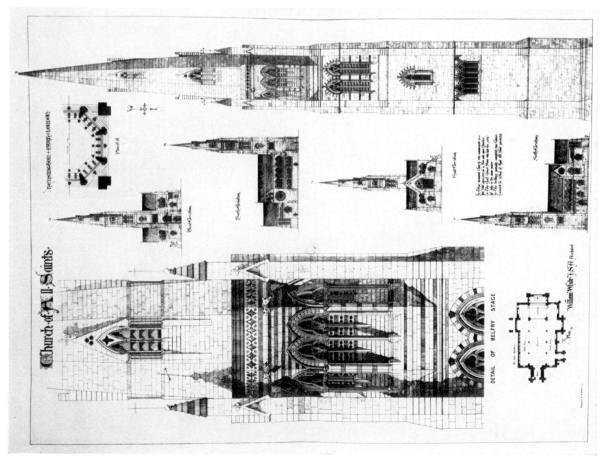

a. White's designs for exterior

ALL SAINTS' CHURCH, TALBOT ROAD, 1852–61. W. White, architect (p. 317)

b. Interior looking west

a. Interior looking east

ALL SAINTS' CHURCH, TALBOT ROAD, 1852–61. W. White, architect (p. 317)

c. Interior

b. Exterior

a. Bassett Keeling's design for exterior

St. Mark's Church, St. Mark's Road, 1863. E. Bassett Keeling, architect (p. 245)

a. Exterior in 1939

b. Interior in 1942

St. George's Church, Aubrey Walk, 1864. E. Bassett Keeling, architect (p. 96)

a

b

c

d

a, *b*. St. Michael and All Angels' Church, Ladbroke Grove, 1870–1. J. and J. S. Edmeston, architects (p. 320)

c. St. Clement's Church, Treadgold Street, 1867. J. P. St. Aubyn, architect (p. 351)

d. Christ Church, Telford Road, 1880–1. J. E. K. Cutts, architect (p. 322). *Demolished*

a, *b*. Temporary iron church, 1855

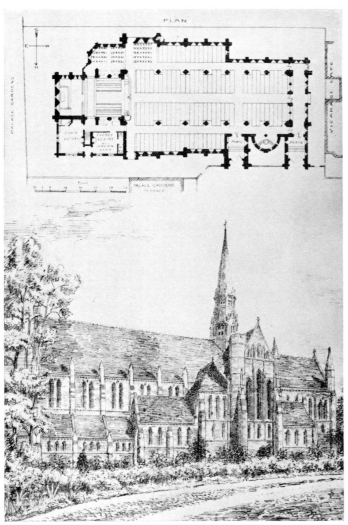

c, *d*. Exterior, plan and interior, 1887–9.   A. Baker, architect

ST. PAUL'S CHURCH, VICARAGE GATE (p. 46).   *Demolished*

20

a. Exterior

b. Brooks's first design for interior

CHURCH OF ST. JOHN THE BAPTIST, HOLLAND ROAD, 1874–1911.
J. Brooks and J. S. Adkins, architects (p. 132)

a, b. CHURCH OF ST. JOHN THE BAPTIST, HOLLAND ROAD, 1874–1911, interior.
J. Brooks and J. S. Adkins, architects (p. 132)

22

a. Interior

b. High altar by Bentley

c. Baptistry by Bentley

Roman Catholic Church of St. Francis of Assisi, Pottery Lane, 1859–61.   H. Clutton, architect: fittings by J. F. Bentley (p. 352)

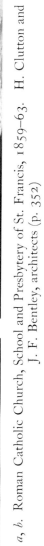

d. Roman Catholic Church of Our Lady of the Holy Souls, Bosworth Road, 1881.   J. F. Bentley, architect (p. 328)

a, b. Roman Catholic Church, School and Presbytery of St. Francis, 1859–63.   H. Clutton and J. F. Bentley, architects (p. 352)

c. Roman Catholic Church of St. Pius X, St. Charles Square, 1908.   P. A. Lamb and R. O'B. North, architects (p. 326)

b. Exterior and garden in 1967

Monastery of the Poor Clares Colettines, Westbourne
Park Road, 1860. H. Clutton, architect (p. 247). *Demolished*

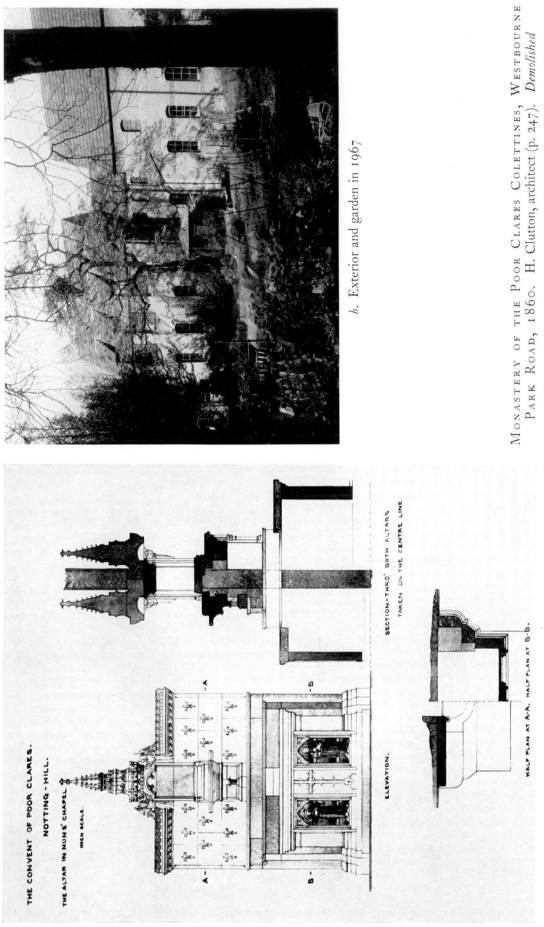

THE CONVENT OF POOR CLARES.

NOTTING-HILL.

THE ALTAR IN NUNS' CHAPEL.

INCH SCALE.

ELEVATION.

SECTION-THRO' BOTH ALTARS

TAKEN ON THE CENTRE LINE.

HALF PLAN AT A-A. HALF PLAN AT B-B.

a. Design for altar by J. F. Bentley

25

a, b. Dominican Convent, Portobello Road, 1862: chapel and cloister. H. Clutton, architect (p. 323)

c. St. Joseph's Home, Portobello Road, 1869 and later. ?F. W. Tasker, architect (p. 326)

a, b. Carmelite Monastery, St. Charles Square, chapel, 1877–8. F. H. Pownall, architect (p. 327)

a, b. West front and south doorway, 1886–7. Goldie, Child and Goldie, architects

c. Priory church, 1959. Sir Giles Scott, architect

CARMELITE PRIORY AND CHURCH, DUKE'S LANE (p. 35)

a. Baptist Chapel, Kensington Place, 1824 (p. 86)
b. Kensington Temple, Kensington Park Road, 1848–9.   J. Tarring,
architect (p. 247)
c. Peniel Chapel, Kensington Park Road, *c*. 1871 (p. 248)
d. Talbot Tabernacle, Talbot Road, 1887.   Habershon and Fawckner,
architects (p. 330)
e, f. Notting Hill Methodist Church, Lancaster Road, 1878–9 (p. 355)

NONCONFORMIST CHAPELS

a. Gateway

b. Church of England chapel

c. Nonconformist chapel

CEMETERY OF ALL SOULS, KENSAL GREEN, 1832–7. J. W. Griffith, architect (p. 335)

a

b

c

d

CEMETERY OF ALL SOULS, KENSAL GREEN: Church of England chapel and vaults, 1836–7.
J. W. Griffith, architect (p. 335)

a. Ducrow family, 1837

b. John St John Long, 1834. R. W. Sievier, sculptor

c. Maj. Gen. Sir William Casement and family, 1844

d. Molyneux family, 1864. J. Gibson, architect

CEMETERY OF ALL SOULS, KENSAL GREEN: monuments

c. W. Mulready, d. 1863

b. Collett family, c. 1840 (left),
and J. Gordon, d. 1840

a. Princess Sophia, d. 1848

f. Families of Elton, c. 1900 (left),
Richardson, c. 1888, and Kiralfy,
c. 1919 (right)

e. John Gibson, architect, d. 1892

d. Mary Gibson, d. 1870

CEMETERY OF ALL SOULS, KENSAL GREEN: monuments

33

f. Monument to J. B. Shaw, St. Barnabas, 1919

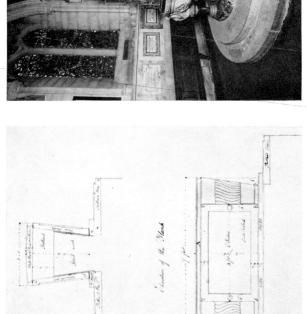

c. St. John's altar, St. Francis, Pottery Lane, 1861, by J. F. Bentley and N. H. J. Westlake

b. Font, St. Mary Abbots, 1872–81, by Sir George Gilbert Scott

a. Tomb of E. Johnstone, St. Mary Abbots, 1784, by (Sir) John Soane

e. Reredos, St. John's, Ladbroke Grove, c. 1890, by (Sir) Aston Webb and Emmeline Halse

d. Monument to G. Shaw, St. Barnabas, 1901, by G. Moira and F. Derwent Wood

CHURCH DETAILS

a, b. Royal Kent Theatre, near Kensington High Street, in *c.* 1834 (p. 37).   *Demolished*

c. Coronet Theatre (now Gaumont Cinema), Notting Hill Gate, 1898, in *c.* 1900.   W. G. R. Sprague, architect (p. 41)

THEATRES

NOTTING HILL GATE METROPOLITAN RAILWAY STATION in *c.* 1868

a. Water Tower, Campden Hill, 1857–8. A. Fraser, architect (p. 99). *Demolished*

b. Tile kiln, Walmer Road, Potteries, rebuilt 1879 (p. 340)

c. St. Marylebone Infirmary (now St. Charles Hospital), Exmoor Street, 1879–81. H. Saxon Snell, architect (p. 330)

d. North Thames Gas Board, Kensington Church Street, 1924–6. H. Austen Hall, architect (p. 30)

a. Vestry Hall, Kensington High Street, 1851–2. B. Broadbridge, architect (p. 37)

b. Town Hall, Kensington High Street, 1878–80. R. Walker, architect (p. 37)

c. Public Library, Ladbroke Grove, 1890–1, in 1900. T. Phillips Figgis and H. Wilson, architects (p. 345n.)

d. Charity School, Kensington High Street, 1711–12. N. Hawksmoor, architect (p. 36). *Demolished*

a. Nos. 9–11 (1838–9) and 13 (*c.* 1760) Holland Street (p. 28)

b. Nos. 16 (rebuilt) and 18–26 even (1727–9) Holland Street (p. 28)

c. No. 89 Peel Street, 1825 (p. 82)

d. Nos. 136 and 138 Kensington Church Street, 1736–7 (p. 39)

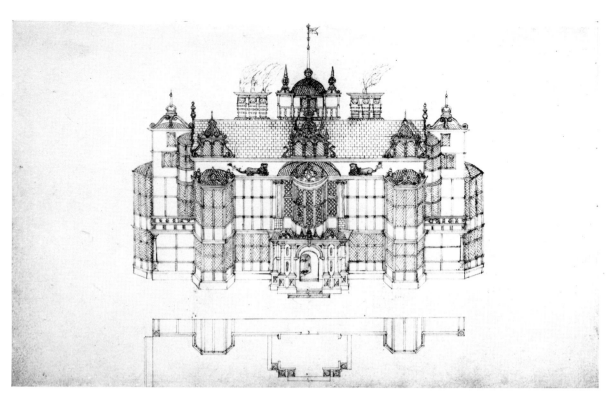

a. Drawing by John Thorpe, probably of original state of Campden House (p. 55)

b. Campden House in *c.* 1660. *Demolished*

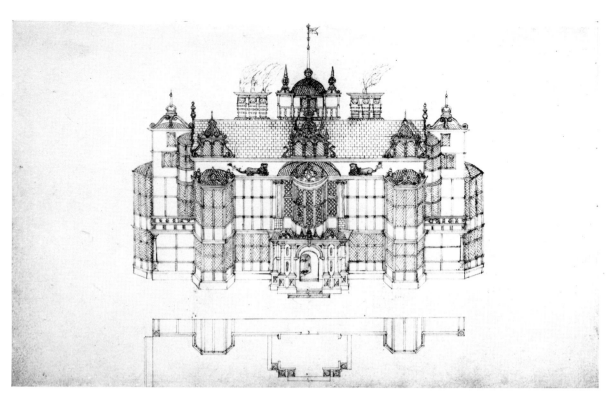

a. No. 54 Sheffield Terrace, 1849. Built and occupied by J. Little, builder (p. 53)

b. No. 38 Sheffield Terrace, 1876–7. A. Waterhouse, architect (p. 56)

c. Gordon Place, 1846 (p. 52)

d. Nos. 14–17 consec. Campden Grove, 1846–7. ?T. Allason, architect (p. 51)

THE PITT ESTATE

a. Little Campden House, *c.* 1690–1700, in 1937 (p. 56).
Demolished

b. Nos. 42–50 even Sheffield Terrace, *c.* 1850.
?T. Allason, architect (p. 51)

c. Nos. 1–19 odd Palace Gardens Terrace, 1860.
W. L. Edwards, builder (p. 44)

d. Nos. 1–3 consec. Inverness Gardens, 1860.
W. L. Edwards, builder (p. 44)

e. Hillgate Place, *c.* 1850–60 (p. 85)

f. Campden House Terrace. Leased to W. A. Daw,
builder, 1898 (p. 54)

42

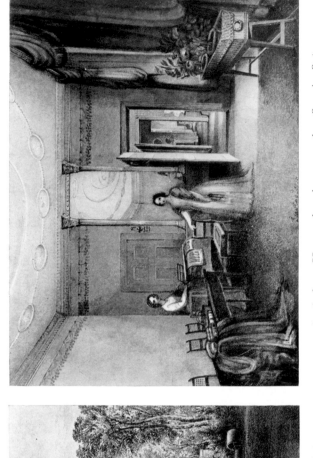

a. Aubrey House, north front in early 19th century (p. 89)

b. Aubrey House, drawing-room in 1817 (p. 89)

c, d. Campden Hill Square, east side, 1826–40 (p. 89)

43

a. Nos. 23–27 odd Holland Park Avenue, 1829. ? R. Cantwell, architect (p. 93)

b. No. 3 Campden Hill Place. Leased to G. Drew, builder, 1862 (p. 95)

c. Aubrey Road looking north (p. 93)

d. Hillsleigh Road looking south (p. 94)

44

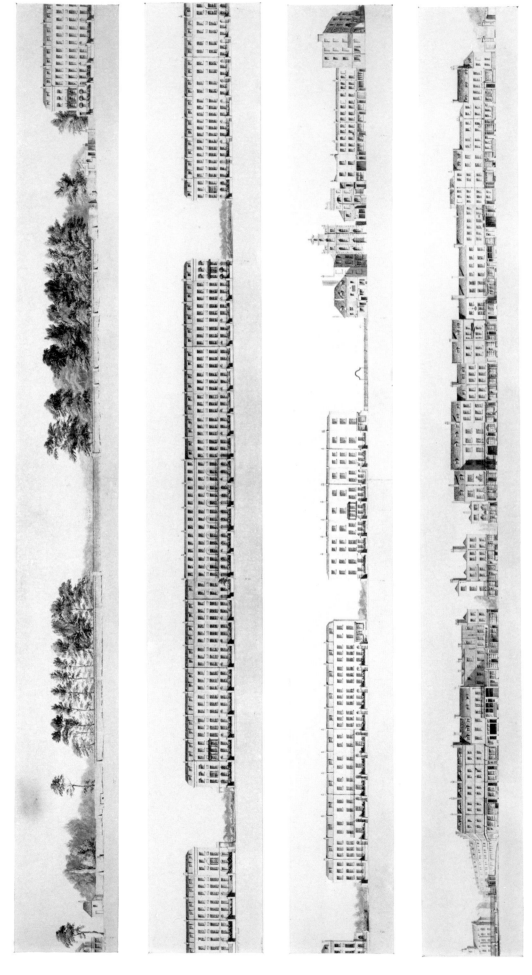

KENSINGTON HIGH STREET, north side in 1811 (*reading from west to east*). *All except two houses now demolished*

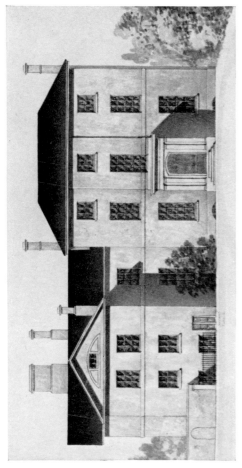

b. North elevation

c. South elevation

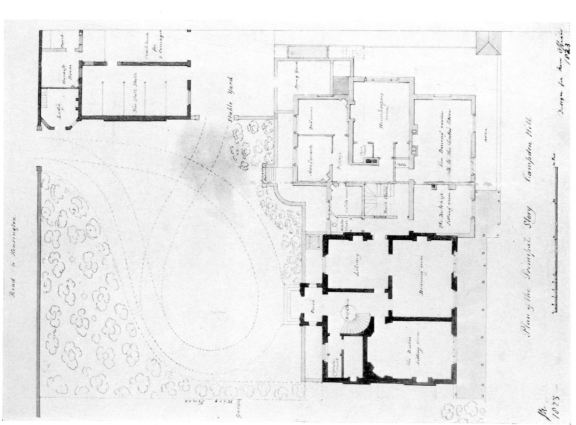

a. Plan

BEDFORD LODGE, CAMPDEN HILL, 1815 (?J. Tasker, architect): designs of 1823 by
Jeffry Wyatt for adding east wing (p. 69). *Demolished*

46

b. Hornton Street, east side looking south, in 1971. F. S. Chesterton, architect (p. 66)

c. Nos. 44 and 46 Holland Street, *c.* 1845. ? J. Duval, builder (p. 74)

a. Hornton Street, east side looking south, in 1903 (p. 61). *Demolished*

THE PHILLIMORE ESTATE

c. Nos. 1–37 odd Hornton Street, 1873–80. T. Cawley and others, builders (p. 74)

b. Nos. 1 and 2 Airlie Gardens, 1881. W. Cooke, builder (addition 1891, p. 66)

THE PHILLIMORE ESTATE

a. Nos. 44 and 45 Phillimore Gardens, 1862. J. G. Davis, builder (p. 64)

48

c. The Abbey, hall, 1879–80 (p. 72). *Demolished*

b. The Abbey, Campden Hill Road, 1879–80 (p. 72). *Demolished*

a. Nos. 6–12 even Phillimore Place, 1861 (p. 64)

THE PHILLIMORE ESTATE: houses designed by H. W. Hayward, architect

b. Nos. 18–22 even Stafford Terrace, 1868–74. J. G. Davis, builder (p. 65)

d. Thorpe Lodge, Campden Hill, landing: W. K. Shirley, architect for embellishments of 1904–12 (p. 70)

THE PHILLIMORE ESTATE

a. Linley Sambourne's house, Stafford Terrace, drawing-room in 1961 (p. 65)

c. Linley Sambourne's house, Stafford Terrace, dining-room in 1961 (p. 65)

b. Nos. 8 and 9 Holland Villas Road. Leased to J. Hall, builder, 1858 (p. 115)

d. Ilchester Place, north side, completed 1928. L. Martin, architect (p. 129)

a. No. 73 Addison Road. Leased to J. Hall, builder, 1853 (p. 113)

c. Nos. 40–94 even Holland Road, 1870–2 (p. 118)

THE HOLLAND ESTATE

b. Same after rebuilding in 1905–8.   C. J. C. Pawley, architect
(p. 128)

a. Corner of Melbury Road and Holland Park Road in *c.* 1905,
before rebuilding (p. 128)

d. Nos. 2–9 consec. Holland Park, 1860–6.   W. and F. Radford,
builders (p. 119)

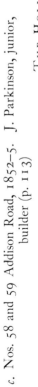

THE HOLLAND ESTATE

c. Nos. 58 and 59 Addison Road, 1852–5.   J. Parkinson, junior,
builder (p. 113)

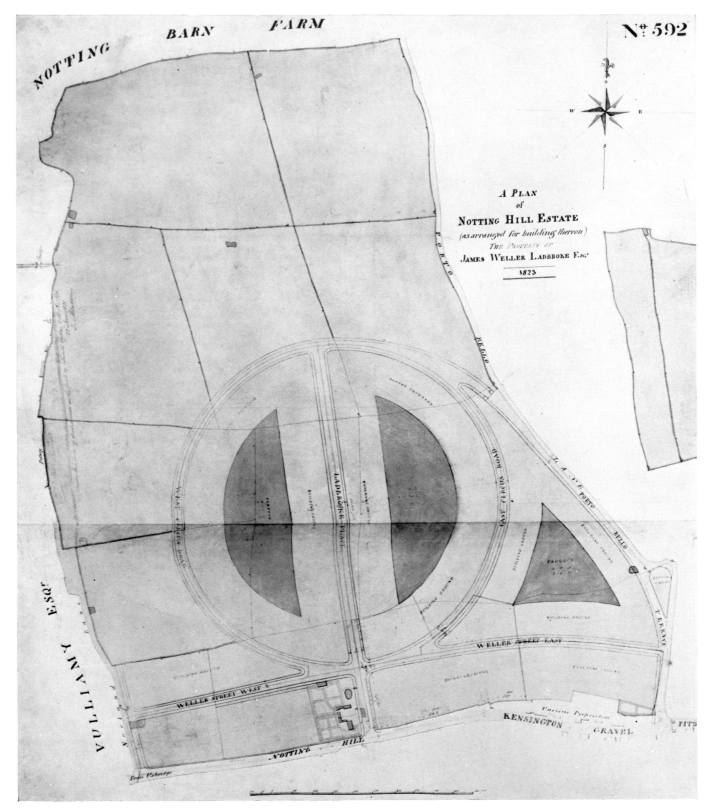

THE LADBROKE ESTATE: plan for building by T. Allason, 1823 (p. 196)

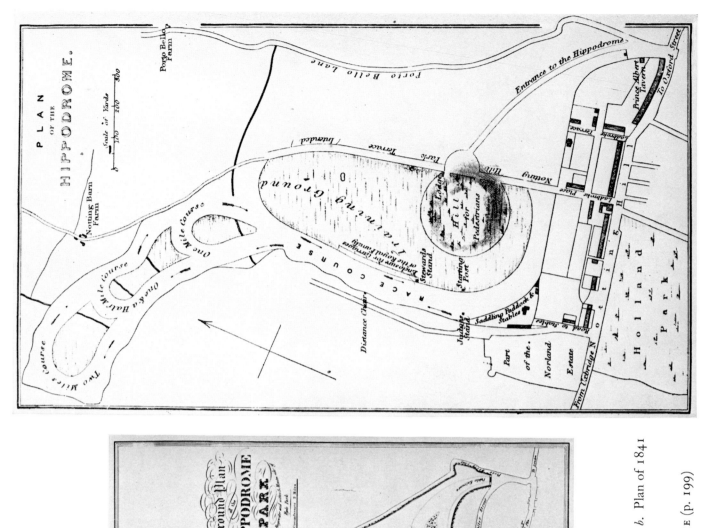

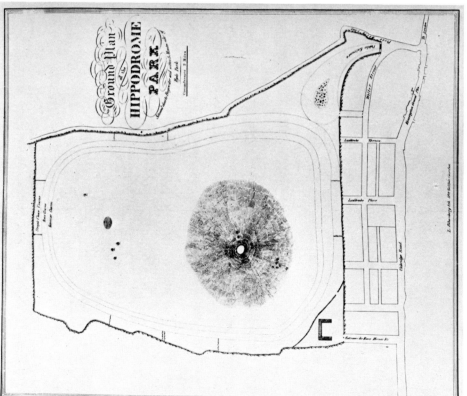

a. Plan of 1837

b. Plan of 1841

THE LADBROKE ESTATE: THE HIPPODROME (p. 199)

54

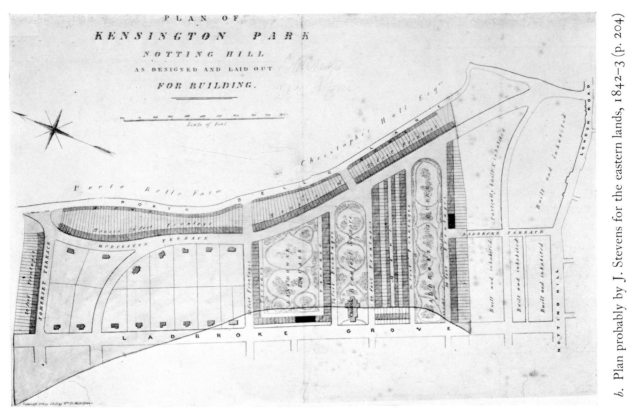

b. Plan probably by J. Stevens for the eastern lands, 1842–3 (p. 204)

a. Plan by J. Thomson for the western lands, 1842 (p. 204)

THE LADBROKE ESTATE

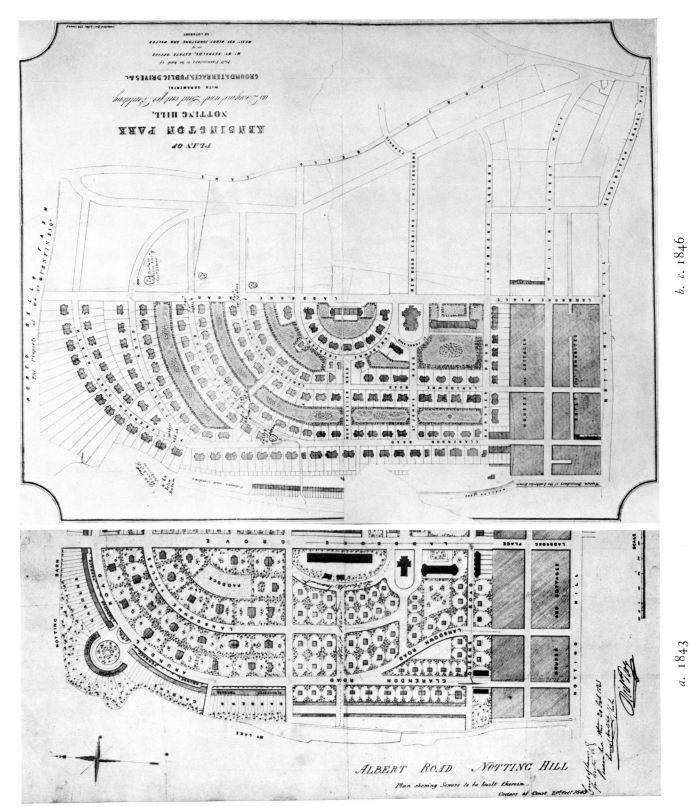

a. 1843

b. c. 1846   Thomson's plan for the western lands (p. 209)

THE LADBROKE ESTATE: modifications of Thomson's plan for the western lands (p. 209)

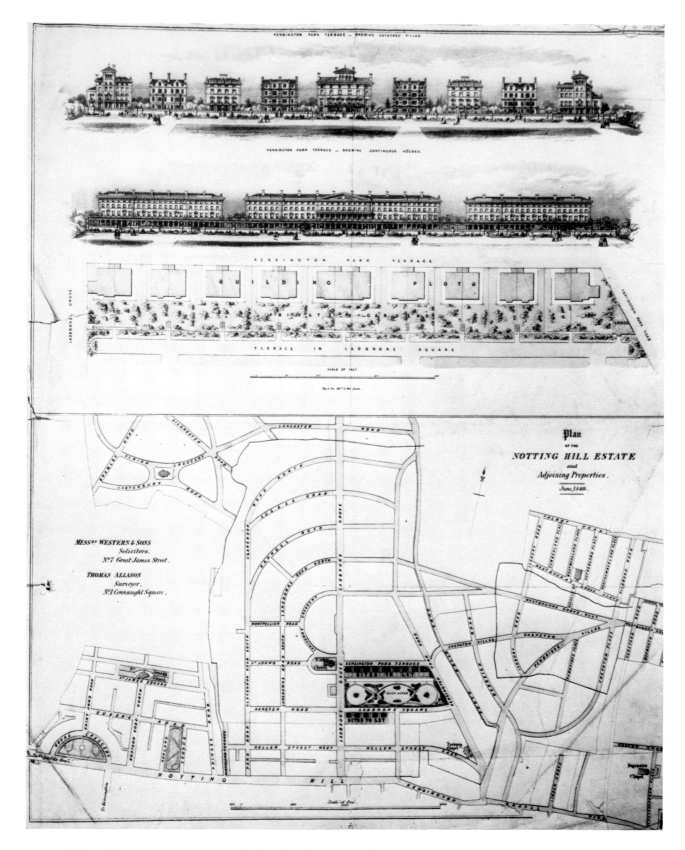

THE LADBROKE ESTATE: design by T. Allason for Kensington Park Gardens, 1849 (p. 223)

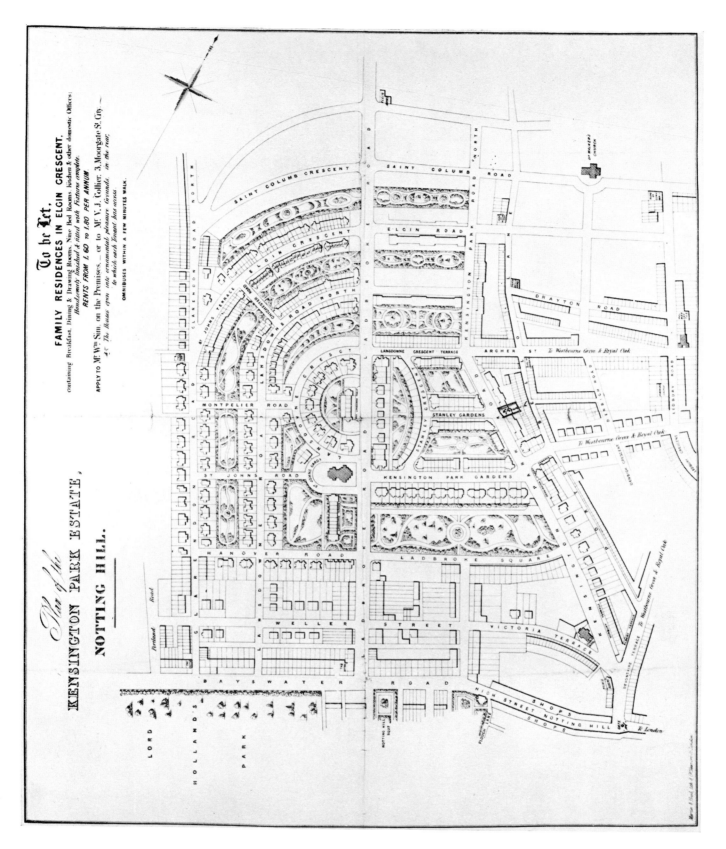

THE LADBROKE ESTATE: plan in c. 1855

58

b. Nos. 2–6 even Holland Park Avenue, 1828. R. Cantwell, architect (p. 197)

d. Nos. 3 and 4 Ladbroke Terrace, 1826. R. Cantwell, architect (p. 197)

a. Nos. 24–28 even Holland Park Avenue, 1828. R. Cantwell, architect (p. 197)

c. Nos. 30–38 even Holland Park Avenue, 1826 (p. 197)

THE LADBROKE ESTATE

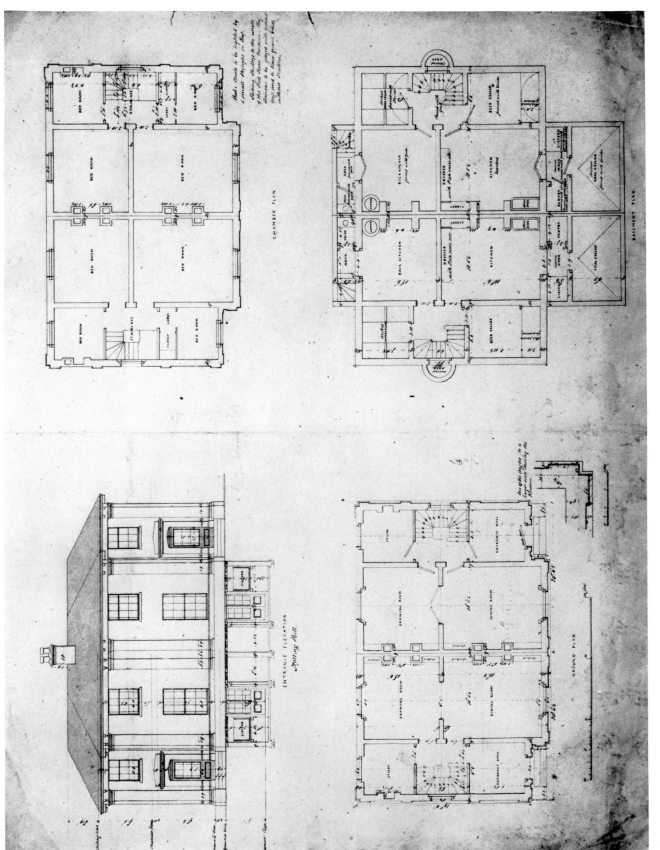

THE LADBROKE ESTATE: plans and elevation by R. Cantwell for 'villas at Notting Hill', relating to
Nos. 3 and 4 Ladbroke Terrace (p. 198)

a. Nos. 16–26 even Clarendon Road

b. No. 39 Clarendon Road

c. Nos. 1–6 consec. Lansdowne Walk

d. Nos. 37–61 odd Ladbroke Grove

e. No. 61 Ladbroke Grove

THE LADBROKE ESTATE: houses designed by J. Thomson, architect, and built under leases of 1842–5 to W. Reynolds, surveyor (p. 208)

a. Nos. 9 and 11 Ladbroke Road. Lessee, W. Chadwick, architect, 1847 (p. 214)

b. No. 14 Ladbroke Road. Lessee, W. Chadwick, 1843 (p. 215)

c. Nos. 13–43 odd Ladbroke Road. Various lessees, 1848–54 (p. 215)

d. Nos. 16 and 18 Ladbroke Road. Lessee, W. Chadwick, 1848 (p. 215)

e. Nos. 23–37 consec. Ladbroke Square, 1843–4. ? J. Stevens, architect (p. 214)

THE LADBROKE ESTATE

a. Nos. 1–11 odd Clarendon Road, 1840–1. *Demolished*

b. Nos. 21–35 odd Ladbroke Grove, 1839–40

c. Nos. 23–29 odd Clarendon Road, 1845

d. Nos. 2–12 even Lansdowne Road, 1843

e. Nos. 12 and 14 Clarendon Road, 1845

f. Nos. 1–3 consec. Kensington Park Gardens, 1849–50

THE LADBROKE ESTATE: houses by W. J. Drew and/or T. Allason (p. 215)

a. Nos. 87 and 89 Clarendon Road, 1849

b. Nos. 43 and 45 Clarendon Road, 1845

c. Nos. 15 and 17 Lansdowne Road, 1846

d. Nos. 37–43 odd Lansdowne Road, 1846

e, f. No. 14 Lansdowne Road, 1844, in *c.* 1860 and 1971 (p. 249)

THE LADBROKE ESTATE: houses built under auspices of R. Roy and/or W. Reynolds (p. 210)

64

a. Design for Kensington Park Gardens, 1853

b. Kensington Park Gardens, north side

c. Kensington Park Gardens, south side from Ladbroke Square

d. Stanley Gardens and St. Peter's Church

THE LADBROKE ESTATE: houses by T. Allom, architect, 1852–*c.* 1857 (p. 225)

a. Nos. 1–3 consec. Ladbroke Gardens

b. No. 1 Stanley Crescent

c. Nos. 10 and 11 Stanley Crescent

THE LADBROKE ESTATE: houses by T. Allom, architect, 1852–*c*. 1857 (p. 225)

a. Nos. 10–12 consec. Kensington Park Gardens

b. No. 24 Kensington Park Gardens, interior

c, d. Nos. 20–22 consec. Stanley Gardens, front and back

THE LADBROKE ESTATE: houses by T. Allom, architect, 1852–*c.* 1857 (p. 225)

a. Nos. 52–56 even Lansdowne Road, 1852–*c.* 1860 (p. 256)

b. Nos. 22–34 consec. Lansdowne Crescent, 1860–2. H. Wyatt, architect (p. 239)

c. Nos. 104–116 even Elgin Crescent, 1852–8 (p. 240)

d. Nos. 84–104 even Lansdowne Road, 1852–64 (p. 239)

e. Nos. 148–158 even Kensington Park Road, 1852 (p. 238)

f. Nos. 80–94 even Ladbroke Grove, 1861. E. Habershon, architect (p. 240)

THE LADBROKE ESTATE

a. No. 21 Dawson Place, 1850. W. Radford, builder (p. 263)

b. Nos. 2 and 4 Chepstow Villas, 1846. W. Reynolds, builder (p. 263)

c. Nos. 1–11 odd Chepstow Villas, 1847–9. G. Passmore, builder (p. 272)

d. Nos. 2–18 even Pembridge Gardens, 1857–9. W. and F. Radford, builders (p. 263)

CHEPSTOW VILLAS AREA

a. Looking east in *c.* 1865

b. Nos. 24–26 consec.

c. Nos. 1–3 consec.

PEMBRIDGE SQUARE, 1856–64. W. and F. Radford, builders (p. 266)

a. Design for Royal Crescent, *c.* 1840. R. Cantwell, architect (p. 280)

b. Design for St. James's Square (now Gardens), *c.* 1847. J. Barnett, architect (p. 288)

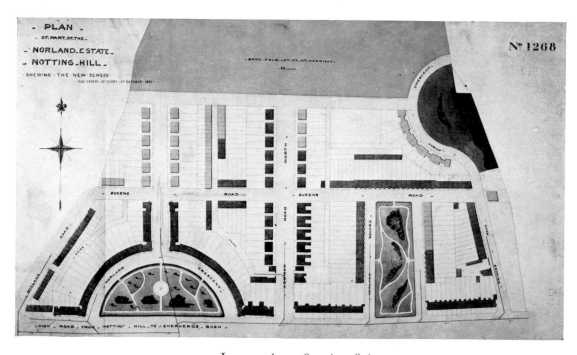

c. Layout plan, 1841 (p. 280)

THE NORLAND ESTATE

b. Norland Square, north side, and Queensdale Road, 1842 onwards (p. 283)

a. Addison Avenue looking north, *c.* 1841–50 (p. 283)

c, d. Nos. 14–24 and 42–46 consec. St. James's Gardens, 1850–1. J. Barnett, architect (p. 288)

THE NORLAND ESTATE

a, b. Nos. 23–36 and 10–12 consec. Royal Crescent, 1842 onwards.   R. Cantwell, architect (p. 282)

c. Princes Place, 1844 (p. 286).   *Part demolished*

d. Nos. 14–30 even St. Ann's Villas, 1845 onwards
(p. 287)

e. No. 12 St. Ann's Villas, 1845 onwards (p. 287)

THE NORLAND ESTATE

a. Linden Lodge, 1827.
T. Allason, architect (p. 269).
Demolished

b. No. 38 Linden Gardens,
1827. T. Allason,
architect (p. 269)

c. Clanricarde Gardens,
1869–73. T. Goodwin
and W. White, builders
(p. 270)

a. St. Ervan's Road. Built *c*. 1866 onwards under aegis of the Land and House Investment Society Ltd. (p. 312)

b. Nos. 1–12A consec. Colville Square, *c*. 1864–75. Built under aegis of G. F. J. Tippett (p. 300)

c. Nos. 177–193 odd Ladbroke Grove, 1868–9. T. Goodwin and W. White, builders (p. 331)

d. Nos. 152–168 even Ladbroke Grove, 1868–70. G. Heritage, sen. and jun., builders (p. 331)

e. Acklam Road. Built *c*. 1866 onwards under aegis of the Land and House Investment Society Ltd. (p. 312). *Left*, elevated motorway, 1970

f. Nos. 154–166 even Oxford Gardens, *c*. 1905–14. Daley and Franklin, builders (p. 317)

THE PORTOBELLO AND ST. QUINTIN ESTATES

a. Prince of Wales, Pottery Lane front (p. 293)

b. Ladbroke Arms, Ladbroke Road

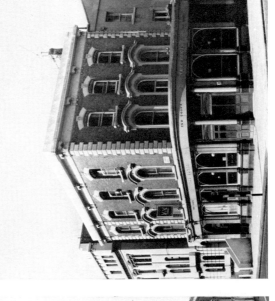

c. Former Clarendon Hotel, Clarendon Road (p. 250)

d. Elgin, Ladbroke Grove

e. Britannia, Clarendon Road

PUBLIC HOUSES

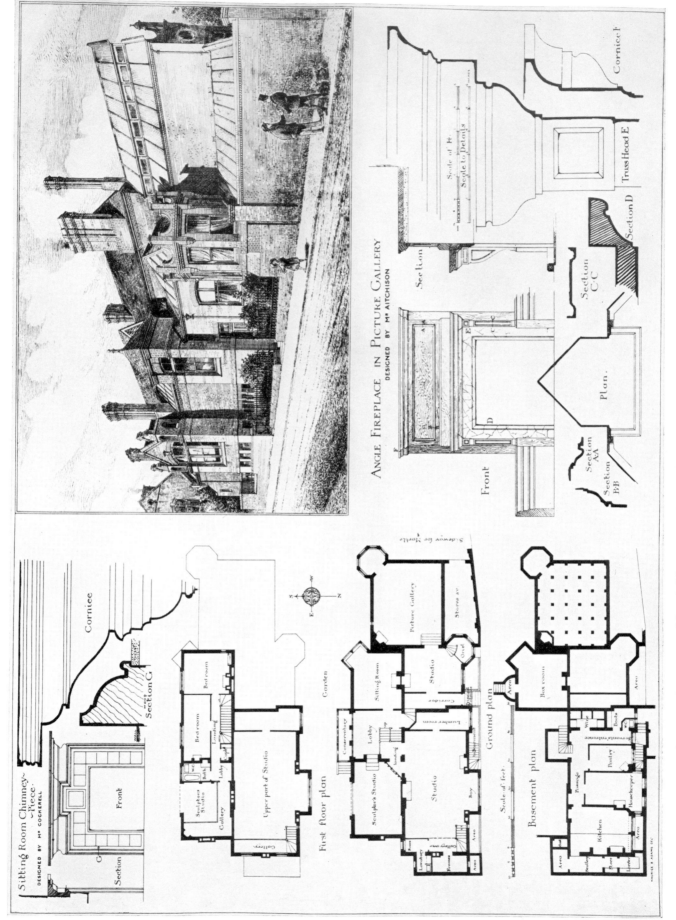

ARTISTS' HOUSES: No. 6 MELBURY ROAD for G. F. Watts, 1875–6. F. P. Cockerell, architect, with additions by G. Aitchison (p. 143). *Demolished*

b. Arab Hall, 1877–9

a. Entrance hall, 1865–6

ARTISTS' HOUSES: LEIGHTON HOUSE, HOLLAND PARK ROAD, 1865 onwards.
G. Aitchison, architect (p. 136)

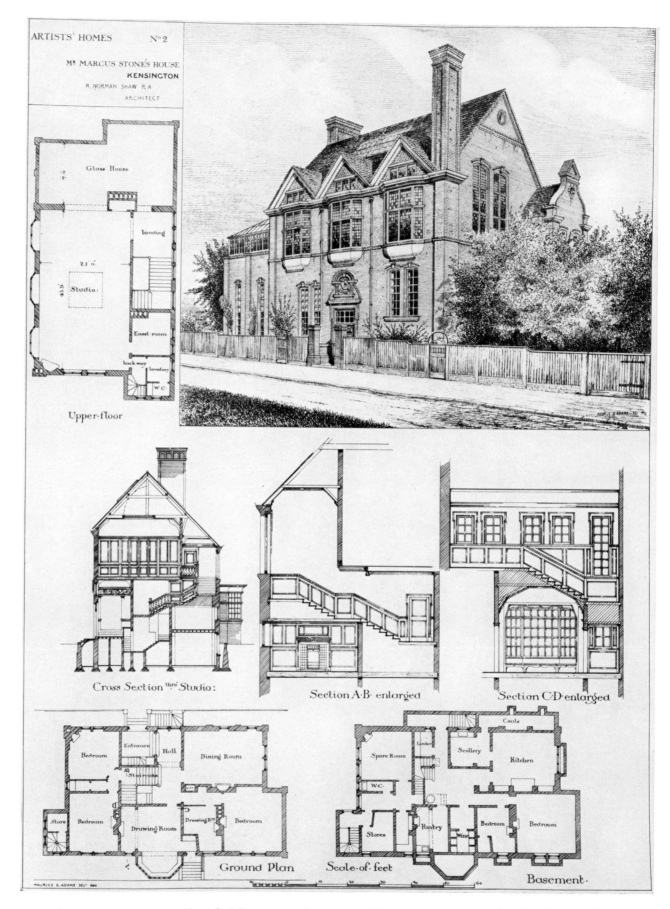

ARTISTS' HOMES   Nº 2

Mʳ MARCUS STONE'S HOUSE
KENSINGTON
R. NORMAN SHAW R.A
ARCHITECT

Glass House

landing

25' 0.

43.9.   Studio.

Easel room

back way   lavatory

W.C.

Upper floor

Cross Section thrᵒ Studio.

Section A·B· enlarged

Section C·D· enlarged

Bedroom   Entrance   Hall   Dining Room

Staircase

Store   Bedroom   Drawing Room   Dressing Rᵐ   Bedroom

Ground Plan

Spare Room   Larder   Scullery   Coals   Kitchen

W·C·

Stores   Pantry   Wine   Bedroom   Bedroom

Scale of feet

Basement.

ARTISTS' HOUSES: No. 8 MELBURY ROAD for Marcus Stone, 1875–6. R. Norman Shaw,
architect (p. 143)

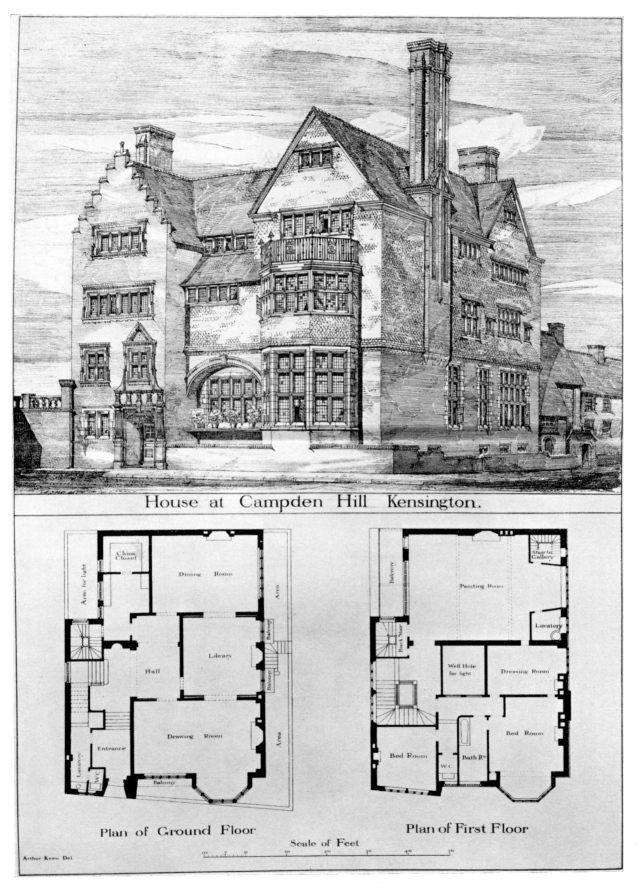

House at Campden Hill Kensington.

Plan of Ground Floor

Plan of First Floor

Scale of Feet

Arthur Keen Del.

ARTISTS' HOUSES: NO. 118 CAMPDEN HILL ROAD for G. H. Boughton, 1876–8. R. Norman Shaw, architect (p. 82)

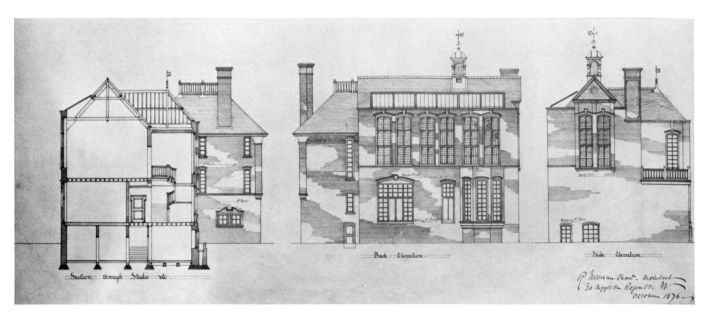

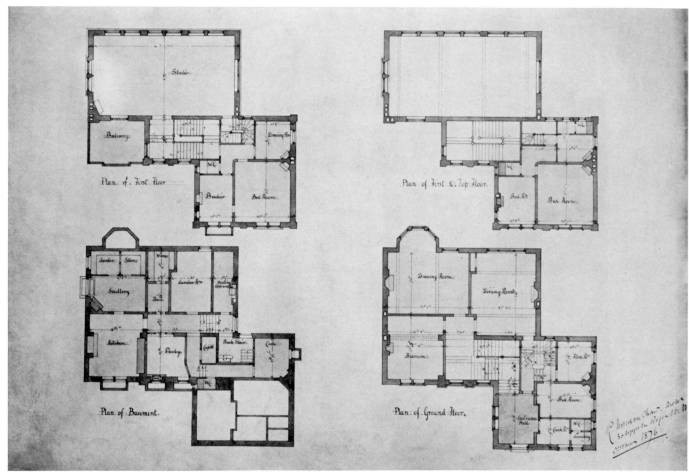

ARTISTS' HOUSES: NO. 31 MELBURY ROAD for (Sir) Luke Fildes, 1876–7. R. Norman Shaw, architect (p. 148)

a. No. 31 Melbury Road

b. View looking north

ARTISTS' HOUSES IN MELBURY ROAD IN *c.* 1900

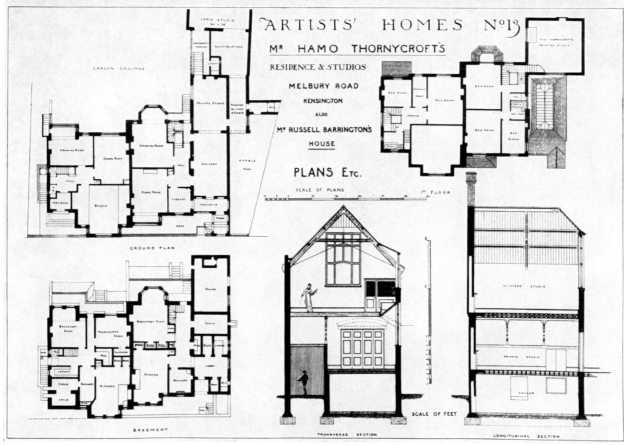

ARTISTS' HOUSES: NOS. 2 AND 4 MELBURY ROAD for (Sir) Hamo Thornycroft, 1876–7. Designed by Thornycroft and J. Belcher (p. 142)

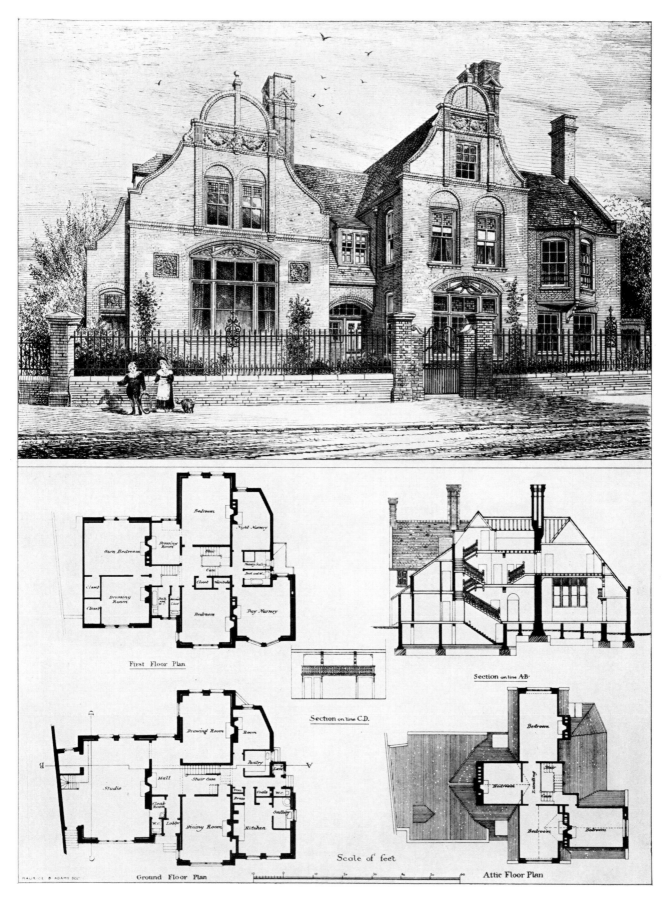

First Floor Plan

Section on line C.D.

Section on line A·B·

Ground Floor Plan

Scale of feet

Attic Floor Plan

ARTISTS' HOUSES: NO. 14 MELBURY ROAD for Colin Hunter, 1876–8.   J. J. Stevenson, architect
(p. 144). *Demolished*

a. No. 47 for W. Graham Robertson, 1892–3. R. D. Oliver, architect. Additions 1912 (p. 149)

b. No. 2B for (Sir) Hamo Thornycroft, 1892. J. Belcher, architect (p. 143)

c. Nos. 55 and 57, 1893–5. Halsey Ricardo, architect (p. 150). *Left,* No. 47

MELBURY ROAD

a. South front

b. North front

TOWER HOUSE, MELBURY ROAD, 1875 onwards, in *c*. 1885. W. Burges,
architect (p. 144)

a. Drawing-room

b. Library

Tower House, Melbury Road, 1875 onwards, in *c*. 1885. W. Burges, architect (p. 144)

a. Guests' bedroom

b. Burges's bedroom

TOWER HOUSE, MELBURY ROAD, 1875 onwards, in *c.* 1885. W. Burges, architect (p. 144)

88

b. Ceiling of Burges's bedroom

a. Dining-room

TOWER HOUSE, MELBURY ROAD, 1875 onwards, in *c.* 1885. W. Burges, architect (p. 144)

b. Chimneypiece in Burges's bedroom

a. Chimneypiece in library

Tower House, Melbury Road, 1875 onwards, in *c.* 1885. W. Burges, architect (p. 144)

a. Entrance vestibule

b. Hall

c. Exterior

No. 8 Addison Road, 1905–7. Halsey Ricardo, architect (p. 135)

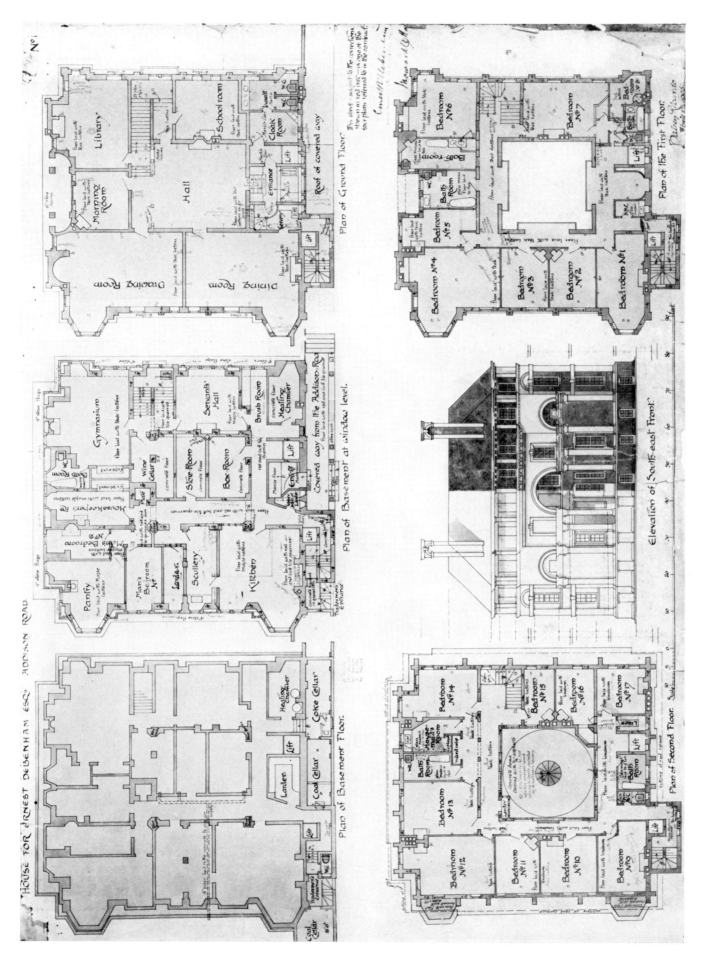

No. 8 Addison Road: contract drawing by Halsey Ricardo, 1905 (p. 135)

a. Houses and gateway at north end as proposed in 1844. T. H. Wyatt and D. Brandon, architects

c. Nos. 8 and 8A, front, in 1938 (p. 164). *Demolished*

b. No. 8, back, 1843–6. Owen Jones, architect (p. 163). *Demolished*

KENSINGTON PALACE GARDENS

b. No. 17, front in 1971

d. Nos. 6 and 7, 1844–6. T. H. Wyatt and D. Brandon, architects (p. 163)

a. No. 17, front, 1844–6. H. E. Kendall, junior, architect (p. 179)

c. No. 26, front, 1844–5. T. H. Wyatt and D. Brandon, architects (p. 184). *Demolished*

KENSINGTON PALACE GARDENS

a. Front

b. Entrance hall

c. Back

No. 12 Kensington Palace Gardens, 1845–6. Designed in (Sir) Charles Barry's office (p. 167)

a. Drawing-room

b. Dining-room

c. Library, by M. D. Wyatt, 1864

d. Billiard-room, by M. D. Wyatt, 1864

No. 12 Kensington Palace Gardens, 1845–6. Designed in (Sir) Charles Barry's office (p. 167)

a. Original front

b. Front with alterations of 1857 by R. R. Banks and C. Barry, junior

No. 20 Kensington Palace Gardens, 1845–6. Designed in (Sir) Charles Barry's office (p. 180)

a

b

a. No. 20, front in 1971 (p. 180)   *b.* No. 24, 1845–*c.* 1849. Owen Jones, architect (p. 183)

KENSINGTON PALACE GARDENS

a

b

c

Nos. 18 and 19 Kensington Palace Gardens, 1845–7. Designed in (Sir) Charles Barry's office (p. 179)

a. No. 21, 1845–6. C. F. Oldfield, architect (p. 182)

b. No. 16, 1846–7. T. H. Wyatt and D. Brandon, architects: additions 1903 (p. 178)

c. No. 21, saloon, by ?W. Flockhart, 1905 (p. 182)

KENSINGTON PALACE GARDENS

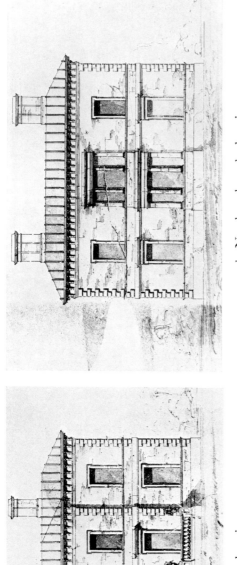

b. North and south elevations

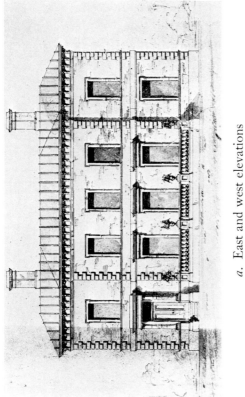

a. East and west elevations

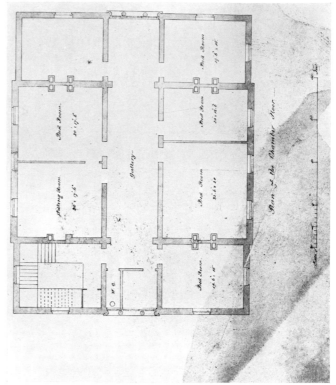

d. First-floor plan

c. Ground-floor plan

No. 10 Kensington Palace Gardens, 1846–*c.* 1849. P. Hardwick, architect (p. 165)

c. Staircase compartment

b. Back

a. Front

No. 10 Kensington Palace Gardens,
1846–*c.* 1849. P. Hardwick, architect. Altered
1896 and 1903–4 (p. 165)

a. Front in 1855

b. South side in 1855

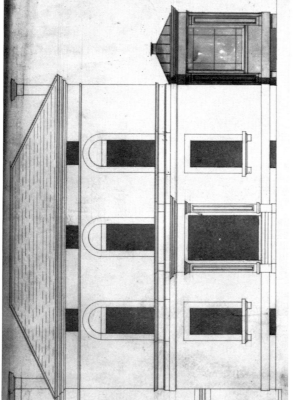

c. Front in 1965

d. Back in 1971

No. 14 KENSINGTON PALACE GARDENS, 1850–1. T. Cubitt, architect.
Altered 1887 and 1908 (p. 173)

c. Front in 1924

a. Front in 1852

b. Saloon in 1870   C. J. Richardson and others, architects (p. 171)

No. 13 Kensington Palace Gardens, 1851–3.

a. No. 22, front, 1851–3. C. F. Oldfield, architect (p. 182)

b. No. 23, front, 1852–4. C. F. Oldfield, architect (p. 182)

c. No. 9, front, 1852–4. S. Smirke, architect (p. 164)

d. No. 9, drawing-room. Panelling inserted 1938 (p. 164)

KENSINGTON PALACE GARDENS

a. Front

b. Back

c. Hall

d. Drawing-room

No. 11 Kensington Palace Gardens, 1852–4. S. Smirke, architect. Roof rebuilt 1874, interior altered 1937 (p. 165)

a. Front

b. Back

c. Library by G. Wellesley and T. Wills, 1937

d. Music-room

No. 15 Kensington Palace Gardens, 1854–6. J. T. Knowles, senior, architect (p. 175)

b. No. 15A, 1852–4. D. Brandon, architect (p. 178)

c. No. 12A, back, 1863–5. J. Murray, architect (p. 170)

a. No. 15, hall

KENSINGTON PALACE GARDENS

c. South front (*now obscured*) in 1905

b. East and north fronts after alterations of 1957 onwards

a. East and north fronts in *c.* 1956

No. 1 Palace Green, 1868–73. Philip Webb, architect (p. 185)

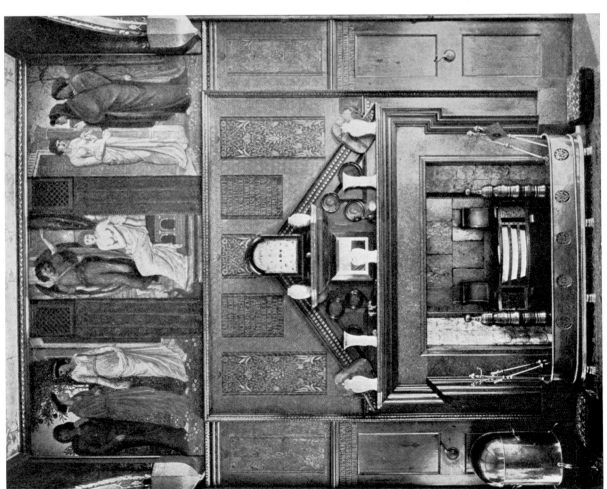

No. 1 PALACE GREEN, morning-room in 1898. Decorations by Burne-Jones, Morris, Walter Crane and Philip Webb (p. 187)

a. No. 4, 1905.   Read and MacDonald, architects

b. No. 5, 1905.   E. P. Warren, architect

c. No. 6, 1910.   Read and MacDonald, architects

d. No. 7, 1913.   Field and Simmons with Faulkner, architects

e. No. 8, 1908.   ?A. Faulkner, architect

f. No. 10, 1905.   E. J. May, architect

PALACE GREEN (p. 190)

a. No. 5, staircase

b. No. 10, hall

c. No. 8, hall

d. No. 8, ground-floor corridor

PALACE GREEN, interiors (p. 190)

a. Campden Houses, Peel Street, 1877–8. E. Evans Cronk, architect (p. 82)

b. Mall Chambers, Kensington Mall, 1865–8. J. Murray, architect (p. 40)

c. Campden Hill Court, Campden Hill Road, 1898–1900. F. and E. C. Pilkington, architects (p. 74)

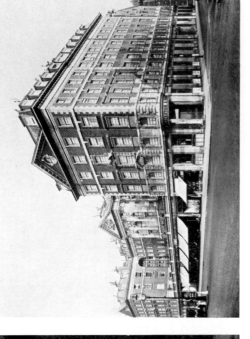

d. Oakwood Court, 1899 onwards. Various architects (p. 129)

e. Hornton Court, Kensington High Street, 1905–7, in *c.* 1912. F. S. Chesterton and J. D. Coleridge, architects (p. 67)

FLATS